Spatial Formats under the Global Condition

Dialectics of the Global

Edited by
Matthias Middell

Volume 1

Spatial Formats under the Global Condition

Edited by
Steffi Marung/Matthias Middell

DE GRUYTER
OLDENBOURG

Funded with help of the DFG, a product of the SFB 1199.

ISBN 978-3-11-076342-3
e-ISBN (PDF) 978-3-11-064300-8
e-ISBN (EPUB) 978-3-11-063941-4

Library of Congress Control Number: 2019941360

Bibliographic information published by the Deutsche Nationalbibliothek
The Deutsche Nationalbibliothek lists this publication in the Deutsche Nationalbibliografie; detailed bibliographic data are available on the Internet at http://dnb.dnb.de.

© 2021 Walter de Gruyter GmbH, Berlin/Boston
This volume is text- and page-identical with the hardback published in 2019.
Typesetting: Integra Software Services Pvt. Ltd.
Printing and binding: CPI books GmbH, Leck
Cover image: Map of traffic on the Atlantic Ocean in 1896
© THEPALMER/gettyimages

www.degruyter.com

Preface

Ever since the 1990s, "globalization" has been a dominant idea and, indeed, ideology. The metanarratives of Cold War victory by the West, the expansion of the market economy, and the boost in productivity through internationalization, digitalization, and the increasing dominance of the finance industry became associated with the promise of a global trickle-down effect that would lead to greater prosperity for ever more people worldwide. Any criticism of this viewpoint was countered with the argument that there was no alternative; globalization was too powerful and thus irreversible. Today, the ideology of "globalization" meets with growing scepticism. An era of exaggerated optimism for global integration has been replaced by an era of doubt and a quest for a return to particularistic sovereignty. However, processes of global integration have not dissipated and the rejection of "globalization" as ideology has not diminished the need to make sense both of the actually existing high level of interdependence and the ideology that gave meaning and justification to it.

The following three dialectics of the global are in the focus of this series:

Multiplicity and Co-Presence: "Globalization" is neither a natural occurrence nor a singular process; on the contrary, there are competing projects of globalization, which must be explained in their own right and compared in order to examine their layering and their interactive composition.

Integration and Fragmentation: Global processes result in de- as well as reterritorialization. They go hand in hand with the dissolution of boundaries, while also producing a respatialization of the world.

Universalism and Particularism: Globalization projects are justified and legitimized through universal claims of validity; however, at the same time they reflect the worldview and/or interest of particular actors.

Contents

Preface —— V

Steffi Marung and Matthias Middell
The Respatialization of the World as one of the Driving Dialectics under the Global Condition —— 1

Part I: Concepts and Historicity

Matthias Middell
Category of Spatial Formats: To What End? —— 15

Bob Jessop
Spatiotemporal Fixes and Multispatial Metagovernance: The Territory, Place, Scale, Network Scheme Revisited —— 48

Judith Miggelbrink
Mapping the Toolbox: Assemblage Thinking as a Heuristic —— 78

Part II: Territories

Frank Schumacher
Reclaiming Territory: The Spatial Contours of Empire in US History —— 107

John Breuilly
Modern Territoriality, the Nation-State, and Nationalism —— 149

Part III: Portals

Geert Castryck
Disentangling the Colonial City: Spatial Separations and Entanglements inside Towns and across the Empire in Colonial Africa and Europe —— 183

Holger Weiss
Hamburg, 8 Rothesoodstrasse: From a Global Space to a Non-place —— 205

Antje Dietze
Visions of the World. Transnational Connections of the Panorama Industry in Leipzig at the Turn of the Twentieth Century —— 228

Part IV: International Spaces

Glenda Sluga
The International History of (International) Sovereignty —— 257

Steffi Marung, Uwe Müller and Stefan Troebst
Monolith or Experiment? The Bloc as a Spatial Format —— 275

Ulf Engel
Regionalisms and Regional Organizations —— 310

Sarah Ruth Sippel and Michaela Böhme
Dis/Articulating Agri-food Spaces: The Multifaceted Logics of Agro-investments —— 334

Hannes Warnecke-Berger
The Spatial Turn and Economics: Migration, Remittances, and Transnational Economic Space —— 360

Authors —— 379

Index —— 382

Steffi Marung and Matthias Middell
The Respatialization of the World as one of the Driving Dialectics under the Global Condition

This volume is the result of intense collaboration among scholars from various disciplines – geography, sociology, history, cultural studies, political science, international studies, and international history – as well as area studies expertise – on Africa, the Americas, and Europe in particular. Furthermore, it is the outcome of various modes of translation across those disciplinary and area boundaries. The invitation to collaborate on the project was to test a conceptual vocabulary. More than a common language, this vocabulary acts as a heuristic repertoire to investigate how the intensification and acceleration of global connectedness has caused reactions by various actors at different times and in varying geographies to deal with these challenges. These reactions have essentially taken spatial forms, not only as efforts to contain, limit, and stem flows of goods, people, or ideas – by establishing borders, circumscribing hermetic spaces of activity, preventing mobility, prohibiting access, or excluding competitors – but also as struggles to manage, redirect, profit from, fuel, and appropriate those flows – by creating networks, promoting hubs, or pushing for more exchange to the benefit of diverse, often conflicting projects. Accordingly, all authors within this volume share an understanding of globalization as a dialectic of flows and controls as well as of de- and reterritorialization, essentially the result of multiple globalization projects, including the activities of actors with specific agendas, resources, and instruments to pursue them.

The role of space in social interaction has attracted rapidly growing interest over the past decades – both in academia in particular and society in general. This interest is certainly maintained through the perception that new technologies and forms of communication – often encapsulated in the term digitalization – as well as new configurations of political affairs at a global scale – often summarized under the notion of the new world order – are about to bring new forms and functions of space into existence. This has led to a proliferation of – often metaphorically used – spatial semantics, which seem to indicate that new phenomena are emerging.

Within the search for an explanation of such new spatial configurations, this newness is related to and even integrated into the most powerful narrative of our times: that being that globalization is both the driving force and the framework for a multitude of societal changes. After a period of overoptimistic speculations that globalization would erase the traditional forms of territoriality to the profit of border-transcending fluidity, the debate has waned in light of real world observations. The nation-state has not disappeared, instead remaining, for example, during the global financial crisis in 2007/08 powerful enough to buy banks that were estimated "too big to fail", or in other words too pivotal for the functioning of societies to be exposed to the rules of a pure market mechanism. But ironically, it were exactly these banks as well as economists convinced of the superiority of such market mechanisms that had propagated in the 1990s a rather borderless world of digitized trade with ever more complex transnational and transregional assets and investments. Some even had spoken of the end of the nation-state and started to search for alternative forms of (global) governance. Such hopes, however, were frustrated at many occasions while, at the same time, an entire world of transnational connections (from communication infrastructures to NGOs) emerged and developed agency.

But the seemingly surprising return of some nation-states to the stage at times of fundamental crisis should not be misinterpreted as the revival of a period when the nation-state not only was the sole spatial format in the world but in fact was also able to assert control over many – if not all – other spatial forms of societal self-organization, from the local to the international. This period can be located in the late nineteenth and early twentieth centuries when the nation-state was recognized as a very efficient tool to regain control over border-crossing flows, which characterized the global condition of the time. This global condition was the product of steam ships and telegraph, together with the slow emergence of the first world markets, an increasing urbanization, and steps into the first and second waves of industrialization. Terms such as "Weltpolitik" or "Weltwirtschaft" indicate that not only German was a recognized cultural context from which experience and aspiration was copied into other societies but above all that also the times of strong nationalization coincided with the discovery of an ever-increasing list of items that were only able to be solved and regulated with the help of transnational regulation and international organizations.

What is interesting to observe is that the most powerful states in a world, which were characterized by globalization and nationalization as a reaction to such border-crossing connections, were not nation-states in the purest sense of the word. What is evident already from the official label for the British Empire was true for the French state as well; it as well applied to the USA and to Belgium and Russia and so on. Until the emergence of the Third French Republic, out of the ashes of a war with Prussia and a revolution in Paris, non-monarchic forms of government were rather to be found in the Americas than in Europe. But even in the case of the USA as well as France, a unique mixture of constitutionalism at home and imperialist behaviour in regions to be conquered or already colonized was characteristic of a spatial format that should not be confined to the definition of a nation-state.

People of the late nineteenth century were convinced that their nation-states or empires would be able to gain control over global flows and therefore built alliances of political, economic, and cultural elites mainly along such national categories to develop appropriate institutions, strategies, and practices for the necessary self-positioning under the global condition. However, World War I already demonstrated the uncertainty of the situation. As recognized by a growing number of critical commentators, the competition between states had led to a deadly and highly destructive four-year period of warfare and stalemate. Furthermore, on the one hand, it had given rise to the understanding that an exponentially rising number of issues could no longer be solved at the national level only. As a consequence, the League of Nations was established and continued ongoing efforts to systematize the actions of international organizations. But, on the other hand, the principle of self-determination of the people – which, concurrently, was a historical echo of the anti-imperial foundation of the USA in the late eighteenth century and an attack on empires still existing in Central Europe – continuously sought solutions to global problems involving sovereign states, but not necessarily nation-states.

Today, the situation seems to have changed – at least to a certain extent. Often heard is the argument that nation-states are too small to find appropriate answers to global challenges as well as to compete with big powers. Regional associations of states have overcome the first period of hesitation between a purely national and a consequently continental approach and have been greatly institutionalized over the last three decades – claiming authority over a series of issues that were before under the complete authority of their member states. Such a shift has not been without conflict, but these conflicts indicate that the number is increasing of those who do not believe any longer that the state is the preeminent actor for controlling global flows. And this holds true despite the fact that major powers seem to fall back into protectionist behaviour that such arguments influence political cultures since they resonate with historical references easy to mobilize.

Multipolarity in international relations, virtual spaces across continents filled with music and tweets, transregional value chains spanning long distances, disconnection between global hubs and their hinterlands, maritime basins for so-called blue industries, and exploration of outer space for industrial use – this is but a short list of seemingly or really new phenomena that are creating new challenges to the dialectics of global flows and control.

The Collaborative Research Centre (SFB) 1199: "Processes of Respatialization under the Global Condition", based at Leipzig University, has chosen this focus for its work. The SFB brings people from many area studies together with scholars from the social sciences, history, and cultural studies. It intends to investigate how different societies in the world and over the past two and half centuries have organized themselves spatially to respond to the emerging and since growing global challenges. In defining globalization, we incorporate the dialectics of de- and reterritorialization affecting non-territorial frames of social interaction. In such an understanding, space and spatial literacy are central to the capacities of individuals as well as collective actors to react to border-crossing flows – both new and old. By space, we do not interpret it as a container within which social interaction just happens. On the contrary, we adopt the insights from the various spatial turns that have affected the participating disciplines – at different times and to different degrees but parallel enough to allow meaningful dialogue – and interpret space as the outcome of the interaction among people and between people and nature. By spatial literacy, we mean the capacity to "read" spatial configurations and to have tools available to make such perceptions visible to others. Cartography is probably the most obvious of such tools, but its history and the history of its critics demonstrate what seems to us to be essential when it comes to spatial literacy: it is not gained once for all, but it has to be appropriated again and again against a changing background. The maps that seemed to provide to our ancestors a realistic visualization of the world as its was look now like an ideological construct to hide more than it shows. Critical cartography or geography as a whole has contributed tremendously to such a deconstructivist approach. When we turn the lessons learned from such interventions into a positive message, then it is exactly the fact that spatial literacy is time specific, and the demand for it has both driven processes of professionalization towards geography at university and high school as well as more recently processes of democratization of knowledge, where technology allows almost everyone to produce his or her own maps on a device that is small enough to fit in our pockets. But spatial literacy is more than having the right map at hand. It is the capacity to orient oneself within the world and to formulate priorities for one's own organization of relevant spaces. What is faraway or close by are not necessarily functions of physical distance nor are they spaces of belonging, but they all demand a decision of how we define them according to our interest and to our daily practices of spatialization. Cosmopolitans may define proximity in very different ways from how nationalists proceed. Hence, their spatial literacies differ, and the subsequent question arises which literacy becomes the dominant one in which society.

Since entering the global condition starting in the mid-eighteenth century, such questions are of utmost importance because the answers to them inform our perspectives on a world that is made up of expanding connectedness without becoming flat or free of conflict. On the contrary, competing visions of world order invite one to see the world differently and, as a consequence, to put emphasis on the one or the other spatial format. This has to do with the fact that such world orders are first of all spatial orders, consisting of different spatial formats. To insist on them or to adapt them to challenges produced by new flows that make existing spatial configurations more and more porous becomes a need for those who would like to continue profiting from established modes of rule, authority, and dominance. But newcomers as well as those dissatisfied with the old order again and again design alternative worlds, free from old borders or protecting people through newly drawn boundaries. New technologies, for example, produce the appetite for new spatial formats and raise in many of these cases a sense of resistance to such innovation.

The contributions in this volume are organized in four parts, reflecting the challenges of this agenda, which is not relevant to only one discipline or one area of expertise. Geographers, for example, will probably discover novel insights into familiar debates as they hopefully find new inspiration through the eyes of their colleagues from international studies and history. And vice versa, historians will encounter currently circulating arguments, reconfigured and conceptualized in an enriching way through the lens of a spatial perspective. This volume is therefore an effort to reintegrate two trends in the organization of "knowledge about the world" that have parted following a fundamental transformation happening in the late eigtheenth and early nineteenth century: geographization and historicization. While historicization is acknowledged and increasingly investigated after the initial conceptualization by Reinhart Koselleck, the fundamental connection between globalization and the attention paid to processes of respatialization has, despite attracting a wide spectrum of interesting research directions, not yet led to its coherent rethinking into one concept.

This also may have to do with the inherent Eurocentrism in both these trends – academically institutionalized in the transatlantic West since the late nineteenth century and becoming the dominant lens through which non-Western societies were forced to perceive themselves. This one-way context is addressed in the contributions to this volume either by taking up the challenge from alternative historical and spatial interpretations of the global condition or by bringing into dialogue empirical findings from non-Western, non-European world regions with dominant narratives about how the spatial order of the modern world has emerged. As critics of Eurocentrism have convincingly demonstrated again and again, the Western experience with both the distinction between *ancien régimes* and modern futures and between traditional and modern forms of respatializing the world when being confronted with the global condition is not necessarily relevant for all parts of the world. But with the emergence of the global condition, these distinctions have become more and more transregionally interrelated given the intensifying dialogue across borders and the growing interdependency of societies bound together by trade, division of labour, migration, communication, etc.

The first section develops the conceptual and theoretical repertoire from a geographer's, a historian's, and a sociologist's perspective, with which to tackle and investigate globalization and its driving dialectics. Bob Jessop does not simply repeat the essence of territory, place, scale, and networks approach he has developed more than a decade ago with colleagues from political geography, but he integrates more recent political affairs challenging any teleology towards supra- or transnational organization of governance and engages with the approach developed by the Leipzig-based SFB around the categories of spatial formats and spatial order. Matthias Middell presents an overview of the ongoing research within the SFB and introduces the central categories of processes of respatialization, spatial formats, and spatial orders in more detail and discusses advantages of bringing a historical and a geographical perspective together. Judith Miggelbrink contributes with idea of assemblages, which can be considered an additional lens through which we can see the effects of collective and individual action in the creation of a spatial configuration that has an impact on all these actors and the, often unintended, consequences of their actions. Against this background, the following sections take up these efforts and apply them to specific historical moments and problems.

The second section addresses the conflictive emergence of territorial spatial formats – particularly empire and nation-state – which are until today the elephants in the room in political and academic debates about the spatiality of globalization. These have long dominated the way we think of how societies have in the past and should in the present be organized to successfully compete in an ever more interconnected world. In a *longue durée* perspective spanning the 1780s to present day and bringing together an impressive range of literature, Frank Schumacher counters established teleological narratives about the transition from empire to nation with a focus on the United States, without engaging in the discussion if the US was an empire or not. Instead, he provides a much more nuanced interpretation of US history in the long term as being driven by the entanglement of imperial and national logics of territorialization. Organized around the pivot of the Civil War, his chapter challenges narratives according to which the US emerged afterwards as a stabilized nation-state.

In contrast, he demonstrates how after this alleged caesura empire and nation remains – though in different ways – deeply intertwined ways of spatializing politics and society in and from the US, ways that were related to questions of gender, race, slavery, migration, and overseas colonialism.

John Breuilly complements this agenda of complicating our understanding of the history of territoriality in an equally long-term perspective from the 1790s until today by disentangling the emergence of territoriality as a more general process from the rise of nation-state territoriality more specifically. Productively and critically engaging with the widely debated arguments of Charles Maier, Breuilly unravels different ways of spatializing state sovereignty, of which territoriality has been a quite influential form of coercive power and yet could be combined with or in competition with non-territorial forms such as economic or ideological power. He, furthermore, emphasizes how territorialization – whose "invention" and earliest institutionalization he historically locates in eighteenth-century Europe, which was afterwards enforced on other world regions through imperial projects – has empirically not been a linear, coherent process but instead characterized and fuelled by reverse movements of deterritorialization. Both authors demonstrate that territorialization in these different variations has concerned not only the "space within" but, out of necessity, also the organization of relations to the "outside". Being a contradictory process, it has led not to one but to a number of different spatial formats, in which elites, citizens, and colonial subjects found themselves bound up in – for example, overseas colonies, segregated areas in the US South, an "informal empire", or "nuclear colonialism" – where they imagined, promoted, and resisted different ways of organizing citizenship and identities.

While this section has concentrated on the transatlantic core, the third section moves to seemingly more marginal spaces in the colonial periphery in Africa and their positionality vis-à-vis the metropoles as well as sub-centres in Central Europe and transnational networks connecting European and non-European radicals. Here, the contributions zoom in on cities as portals of globalization, which can both be applied heuristically as spatial formats in their own right as well as be used as a lens through which to observe the *relationality* of spatial formats – such as the empire, the nation-state, or transnational networks. All three contributions in this section consider relationality not only by disentangling the city as a container but also by investigating specific sites, places, and actors in the city, who engage in the reading, imagining, and producing of different spatial formats. To this end, they demonstrate how parts of such cities – not necessarily the city as a whole – are themselves embedded in larger spatial orders, such as the colonial order of Berlin's Africa, the German Empire, or international communism. The conceptual lens of portals of globalization turns out to be particularly productive for investigating the relationality of spatial formats and their consolidation into spatial orders.

As a comparative tour de force of different colonial cities in Berlin's Africa that connects them to imperial metropoles in which the colonial city is situated itself, Geert Castryck's chapter demonstrates not only how colonial elites imagined and aimed to implement the colonial city as an imperial project, but also how it was appropriated by inhabitants of these towns, inhabitants that were themselves often mobile and well connected to communities outside of it, thereby becoming established as key actors for making the connections across the empire work. In this way, it becomes possible to integrate the metropole and the colony into one spatial format of the colonial city by accounting for the different positionalities of actors in relation to the spatial order of colonialism. In a similar manner, in order to comprehend the making and relating of spatial formats, the contributions by Holger Weiß and Antje Dietze focus on actors, the distribution of varying resources, and being situated in often unequal ways in a larger spatial order.

Concentrating on the intense decade of the mid-1920s to mid-1930s at a very specific site in Hamburg, Holger Weiß uncovers multiple and competing projects of institutionalizing radical networks addressing questions of social, racial, economic, and political marginalization. On different scales – international, regional, national, and local – and within varying geographies – addressing different parts of Europe, the US, as well as Asia and Africa – actors such as Albert Walter, James W. Ford, or George Padmore pursued their radical emancipatory projects by establishing places and networks that turned 8 Rothesoodstrasse not only into a hub of Moscow-orchestrated international communism but also into the – not necessarily congruent – struggle of internationally mobile workers as well as black activists from the US and Africa. The focus on this particular site of overlapping struggles and resistance movements enables us to discern the relationality of spatial formats as well as the conflictive ways of their production in the context of a spatial order in transition.

In a similar line of argument, Antje Dietze substantiates the centrality of popular culture as a mode through which spatial formats are imagined, negotiated, as well as related to each other. Examining the panorama industry in Leipzig since the early nineteenth century, with a focus on the final decades of the century, she highlights the role of urban actors – businessmen in particular – as mediators between different economic and cultural circulations and transfers. Combining the analysis of business networks of the panorama industry with an investigation of the form and content of the panoramas themselves, she draws our attention to the methodological implications for the investigation of processes of spatialization under the global condition. She positions the panorama industry as a productive empirical lens through which to investigate the relationality of spatial formats – in her case the empire and the nation – and the connected and fragmented geographies of circulation on a regional and transatlantic scale.

The fourth and final section moves further into the present, focussing on moments and sites in which new spatial formats are imagined, institutionalized, and struggled with, when older spatial orders – be it formed by empires or nation-states – become contested and as a result fragile. As Glenda Sluga shows, the spatial imaginary of "international spaces" is not only invoked by scholars and intellectuals but also partially institutionalized politically and economically in frontier zones and in moments of crisis. Here, actors either aim to defend an already introduced spatial format, such as the empire, or to further strengthen, adapt, and stabilize fledgling proposals such as the nation-state, by using internationalization to assert sovereignty.

A similar dialectic seems to explain the rise of new regionalisms in the Global South, as Ulf Engel demonstrates. Even though regionalization and the establishing of regional organizations are far from new phenomena, dating back to the early nineteenth century, these processes have been appropriated – under conditions of post-colonial state-building and changing forms of territorialization in the second half of the twentieth century in the transatlantic West – by actors in the Global South to legitimize alternative ways of imagining and implementing territorial sovereignty. While these efforts seem to have blossomed after the end of the Cold War, this period saw significant experimentation with new spatial formats as well as the translation and adaptation of the world of empires with logics of national and transnational spatializations, as Steffi Marung, Uwe Müller, and Stephan Troebst argue in their chapter about the bloc. Its emergence as a political and an analytical concept, which has been characterized by massive tensions, has been the result of the efforts of actors within and outside the bloc to reorganize a post-colonial world in Eastern Europe and to develop new ways of connecting to societies in the Global South.

Sarah Ruth Sippel and Michaela Böhme investigate the consequences of new transregional ties between large suppliers of agricultural goods in Australia and the growing appetite of an urban Chinese population for meat and new crops. What appears to some as a self-evident match of supply and demand is for others a dangerous occupation of land by foreigners or an inadequate marketization of natural resources. Imaginations of what land may mean cross the flows of capital and food in a conflictual way and the encounter produces new ideas about the "right" spatialization at times of demographic pressure on food supply, of increasing financialization of agri-food industries and a transformation brought about by the continued digitalization in this business.

Another process that hints at the same direction is analysed by Hannes Warnecke-Berger, who takes a closer look at remittances that come with labour migration and have reached a point where entire former national economies depend largely, or even predominantly, on income resulting from such transfers from abroad. Investigating the effect of these transfers on the macroeconomic development of the countries concerned, he further asks how these connections between migrants and their families or village communities/urban neighbourhoods at home are morally embedded. His main finding is the robust structure of what looks at first like simply an economic transaction through mutual moral dependency, for which he introduces the term moral economy, borrowed from historical research of proto-capitalist periods. Both cases presented by Sippel and Böhme as well as by Warnecke-Berger demonstrate that there is no exclusive relationship between economic and cultural dimensions of respatialization.

Overall, this is a first step into a new field. We are far from an all-encompassing typology, and it may be that we never reach it because the processes of respatialization will not end producing new spatial formats and, as a consequence, also new spatial orders. However, we can conclude from the examples given in this volume that two sorts of spatial formats can be encountered: those building on the achievements of a process of territorialization and those making use of border-crossing connections between individual places or sites.

The first sort of spatial formats has its ideal type in the complete nation-state, with the vast majority of economic as well as cultural activities and social relations being organized within the territory of such a state. It becomes evident that this ideal type cannot be found in reality for both historical and systematic reasons. On the one hand, it is a very rare exception if not an impossibility that all social interactions happen (even the majority) on only one territory, given the historical connectedness that dates back to millennia of mobility. Fantasies of ethnic purity or of economic autarky may occur, but they are in conflict with omnipresent effects of entanglements. Wherever territorialization has not reached the point of absolute completion, we can witness asymmetries in power between all kinds of minorities and those claiming to be the ruling majority. Projections of this configuration result in imperialist behaviour towards people in occupied lands and colonies. On the other hand, the creation of nation-states has not happened ex nihilo but has been a reaction to global challenges, as argued above. Therefore, it coexists *systematically* with global connections to which it reacts and within which it is embedded.

The other ideal type of spatial formats is probably the value chain, connecting sites of production across the globe. They are often imagined as completely disentangled from their hinterlands and in some cases – for example, with some, but by far not all, special economic zones – powerful actors are able to ensure this disconnection to a certain degree in order to profit from such deterritorialization. But even in the most exceptional of such cases, family ties persist, dependencies on political stability count, and people drudging in the factories use the infrastructures of territories after work is done.

For the sake of a typology, it makes sense to distinguish between these two ideal types; however, for a historical explanation of changes in the spatial order, it seems more fruitful to look at the interactions between the various spatial formats and their combination for the profit of certain projects of globalization, which are always at the same time projects of respatialization of the world. The described ideal types should not be confused with historical accounts of a single national or regional development, but still they certainly have an extraordinary importance for the imaginations of existing world orders or proclaimed alternatives. They inspire fantasies of how the world should be spatially organized and mobilize enormous societal energies.

Part I: **Concepts and Historicity**

Matthias Middell
Category of Spatial Formats: To What End?

Starting Point: Space as an Indispensable Dimension of Social Relations

Human actions – individual and collective – occur in space and time. Thus, space is a central dimension of social interaction and the resulting social relations.[1] Actors make use of geographic space when representing the spatial dimensions of their actions, when they apply widely accepted categories for framing and structuring these spaces, and when they create spaces through their social relations.

Conversely, one could say that every social interaction has, at least, one spatial dimension and often multiple dimensions. The French sociologist and philosopher Henri Lefebvre developed his memorable spatial triad to capture typologically the various spatial dimensions that can be found in one social interaction: *espace perçu* (the tangible, materialized, socially-produced space[2]), *espace conçu* (the totality of linguistic, visual, and other codifications that actors use to represent space), and *espace vécu* (lived space). While one may disagree with Lefebvre's classificatory system, its basic premise is undeniable: the diversity of spatial dimensions that accompany and characterize social relations cannot be reduced to any one dimension nor to the sum of its parts.

Spaces and Spatial Formats

This basic premise helps us comprehend why it is so difficult to develop a systematic understanding of the various spatial dimensions. This, certainly, does not mean that these spatial dimensions are a recent invention of the social sciences, which were overlooked in the past. Earlier theorists understood, for example, that battles took place at specific sites because these sites were of geostrategic significance; they understood that shipping lanes developed along

---
[1] B. Werlen, *Gesellschaft und Raum*, Stuttgart: Franz Steiner Verlag, 1988.
[2] "This is the materialized, socially-produced space that exists empirically. It is directly sensible or perceivable – open to measurement and description. It is both the medium and the outcome of human activity, behaviour and experience" (H. Lefebvre, *The Production of Space*, Oxford: Blackwell Publishing, 1991).

specific routes and to certain destinations because experience had taught that there wind and sea conditions were favourable and a profit could be made. But social action is not determined by only a few geographical characteristics, and the resulting complexity can be perceived as being contingent, rather than accidental, on the location of an event or a geographical frame. The production of space most often is the result of many interfering processes of spatialization, therefore making it difficult to decipher. At times where the world appears as increasingly interconnected, this complexity causes tension since old hierarchies of such spatial frames are dissolving and without necessarily being replaced by new clear-cut hierarchies of important and less important spatial frames of social interaction. It is no wonder that the debate about "globalization" has also brought about a new spatial turn, stretching over many different academic disciplines and problematizing in very different ways the relationship between revised societal theories – or narratives – that take their point of departure from the category of modern globalization and observations of processes of spatialization.

That said, our understanding of experiences of spatiality has evolved over time. Thus, it is valid to enquire into caesuras of our understanding and to investigate the origins of our current categories for describing processes of space-making. This leads to the broad sphere of enquiry addressed by the various lines of geographic history.[3] Within these lines, abstract concepts have been developed to capture the spatial dimension of social relations; these concepts have been quickly translated into worldviews, from which multiple distinct cartographic languages and spatial semantics have emerged. But the suitability and usefulness of these representations have been repeatedly called into question and thus have been subject to near constant renewal.[4] This dissatisfaction has accompanied the development of different cartographic languages and persists today.

The preference for representing spatial relations in visual images went hand in hand with the use of a rich metaphoric language and analogies drawn from the available knowledge, experiences, and ideologies. For example, in describing imperial space, early modern European theorists drew on the experience of the

---

[3] W.E. Murray, *Geographies of Globalization*, Abingdon: Routledge, 2006; I. Schröder, *Das Wissen von der ganzen Welt: Globale Geografien und räumliche Ordnungen Afrikas und Europas, 1790–1870*, Paderborn: Verlag Ferdinand Schöningh, 2011; J.D. Sidaway et al., "Area Studies and Geography: Trajectories and Manifesto", *Environment and Planning D: Society and Space* 34 (2016) 5, pp. 777–790.
[4] C. Grataloup, *L'invention des continents: Comment l'Europe a découpé le Monde*, Paris: Larousse, 2009; C. Grataloup, *Géohistoire de la mondialisation*, Paris: Armand Colin, 2010.

Roman Empire.[5] This development cannot be explored in depth here, suffice it to say that the cartographic languages and spatial semantics, still available to us today, are the product of various earlier stages of reimagining the world or parts of it.[6] Yet, spatialization has eluded any conclusive systemization, instead repeatedly being subject to scrutiny. Historically, we have seen periods in which spatial semantics acquired a degree of stability. But these periods were always replaced by less stable ones, in which reflection on new issues precipitated a rapid expansion in spatial semantics and technological advancements as well as produced new forms of map-making and standards of cartographic representation.[7]

The last three decades certainly fall into the latter category; with the intensification of cross-border, transnational, transregional, and even global processes, the spatial dimensions of social relations have become more and more complex. This complexity has led to a devaluation of established spatial relations, along with a growing interest among some actors in reimagining space. As a result, traditional strategies for reducing the (ever-present) complexity of processes of space-making have come under attack, prompting a proliferation of spatial metaphors, in which the word "space" has frequently been combined with other social dimensions to indicate the applicable perspective. A steady stream of books and essays, since the 1990s, have described or posited the emergence or increased relevance of a plethora of "new spaces", inter alia, social and political spaces, literary spaces, spaces of violence and of peace, border regions and deterritorialized spaces, imperial and transnational spaces, spaces of knowledge, global spaces, geographic spaces, spaces of entanglement, and interstitial spaces.

---

5 A. Pagden, *The Burdens of Empire: 1539 to the Present*, Cambridge: Cambridge University Press, 2015.
6 A. Ramachandran, *The Worldmakers: Global Imagining in Early Modern Europe*, Chicago: University of Chicago Press, 2015.
7 K. Wigen, "Cartographies of Connection: Ocean Maps as Metaphors for Interarea History", in: J.H. Bentley, R. Bridenthal and A.A. Yang (eds.), *Interactions: Transregional Perspectives on World History*, Honolulu: University of Hawai'i Press, 2005, pp. 150–166; G. Pápay, "Kartographie", in: S. Günzel (ed.), *Raumwissenschaften*, Frankfurt/Main: Suhrkamp, 2009, pp. 175–191; B. Schellhase and U. Wardenga, "'Inzwischen spricht die Karte für sich selbst': Transformation von Wissen im Prozess der Kartenproduktion", in: S. Siegel (ed.), *Kartographieren: Materialien und Praktiken visueller Welterzeugung*, Berlin: De Gruyter, 2011; M. Picker, V. Maleval and F. Gabaude (eds.), *Die Zukunft der Kartographie: Neue und nicht so neue epistemologische Krisen*, Bielefeld: transcript Verlag, 2013; W. Rankin, *After the Map: Cartography, Navigation, and the Transformation of Territory in the Twentieth Century*, Chicago: University of Chicago Press, 2016; A. Kent and P. Vujakovic (eds.), *The Routledge Handbook of Mapping and Cartography*, Abingdon: Routledge, 2018.

This is not to say that these metaphors are not expressing a theoretically coherent framework, at which they may imply. Instead, they are occasionally used as categories for theoretical generalizations. They express an often empirically based understanding, in that all social interactions (including those addressed in such studies) involve processes of space-making. That said, studies of such "hyphenated spaces" too often focus on space as a container for a specific type of social relation, thereby failing to consider how spatial relations and representations of those relations continually stabilize, destabilize, and change these spaces.

At the same time, this proliferation signals an increasing understanding among observers that customary patterns of spatiality are being challenged. They are losing their legitimacy and/or relevance and others are gaining currency. The increased presence of metaphors in the spatial semantics points to a change in the way processes of space-making are conceived, ordered, institutionalized, and normalized.

A proliferation of new and metaphorical spatial semantics should not be equated with increased clarity. On the contrary, the amplification of discourse about "space", we argue, signifies a growing mindfulness to two fundamental issues of our age (the significance of spatial relations and the transformation of traditional forms of spatial relations) – without any corresponding greater insight into fundamental questions about what characterizes these spaces, how they relate to one another, or whether resulting spatial orders are becoming increasingly complex within the context of processes of globalization. In short, simply postulating new "spaces", we contend, no longer represents a promising strategy for answering the above questions.

The following essay seeks to explore paths to a heuristic approach that is inspired by the various strands of the current debate, but which moves beyond postulating new hyphenated spaces. To this end, we propose two concepts – spatial format and spatial order – which, we think, can help elucidate the co-constitution of processes of space-making and the global condition.

If in every situation involving social interaction, multiple spatial dimensions are brought into play; we must first ask by whom. Spatial dimensions do not exist in the abstract; instead they result from the spatializing actions of individual and collective actors. These actions are multifaceted and fleeting. Field research inspired by ethnographic methods, that is to say a precise and detailed description of the observed, is the closest that we can come to capturing them. Nevertheless, this methodology has its limits, as we are soon confronted with a huge variety of more or less consequential observations. Consequently, attention to scale and societal relevance is critical; only in their standardized form do processes of space-making take on significance for society as a whole and thus are useful in analysing collective processes of space-making.

Accordingly, we can say that processes of space-making, *firstly*, result in routines that stabilize over time. But, *secondly*, only some of these stabilized routines become institutionalized; they are defined and validated as well as assume relevance in the public sphere. For this to happen, not only must these processes of space-making occur repeatedly over a lengthy period of time, they must also converge in relation to a format and the apprehension of this format must be collectively shared. This includes also, *thirdly*, that such formats are named and that a collective acceptance as such emerges. Spatializing activities have, *fourthly*, to be performed and have to be performative in order to become accepted and therefore successful and powerful as spatial formats in a given social context.[8]

Our proposed concept for describing the results of such processes of space-making, which are characterized by long-term repetition, standardization, performativity, and institutionalization, as well as by the collective imaginings of their stability, is spatial format. Spatial formats by no means only result from political space-making. They can also be the product of cultural and economic activities. But most importantly, because of their institutional component and the imaginations associated with their formation, they are often connected to politico-administrative processes and respectively ideological interpretations.

One example that comes to mind is the German notion of *Volkswirtschaft*, which may translated as national economy and which addresses the fact that economic actors found it an increasingly attractive way (in the second half of the nineteenth as well as in large parts of the twentieth centuries) to conceive of their market-driven interaction within the spatial framework of a nation-state and to rely on statistics and other information focusing on this framework. The term *Volkswirtschaft* hints at the fact that this format became important even before the official establishment of the German Empire as nation-state in 1871 and during a period when culture and assumed ethnic roots helped in defining the space of ever-intensified economic interaction.

---

8 As a good introduction, both historical and systematic, to the performative turn, see J. Martschukat and S. Patzold (eds.), *Geschichtswissenschaft und "Performative Turn": Ritual, Inszenierung und Performanz vom Mittelalter bis zur Neuzeit*, Cologne: Böhlau Verlag, 2003. The authors argue that this performative turn took inspiration from speech act theory, theatre studies understood as cultural studies, the investigation of ritual beyond its framework of religious studies, and finally gender studies ("doing gender"). A parallel strand of interest in performativity developed within cultural geography with the concept of doing space.

Politico-administrative and economic forms of space-making converge and stabilize each other mutually.

The convergence of multiple processes of space-making into a spatial format, without a doubt, does not take place in a vacuum. There is always a pre-existing world, which spatial formats interpret and in which the social interactions are integrated. In many cases, when certain processes of space-making lose importance or even come to an end, it does not challenge existing spatial formats, but rather confirms them. This is either because the now acting subjects adjust their renewed processes of space-making to the spatial formats they encounter or because they do not want their ideas about the relevant spatial formats to appear to blatantly contradict socially accepted ideas. This dialectic in which existing and imagined spatial formats are juxtaposed, synthesized, and reconciled leads to the stabilization of the generated spatial formats over the course of long historical phases. Cities or regions may serve as examples here since the perceived continuity of their existence hides – only artificially – that central actors, primary directions, and important functionalities of space-making processes have changed dramatically while slipping into an already accepted and seemingly continued shell.

In contrast to the above situation, there are situations in which spatial formats are explicitly challenged and are no longer considered adequate. This type of challenge initiates a period of uncertainty and a search for new spatial formats capable of remedying the identified deficiencies of older spatial formats. Once such new formats are found, the previously described process of stabilization and legitimation begins.

Spatial formats originate from processes of space-making and have the following characteristics:
- A positive or negative association with an existing set of spatial formats (action-driven imaginations of the appropriate spatial formats for the realization of processes of space-making);
- Multiple institutionalizations (including the establishment of an infrastructure that facilitates stabilization and makes it visible);
- A conspicuous charge in importance through description, designation, and functional assignment;
- A certain historical stability over longer periods of time;
- They are performed in multiple ways and by multiple actors to the end that they are deeply rooted in the perception of daily-life routines of the many.

Spatial formats are thus both structures that shape social actions and imaginations that guide social actions. They do not become powerful drivers of both action and imagination if they are not being performed through speech acts, rituals, and other performative acts or having a strong connection to influential narratives circulating in the concerned community.

From a systematic point of view, spatial formats originate from the multiplicity of processes of space-making and from a historical point of view; they replace, complement, or compete with already existing spatial formats.

Abstraction and Ideal Types

Spatial formats, thus, are directly related to tangible actions, but at the same time are the products of a process of abstraction. To borrow Max Weber's terminology, spatial formats simultaneously bear the traits of the actual and the ideal type. As a result, there was much confusion in earlier histories of science addressing spatiality – the most impressive example being the notion that the nation-state represented the culmination of historical development and the optimal spatial format for meeting the challenges of modern globalization. This idea, which gained currency in the last third of the nineteenth century, is now labelled methodological nationalism and is rejected by most social scientists as a particular feature of Eurocentrism.[9] And yet, methodological nationalism and Eurocentrism respectively have proven stubbornly resilient, continuing to influence thinking about processes of space-making. Overcoming this bias, as discussions have shown, requires that we consider empirical evidence that extends beyond the West. This does not mean that we should replace one centrism with another, but rather we must advance a heuristic firmly grounded in multiperspectivity.

The territory, place, scale, and networks (TPSN) framework, as outlined by Jessop, Brenner, and Jones,[10] tackles these inherited, unreflective geographic assumptions through the elaboration of abstract concepts describing ideal typical components of four key dimensions of sociospatial relations. In devising these concepts, Jessop, Brenner, and Jones painstakingly attempt to distance themselves from actual historical-social processes of space-making. The abstracted concepts are then used as heuristic devices for assessing the current or historical

---

[9] A. Wimmer and N. Glick-Schiller, "Methodological Nationalism and Beyond: Nation-State Building, Migration and the Social Sciences", *Global Networks* 2 (2002) 4, pp. 301–334; A. Amelina (ed.), *Beyond Methodological Nationalism: Research Methodologies for Cross-border Studies*, Abingdon: Routledge, 2012.

[10] B. Jessop, N. Brenner and M. Jones, "Theorizing Sociospatial Relations", *Environment and Planning D: Society and Space* 26 (2008) 3, pp. 389–401; B. Jessop, "Territory, Politics, Governance and Multispatial Metagovernance", *Territory, Politics, Governance* 4 (2016) 1, pp. 8–32.

sociospatial landscape. But what the authors fail to consider is that the construction of ideal types is always done from a certain perspective, hence clashing with post-structuralist doubts about science's claim of objectivity.

The strength of the ideal type approach is not multiperspectivity. This becomes apparent in the descriptions used by the TPSN approach, which rely on a particular system of linguistic conventions and so could not be easily applied, for example, in languages used by non-Europeans, who insist on the particularity of their own intellectual traditions and historical roots. Additionally, ideal types effectively bring time to a standstill, in that they are always formulated from the perspective of a particular present. Thus, the path dependency and alternativity of historical developments are obfuscated. Again, this expresses itself as a problem of language, this time of its historical charge by certain experiences tied to a historical situation (such as the Europe of the late nineteenth century).

Intentionality

Processes of space-making arise from the actions, thoughts, and feelings of individuals as well as from every type of social organization as an expression of collective action. However, to reduce all of these to intentional spatializations would fall short of the mark. Processes of space-making that lack intentionality, in many cases, leave no long-term traces on collective perception (albeit they may have a lasting impact on certain individuals), and so are subject to little or no analysis.

Consequently, we need to make an important distinction. Certain forms of action address the spatial dimension directly and so are investigated in many academic disciplines as processes of space-making (including geopolitics). However, in other social interactions, the spatial dimension remains in the background. Processes of space-making are not explicitly addressed by actor but disappear in the face of other concerns, be they of an economic, a cultural, or a political nature.[11] But when these spatial structures, created or changed by these social interactions, are mobilized by existing power structures,[12] it prompts a closer examination (beyond academic interest in the geography) of

---

[11] This is discussed in greater detail and with reference to an abundant political science literature by H. Zinecker, "Maras as Producers of Translocal Spaces of Violence: Theoretical Model and Structure of Argument", SFB Working Paper 1 (2018).

[12] N. Thrift, "On the Determination of Social Action in Space and Time", *Environment and Planning D: Society and Space* 1 (1983) 1, pp. 23–56; N. Thrift, *Spatial Formations*, London: Sage, 1996.

the involved processes of space-making. While they are no longer taken for granted, a certain reductionism takes place. The space that ostensibly structures action is reduced to a mere container, which – although not limiting the observed action – requires no further investigation. This negligence in determining more precisely the relationship between action and space-making has been broached by various parties.[13]

Already in 1967, Michel Foucault had intuited:

> The great obsession of the nineteenth century was, as we know, history: with its themes of development and of suspension, of crisis and cycle, themes of the ever-accumulating past, with its great preponderance of dead men and the menacing glaciation of the world. [...] The present epoch perhaps will be above all the epoch of space. We are in the epoch of simultaneity: we are in the epoch of juxtaposition, the epoch of the near and far, of the side-by-side, of the dispersed. We are at a moment, I believe, when our experience of the world is less that of a long life developing through time than that of a network that connects points and intersects with its own skein.[14]

It seems to us not by chance that the French theorist rejected a temporalization of spatiallydefinable differences. As was typical of modernization theory, his theory was formulated at the intersection of two trends, symbolized by the looming defeat of technologically superior US troops in Vietnam and the emergence of the Internet. The idea that one could translate synchronous difference into diachronic difference became less and less convincing, especially after the war in Vietnam had been lost.[15] Moreover, the revolutionary acceleration of communication initiated by the Internet (comparable to the introduction of the telegraph in the mid-nineteenth century) quickly upended the technological advantages that had underpinned the rigid order of the First, Second, and Third Worlds.

Admittedly, Foucault's premonition has not materialized as quickly as catchphrases of the current epoch would suggest. In 2000, the American historian Charles Maier repeated Foucault's conjecture, but by now the tone was one of confirmed diagnosis:

> The concept of hierarchically organized Fordist production based on a national territory was supplanted by the imagery, if not always the reality, of globally coordinated

---

[13] Various authors have written essays attempting to introduce this turn in the social sciences. See, e.g., R. Kosselleck, *Zeitschichten: Studien zur Historik*, Frankfurt/Main: Suhrkamp, 2000, pp. 78–96.
[14] See J.W. Crampton and S. Elden (eds.), *Space, Knowledge and Power: Foucault and Geography*, Abingdon: Routledge, 2007.
[15] D. Milne, *America's Rasputin: Walt Rostow and the Vietnam War*, New York: Hill & Wang, 2008.

networks of information, mobile capital and migratory labour. [...] Decisive resources will not be those of space but of networks and interaction, regardless of the area over which they take place.[16]

Spatial Turn and Spatial Literacy

The late 1960s witnessed an expanding scholarly interest in space and processes of space-making. This interest, which continues today, has been labelled the "spatial turn", creating the mistaken impression that this was the first time that scholars had taken note of space and spatial processes.[17] This, certainly, is not true for geography, an academic discipline that owed its existence to a series of developments in knowledge systems, most notably the transition from the Newtonian concept of absolute space to a relational understanding of space at the turn of the twentieth century.[18] Thus, instead of speaking of a singular spatial turn, it would be more productive to assume multiple epistemological breaks. The long history of geographic imaginations and ideologies clearly indicate that the epistemological and experiential foundations of our current interest in space are not limited to the last quarter of the twentieth century.[19] As Benno Werlen notes:

---

16 C.S. Maier, "Consigning the 20th Century to History: Alternative Narratives for the Modern Era", *American Historical Review* 105 (2000) 3, pp. 807–831.

17 See, e.g., J. Döring and T. Thielmann, *Spatial Turn: Das Raumparadigma in den Kultur- und Sozialwissenschaften*, Bielefeld: transcript Verlag, 2008; B. Warf and S. Arias (eds.), *Spatial Turn: Interdisciplinary Perspectives*, Abingdon: Routledge, 2009; F. Williamson, "The Spatial Turn of Social and Cultural History: A Review of the Current Field", *European History Quarterly* 44 (2014) 4, pp. 703–717.

18 We do not wish to give the erroneous impression that the history of spatial turns started in or was limited to Europe. Presumably, the formation of larger social units on the basis of tribe or ethnicity had already attracted attention to the issue of claimed space and its limitations, as had confrontations between nomadic and settler communities. However, documentation, at best is rudimentary and thus research is difficult. Documentation is better with the emergence of large empires, as various reference works have now addressed comparatively: P.F. Bang and C.A. Bayly (eds.), *Tributary Empires in Global History*, Basingstoke: Palgrave Macmillan, 2011; P.F. Bang and D. Kołodziejczyk (eds.), *Universal Empire: A Comparative Approach to Imperial Culture and Representation in Eurasian History*, Cambridge: Cambridge University Press, 2012; P.F. Bang and W. Scheidel (eds.), *The Oxford Handbook of the State in the Ancient Near East and Mediterranean*, Oxford: Oxford University Press, 2013.

19 M.W. Lewis and K. Wigen, *The Myth of Continents: A Critique of Metageography*, Berkeley: University of California Press, 1997.

Socio-spatial relations have always been and remain above all changeable. They are socio-cultural and artificial in nature. Thus, the current shift does not indicate the "end" or the collapse of "true geography" that should be prevented. Rather, the challenge for scientific geography is to make this new geographic reality comprehensible. It is surely one of the most important and noble duties of this discipline to prepare present and future generations for a life under new geographic conditions and thus to focus on processes of globalization – with their positive as well as problematic implications.[20]

Clearly, political, economic, or social spatial formats cannot be easily separated from spatial imaginations, even if for analytical purposes this is necessary.

Spatial imaginations – along with associated speech acts and symbolic forms – are important, but by themselves they do not suffice to explain changing spatial formats and spatial orders under the global condition, past or present. Changes in spatial semantics and shifts in the significance of spatial imaginations indicate that new processes of space-making have been proposed or gained currency. New spatial imaginations or the re-evaluation of current or past spatial imaginations are attempts at creating a new spatial literacy that is capable of describing changed spatial structures. In other words, it is an effort to interpret changing spatial conditions and make them the basis of action. As scholars, we participate in these processes of creating and transforming current spatial literacy. Thus, rather than describing an abstract orientation or an ability to read maps – uncritically put forward as timeless – spatial literacy is an intellectual awareness of changes in the processes of space-making that is historically conditioned and mutable. Spatial literacy, therefore, can be seen as a kind of crisis management initiative that allows societies to adapt to a new stage of global connectivity.

Critical Junctures of Globalization

Recent debates on sociospatial theory suggest that the "spatial turn", beginning in the 1970s, was not the first such turn:
1. Research on the origins of the category "territory" suggests a comparable shock in understandings of space in the late sixteenth century[21] and has allowed for a new conceptualization of the relationship between empire and practices of territorialization.

---

20 B. Werlen, *Gesellschaft, Handlung, Raum*, Stuttgart: Franz Steiner Verlag, 2017.
21 S. Elden, *The Birth of Territory*, Chicago: University of Chicago Press, 2013.

2. The nationalization of language, which calls to mind the crisis of empire in the late eighteenth and early nineteenth centuries, can also be seen as a comparable crisis, in which the semantics of space changed dramatically.
3. The late nineteenth century produced a new language of space addressing world markets, global politics, as well as transnational nations. This development reflected that a "trivial" nationalization was no longer viewed as providing an adequate description of spatial relations.[22]
4. The change in spatial semantics in the last three decades, now with explicit references to the concept of globalization, goes hand in hand with an intensified scientific debate as well as with exploratory movements by political, cultural, and economic actors seeking to find an appropriate response to new challenges of the spatial order after the end of the seeming stability of the Cold War.

These phases in which changing spatial dynamics are perceived as extremely unsettling are replaced by those in which the understanding of sociospatial relations stabilize. In this latter phase, something akin to the idea of a "correct" geography, that is to say a representation of spatial relations justified by the experiences of large groups of people in different regions, emerges. But it is during the periods of intense uncertainty, transformation, and even upheaval that our understanding of spatial relations adapts to new global connections. We can call them critical junctures of globalization since they are all to a certain degree moments and arenas of a rearrangement (often accompanied by violence) between border-crossing flows and the attempt to regain control over such flows while making use of their profitability.[23]

---

[22] J. Osterhammel, "Raumbeziehungen: Internationale Geschichte, Geopolitik und historische Geographie", in: W. Loth and J. Osterhammel (eds.), *Internationale Geschichte: Themen-Ergebnisse-Aussichten*, Berlin: De Gruyter, 2000, pp. 287–308; J. Osterhammel, "Raumerfassung und Universalgeschichte", in: J. Osterhammel (ed.), *Geschichtswissenschaft jenseits des Nationalstaats. Studien zu Beziehungsgeschichte und Zivilisationsvergleich*, Göttingen: Vandenhoeck & Ruprecht, 2001, pp. 151–169; on Randolph Bourne's "Trans-National America" (1916), see the analysis of K. K. Patel, "Nach der Nationalfixiertheit: Perspektiven einer transnationalen Geschichte", Inaugural lecture, Faculty of Philosophy of Humboldt University of Berlin, 12 January 2004, https://edoc.hu-berlin.de/bitstream/handle/18452/2330/Patel.pdf?sequence=1.

[23] See U. Engel and M. Middell, "Bruchzonen der Globalisierung, globale Krisen und Territorialitätsregimes – Kategorien einer Globalgeschichtsschreibung", *Comparativ: Zeitschrift für Globalgeschichte und vergleichende Gesellschaftsforschung* 15 (2005), 5–6, pp. 5–38; M. Middell and K. Naumann, "Global History and the Spatial Turn: From the Impact of Area Studies to the Study of Critical Junctures of Globalisation", *Journal of Global History* 5 (2010) 1, pp. 149–170.

Spatial Formats and Spatial Order(s)

These spatial conditions, subject to constant negotiation, are based on the development of new spatial formats, on the revaluation of old formats, and on the joining of these spatial formats in a spatial order, whose scale is still to be determined. These thoughts are based on four observations:

1. All social actions and interactions have one or more spatial dimensions. Only a small percentage of the routines resulting from such processes of space-making become (relatively) stable spatial formats. This stability is achieved through repetition, institutionalization, performance, and reflexivity (definition and authentication).
2. Spatial formats that emerge from specific processes of space-making never exist in isolation. Instead they exist in specific relationships with other spatial formats (in competition with, complementary to, or parallel with). Together with other formats, they form a structure consisting of all the spatial dimensions of social interaction. This structure we call spatial order. For analytical purposes, these spatial orders can be treated as distinct sectors (e.g. Argentina, Eurasia, or the free trade zone in colonized Africa established by the Berlin conference in the late nineteenth century). To investigate the one or the other of these configurations, it makes sense to treat it as a spatial order in its own right. Nevertheless, we realize that such spatial orders are increasingly interconnected and cannot be completely understood without taking into consideration the different linkages it has with other parts of the world – be it mutual influence, strong opposition, or an asymmetric power relation. Therefore, in principle it must be assumed that under the global condition all spatial orders – regional (including supra- and intra-regional) and national – are increasingly interdependent.[24] If they merge into one global spatial order or continue, at least partly, to follow their own logics is a question for further conceptual debate as well as empirical investigation. The fact that some dream of a world order guaranteed by a few, or even only one remaining, superpowers and others insist on the necessity of a one-world approach to save the world from self-destructive forces of mankind is not reason enough to echo these dreams in scholarly contributions that support constructing such a worldwide spatial order. It might be that imagination differs from the real integration of spatial formats and different

---

24 M. Castells, *The Rise of the Network Society*, Hoboken: Wiley-Blackwell, 2010.

spatial orders into one.[25] What becomes clear from recent scholarship is that this does not mean that this process results in a homogenous spatial order, in which networking is increasingly linear. On the contrary, interdependencies tend to increase imbalances in resources, power, and perceived proximity. The concept of spatial order should not be confused with the assumption of a single world society devoid of inequalities and asymmetries of power.[26]

3. The resulting constellation of spatial formats – the spatial order – periodically enters a critical phase of contestation, precipitating a search for new spatial forms, which can reconcile the spatial dimension of social action with the changing interests and ideas of the actors involved. During such phases of uncertainty, we often see a proliferation of spatial semantics. But this proliferation of spatial semantics does not necessarily indicate a proliferation of spatial formats; instead, it can also indicate that existing spatial format(s) require a new intellectual foundation or a new position within the spatial order.
4. This dynamic is further fuelled by the increase in global flows and efforts to regain control of them, so that with the entry into the global era the intervals between phases in which we see a proliferation of spatial semantics and increased uncertainty over the continued existence of established spatial formats shorten.

Case Studies

Studying such processes via a selection of case studies as in the Collaborative Research Centre (SFB) 1199: "Processes of Spatialization under the Global Condition",[27] cannot be limited to a specific region of the world (e.g. the Global

---

[25] N. Luhmann, "Die Weltgesellschaft", in: N. Luhmann, *Soziologische Aufklärung*, vol. II, Wiesbaden: VS Verlag für Sozialwissenschaften, 1975, pp. 63–88.

[26] R. Stichweh, *Die Weltgesellschaft: Soziologische Analysen*, Frankfurt/Main: Suhrkamp, 2000; S. Vietta, *Die Weltgesellschaft: Wie die abendländische Rationalität die Welt erobert und verändert hat*, Baden-Baden: Nomos, 2016.

[27] Such case studies are currently conducted in the framework of individual subprojects of the Leipzig-based Collaborative Research Centre (SFB) 1199: "Processes of Spatialization under the Global Condition" (for details, see SFB 1199, "Welcome", <http://research.uni-leipzig.de/~sfb1199/index.php?id=7> (accessed 14 December 2018) and as dissertations that are part of the doctoral programme of the Graduate School Global and Area Studies (see Graduate School Global and Area Studies, "Home", <https://home.uni-leipzig.de/~gsgas> (accessed 14 December 2018)).

North) nor can it be reduced to the very recent past[28]; it requires investigating processes over lengthy periods of time. But this is much more than the illustration of diversity over space and time. In contrast to a purely inductive approach to theorizing, it is important for this project to acknowledge that the totality of spatial formats cannot be determined. Our case studies, for this reason, do not endeavour to classify understudied historic situations according to a fixed theoretical framework having a limited number of categories; instead, we seek to discover spatial formats previously not recognized as such. In so doing, the research initially participated in the above-mentioned proliferation of spatial semantics, but now, through its inductive approach, has turned to examining to what extent the identified spatial formats are novel or represent a variation on spatial formats found elsewhere.

A deductive approach that starts with defining the totality of spatial formats does not, however, seem appropriate for a multitude of reasons. First, our current understanding of the object of research is rudimentary both regarding past historical eras and the present. This is due in no small measure to the fact that only recently have categories for spatial formats and spatial orders been proposed. Thus, existing research must first be scrutinized to determine to what extent past findings are transferable to this concept. One of the central challenges is identifying transitions from processes of space-making to the establishment of spatial formats, based on the previously outlined criteria of stabilization, scale, performativity, and reflexivity. In addition, we need to undertake a comparable empirical effort aimed at identifying which spatial semantics circulate beyond the borders of a particular world region and the extent to which this suggests that similar spatial formats are establishing themselves in different parts of the world.[29]

---

[28] For a still valid collection of critical viewpoints and responses to them, see J.M. Blaut, *The Colonizer's Model of the World: Geographical Diffusionism and Eurocentric History*, New York: Guilford, 1993; A. Dirlik, "Is there History after Eurocentrism? Globalism, Postcolonialism, and the Disavowal of History", *Cultural Critique* 42 (1999) 2, pp. 1–34; D. Chakrabarty, *Provincializing Europe: Postcolonial Thought and Historical Difference*, Princeton: Princeton University Press, 2000; S. Conrad and S. Randeria (eds.), *Jenseits des Eurozentrismus: Postkoloniale Perspektiven in den Geschichts- und Kulturwissenschaften*, Frankfurt/Main: Campus, 2002.

[29] For some spatial formats, such as empire and nation-state, there is a widespread assumption that they are universal. However, the objection has been raised that one must closely examine the actors advancing this idea of universality: Is their assumption based on an unreflective Eurocentrism, or is it an appropriation by elites in other parts of the world who use these spatial semantics to legitimize their sometimes completely different interests? The debate about "weak or failed nation-states" contains numerous indications both that it is

These first two issues could, as one may argue, more or less easily be resolved through an appropriate research effort. But the third reason why we cannot ascertain the totality of spatial formats is contained within the definition itself. The formation of new spatial formats comprises an innovative response on the part of individual and collective actors to the challenges of transregional and global interactions. As such, there is high likelihood that ongoing searches for solutions to these challenges will continue to produce new spatial formats. The very open-endedness of the process precludes the formulation of a finite list of spatial formats.

Where to Begin?

Conceivably our analysis of social interactions and associated processes of space-making could start with the migration of our distant ancestors out of Africa. Such a long-term perspective would allow us to demonstrate unequivocally that space-making is not synonymous with modern mobility and that spatial formats predate the formation of empires and nation-states. Such an endeavour would require the specialized knowledge of historians, anthropologists, archaeologists, and palaeographers versed in sources even before any written documentation. Although information and materials generally are available for these distant periods, the challenge of imposing a rigorous comparative methodology are immense. Yet, early spatial formats – whether villages, city states, transcontinental trade routes, or the spaces of nomadic movement – have shown themselves to be surprisingly resilient, despite having undergone countless redefinitions in relation to other spatial formats.[30] Interest in this long history of global connectivity and space-making received a boost in the wake of renewed interest in world history in the 1980s.[31]

Global or transregional connectivity does not look the same across all historical epochs. Thus, scholars have developed various classificatory systems to

---

a transplanted normative concept and that a participatory nation-state was seldom the primary goal of state independence. See J.C. Scott, *Seeing like a State: How Certain Schemes to Improve the Human Condition have Failed*, New Haven: Yale University Press, 1998.

30 For an impressive description of such continuities, see J.R. McNeill and W.H. McNeill, *The Human Web: A Bird's-eye View of World History*, New York: W.W. Norton & Co., 2003.

31 Noteworthy summaries of this history include J.H. Bentley and H.F. Ziegler, *Traditions & Encounters: A Global Perspective on the Past*, New York: McGraw-Hill, 2000 and M.E. Wiesner-Hanks (ed.), *The Cambridge World History*, 9 vols., Cambridge: Cambridge University Press, 2015, vol. I.

describe the defining features of global interpenetration for various historical periods. For example, the British historian Christopher Bayly employs the terms archaic globalization and modern globalization.[32] However, in making this distinction, Bayly does not posit an abrupt shift from less sophisticated features of global connectivity to more sophisticated patterns of globalization. Instead, he identifies a lengthy transitional period from 1750 to 1850, in which old forms of globality were slowly replaced by new forms: "The argument is that the period saw the subordination of older forms of globalization to new and yet inchoate ones emerging from Euro-American capitalism and the nation-state. An essential feature of this proto-globalization was its continued utilization, or 'cannibalization' of forms of archaic globalization."[33] For Bayly, it was the underlying ideology that distinguishes the two eras of global connectivity. In the archaic era, the dominant ideologies were "cosmic kinship, universal religion and humoral understandings of the body and land," and in the modern era, they are nationalism, capitalism, democracy, and consumerism. Bayly argues that the idea of "cosmic kinship" is diametrically opposed to the sweeping territoriality of the modern era. Unlike ideological differences, cultural differences, including patterns of consumption, were not consistently based on normative structures and thus evolved more slowly. Under archaic globalization, a ruler dominated a vast array of living conditions and the exchange of exotic foodstuffs was intensified across the entire area of dominion. Despite the integration of large empires, archaic globalization was based on extensive regionalization. The available means of transport and communication lacked the leverage to overcome the regional quality of global connectivity.

Circa 1650, a new period of globalization (proto-globalization), defined by the emergence of the plantation economy and the use of slave labour, witnessed increased specialization in the production and trade of predominantly luxury goods, such as spices, sugar, coffee, and later cotton. The increase in the interregional exchange of labour and goods stimulated gold and silver trade between Latin America and East Asia. This development, in turn, accelerated the monetization of exchange and thus the ability of states to raise money by levying taxes. With additional funds, states were able to expand central functions, such as administrative control and military forces. The nexus between the expansion of state control over vast empires (and the use of armies to compete against other empires for influence) and the extraction of resources

---

[32] C.A. Bayly, "'Archaic' and 'Modern' Globalization in the Eurasian and African Arena, c. 1750–1850", in: A.G. Hopkins (ed.), *Globalization in World History*, New York: Penguin Books, 2002, pp. 47–73.
[33] Ibid., p. 50.

from the subordinated territories widened the scope of state intervention. The modern military state became a fiscal state and expanded its access to economic resources. England, despite its loss of the American colonies during this period, achieved great success in the race for global influence.[34] Meanwhile, its competitor France experienced bankruptcy and underwent a revolutionary restructuring before re-entering the fray (at least briefly) under Napoleon.[35]

Yet changes in political, cultural, and economic structures, as Bayly notes, did not trigger an epochal break. Continuities with the archaic model of global connectivity could still be seen. For example, rulers continued to use nomadic warrior peoples for modern military conflicts and diasporic communities that specialized in banking and trade (over land and by sea) survived in the steppes and deserts of Eurasia and Africa. But it is not enough to see these developments as proof of the early onset of global connectivity or to use them to highlight continuities with the past – a frequent occurrence in much research on the medieval and early modern era. Instead, what makes these developments so interesting is the ways in which they are integrated, improved upon, or subordinated by nineteenth-century globalization[36] and consequently the spatial formats that they represent.

Over the course of the nineteenth century, the (relatively) small-scale trade in luxury goods was replaced by the mass production and consumption of comparatively inexpensive goods. This shift was facilitated by a transregional division of labour between raw materials–extracting peripheries and emerging centres of industry. Textile production (albeit without the complete loss of highly specialized production centres, for example, in India[37] or production for local needs) was the first affected by this shift.[38] This division soon spread to other areas of production, including the food sector.[39]

---

[34] P.K. O'Brien, "Fiscal and Financial Preconditions for the Rise of British Naval Hegemony, 1485–1815", LSE Working Paper 91 (2005), http://www.lse.ac.uk/Economic-History/Assets/Documents/WorkingPapers/Economic-History/2005/WP9105.pdf

[35] A. Forrest and M. Middell (eds.), *The Routledge Companion to the French Revolution in World History*, Abingdon: Routledge, 2015.

[36] Bayly, "'Archaic' and 'Modern'", p. 62 sq.

[37] For detailed account of the role of state in subordinating traditional quality production to the rational of mass production of cheap textiles, see P. Parthasarathi, *Why Europe Grew Rich and Asia Did Not: Global Economic Divergence, 1600–1850*, Cambridge: Cambridge University Press, 2011.

[38] A. Nützenadel and F. Trentmann (eds.), *Food and Globalization: Consumption, Markets and Politics in the Modern World*, London: Bloomsbury, 2008.

[39] For a critical assessment of the concept of world markets, see G.M. Winder, "Conceptualizing the World Economy", in: M. Middell (ed.), *Routledge Handbook of Transregional Studies*, Abingdon: Routledge, 2018, pp. 221–234.

The emergence of "world markets" was closely tied to quicker and more reliable access to market information, such as on pricing, and supply and demand, which allowed investors to reduce financial risks and improve outcomes. At the same time, improvements in the speed and modes of transport allowed investors to benefit more from the transregional division of labour. Hence, the development of the telegraph, steam shipping, and later railway networks were essential for the growth of world markets. But these new infrastructures required guarantees that neither the old spatial formats nor private investors could provide. Consequently, by the late eighteenth century, intense debates had erupted on the reimagining of spatial relations in the world – from the constitutional discussions in the United States and France, which revised the concept of nation and nation-state,[40] to geopolitical considerations, which resulted in the development of land and submarine cable systems in the nineteenth century.[41] The dynamics of a new spatial format – the national state – gradually overtook other spatial formats, as initially it appeared the ideal structure for mobilizing resources (e.g. the taxing of French estates, previously exempt, in the name of national interest) and for safeguarding sovereignty. Nations were actors engaged in global competition, not the baubles of dynastic interests. The loss of diversity within the nation and its clear demarcation from outside territories seemed a reasonable price to pay for these advantages. But the costs soon became apparent, as it was difficult to reconcile the idea of the nation with imperial control over remote regions or the subjugation of colonial peoples. This dissonance soon took a concrete form when French planters refused to grant free men of colour citizenship in Saint-Dominique, and a rebellion broke out on France's most valuable island possession.

The transition to modern globalization has not led to the dissolution of all borders nor has it led (as it was sometimes presumed) to a world of national states in which bilateral and multilateral negotiations of connectivity are free of power imbalances. The reality is much more complex and underlines the emergence of diverse and conflicting spatial formats – a topic to which we will return later.

---

[40] D. Armitage, *The Declaration of Independence: A Global History*, Cambridge: Harvard University Press, 2007.
[41] P.J. Hugill, "The Geopolitical Implications of Communication Under the Seas", in: B.S. Finn and D. Yang (eds.), *Communications Under the Seas: The Evolving Cable Network and Its Implications*, Cambridge: Massachusetts Institute of Technology Press, 2009, pp. 257–278.

Territory-Place-Scale-Networks

What distinguishes our approach from other systematic efforts to theorize sociospatial relations is that our approach is firmly anchored in historical research. The TPSN framework, developed by Jessop, Brenner, and Jones in the late 1990s and revised in 2008, has gained particular prominence.[42] The starting point for TPSN – like the "new political geography" in general[43] – was the observation that methodological territorialism, that is to say the subsuming of all aspects of spatial relations under the rubric of territoriality, did not suffice for theorizing the polymorphy of sociospatial relations. In this respect, the TPSN framework should be commended because it moved beyond a one-dimensional approach that threatened to overlook other important processes of space-making.[44] The TPSN framework calls for a multidimensional, polymorphous account based on four dimensions of sociospatial relations: territory, place, scale, and networks/reticulation, and it was linked to a series of very powerful globalization narratives that emerged in the 1990s and gained dominance in the early 2000s. The added focus on place has its origin in the categories of glocalization,[45] developed by Roland Robertson in 1992, and supports the local investigation of global processes. The concept of scale reflects the experience of multilevel governance as well as the notion that increasingly borders of every kind would be traversed.[46] Networks demonstrate new forms of connectivity between remote locales, rather than to the hinterlands, and help to explain reduced enthusiasm for a world dominated by outsourcing and global players.[47]

The "new political geography", and particularly TPSN, has been so effective because it classifies crucial new experiences with processes of space-making according to categories. Rather than simply comparing these processes, it maps them as part of one system. In short, it provides a toolkit for

---

[42] B. Jessop, N. Brenner and M. Jones, "Theorizing Sociospatial Relations", *Environment and Planning D: Society and Space* 26 (2008) 3, pp. 389–401. See also the contribution by Bob Jessop in this volume, which is based on the lecture at the annual conference of the SFB 1199 and partly delves into the theoretical considerations outlined here.
[43] J.A. Agnew et al. (eds.), *The Wiley Blackwell Companion to Political Geography*, Hoboken: Wiley-Blackwell, 2015.
[44] J. Agnew, "The Territorial Trap: The Geographical Assumptions of International Relations Theory", *Review of International Political Economy* 1 (1994) 1, pp. 53–80.
[45] R. Robertson, "Glocalization: Time-Space and Homogeneity-Heterogeneity", in: M. Featherstone, S. Lash and R. Robertson (eds.), *Global Modernities*, London: Sage, 1995, pp. 25–44.
[46] M. Zürn, "Global Governance as Multi-Level Governance", in: D. Levi-Faur (ed.), *The Oxford Handbook of Governance*, Oxford: Oxford University Press, 2012, pp. 730–744.
[47] R.J. Holton, *Global Networks*, Basingstoke: Palgrave Macmillan, 2008.

undertaking a comprehensive analysis of a new and complex social reality. To do this, its definitions of territory, place, scale, and networks are broad enough that they can be applied to many spatial configurations in the world. The underlying assumption is that these four elements can be used to explain every situation, although the mix of the four features in each situation will vary. Although the TPSN framework says very little about the temporal dimension, the implication is that these categories could be used to explain contemporary situations and their historical antecedents. Whether this framework is useful for describing historical processes has not been critically tested, because analysts of the contemporary situation have shown much more interest in the TPSN framework than historians.

The historical applicability of the TPSN framework is the starting point of our critique. TPSN assumes a pronounced contrast between present and past, meaning the defining feature of the present situation is that the terminology of an earlier situation is no longer adequate for describing it. This delineation is made without clarifying the starting point of the "present", defining what constitutes the "past" – a world presumably circumscribed by the unfolding of territoriality – explaining how or when the transformation from "past" to "present" took place, or even if the "past" experienced any transformations relevant for the analysis of the "present".

These shortcomings are not peculiar to TPSN; one sees in the social sciences many analyses of contemporary globalization that disregard the history of global connectivity. And yet, these analyses often implicitly adopt a historical narrative. For example, they may define the contemporary world in opposition to the world of sovereign national states presumably created by the Peace of Westphalia (1648), or they may postulate a contemporary world characterized by global flows and fluid networks, contrasting these to earlier structuring territories. In most of these narratives, a discourse of newness dominates.[48] A modified version of the above approach is offered by Ulrich Beck. While he still emphasizes the novelty of the present, he constructs a triptych in which there is a linear progression from the early modern world of networks to immobilization in the age of national states to today's global mobility and hybridity.[49]

---

[48] U. Engel and M. Middell (eds.), *Theoretiker der Globalisierung*, Leipzig: Leipziger Universitätsverlag, 2010.
[49] U. Beck, *Was ist Globalisierung? Irrtümer des Globalismus – Antworten auf Globalisierung*, Frankfurt/Main: Suhrkamp, 2002.

A Contextualized and Historicized Approach

Propelled by a similar interest in understanding the contemporary global condition, our approach, as noted earlier, is firmly and consistently anchored in historical research. This historicized approach entails examining the different historical contexts in which proliferations of spatial semantics have taken place as well as historicizing the changes in the spatial order(s) resulting from the contestation of various actors. The construction of new and alternative spaces does not involve a linear unfolding of a problem in time, but rather a succession of interconnected phases. Phases in which various actors become dissatisfied with the spatial relations of parts of a society, individual societies, or the world as a whole and respond by proposing new spatial formats or the reorganization of existing ones are followed by phases in which spatiality receives little or no attention. Following the time period from 1750 to 1850, described by Reinhart Koselleck as a "saddle era" (based mostly on European experiences),[50] the intervals between the two phases have become shorter, primarily due to increased interconnections between world regions in which neither the processes of space-making nor the imaginations of those processes were in sync.

The call for greater attention to the relationship between contemporary processes and past transformations did not result in historians immediately abandoning their long-held tendency to neglect the spatial dimension of social actions. As late as 2010, one of the founders of spatial history Richard White complained, "[h]istorians still routinely write about political change, social change, class relations, gender relations, cultural change as if the spatial dimensions of these issues matter little if at all."[51] But in recent years, this situation has improved considerably; today, numerous empirically grounded accounts and theoretical studies[52] are available that can facilitate a comparison between contemporary processes that appear new as well as historical processes.

---

[50] R. Koselleck, "Einleitung", in: O. Brunner, W. Conze and R. Koselleck (eds.), *Geschichtliche Grundbegriffe*, vol. I, Stuttgart: Klett Cotta, 1979. On the subsequent debates of the term in German and French historiographies, see E. Décultot and D. Fulda (eds.), *Sattelzeit: Historiographiegeschichtliche Revisionen*, Berlin: De Gruyter, 2016.

[51] R. White, "What is Spatial History?", Stanford Spatial History Lab Working Paper (2010), https://web.stanford.edu/group/spatialhistory/cgi-bin/site/pub.php?id=29

[52] Important not only for German historiography was the book by the Frankfurt scholar Karl Schlögel, which went in the direction of detailed description and theoretical conclusions: K. Schlögel, *Im Raume lesen wir die Zeit: Über Zivilisationsgeschichte und Geopolitik*, Munich: Carl Hanser Verlag, 2003. It seems no coincidence that its appareance coincided with Jürgen Osterhammel's study of geopolitics as a dimension of universal-historical thinking: J. Osterhammel, "Raumerfassung und Universalgeschichte", in: J. Osterhammel

This literature has continued to expand as historians' interest in space, borders, and the traversing of borders has intensified. From this body of literature, the impression – still to be tested – emerges that throughout history, the number of spatial formats has remained relatively small. Instead of a plethora of new spatial formats, a small number of spatial formats have been given different characteristics, functionalities, and positions in a more or less hierarchically organized spatial order.

With a historicized approach, not only are we able to observe long-lasting processes of space-making and their effects on the configuration of spatial orders, we are also able to examine the processual nature of space-making. While many systematic studies offer exhaustive comparisons of new and old conditions, it goes unnoticed that the emergence of new spatial formats and spatial orders is one of their essential features. A truism for historians that new conditions have a more or less pronounced path dependency on past conditions becomes of critical significance when we undertake an interregional comparative study of space-making under global conditions. In this scenario, two operations must be combined: the quasi-vertical investigation of spatial formats relevant to a particular society or larger region and the horizontal analysis of the circulation of ideas regarding the form and function of such spatial formats.[53] Circulation, however, should not be understood as a unidirectional flow from the place of origin or centre to the periphery, as is often assumed in the literature on the dissemination of the nation-state model.[54] Instead, circulation is understood as multidirectional, in which through translation and intercultural transfers, a creative appropriation and adaptation of spatial semantics and spatial formats to historical requirements and contemporary needs takes place.[55]

(ed.), *Geschichtswissenschaft jenseits des Nationalstaats*, Göttingen: Vandenhoeck & Ruprecht, 2001, pp. 151–169.

53 Interestingly, despite the many cultural phenomena previously explored by specialists in connected, shared, and transnational history, histoire croisée or intercultural studies, the field of spatial semantics and spatial imaginations has received relatively little attention, although some insights are slowly being made. The interdependencies do not play out between fixed units, but rather constitute them, making the investigation of intercultural transfers an extremely important spatial dimension of its own.

54 For an excellent overview of the literature on nationalism, see J. Breuilly (ed.), *The Oxford Handbook of the History of Nationalism*, Oxford: Oxford University Press, 2013.

55 On this methodological problem, see, e.g., B. Neumann and A. Nünning (eds.), *Travelling Concepts for the Study of Culture*, Berlin: De Gruyter, 2012; D. Bachmann-Medick (ed.), *The Trans/National Study of Culture: A Translational Perspective*, Berlin: De Gruyter, 2014; T. Adam (ed.), *Yearbook of Transnational History*, vol. I, Madison: Fairleigh Dickinson University Press, 2018.

A List of Potential Spatial Formats for a Historical Narrative

As already noted, our approach does not allow for a complete list of historically observable spatial formats. In this respect, it lacks the elegant brevity of the TPSN framework, in which only two classes of spatial formats are delineated – those associated with processes of territorialization and those based on connections and interdependencies between two or more points or places. The problem, however, with this framework is that it assumes the universality of territorialization rather instead of seeing it as a relational and historical process. In contrast, our approach does not reduce territoriality to a static and timeless container. Moreover, in defining networks, it allows us to avoid anachronistic analogies between today's often technologically advanced networks and the networks of earlier historical epochs.

The period from circa 1450 to 1800 was characterized by highly diverse processes of space-making and an incremental acceleration in communication.[56] During this period, we can identify four spatial formats which played a critical role in structuring human life[57]:

1. Empires (as well as some larger kingdoms), many of which had tax-paying provinces or tributary client kingdoms – the internal and external borders of which were poorly defined.[58] These empires lacked a strong centralized administration capable of unifying the heterogeneous populations over which they ruled. Claims to authority were based on personal ties and loyalty rather than defined boundaries. However, beginning in the seventeenth century, we see a gradual shift towards territoriality. This shift – an expression of rising dissatisfaction with border regions where neither geography nor political treatises provided clear lines of demarcation and so remained areas of

---

[56] R. Koselleck, "'Neuzeit': Zur Semantik moderner Bewegungsbegriffe", in: R. Koselleck, *Vergangene Zukunft: Semantik geschichtlicher Zeiten*, Frankfurt/Main: Suhrkamp, 1979, pp. 300–348, at 302–303.

[57] Here as elsewhere a double disclaimer is needed. The state of research for different parts of the world varies; so there is a danger that those areas that have been researched better will be overrepresented. Also, despite efforts to limit conceptual Eurocentrism, the historiography on which these observations are based has not completely shed their Eurocentric perspectives. These problems cannot be overcome in a single essay, but only by the targeted organization of multiperspectivity in a collective, even controversial, volume.

[58] J. Burbank and F. Cooper, *Empires in World History: Power and the Politics of Difference*, Princeton: Princeton University Press, 2010.

contention – entailed surveying lands and peoples in an effort to consolidate authority.
2. Maritime trade centres in particular, but also land-based ones (such as in the Sahara and along the Silk Road) merged into trade networks. In some instances, these networks were global, but typically they were rather regional in scale.[59] They functioned as portals of archaic globalization and as such developed a distinctive culture of transregional mobility.[60]
3. The town/village formed the basic unit of most societies, some of which had far-reaching privileges that created favourable conditions for networking beyond the boundaries of a particular empire. Frequently, land and natural resources were owned in common; this arrangement shielded affected persons from the devastation of crop failures and market fluctuations.
4. Translocal intellectual networks facilitated the communication of new knowledge between locales and the preservation of ancient knowledge from Greek and Roman times as well as from the early golden ages of India and China.

Undoubtedly, the list of spatial formats for this time period will expand as research continues, but based on its current form, at least two conclusions can be made:
a) Spatial formats were not solely the product of processes of space-making initiated by political actors.
b) Actors with ties to state-building were particularly successful in asserting the relevance of the spatial formats they created.

By the mid-eighteenth century, the seeming stability of the above spatial order was shaken by the transnational competition between some empires. In particular, the Seven Years' War (1756–1763), fought on three continents and considered by some as the "first world war", made clear that this competition had sparked irreversible internal transformations.[61] From this point forward, empires introduced various techniques of territorialization to minimize internal

---

[59] On this, see Braudel's classic and still relevant study: F. Braudel, *Civilisation matérielle, économie et capitalisme, XVe-XVIIIe siècle*, Paris: Le Livre de Poche, 1979. See also G. Garner and M. Middell (eds.), *Aufbruch in die Weltwirtschaft: Braudel wiedergelesen*, Leipzig: Leipziger Universitätsverlag, 2012.
[60] M. Middell, "Portals of Globalization as Lieux de Mémoire", *Comparativ: Zeitschrift für Globalgeschichte und vergleichende Gesellschaftsforschung* 27 (2017) 3–4, pp. 58–77. See also the contribution by Geert Castryck to this volume.
[61] F. McLynn, *1759: The Year Britain became Master of the World*, New York: Grove Press, 2004; S. Externbrink (eds.), *Der Siebenjährige Krieg (1756–1763): Ein europäischer Weltkrieg im Zeitalter der Aufklärung*, Berlin: De Gruyter, 2008; M. Füssel, *Der Siebenjährige Krieg: Ein Weltkrieg im 18. Jahrhundert*, Munich: C.H. Beck, 2010.

conflicts and to mobilize resources for competing with other states: land reform, restrictions on aristocratic privileges, the consolidation of territory, increased tax rates as well as efforts at widening the tax base, and the professionalization of government administration.[62] This partial territorialization of empire in the mid-eighteenth century owed its origins in part to transregional discussions about the crisis of empire and a developing body of knowledge exhibiting the benefits of territorialization.

Although this partial territorialization reduced the relevance of the interior borders, it had less impact on external borders, which remained vague in places where they did not coincide with natural boundaries. It also did not make all imperial subjects equal. Even as these processes of space-making unfolded in the metropole, a host of very different projects were initiated in the colonized spaces (e.g. settler colonialism, the plantation system, and trading posts and territorial concessions[63]). These projects, loosely associated with the remaking of space in the metropole, were intended to maintain and consolidate imperial power in the colonized spaces.

The first phase of transformation from 1776 to 1826 remade the spatial order of the world in three ways:

1. The revolutions in North America and South America as well as in the Caribbean led to the formation of new states that established their independence from empire, thus introducing a new geopolitical situation.[64] The success of these states ensured that anti-imperialist rhetoric continued to gain momentum.[65]
2. The principles underpinning the spatial format of the nation-state became embedded in constitutional doctrine and institutionalized. Following this point, the imagined spatial format of the nation-state became a model for multiple processes of space-making in other parts of the world.

---

[62] For a more detailed account of this process, focusing on overlapping empires of East-Central Europe, see S. Marung, M. Middell and U. Müller, "Territorialisierung in Ostmitteleuropa bis zum Ersten Weltkrieg", in: F. Hadler and M. Middell (eds.), *Handbuch einer transnationalen Geschichte Ostmitteleuropas*, vol. I, Göttingen: Vandenhoeck & Ruprecht, 2017, pp. 37–128.

[63] On the typologies of colonialism, see e.g., J. Osterhammel & J.C. Jansen, *Kolonialismus: Geschichte, Formen, Folgen*, Munich: C.H. Beck, 2012.

[64] J. Adelman, *Sovereignty and Revolution in the Iberian Atlantic*, Princeton: Princeton University Press, 2009; P. Frymer, *Building an American Empire: The Era of Territorial and Political Expansion*, Princeton: Princeton University Press, 2017.

[65] I.R. Tyrrell, J. Sexton and P.S. Onuf (eds.), *Empire's Twin: U.S. Anti-imperialism From the Founding Era to the Age of Terrorism*, Ithaca: Cornell University Press, 2015.

3. The considerable autonomy of many old trade networks was shaken by these and other political and economic developments. The emerging manufacturing and industrial bourgeoisie became less maritime oriented than the old commercial bourgeoisie. This reorientation developed slowly as national markets promised increased profits due to the continued commodification of agriculture and advancing urbanization. This reorientation of the market was part of the integration of old spatial formats into new ones.

But the changes introduced during this first phase of transformations rarely resulted in the creation of national states; instead what we see are variations on the nation-state format:
- Nationalized and partially democratized imperial states (e.g. Great Britain, France, Spain, Portugal, USA, and Brazil)[66];
- Post-imperial statehood followed by a slow transition to a national state (e.g. Latin America)[67];
- Empires that territorialized and absorbed aspects of nationalization without recognizing civil rights (e.g. Russian, Habsburg, Chinese, Japanese, and Ethiopian).

A second phase of transformation from 1840 to 1880 was characterized by a revolution in transportation and communication, which again prompted a new space-making of the world.[68] During this phase, we see:
- The expansion of imperial spaces based on previously introduced spatial formats, such as settler colonies, plantation colonies, territorial concessions, trade bases, and free trade zones. This expansion went hand in hand with the consolidation of federations of states (e.g. the German Empire and Kingdom of Italy). This twofold process represented another step in the transformation of empires, which were unable to avoid expanding participatory rights in the metropole but did not extend these rights to their colonies and peripheries.[69]

---

66 On the USA, see the broad overview given by Frank Schumacher in his contribution to this volume.
67 J. Adelman, "An Age of Imperial Revolutions", *American Historical Review* 113 (2008) 2, pp. 319–340.
68 R. Wenzlhuemer, *Connecting the Nineteenth-Century World: The Telegraph and Globalization*, Cambridge: Cambridge University Press, 2013.
69 This contradiction cannot be interpreted as the teleology of empire to nation-state, but at best as a multistage process of adapting the spatial format of the empire to a changing spatial order as recent research has shown. See J. Esherick, H. Kayalı and E. van Young (eds.), *Empire*

- The emergence of world markets for goods and labour led to transregional regimes of migration[70] and transnational trade and value chains.[71] The ramifications of the latter extended beyond traditional economic sectors affecting many other sectors of society (e.g. the cultural realm) that became subject to commercialization. Cross-border trade in goods and value chains typically were associated with national economic units.[72]
- International organizations emerged as a new spatial format to regulate mobility and its associated problems. This mobility reached unprecedented speeds during this phase.[73]

Yet another phase of transformation took place between 1918 and 1961. This phase was defined by challenges to the legitimacy of the dominant political spatial formats – that is to say the empire, the nation-state, and imperial national states – owing to increased competition in the international system and growing interconnectivity. Because of these challenges, this phase is characterized by experimentation in spatial formats:
- The early years of the Soviet Union witnessed an effort to create a completely new spatial format by drawing on the anti-imperialist impulse. This project soon failed due to its conflicting ambitions. The Treaty on the Creation of the Soviet Union (1922) and the Soviet Constitution (1924) attempted a precarious balancing act; in one spatial format, they tried to incorporate the internationalist and anti-nationalist legacy of the socialist movement, reconciling

---

to Nation: Historical Perspectives on the Making of the Modern World, Lanham: Rowman & Littlefield, 2006.
70 A. McKeown, "Global Migration 1846–1940", Journal of World History 15 (2004) 2, pp. 155–189.
71 For the time being, it must be left open whether these chains are primarily transnational as previous research suggested or whether they are better characterized as transregional as numerous examples suggest, but which have not yet been taken up by theory. On this topic, see, e.g., C. Dejung and N.P. Petersson (eds.), *The Foundations of Worldwide Economic Integration: Power, Institutions, and Global Markets, 1850–1930*, Cambridge: Cambridge University Press, 2013; in the case of trade networks, their transregional character is clearer, see C. Dejung, *Commodity Trading, Globalization and the Colonial World: Spinning the Web of the Global Market*, Abingdon: Routledge, 2018.
72 For an impressive example and an excellent synopsis of the research literature on product chains and cluster analysis, see R. Declercq, *World Market Transformation: Inside the German Fur Capital Leipzig 1870 and 1939*, Abingdon: Routledge, 2017.
73 A. Iriye, *Global Community: The Role of International Organizations in the Making of the Contemporary World*, Berkeley: University of California Press, 2002; M. Herren, *Internationale Organisationen seit 1865: Eine Globalgeschichte der internationalen Ordnung*, Darmstadt: wbg Academic, 2009.

federalist elements with an imperial tradition, and at the same time deepen the state's monopoly on trade with foreign entities. Ultimately, the union of such diverse aims in one spatial format did not succeed; the rebellion of some Soviet states in 1989/90 exhibited quite clearly the flaws of this model.[74]
- Fascism can also be read as a failed attempt – ending in 1945 – at a radicalized return to the imperial spatial format.[75]
- The 1918 idea of national self-determination slowly transitioned into a process of decolonization.[76] Decolonization produced numerous nation-states, which in turn became integrated into the spatial format of (post-colonial) transregional organizations,[77] such as the Commonwealth[78] or International Organization of the Francophonie (Organisation Internationale de la Francophonie).[79]
- The Cold War blocs and the Non-aligned Movement constituted similar integrations to the one described above.[80]
- The liberation of business and civil society from the omnipresence of the national state spatial format facilitated the emergence of numerous diverse transnational spaces.
- The Berlin Africa Conference (1884/85) had established, among other things, a free trade zone in Africa. "Berlin's Africa"[81] allowed various colonial powers

---

74 H. Carrère d'Encausse: *L'empire éclaté: La révolte des nations en U.R.S.S.*, Paris: Le Livre de Poche, 1978; I.V. Gerasimov, *Novaja imperskaja istorija postsovetskogo prostranstva: Sbornik statej*, Kasan: Tatarskoe gazetno-Iurnal'noe izdatel'stvo, 2004; T.R. Weeks, "Nationality, Empire, and Politics in the Russian Empire and USSR: An Overview of Recent Publications", *H-Soz-Kult*, 29 October 2012, http://www.hsozkult.de/literaturereview/id/forschungsberichte-1134; and the rich literature that deals with Central Asia's position within the Soviet Union and has been published over the past decade.
75 R.J.B. Bosworth (ed.), *The Oxford Handbook of Fascism*, Oxford: Oxford University Press, 2010.
76 S. Kunkel and C. Meyer, *Aufbruch ins Postkoloniale Zeitalter: Globalisierung und die Außereuropäische Welt in den 1920er und 1930er-Jahren*, Frankfurt/Main: Campus, 2012.
77 U. Engel, Regionalismen, Berlin: De Gruyter, 2018.
78 T.M. Shaw, *Commonwealth: Inter- and Non-State Contributions to Global Governance*, Abingdon: Routledge, 2008.
79 J. Erfurt, *Frankophonie: Sprache, Diskurs, Politik*, Stuttgart: UTB, 2005; G. Glasze, *Politische Räume: Die diskursive Konstitution eines "geokulturellen Raums" – die Frankophonie*, Bielefeld: transcript Verlag, 2009.
80 See the contribution in this volume on the Eastern bloc by Steffi Marung, Uwe Müller, and Stefan Troebst.
81 P. Nugent and A.I. Asiwaju (eds.), *African Boundaries: Barriers, Conduits, and Opportunities*, London: Bloomsbury, 1996; G. Castryck (ed.), "The Bounds of Berlin's Africa: Space-Making and Multiple Territorialities in East and Central Africa", *International Journal of African Historical Studies* 52, (2019) 1 (forthcoming).

to access resources and develop infrastructure projects.[82] This spatial format clearly illustrates how multiple actors – established powers, newly emerging powers, and local elites – participated in negotiating actual spatial practices. The motives for creating such zones of limited sovereignty and overlapping access were varied. But these zones served as the foundation for another spatial format, special economic zones (SEZ). An SEZ is a geographically delineated area inside a nation that, for the purposes of trade, business operations, duties, and tariffs, is deemed a foreign territory. The economic laws applicable in these zones, for example taxation and labour laws, are less stringent than those in the rest of the country in order to encourage foreign investment. The acronym SEZ covers a wide range of zones, including, but not limited to, export-processing zones, development zones, extractive industry enclaves, industrial parks, and science and innovation parks.[83]

In addition to these three phases, some scholars identify the post-1989 period as a fourth phase of transformation and for good reason. But because this fourth phase is ongoing, its features are more difficult to pinpoint. Digitalization, the standardization and containerization of transport, and the transregional expansion of value/supply chains (outsourcing of classic industries, asymmetry of profits by positions in the value/supply change) have all posed new challenges for existing spatial formats.

Countless studies have addressed the issue of deterritorialization. Similarly, multiple prognoses have been made concerning the emergence of new spatial formats. But too often, these analyses have been closely linked to various political projects aimed at valorizing or assisting the ascendancy of a particular spatial format.

– Observing that large cities will play an increasingly important role in resolving global problems is hardly surprising given the exponential growth in people living in urban centres. This claim, however, has been closely tied to demands by transnationally connected cities for their emancipation from a hierarchical spatial order that privileges the nation-state.[84] In the context

---

[82] D. van Laak, *Imperiale Infrastruktur, Deutsche Planungen für eine Erschließung Afrikas 1880 bis 1960*, Paderborn: Verlag Ferdinand Schöningh, 2004.

[83] M. Maruschke, *Portals of Globalization: Repositioning Mumbai's Ports and Zones 1833–2014* (Dialectics of the Global, vol. II), Berlin: De Gruyter, 2018.

[84] P.J. Taylor, "World Cities and Territorial States: The Rise and Fall of Their Mutuality", in: P.J. Taylor and P.L. Knox (eds.), *World Cities in a World-System*, Cambridge: Cambridge University Press, 1995, pp. 48–62; S. Sassen, *The Global City: New York, London, Tokyo*, Princeton: Princeton University Press, 2001.

of the debate on global cities, the thesis has emerged that these cities are both the command centres of globalized capitalism and the social arena in which future decisions about distribution of power and resources will be made – the fact that this analysis was produced by municipal advisory councils and think tanks, such as the Brookings Institution,[85] highlights the often close relationship between analysis and political agendas. Beyond the role these cities may play, it is also important that we consider whether the significance of contemporary "global" cities is something new or a continuity with that of former centres of trade and power.[86] Such a continuity, we believe, cannot be reduced to these cities' control function under global capitalism. In this respect, the category – portal of globalization – seems more appropriate than command centres as it can encompass both a central position in global exchanges and a profound cultural influence owing to these cities' very positioning at the interface between cross-border networking and regional or national territorialization.[87] Whether such features would ever lead to a world ruled by mayors remains an open question.

- After the late eighteenth century, transnational spaces expanded into transregional ones as a result of new infrastructures and especially digitalization. Together, these two developments produced a qualitative change in outsourcing. Longer supply chains allowed global companies to take advantage of closer proximity to raw material sources, relevant knowledge stores, and the combination of a highly qualified and cheap labour force. However, both mounting social costs and the loss of control over

---

[85] S. Sassen, "A Global City", in: C. Madigan (ed.), *Global Chicago*, Champaign: University of Illinois Press, 2004, pp. 15–34; G. Clark, *Global Cities: A Short History*, Washington, DC: Brookings Institution Press, 2016.

[86] Sassen energetically denies this claim: "In this sense, global cities are different from the old capitals of erstwhile empires, in that they are a function of crossborder networks rather than simply the most powerful city of an empire. There is, in my conceptualization, no such entity as a single global city as there could be a single capital of an empire; the category global city only makes sense as a component of a global network of strategic sites. The corporate subsector which contains the global control and command functions is partly embedded in this network" (S. Sassen, "The Global City: Introducing a Concept", *Brown Journal of World Affairs* 11 (2005) 2, pp. 27–43, at 41). In contrast, Clark draws attention to multiple shifts in the relationship between central cities and global interconnections. This perspective is keeping with growing urban historical research that increasingly transcends the framework of individual nations and of the West.

[87] On this, see M. Middell, "Portals of Globalization as Lieux de Mémoire", *Comparativ: Zeitschrift für Globalgeschichte und vergleichende Gesellschaftsforschung* 27 (2017) 3–4, pp. 58–77.

intellectual property has long since dampened the initial euphoria over such benefits. It is no coincidence, for example, that in the United States the rise of populism under President Trump coincides with heated polemics on the outsourcing of manufacturing to China and the resulting trade deficit.
- Like other spatial formats put forward as solutions to the challenges of globalization, the initial enthusiasm surrounding regionalism[88] has waned. The idea that regional integration would facilitate global governance (for example, within the framework of United Nations system) found considerable acceptance in academic and political circles, including a body of literature on "new regionalism".[89] New regionalism highlighted the consolidation of regional organizations and the expansion of their range of policy objectives. It covered a whole range of phenomena previously ignored by theorists of regionalism, such as non-state actors and informal flows. But new regionalism was centred on the European Union (EU), raising the EU up as a model to be emulated by regional organizations in other parts of the world. This optimism, nevertheless, was dampened by the EU's inability to overcome member states' fears of relinquishing sovereignty and by its extreme doubts about the appropriate strategy for future integration: enlargement or consolidation, a confederation (union of sovereign states) or federation state, or multilevel democratic governance or a commitment to subsidiarity.
- When neither transregional connections nor regionalism provided a comprehensive solution for regaining political control over the current global flows, a quasi-neo-imperial behaviour emerged, that is to say the attempt to return parts of the world to the status of an imperial subsidiary space,[90] despite the seeming demise of this format with the conclusion of the Cold War.

This list is by no means exhaustive and because spatial relations are always subject to renegotiation, it cannot be. Nonetheless, it can serve as a point of departure for further empirical research, for comparisons across world regions, and for the formulation of a historically grounded theoretical model.

---

[88] Engel, *Regionalismus*.
[89] T.A. Börzel and T. Risse (eds.), *The Oxford Handbook of Comparative Regionalism*, Oxford: Oxford University Press, 2016.
[90] Most strikingly, the annexation of Crimea by Russia in 2014 as well as the Syrian theatre of war invite corresponding investigations with regard to the openness of power relations.

Conclusion

Our goal was to develop a heuristic tool that may help with explaining in their historical context processes of space-making under the global condition that became characteristic of modern globalization. For this, we start from a multilevel compression: Spatialization must first be understood as an essential dimension of every social interaction. The term spatial format is used to describe the results of those processes of space-making that achieve stability for longer periods of time. Through a process of collective reflection, spatial formats are assigned a function in controlling new experiences of spatiality. Accordingly, spatial formats have more than one dimension: they are imagined, and they inspire a praxis of spatial structuring. By examining spatial imaginations and practices of spatialization in which spatial formats are consolidated, we also acknowledge and comprehend the individual and collective actors who attach their interests and imaginations to certain spatial formats.

Spatial formats, however, are not created ex nihilo but are always based on an already existing spatial order, which in turn is formed through the juxtaposition or superimposition of several spatial formats. At the latest, with the transition to modern globalization (circa 1750 to 1850), there is a linking of previous separate spatial orders. However, this linking did not result in a homogenizing integration into a single world society. The global spatial order, therefore, remains the vanishing point of interdependent action in a still fragmented world. Depending on the positionality of individual societies or actors in this fragmented world, different spatial formats seem more or less important. Determining spatial formats' scope of relevance and understanding their causation offers an important heuristic for analysing global integration and the multipolarity of the contemporary world.

Bob Jessop
Spatiotemporal Fixes and Multispatial Metagovernance: The Territory, Place, Scale, Network Scheme Revisited

This chapter presents a strategic-relational approach to spatiotemporality and proposes a set of interrelated concepts relevant to the Leipzig project's three key organizing themes: spatialization, spatial formats, and spatial orders. The argument unfolds in six steps. First, it considers what is at stake in spatial (re-) turns in social analysis and calls for a rigorous ontological spatial turn. Second, it outlines four recent turns in geographical enquiry, their motivations, and some of their limits in grasping the complexities of sociospatial organization.

Third, it presents the territory, place, scale, and networks (TPSN) schema as a considered theoretical response to one-dimensional spatial turns. This highlights the structuring role of four corresponding spatialization practices as well as their relation to spatial imaginaries that guide the construction of sociospatial relations and their articulation into larger spatial orders. Fourth, while a general spatial turn occurred in response to overemphasis on the temporality of social relations, a justified "bending of the stick in the other direction" should be tempered by recognition that sociospatial patterns also have temporal aspects. In this spirit, I introduce the concept of spatiotemporal fixes and explore some of their key strategic-relational aspects. This involves addressing their structural, discursive, governmental, and agential aspects. Fifth, building on the TPSN schema and its relation to spatiotemporal fixes, I discuss the government, governance, and metagovernance of sociospatial relations. On this basis, I then elaborate the notion of multispatial metagovernance and illustrate its role in the recent development of the European Union (EU). Sixth, and final, the chapter offers some general comments on what this approach implies for work on spatialization, spatial formats, and spatial orders.

What is at Stake in Making Spatial (Re)turns?

Actors are forced (usually unwittingly) to reduce the complexity of the natural and social world to "go on" within it by taking some aspects as more meaningful or important than others. A fortiori, this holds for the complexity of geophysical and sociospatial relations. Hence actors approach them through

https://doi.org/10.1515/9783110643008-003

spatial imaginaries that frame their spatial understandings, projects, and experiences or, at least, through other kinds of social imaginary that have significant spatial presuppositions and implications.[1] This holds not only for active or passive participants in the social world but also for disinterested observers. All spatial imaginaries are selective, however. Those adopting a given imaginary cannot see what it cannot see without requisite sensitivity and self-reflection on the implications of adopting one or another spatial imaginary. This is one basis of spatial turns in the humanities and social and natural sciences as scholars reflect on the limits of prevailing approaches to sociospatiality and, perhaps, develop new research programmes. More generally, it follows that, while selective imaginaries are necessary to facilitate going on in the world, they also limit possibilities for action. If, and when, they prove inadequate, this may lead to revivals, revisions, renewals, or radically novel imaginaries and patterns of conduct.

Another dimension of complexity reduction is structuration. This sets limits to compossible combinations of relations among relations, so that not everything that is considered possible in isolation from its place in space-time is compossible in a specific historical context.[2] Compossibility is always relative to specific time-space structures and horizons of action, power geometries of time-space compression, and the constraints of specific time-space envelopes.[3] It is also a dynamic relation among relations rather than a static one. Its effects can be benign and/or pathological and are typically asymmetrical. Relations of imperial domination or economic dependency illustrate this and often generate resistance where these asymmetries are not accepted as legitimate. There can be many simultaneous attempts to limit what is compossible at different sites and scales and few attempts succeed at a macrolevel. Thus, if some structural coherence and a strategic line do emerge, even in a provisional, partial, and unstable way, this result cannot be attributed to a single master subject. It is a contingently necessary outcome of the asymmetrical interaction of competing

---

[1] Cf. on the dialectical relations among conceived, perceived, and lived space, see H. Lefebvre, *The Production of Space*, Oxford: Blackwell Publishing 1991; on imagined places, see R. Shields, *Places on the Margin: Alternative Geographies of Modernity*, Abingdon: Routledge, 1991; and E. Soja, *Thirdspace Journeys to Los Angeles and Other Real and Imagined Places*, Oxford: Blackwell Publishing, 1996.

[2] On compossibility, see M.R. Jones and B. Jessop, "Thinking State/Space Incompossibly", *Antipode* 42 (2010), pp. 1119–1149.

[3] On the latter two concepts, see D. Massey, "Power-Geometry and a Progressive Sense of Place", in: J. Bird et al. (eds), *Mapping the Futures*, Abingdon: Routledge, 1993, pp. 59–69; D. Massey, *Time, Place, and Gender*, Minneapolis: University of Minnesota Press, 1994.

structuration attempts and, even where there is a hegemonic or dominant sociospatial strategy, its results are partly due to blind co-evolution.[4]

Compossibility is inherently spatiotemporal because social relations, especially those that are sedimented or institutionalized, are themselves inherently spatiotemporal (see below on institutional and spatiotemporal fixes). Exploring this requires going beyond time and space as external parameters of action to explore how specific spatial arrangements and formats entail specific spatiotemporal selectivities. As Doreen Massey notes:

> All attempts to institute horizons, to establish boundaries, to secure the identity of places, can in this sense therefore be seen to be *attempts to stabilize the meaning of particular envelopes of space-time* [original emphasis]. They are attempts to get to grips with the unutterable mobility and contingency of space-time. Moreover, however common, and however understandable, they may be, it is important to recognize them as such. For such attempts at the stabilization of meaning are constantly the site of social contest, battles over the power to label space-time, to impose the meaning to be attributed to a space, for however long or short a span of time.[5]

Spatial arrangements or formats can be examined in several ways. (1) They can be considered in terms of embedded spatialities and temporalities as emergent, regularized results of social interaction and spatial and temporal imaginaries. (2) They can be seen as the structurally inscribed strategic spatiotemporal selectivities involved in these emergent spatial configurations – or formats – and, again, the kinds of spatiotemporally oriented strategic horizons of action and modes of calculations that may be oriented to maintaining, subverting, or overthrowing them. (3) They can be regarded as the sedimentation of reflexively reorganized spatiotemporal matrices or spatial orders as processes of variation, selection, and retention lead to the partial, temporary, and provisional consolidation of specific spatiotemporal arrangements and, concomitantly — but potentially discordantly or disjunctively, recursively selected strategies and tactics concerned with chronotopic governance, the use of history to make history (historicity), and capacities to relocate, jump or bend scales, rearticulate networks, and so on – or, indeed, to subvert, undermine, or overthrow these spatiotemporal constraints. And (4) they can be considered the recursive reproduction of spatiotemporal orders that results

---

[4] B. Jessop, *State Power: A Strategic-Relational Approach*, Cambridge: Polity, 2007; cf. M. Foucault, *Security, Territory, Population, Lectures at the Collège de France, 1977–1978*, Basingstoke: Picador, 2007; M. Foucault, *The Birth of Biopolitics: Lectures at the Collège de France, 1978–1979*, Basingstoke: Picador, 2008; see also the discussion in the section on "Spatial Formats and Spatiotemporal Fixes".

[5] Massey, *Time, Place, and Gender*, p. 5.

from the interaction of these analytically distinct but empirically interacting levels of spatiotemporal organization. Figure 1 maps the strategic-relational dialectic that connects these levels of analysis. Note, however, that the first level of analysis – depicting a simple dichotomy between external, absolute time-space and an idealist, universal affirmation of time-space as Kantian a prioris – is ruled out by acceptance that space and time are socially produced and reproduced, including the metrics in and through which they are perceived. Thus, this row in Figure 1 serves merely as a *negative heuristic* (avoid such a prioris) before showing how increasingly interesting and *positive productive* concepts can be generated through the stepwise articulation of concepts from one column in a given row into those from its correlative column in the same row. In this way it is possible to overcome the limits of simple dualities by moving to dialectically interrelated dualities and, in a further step, introducing the greater or less capacity of all or some agents to reflect on and transform sociospatial relations along with the mechanisms of variation, selection, and retention that contribute to the selection of organic (and composable) spatial orders.

Four Basic Kinds of Spatial Turn

Building on these preliminary remarks, I now comment on the four main kinds of spatial turns that are relevant in this contribution: thematic, methodological, ontological, and reflexive.[6] Regarding spatiality, they can be characterized as follows. First, a thematic turn occurs when previous research topics are downplayed in favour of (re)focusing on intrinsically or contingently spatial issues. These would include the simplest of the three Leipzig project concepts, namely, spatializations and their various dimensions, emphasizing the mobile (cf. Massey), processual, and variable nature of spatial arrangements. Second, a methodological turn privileges some aspects of sociospatiality as an initial entry point to – a spatial lens on – the study of complex phenomena and uses appropriate theoretical concepts and research methods to this end. The concept of spatial formats could well be located here: it suggests a set of spatial entry-points for the study of phenomena that are often studied without specific regard or, indeed, any regard to their spatial aspects and thereby aims to

---

6 Cf. B. Jessop, "Institutional (Re)turns and the Strategic–Relational Approach", *Environment and Planning A* 33 (2001) 7, pp. 1213–1237; B. Jessop, "Critical Semiotic Analysis and Cultural Political Economy", *Critical Discourse Studies* 1 (2004) 2, pp. 159–174; B. Jessop, N. Brenner and M.R. Jones, "Theorizing Sociospatial Relations", *Environment and Planning D* 26 (2008) 3, pp. 381–401.

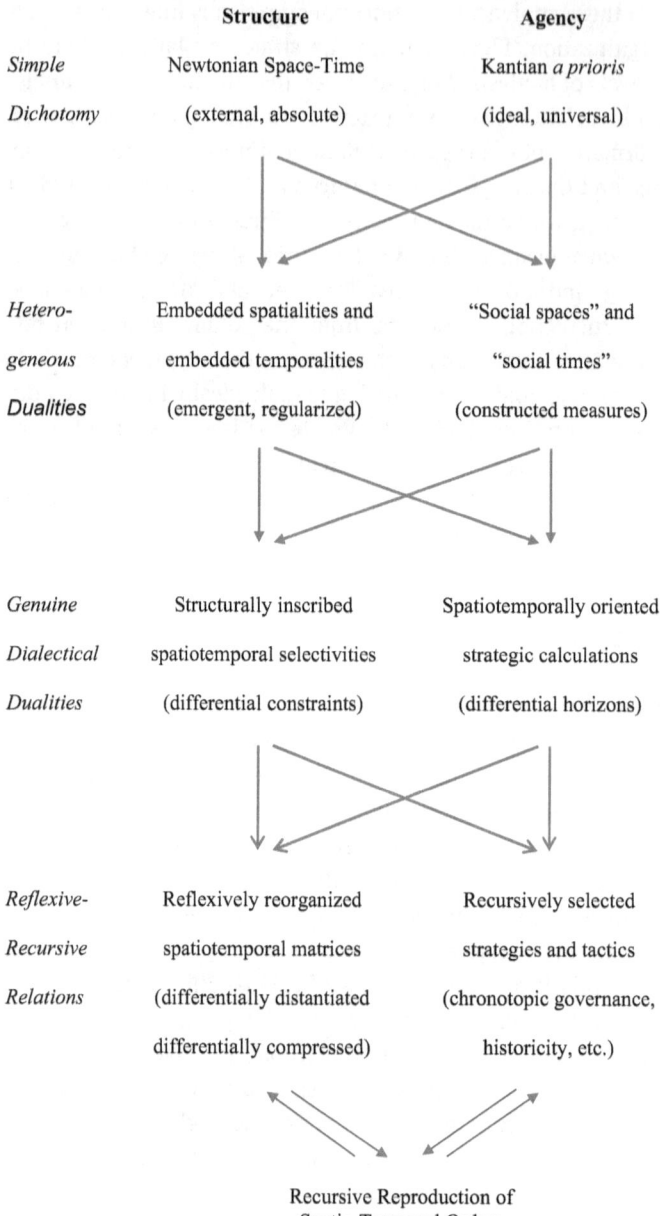

Figure 1: A Strategic-Relational Approach to Spatiotemporality.
Modified version of Figure 1.2 in N.L. Sum and B. Jessop, *Towards a Cultural Political Economy: Putting Culture in its Place in Political Economy*, Cheltenham: Edward Elgar, 2013, p. 63.

provide descriptive and explanatory value-added to the understanding of these phenomena. Whether spatial formats then operate in the manner of Marxian rational abstractions, Weberian ideal types, or some other kind of comparative lens would depend on how the investigator constructs the explanandum and the development of the overall spatial formats approach. Methodological turns are often more productive when the entry point differs from the exit point as other aspects of the social order are introduced into a more complex investigation. This would seem to hold when spatial formats are adopted as an entry-point into the relevant phenomena, enabling their spatial complexity to be discovered.

Third, an ontological turn occurs when spatiality is regarded as a fundamental aspect of the natural and social worlds, such that any attempt to describe or explain these worlds that neglects spatiality is bound to be defective. At stake in such a turn is the recognition that social relations are always already spatial and that their sociospatiality matters as much as their sociotemporal features. This said, it is crucial to avoid a radical ontologization of space (especially vis-à-vis time) because this easily leads to an empty spatial fetishism that abstracts from other salient features of social relations to focus on spatiality as such. Yet space in general does not exist – except as an abstract horizon of action waiting to be given concrete spatial content or as abstract geometrical or topological representations of points, lines, or three-dimensional spatial relations devoid of content. Without attention to specific spatial formats, imaginaries, and strategies, spatial fetishism assigns causal power to space per se as a determinant of human action. But even such causal powers are relational – relative to specific spatiotemporal horizons of action and technologies for conquering time-space; otherwise it amounts to no more than the claim that space matters. As Andrew Sayer argues, researchers must examine *how* space makes a difference and, we might add, bringing in the issue of agency, how it can be made to make a difference. This requires attention not only to the abstract moments of sociospatiality but also to their contingent articulation such that specific "spatial effects" are produced. The study of spatial orders, the most complex-concrete concept in the Leipzig trinity, implies strong ontological commitments to the inherent spatiality of the social and natural world and their interrelations once humankind began to walk the earth.[7]

---

[7] A. Sayer, "The Difference that Space Makes", in: D. Gregory and J. Urry (eds.), *Social Relations and Spatial Structures*, Basingstoke: Palgrave Macmillan, 1985, pp. 49–66.

Fourth, a reflexive turn focuses on the contingencies of spatial imaginaries and accounts of sociospatiality. It may compare and critically evaluate different imaginaries and their implications for action and research, identify their respective strengths and blind spots, seek to render them commensurable, or, at least, identify where and why they differ and remain contested. It may also explore specific spatial imaginaries, putting them into their historical context, explaining their uneven adoption or recontextualization in different fields, disciplines, or research programmes, how they get sedimented through normal scientific routines or are challenged and replaced in scientific revolutions, how they "travel" in space-time and with what effects, and so on. The history and sociology of geographical enquiry, the production of geographical knowledge, and its embedding in wider sets of social relations illustrate this turn.[8] Projects that provincialize hegemonic imaginaries, knowledges, and epistemologies are also relevant here. In short, a reflexive turn involves metatheoretical reflection on the development, reception, and effects of specific spatial imaginaries, spatial themes, spatial research methods, and ontological assumptions about sociospatiality.

The Social Production of Spatiality

The starting point for a concern with spatialization is the recognition, now widespread, of course, that space is socially produced through engagement with, refusal of, or resistance to situated social interaction.[9] Space comprises socially constructed grids and horizons of social action that divide and organize the natural, social, and imaginary world(s) and orient actions in the light of such divisions. These grids and horizons provide "spaces of interaction" that may lead to the emergence and consolidation of specific sociospatial arrangements (or spatial formats). These spaces of interaction can be approached from three perspectives: first, as *asymmetrical sites of social action* that factitiously privilege some kinds of spatial orientation and action over others; second, as *objects of sociospatial ordering strategies* deliberately oriented to fixing, manipulating, reordering, and relaxing material, social, and symbolic borders, boundaries, frontiers, and liminal spaces; and, third, as *governmental technologies used to steer action by sedimenting sites of action*

---

8 See, e.g., M. Middell (ed.), *Self–Reflexive Area Studies*, Leipzig: Leipziger Universitätsverlag, 2013; T. Loschke, *Area Studies Revisited: Die Geschichte der Lateinamerikastudien in den USA, 1940 bis 1970*, Göttingen: Vandenhoek & Ruprecht, 2016.
9 Cf. D. Massey, *For Space*, London: Sage, 2005.

and establishing hegemonic or dominant spatial horizons of action and/or mobilizing resistance thereto.

An important theoretical precondition for exploring spatialization is to distinguish between its initial "raw material" and the sociospatial relations that result from its appropriation and transformation through diverse spatialization processes and practices. This distinction is most often made in relation to the terrestrial and the territorial. The former term refers, in everyday parlance, to the earth, water, and sky within and beyond human reach. More specifically, it comprises *terra*, or "land", in its broadest sense: land and its subterranean substratum, the sea, its depths and seabed, the air above, and, where relevant, outer space provide the geophysical and socially appropriated "raw materials" or general substratum for territorialization and other forms of spatialization. Before *Homo sapiens* emerged, these raw materials had already been transformed through geophysical processes and the interactions of flora and fauna. These legacies constitute the "first nature" that is transformed through human action as the basis for "second nature" as it becomes subject to different spatialization practices and transformed materially and in terms of its social significance. In this sense, the production of nature is an integral part of the production of space. As Neil Smith notes, "when this immediate appearance of nature is placed in a historical context, the development of the material landscape presents itself as a process of the production of nature".[10] How much and how far earth, water, and sky are so transformed depends on available spatialization and other technologies, past and present spatial imaginaries, and past and present social practices. Conversely, variations in first and second nature also constitute the grounds (pun intended) for ethnogenesis, as different terrains favour different corporeal and mental adaptations, leading to diverse human communities and cultures.[11] These variations also provide the basis for enduring divisions that can constitute the basis for conflict or cooperation, for example between hill peoples and plain dwellers or nomads and sedentary peoples.[12]

The occupation and transformation of the terrestrial is often studied in terms of place-making and/or territorialization. Even nomads usually have recognized

---

10 N. Smith, *Uneven Development: Nature, Capital and the Production of Space*, Oxford: Blackwell Publishing, 1984, pp. 34, 34–65.
11 For a brief survey, see K. van der Pijl, *Nomads, Empires and States: Modes of Foreign Relations and Political Economy*, vol. I, London: Pluto Press, 2007, pp. 25–44.
12 See Ibid.; J.C. Scott, *The Art of Not Being Governed: An Anarchist History of Upland Southeast Asia*, New Haven: Yale University Press, 2009; J.C. Scott, *Against the Grain: A Deep History of the Earliest States*, New Haven: Yale University Press, 2017.

porous regions within which they roam, setting up temporary homes and returning to central places for social purposes.[13] Territorialization in general involves settlement and boundary-drawing, that is the constitution of frontiers, borders, and lines that serve to demarcate, "contain", *and* connect social relations. There is also a rich history of interactions between nomads, empires, and states.[14] A more restricted meaning of territorialization concerns the demarcation of the exercise of political power. This can take the form of simple or complex chiefdoms, the rise of city-states, and other forms of statehood.[15] The territorial national (Westphalian) state is only *one* form of territorialization of political power and, as the reference to the Peace of Westphalia (1648) indicates, is historically very recent and, indeed, a long-time in the making even after that date.[16] Other state forms have existed and some still survive: city-states, small states, empire, suzerainty, satrapy, client states, trust territories, colonies, protectorate, mandates, etc. Other forms of political power are only loosely related to distinct territories or not directly territorial at all (e.g. stateless societies, nomadic and snowball states, virtual regions, networked governance, and so on).

Seen in terms of its juridico-political construction, the terrestrial may be *terra nullius* and/or divided among territorial powers ("extra-territoriality"). The geophysical character of land, sea, and sky conditions claims to sovereignty, underpins different kinds of territorial organization and political imaginaries and strategies, triggers different kinds of territorial disputes, influences the formation and development of land-based and maritime empires, and shapes international law. The main result of territorialization is to divide the landmass into delimited areas governed by a political authority (especially one or another kind of state) that makes binding decisions on residents and defends its

---

13 M.J. Casimir and A. Rao (eds.), *Mobility and Territoriality: Social and Spatial Boundaries among Foragers, Fishers, Pastoralists and Peripatetics*, Oxford: Berg Publishers, 1992; van der Pijl, *Nomads, Empires and States*.
14 See, e.g., R. Amitai-Preiss and D.O. Morgan, *The Mongol Empire and Its Legacy*, Leiden: Brill, 2000; T J. Barfield, "The Shadow Empires: Imperial State Formation along the Chinese–Nomad Frontier", in: C.M. Sinopoli and T.N.D'Altroy (eds.), *Empires: Perspectives from Archaeology and History*, Cambridge: Cambridge University Press, 2001, pp. 8–41; L. Kwanten, *Imperial Nomads: A History of Central Asia, 500–1500*, Philadelphia: University of Pennsylvania Press, 1979; van der Pijl, *Nomads, Empires and States*; J. Rennstich, "Nomads of the Land and Sea: Stateless State-Challengers in World System Evolution", Presented paper, 58th Annual Meeting of the International Studies Association, Baltimore, 22–25 February 2017.
15 See B. Jessop, *The State: Past, Present, Future*, Cambridge: Polity, 2015.
16 B. Teschke, *The Myth of 1648: Class, Geopolitics, and the Making of Modern International Relations*, London: Verso, 2003.

authority against internal and external threats. For different reasons, the "high seas" and some terrestrial areas (notably the Antarctic, currently legally defined as *terra nullius*, i.e. land without a sovereign) escape territorialization.

From the Taken-for-Grantedness of Territory to other Spatial Dimensions

If we consider the development of geography as the main discipline that takes spatiality – as opposed to other dimensions of the natural and social world – as its self-described core focus and, hence, as its *ontological* starting point, we can observe three recent *thematic* and/or *methodological* spatial turns in mainstream scholarship. Schematically, these are a concern with places (including regions) as opposed to territory, a scalar turn, and a network turn. This observation implies that territory was the taken-for-granted framework for geographical enquiry based on the transformation of the terrestrial into territory due to some kind of "territorial imperative" that implies that nomadism is savage, primitive, or primordial. Recent mass migrations have called this assumption into question even as they are seen to threaten the territorial integrity of states and prompt new political responses and new fields of study. This concern with territory was criticized on several grounds in the 1970s and 1980s. This was probably related to the growing concern with globalization in the post-war world as an allegedly new process.

There were two main criticisms of territorial analysis. First, there was the "territorial trap", that is the Westphalian temptation to assume that states are sovereign within their territory, that the "domestic-foreign" distinction is a fixed feature of the modern interstate system, and that states are static, timeless, territorial power containers.[17] Second, the charge of "methodological nationalism" criticized the view that *territorialization* is confined to the building of national boundaries by national states and thereby defines societies in national terms. These claims prompted productive debates on the changing territorialities – and, more generally, spatialities – of statehood[18] as well as a turn to other sociospatial themes. Different forms of territorialized political power coexist and are complemented/undermined by diverse forms of extra-territoriality in and

---

[17] J. Agnew, "The Territorial Trap: The Geographical Assumptions of International Relations Theory", *International Political Economy* 1 (1994) 1, pp. 53–80; P.J. Taylor, "The State as Container: Territoriality in the Modern World-System", *Progress in Human Geography* 18 (1994) 2, pp. 151–162.
[18] N. Brenner et al. (eds.), *State/Space: A Reader*, Oxford: Blackwell Publishing, 2003.

beyond states. We can call this a territorial turn insofar as it examined what was previously taken for granted and led to new ways to study the complexities of territorialization, its contradictions, and its crisis tendencies across space-time.

Another response to the territorial trap and methodological nationalism was growing concern with places, localities, and regions as non-territorial forms of spatial organization. This turn also had its internal critiques, which generated lively debates. Specifically, geographers began to reject the notion that *place* (or locale) was a fixed, areal, and self-contained building block of sociospatial organization. Initially, grounded in studies of spatial divisions of labour and local or regional economic restructuring in the 1980s as uneven development became more characteristic of advanced industrial economies, geographers rejected the taken-for-grantedness of place. They emphasized that its boundaries are contingent and relational and serve both to contain and to connect interactions across places and spaces at diverse scales. Moreover, the social significance of place is usually closely tied to everyday life, has layered and differential temporal depth, and is linked to collective memory and social identity. The naming, delimitation, and meaning of places are contested and changeable and the coordinates of any given physical space can be connected to multiple places with different identities, spatiotemporal boundaries, and social significance. In other words, places were seen as emerging from relationally constituted, polyvalent processes that were embedded in broader sets of social relations.[19]

A second turn occurred around scale in the 1990s. This was conventionally conceived as a nested hierarchy of bounded spaces of differing size and, in territorial terms, was related to different tiers of government. The scalar turn questioned such conceptions. It arose from efforts to discover how global, continental, national, regional, and local relations were being recalibrated through capitalist restructuring, state transformation, and changes in "civil society" and its mobilization. Scholars addressed the (potentially tangled and divergent) processes of scale-making, rescaling, and scale-jumping and how they affected hierarchical relations among various intertwined forms of sociospatial organization, such as market exchange, state institutions, urban forms, and citizenship regimes.[20] The

---

[19] T. Cresswell, *Place: A Short Introduction*, Oxford: Blackwell Publishing, 2004; R. Hudson, *Producing Places*, New York: Guilford Press, 2002; Massey, "Power-Geometry and a Progressive Sense of Place"; Massey, *For Space*.

[20] C. Collinge, "Self–Organization of Society by Scale: A Spatial Reworking of Regulation Theory", *Environment and Planning D: Society & Space* 17 (1999), pp. 557–574; R. Keil and R. Mahon (eds.), *Leviathan Undone? Towards a Political Economy of Scale*, Vancouver:

resulting rich analyses of scalar relations had two rather contradictory outcomes. One was a bandwagon effect in which ever more sociospatial themes were subsumed under a scalar rubric; the other was advocacy of a "flat ontology" that denied the relevance of territoriality as a hierarchical structuring principle and treated scale as somehow akin to horizontal networks. This ignored the complexity of the links among different scales of action, which could be linked vertically, horizontally, and transversally as well as centripetally and centrifugally.

A third turn focused on networking as a structuring principle and pattern of conduct. It examined *flat, decentred* sets of social relations that are organized on functional or flow lines and characterized by "symmetrical connectivity".[21] Scholars explored networks, stressing transversal, "rhizomatic" forms of interspatial interconnectivity, and studied network geographies in such fields as commodity chains, interfirm interdependencies, cross-border governance systems, interurban relations, and social movements.[22] This fed broader interest in networks and their relation to old and/or new territorial, place-based, and scalar formations.[23] Nonetheless, such "flat ontologies" risk neglecting the hierarchical relations that often exist within and among networks. For, even if power relations within all networks were egalitarian and symmetrical, inequality and asymmetry could still occur in network-network relations, as expressed in the uneven capacities of networked agents to pursue their own interests and strategies. Such asymmetries and inequalities can (and do) arise from the place-based grounding of networks (global cities or marginal places), the scales at and across which they operate (e.g. dominant, nodal, or marginal), and their territorial (dis)embedding (e.g. colonies, empires, or strong vs. weak states).

University of British Columbia Press, 2009; E. Sheppard and R. McMaster (eds.), *Scale and Geographic Inquiry: Nature, Society, and Method*, Hoboken: Wiley-Blackwell, 2004; N. Smith, "Remaking Scale: Competition and Cooperation in Prenational and Postnational Europe", in: H. Eskelinen and F. Snickars (eds.), *Competitive European Peripheries*, Berlin: Springer, 1995, pp. 59–74; E.A. Swyngedouw, "Neither Global nor Local: 'Glocalization' and the Politics of Scale", in: K. Cox (ed.), *Spaces of Globalization: Reasserting the Power of the Local*, New York: Guilford, 1997, pp. 137–166.

21 M. Castells, *The Rise of the Network Society*, Oxford: Blackwell Publishing, 1996.
22 G. Grabher, "Trading Routes, Bypasses and Risky Intersections: Mapping the Travels of 'Networks' between Economic Sociology and Economic Geography", *Progress in Human Geography* 30 (2006), pp. 1–27.
23 A. Amin, "Regions Unbound: Towards a New Politics of Place", *Geografiska Annaler: Series B* 86 (2004) 1, pp. 33–44; S.A. Marston, J.P. Jones III and K. Woodward, "Human Geography without Scale", *Transactions of the Institute of British Geographers* 30 (2005), pp. 416–432.

These turns were sometimes pushed too far and interpreted in one-dimensional terms. Some scholars fell into the metonymic trap of conflating a part (territory, place, scale, or networks) with the whole (the totality of sociospatial organization), whether this was due to conceptual imprecision, an overly narrow analytical focus, or ontological (quasi-)reductionism. Examples include (1) *methodological territorialism*, which, as noted, subsumes all aspects of sociospatial relations under the rubric of (politicized) territoriality; (2) *place-centrism*, which treats places as discrete, largely self-contained, socioecological assemblages and/or relies excessively on the lexicon of place to interpret sociospatial relations; (3) *scale-centrism* treats scale as the primary axis around which other sociospatial dimensions are organized, or alternatively, subsumes more and more sociospatial relations under an increasingly sophisticated scalar rubric[24]; and (4) a one-sided, *network-centric* focus on the horizontal, rhizomatic, topological, and transversal interconnections of networks located in frictionless spaces of flows and marked by accelerating mobility.[25]

The TPSN Framework

Jessop, Brenner, and Jones offer a distinctive response to these often one-dimensional ontological and methodological turns.[26] Rather than making a similar turn to highlight another sociospatial moment, they proposed a heuristic framework that, due to its focus on territory (T), place (P), scale (S), and networks (N), was termed the TPSN framework. It was concerned with revealing the complex, multidimensional nature of sociospatial configurations. This framework is an abstract taxonomic tool that can be populated by actual spatial imaginaries, representations, objects of strategic intervention, and (un)intended outcomes. In this way, it can also provide a bridge between actors' perspectives and observers' interpretations. It is also useful for discussing different sociospatial priorities of different accumulation regimes and modes of regulation. In addition to their general spatial awareness, participants and observers deploy more specific grids and horizons of action. While other principles certainly exist, these four were the most salient in the 1980s–2000s. How they

---

24 See, e.g., S.A. Marston, "The Social Construction of Scale", *Progress in Human Geography* 24 (2000) 2, pp. 219–242.
25 M. Sheller and J. Urry, "The New Mobilities Paradigm", *Environment and Planning A* 38 (2006), 207–226.
26 Jessop, Brenner and Jones, "Theorizing Sociospatial Relations".

might apply to cyberspace, virtual space, or digital space remains to be explored by the original proponents of the TPSN scheme.

Table 1 cross-tabulates all four sociospatial dimensions regarded, first, as *structuring principles* and, second, as fields open to *structuration* through one or other principle. It shows that structuring principles do not just apply to themselves – a route to mutually isolated forms of one-dimensionalism – but to other sociospatial fields too. The concepts presented in each cell were (and remain) illustrative, intended to spur research strategies on sociospatial polymorphy. Serious research must also overcome the two-dimensionalism of this table to give a richer account of specific TPSN landscapes, spatial formats, and spatial orders.

Table 1: Towards a Multidimensional Analysis of Sociospatiality.

Structuring practices	Fields of Operation			
	TERRITORY	PLACE	SCALE	NETWORKS
TERRITORI-ALIZATION	States as "power containers" defined by their frontiers or boundaries	Integrating places into a territory, managing uneven growth in a state	Intergovernmental arrangements for coordinating different scales	State alliances, consociational democracies, multiarea government
PLACE-MAKING	Core-periphery relations, land-based empires, borderlands	Locales, milieux, cities, regions, localities, globalities	Glocalization, glurbanization (global-local and urban-global ties)	Local, urban, regional governance or partnerships
RESCALING	Scaled political authority (multilevel government, federal states)	Local↔global articulations, areal (spatial) division of labour	Nested or tangled scalar hierarchies, scale-jumping, re and descaling	Parallel power networks, private international regimes
NETWORK-ING	Cross-border region, virtual regions, nomadic shadow empires	Global city networks, polynucleated cities, overseas trading companies	"Soft spaces", networks of differently scaled places	Networks of networks, spaces of flows, maritime empires

Greatly modified version of Table 3.2 in Jessop, Brenner and Jones, "Theorizing Sociospatial Relations".

Taking territory to illustrate these points, this matrix shows that each sociospatial concept can be deployed in three ways:
- *in itself* as a product of (re)bordering strategies that operated on the existing territorial landscape (this read the matrix diagonally, hence territorialization ⟷ territory);
- as a *structuring practice* (or causal process) that impacts other already structured fields of sociospatial relations that may be undergoing restructuring in other respects too (this reads the matrix horizontally, hence: territorialization → place; territorialization → scale; territorialization → network);
- as a *structured field*, produced in part through the impact of other sociospatial structuring principles on territorial dynamics (here the matrix is read vertically to consider: place → territorialization; scale → territorialization; and network → territorialization).

The same points hold for the three other moments in this schema. It thereby suggests that sociospatial configurations can be interpreted as contingent expressions of efforts at strategic coordination and structural coupling in specific spatiotemporal contexts. This highlights the heuristic value of adopting a strategic-relational approach.

First, these configurations can be the *site* for elaborating spatiotemporal strategies and fixes, that is sites where strategies and fixes are elaborated and pursued. In this regard, they provide reference points for diverse spatial identities, imaginaries, interests, and associated strategies. These could privilege one axis of spatial organization or involve two or more axes (e.g. states, land-based empires, global city networks, and virtual regions such as the Brazil, Russia, India, and China economic quartet known as BRIC and later, with the addition of South Africa, the BRICS).

Second, they can be the *object* of spatiotemporal strategies and fixes, that is, become the object of recalibration, reorganization, collibration, and so on either in their current form (e.g. by rebalancing the different structuring principles) or as future objects yet to be formed (e.g. the One Belt, One Road project, now officially known as the Belt and Road Initiative, promoted by China to reconnect the Eurasian heartland).

Third, they can have different roles *as means* in securing, modifying, or disrupting the coherence of spatiotemporal relations in social formations in different stages of development, historical contexts, and specific conjunctures. For example, guerrilla networks could be deployed to create conditions in which the countryside surrounds towns as fixed places in a revolutionary struggle, or dense institutional networks can be established to strengthen the competitiveness of polycentric urban regions considered as an interconnected set of places.

Fourth, different structuring principles may be conducive to different kinds of sociospatial governance. Territorialization is closely associated with a hierarchical state logic, in which sovereign states govern their respective territories – considered as power containers that are not subject to external authority – and seek to manage interstate relations by using state resources and capacities. Place-based governance could become the basis of local democracy based on community and solidarity and act as a counterweight to centralized territorial power, or, where mobility is limited, it could be a means of subordinating marginal groups. Interscalar articulation is associated with multilevel government or governance. A scalar and/or reticular logic is appropriate to balancing spatial fixity and motion within a space of flows across continuous space-time with a greater emphasis on negotiation and decentred steering. These strategies are not mutually exclusive. Indeed, because different forms of spatialization can be combined to produce different spatial formats, more complex spatial governance strategies exist, with or without internal tensions. Two-dimensional examples include multilevel governance arrangements that combine territory and scale; core-periphery relations based on asymmetrical relations among places in a territory; polynucleated cities based on networked places; and networked territories such as cross-border regions. An interesting case found at different scales is the balancing of a state-centred logic oriented to territorial governance and a capitalist logic oriented to managing the space of flows.[27] Free trade zones, gateway cities, transregional economic corridors, customs unions, and global trade regimes organized in the shadow of a hegemonic state provide examples of such arrangements. These forms of governance can be combined in more complex forms of multispatial metagovernance targeted at specific spatial sites or their differential articulation in pursuit of larger sociospatial projects (see below the section on "Multispatial Metagovernance").

Fifth, relatedly but more generally, we might explore whether the relative weight of the four "pure" TPSN moments of spatialization is associated with the relative stability of different spatial formats and/or emergent spatial orders. For

---

27 See G. Arrighi, *The Long Twentieth Century: Money, Power and the Origins of Our Times*, London: Verso, 1994; D. Harvey, *The New Imperialism*, Oxford: Oxford University Press, 2003. Indeed, Harvey suggests that each logic generates contradictions that must be contained by the other. If the territorial logic blocks the logic of capital, there is a risk of economic crisis; if capitalist logic undermines territorial logic, there is a risk of political crisis. Overall, this generates a spiral movement of uneven geographical development as contradictions are displaced from one logic to the other in a process of mutual adjustment and reaction (Harvey, *The New Imperialism*, p. 140).

example, the Atlantic Fordist accumulation regime, its mode of regulation, and its societal paradigm tended to prioritize territory and place as core organizing principles. This regime resulted from relatively successful efforts to construct and steer the development of a national economy, national territorial state, and national society, and it involved consistent efforts to reduce uneven local and regional development and core-periphery relations that were generated by Fordist growth dynamics through mechanisms that Neil Brenner described as spatial Keynesianism.[28] In turn, the crisis of Atlantic Fordism was strongly related to growing economic internationalization, which undermined the structured coherence of economic spaces organized within national borders and weakened the state's ability to secure full employment and manage uneven development through Keynesian welfare techniques. Two economic imaginaries came to hegemonize post-Fordist scenarios and strategies. First, an economic regime dominated by the transition to a "knowledge-based economy" would prioritize networks and scale over securing territorial integrity and governing specific places. The focus would be building knowledge-intensive value chains and inserting networks into a scalar as well as spatial division of labour by reducing the frictions of national borders. Second, a neo-liberal, finance-dominated accumulation regime would prioritize the telematic space of flows over territory and promote scalar networks of financial hubs.

Sixth, each sociospatial organizing principle has its own forms of inclusion/exclusion and entails differential capacities to exercise state powers. This opens a strategic field in which social forces seek to privilege different modes of sociospatial organization to privilege their ideal and material interests. Regarding the state in its narrow, juridico-political sense, examples include gerrymandering constituency boundaries, voter suppression, promoting or weakening place-based uneven development and centre-periphery inequalities, reordering scalar hierarchies and scale-jumping, and organizing parallel power networks that cut across formal vertical and horizontal divisions of power within and beyond the state. Some social forces are marginalized, excluded, or subject to coercion, leading to social and political blowback against the forms of marginalization, exclusion, and inequality associated with given spatial formats.

Seventh, as two of its proponents have argue, the TPSN approach also offers a research method that is sensitive to the *"geographies of compossibility* [original emphasis]*"*.[29] These exist because not every sociospatial arrangement that seems

---

28 N. Brenner, *New State Spaces: Urban Governance and the Rescaling of Statehood*, Oxford: Oxford University Press, 2004.
29 Jessop and Jones, "Thinking State/Space Incompossibly".

possible when judged in isolation can be combined with all other individually feasible arrangements when seen in terms of their articulation in specific spatiotemporal envelopes. In short, not everything that is *possible* is *compossible*. Which arrangements are eventually combined depends on discursive-material interactions among co-evolving sociospatial configurations in specific contexts. Some strange combinations do survive – witness long-lasting interactions between nomads and empires, which sometimes have mutually beneficial and sometimes pathological effects. This is linked to diverse contradictions, conflicts, dilemmas, marginalization, exclusion, and volatility, both within and among these sociospatial forms. These arrangements must be analysed in space-time because (in)compossibility does not have fixed and absolute properties of spatial orders (see below the section on "Spatial Formats and Spatiotemporal Fixes").

Eighth, the transition between different spatial formats is rarely smooth because it involves uneven development, institution-building, and the promotion and consolidation of new geoeconomic or geopolitical spatial imaginaries. Crises and attempts at crisis resolution may both reorder the relative weight of the four principles and their institutional expressions and, hence, modify their respective roles in displacing or deferring crisis tendencies and contradictions in one or another spatiotemporal fix. They may also alter the prospects of sub- or counter-hegemonic projects (e.g. the social economy or Occupy movements). Moreover, as such transitions also create winners and losers, they can lead to resistance and other challenges.

Ninth, the TPSN schema can be used to categorize the spatial dimensions and dynamics of resistance. Table 2 presents a thought experiment to illustrate how this might be explored.

Spatiotemporal Fixes and Spatial Formats

Building on the taxonomy presented above, this section draws on my previous strategic-relational work on conjunctural analysis, cultural political economy, and institutional analyses to reflect on how spatial formats characterized by the articulation of different sociospatial moments come to be stabilized, even if only in a provisional, partial, and relative way. This poses the question of semiotic fixes, institutional fixes, and spatiotemporal fixes.

A semiotic fix involves the sedimentation of a specific spatial, spatialized, or spatially relevant imaginary so that it becomes the taken-for-granted reference point for social action, institution-building, and spatialization strategies. Sedimentation is a process that occurs through variation in and the subsequent selection and retention of rival spatial imaginaries, such that one imaginary

Table 2: A TPSN Matrix of Resistance.

	The TSPN of Resistance			
	TERRITORY	**PLACE**	**SCALE**	**NETWORKS**
TERRITORY	NOMADISM	Secession, separatism, irredentism	Dual power, anti-imperialism	Wars of position
PLACE	Peasant wars, migration, asylum	RED BASES, SURVIVALISM	Council communism, soviets, communes	Militant particularism
SCALE	Subsidiarity	Countryside surrounds towns, siege warfare	SCALE-JUMPING	World Social Forum International Solidarity Movement
NETWORKS	Mobile tactics	Movements of homeless and dispossessed	Localism, factory egoism, anarchism	MULTITUDE

becomes the naturalized or hegemonic framework of spatial identities, interests, and strategies. As such, it defines appropriate objects of spatial observation, calculation, management, governance, or guidance, and thereby frames the competition, rivalries, and struggles that occur around spatialization within its parameters. Such fixes are never fully closed or sedimented, of course: even hegemonic spatial imaginaries are contested. They often depend on complementary sub-hegemonic spatial imaginaries with different sociospatial bases of support or sites of spatialization; and they are all vulnerable to counter-hegemonic spatial imaginaries. Semiotic fixes are most effective when they connect different spheres, scales, and sites of social action and have in-built sources of redundancy and flexibility that can be mobilized in the face of instability or crisis. They can be studied in terms of historical semantics, pragmatic conceptual history, critical discourse analysis, and other forms of semiotic enquiry, on condition that extra-semiotic factors as well as internal semiotic factors are brought into the explanation of the development, reception, and effects of competing imaginaries.[30]

---

[30] For a more detailed account of the theoretical and methodological foundations for exploring the variation, selection, and sedimented retention of semiotic fixes, see Sum and Jessop, *Towards a Cultural Political Economy*.

Two other key concepts that highlight the role of agency and strategy in resolving contradictions and dilemmas are "institutional fix" and "spatiotemporal fix". Like semiotic fixes, these also emerge, to the extent that they do, in a contested, trial-and-error process, involving different social forces and diverse strategies and projects. In addition, they typically rest on an institutionalized, unstable equilibrium of compromise.

An institutional fix is a complementary set of institutions that – via institutional design, imitation, imposition, or chance evolution – offer (within given parametric limits) a temporary, partial, and relatively stable solution to the coordination problems involved in securing economic, political, or social order. Nonetheless, it is not purely technical and, rather than providing a post hoc solution to pre-given coordination problems, it is partly constitutive of this order. It rests on an institutionalized, unstable equilibrium of compromise or, in extremis, an open use of force. As noted regarding the more general notion of compossibility, institutional fixes (as with semiotic and spatiotemporal fixes) can have benign or pathological effects and are typically asymmetrical in their strategically selective impact on the capacities and vulnerabilities of different social forces.

An institutional fix can also be examined as a spatiotemporal fix (or STF), and vice versa.[31] This is because institutions are inherently spatiotemporal. They emerge in specific places and at specific times, operate on one or more scales of action and specific temporal horizons, and develop their own specific capacities to stretch social relations and to compress events in space and time, and, hence, they have their own specific spatial and temporal rhythms. These spatiotemporal features are not accidental or secondary features of institutions but constitutive properties that help to distinguish one organization, institution, or institutional order from another.[32] In turn, a spatiotemporal fix consists in a specific configuration of the material, social, and spatiotemporal aspects of a given set of social relations in a specific "time-space envelope". STFs establish the TPSN spatial formats and temporal boundaries within which the always relative, incomplete, and provisional structural coherence (and hence the institutional complementarities) of a given social order are secured – to the extent that this is ever the case. Such fixes delimit the main spatial and temporal

---

[31] The following definition differs from that offered by D. Harvey, *The Limits to Capital*, Oxford: Blackwell Publishing, 1982; for an explanation, see B. Jessop, "Spatial Fixes, Temporal Fixes, and Spatio-Temporal Fixes", in: N. Castree and D. Gregory (eds.), *David Harvey: A Critical Reader*, Oxford: Blackwell Publishing, 2006, pp. 142–166.
[32] Cf. P. Pierson, *Politics in Time: History, Institutions and Social Analysis*, Princeton: Princeton University Press, 2004.

boundaries within which the relative structural coherence of sociospatial relations is secured and displace certain costs of securing this coherence beyond these boundaries. A key contribution of STFs is externalizing the material and social costs of securing such coherence beyond the spatial, temporal, and social boundaries of the institutional fix by *displacing* and/or *deferring* them. These fixes externalize the material and social costs of securing coherence beyond specific spatial, temporal, and social boundaries, such that zones of relative stability depend on instability elsewhere.

Two corollaries are that *current* zones of *stability* imply *future* zones of *instability* and that zones of stability *in this place* imply zones of instability *in other places* – including within a given zone of stability that is internally differentiated and stratified. Even within the "internal" boundaries of a given STF, some classes, class fractions, social categories, or other social forces located within these spatiotemporal boundaries are marginalized, excluded, or subject to coercion. STFs thereby only *appear* to harmonize contradictions, which persist in one or another form. Such regimes are partial, provisional, and unstable and attempts to impose them can lead to "blowback" at home as well as abroad. The primary sociospatial moments and temporal horizons around which fixes are built and their coherence vary widely over time. This is reflected in the variable coincidence of different boundaries, borders or frontiers of action and the changing primacy of different scales in complex configurations of territory-place-scale-network relations.

This is a contested process, involving different economic, political, and social forces and diverse strategies and projects and this, in turn, is one source of the instability of institutional and spatiotemporal fixes that are consolidated, if at all, only provisionally and partially and that are always the product of a temporary unstable equilibrium of compromise. It is also fractal. That is, at whatever scale of analysis we adopt, we find competing, contrary, and contradictory attempts to establish organizational, institutional, and spatiotemporal fixes on many sites, with alternative targets of government and/or governance, using different kinds and combinations of sociospatial organizing principles and strategies, intended to serve different kinds of ideal and material interests, and reflecting different sets of social forces.

Regions and Territories

Regions can be located through the TPSN scheme in various ways. Interestingly, Ansi Paasi and Jacob Metzger found this puzzling in a recent article on regions, noting that the ambiguity of regions meant that my colleagues and I could not locate it in the TPSN matrix.[33] My reply would be that regions can be located in the matrix – but in several ways rather than one unambiguous way. Specifically, they can be defined in terms of territory, that is, as divisions within politically organized terrestrial space. Referring to Table 1, such regions would be located in the vertical territory column. They would comprise a kind of territory that has been shaped by effects of place-making, scalar articulation, and networking. Regions can also be explored in terms of the organization of spaces in terms of place, that is based on lived experience, collective memory, regional identity, and so on. Issues of scale can also arise. Thus, regions can vary in size of scale from micro-regions through urban or metropolitan regions to the Europe of regions or macroregions (often networked) and also include virtual regions (an example is the Four Motors for Europe region) or virtual macroregions (an example is the collaboration and partial integration of the four BRIC economic-political spaces). These remarks indicate the complex relational geography of regions in which different regional imaginaries and different principles of regional organization are in play and in which, moreover, regions operate not only as containers but also as connectors through a range of cross-regional networks. In this sense, regions exist in a space characterized by the tension between containment and connection, fixity and flow, imagined identity and actual connectedness.

The emergence, consolidation, and subsequent disarray of the virtual region comprising the BRIC economies suggest the complex and tangled hierarchy of regions in world society. This hierarchy should not be understood politically, as a hierarchy of power, in terms of a more-or-less significant fields of geoeconomic and geopolitical contestation.

The twin peaks of this hierarchy comprise two broad geostrategic realms: first, a maritime realm formed by Western Europe, North America, maritime East Asia, Australia, and the Mediterranean littoral, and, second, the Eurasian continental realm, including the former Soviet Union and China.[34] Next come subordinate geopolitical regions (e.g. Europe, Japan, and North America) and independent geopolitical regions outside the two main geostrategic realms (e.g. South Asia). And below these are individual national states followed by subnational and cross-border regions.[35] Among these types of region, we find different and changing degrees of hegemony and hierarchy, overlapping spheres of

---

33 See A. Paasi and J. Metzger, (2016): "Foregrounding the Region", *Regional Studies*, 51 (2016) 1, pp. 19–30.
34 Mackinder describes this grouping as the Eurasian heartland (H. Mackinder, "The Geographical Pivot of History", *The Geographical Journal* 170 (1904) 4, pp. 421–444).
35 S.B. Cohen, *Geopolitics of the World System*, Lanham: Rowman & Littlefield, 2003.

influence, national components and transnational influences, interdependencies, pockets of self-containment, embryonic and dying regions, marginal spheres, and areas of confrontation. This is reflected not only in shifts in national economic fortunes but also in the rise and fall of regions, new "North-South" divides, and so on. There are continuing complex rearticulations of global-regional-national-local economies, with uneven effects. Thus, in addition to the heterogeneous ensemble of regional spaces, we find mosaics of cross-border alliances organized within and across regions and continents, sometimes based on intergovernmental cooperation, sometimes on pooled sovereignty, or sometimes on hidden forms of (neo-)imperial domination. This complicates regional dynamics and the prospects of regional economic strategies. Indeed, it would be more apt, if convoluted, to discuss pluri-spatial, multitemporal, and poly-contextual modes of imagining, constituting, and governing regional economies and their always relative, provisional, and unstable integration into more encompassing economic spaces, right up to the world market.

The choice of spatial scale at which regional economic development should be pursued is inherently strategic. It depends on various political, economic, and social specificities of an urban and regional context at a given conjuncture. The temporal and spatial are closely connected here. The choice of time horizon will influence the appropriate spatial scale for development strategies. Likewise, the chosen spatial scale will influence the time horizon for pursuing these strategies. This is quite explicit in many regional economic strategy documents – with powerful players seeking to shape both the spatial and temporal horizons to which economic and political decisions are oriented so that the economic and political benefits are "optimized". When space and time horizons complement each other, it is possible for economic development to occur in relatively stable "time-space envelopes".[36]

In this context, considering the relativization of scale that followed the loss of primacy of the national scale when no new primary scale has yet been consolidated, new kinds of regional strategy have become possible. These can be understood in TPSN terms. For example:
- Seeking to locate a given place or region within a vertical hierarchy to maximize the advantages accruing from its relations to each point in the scale;

---

[36] Cf. Massey, *Time, Place, and Gender*; N.L. Sum, "'Time-space Embeddedness' and 'Geo-governance' of Cross-border Regional Modes of Growth: Their Nature and Dynamics in East Asian Cases", in: A. Amin and J. Hausner (eds.), *Beyond Market and Hierarchy*, Cheltenham: Edward Elgar, 1997, pp. 159–195.

- Developing horizontal linkages among places or regions of similar type, ignoring the vertical dimension in favour of network building (global city networks are one example, cross-border regions another);
- Building "transversal" linkages, that is to say bypassing one or more immediately neighbouring scale(s) to engage with processes on other scales. Examples are growth triangles, export processing zones, free ports, and regional gateways;
- Trying to escape from scalar or place-bound constraints by locating one's activities in a borderless space of flows or moving into "cyberspace".

These options may be combined in more complex strategies, which can be explored from three viewpoints. (1) The first is the nature of the interscalar articulation involved – vertical (up and/or down), lateral (extraversion or introversion), transversal, etc. (2) The second is their primary carriers – private economic agents (e.g. firms, banks, chambers of commerce, or private equity funds), public bodies (e.g. different tiers of government, local or regional associations, or quangos), or social movements of various kinds (e.g. diasporas, civic associations, ethnic communities, nationalist movements, movements mobilized behind the right to the city or assertion of cultural identity, etc.). (3) The third is the relative primacy of the logics of the de- and reterritorialization of political power, usually associated with state actors or forces dependent on the state, and the rescaling and reorganization of the space of flows, usually associated with economic actors seeking to optimize profits without regard to territorial boundaries

Seen in these terms, regional imaginaries could aim to strengthen regional political institutions and capacities to govern regional economic space and/or to find ways to capture flows through specific spatial fixes (e.g. infrastructure provision) or reducing frictions (e.g. deregulation, liberalization, or flexibilization). This raises an interesting question about how the logics of territorialization and flows are combined in specific cases of regionalization and how, if at all, these sometimes complementary, sometimes antagonistic, logics can be governed.

Multispatial Metagovernance

Viewed in TPSN terms, the European Union has been described and approached strategically in various ways: territorially, as the *Europe des patries* (or nation-states); in place terms, as a Europe of cities or regions (including cross-border regions); in scalar terms, as a space of multilevel government or governance; and, finally, as a space of network governance oriented to a space of flows. Here I focus on the last two mappings.

Multilevel government denotes a political regime characterized by imperative coordination through a territorial state – with a multilevel but unified hierarchy of command – that claims responsibility for managing relations among bounded areas under its exclusive control. This state can be a single territorial state – with at least two tiers of government – or a confederation of such states that has delegated at least some competences to one or more supranational political instances. The former arrangement is typically analysed in terms of public administration and federalism. The latter has re-emerged as an analytical or strategic problem in two contexts: (1) the decomposition of the Soviet Union – *a multi-state imperial regime dominated by Russia* – and its reorganization into a commonwealth of independent states that is seeking a new equilibrium of powers and competencies across economic spaces and states that were previously poorly integrated under central command; and (2) the expansion of the European Union as a *multi-tiered federal state in the process of formation*, in which the relationship among its political tiers (cities, regions, national states, and European institutions) is not yet settled and has evolved hitherto through a mix of incremental innovation in stable periods and crisis-induced radical integration in turbulent periods. Thus, whereas the Europe of Cities and the Europe of Regions are more incremental developments, recent proposals for tighter fisco-financial integration and centralized budgetary oversight are responses to the Eurozone crisis. The overall process of integration is a complex, hybrid process with different forms of government and governance in different policy fields and in different periods.

Theoretical and policy debates about multilevel government (hereafter MLG) range between two poles. At one pole, we find arguments for multilevel government based on a commitment to subsidiarity, that is to say maximum possible devolution of powers and competences to the lowest tier of government, with higher tiers responsible for policy problems that cannot be settled at lower levels. At the other pole, we find calls for a United States of Europe with power concentrated in European-level institutions and lower tiers acting as relays for decisions made at the European level. Situated between these poles are many other proposals and, more importantly, competing tendencies or developmental trends. Interestingly, the MLG concept occupies just two cells in Table 1: those concerned with territorial ordering along scalar lines and the (re)scaling of territorial relations. Likewise, the narrow descriptive and explanatory power of the alternative concept of multiscalar metagovernance compared with the potential range of multidimensional sociospatial governance arrangements also shows the limits of this alternative concept. For, while it transcends government and governance, it merely substitutes scale for level as the site of metagovernance practices.

Network governance relies on a mix of well-ordered market relations (economic exchange), commitment to negotiation (consensus-oriented deliberation), and solidarity (credible commitments to cooperation). It can emerge spontaneously, in response to initiatives by key stakeholders, or from state initiatives to reduce the burdens of government by pooling sovereignty and/or sharing responsibilities for governing complex problems with diverse public, private, and third-sector partners. Network governance aims to secure the conditions for the flow of goods, services, technologies, capital, and people across different territories, for connecting different places in new divisions of labour (e.g. networks of cities, interdependent centres of production, or different forms of centre-periphery relation), over different scales of social organization (that may not coincide with territorial boundaries), and different sets of social bonds based on mutual trust. This pattern is less concerned with the integration of government in an emerging supranational or federal state system than with creating the conditions for integrated markets with agreed upon governance arrangements but no overall coordination. It is closer to the open regionalism model that has been suggested for East Asia and the Pacific region more generally. In the European Union, this governance pattern is seen in, inter alia, the open method of coordination.

Multilevel government and network governance are prone to the tensions and crisis tendencies in the more general oscillation between territorial government and the governance of flows. Thus, the hybrid character of government-cum-governance in the European Union combines elements of both forms plus other transversal arrangements – further complicated in the last few years by the development of a new political axis based on Franco-German interest in keeping the Eurozone intact, with decisions being imposed on weaker member states, notably Greece but also with Portugal and Italy being subject to Franco-German dictates. In this sense, the EU is a major and, indeed, increasingly important, supranational instance of *multispatial metagovernance* in relation to a wide range of complex and interrelated problems. Indeed, because the sources and reach of these problems go well beyond the territorial space occupied by its member states, the EU is an important, if complex, point of intersection in the emerging, hypercomplex, and chaotic system of global governance (or, better, global metagovernance). As such, it cannot be fully understood without taking account of its complex relations with other nodes above, below, and transversal to the European Union. Indeed, while one might hypothesize that the European scale is becoming increasingly dominant within the EU's multispatial metagovernance regime, it is merely nodal in the emerging global multiscalar metagovernance regimes that are developing under the (increasingly crisis-prone) dominance of the United States.

This suggests that multilevel government and/or multiscalar governance should be put in their place in a broader multispatial metagovernance approach and that its agents should be sought not only in a multilevel or multiscalar division of labour but also in relation to their positioning in territorial, place-based, and network-mediated forms and modes of agency. Admittedly, in practice, much work presented under the rubric of MLG (whether the third letter in the acronym is interpreted as government or governance) does consider some of these complexities, usually in presenting findings rather than in any prior theoretical analysis. In this sense, terminologically, MLG is a misleading and oversimplified self-designation of work in this field. Unsurprisingly, this has triggered many attempts to clarify different meanings and dimensions of MLG.

One alternative, drawing on the TPSN schema, is *multispatial metagovernance*.[37] This is relevant not only to the MLG literature but also to other issues of governing complex social relations that exist in and across several spatiotemporal social fields. Multispatial metagovernance has four advantages over multilevel government, network governance, multilevel governance, and other widely used concepts.

First, it affirms the irreducible plurality of territorial areas, social scales, networks, and places to be addressed in attempts at governance. It notes the complex interrelations between territorial organization, multiple scalar divisions of labour (and other practices), networked forms of social interaction, and the importance of place as a meeting point of functional operations and the conduct of personal life. Second, it recognizes the complex, tangled, and interwoven nature of the relevant political relations, which include important horizontal and transversal linkages – indicated in notions such as "network state" or "network polity" – as well as the vertical linkages implied in multilevel government and/or governance.

Third, in contrast to a one-sided emphasis on heterarchic coordination, it introduces metagovernance considered as the reflexive art of balancing government and other forms of governance to create requisite variety, flexibility, and adaptability in coordinated policy-formulation, policy-making, and implementation. Fourth, it stresses the plurality and heterogeneity of actors involved in such institutions and practices, which stretch well beyond tiers of government and the limits of any given administrative, political, or economic space.

---

[37] B. Jessop, "Territory, Politics, Governance and Multispatial Metagovernance", *Territory, Politics, Governance* 4 (2016) 1, pp. 8–32.

Conclusions

This chapter has covered a large spatial field at breakneck speed. Its aim was to clarify theoretically what is at stake in studying spatialization thematically, methodologically, and ontologically as a contingent, multi-dimensional, and unevenly developing process. It also aimed to provide means for a reflexive turn in the study of spatialization by indicating some of the complexities of spatialization. By introducing the TPSN schema and showing how it can be deployed to think through the differential articulation of different kinds of spatial structuring principles and their role in (re)ordering different spatial "raw materials", I hope to have shown the limitations of one-sided, one-dimensional analyses and to have shown how structure and agency can be explored in and through the same basic theoretical framework. I want to emphasize here that the heuristic potential of the TPSN schema has been exemplified to render it plausible rather than fully demonstrated. For, not only were the cells in Tables 1 and 2 occupied by illustrative concepts rather than the full set of extant possibilities in the relevant literatures – such that other concepts could have been used; but, in addition, the two tables were only two-dimensional when spatializations, spatial formats, and spatial orders in the "real world" are multi-dimensional. This is one reason why I emphasized above that, while one must choose an entry-point (and, it might be added, perhaps a standpoint too) when embarking on research into spatializations, the exit point is likely to be different. Further research in this area, perhaps in the framework of the Leipzig project, would certainly benefit from adopting three-dimensional analyses.

For example, in commenting on the first draft of this chapter, Matthias Middell suggested that it is important not to take contemporary networks as the model for studying networks in earlier periods or, again, the relation among places in contemporary transregional frameworks as a paradigm for the relations among, say, city-states in Mesopotamia. This caution is very germane to the productive use of the TPSN scheme. Table 1 includes seven cells in which different kinds of network appear – either in terms of the effects of networking as a structuring principle and/or in terms of networks as the spatial field on which territorialization, place-making, or (re)scaling operate. Thus, nomadic empires that existed sometimes in the shadow of, or were even parasitic upon, sedentary empires[38] are in one cell; maritime empires are in another; the Eurasian Mongol Empire, together with its vassal states, would belong in

---

38 See, for example, T.J. Barfield, "The Shadow Empires". In: Sinopoli and D'Altroy (eds.) *Empires*. Cambridge: Cambridge University Press, 2001, pp. 8–41.

a third, namely, the place-territory cell illustrated – but not exhausted – by the cases of land-based empires, centre-periphery relations, and borderlands.[39] Similarly, regarding place, there are seven place-related two-dimensional cells, with global city networks located in a different cell from inter-(city-)state relations and alliances. How one might locate relations among Mesopotamian city-states in this grid will depend on the changing outcomes of cycles of territorial expansion and retreat among early statelets and the first rival pristine states, efforts to expand control over the respective peripheries of city-states, the effects of the first (Akkadian) and subsequent attempts to build empires, and so forth.[40] This cannot be prejudged by a conceptual schema such as the TPSN paradigm – but the latter can help to interpret the results of theoretically-informed historical research. More generally, these questions point to the potential of the TPSN scheme to open space to study varieties of colonialism or imperialism, world history, and variegated colonialism and/or imperialism as structurally coupled, co-evolving forms of spatial organization. There are interesting developments in this area with the increasing attention being paid not just to varieties of colonialism and imperialism but also to their mutual imbrication and, for certain periods, compossibility rather than conflict.[41]

Middell also posed a further set of questions, concerning how subaltern groups, territories, places, and networks can be located in this schema.[42] A first response might be to invoke Michel de Certeau's remark that the powerful use space to exercise control, the powerless use time to express their resistance.[43]

---

[39] For a long-run perspective on the conflicts between land-based and maritime empires, see C. Schmitt, *Land and Sea: A World Historical Meditation*, Candor, NY: Telos Press, 2015 <originally 1942>. This text could easily be mined for many other two- and three-dimensional spatial orders.

[40] For a magisterial survey of Mesopotamian city-state formation and inter-state relations, see J.C. Scott, *Against the Grain: A Deep History of the Earliest States*, New Haven: Yale University Press, 2017. See also N. Yoffee, *Myths of the Archaic State: Evolution of the Earliest Cities, States, and Civilizations*, Cambridge: Cambridge University Press, 2005.

[41] For some interesting preliminary observations on this issue, see S.J. Potter and J. Saha, "Global history, imperial history and connected histories", *Journal of Colonialism and Colonial History*, 16 (2015) 1, http://muse.jhu.edu/journals/journal_of_colonialism_and_colonial_history/v016/16.1.potter.html

[42] In fact, he referred, loosely, to the Global South; I have expanded his question to include other kinds of relatively powerless social forces. For a critique of the concept of Global South from a strategic-relational perspective, see B. Jessop, "'The world market, North-South relations, neoliberalism", *Alternate Routes: A Journal of Critical Social Research*, 29, 2018, pp. 207–28.

[43] See M. de Certeau, *The Practice of Everyday Life*, Berkeley: University of California Press, 1985, pp. 35–37 and *passim*.

A second response would be to refer to Table 2, which locates different kinds of resistance within the TPSN matrix. A more satisfactory response, able to integrate the other two, would involve developing the strategic-relational approach (SRA)[44] that informs the TPSN schema. The SRA posits that sociospatial configurations can be construed not only as contingent expressions of competing efforts at strategic coordination and structural coupling in specific spatiotemporal contexts but also that every such configuration differentially privileges some forces, some interests, some spatio-temporal horizons of action, some strategies and tactics, and so forth, over others. They are inherently asymmetrical, and this poses crucial questions about the conditions in which these asymmetries are reproduced, contested, and transformed. The interrelated concepts of semantic fix, institutional fix, and spatio-temporal fix are relevant here – but, as also noted above, more work is required on the forms, modalities, and conditions for success of sub-hegemonic and counter-hegemonic resistance.

In short, the schema presented above is intended both as a negative heuristic, identifying approaches to avoid in the study of spatializations, spatial formats, and spatial orders, and as a positive heuristic, indicating fruitful lines of inquiry into the complexities of these phenomena. The TPSN schema does not offer a theory but a useful conceptual framework that can be linked to other concepts and be employed in historical research. And, like any other intervention into scientific discussion, it is fallible and open to revision. The Leipzig project could provide a fertile ground for evaluating its utility in comparison with other approaches.

---

[44] On this approach, see B. Jessop, *State Power: A Strategic-Relational Approach*, Cambridge, Polity, 2007.

Judith Miggelbrink
Mapping the Toolbox: Assemblage Thinking as a Heuristic

Introduction

Assemblage is a concept that has received contrary responses in a number of scientific communities.[1] On the one hand, adaptations of assemblage thinking have been bound up with hopes to achieve a better understanding of newly emerging social phenomena traded under the heading of "globalization".[2] It offers, as Collier and Ong put it, "analytical and critical insight into global forms by examining how actors reflect upon them or call them into question".[3] Others, such as DeLanda, promote assemblage thinking as it, according to those that use it, provides an epistemological tool that goes beyond established relations of micro- and macrostructures, stresses the relation of volatility and

---

[1] The paper is part of a project that investigates medical practices as a field of mundane social practices that is assumed to be suited for revealing processes of spatialization under the global condition. Medical treatment is a social practice "the state" is intensely involved in – in terms of legislation (e.g. approval of physicians; licensing or proscribing active substances, therapies, and medical appliances; and regulation of the health insurance sector), in terms of infrastructural provision (e.g. hospitals and policlinics), and in terms of research investment, public health control, etc. Albeit with remarkable differences among countries, one can state that almost every moment, every movement and decision in any treatment situation is – to a greater or lesser extent – regulated, defined, enabled, formed, limited, structured, and, hence, captured by the presence of "the state". However, at its fringes, a broad range of heterogeneous activities have been observed, such as patients looking for therapies that are not available (e.g. reproductive therapies or organ transplantation) or not affordable (e.g. dental care) in their home country, health insurance companies actively propagating medical treatment abroad under special payment schemes, as well as new forms programmes promoting cooperation of hospitals, doctors, and insurances across European borders.
[2] See, e.g., C.R. Janes and K.K. Corbett, "Anthropology and Global Health", *Annual Review of Anthropology* 38 (2009), pp. 167–183; S. Legg, "Of Scales, Networks and Assemblages: The League of Nations Apparatus and the Scalar Sovereignty of the Government of India", *Transaction of the Institute of British Geographers* 34 (2009), pp. 234–253; S. Sassen, *Territory, Authority, Rights: From Medieval to Global Assemblages*, 2nd edn., Princeton: Princeton University Press, 2008.
[3] S.J. Collier and A. Ong, "Global Assemblages, Anthropological Problems", in: S.J. Collier and A. Ong (eds.), *Global Assemblages: Technology, Politics, and Ethics as Anthropological Problems*, Hoboken: Wiley-Blackwell, 2005, pp. 3–21, at 14.

https://doi.org/10.1515/9783110643008-004

stability, and cuts through the distinction of "things" and "enunciations".[4] Extending to the realm of the pre-discursive and being rooted in psycho-analytical thinking, it offers emancipation from established ways of conceptually framing empirical research through the epistemological imaginary it provides. It is particularly expected to comprehend emerging practices that cut across established boundaries and contexts and, at the same time, unite *different* contexts and thus link allegedly separated fields. Moreover, it has been discussed as an epistemological key tool to regain conceptual access to the material and materiality in geography.[5]

On the other hand, assemblage has been criticized as an ambitious, fuzzy, and overloaded concept that (in the best case) mediates a "playful and critical aesthetics".[6] Located at the crossroads of analysis and aesthetics, its lack of analytical rigour has been acknowledged several times – a quality that might also be mirrored by the ease with which the term has crossed disciplinary boundaries from psychoanalysis/schizoanalysis to anthropology, geography, sociology, political sciences, etc. It is not surprising that some harsher comments consider the term "an odd, irregular, time-limited object for contemplation"[7] and underline "the built-in obsolescence of the term in the global futures market of academic authority"[8] – not least because of some "more obfuscatory theoretical formulations of the term by anthropologists referencing (but not always reading) Deleuze and Guattari".[9] John Allen, a geographer working on topological concepts in geography, however, regards assemblage as a term that "should perhaps allow us to do certain things and enable us to think in certain ways that were not possible before".[10]

In order to explore some of the analytical perspectives that might be offered by assemblage thinking for the study of processes of spatialization under the global condition, this chapter assesses four bodies of assemblage-centred literature that employ the concept for rather different, though partly interrelated, purposes: (1) assemblage thinking as an anti-holistic paradigm, (2) assemblage as a concept addressing conduct and directionality, (3) assemblage

---

4 M. DeLanda, *Assemblage Theory*, Edinburgh: Edinburgh University Press, 2016.
5 C. McFarlane, "The City As Assemblage: Dwelling and Urban Space", *Environment and Planning D: Society and Space* 29 (2011) 4, pp. 649–671.
6 G.E. Marcus and E. Saka, "Assemblage", *Theory, Culture & Society* 23 (2006) 2–3, pp. 101–106, at 103.
7 Ibid., p. 102.
8 M. Sparke, "Triangulating Globalization", review of *Territory, Authority, Rights: From Medieval to Global Assemblages* by S. Sassen, pp. 1–7, at 2, (accessed 16 March 2014)
9 Ibid.
10 J. Allen, "Powerful Assemblages?", *Area* 43 (2011) 2, pp. 154–157, at 154.

as a methodological strategy to dissect socio-biological entities, and (4) assemblage as a concept comprehending globalization. From that, I suggest employing assemblage thinking not as a coherent theoretical body but to use it as a heuristic that allows entities to be addressed by focusing attention on their formation processes through "relations of exteriority",[11] their heterogeneous nature, and their potential directionality. In the following part, I discuss the problem of methodological underdetermination that is of particular relevance for the empirical scope of the concept. Finally, the paper takes a brief look at some implications assemblage thinking could have concerning the analysis of processes of spatialization.

Mapping Strands of Assemblage Thinking

Strands

Having become a concept that jumps remarkably easily across disciplinary boundaries, the term assemblage is subject to a broad range of interpretations. The following section, however, is confined to four fields of debate that are summarized as anti-holistic approach, conduct and directionality, the human body as terrain, and performing globalization.

Anti-holistic Approach

Though primarily rooted in psychoanalysis/schizoanalysis, Deleuze and Guattari's elaboration on assemblage serves as the main source for a social-scientific adaption of the concept. Manuel DeLanda's interpretation epitomizes this first strand.[12] In his interpretation, which is confined to the understanding of "social wholes",[13] assemblage is introduced to discuss the complex nature of social entities by pointing to the way these entities are produced through relations. Assemblages, thus, are temporary stable formations emerging from certain so-called "strata" through "*objective articulatory processes* [original

---

[11] Referring to Deleuze, M. DeLanda, *A New Philosophy of Society: Assemblage Theory And Social Complexity*, London: Continuum, 2006, p. 10; see also DeLanda, *Assemblage Theory*, p. 2.
[12] DeLanda, *A New Philosophy of Society*; DeLanda, *Assemblage Theory*.
[13] DeLanda, *Assemblage Theory*, p. 22.

emphasis] that yield a molar whole from a population of molecular parts".[14] Upon emergence, an assemblage is assumed to produce effects on the components it consists of as "it immediately starts acting as a source of limitations and opportunities for its components".[15] This is called "downward causality".[16] Not only is an assemblage irreducible to its parts, its parts are merely formed and called into existence through the assembling process.[17]

In this rather abstract theoretical imagination, assemblages are characterized by two features, or parameters: the degree "to which an assemblages homogenises its own components"[18] – its degree of *territorialization*, as it is called by Deleuze and Guattari – and the degree to which the identity of the emerging entity is formed by certain "expressive components"[19] – its degree of *coding and decoding*. A despotic state apparatus, as he exemplifies, develops a stronger regime of coding of manners, property, trade, etc. than a liberal one.[20] By "parameters" – or "knobs" as he calls it elsewhere – DeLanda indicates that a certain arrangement might be more or less territorialized and more or less coded. Assemblages and strata are not opposites but rather phases that can be transformed into the other. In terms of parametric thinking, a strata is the "phase" when both parameters "have high values",[21] that is to say it is highly territorialized (homogenized) as well as highly coded.

Considered to be opposed to holistic concepts, this first strand of assemblage thinking focuses on articulatory processes instead of pre-existing entities, on constant reshaping, and on the mutual definition of elements through relations. Furthermore, it underlines that the identity of "elements" and "entities" are defined through relations and, thus, are extrinsic instead of being intrinsic. In order to illustrate parametrical thinking of this type, DeLanda refers to Deleuze's discussion – though not fully elaborated – of the subject/subjectivity. Deterritorialization, thus, would mean a process that "takes the subject back to the state it had prior to the creation of fixed associations between ideas, that is, the state in which ideas and sensations are connected as in a *delirium* [original emphasis]".[22] This first strand applies assemblage as an abstract theoretical

---

14 Ibid., p. 23.
15 Ibid., p. 21.
16 Ibid.
17 Ibid.
18 Ibid., p. 22.
19 Ibid.
20 Ibid., p. 23.
21 Ibid., p. 26.
22 Ibid., p. 27.

imagination that facilitates the application of a certain explanatory mechanic to a broad range of formation processes of certain entities – spanning a steel plant,[23] Marina Bay of Singapore,[24] Iceland as an island laboratory,[25] community forest management,[26] land as a resource,[27] the sea,[28] Irish holy wells,[29] the climate,[30] carbonscapes,[31] and international relations.[32] Though the studies vary remarkably regarding the entities they discuss, there seems to be an underlying consent for the fruitful perspectives it derives from the role it plays in *dissecting established entities*.

Conduct and Directionality

A second strand of assemblage-oriented approaches revolves around conduct and directionality. Several scholars mention in their works that assemblage thinking has some parallels and interconnections to literature focusing on the problems of governing raised in Foucault's work on biopolitics.[33] Being occupied with the question of how political reason (*raison d'État*) is implemented in Western societies, Foucault introduced the notion of assemblage to identify and highlight a distinctive combination of political knowledge and technology that allows a population to be governed[34]: the military-diplomatic apparatus

---

[23] D. Swanton, "The Steel Plant as Assemblage", *Geoforum* 44 (2013), pp. 282–291.
[24] E.X.Y. Yap, "The Transnational Assembling of Marina Bay, Singapore", *Singapore Journal of Tropical Geography* 34 (2013), pp. 390–406.
[25] B. Greenhough, "Assembling an Island Laboratory", *Area* 43 (2011) 2, pp. 134–138.
[26] T. Murray Li, "Practices of Assemblage and Community Forest Management", *Economy and Society* 36 (2007), pp. 263–293.
[27] T. Murray Li, "What is Land? Assembling a Resource for Global Investment", *Transaction of the Institute of British Geographers* 39 (2014), pp. 589–602.
[28] C. Bear, "Assembling the Sea: Materiality, Movement and Regulatory Practices in the Cardigan Bay Scallop Fishery", *Cultural Geographies* 20 (2013), pp. 21–41.
[29] R. Foley, "Performing Health in Place: The Holy Well as a Therapeutic Assemblage", *Health and Place* 17 (2011) 2, pp. 470–479.
[30] S. Arora-Jonsson et al., "Carbon and Cash in Climate Assemblages: The Making of a New Global Citizenship", *Antipode* 48 (2016) 1, pp. 74–96.
[31] H. Haarstad and T.I. Wanvik, "Carbonscapes and Beyond: Conceptualizing the Instability of Oil Landscapes", *Progress in Human Geography* (2016) preprint, pp. 1–19.
[32] M. Acuto and S. Curtis (eds.), *Reassembling International Theory: Assemblage Thinking and International Relations*, Wiesbaden: Springer, 2013.
[33] See, e.g., Legg, "Of Scales, Networks and Assemblages".
[34] M. Foucault, *Security, Territory, Population: Lectures at the Collège de France 1977–78*, Basingstoke: Palgrave Macmillan, 2009, p. 384; the course summary (p. 437) speaks of "technologies".

and the apparatus of police. Their function is "to maintain a relation of forces" and to enable "the growth of each of the forces without the break-up of the whole".³⁵ From this ontological³⁶ understanding of assemblage as the distinctive (and actual/tangible) technologies and knowledge through which a *raison d'État* takes shape and unfolds follows an explicative interest how a certain assemblage has been arranged and develops in order to successfully serve these functions.

The notion of assemblage does not mirror a general or abstract interest in processes of emergence at first hand, but a more reconstructive interest in the "internal forces" – the mechanisms of security – ensuring the functioning of a "state" and the management of its population at a certain point of time. Directly referring to Foucault, Miller and Rose develop their interpretation of assemblages precisely from the problem of how governing is realized through conduct and "conducting of conduct"³⁷ and, consequently, provide an explanation of assemblages that "bring persons, organizations and objectives into alignment".³⁸ With the notion of assemblage, the authors comprehend the functionality and value of certain "elements" – or rather instruments – of the social world through which government can be exerted:

> devices, tools, techniques, personnel, material, and apparatuses that *enable authorities to imagine and act upon the conduct of persons* [emphasis added], individually and collectively and in locals that were often distant. These were assemblages that enabled what we termed, borrowing loosely from the writings of Bruno Latour, "government at a distance".³⁹

Taking up the idea of directionality, Barry, in his study on technological zones, offers a more pronounced version of "agencement or assemblage" by defining it as a zone "that accelerates and intensifies agency in particular directions, and with unpredictable and dynamic effects".⁴⁰ He speaks of "a structuring of relations, which has a normative force, but one which does not necessarily take

---

35 However, assemblage is not a very prominent or stabilized term in this case; the table of content of the English translation, for instance, uses both "assemblage" and "ensemble" to point to the role of technologies for implementing governmental rationality.
36 Here, I refer to Searle's understanding of the ontologically subjective: J. Searle, *Die Konstruktion gesellschaftlicher Wirklichkeit: Zur Ontologie sozialer Tatsachen*, Reinbek: Rowohlt, 1997.
37 P. Miller and N. Rose, *Governing the Present: Administering Economic, Social and Personal Life*, Cambridge: Polity, 2008, p. 16.
38 Ibid., pp. 21–22.
39 Ibid., p. 16.
40 A. Barry, "Technological Zones", *European Journal of Social Theory* 9 (2006) 2, pp. 239–253, at 241.

a disciplinary form".[41] In doing so, he, on the one hand, underlines the directing, controlling, or regulating effects of an assemblage, but, on the other hand, he avoids an overly deterministic perspective by emphasizing the *unpredictability* of effects. Structuring and alignment of agency within a formation is, however, not considered to be an open, self-organizing process but is assumed to result from a directionality that "during recent decades [...] has been justified, in part, by the neoliberal rationality of market liberalization and economic freedom".[42] This allows for an actual reading of assemblage to be undertaken that comes close to more structuralist perspectives, such as "apparatus" and "dispositive". It problematizes the production of relative stability and the maintenance of forces through technology and knowledge.[43] To extract a conclusion from these observations on the usage of "assemblage" in the field of governing, I assume that considering governing through an assemblage heuristic might broaden the perspective towards the fundamental heterogeneity of "things" through which governance is performed, maintained, and reproduced. Its conceptual plasticity might facilitate comparative approaches towards governance but perhaps at the expense of an empirical vagueness.

The Human Body as Terrain

Thirdly, assemblage thinking has been adapted to the discussion of the fabrication of the human body and its constant repositioning through knowledge, technology, science, and politics. In this field of enquiry, assemblage is developed as a means of "thinking bodies other than through oppositional categories which necessarily reframes our understandings of the encounters between bodies and other objects, including the technological", as Dianne Currier states by referring to the work of Elizabeth Grosz and other thinkers in the field of feminist theories and intersectional approaches.[44] Such a use of assemblage aims at disentangling the alleged identity[45] of the human body and instead introduces

---

41 Ibid.
42 Ibid.
43 Legg, "Of Scales, Networks and Assemblages", p. 239.
44 D. Currier, "Feminist Technological Futures: Deleuze and Body/Technology Assemblages", *Feminist Theory* 4 (2003) 3, pp. 321–338, at 325.
45 Interestingly, it has been argued that, finally, Haraway's concept of the cyborg as an amalgamation fails to break with the concept of identity precisely at the point where it is produced – at "the intersection of bodies and technologies"– as it logically presupposes (and thereby constructs) the identity it aims to overcome. See Currier, "Feminist Technological Futures", p. 323.

an idea of the human body as an assemblage that is, moreover, part of other assemblages. Though she does not work with an assemblage-related terminology, the intellectual technique Donna Haraway unfolds in her seminal work on *Simians, Cyborgs, and Women* is foundational to this debate as it offers a strategy for comprehending processes of disintegrating and decentring of the human body by questioning allegedly given boundaries and binaries, such as human/non-human, nature/technology, human/machine, and body/environment. Interestingly, her argument is based on an analysis of "the apparatus of bodily production" since the 1980s: the discovery of immunological reactions in the 1960s and the subsequent invention of the immune system as a pivot of biomedicine and biotechnology in the 1980s marks (to her) a turning point in the construction of bodies and selfs, making the immune system an "elaborate icon for principal systems of symbolic and material 'difference' in late capitalism".[46] "Bodies", as Haraway concludes, "are not born; but they are made."[47] Moreover, the body is always "a historically specific terrain".[48]

The actual terrain comes from the biomedicalization that is "made possible by such technoscientific innovations as molecular biology, biotechnologies, genomization, transplant medicine, and new medical technologies".[49] Bodies, therefore, are neither stable entities nor do they have *one* clear and identifiable boundary; instead, Haraway describes them as "material-semiotic generative nodes" with boundaries that "materialize in social interaction; 'objects' like the bodies do not pre-exist as such".[50] As Currier states, Haraway's reformulation of the body can be read as a reconstitution of "the body as an object of knowledge primarily as an information construct".[51] However, the "historically specific terrain" is not only the terrain of technoscientific knowledge but also a terrain of ethical and juridical struggles about the implications and boundaries of technoscientific inventions.

As a conclusion from this body of research, assemblage thinking here serves as a mode to develop a new perspective on the human body that challenges the very idea of its pre-given, natural integrity or identity. By subjecting the body to new biomedical technologies, not only has its discursive production

---

46 D.J. Haraway, *Simians, Cyborgs, and Women: The Reinvention of Nature*, Abingdon: Routledge, 1991, p. 204.
47 Ibid., p. 208.
48 Ibid.
49 A. Clarke et al., "Biomedicalization: Technoscientific Transformations of Health, Illness, and U.S. Biomedicine", *American Sociological Review* 68 (2003), pp. 161–194, at 162.
50 Haraway, *Simians, Cyborgs, and Women*, p. 208.
51 Currier, "Feminist Technological Futures", p. 322.

take on a new quality but it has also revealed the need to conceptually address the human body in a way that takes into account the dynamics of its constant production through a multitude of external conditions.

Performing Globalization

A fourth field of using assemblage revolves around globalization and globalized practices. Whereas the Foucauldian usage of assemblage is mainly restricted to his interest in the emerging "modern" technologies of governing a population – and thus does not struggle with "globalization" – the concept recently has received remarkable attention in the field of globalization. Here, I discuss two of them: The role of assemblage in Saskia Sassen's 2006 book on *Territory, Authority, Rights: From Medieval to Global Assemblages*, and in her 2010 article entitled "When the City Itself Becomes a Technology of War", as well as in Stephen Collier and Aihwa Ong's 2005 volume on *Global Assemblages*. These scholars, nevertheless, apply assemblage thinking in quite contrasting ways: Sassen's work, on the one hand, focuses mainly on what she identifies as a substantial altering of conditions of urban order that manifest in "asymmetric wars" localized "in the larger assemblages of territory, authority and rights within which they take place".[52] In framing these new conditions, Sassen depicts a rather dystopic scenario of cities, which become targets of terrorist attacks as well as mediating sites of asymmetric wars spawning all kinds of social and distributive battles around the provision and basic supply of water, food, and energy – fuelled by climate change and global warming:

> We are seeing the multiplication of a broad range of partial, often highly specialized or obscure, assemblages of bits of territory, authority and rights once firmly ensconced in national and interstate institutional frames. These assemblages cut across the binary of inside and outside, our and theirs, national versus global. They arise out of and can inhabit national institutional and territorial settings; they can also arise out of mixes of national and global elements and span the globe in what are largely trans-local geographies connecting multiple sub-national spaces.[53]

Assemblage, here, mainly denotes a certain observational awareness of changing relations between certain dimensions through which sociopolitical realities unfold. Assemblages emerge from – or even take over – established arrangements

---

[52] S. Sassen, "When the City Itself Becomes a Technology of War", *Theory, Culture & Society* 27 (2010), pp. 33–50, at 34.
[53] Ibid., pp. 45–46.

that have mainly unfolded through territorial logics, which are now increasingly being substituted by non-territorial spatialities. Sassen declares her usage of the term as purely descriptive, thereby implicitly denying any explanatory capacity. In summarizing her position, Mather aptly states that for Sassen assemblage is a

> descriptive tool that allows her to illuminate the variety of ways in which territory, authority and rights are assembled – or disassembled – in particular places. It does not, however, carry theoretical weight: she writes, "I locate my theorization elsewhere" (Sassen, 2006: 5). In other words, her *explanation* happens elsewhere.[54]

Notwithstanding, this description is not entirely pre-explanatory, even if it is meant to serve as a neutral, pre-theoretical, and innocent term. In a very fundamental sense, detaching description from explanation denies that there is no formation of a subject of enquiry without presuppositions. Any description is inevitably written from "somewhere"; relies on choices, inclusions, and, omissions; and comprises order and arrangements at least in a rudimentary way. In a more specific sense, the descriptive dimension the concept of assemblage undoubtedly entails is substantiated by epistemological considerations. Furthermore, abandoning any explanatory capacity also distracts the usage of the concept from its Foucauldian role in understanding the history of political reason and governing, which was to reveal processes of forming "associations" of heterogeneous objects, such as institutions, inventions, techniques, etc.[55]

In contrast to Sassen's "refreshingly frank refusal to play around",[56] in their debate on the analytical capacities of the term Collier and Ong explicitly present assemblage as an analytical response to what is experienced as globalization.[57] Global assemblages, as they call this group or class of emerging forms, are reactions to certain problems; they are defined as "sites for the formation and reformation of what we will call [...] *anthropological problems* [original emphasis]".[58] The authors argue – reminding us of Foucault's notion of problematization – that new assemblages originate from a distinctive class of problems

---

54 C. Mather, "Assembling Geographies of Global Crisis", *Dialogues in Human Geography* 1 (2011), pp. 342–345, at 344.
55 In retreating from a discussion of its analytical capacities, Sassen's implementation of the concept, hence – as Anderson et al. put it – "loses sight of what we take to be the key starting point of an assemblage-based analysis of the social: to understand assembling as an ongoing process of forming and sustaining associations between diverse constituents" (B. Anderson et al., "On Assemblages and Geography", *Dialogues in Human Geography* 2 (2012) 2, pp. 171–189, at 174).
56 Sparke, "Triangulating Globalization", p. 2.
57 Collier and Ong, "Global Assemblages, Anthropological Problems", p. 3.
58 Ibid., p. 4.

that arise from "forms and values of individual and collective existence [...] that [...] are subject to technological, political, and ethical reflection and intervention".[59] Therefore, globalization does not focus on "broad structural formations or new configurations of society and culture", but rather "examines a range of phenomena that articulate such shifts: technoscience, circuits of licit and illicit exchange, systems of administration or governance, and regimes of ethics and values".[60]

The "global" in global assemblages is given a double meaning by the authors. By considering certain phenomena as "global", "we meant to emphasize a peculiar characteristic of their conditions of possibility", which lies in their "distinctive capacity for decontextualization and recontextualization, abstractability and movement, across diverse social and cultural situations and spheres of life".[61] This allows a twofold perspective to be taken on the phenomena in question. The definition might be applied to phenomena that have already been disseminated and, thereby, transformed social conditions as they rely on "global" social forms that are "abstractable, mobile, and dynamic, moving across and reconstituting 'society,' 'culture,' and 'economy,'".[62] Beyond a reconstructive interest, there is also a speculative dimension in the definition, insofar that it focuses on the *potential* material technologies or specialized social expertise that *might unfold* to foster cross-contextual mobility and movement. From that, a definition of assemblage is derived that includes both the effect and the process, thereby invoking the double notion of stability and permanent shifts or recombinations:

> An assemblage is the product of multiple determinations that are not reducible to a single logic. The temporality of an assemblage is emergent. It does not always involve new forms, but forms that are shifting, in formation, or at stake. As a composite concept, the term "*global assemblage*" [original emphasis] suggests inherent tensions: global implies broadly encompassing, seamless, and mobile; assemblage implies heterogeneous, contingent, unstable, partial and situated.[63]

This line of debate essentially scrutinizes mobilization and circulation by targeting processes that cross boundaries that have been recognized/proven as being relatively stable. Consequently, this notion of assemblage brings into

---

[59] Ibid.
[60] Ibid.
[61] Ibid., pp. 10–11.
[62] Ibid., p. 11.
[63] Ibid., p. 12.

view tension between "entity" and "process", between formation and the formed without privileging the one over the other.

Conceptual Convergences, Flat Epistemologies

Without claiming to provide an entire picture here, the four strands depicted above show some similarities if not convergences. Firstly, assemblage thinking considers formation *processes*, that is to say fluidity, changes, dynamics, and instabilities. These are addressed in two ways: On the one hand, by focusing on networked formations and emergence, assemblage thinking offers a procedural perspective on the relevance of technology in societal change. However, it not only (re)instates the relevance of "materiality", "technique", and "infrastructure" but also acknowledges that "materials experience an emancipation from their role as passive recipients and start to co-articulate agency and shape political practices".[64] On the other hand (and more generally), assemblage thinking challenges the idea of pre-givenness, unchangeability, and immutability – a perspective that it clearly shares with other sociotheoretical perspectives. What it might add to existing debates is a greater focus on the problem of stabilization and destabilization of entities.

Secondly, assemblages are considered *relational*[65] because the formation process – yielding a (new) "whole" or "entity" – is assumed to have effects on the elements it incorporates and aligns, while – in turn – elements are never completely absorbed, determined, or aligned by a certain assemblage. Hence, not only an assemblage itself is mutable, but also its networked elements are constantly transformed through their relational combination and joining of other assemblages. Consequently, in the light of assemblage thinking, causality needs to be reconsidered as it can be conceived of as neither macro-driven nor micro-driven but as inherent to formation processes. This does not mean that there is no causality at all but rather that causality is neither confined to a certain causal structure, a single centre, or some kind of upward and downward stream of causation nor to another kind of "invisible hand". At this point, the attention paid

---

64 M. Müller, "Assemblages and Actor-Networks: Rethinking Socio-material Power, Politics and Space", *Geography Compass* 9 (2015) 1, pp. 27–41, at 34.
65 See, e.g., DeLanda, *A New Philosophy of Society*; DeLanda, *Assemblage Theory*; D. Featherstone, "On Assemblage and Articulation", *Area* 43 (2011) 2, pp. 139–142; Müller, "Assemblages and Actor-Networks".

by assemblage thinking to relationality might help to go beyond what Hirshman and Reed call "the limitations of traditional forcing-cause arguments" and broaden – methodologically as well as empirically – what is taken into consideration to explain social realities.[66] This, however, requires a closer look at what "inherent" could mean.

Thirdly, assemblages are conceived of as being *responsive* – to a demand, a deficit, or an affordance that has become a problem from a certain perspective. Throughout the strands of debates, assemblages have been related to specific moments of inventions that supposedly reveal a new quality, in that they might fundamentally change human/social life: for example, when new modes of governing are invented, when new technologies and procedures of treating the human body arrive, or when new types of conflict emerge. Though assemblage thinking refuses monocausal models of explanation, it identifies certain generative moments: *potentialities* of technologies, *problems* of governing, and human *desires*.[67] Such a problematization, as Rabinow states, "is both a kind of general historical and social situation – saturated with power relations, as are all situations, and imbued with the relational 'play of truth and false', a diacritic marking a subclass of situations – as well as a nexus of responses to that situation".[68] Despite the question how these problematizations can be dealt with in terms of social, political, psychoanalytical, anthropological, geographical, or other ways of reasoning, it can be concluded at this point that assemblages are widely conceived of as responsive formations but presumably not in a direct or unilineal "problem solving" manner. Accordingly, the military-diplomatic apparatus and the apparatus of police react to a certain problem of governing but, however, cannot be reduced to it. Also, organ transplantation has been enabled through technical-surgical and biomedical invention as well as a steady accumulation of knowledge and expertise but, however, cannot be reduced to it.

---

[66] D. Hirshman and I.A. Reed, "Formation Stories and Causality in Sociology", *Sociological Theory* 32 (2014) 4, pp. 259–282, at 260.
[67] Assemblages are "*desired* [original emphasis]", as Müller puts it referring to Deleuze; they do not emerge from a nowhere but "have a corporeal component" (Müller, "Assemblages and Actor-Networks", p. 34).
[68] P. Rabinow, "Midst Anthropology's Problems", in: S.J. Collier, A. Ong (eds.): *Global Assemblages: Technology, Politics, and Ethics as Anthropological Problems*, Hoboken: Wiley-Blackwell, 2005, pp. 40–54, at 44.

Assemblage Thinking as Epistemological Tool

Assemblage as a Heuristic

As a consequence of the preceding discussion, I suggest to employ assemblage not as a theory but as a heuristic, that is to say a strategy to address entities by directing attention at their formation processes through "relations of exteriority",[69] their heterogeneous nature, and their potential directionality. As an entity, I consider a "thing", an "object", an "event", or a "practice" that is regarded, acknowledged, addressed, and treated as a whole. I furthermore assume that – according to the "variable ontology of the social"[70] – entities possess different qualities that need to be traced. This has two relevant implications: although the entity is produced relationally, elements do not have predetermined meanings or positions but – being captured by different assemblages – instead might act in completely different ways. Accordingly, "meaning" and "position" depend entirely on the emergence of an assemblage. Furthermore, the role of an element varies, as DeLanda underlines, from "purely *material*" to "purely *expressive*".[71] Though one might object that even talking about a "purely material" role necessarily relies on expressivity, the assumed variability shifts the attention from assemblage as an entity *towards processes and acts of formation*, or *assembling*.

Furthermore, it presupposes an instance that identifies the entity standing out against an undifferentiated background; the entity is produced and, hence, necessarily becomes an imagined and represented entity. "Imagined and represented" means that the entity is perceived, that is to say seen or named an entity, as well as conceived of, that is deliberately or strategically produced. Imagination and representation of the entity – in law, arts, mass and social media, politics, literature, religion, etc. – are part of its formation.[72]

Notwithstanding, this does not mean that using the same word(s) for an entity automatically implies the same entity, quite the contrary. Law and Mol, in their study of foot and mouth disease, argue that there are three ontologically different diseases behind the same terminology – each one having its own qualities, spatialities, and temporalities. This highlights the need to

---

69 DeLanda, *A New Philosophy of Society*, p. 10; referring to Deleuze, see DeLanda, *Assemblage Theory*, p. 2.
70 DeLanda, *Assemblage Theory*, p. 267.
71 DeLanda, *A New Philosophy of Society*, p. 12.
72 For that, I would borrow the term re-entry from systems theory to describe that a topic once identified, named, and represented necessarily becomes an element in the sequence of following social acts, gaining, losing, and shifting meaning.

consider formation processes of entities not as universal but as relational and contextual. "Relations of exteriority" consider formation processes of social entities that are rooted in multiple logics, networks, and resources and, hence, cannot be traced back to some internal characteristics of the entity, a single causal mechanism, or another kind of linearity.[73]

"Directionality", finally, involves two aspects regarding the functioning of social entities. First, it refers to the generative, productive capacity of an entity-in-the-making to drag "elements" into it, to define these elements as elements as well as the relations between these elements, and to align them. Second, it refers to the productive capacity of entities to "have an influence" over something and generate "effects" without assuming a deterministic or linear cause-and-effect mechanism. Instead, "directionality" draws attention to the question how an entity becomes stable enough to gain an influence over social relations and to make certain outcomes probable. Focusing on directionality, thus, emphasizes the role of entity *formation* in attempts of purposeful structuring and aligning elements in a certain field.[74]

Methodological Underdetermination

One major problem of assemblage-oriented approaches arises precisely from what it is valued for: its esteem for a *naked (flat) epistemology*. Assemblages are routinely described as being composed of "heterogeneous elements".[75] Analytically, this type of study starts with addressing an allegedly stable entity (such as a production plant) and enumerates the processes of "gathering, coherence and dispersion"[76] of the respective entity. In terms of social science, the required conceptual approach is very reconstructive as "assemblage views social entities [...] as being formed through the connection of heterogeneous components".[77] Though offering a powerful imagination, notions of "connection", "composition", and "relation" seem to be under-conceptualized in terms of an

---

[73] J. Law and A. Mol, "Veterinary Realities: What is Foot and Mouth Disease?", *Sociologia Ruralis* 51 (2011), pp. 1–16, at 2.
[74] Müller, "Assemblages and Actor-Networks"; Murray Li, "Practices of Assemblage and Community Forest Management".
[75] Collier and Ong, "Global Assemblages, Anthropological Problems", p. 5; Murray Li, "Practices of Assemblage and Community Forest Management", p. 264; Anderson et al., "On Assemblages and Geography", p. 124; Mather, "Assembling Geographies of Global Crisis", p. 343.
[76] Bear, "Assembling the Sea", p. 4.
[77] Swanton, "The Steel Plant as Assemblage", p. 286.

explicit definition of the spectre of connecting and relating processes. Positively said, assemblage-oriented approaches avoid any a priori constriction or reductionism of explanation because "assemblage" "is relatively agnostic about the kinds of 'stuff' that can come together in a formation story".[78] Such "stuff" includes "actions, communications, various kinds of material stuff, and a wide variety of mediations in a way that challenges traditional understandings of levels of analysis".[79] Assemblage offers, as Swanton puts it in his analysis of the assemblage of a steel plant, a "tool that copes with the overwhelming array of technologies, materials and cultures that must hold together for a steel plant to function and recognises the agency of matter". This comprises "all kinds of routine, reproduction work – health and safety, repair and maintenance, monitoring and inspection – [which] are fundamental to production".[80]

Accordingly, assemblage serves complementarily both a demand for structural but not a structuralist understanding of society and a demand for a relatively unspecific conceptual framework that provides room for manoeuvre to address the heterogeneous. Methodologically, it operates between the assumption of stable structures and the realm of pure fluidity – "heterogeneity" or "potentiality", as Anderson et al. term it referring to DeLanda.[81] From an analytical point, therefore, the answer to the question what an actual assemblage comprises is, out of necessity, open ended and non-enumerative. Indeed, it could be literally everything that serves the function of governing – which would be, in Foucault's example, the whole military-diplomatic apparatus and the apparatus of police and, in Savage's example, "everything" ("every technology") that functions as a descriptive tool. If adopted as a term for addressing processes of formation, assemblage does not privilege any "thing" but spans the spectrum from "the material", "the social", and "the affective" to "the ideological" and further on as it simply does not provide criteria to place "things" aside. Assemblage is conceptually mouldable or, as Marcus and Saka declare, it is "an experimental genre form that thus is organic to the contours of the object of study".[82] Negatively said, its non-enumerative, example-driven, and potentially random way of considering forming elements and relations does not offer a transparent basis for operationalization but, instead, runs the risk either to deliberately combine moments of explanation at disposal or to

---

[78] Hirshman and I.A. Reed, "Formation Stories and Causality in Sociology", p. 268.
[79] Ibid.
[80] Swanton, "The Steel Plant as Assemblage", p. 283.
[81] C. McFarlane and B. Anderson, "Assemblage and Geography", *Area* 43 (2011) 2, pp. 124–127, at 125; Anderson et al., "On Assemblages and Geography", p. 184.
[82] Marcus and Saka, "Assemblage", p. 103.

fall back in some (supposed to be overcome) disciplinary routines of constructing explanation.

To overcome its methodological underdetermination, scholars have opted both for a Latourian-inspired as well as actor-network theory (ANT)-oriented as well as a Foucauldian-based explication of assemblage thinking.[83] One example for the latter can be derived from Murray Li's work on community forest management in Canada. Assemblage enriches her observational perspective as it "enables the expansion of the analytic of governmentality" and "finesse questions of agency by recognizing the situated subjects who do the work of pulling together the heterogeneous elements". First – instead of explicating the heterogeneity to which she also refers in the beginning – she identifies a number of practices through which the "continuous work of pulling disparate things together" (ibid.) is performed. The practices she explicitly names are (1) forging alignment, (2) rendering technical, (3) authorizing knowledge, (4) managing failures and contradictions, (5) anti-politics, and (6) reassembling.[84]

Forging alignment refers to practices that show a "will to govern as point of convergence and fracture" and covers the work of linking objectives and interests of parties involved. Concerning *rendering technical*, she identifies those practices that extract the problem "from the messiness of the social world" as well as those techniques that shape the problem, present the possibility of intervention, and demonstrate the benefit. *Authorizing practices* revolve around the identification of the "requisite body of knowledge". Another type of practices comprises *managing failures and contradictions*, which – for the sake of governing them – might be presented as "rectifiable deficiencies" that can be smoothed out. *Anti-politics*, then, addresses a specific mode of dealing with problems by rendering "them as a matter of techniques" and locating them in arenas of administration and expertise instead of political debate. *Reassembling*, finally, refers to a constant "grafting on new elements, reworking old ones, [and] transposing the meaning of old terms".[85]

Though it is not entirely clear if the set of practices and the categories of elements are deduced from a theoretical perspective or inductively extracted from fieldwork, the selection is informed by a Foucauldian-based interest in social struggles through which modes of governing practice unfold. By this, Murray Li offers an approach to the black box of the heterogeneous as she

---

[83] For an ANT-oriented approach, see Müller, "Assemblages and Actor-Networks"; for a Foucauldian-based explication of assemblage thinking, see Legg, "Of Scales, Networks and Assemblages".
[84] Murray Li, "Practices of Assemblage and Community Forest Management", p. 264–267.
[85] Ibid.

focuses on "everything" that supports – in a broad sense – the will to govern. Likewise, anti-politics can be framed as a strategy serving an interest in governing people, relations, and problems in a different way. The "multitude" is reduced to specific aspects of practices that employ a range of elements identified as *things*, being material objects such as trees, logs, non-timber forest products, etc.; *situated subjects*, such as villagers, labourers, entrepreneurs, officials, activists; *objectives*, such as profit, pay, livelihood, control, property, etc.; and *arrays of* "knowledge, discourses, institutions, laws and regulatory regimes".[86] However, as elements-in-practice(s), they all are subject to the representational dynamics of the formation process, including the *perceived* ontological status of the respective element. Though reductive in the sense of concentrating on practices and techniques of governance, Murray Li offers a perspective that is neither reductive in terms of methodologically predetermined boundaries, elements, and relations of the assumed entity nor does it assume a consistent and durable entity.[87]

Though assemblage thinking deserves a deeper examination of the ways it has been combined with entirely different approaches to space, the last section focuses on three aspects: (1) the spatial/non-spatial interpretation of de-/territorialization in the Deleuzoguattarian strand of assemblage thinking, (2) its attractiveness for geography, which results from its parallels to the idea of ideographic reconstruction of geographic entities, and (3) the closeness of assemblage thinking to topological concepts of space.

Slippery Slopes: Addressing "Space" in Strands of Assemblage Thinking

Territorialization

Territorialization is, according to DeLanda, a key term in the work of Deleuze and Guattari that has a very specific meaning within the parametric description of an assemblage. In DeLanda's interpretation,

---

[86] Ibid.
[87] D. Massey, "Spacetime, 'Science' and the Relationship between Physical Geography and Human Geography", *Transactions of the Institute of British Geographers* 24 (1999), pp. 261–276, at 269; Murray Li, "What is Land?", p. 590.

> [t]erritorialisation refers not only to the determination of the spatial boundaries of a whole – as in the territory of a community, city, or nation-state – but also to the degree to which as assemblage's component parts are drawn from a homogeneous repertoire, or the degree to which an assemblage homogenises its own components.[88]

DeLanda defines it as "an important parameter, or *variable coefficient*" [original emphasis] of a social whole. By referring to Deleuze and Guattari, he uses parametrical thinking in order to use the idea that the two different kinds of social wholes, stratum, or assemblage should be understood not as opposites but as phases – like substances taking on a certain aggregate state. Transition between phases is regulated through parameters. Territorializing, thus, refers to the degree to which an assemblage is homogenized; it refers "to the degree to which an assemblage's component parts are drawn from a homogeneous repertoire, or the degree to which an assemblage homogenises its own components".[89]

However, the "not only" in DeLanda's quote is telling; though primarily non-spatial, de-/territorialization apparently can work through spatial means, that is to say through the determination of spatial boundaries. Notwithstanding the double notion of territorialization with its spatial and non-spatial interpretations, geographers (not surprisingly) tend to emphasize the spatial implication. Territorialization is, as Bear in an article entitled "Assembling the Sea" underlines, "first about the acquisition, definition and reinforcement of spatial boundaries"– "whether through networks [...] or through the jurisdictional boundaries of governmental organization",[90] as he continues in quoting Braun. Consequently, territorialization is understood as "implicitly exclusionary".[91] However, the understanding of territorializing and deterritorializing developed by Bear goes beyond the expression of a political will, objective, or interest. And – as territorialization is not confined to human beings – Bear's understanding also goes beyond an animal's or a group of animals' attempt at controlling movement, proximity, and distance, including deterritorializing effects through movement caused by non-living objects like currents. Together with fish and dolphins, they are the deterritorializing elements of the assemblage, whereas fishery mainly exerts territorializing impulses. Territorialization, as Bear states, "can also refer to 'non-spatial processes which increase the internal

---

[88] DeLanda, *Assemblage Theory*, p. 22.
[89] Ibid., pp. 19–22.
[90] Bear, "Assembling the Sea", p. 4.
[91] B. Braun, "Environmental Issues: Global Natures in the Space of Assemblage", *Progress in Human Geography* 30 (2006) 5, pp. 644–654.

homogeneity of an assemblage'".[92] A conflict, for instance, might increase the degree of territorialization of a community in terms of exaggerating differences perceived between "us" and "them" and manifest boundary-drawing.

From this perspective follows, first, that assemblages can stimulate transformative processes and change the elements through which they are formed (armies, or "war machines", are one example deployed by Deleuze and Guattari as well as by DeLanda). Assemblages not only have top-down effects on their parts in terms of changing the component parts, they are also built of (DeLanda 2016:71) but, moreover, causality is directly linked to (depends on?) the degree of territorialization. It follows, second, that homogenizing might be accomplished through spatial means *but not necessarily has to be*, that is to say through defining areas, spatial remits, and borders performing processes of homogenizing and exclusion as two sides of the same coin.[93]

Attractiveness to Geography

The way assemblage is understood as the effect or resultant of processes of the formation of heterogeneous elements from physical substrates, living creatures, buildings, human and non-human beings, interactions, and infrastructures to emotions and ideologies reveals parallels to older concepts of holism that have been quite popular in the history of geographical thinking. Specifically, the "notion of heterogeneous actants"[94] seems to provide some continuity or recovery in geographical reasoning. Though there might be an important difference of how the *Allzusammenhang der Dinge* – a figure of thought many geographers are familiar with – has been treated as objectivity or as potentiality, there are resemblances.[95] At least with regard to geography, assemblage permits a re-entering and justification of the old menagerie of objects of different ontological status, such as material, natural, and artificial objects as well as mental objects and objective knowledge. Another parallel lies in the idea of individuation and an ideographic approach in geography. Simplified to the extreme, an ideographic approach in geography refers to the uniqueness of geographic objects such as certain landscapes, whose characteristic cannot be understood fully by applying nomothetic rules as they have an expressive quality that

---

92 Ibid., p. 40.
93 DeLanda, *Assemblage Theory*, p. 71.
94 Bear, "Assembling the Sea", p. 3.
95 There is, of course, a fundamental difference in the way stability is thought of being existent or something that is constantly in "becoming".

results from a close interaction of a potential multitude of elements. If we reduce this ideographic approach to its essence, apparently there is a similarity to DeLanda's interpretation of the entity of an assemblage:

> Communities and organisations are historically individual entities, as much so as the persons that compose them. While it is true that the term "individual" has come to refer to persons (or organisms in the case of animals and plants), it is not incoherent to speak of individual communities, individual organisations, individual cities, or individual countries. The term "individual" has no preferential affinity for a particular scale (persons or organisms) but refers to an entity that is historically unique.[96]

Besides permitting a re-entry of holistic thinking through the backdoor, reading assemblage theory this way can easily be taken as a justification for identifying "classical" geographic objects such as the Alps, the Great Plains, or the Steppe as emergent entities that can be traced backed in terms of their respective processes of individuation. Though DeLanda does not go into detail at this point, we can at least state that assemblage thinking *this way* sets the stage for a resuscitation of encompassing geographic concepts, such as a certain landscape or city or any other ideographic entity "out there". Indeed, at first glance, this could be read as a call for a historical reconstruction of "geographic" entities. However, this is not the primary aim if we follow Bear quoting Braun's "brief exposition of geographies of assemblage [that] comes through understanding that "entities [...] may be usefully treated as products of historical processes'".[97] This, as Bear continues, "relates to Cresswell's call to re-focus "on the vertical aspects of place – the "thereness" of a particular location and locale that is both the product of horizontal flows and a reason for those flows combining precisely there". From a disciplinary perspective, assemblage-based notion of entities come close to an understanding of "place specificity" that has been developed by Doreen Massey in her elaboration on power geometries. Here, she suggests considering "what gives a place its specificity is not some long internalized history but the fact that it is constructed out of a particular constellation of relations, articulated together at a particular locus". A certain representational trope, hence, should not be conflated, neither with the extent of a formation process nor with its alleged coherence.[98]

---

96 DeLanda, *Assemblage Theory*, p. 13.
97 Bear, "Assembling the Sea", p. 15.
98 D. Massey, "Power-geometry and a Progressive Sense of Place", in: J. Bird et al. (eds.), *Mapping the Futures: Local Cultures, Global Change*, Abingdon: Routledge, 1993, pp. 59–69, at 66.

Topology

Though assemblage thinking does not propose a single or uniform concept of space, I would follow Müller in his assumption that "[p]erhaps the most immediately spatial implication of adopting an assemblage [...] perspective is [its] view of space as topological".[99] In echoing the debate mainly sparked by John Allen's contributions to geography's adaptation of topology,[100] Müller suggests to read assemblage thinking and its potential spatial implication through the lens of a broader debate on non-metric concepts of space that is not limited to assemblage thinking but also includes geographic adaptations of actor-network theory and (as we will see later on) notions of relational space.[101]

In order to prepare the ground for topological thinking, Müller uses the picture of a handkerchief "whose ends, if laid out flat on a table, are far from each other but end up close together when scrunched"[102] – a picture that is already applied by Serres and Latour and, later on, taken up by Allen to understand the conceptual approach of actor-network theory towards "space".[103] If we abstract from the handkerchief, we get the idea of a flat grid evenly and potentially endlessly stretched in two directions (though the handkerchief, of course, has four edges). Every point of this structure is clearly defined by grid-related coordinates. "Scrunching up", then, means any *de*formation or *trans*formation of the primary structure of the grid by which distant points become contiguous or overlapping, and, consequently, the primary form is transformed into another. The general idea of transformation is intuitively accessible if we think of two- or three-dimensional forms as they correspond to the space of our experience. However, transformation loses immediate comprehensibility if expressed set theoretically, geometrically, or algebraically. Yet, a topological approach to space is utilized

---

99 Müller, "Assemblages and Actor-Networks", p. 35.
100 J. Allen, "Powerful Geographies: Spatial Shifts in the Architecture of Globalization", in: S. Clegg and C. Haugaard (eds.), *The Handbook of Power*, London: Sage, 2008, pp. 157–173; J. Allen, "Three Spaces of Power: Territory, Networks, plus a Topological Twist in the Tale of Domination and Authority", *Journal of Power* 2 (2009) 2, pp. 197–212; J. Allen, "Making Space for Topology", *Dialogues in Human Geography* 1 (2011) 3, pp. 316–318; J. Allen, "Powerful Assemblages?", *Area* 43 (2011) 2, pp. 154–157; J. Allen, "Topological Twists", *Dialogues in Human Geography* 1 (2011) 3, pp. 283–298; A. Latham, "Topologies and the Multiplicities of Space-Time", *Dialogues in Human Geography* 1 (2011) 3, pp. 312–315, at 313
101 D. Massey, *For Space*, London: Sage, 2005; J. Murdoch, "The Spaces of Actor-Network-Theory", *Geoforum* 29 (1998) 4, pp. 357–374; Müller, "Assemblages and Actor-Networks".
102 Müller, "Assemblages and Actor-Networks", p. 35.
103 For Serres and Latour, see Murdoch, "The Spaces of Actor-Network-Theory", p. 360; Allen, "Topological Twists", p. 285.

not to make the depth of a mathematical field productive for social sciences but to imaginatively oppose the idea of geometric space rendered in terms of Euclidian geometry. The potential abstractness of a topological notion is countered by a sensorial, perceptual grounding. Meant to capture "the disruption to our sense of what is near and what is far",[104] the topological imagination challenges the alleged hegemonic idea of geometric and topographic notions of space by claiming that a Euclidean, metric space is not the only spatiality geographers should be aware of. A topological approach is, hence, characterized by its opposition to metric space, or, more precisely, by the assumption that proximity is not determined by metric variables.

In geography, Euclidean geometry has broadly been associated with models of *metric* (or *physical*) distance, extension, dispersion, and (physical) limitation. Corresponding with a Euclidian approach to space, scholars have emphasized that the *measurement of space* and *governing via spatial means* have amalgamated in the specific form of a power technology pursuing the modern state.[105] Metric space, equated with the measured and mapped "territory", and "territory", equated with "space", per se makes metric space the hegemonic form of social spatiality. Concepts of metric space in this broadened sense offer a perspective on human action and social order that is limited by the question in how far metrics (distances, extensions, limits) could claim any explanatory power. And indeed, there has been a substantial critique even in the heyday of quantified geographical models operating in the logics of metrisized space with regard to the limited analytical range and potential reductionism of metric projections of social facts. A taken-for-granted conceptualization of space as metric space equated with territory, thus, has been blamed both for its (limited and even more) shrinking capacity to deal with the complexity of "real world" transformations as well as for its methodologically privileging sociopolitical orders that are built on absolute space, such as the modern nation-state.[106]

At this point, a topological notion of space provides, presumedly, a theoretical means to prepare ground for non-metric concepts of addressing social spatialities, which, as Latham postulates, "allows us to account for the complex orderings of

---

[104] Allen, "Topological Twists", p. 284–290.
[105] R. Sack, *Human Territoriality: Its Theory and History*, Cambridge: Cambridge University Press, 1986, p. 218; S. Elden, "Governmentality, Calculation, Territory", *Environment and Planning D: Society and Space* 25 (2007), pp. 562–580.
[106] J. Agnew, "The Territorial Trap: The Geographical Assumptions of International Relations Theory", *International Political Economy* 1 (1994) 1, pp. 53–80.

everyday spaces in novel ways".[107] It is expected to free spatial reasoning from a preoccupation with – literally – *geometric* space, that is to say points, lines, and areas projected on the earth surface, and, hence, to avoid a preselection of certain spatialities, such as the bounded space of the nation-state and its subdivisions. Indeed, the examples presented in the literature – for example, transnational social movements – emphasize a reconceptualization of space beyond the idea of territorial fixation and durability and, instead, shift towards the analysis of flexible alignments of distant elements without stepping into the trap of a binary opposition of "the global" and "the local".[108]

(1) Topology as diagnosis: The way topology is adapted by Allen implies that we are witnessing a fundamental change in society regarding its underlying spatiality. Whereas modern society – how vague and in need of explanation this notion may be – was performed through an absolute and abstract concept of space[109] epitomized in the fixed and distinct territorial geometries of nation-states that, in turn, became the hegemonic concept of space, today's world society works *differently*. Topology, thus, is assumed to be a/ the contemporary spatial form of a globalized world. This notion of topology points to empirico-historical processes of transformation, through which established networks based on metric relations and territorial proximities are shattered and which networks arrive that are built on new forms of relationality. In this perspective, a topological or relational space is the result of seminal processes of transformation for which territorial forms of the social are mere legacies, as the following quote illustrates:

> The varied processes of spatial stretching, inter-dependence and flow, combine in situ trajectories of sociospatial evolution and change, to propose place – the city, region or rural area – as a site of intersection between network topologies and territorial legacies. The result is no simple displacement of the local by the global, of place by space, of history by simultaneity and flow, of small by big scale, or of the proximate by the remote. Instead, it is a subtle folding together of the distant and the proximate, the virtual and the material, presence and absence, flow and stasis, into a single ontological plane upon which location – a place on the map – has come to be relationally and topologically defined.[110]

---

107 Latham, "Topologies and the Multiplicities of Space-Time", p. 313.
108 Müller, "Assemblages and Actor-Networks", p. 35.
109 "An abstract space and time provide the economy with a powerful, practical, and easily manipulated framework to organize people and resources for a mass society" (Sack, *Human Territoriality*, p. 218).
110 M. Jones, "Phase Space: Geography, Relational Thinking and Beyond", *Progress in Human Geography* 33 (2009) 4, pp. 487–506, at 487.

Topology as diagnosis resonates with the third form of assemblage thinking by focusing on emergent effects of certain global forms crossing established boundaries and contexts through their abstractedness.

(2) Topology as methodology: There is, however, a second notion of topology at work in assemblage thinking that is distinct from its diagnostic claim. Topology also refers to the idea of relationality, which is as well present in relational geographies and especially in ANT, as Murdoch underlines:

> What ANT adds to the more commonplace understandings of relational spaces is a concern with network. While the term network is commonly utilised in social science to describe technological relations, economic forms, political structures and social processes, ANT uses the term in a way which is quite distinct from such applications. Or rather, it might be argued that ANT bundles all these network applications together for it concerns itself with the heterogeneity of networks; that is, ANT seeks to analyse how social and material processes (subjects, objects and relations) become seamlessly entwined within complex sets of association. This leads on to an interest in "network topologies", with the ways that spaces emerge as socio-material relations are arranged into orders and hierarchies.[111]

Here, topology does not serve to mark the gap between an already conventionalized territorial concept of space, on the one hand, and a newly emerging spatiality, on the other, but to blend the concepts of relationality and spatiality in one new conceptual approach that is called "network topology". This second notion of topology resonates with a broader strand of what has been called "thinking space relationally" and is already present in Jones' quote above – indicating that witnessing major transformation processes often come along with methodological changes, with none of them being superior to the other.[112] As "relational thinking" "dissolves the boundaries between objects and space, and rejects forms of spatial totality", he concludes that "objects *are* space, space *is* objects, and moreover objects can be understood *only* [all original emphasis] in relation to other objects – with all this being a perpetual becoming of heterogeneous networks and events that connect internal spatiotemporal relations".[113] Topology, here, refers to the form of social, economic, and political relations and arrangements that inherently (by definition) *is* spatial. "Scrunching up", then, promotes an existing form that can be rearranged with/without getting destroyed.

---

111 Murdoch, "The Spaces of Actor-Network-Theory", p. 359.
112 Jones, "Phase Space", p. 488.
113 Ibid., p. 491.

Both approaches have different consequences for assemblage as a heuristic: The former suggests to discuss formation processes with regard to their capacities to align and to transform practices and to drag "things" into new networks, irrespective of the sociospatial embeddedness due to the transcontextual portability of key features ("global forms") of the formation process (e.g. standardization processes and homogenization of norms). By applying the latter, the focus shifts towards an understanding of spatialization as an inherent quality of any kind of relatedness and relation-building.[114]

Making the Heuristic Productive for the Analysis of Processes of Spatialization: Some Preliminary Thoughts

Assemblage, indeed, is a playful conceptual world in which one can get lost. It can be mapped in different strands – not only the four I sketched in the first part – and even if broken down to a heuristic device as I suggested above, it is methodologically underdetermined and has ambivalent relations to any conceptual notion of "space". Despite the methodological concerns that I termed as underdetermination, based on a heuristic understanding of assemblage it could provide some useful starting point for further debates:

a) As the concept operates between a potentially overdeterministic assumption of stable structures and a similar problematic proclivity for fluidity and "pure potentiality",[115] it might serve as an approach to a closer examination of (in)stability and durability/ephemerality of entities. Formation processes are always nested in social practices; conglomerates of decisions and perceptions, rules, and norms; material objects and ideas; emotions and effects; as well as technologies and infrastructures. Here, a similar "open" concept supports a broader discussion how potentiality turns into actuality and back to potentiality again.

b) The concept might stimulate comparative analysis insofar as it allows the "mechanics" of formation processes of emergent entities to be dissected. As Collier and Ong demonstrate in their edited volume, seemingly different formation processes share certain key features, for example their abstractability,

---

114 See Jones, "Phase Space".
115 Anderson et al., "On Assemblages and Geography", p. 184.

allowing de- and recontextualization. The assemblage heuristic could, hence, be read as a comparative heuristic.

c) Assemblage thinking also serves to challenge established, conventionalized notions of space as a measurable, mappable dimension of social life and, instead, points to the temporality of these notions of space. However, in considering the parallels between ANT as well as relational geography, it echoes a broader debate on topology. In doing so, assemblage thinking complements a line of debate that has criticized a tendency to separate the social from the spatial.

Part II: **Territories**

Frank Schumacher
Reclaiming Territory: The Spatial Contours of Empire in US History

Contested Imperial Terrain

Walter Lippmann was an astute observer of American politics and society. In 1927, the journalist and author diagnosed a profound disjunction between international views of the United States as an empire and American self-perceptions of their nation as an anti-colonial beacon of liberty. Lippmann wrote: "We have learned to think of empires as troublesome and as immoral, and to admit that we have an empire still seems to most Americans like admitting that they have [...] lost their political chastity."[1] As a consequence, Lippmann observed that "we go on creating what mankind calls an empire while we continue to believe quite sincerely that it is not an empire because it does not feel to us the way an empire ought to feel."[2]

The practice of empire was of course not merely the product of perception and emotional recognition. In their ideal type, empires were large-scale political organizations like nation-states but in contrast emphasized expansion over consolidation and difference over social or ethnocultural homogeneity. According to Charles Maier, "[e]mpire has a function of stabilizing inequality or, perhaps more precisely, reconciling some rituals and forms of equality with the preservation of vast inequality." Jane Burbank and Frederick Cooper have underlined this imperial proclivity to difference: "The nation-state proclaims the commonality of its people [...] while the empire-state declares the non-equivalence of multiple populations."[3]

Lippmann's observations of an emotive-cognitive disconnect between the practice of empire and its denial is thus not surprising considering the conceptual emphasis of imperial rule on "distinction and hierarchy". These anti-republican characteristics were further enhanced by negative connotations of imperialism as a practice of subjugation and exploitation and contrasted with

---

[1] W. Lippmann, "Empire: The Days of Our Nonage Are Over", in: W. Lippmann, *Men of Destiny*, New Brunswick: Transaction Publishers, 2003, pp. 215–222, at 216.
[2] Ibid., 217.
[3] J. Burbank and F. Cooper, *Empires in World History: Power and the Politics of Difference*, Princeton: Princeton University Press, 2010, p. 8; C.S. Maier, *Among Empires: American Ascendancy and Its Predecessors*, Cambridge: Harvard University Press, 2006, p. 23.

the purported equalizing and integrative force of the nation-state. Such binary constructs of empire and nation have consistently fuelled a widespread refusal to acknowledge the imperial characteristics of the American polity.[4]

In contrast to public discourses and perceptions, however, there is much consensus among historians today that the United States has been an empire at certain stages in history. For decades now a vibrant, innovative, and robust historiography has explored many of the driving forces, manifestations, and repercussions of this empire in a variety of geographic and temporal contexts. At the sametime, however, controversy persists over the extent, iterations, and temporal sequence of this empire and its wider implications for the writing of US and global history.[5]

At the heart of the matter is the frequent discursive *dis*location of this empire from its concrete spatial underpinnings and manifestations. Whereas the conquest of vast transcontinental spaces, for example, has frequently been interpreted as settler imperialism, its final political form – the nation-state – is commonly juxtaposed with empire thus obfuscating the systemic overlap and temporal longevity of both forms of political organization. Furthermore, the contours and foundational dynamics of US imperial engagement with the world are persistently characterized as non-territorial, thereby exceptionalizing the American Empire from historical precedent, disconnecting it from the imperial nation, and marginalizing the life experiences of millions of inhabitants of the imperial territories abroad.

As a consequence, this dismissal of the spatial dimension of empire in US history has undermined widespread efforts to neutralize the "intellectual contortions" of nationalist exceptionalism and its enduring grip on public discourses on power, race, and liberty.[6] But in the absence of an interpretative

---

[4] P. Ther, "'Imperial Nationalism' as a Challenge for the Study of Nationalism", in: S. Berger and A. Miller (eds.), *Nationalizing Empires*, Budapest: Central European University Press, 2015, pp. 573–591, at 574.

[5] For a theoretically reflective historiographical overview, see P.A. Kramer, "Power and Connection: Imperial Histories of the United States in the World", *American Historical Review* 116 (2011) 5, pp. 1348–1391; and more recently, see P.A. Kramer, "How Not to Write the History of U.S. Empire", *Diplomatic History* (October 2018), advance article in the meantime published: Diplomatic History 42 (2018) 5, pp. 911-931.

[6] On "intellectual contortions", see C. Altman, "The International Context: An Imperial Perspective on American Legal History", in: S.E. Hadden and A.L. Brophy (eds.), *A Companion to American Legal History*, Hoboken: Wiley-Blackwell, 2013, pp. 543–561, at 543; a recent example for an exceptionalist narrative: E.C. Hoffman, *American Umpire*, Cambridge: Harvard University Press, 2013.

synthesis of the deep interconnectivity of empire and nation in US history, and despite all specialized knowledge of America's imperial past, Lippmann's observation about imperial disconnect remains in many respects as valid today as it was ninety years ago.

Based on a wide reading of historical sociology, cultural geography, legal history, political theory, and cultural studies, this chapter takes issue with such obfuscating non-territorial understandings of US power. It suggests instead that empire in US and global history developed in part along a bandwidth of overlapping manifestations and imaginations of imperial territoriality in a variety of spatial formats, including but not limited to colonies. The exclusive conflation of empire and colonialism obscures the great variance of imperial spatial settings, territorialized power differentials, and geographic interconnectivities through the American polity's "capillaries of empire".[7]

The analytical focus on a broadly conceptualized imagination and practice of imperial territoriality not only increases the visibility and tangibility of empire but also unravels widely accepted sequential logics in narratives of US history; according to such streamlined perspectives, the United States was born out of an anti-colonial struggle, created a transcontinental nation-state, and acquired a modest colonial empire by the late nineteenth century but quickly advanced decolonization during the interwar years before it substituted territoriality with preponderant political, military, economic, and cultural power and prestige in its quest for global leadership.

Instead, this chapter suggests an alternative chronology by which empire, nation, and global engagement have always intersected from the eighteenth century onwards until today and created a polity whose metropolitan core consisted of both empire and nation while its engagement with global frontiers displayed a remarkably consistent reliance on formats of imperial territoriality. By *relocating* the American Empire in spatial settings at home and abroad over the *longue durée*, this chapter breaks down artificial boundaries between the domestic and the foreign, conceptually integrates empire and nation and their respective historiographies, and probes the utility of imperial territoriality as a potentially synthesizing analytical framework for the writing of US history in its global contexts.

---

7 On "capillaries of empire", see A.W. McCoy, *Policing America's Empire: The United States, the Philippines, and the Rise of the Surveillance State*, Madison: University of Wisconsin Press, 2009, p. 15; on territoriality, see also D. Immerwahr, "The Greater United States: Territory and Empire in U.S. History", *Diplomatic History* 40 (2016) 3, pp. 373–391; for a scathing critique, see Kramer, "How Not to Write the History of U.S. Empire".

Imperial Horizons, 1780s to 1860s

On 4 July 1776, 13 for stylistic and aesthetic reasons replace with thirteen North American colonies announced their separation from the British Empire and created a federal union of loosely associated states. Their declaration of independence outlined a list of grievances against the British crown, reiterated their frustration with London's unwillingness to reform the empire along colonial demands, and underlined the new polity's foundational promise of equal rights to "life, liberty, and the pursuit of happiness".[8] Later generations have often misinterpreted this remarkable document and the act of separation from Britain as a manifesto for decolonization and a repudiation of empire.

But powerful imperial imaginations dominated the world views of the founding generations and influenced how Americans perceived their political and natural environment and imagined their polity's developmental trajectory. The term empire was frequently invoked by contemporaries for a polity with control over expanding territory but without carrying any of the negative connotations that later generations would associate with its practice.[9] It appeared as a natural choice for political organization to ensure that the new state could assume a sovereign and equal position among the "powers of the earth".[10]

Such positive associations were the result of a conceptual distinction in the colonies between empires as organizational ideal types from their specific colonial experiences. After the mid-eighteenth century, the colonists had tried to convince London of the need for greater local control. Their goal had not been separation but further integration into an empire that they hoped would become more responsive to the circumstances and needs of the imperial periphery. Much of the subsequent struggle with the British Empire was thus less the result of an anti-British American identity and a rejection of empire per se, but more the consequence of specific disputes over imperial organization. These disputes evolved into the development of an alternative model of empire with more diffusion of authority than Britain was willing to concede. "The problem

---

[8] Text and impact are discussed in D. Armitage, *The Declaration of Independence: A Global History*, Cambridge: Harvard University Press, 2008.
[9] R.H. Immerman, *Empire for Liberty: A History of American Imperialism from Benjamin Franklin to Paul Wolfowitz*, Princeton: Princeton University Press, 2010, pp. 6–7.
[10] E.H. Gould, *Among the Powers of the Earth: The American Revolution and the Making of a New World Empire*, Cambridge: Harvard University Press, 2012.

for American colonials wasn"t that they didn"t want to be a part of the British Empire; it was that they weren"t being treated as full members of it."[11]

The second reason for the positive assessment of empire had its origins in American understandings of the international environment. Empires constituted the organizational norm of eighteenth-century international relations and set the political and legal standards for state interaction, dominated global economics, and nominally controlled vast North American territory. These empires possessed the means to not only frustrate any expansionist designs of the new state but to challenge its very existence. In addition, hundreds of indigenous polities populated areas within and beyond spaces to which Britain, France, Spain, or Russia claimed sovereignty. The Comanche and Lakota developed extensive "kinetic empires", whose power was based on speed and mobility and persistently resisted Euro-American colonization.[12] By the early nineteenth century, Americans had only encountered a fraction of these civilizations and during those encounters cooperated with some while being hostile to most.

These potential roadblocks to territorial expansion reminded Americans that their polity was a vulnerable and dependent junior state on a global periphery dominated by indigenous and European powers. For many contemporaries, such threat perceptions confirmed their imperial ambitions and reinforced the belief that territorial growth with demographic, agricultural, and commercial development constituted the most fundamental precondition to ensure survival and simultaneous acceptance by dominant international actors.[13]

Geographic imaginations constituted a reassuring and uniting dimension of American deliberations on empire. They found their expression in literature, paintings, cartography, the "social life of maps", and the widespread political use of spatial tropes, which often fused religious and geographic metaphors.[14]

---

11 E. Larkin, *The American School of Empire*, Cambridge: Cambridge University Press, 2016, p. 5; L.B.A. Hatter recently underlined that "[i]t is no longer possible to think of the Revolution as a fork in the road when the founders wisely chose a unique path to the future that would set the United States apart from the rest of the world" (L.B.A. Hatter, "Taking Exception to Exceptionalism: Geopolitics and the Founding of an American Empire", *Journal of the Early Republic* 34 (2014) 4, pp. 653–660, at 660).
12 P. Hämäläinen, "What's in a Concept? The Kinetic Empire of the Comanches", *History and Theory* 52 (2013), pp. 81–90, at 85; for a detailed analysis, see P. Hämäläinen, *The Comanche Empire*, New Haven: Yale University Press, 2008.
13 W.O. Walker III, *National Security and Core Values in American History*, Cambridge: Cambridge University Press, 2009, pp. 1–44.
14 For early nineteenth-century geographic imaginations, see C.C. Apap, *The Genius of Place: The Geographic Imagination in the Early Republic*, Durham: University of New Hampshire Press, 2016; for early US cartography, see M. Brückner, *The Geographic Revolution in Early America:*

In much of those imperial imaginaries, the ultimate spatial contours of the polity remained unclear and steadily expanded as Americans spread westward in the quest for land and resources. In a mutually reinforcing process between imagination and practice, this outreach was informed by notions of "manifest destiny" and "continentalism".[15]

Both concepts advanced a territorially expansive vision for the polity's developmental trajectory based on the conviction that the new state would dominate North America and might even encompass Canada and the Caribbean Basin. This maximalist vision had its origins in colonial times when Euro-American settlers began to refer to their collective as "the continent".[16] It gained further popularity during the process of separation when Americans measured the legitimacy of their claims by spatial comparisons between "their" continent and the small British Isles.[17] Towards the mid-nineteenth century, advocates of expansion such as William Henry Seward, who served as secretary of state during the Lincoln and Johnson administrations from 1861 to 1869, developed "continentalism" into a coherent geostrategic framework. For Seward, an extensive land-based empire was a strategic precondition for oceanic control, global commercial and political outreach, and the ultimate displacement of Britain's international primacy.[18]

The ability of indigenous polities to successfully challenge US expansion was steadily downgraded in such geopolitical imaginations obsessed with potential Old World rivals. While exploratory mapping expeditions had provided great detail about the spatial spread and configuration of often complex indigenous

---

Maps, Literacy & National Identity, Chapel Hill: University of North Carolina Press, 2006 and M. Brückner, *The Social Life of Maps in America, 1750–1860*, Chapel Hill: University of North Carolina Press, 2017; geographic tropes and the imperial imagination are explored in L. Benton, *A Search for Sovereignty: Law and Geography in European Empires, 1400–1900*, Cambridge: Cambridge University Press, 2010, pp. 14–15.

15 A. Stephanson, *Manifest Destiny: American Expansionism and the Empire of Right*, New York: Hill & Wang, 1995; on "continentalism", see D.W. Meinig, *The Shaping of America: Continental America, 1800–1867*, vol. II, New Haven: Yale University Press, 1993, pp. 211–218; C. Vevier, "American Continentalism: An Idea of Expansion: 1845–1910", *American Historical Review* 65 (1960) 2, pp. 323–335.

16 J.D. Drake, *The Nation's Nature: How Continental Presumptions Gave Rise to the United States of America*, Charlottesville: University of Virginia Press, 2011, p. 154.

17 In 1775/76, Thomas Paine wrote: "small islands not capable of protecting themselves, are the proper objects for kingdoms to take under their care; but there is something very absurd, in supposing a continent to be perpetually governed by an island" (T. Paine, *Common Sense*, New York: Penguin Books, 1976, pp. 90–91).

18 Immerman, *Empire for Liberty*, pp. 98–127; E.N. Paolino, *The Foundations of the American Empire: William Henry Seward and U.S. Foreign Policy*, Ithaca: Cornell University Press, 1973; W. Stahr, *Seward: Lincoln's Indispensable Man*, New York: Simon & Schuster, 2012.

political organizations, many Americans denied that such polities possessed legitimate territorial sovereignty. This denial reflected traditional racialized alterities between self and other to which Americans had been acculturated since colonial times. This habitual ethnocultural disdain informed much of the legitimizing discourse on territorial conquest and laid the imaginative foundations for the settler empire's "eliminationist assault" on indigenous civilizations.[19]

The severity of this century-long war has largely been obscured by national narratives that marginalize the violent dimensions of territorial conquest and emphasize the seemingly orderly interimperial transfer of spatial sovereignty by purchase. In this privileged narrative, the United States utilized Old World interimperial rivalries to buy vast portions of the North American continent, such as the Louisiana Territory from France in 1803 or Alaska from Russia in 1867. Such transfers have widely been considered an exceptionally benign hallmark of US expansion. In the words of historian Jeremy Black: "American advance was within areas whose sovereignty had already been ceded to America. There was not the need to advance and fight in order to gain sovereignty [...] Americans faced no resistance from a large and resilient population."[20]

Such retrospective obfuscations of imperial violence have a long history and were deeply embedded in contemporary practices of empire-building. The United States, for example, followed the British practice of complementing such land transfers among empires with corresponding treaties with indigenous polities, which were treated by Washington as sovereign foreign nations until the 1830s.[21] This procedure signalled US compliance with international imperial legal traditions, upheld the illusion of fair negotiations over

---

[19] Daniel Jonah Goldhagen has coined the term "eliminationist assaults" in D.J. Goldhagen, *Worse Than War: Genocide, Eliminationism, and the Ongoing Assault on Humanity*, New York: Public Affairs, 2009, p. 59; on alterities, see M.P. Cullinane and D. Ryan (eds.), *U.S. Foreign Policy and the Other*, New York: Berghahn Books, 2014.

[20] J. Black, *America as a Military Power: From the American Revolution to the Civil War*, Westport: Praeger, 2002, p. 100; Dominic Alessio and Wesley B. Renfro emphasized that "this method of empire building by acquisition could help to explain why the United States, unlike its European and Japanese counterparts, is not generally considered to be an imperial power, at least not a nineteenth-century one [...] this method of expansion by purchase is often viewed as more palatable and benevolent than conquest [...] it is not even considered an imperial process at all" (D. Alessio and W.B. Renfro, "The Voldemort of Imperial History: Rethinking Empire and US History", *International Studies Perspectives* 17 [2016], pp. 250–266, at 254); for the broader context, see also D. Alessio, "'Territorial Acquisitions are among the Landmarks of our History': The Buying and Leasing of Imperial Territory", *Global Discourse* 3 (2013) 1, pp. 74–96.

[21] Land titles, transfers, and sovereignty are discussed in S. Banner, *How the Indians Lost Their Land: Law and Power on the Frontier*, Cambridge: Harvard University Press, 2005.

territorial sovereignty, and provided large-scale land grabs with a veneer of legal respectability.

At the same time, Americans also drew on European traditions of international law and colonial cultural reservoirs of racial binaries to erode indigenous sovereignty, which was strictly defined as effective territorial control. Conveniently streamlining a wide variety of indigenous ethnocultural groups, contemporaries emphasized and generalized nomadic characteristics, which to their mind precluded territorially based sovereignty. Supported by contemporary legal imperialism, the federal government steadily invalidated indigenous land titles, paved the way for their territorial dispossession, and downgraded indigenous status from that of foreign nations to dependent wards of the United States.[22]

The enforcement of US land claims and the legalized dispossession of indigenous polities unveiled the full spectrum of violence employed by the imperial state to advance its most important project of territorial aggrandizement. Prolonged warfare was accompanied by frequent massacres, "ethnic cleansing" and large-scale forced resettlements (such as the Cherokee removal), genocide (as against the Yuki of northern California), and forced acculturation programmes.[23] The federal government devoted enormous resources to the creation of a military infrastructure and the management of captive peoples in holding zones and reservations.[24] Such infrastructure needs escalated after the Indian Removal Act (1830), which initiated a period of large-scale forced population transfers to the so-called Indian Territory, in present-day Oklahoma.

---

[22] In *Cherokee Nation v. Georgia* (1831), the majority opinion of the US Supreme Court concluded that, while the Cherokee constituted a polity, they were not a state according to contemporary legal convention because they lacked territorial sovereignty. The court underlined that the Cherokee "occupy a territory to which we assert a title independent of their will", quoted in: K. Raustiala, *Does the Constitution Follow the Flag? The Evolution of Territoriality in American Law*, Oxford: Oxford University Press, 2009, p. 40.

[23] B. Madley, *An American Genocide. The United States and the California Indian Catastrophe, 1846–1873*, New Haven: Yale University Press, 2016; for a critical perspective on the utility of the genocide concept, see G.C. Anderson, *Ethnic Cleansing and the Indian: The Crime That Should Haunt America*, Norman: University of Oklahoma Press, 2014.

[24] Historian Robert Lee estimates that the federal government allocated roughly 10 per cent of its budget to Indian affairs during much of the nineteenth century (R. Lee, "Accounting for Conquest: The Price of the Louisiana Purchase of Indian Country", *Journal of American History* 103 [2017] 4, pp. 921–942); on US army operations most recently, see R. Wooster, *The American Military Frontiers: The United States Army in the West, 1783–1900*, Albuquerque: University of New Mexico Press, 2009; on the political economy of western conquest, see P.A.C. Koistinen, *Beating Plowshares into Swords: The Political Economy of American Warfare, 1606–1865*, Lawrence: University Press of Kansas, 1996.

Despite the severity of the imperial onslaught on their societies, indigenous polities remained active participants in the struggle for control of North America. Their strategies and policies often intersected with interimperial wars and their respective alliances. During the failed American invasion of Canada (1812–1814), indigenous polities along the lower Great Lakes played an important role in the defence of British North America. In the US war with Mexico (1846–1848), decades of indigenous empire-building in the south-western borderlands weakened Mexico's military and economic ability to defend its territory against the United States. The American Empire drew on these borderland struggles to legitimize its invasion and subsequent territorial annexation of 1.3 million km^2 as a purported spatial projection of order and stability.[25]

Although the focus of US empire-building was on North America, the overall spatial horizons of its imperial engagement quickly expanded into the global arena, with a particular emphasis on the Caribbean Basin and the Asia Pacific region.[26] According to historian Konstantin Dierks, the United States involved itself actively in many parts of the world with a "will to superiority, will to reach, will to intrusion, will to coercion, will to mastery, [and] will to domination."[27] The incongruence between aspirations and abilities during the first half of the nineteenth century, however, did not deter the United States from actively seeking opportunities for further advancement in hemispheric and global contexts – without losing sight of existing power differentials. In the global jockeying for imperial positions, the United States balanced confrontation and conciliation through rhetorical demarcation from Old World imperialism, accelerated development of naval and diplomatic capabilities, and transimperial cooperation.

---

25 S. Shuck-Hall, "The Battle for Ancestral Homeland: An Examination of American Indians in the War of 1812", *Revue Française D'Études Américaines* 139 (2014), pp. 30–41; for the Mexican War, see B. DeLay, *War of a Thousand Deserts: Indian Raids and the US-Mexican War*, New Haven: Yale University Press, 2008 and A.S. Greenberg, *A Wicked War: Polk, Clay, Lincoln, and the 1846 Invasion of Mexico*, New York: Knopf, 2012.

26 "Interchange: Globalization and Its Limits between the American Revolution and the Civil War", *Journal of American History* 103 (2016) 2, pp. 400–433; see also R. Zagarri, "The Significance of the 'Global Turn' for the Early American Republic: Globalization in the Age of Nation-Building", *Journal of the Early Republic* 31 (2001) 1, pp. 1–37.

27 K. Dierks, "Americans Overseas in the Early American Republic", *Diplomatic History* 42 (2018) 1, 17–35, at 35; Dierks' digital history project "Mapping History: Reflections on the Globalization of the United States: 1789–1861 Digital Project" traces US activities abroad to map the global engagements of antebellum Americans: http://common-place.org/book/mapping-history-reflections-on-the-globalization-of-the-united-states-1789-1861-digital-project/ (accessed 4 December 2018).

President James Monroe's message to Congress in 1823 constituted a hallmark of this flexible imperial strategy. Later elevated to doctrinal status, this quintessential American geopolitical statement warned European powers against further colonization or recolonization in the Americas and simultaneously pledged non-interference in European affairs.[28] Over time, the Monroe Doctrine would frequently be invoked to underwrite spatial claims. By the 1820s, however, Monroe's rhetorical demarcations of spheres of interest anticipated abilities to shape global affairs more than it reflected US strategic capabilities.

Despite such shortcomings, the statement provided an important crystallization point for the ideological advancement of "imperial anti-colonialism", which laid the imaginary groundwork for the obfuscation of America's imperial ambitions. The United States declared itself a champion of post-colonial nations, claimed exception to Old World imperialism, and implied that its own expansive empire merely served as anti-colonial security measure.[29]

To match its aspiration, the United States steadily expanded its naval and diplomatic capabilities. Twenty years after Monroe's address, US navy forward deployments already consisted of seven station squadrons that operated in specific world regions (West Indies, Pacific, North Atlantic, South Atlantic, Mediterranean, Africa, and Asia). Before the age of steam, such squadrons of 5–6 ships sailed the seas without need for fuel. Supplies were made available by 18 commercial depots around the world from Buenos Aires to Yokohama.[30] This interventionist infrastructure enabled the United States: "to take punitive military action anywhere in the world, a projection of power that few other countries could muster at the time."[31] In addition, an increasing number of US consular posts ensured that American interests were adequately represented

---

[28] For a thorough interpretation of the Monroe Doctrine and its multiple iterations, see J. Sexton, *The Monroe Doctrine: Empire and Nation in Nineteenth-Century America*, New York: Hill & Wang, 2011.

[29] On "imperial anti-colonialism", see W. Appleman Williams, *The Tragedy of American Diplomacy. Revised and Enlarged Edition*, New York: Dell Publishing, 1972, p. 16; according to Walter LaFeber, the demand for decolonization served as "a device for conquering a continental empire. In nineteenth-century US foreign policy, decolonization became less an act of altruism [...] than an integral and successful part of the nation's most aggressive self-interest" (W. LaFeber, "The American View of Decolonization 1776–1920: an Ironic Legacy", in: D. Ryan and V. Pungong (eds.), *The United States and Decolonization: Power and Freedom*, New York: St. Martin's Press, 2000, pp. 24–40, at 29).

[30] S.L. Pettyjohn, *U.S. Global Defense Posture, 1783–2011*, RAND Project Air Force, Santa Monica: RAND Corporation, 2012, pp. 19–24.

[31] Dierks, "Americans Overseas", p. 33.

around the world.³² This combined network of consular posts, naval stations, and resupply bases provided the necessary infrastructure for the global projection and forward deployment of forces to protect commercial shipping against pirates, support scientific expeditions, and claim territorial interests for the United States.³³

Even though not every American activity abroad was empire-building, such outpost networks often closely shadowed European imperial engagements.³⁴ In the Pacific and in Asia, for example, the United States closely accompanied the incursions of seasoned imperial powers in attitude and practice to ensure its fair share of political influence, trade, and commerce. This world region constituted a central geographical axis for US imperial outreach and complemented the simultaneous continental thrust to the Pacific coast. In the Pacific, considered the gateway to Asia, US interests focused on the Hawaiian archipelago, which served as a hub for whalers, traders, explorers, and missionaries. After the 1820s, the United States steadily extended its commercial, political, and cultural footprint in the islands against competing empires and slowly transformed Hawaii into a dependent satellite of the American Empire.³⁵

In China and Japan, the United States combined missionary activities, exploratory expeditions, unequal trade treaties, and the establishment of extraterritorial zones and enclaves to take its place alongside the Old World empires.³⁶

---

32 By the 1790s, most of the 18 US consular posts had been located in Europe; by 1860, 350 consulates and another 200 consular agencies spanned the globe and represented the imperial state on every continent. Numbers can be found in W. Burges Smith, *American Diplomats and Consuls of 1776–1865*, Arlington: Foreign Service Institute, US Department of State, 1986, p. 8; C.S. Kennedy, *The American Consul: A History of the United States Consular Service, 1776–1924*, Washington, DC: New Academia, 2015; Nicole Phelps has mapped the evolution of the US consular service: http://blog.uvm.edu/nphelps/ (accessed January 5 2018).

33 Until the mid-nineteenth century, such naval engagements and force deployments encompassed military interventions in North Africa, the West Indies, Central America, South America, West Asia, East Asia, and the Pacific Ocean. For a complete list, see B. Salazar Torreon, *Instances of Use of United States Armed Forces Abroad, 1798–2017*, Congressional Research Service Report 7-5700, October 2017, https://fas.org/sgp/crs/natsec/R42738.pdf (accessed 5 January 2018).

34 For a criticism of the empire label, see N. Shoemaker, "The Extraterritorial United States to 1860", *Diplomatic History* 42 (2018) 1, pp. 36–54; in support, see B. Blower, "Nation of Outposts: Forts, Factories, Bases, and the Making of American Power", *Diplomatic History* 41 (2017) 3, pp. 439–459.

35 In 1842, Secretary of State Daniel Webster warned Britain and France to refrain from colonization in the Hawaiian Islands by extending the Monroe Doctrine into the Pacific (Sexton, *The Monroe Doctrine*, p. 112).

36 US geostrategic perceptions of the Asia-Pacific region are discussed in M.J. Green, *By More Than Providence: Grand Strategy and American Power in the Asia Pacific since 1783*, New York:

In contrast to Monroe's emphasis on the fundamental differences between America and Europe, US practices in Asia underlined the close proximity of their respective imperial projects. Until the mid-twentieth century, the United States moved in the imperial slipstream of globally active European powers and operated within a framework and according to political, diplomatic, legal, and commercial standards set by more experienced, prestigious, and powerful empires. Frank Ninkovich has described this US junior role in empire-building in Asia as "hitchhiking imperialism".[37]

The Caribbean Basin constituted a second geographic focus of US imperial outreach. Considered by many contemporaries as the "American Mediterranean", Caribbean islands and territories in Central America had long been an object of Washington's imperial desire after the conquest of Florida and victory in the Mexican War. Numerous attempts were made to purchase Cuba from the Spanish Empire and to gain control over the possible building site for an interoceanic canal in Central America. Some imperialists like William Henry Seward even advocated moving the US capital to Mexico City. Others imagined a giant imperial republic that would extend as far south as Brazil. In addition, private empire-builders like William Walker operated across vast spaces in Mexico, Cuba, Nicaragua, Honduras, and Ecuador during the 1840s and 1850s. These so-called "filibusters" planned private imperial enclaves, often to extend Southern-style slave plantations into the tropics and hoped that their domains would subsequently be annexed by the United States. Most of these adventure schemes ended in disaster and found mixed reception in the United States.[38]

Columbia University Press, 2017; on missionary activities, see E. Conroy-Krutz, *Christian Imperialism: Converting the World in the Early American Republic*, Ithaca: Cornell University Press, 2015; on extraterritoriality in China and Japan, see T. Ruskola, "Canton is not Boston: The Invention of American Imperial Sovereignty", *American Quarterly* 57 (2005) 3, pp. 859–884; E. Scully, *Bargaining with the State from Afar: American Citizenship in Treaty Port China, 1844–1942*, New York: Columbia University Press, 2001; Raustiala, *Does the Constitution follow the Flag?*, pp. 63–68.

37 F. Ninkovich, *The United States and Imperialism*, Hoboken: Wiley-Blackwell, 2001, p. 158.

38 M. Gobat, *Empire by Invitation: William Walker and Empire in Central America*, Cambridge, MA: Harvard University Press, 2018; A.S. Greenberg, *Manifest Manhood and the Antebellum American Empire*, Cambridge: Cambridge University Press, 2015; R.E. May, *Manifest Destiny's Underworld: Filibustering in Antebellum America*, Chapel Hill: University of North Carolina Press, 2002; for Southern conceptions of empire, see M. Karp, *This Vast Southern Empire: Slaveholders at the Helm of American Foreign Policy*, Cambridge: Harvard University Press, 2016 and R.E. May, *The Southern Dream of Caribbean Empire*, Baton Rouge: Louisiana State University Press, 1973.

In contrast to those expansion schemes, however, the United States did not acquire colonies in the Caribbean during this first phase of empire-building, much to the disappointment of many imperialists. But the Caribbean Basin was a world region of intense interimperial competition, in which the United States was still merely a junior participant and whose economic and political well-being depended to a large degree on a cooperative relationship with Old World powers, in particular with the British Empire.[39]

In addition, Americans were also split on the wisdom of acquiring territory beyond the continent. Some objected on principle grounds, invoking Montesquieu's dictum that imperial expansion produced corruption, despotism, and decay.[40] Others were less concerned about territory and more about its inhabitants, arguing that ethnocultural diversity would undermine the polity's stability. They insisted that only territory with a Euro-American majority, or spaces that had been "cleared" for settlement through forced relocations, should be incorporated into the empire.[41] Like most Americans, they envisioned the United States as a racially homogenous Anglo-Saxon nation and tied their polity's future to its ability to exclude non-whites from the imperial state.[42]

Finally, abolitionist opponents to further territorial expansion also worried about the impact of a Caribbean empire on the domestic balance of power

---

39 On US dependency, see A.G. Hopkins, "The United States 1783–1861: Britain's Honorary Dominion?" *Britain and the World* 4 (2011) 2, pp. 232–246 and S.W. Haynes, *Unfinished Revolution: The Early American Republic in a British World*, Charlottesville: University of Virginia Press, 2010.

40 A.G. Hopkins, *American Empire: A Global History*, Princeton: Princeton University Press, 2018, pp. 32–33; on opposition to westward expansion, see D. Mayers, *Dissenting Voices in America's Rise to Power*, Cambridge: Cambridge University Press, 2007, pp. 13–108.

41 Lewis Cass, Democratic (member of the Democratic Party) democratic senator from Michigan, exemplified this discursive simultaneity of imperial advocacy for new territory and nationalist desire for exclusive racial homogeneity when he demanded: "We do not want the people of Mexico, either as citizens or subjects. All we want is a portion of territory which they nominally hold, generally uninhabited, or, where inhabited at all, sparsely so, and with population which will soon recede, or identify itself with ours", quoted in Burbank and Cooper, *Empires*, p. 265; such racialized critiques of Mexican territorial annexations, are explored in: R. Horsman, *Race and Manifest Destiny: The Origins of American Racial Anglo-Saxonism*, Cambridge: Harvard University Press, 1981, pp. 229–248; Mayers, *Dissenting Voices*, pp. 109–137.

42 For US expansion as a project of racial exclusivity most recently, see P. Frymer, *Building an American Empire: The Era of Territorial and Political Expansion*, Princeton: Princeton University Press, 2017; for the extent of racial hierarchies in the imperial state, see M.-K. Jung, "Constituting the US Empire-State and White Supremacy: The Early Years", in: M.-K. Jung, J.H. Costa Vargas and E. Bonilla-Silva (eds.), *State of White Supremacy: Racism, Governance, and the United States*, Paolo Alto: Stanford University Press, 2011, pp. 1–23.

between free and slave labour states. Since the polity's founding, Northern and Southern states had widely agreed on the need for further territory. But while they shared negative dispositions towards indigenous cultures, they also pursued different imperial trajectories. The South envisioned a territorially expansive slave-based plantation empire, whereas the North advanced its vision of an ever-expanding system settler empire of free labour. Each territorial addition exasperated the contradiction between those mutually exclusive imperial visions within the polity and its frail compromises regarding the spatial delineation of slavery. It also intensified the opposition of abolitionists and reformers to territorial aggrandizement in the Caribbean.

By the mid-nineteenth century, the United States controlled a vast transcontinental empire that encompassed an imperial core of 33 states and a federal district as well as a periphery of 7 large territories that made up more than half of the polity's size. Extraterritorial outposts and exceptional zones at home and abroad complemented this spatial imperial mosaic.[43] The rise of this empire came at the expense of indigenous polities, whose territorial sovereignty dwindled from 80 per cent in the 1770s to less than 5 per cent a century later.[44] The settler imperial dynamic of constant warfare and aggressive land and population management underlined that the United States was an empire long before it became a consolidated nation-state in the second half of the nineteenth century.[45] Territorial conquest was the lifeblood of this new polity and deeply shaped its self-perceptions, cultural production, and global outlooks.

Imperial Trajectories, 1860s to 1940s

The second phase of the American Empire was bracketed by two wars with imperial characteristics that posed powerful interior and exterior challenges to the territorial integrity of the United States. During the mid-nineteenth century, Civil War Southern states left the shared polity and created a competing empire-state

---

[43] For data see G. Ripley and C.A. Dana (eds.), *The American Cyclopedia: Popular Dictionary of General Knowledge*, vol. XIV, New York: D. Appleton & Co., 1863, p. 784, table 1.

[44] For numbers, see B. DeLay, "Indian Polities, Empire, and the History of American Foreign Relations", *Diplomatic History* 39 (2015) 5, pp. 927–942, at 932.

[45] S. Hahn, *A Nation Without Borders. The United States and Its World in the Age of Civil Wars 1830–1910: The Penguin History of the United States*, New York: Viking, 2016, p. 2; for the importance of war to empire-building, see F. Anderson and A. Cayton, *The Dominion of War: Empire and Liberty in North America 1500–2000*, New York: Viking, 2005; on federal land policy, population management, and empire, see Frymer, *Building an American Empire*.

in the struggle for North American dominance. Roughly eighty years later, during the Second World War, three rivalling empires in Europe and Asia challenged the global position of the United States in their quest for international primacy.

In both cases territorial empire exacerbated rather than contained potential challenges: instead of enhancing the polity's cohesion, pre–Civil War expansion accelerated its fragmentation; and instead of providing simultaneous imperial territorial strong points and external security, the post–Civil War US overseas empire and its global outreach created interimperial frictions and enhanced national vulnerabilities. The intervening decades were characterized by three intersecting dynamics of the American Empire in continental, hemispheric, and global contexts: the consolidation of an imperial nation, empire-building beyond the continent, and the quest for global primacy.

Territorial consolidation after the Civil War rested on the polity's ability to successfully reintegrate 11 former enemy states into the Union. This process of reconstruction was driven by the desire to transform rivalling imperial outlooks into a coherent nation-state and was accompanied by intense cultural and ideological nationalism.[46] But talk of the nation and its promise of freedom did neither disqualify nor end imperial practice. On the contrary, this policy of national unification had enduring spatial implications for the United States and the continent, which limited the transformative power of Southern reconstruction and further anchored and embedded imperial rule by difference, exclusion, and subjugation in the American polity.

In at least five ways, empire and nation remained deeply intertwined and mutually reinforcing trajectories in the post-war territorial development of the reunited States: first, while imperial characteristics had shaped the causes and conduct of the Civil War, they also framed the initial post-war relationship between the North and South in the polity's approach to "securing the peace".[47] The former Confederate states were militarily occupied for more than a decade to supervise their gradual readmission into the United States. The political integration was based on their support for constitutional amendments that abolished slavery

---

46 For the cultural discourse on memory, war, and nation, see S.W. Gold, *The Unfinished Exhibition: Visualizing Myth, Memory, and the Shadow of the Civil War in Centennial America*, Abingdon: Routledge, 2017; A. Böger, *Envisioning the Nation: The Early American World's Fairs and the Formation of Culture*, Frankfurt/Main: Campus, 2010, pp. 61–108.

47 M. Duffy Toft, *Securing the Peace: The Durable Settlement of Civil Wars*, Princeton: Princeton University Press, 2009; for the imperial dynamics of this war, see also J.C. Hammond, "Slavery, Sovereignty, and Empires: North American Borderlands and the American Civil War, 1660-1860", *The Journal of the Civil War Era* 4 (2014) 2, pp. 264–298; on reconstruction still, E. Foner, *Reconstruction: America's Unfinished Revolution, 1863–1877*, New York: Harper & Row, 1988.

as well as codified birthright citizenship and the entitlement of all citizens to equal protection and due legal process. During this phase of reconstruction, "the entire South became, in effect, a new imperial holding, and it displayed many features common to such conquered, captive territories."[48]

The ultimate failure of reconstruction created a second imperial trajectory within the national core through the establishment of a spatially delineated race regime in the US South. This zone of violence flourished because of the steady erosion of civic nationalism, the resurgence of pre-war Southern elites, and the Northern decision to prioritize territorial integrity and federal dominance over the enforcement of liberty and inclusion.[49] The brutal oppression of African Americans and their systematic exclusion from the polity for almost a century not only highlighted the imperial characteristics of the post–Civil War state but also informed European colonial ventures in Africa and the 1935 Nuremberg race laws.[50]

Imperial subjugation and exclusion also shaped nation-building in the western borderlands, which had played an important role during the Civil War.[51] In this third spatial trajectory of the imperial state, the federal government accelerated the military conquest of indigenous polities and intensified land appropriations, legal exclusion, and "ethnic cleansing". Total war against indigenous resistance employed Civil War tactics and was accompanied by the cultural assault on indigenous communities through a wide range of forced acculturation programmes, which included further territorial dispossession in exchange for citizenship by 1924.[52]

---

48 D.W. Meinig, *The Shaping of America: Transcontinental America, 1850–1915*, vol. III, New Haven: Yale University Press, 1993, p. 189; M.L. Bradley, *The Army and Reconstruction, 1865–1877*, Washington, DC: Center for Military History, 2015; P.M.R. Stirk, *A History of Military Occupation from 1792 to 1914*, Edinburgh: Edinburgh University Press, 2016, pp. 146–187.
49 T. Bender, *A Nation Among Nations: America's Place in World History*, New York: Hill & Wang, 2006, p. 180.
50 On the post-war US South as transimperial inspiration, see J. Whitman, *Hitler's American Model: The United States and the Making of Nazi Race Law*, Princeton: Princeton University Press, 2017; A. Zimmerman, *Alabama in Africa: Booker T. Washington, the German Empire, and the Globalization of the New South*, Princeton: Princeton University Press, 2010; on racial violence, see M. Berg, *Popular Justice: A History of Lynching in America*, Chicago: I.R. Dee, 2011 and M.J. Pfeifer, *Lynching and American Society, 1874–1947*, Champaign: University of Illinois Press, 2004.
51 On connections between Civil War and western conquest, see A. Arenson and A.R. Graybill (eds.), *Civil War Wests: Testing the Limits of the United States*, Berkeley: University of California Press, 2015; V. Scharff (ed.), *Empire and Liberty: The Civil War and the West*, Berkeley: University of California Press, 2015.
52 On conceptual linkages between the Civil War and the Indian Wars, see B. Cothran and A. Kelman, "How the Civil War became the Indian Wars", *New York Times*, 25 May 2015, https://

In a fourth imperial trajectory, rule by difference also shaped the political and legal relationship between the national core and its western borderlands. In accordance with the Northwest Ordinance (1787), territories had to pass through congressionally approved stages of development to reach statehood in the polity.[53] Territorial residents were ruled by military or civil governors and enjoyed neither voting rights nor full constitutional protection. For many territories, this "purgatory" of colonial dependency often lasted for half a century and prompted frequent protests by settlers, who compared their territorial status to that of a subjugated imperial province.[54] This coexistence and slow harmonization of spatial formats with diverging legitimacies of rule within one polity was the hallmark of an "empire-state", whose national characteristics steadily gained ground to complement its imperial dimensions.[55] For most territories, this harmonization process of territorial conversion to statehood was completed by World War I when 48 contiguous states formed the core of the American imperial nation.[56]

---

opinionator.blogs.nytimes.com/2015/05/25/how-the-civil-war-became-the-indian-wars/ (accessed 20 March 2018); A. Kelman, *A Misplaced Massacre: Struggling over the Memory of Sand Creek*, Cambridge: Harvard University Press, 2013; R.M. Utley, "Total War on the American Indian Frontier", in: M.F. Boemeke, R. Chickering and S. Förster (eds.), *Anticipating Total War: The German and American Experiences, 1871–1914*, Cambridge: Cambridge University Press, 1999, pp. 399–414; on acculturation programmes, see D.W. Adams, *Education for Extinction: American Indians and the Boarding School Experience, 1875–1928*, Lawrence: University Press of Kansas, 1995; C.J. Genetin-Pilawa, *Crooked Paths to Allotment: The Fight over Federal Indian Policy after the Civil War*, Chapel Hill: University of North Carolina Press, 2012.

53 G. Lawson and G. Seidman, *The Constitution of Empire: Territorial Expansion and American Legal History*, New Haven: Yale University Press, 2004, especially part II; P.S. Onuf, *Statehood and Union: A History of the Northwest Ordinance*, Bloomington: Indiana University Press, 1987; for the imperial character of territorial government, see J.E. Eblen, *The First and Second United States Empires: Governors and Territorial Government, 1784–1912*, Pittsburgh: University of Pittsburgh Press, 1968.

54 Martin Maginnis from the Montana Territory, for example, described territorial rule in 1884 as "the most infamous system of colonial government that was ever seen on the face of the globe", quoted in: J. Go, *Patterns of Empire: The British and American Empires, 1688 to the Present*, Cambridge: Cambridge University Press, 2011, p. 49; on "purgatory", see D. Immerwahr, "The Greater United States: Territory and Empire in US History", *Diplomatic History* 40 (2016) 3, pp. 373–391, at 384.

55 Go argues that "[i]t follows that the United States has never been a 'nation of states' with equal standing. For nearly all of its history, it has had territories alongside its states. The United States has been primarily an *empire-state* rather than a nation-state" (Go, *Patterns of Empire*, p. 49).

56 For the history of this conversion process, see B.F. Shearer, *The Uniting States: The Story of Statehood for the Fifty United States*, 3 vols., Westport: Greenwood, 2004.

But imperial characteristics also continued to interlace national development in a fifth trajectory, which encompassed a wide range of measures such as citizenship laws, immigration restrictions, and disenfranchisement to exclude large parts of the population from the polity on the basis of race and gender. Although women received voting rights at the federal level in 1920, their citizenship status remained tied to race-based marriage laws into the 1930s. Such ethnocultural and gender-based restrictions varied in their intensity throughout the national territory and found further spatial expression in reservations, a southern zone of disenfranchisement, migratory restrictions in the western states, urban ghettos, or internment camps during World War II.[57]

These five trajectories highlight how deeply imperial practices were embedded in US nation-building between the 1860s and 1940s. But while the hybrid character of the imperial nation maintained political and legal difference within the polity, it also intensified its technological and ideological integration to secure territorial sovereignty. Aggressive nationalism emphasized reconciliation, identified diversity as a weakness, and interpreted expansive territoriality as a precondition for national and international greatness. While the "Americanization" movement, its accompanying ideology of Americanism, and extensive campaigns for social engineering addressed the question of how to turn a nation of diverse ethnocultural immigrants into a homogeneous polity, geospatial interpretations of the frontier provided an influential interpretative framework for the historical trajectory of the American polity.[58]

The most prominent and culturally significant example for this metanarrative in the United States was historian Frederick Jackson Turner's 1893 frontier thesis, which advanced an environmentalist framework to explain the rise of an

---

57 On immigration, see D.R. Gabaccia, *Foreign Relations: American Immigration in Global Perspective*, Princeton: Princeton University Press, 2012; P.A. Kramer, "The Geopolitics of Mobility: Immigration Policy and American Global Power in the Long Twentieth Century", *American Historical Review* 123 (2018) 2, pp. 393–438; Stefan Heumann argues that legal differentiation without an expansive territorial logic did not qualify the US as an empire (S. Heumann, "State, Nation, and Empire: The Formation of the US", *Journal of Political Power* 4 [2011] 3, pp. 375–393); Julian Go, on the other hand, suggests that racialized exclusion requires no expansive territorial logic for a liberal state to qualify as empire (J. Go, "Myths of Nation and Empire: The Logic of America's Liberal Empire-State", *Thesis Eleven* 139 [2017] 1, pp. 69–83).

58 D. Herrmann, *"Be an American": Amerikanisierungsbewegung und Theorien der Einwanderungsintegration*, Frankfurt/Main: Campus, 1996; A. v. Saldern, *Amerikanismus: Kulturelle Abgrenzung von Europa und US-Nationalismus im frühen 20. Jahrhundert*, Stuttgart: Franz Steiner Verlag, 2013; C.A. Ziegler-McPherson, *Americanization in the States: Immigrant Social Welfare Policy, Citizenship & National Identity in the United States, 1908–1929*, Gainesville: University Press of Florida, 2009.

American nation.⁵⁹ According to Turner, European settlers were turned into self-reliant, democratic, and resilient Americans on the frontier in the struggle for "civilization and order" over nature and chaos. Neither indigenous cultures nor the legal or political particulars of territorial conquest were of interest to Turner but the transformative dynamic of spatial appropriation which he interpreted as the exceptional cultural foundation for self-governing and self-reliant Americans and their polity.⁶⁰ Even though such spatial logics and corresponding ethnocentric national narratives were not unique in a world of settler empires, Turner's arguments resonated widely at home and abroad as an interpretative lens for American nationalism as they obfuscated imperial conquest as nation-building and expressed deep-seated anxieties about how an end to the dynamic frontier would affect the stability of the American polity.⁶¹

While Turner remained vague about the need for further territory, advocates of empire-building abroad viewed continued spatial expansion as central to US stability and security. They hoped that new territory would provide access to raw materials and new markets for industrial goods, neutralize destabilizing tensions of industrial modernity, and ultimately advance a *Pax Americana*. While this trust in the bonding qualities and security-inducing effects of territorial expansion was partially fuelled by anxieties about the closing of the transcontinental frontier, it also reflected an imperial perspective on the world – informed by a vast territorial domain, the emergence of a powerful regulatory state, a dynamic industrial economy, a modernized military, and an expansive nationalist ideology.⁶²

---

59 F.J. Turner, *The Significance of the Frontier in American History*, Madison: State Historical Society of Wisconsin, 1894; the cultural significance of the "frontier" myth has been explored by Richard Slotkin in R. Slotkin, *Regeneration through Violence: The Mythology of the American Frontier, 1600–1860*, Middleton: Wesleyan University Press, 1973; R. Slotkin, *The Fatal Environment: The Myth of the Frontier in the Age of Industrialization, 1800–1890*, New York: Atheneum, 1985; R. Slotkin, *Gunfighter Nation: The Myth of the Frontier in Twentieth-Century America*, New York: Atheneum, 1992.
60 B. Saler, *The Settler's Empire: Colonialism and State Formation in America's Old Northwest*, Philadelphia: University of Philadelphia Press, 2015, pp. 306–307.
61 For a Russian interpretation of empire and nation in the writings of Sergei Mikhailovich Solov'ev, which preceded Turner, see M. Bassin, "Turner, Solov'ev, and the 'Frontier Hypothesis': The Nationalist Significance of Open Spaces", *Journal of Modern History* 65 (1993) 3, pp. 473–511; I am grateful to Steffi Marung, Leipzig, for bringing this to my attention.
62 On this transformative dynamic, see K. Shake, *Safe Passage: The Transition from British to American Hegemony*, Cambridge: Harvard University Press, 2017, pp. 120–123; for a critical perspective, see G. Gerstle, "The Civil War and State-Building: A Reconsideration", *Journal of the Civil War Era* 7 (2017) 1, p. 8.

This advocacy for further empire found its most concise expression in the geopolitical writings of naval officer Alfred Thayer Mahan. In his bestseller, *The Influence of Seapower Upon History* (1890), Mahan encouraged the United States to emulate British imperial success by gaining control of oceanic spaces through a powerful navy, an interoceanic canal in Central America, insular outposts as coaling stations and communication relays, and some colonies for raw materials and as surplus markets.[63] Although Mahan advocated the creation of a sea-based empire, he remained ambivalent about the extent of territory required for international primacy and repeatedly highlighted the ability of British sea power to project force over vast regions through the control of a minimalist network of bases and strong points.[64] This spatial "modesty" reflected strategic efficiency as much as it echoed contemporary insecurities about overseas colonial conquests, which many deemed expensive to maintain, difficult to defend, and hard to justify for a nation whose credibility hinged on the obfuscation of its imperialism as altruism.[65]

In practice, the United States initially steered a middle ground: it annexed resource-rich Alaska by interimperial transfer from Russia in 1867 to gain control over Canada's western provinces, which would have turned Alaska into a contiguous settlement frontier with exclusive access to North America's Pacific coast.[66] Beyond the continent, the United States focused on the extension of extraterritorial zones in Korea and the annexation of uninhabited or thinly populated insular strong points, harbours, and bases in the Midway Atoll (1867), Samoa (1872), and Hawaii (1887). After the 1850s, the US also claimed more than 70 islets in the Pacific and the Caribbean to mine the natural fertilizer guano.[67] All of these insular additions to the empire constituted strategic links

---

[63] A. Thayer Mahan, *The Influence of Sea Power Upon History, 1660–1783*, Boston: Little, Brown and Co., 1890; on Mahan's geopolitical influence, see D. Milne, *Worldmaking: The Art and Science of American Diplomacy*, New York: Farrar, Straus and Giroux, 2015, pp. 21–68.

[64] Milne, *Worldmaking*, p. 39.

[65] S. Ricard, "The Exceptionalist Syndrome in U.S. Continental and Overseas Expansion", in: D.K. Adams and C. A. van Minnen (eds.), *Reflections on American Exceptionalism*, Keele: Keele University Press, 1994, pp. 73–82.

[66] W. Nugent, *Habits of Empire: A History of American Expansion*, New York: Alfred E. Knopf, 2008, pp. 244–251; M.A. Cook, "Manifest Opportunity: The Alaska Purchase as a Bridge between United States Expansion and Imperialism", *Alaska History* 26 (2011) 1, pp. 1–10; S. Haycox, *Alaska: An American Colony*, Seattle: University of Washington Press, 2015.

[67] J.M. Skaggs, *The Great Guano Rush: Entrepreneurs and American Overseas Expansion*, New York: St. Martin's Press, 1994.

disproportionate to their size in a transportation and communication chain that connected the North American Pacific coast to the Asian mainland.[68]

But this integrative respatialization was simultaneously obfuscated by legal barriers between the imperial metropole and its insular territories. Designed to contain potential opposition and enable the United States to enjoy the benefits of imperial ownership without the political or constitutional implications of sovereignty, such legal smokescreens mirrored European practices.[69] They were first used by the American Empire in the Guano Islands Act (1856), which acknowledged ownership but denied US sovereignty over the islets and described their legal status as "appertaining to the United States".[70]

Such conceptual building blocks for an "empire by stealth" proved less effective in debates over the annexation and potential inclusion of larger and ethnoculturally diverse territories such as Cuba, the Dominican Republic, or Hawaii, all where Euro-American settlers could not easily displace local residents.[71] The traditional tension between imperial ambition and concerns over the potential incorporation of substantial non-white populations into the polity reached a further climax after US victory in the Spanish-American War (1898) and the subsequent debate over the annexation of former Spanish colonies.

At the heart of the controversy were diverging interpretations of the potential consequences of colonial rule over non-contiguous territories for the American polity. Imperialists viewed the extension of empire abroad as a commercial opportunity; reinforcement of existing territorial empire; ideological fulfilment; historical obligation; opportunity for national reconciliation, pride, and unity; and geostrategic necessity in denying imperial power competitors, in particular Germany and Japan, further inroads into the Caribbean and Pacific Ocean.[72]

---

68 M.J. Green, *By More Than Providence: Grand Strategy and American Power in the Asia Pacific since 1783*, New York: Columbia University Press, 2017, p. 69.
69 For the benefits of ownership without acknowledged sovereignty, see C. Duffy Burnett, "The Edges of Empire and the Limits of Sovereignty: American Guano Islands", *American Quarterly* 57 (2005) 3, pp. 779–803; for the European tradition, see M. Koskenniemi, *The Gentle Civilizer of Nations: The Rise and Fall of International Law, 1870–1960*, Cambridge: Cambridge University Press, 2001, pp. 98–166.
70 A. Burns, *American Imperialism: The Territorial Expansion of the United States*, Edinburgh: Edinburgh University Press, 2017, p. 57.
71 On race as an inhibitor to expansion, see P. Frymer, "'A Rush and a Push and the Land is Ours': Territorial Expansion, Land Policy, and U.S. State Formation", *Perspectives on Politics* 12 (2014) 1, pp. 119–144; E.T. Love, *Race over Empire: Racism and U.S. Imperialism, 1865–1900*, Chapel Hill: University of North Carolina Press, 2004.
72 F. Hilfrich, *Debating American Exceptionalism: Empire and Democracy in the Wake of the Spanish-American War*, Basingstoke: Palgrave Macmillan, 2012; D. C. Hendrickson, *Union*,

The critics of further colonial empire interpreted the territorial gain not as a benefit but as a potential burden for the polity. They drew on traditional arguments against expansion and activated long-standing racial apprehensions about territories with ethnoculturally diverse populations and their impact on the fabric and stability of the American polity. They rejected the need for spatial extensions beyond the contiguous empire, feared the eventual inclusion of non-white populations into the polity, and warned of imperial overstretch, socioeconomic ruin, militarism, and dangerous interimperial competition.[73]

Both advocates and opponents contextualized their understanding of imperial territory through a close reading of the nation's history of expansion. In their view, the post-1898 quest for imperial outreach did not constitute an aberration, as later generations would shamefully argue, but the continuation of an established historical pattern of imperial territoriality. For advocates of expansion, habitual settler imperial outlooks provided a reassuring analytical matrix and cultural archive from which the new tropical frontier was interpreted as a seamless complement to the continental empire.[74] Although many critics

---

Nation, or Empire: The American Debate over International Relations, 1789–1941, Lawrence: University Press of Kansas, 2009.

[73] I. Tyrell and J. Sexton (eds.), *Empire's Twin: U.S. Anti-Imperialism from the Founding Era to the Age of Terrorism*, Ithaca: Cornell University Press, 2015; Hilfrich, *Debating American Exceptionalism*; M.P. Cullinane, *Liberty and American Anti-Imperialism, 1898–1909*, Basingstoke: Palgrave Macmillan, 2012; J. Zwick, "The Anti-Imperialist Movement, 1898–1921", in: V.M. Bouvier (ed.), *Whose America? The War of 1898 and the Battle to Define the Nation*, Westport: Praeger, 2001, pp. 171–192.

[74] On overseas settler colonialism, conceptual continuities, and cultural archives, see K. Bjork, "Prairie Imperialists: The Bureau of Insular Affairs and Continuities in Colonial Expansion from Nebraska to Cuba and the Philippines", *Nebraska History* 95 (2014), pp. 216–229; C.J. Chanco, "Frontier Polities and Imaginaries: The Reproduction of Settler Colonial Space in the Southern Philippines", *Settler Colonial Studies* 7 (2017) 1, pp. 111–133; C.D. Deere, "Here Come the Yankees! The Rise and Decline of United States Colonies in Cuba, 1898–1930", *Hispanic American Historical Review* 78 (1998) 4: pp. 729–765; S. D. Halili Jr., *Iconography of the New Empire. Race and Gender Images and the American Colonization of the Philippines*, Diliman: University of the Philippines Press, 2006; A. Ignacio et al., *The Forbidden Book: The Philippine-American War in Political Cartoons*, San Francisco: T'Boli Publishing, 2004; B.M. Miller, *From Liberation to Conquest: The Visual and Popular Cultures of the Spanish-American War of 1898*, Amherst: University of Massachusetts Press, 2011; M.E. Neagle, *America's Forgotten Colony: Cuba's Isle of Pines*, Cambridge: Cambridge University Press, 2016; A. Paulet, "To Change the World: The Use of American Indian Education in the Philippines", *History of Education Quarterly* 47 (2007) 2, pp. 173–202; W.L. Williams, "United States Indian Policy and the Debate over Philippine Annexation: Implications for the Origins of American Imperialism", *Journal of American History* 66 (1980) 4, pp. 810–831.

shared such cultural and racial predispositions, they also emphasized the underside of "empire as a way of life" through a discursive connection of victims of imperial respatializations at home and abroad.[75]

This contextualization of the post-1898 annexations in the *longue durée* of US empire-building also debated if the new possessions could be integrated into the polity along a trajectory to statehood plotted by the Northwest Ordinance. While critics claimed that the US Constitution required ultimate incorporation and thus objected to colonial annexations, imperialists denied such legal automatisms, emphasized that territorial possession held neither constitutional nor political obligations, described US rule as a temporary "developmental project", and systematically obfuscated the true extent of this empire through semantic conventions, administrative variance, and murky legal demarcations between core and periphery.[76]

Such obfuscations contributed to the containment of anti-colonial opposition and the success of the imperialist agenda as the United States assumed control of the former Spanish colonies Puerto Rico, Guam, and the Philippines in 1898.[77] While Cuba became a long-term protectorate, the US also annexed Hawaii, Wake Island, and Eastern Samoa and later added the Panama Canal Zone and the Danish West Indies to its empire. Legal and semantic detractions laid the foundations for the enduring myth that this overseas empire was all but a brief and an insignificant "detour" from an otherwise anti-colonial national trajectory.

Despite such disagreements on the potential implications of overseas colonial rule, both advocates and opponents often shared similar racialized outlooks on international affairs and the benefits of global integration. In this context, imperial territoriality intensified the simultaneous globalizing of the United States and its further globalization in multiple ways: empire inspired imaginations of global leadership, internationalized both advocates and critics of colonialism

---

75 W.A. Williams, *Empire as a Way of Life: An Essay on the Causes and Character of America's Present Predicament along with a Few Thoughts About an Alternative*, Oxford: Oxford University Press, 1980.
76 For constitutional deliberations on colonial territoriality, see C. Duffy Burnett and B. Marshall (eds.), *Foreign in a Domestic Sense: Puerto Rico, American Expansion, and the Constitution*, Durham: Duke University Press, 2001; C. Duffy Burnett, "Untied States: American Expansion and Territorial Deannexation", *The University of Chicago Law Review* 72 (2005) 3, pp. 797–879; B.H. Sparrow, *The Insular Cases and the Emergence of the American Empire*, Lawrence: University Press of Kansas, 2006.
77 The concerted efforts of imperialists at opinion management are discussed in C.D. Moore, *American Imperialism and the State 1893–1921*, Cambridge: Cambridge University Press, 2017.

through transimperial cooperation, and encouraged the rise of societal global outlooks, internationalist practices, and transnational alliances.[78]

The close spatial proximity of US, European, and Japanese colonies deeply embedded the United States in dense networks of interimperial circulations of people, goods, and ideas.[79] Empire also provided an important rationale and framework for the steadily expanded presence of Americans abroad for business, colonial service, tourism, exploration, and missionary work. A stream of travelogues about their experiences, the professionalization and popularization of geography and geopolitics, the internationalization of domestic consumption patterns, and frequent exoticized spectacles of colonial presence in the imperial metropole further advanced the formation of powerful global outlooks in the American Empire.[80]

Such outlooks accelerated and accompanied the integration of the United States into international policy agreements on standards, and governmental and non-governmental knowledge networks to remedy perceived national and imperial shortcomings.[81] These encounters with the global frontiers increasingly

---

[78] Daniel Gorman has suggested the complementary nature of both imperialism and internationalism: "Imperialists could present empire as a form of internationalism, whereas internationalists could draw from imperialism practical and theoretical lessons", *The Emergence of International Society in the 1920s*, Cambridge: Cambridge University Press, 2012, p. 319.

[79] On interimperial networks, see T. Ballantyne and A. Burton, *Empires and the Reach of the Global, 1870–1945*, Cambridge: Harvard University Press, 2014; V. Barth and R. Cvetkovski (eds.), *Imperial Co-operation and Transfer, 1870–1930*, London: Bloomsbury, 2015; for the American search of colonial expertise in these networks, see F. Schumacher, "Embedded Empire: The United States and Colonialism", *Journal of Modern European History* 14 (2016) 2, pp. 202–224; on anti-colonial alliances, see B. Anderson, *The Age of Globalization: Anarchists and the Anticolonial Imagination*, London: Verso, 2013; K. Hagimoto, *Between Empires: Marti, Rizal, and the Intercolonial Alliance*, Basingstoke: Palgrave Macmillan, 2013.

[80] For post-Civil War global outlooks and activities, see Oliver Charbonneau, "Visiting the Metropole: Muslim Colonial Subjects in the United States, 1904–1927", *Diplomatic History* 42 (2018) 2, pp. 204–227; C. Endy, "Travel and World Power: Americans in Europe, 1890–1917", *Diplomatic History* 22 (1998) 4, pp. 565–594; K.L. Hoganson, *Consumer's Imperialism: The Global Production of American Domesticity, 1865–1920*, Chapel Hill: University of North Carolina Press, 2007; D. Hollinger, *Protestants Abroad: How Missionaries tried to Change the World but Changed America*, Princeton: Princeton University Press, 2017; F. Ninkovich, *Global Dawn: The Cultural Foundations of American Internationalism, 1865–1890*, Cambridge: Harvard University Press, 2009; T.Y. Rothenberg, *Presenting America's World: Strategies of Innocence in National Geographic Magazine, 1888–1945*, Abingdon: Routledge, 2007; I. Tyrell, *Reforming the World: The Creation of America's Moral Empire*, Princeton: Princeton University Press, 2010.

[81] M. Herren, *Hintertüren zur Macht: Internationalismus und modernisierungsorientierte Außenpolitik in Belgien, der Schweiz und den USA, 1865–1914*, Munich: Oldenbourg Verlag, 2000, pp. 371–505; D.T. Rodgers, *Atlantic Crossings: Social Politics in a Progressive Age*,

conflated empire, nation, and globalism and imagined the United States as a new and competing centre of gravity in global affairs destined to replace British primacy. A popular joke from the late 1920s in which a customer announced his intention to purchase a "globe of the United States" not only caricatured parochial reductionism but also indicated how natural expansive visions of a globalized America had become in the early twentieth century.[82] But while imperial territoriality enabled the global projection of US strength and prestige, it also engendered anxieties about territorial integrity, rationalized mushrooming demands for further annexations, provoked pushback from imperial power competitors, and produced public criticism at home and abroad.

The duality of spatial power as an asset and a liability was particularly visible in Central America, where the US Empire encompassed a patchwork of colonies, protectorates, naval bases, infrastructure networks, client regimes, and agricultural production and resource extraction zones.[83] Much of this empire complemented the Panama Canal constructed between 1904 and 1914.[84] This marvel of imperial infrastructure and social engineering was a key geostrategic asset for the United States, which interlinked the imperial nation with its Caribbean and Pacific colonies and global frontiers. It allowed for quick naval redeployments between US coasts and completed transcontinental transportation networks. Finally, the canal positioned the United States at the crossroads between Europe and Asia, respatialized traditional Spanish trade and migration

---

Cambridge: Harvard University Press, 1998; A.R. Schäfer, *American Progressives and German Social Reform, 1875–1920: Social Ethics, Moral Control, and the Regulatory State in a Transatlantic Context*, Stuttgart: Franz Steiner Verlag, 2000.

[82] E.M. Pahlow, "Why World History", *Education* 53 (1932), pp. 133–199, at 193, quoted in: B. Stuchtey and E. Fuchs (eds.), *Writing World History 1800–2000*, Oxford: Oxford University Press, 2003, p. 1.

[83] J.M. Colby, *The Business of Empire: United Fruit, Race, and U.S. Expansion in Central America*, Cornell: Cornell University Press, 2011; M.E. Donoghue, *Borderland on the Isthmus: Race, Culture, and the Struggle for the Canal Zone*, Durham: Duke University Press, 2014; M. Gobat, *Confronting the American Dream: Nicaragua under U.S. Imperial Rule*, Durham: Duke University Press, 2005; A. McPherson, *The Invaded: How Latin Americans and Their Allies Fought and Ended U.S. Occupations*, Oxford: Oxford University Press, 2014; M. Renda, *Taking Haiti: Military Occupation and the Culture of U.S. Imperialism*, Chapel Hill: University of North Carolina Press, 2001; E.S. Rosenberg, *Financial Missionaries to the World: The Politics and Culture of Dollar Diplomacy, 1900–1950*, Durham: Duke University Press, 2003.

[84] Donoghue, *Borderland on the Isthmus*; J. Greene, *The Canal Builders: Making America's Empire at the Panama Canal*, New York: Penguin Books, 2009; A. Missal, *Seaway to the Future: American Social Visions and the Construction of the Panama Canal*, Madison: University of Wisconsin Press, 2008.

patterns, and recalibrated political, commercial, and cultural influence in the Atlantic world.[85]

The successful construction project, however, not only reinforced racialized cultural discourses of imperial pride and global pre-eminence but also fuelled concerns about external and internal threats to US sovereignty over the canal and its oceanic access lanes. This security discourse informed the steady spatial recalibration of the Monroe Doctrine, rationalized the quest for hemispheric dominance, and encouraged the extension of imperial territoriality through the annexation of new colonies in the West Indies, the creation of protectorates in Central America and the Caribbean, and the development of military and naval bases in the region to ensure firm spatial control over the Isthmus of Panama.[86] The advent of the air age further exacerbated insecurities about the canal and resulted in the creation of a vast network of US-controlled airfields in the Americas, West Africa, and the Pacific Ocean in support of continuously expanding geostrategic imaginations of the western hemisphere.[87]

But empire-building, as the Panama Canal amply illustrates, not only served just geostrategic purposes but was also intended to enhance US commercial power. The spatiality of empire reflected this dual thrust, and its mélange of corporate and government interests which often manifested itself in extensive private-public partnerships. Investment protection increasingly developed into a second dimension of the security discourse and advanced geostrategic and economic considerations as mutually reinforcing rationalizations for US territorial control in the Caribbean Basin and beyond.[88] Such

---

85 Meinig, *The Shaping of America*, pp. 380–394; on visualizations of this spatial "centering" of the United States, see map in J.C. Fernald, *The Imperial Republic*, New York: Funk & Wagnalls Co., 1899, p. 100; on Spanish networks, see R.B. Buschmann, E.R. Slack Jr. and J.B. Tueller (eds.), *Navigating the Spanish Lake: The Pacific in the Iberian World, 1521–1898*, Honolulu: University of Hawaii Press, 2014.

86 On discourses of global preeminence, see S.J. Moore, *Empire on Display: San Francisco's Panama-Pacific International Exposition of 1915*, Norman: University of Oklahoma Press, 2013; Missal, *Seaway to the Future*; on geopolitical expansion of the Monroe Doctrine, see S. Ricard, "The Roosevelt Corollary", *Presidential Studies Quarterly* 36 (2006) 1, pp. 17–26; Sexton, *The Monroe Doctrine*, pp. 211–239;

87 J. Van Vleck, *Empire of the Air: Aviation and the American Ascendancy*, Cambridge: Harvard University Press, 2013; on discourses on hemispheric security, see U. Lübken, "'What is the Western Hemisphere?' Spatial Dimensions of United States Interventionist Policy, 1938–1941", in: A. Ortlepp and C. Ribbat (eds.), *Taking Up Space: New Approaches to American History*, Trier: WVT Verlag, 2004, pp. 89–108.

88 Colby, *The Business of Empire*; E.S. Rosenberg, *Financial Missionaries to the World*; C. Veeser, *A World Safe for Capitalism: Dollar Diplomacy and America's Rise to Global Power*, New York: Columbia University Press, 2012.

explanations for the "New Rome's" imperialism during the interwar years were frequently denounced as hypocritical, vulgar, and counterproductive.[89]

The architects of empire responded with the time-tested nationalist narrative of America as a selfless anti-colonial power and devised a discursive strategy to enhance the nation's prestige and credibility by obfuscating its imperial territoriality.[90] In 1924, for example, US diplomats and international lawyers launched a consolidated political campaign to force the editors of the widely respected handbook *Almanach de Gotha* to retract its claim that Cuba, Panama, Liberia, Haiti, and the Dominican Republic constituted US protectorates.[91] The United States further intensified this discursive disassociation from territorial imperialism by somewhat ironically presenting itself as the benchmark for anti-colonial development at the Paris Colonial Exposition in 1931. At the same time, acknowledged colonies alone placed the US fifth among the world's empires, with almost 20 million colonial subjects abroad, or roughly 13 per cent of the polity's population.[92]

But while the insistence on non-territorial aspirations failed to convince many critics at the time, it provided analytical impetus for the concept of "informal" empire in the long run. Informality in this context characterizes power differentials and forms of domination below the benchmark of "direct" territorial control and acknowledged colonial rule.[93] This discursively powerful perspective has emphasized that US actions in the Caribbean were characterized by brief military interventions in a "bash and run" approach, investments, and

---

89 On "New Rome" analogies, see M. Ugarte, *The Destiny of a Continent*, New York: Alfred E. Knopf, 1925; for opposition, see A. McPherson, *The Invaded*, pp. 194–212; Rosenberg, *Financial Missionaries to the World*, pp. 122–150.

90 On prestige and international relations, see R. Gilpin, *War and Change in World Politics*, Cambridge: Cambridge University Press, 1981, p. 30–42; on the "credibility imperative", see R. J. McMahon, "Credibility and World Power: Exploring the Psychological Dimensions in Postwar American Diplomacy", *Diplomatic History* 15 (1991) 4, pp. 455–472.

91 James Brown Scott, a scholar of international law and director of the international law division of the Carnegie Endowment for International Peace, was the driving force behind the American pushback (P. Amorosa, "The American Project and the Politics of History: James Brown Scott and the Origins of International Law", dissertation, University of Helsinki: Faculty of Law, 2018, pp. 91–95); on protectorates, see L. Benton, A. Clulow and B. Attwood (eds.), *Protection and Empire: A Global History*, Cambridge: Cambridge University Press, 2018.

92 Schumacher, "Embedded Empire", p. 220; for figures, see Immerwahr, "The Greater United States", pp. 376–377.

93 J. Osterhammel, *Colonialism: A Theoretical Overview*, Princeton: Markus Wiener Publishers, 2005.

economic oversight to dominate this region without the responsibilities of "formal" rule, except for Puerto Rico and the Virgin Islands.[94]

Over time, this emphasis on "informal" and non-territorial power relations served as the logical corollary and precondition for the benign reassessment of US colonialism as it enabled its presentation as a short-lived, territorially insignificant, and historically atypical manifestation of US power. But the juxtaposition of "formal" and "informal" facets of empire imaginatively exaggerated the degree of control in the former while minimizing its extent in the latter, and thus analytically transposed a non-acknowledged colonial relationship into hegemony or "empire light".[95] The steady transformation and respatialization of the Caribbean Basin into a US imperial domain belied such widespread retrospective mythology driven by exceptionalist national narratives. Neither Woodrow Wilson nor his immediate successor administrations and contemporary public discourses foreclosed imperial territoriality or advanced decolonization. Instead, the United States further extended control over territory in a wide range of spatial formats through long-term military occupation and deeply intrusive administrative, legal, economic, and cultural respatializations, whose intensity and extent contradicted their purported "informality".[96]

Even though such obfuscations of imperial territoriality discursively reconciled empire and advocacy for decolonization at home, they did little to distract the focus of imperial competitors on territorial expansion abroad. These rival states interpreted expansive, resource-rich spaces as the nexus between industrial production, market dominance, and global primacy and

---

[94] On "bash and run", see F. Cooper, *Colonialism in Question: Theory, Knowledge, History*, Berkeley: University of California Press, 2005, p. 196.

[95] On empire and hegemony, see Maier, *Among Empires*, p. 59; M.W. Doyle, *Empires*, Ithaca: Cornell University Press, 1986, pp. 37–38; Ann Laura Stoler has rightfully described indirect rule and informal empire as "unhelpful euphemisms, not working concepts" in A.L. Stoler "On Degrees of Imperial Sovereignty", *Public Culture* 18 (2006)1, pp. 125–146, at 136; on the interconnections between commercial power and territorial state power, see P. Kramer "Embedding Capital: Political-Economic History, the United States, and the World", *Journal of the Gilded Age and Progressive Era* 15 (2016), pp. 331–362.

[96] On Wilson and colonial empire, see E. Rosenberg, "World War I, Wilsonianism, and Challenges to U.S. Empire", *Diplomatic History* 38 (2014) 4, pp. 852–863; a critique and emphasis on deterritorialization, see R. Gerwarth and E. Manela, "The Great War as a Global War: Imperial Conflict and the Reconfiguration of World Order, 1911–1923", *Diplomatic History* 38 (2014) 4, pp. 786–800; on Wilson and the hope for decolonization, see E. Manela, *The Wilsonian Moment: Self-Determination and the International Origins of Anti-Colonial Nationalism*, Oxford: Oxford University Press, 2007.

strove to emulate the United States since the early twentieth century.[97] After the global contraction of industrial capitalism during the 1930s, Germany, Italy, and Japan embarked on a worldwide campaign of expansion to achieve economic autarky through the conquest of resource-rich regions in Europe, Africa, Asia, and the Pacific, thus confronting the United States for the second time in a generation with a fundamental challenge to its own "territorialized power".

After roughly eight decades of imperial outreach, this second phase of the American Empire thus ended as it had begun, with an assault on the territorial integrity of the United States. This time the assault emanated from outside the polity through the Japanese attack on US colonies and territories in the Pacific and North America (Aleutians) and German attempts for dominance in the Atlantic world. The subsequent global war neither discredited nor ended US reliance on territorialized power during the further development of the American Empire. On the contrary, revolutionary developments in weapons technology, challenges to Washington's quest for post-war international leadership, and the inherent paradoxes of territorialized power, intensified the traditional reliance on imperial integration and reinforced the strategic centrality of space to the US quest for global dominance.

Imperial Contours, 1940s to the Present

The end of World War II constituted a moment of unsurpassed strength for the United States in its ability to shape global conditions.[98] Such pre-eminence had confidently been anticipated by a wide range of contemporary observers from airpower enthusiasts to political commentators. They had predicted an "American Century" in which the United States would replace the British Empire to advance a liberal-democratic-capitalist international system conducive to its global aspirations. Although such views often envisioned America as an age-defining empire, they remained remarkably silent as to its territorial configurations and denied the significance of imperial geography; instead, they suggested that US economic dominance and the pervasive influence of its popular and material culture rendered territoriality irrelevant and

---

[97] S. Beckert, "American Danger: United States Empire, Eurafrica, and the Territorialization of Industrial Capitalism, 1870–1950", *American Historical Review* 122 (2017) 4, pp. 1137–1169.
[98] G. Lundestad, *The Rise and Decline of the American "Empire": Power and Its Limits in Comparative Perspective*, Oxford: Oxford University Press, 2012, pp. 11–12.

helped ensure American leadership as it masked imperial ambition as abstract universalism.[99]

This foregrounding of a territorially unbound global America has resonated with many subsequent interpretations of the *Pax Americana* as a projection of wealth, industrial productivity, scientific and technological innovation, military strength, and international prestige on a historically unprecedented scale in support of a hierarchical global order defined by the United States.[100] Such deterritorialized understandings of the modern American Empire drew on notions of "informal rule", frequently conflated globalization and US power, and inflated differences between the American Empire and great empires of the past. From such a perspective, the United States emerges as an exceptionally powerful even imperial yet spatially disinterested advocate and driver of globally beneficial economic and technological integration.

But such world-spanning iterations of US power remained deeply grounded in various overlapping, reinforcing, and sometimes contradictory formats of imperial territoriality and spatial rationales. The logic of territorial power delineated imperial practices in the nation-state, ensured the continuity of overseas colonialism, shaped the polity's geopolitical outlooks, and accelerated the expansion of a vast global network of military and economic imperial outposts.

The post-war imperial state displayed contradictory tendencies: on the one hand, it further integrated the national core by steadily eliminating differentiated rule; on the other hand, it also continued the imperial logic of such difference through its racialized marginalization of non–Euro-American populations in various spatial settings, from internment camps to zones of disenfranchisement and spaces of nuclear resource colonialism. Over time, these imperial threads in the nation-state's fabric transcended these zones in a variety of "imperial formations", from surveillance regimes to immigration restrictions, and the continuous erosion of democracy in the age of an "imperial presidency".[101]

---

[99] D. Harvey, *The New Imperialism*, Oxford: Oxford University Press, 2003, p. 50; on denial of territoriality, see N. Smith, *American Empire: Roosevelt's Geographer and the Prelude to Globalization*, Berkeley: University of California Press, 2003, pp. 19–21; Van Vleck, *Empire of the Air*, pp. 118–130; among political commentary, see W. Lippmann, "The American Destiny", *Life Magazine*, 5 June 1939, pp. 47–53 and 72–73; H.R. Luce, "The American Century" *Diplomatic History* 23 (1941/1999) 2, pp. 159–171.

[100] D.J. Sargent, "Pax Americana: Sketches for an Undiplomatic History", *Diplomatic History* 42 (2018) 3, pp. 357–376.

[101] On "imperial formations", see A.L. Stoler, "Introduction: 'The Rot Remains': From Ruins to Ruination", in: A.L. Stoler (ed.), *Imperial Debris: On Ruins and Ruination*, Durham: Duke University Press, 2013, pp. 1–38, at 8; the term "imperial presidency" is taken from A.M. Schlesinger Jr., *The Imperial Presidency*, New York: Houghton Mifflin, 1973; on challenges to

This overlap of empire and nation intensified under the umbrella of the steadily expanding national security state. Over eight decades from World War II through the Cold War to the so-called "War on Terror", rule by difference in the polity often found discursive legitimacy in the threat horizons of nearly permanent war. If war constituted "the substance of American history", empire was its steady companion and served as the mould for its violent dynamic.[102]

Under the ever-present rationale of national security, empire often found its most visible expression in "anomalous" or "exceptional zones", which delineated the inequitable treatment of the empire's spatial components. The continued colonial disenfranchisement of residents in the District of Columbia constituted an example of such a zone.[103] Furthermore, the concept of exceptionality also applied to spaces in which constitutional rights were temporarily suspended in response to perceived external or internal threats, such as the removal and interment of more than 120,000 people of Japanese and Aleut descent from the US West Coast and Alaskan islands during World War II. But the notion that imperial differentiations constituted a mere temporary anomaly under exceptional security circumstances rather than a structural phenomenon was contradicted not only by the polity's near-permanent state of war but also by the longevity of its disenfranchisement and violent marginalization of non-Euro-American populations in legally sanctioned formats.

At the heart of this disenfranchisement was the persistent racial segregation in the "empire of Jim Crow".[104] This post-Civil War apartheid regime lasted until the 1960s and encompassed a wide range of state and municipal laws and regulations to exclude African Americans from political participation through voting restrictions; it also enforced strict spatial separation regimes across all aspects of life, from schools to hospitals to housing and places of worship.

---

citizenship during the Cold War, see A. Friedman, *Citizenship in Cold War America: The National Security State and the Possibility of Dissent*, Amherst: University of Massachusetts Press, 2014.

102 M.B. Young, "I was thinking, as I often do these days, of war: The United States in the Twenty-First Century", *Diplomatic History* 36 (2012) 1, pp. 1–15, at 1; on the impact of war on modern US history, see M.S. Sherry, *In the Shadow of War: The United States since the 1930s*, New Haven: Yale University Press, 1995.

103 G. Neumann, "Surveying Law and Border: Anomalous Zones", *Stanford Law Review* 48 (1996) 5, pp. 1197–1234.

104 The "empire of Jim Crow" is from a speech by US Secretary of State Condoleezza Rice on 21 October 2005 at the University of Alabama, quoted in: N. Pal Singh, "Beyond the 'Empire of Jim Crow': Race and War in Contemporary U.S. Globalism", *The Japanese Journal of American Studies* 20 (2009), pp. 89–111, at 89.

The purported constitutionality of this empire within the state had been upheld by the US Supreme Court since the late nineteenth century. Furthermore, the court and the federal government also sanctioned the persistence of racialized colonial violence in its widespread practice of lynching through purposeful neglect and non-interference. Instead of legal intervention and enforcement of constitutional protection, all three branches of government embarked on a path of "constitutional anarchy" by resigning territory in the polity to "legally bounded regions of lawlessness" and "zones of permissiveness".[105] For almost a century, the American state thus legitimized and encouraged the maintenance of a "a white supremacist 'racial order' within its borders."[106]

This race regime was not limited to the American South but manifested itself to varying degrees throughout the polity. While landmark laws such as Civil Rights Act (1964) and Voting Rights Act (1965) ended segregation in the mid-1960, they did not end imperial characteristics in the management of the nation's ethnocultural diversity through marginalization and exclusion.

In this context, Western indigenous polities remained a persistent target of resource extraction imperialism throughout the Cold War and beyond. With more than 60 per cent of uranium deposits on reservation land and up to 90 per cent of uranium mining and milling on or in close proximity to reservations, "nuclear colonialism" drew on standard repertoires of disenfranchisement. These were disguised as national security paradigms to uphold a "system of domination through which governments and corporations target indigenous peoples and their land to maintain the nuclear production process".[107]

While the settler imperial logic continued to affect indigenous cultures, national security imperatives also consistently widened the spectre of differentiated rule and suspended constitutionality for growing segments of the polity.

---

[105] D. Kato, "Contitutionalizing Anarchy: Liberalism, Lynching, and the Law", *Journal of Hate Studies* 10 (2012)1, pp. 143–172; see also D. Kato, *Liberalizing Lynching: Building a New Racialized State*, Oxford: Oxford University Press, 2015; on violence, see Pfeifer, *Lynching and American Society*; Berg, *Popular Justice*.

[106] D. King and R. Lieberman, "The American State", in: R. Valelly, S. Mettler and R. Lieberman (eds.), *Oxford Handbook of American Political Development*, Oxford: Oxford University Press, 2016, pp. 231–258, at 247–248.

[107] T. Brynne Voyles, *Wastelanding: Legacies of Uranium Mining in Navajo Country*, Minneapolis: University of Minnesota Press, 2015; D. Endres, "The Rhetoric of Nuclear Colonialism: Rhetorical Exclusion of American Indian Arguments in the Yucca Mountain Nuclear Waste Siting Decision", *Communication and Critical/Cultural Studies* 6 (2009) 1, pp. 39–60, at 40; A. Moore-Nall, "The Legacy of Uranium Development on or Near Indian Reservations and Health Implications Rekindling Public Awareness", *Geoscience* 5 (2015), pp. 15–29.

And while racialized marginalization continued to shape incarceration regimes and framed legal discourses on exclusion from the polity, "imperial formations" increasingly transcended their racial groundings in the normalization of "anomaly" in the security state.[108]

Regimes of fear from thermonuclear annihilation to terrorism now complemented regimes of race as "states of exception" became spatially amorphous and polyvalent formats of simultaneous integration and the maintenance of difference. The integration of a seemingly beleaguered "Fortress America" utilized fear-induced disengagement from the polity while it simultaneously reinforced a strong executive, eroded democratic institution, steadily expanded surveillance regimes, and often arbitrarily suspended civil liberties and constitutional protections. Although never uncontested, this dynamic ensured the composite continuity of the modern American state as imperial nation.[109]

The imperial frontiers abroad underwent similarly contradictory developments in size, composition, and direction. Large territories were integrated into an expanded nation-state with the admission of Alaska and Hawaii to the Union in 1959. In addition, the United States also ended its rule over some territories and protectorates, such as the Philippines in 1946, Cuba in 1959, and the Panama Canal Zone in 1999.

On the other hand, Washington retained not only imperial outposts in those "decolonized" spaces, such as Guantanamo Bay in Cuba, but also extended its territorial rule in the Pacific over most of Micronesia's two thousand islands, which had been a site of intense interimperial competition since the nineteenth century. Between 1947 and 1986, Micronesia was a United Nations (UN) trust territory administered by the United States. Since the end of the trust status, the Northern Mariana Islands have been ruled as a colony with a commonwealth status, while the United States maintains contractually secured protectorates over the nominally independent Federated States of Micronesia, the Republic of Palau, and the Republic of the Marshall Islands. Until today, the Micronesian archipelago has remained a central outpost in a forward territorial perimeter designed to protect and project the polity's imperial power.

In contrast to the decolonizing dynamic of imperial respatialization, these territorial extensions have received scant attention, an oversight that reinforces the perception that colonialism ended with the admission of Alaska and Hawaii

---

108 On incarceration regimes, see C. Hayes, *A Colony in a Nation*, New York: W.W. Norton & Co., 2017.
109 On the politics of fear most recently, see E. Tyler May, *Fortress America: How We Embraced Fear and Abandoned Democracy*, New York: Basic Books, 2017.

to the Union in 1959.[110] While nineteenth-century style colonial empires may have lost appeal as the sine qua non of great power status, the United States has still maintained such an empire in the Caribbean and the Pacific until today, not least because its imperial strategic utility was largely obscured by its low visibility.

This reduced profile was in part the result of its small demographic size and in part a consequence of its overwhelmingly insular character and geographic dispersion.[111] In a spatial logic that equated size with influence, this reductionist geographical imagination juxtaposed scale differentials of large land-based empires with archipelagic sea-based empire frequently, in favour of the former over the latter and thereby ignoring that America's imperial formations rested on both land and sea.[112] The spatial dispersal of this "pointillist empire" over extensive oceanic surface areas and the vast geographic distance of many islands to the imperial metropole further obscured their geostrategic relevance and colonized realities from the public gaze.[113] In addition, the great variance of legal status classifications for these colonies and their euphemistic descriptors further contributed to the widespread perception that overseas empire was inconsequential to the polity while it simultaneously obscured the colonies' shared experience of disenfranchisement.[114]

Despite a combination of imperial neglect and deliberate efforts to mask the persistence of colonial disenfranchisement and its mutations over time, some of the empire's defining features remained surprisingly consistent. In addition to its longevity, discursive conventions, geographic spread, and deep interconnections to the nation-state's "imperial formations", the post-war

---

110 Hopkins' recent one-thousand page American Empire: A Global History devotes one half-sentence to US rule in Micronesia.

111 S.J. La Croix, "Outlying Areas" (Chapter Ef, vol. V) in: S.B. Carter et al. (eds.), *Historical Statistics of the United States, Earliest Times to the Present, Millennial Edition*, 5 vols., Cambridge: Cambridge University Press, 2006, pp. 587–595.

112 B. Russell Roberts and M.A. Stephens, "Introduction: Decontinentalizing the Study of American Culture", in: B. Russell Roberts and M.A. Stephens (eds.), *Archipelagic American Studies*, Durham: Duke University Press, 2017, p. 12; on the persistence of insular marginalization, see J. Letman, "Just 'An Island in the Pacific': How Washington Demeans Its Colonial Conquests", *Foreign Policy in Focus*, 26 April 2017, https://fpif.org/just-an-island-in-the-pacific-how-washington-demeans-its-colonial-conquests/ (accessed 5 May 2018).

113 On "pointillist empire", see D. Immerwahr, "The Greater United States", p. 390.

114 Burns, *American Imperialism*, pp. 163–165; A.H. Leibowitz, *Defining Status: A Comprehensive Analysis of United States Territorial Relations*, Dordrecht: Martin Nijhoff Publishers, 1986, pp. 520–704; contemporary colonial denial is discussed in V. Bulmer-Thomas, *Empire in Retreat: The Past, Present, and Future of the United States*, New Haven: Yale University Press, 2018, p. 99.

overseas empire continued to serve as a highly militarized territorial platform for the defence and geostrategic aspirations of an imperial state engaged in permanent war. The longevity of colonial empire was thus a direct function of the prioritization of militarized power and its demand for unobstructed land use over the rights of territorial residents.[115]

This process was particularly pronounced in Micronesia, whose archipelagos extended across a vast oceanic surface comparable to the size of the continental United States.[116] Under pressure from Washington, the UN designated these islands a "strategic trust", which enabled their extensive militarization without international inspection, intrusion, or intervention.[117] In the spatial logic of empire, the strategic value of such distant islands was twofold: on the one hand, Micronesia and especially the Marshall Islands provided a staging platform for US force projection into Asia; on the other hand, these archipelagos served as a testing ground for nuclear and thermonuclear weapons and their respective missile delivery systems.

Even though the militarization of the broader Pacific was a transimperial project, its nuclear colonialism was advanced most decisively by the United States.[118] Between 1946 and 1962, atoll communities such as Bikini, Enewetak,

---

[115] D. Vine, "Most Countries Have Given Up Their Colonies. Why Hasn't America?" *Washington Post*, 28 September 2017, https://www.washingtonpost.com/news/made-by-history/wp/2017/09/28/most-countries-have-given-up-their-colonies-why-hasnt-america/?utm_term=.18c38c6c4b1a (accessed 12 May 2018).

[116] H.M. Friedman, *Creating an American Lake: United States Imperialism and Strategic Security in the Pacific Basin, 1945–1947*, Westport: Greenwood Press, 2001, p. 1; D.W. Meinig, *Global America, 1915–2000, The Shaping of America*, vol. IV, New Haven: Yale University Press, 2004, p. 387; on US wartime planning for a Pacific empire, see Louis, *Imperialism at Bay*, pp. 259–273.

[117] L. Hirshberg "Navigating Sovereignty under a Cold War Military Industrial Colonial Complex: US Military Empire and Marshallese Decolonization", *History and Technology* 31 (2015) 3, pp. 259–274; V. Pungong, "The United States and the International Trusteeship System", in: D. Ryan and V. Pungong (eds.), *The United States and Decolonization*, 2000, pp. 85–101.

[118] Hirshberg, "Navigating Sovereignty", p. 260; R. Jacobs, "Nuclear Conquistadors: Military Colonialism in Nuclear Test Site Selection during the Cold War", *Asian Journal of Peacebuilding* 1 (2013) 2, pp. 157–177; M.D. Merlin, R.M. Gonzales, "Environmental Impact of Nuclear Testing in Remote Oceania, 1946–1996", in: J.R. McNeill and C.R. Unger (eds.), *Environmental Histories of the Cold War*, Cambridge: Cambridge University Press, 2010, pp. 167–202; on nuclear colonialism, see G. Hecht, "Introduction", in: G. Hecht (ed.), *Entangled Geographies: Empire and Technopolitics in the Global Cold War*, Cambridge: Massachusetts Institute of Technology Press, 2011, pp. 4–5; A. Smith, "Colonialism and the Bomb in the Pacific", in: J. Schofield and W. Cocroft (eds.), *A Fearsome Heritage: Diverse Legacies of the Cold War*, Walnut Creek: Left Coast Press, 2007, pp. 51–71.

Rongelap, or Rongerik were part of the "US Pacific Proving Grounds", where the United States conducted more than 100 atmospheric and underwater nuclear tests, while the Kwajalein Atoll still provides the US military with its principal missile test site. Since the 1960s, some islands, such as Runit, have been used as nuclear waste depositories to store deadly "imperial debris" from a variety of test sites.[119]

The extensive territorial dispossession of the islanders was complemented by their frequent and extensive exposure to radioactive fallout and their abuse as colonial scientific subjects in longitudinal radiation studies such as "Project 4.1" directed by the US Department of Energy.[120] Reminiscent of the treatment of indigenous polities in the American West, the Marshallese were frequently described as insignificant, incapable, and "expendable".[121] The tenor of this colonial marginalization was summed up by National Security Advisor Henry A. Kissinger in 1969 in response to requests for Micronesian compensation for land appropriations: "There are only 90,000 people out there. Who gives a damn?"[122]

This dismissive imperial attitude reflects the empire's racialized desire to control territory without the "complications" of colonial rule. Local populations were perceived by the imperial metropole as unwelcomed additions to strategically valued platforms for force projection, defence, or resource extraction. The treatment of Puerto Rico by the federal government in the wake of tropical cyclone Maria in 2017 was a stark reminder of the persistence of such imperial outlooks and the continuity of colonialism in the American polity.[123]

But the near omnipresence of the United States in global affairs over the last eight decades has often overshadowed such continuities as national and international attention has focused on US intentions, capabilities, and

---

[119] C. Jose, K. Wall and J.H. Hinzel, "This Dome in the Pacific Houses Tons of Radioactive Waste – And It's Leaking", *The Guardian*, 3 July 2015, https://www.theguardian.com/world/2015/jul/03/runit-dome-pacific-radioactive-waste (accessed 10 March 2018); for a conceptual analysis of imperial debris and ruins, see A.L. Stoler, *Duress: Imperial Durabilities in Our Time*, Durham: Duke University Press, 2006, pp. 336–379.

[120] B. Rose Johnston, H.M. Barker, *Consequential Damages of Nuclear War: The Rongelap Report*, Abingdon: Routledge, 2008, pp. 103–107.

[121] A. Kearney, *Violence in Place: Cultural and Environmental Wounding*, Abingdon: Routledge, 2016, p. 167.

[122] Kissinger quoted in: W.J. Hickel, *Who Owns America?* Englewood Cliffs: Prentice-Hall, 1971, p. 208.

[123] M. William Palen, "Decisions more than a Century ago Explain Why the U.S. has failed Puerto Rico in its Time of Need. Fears about Trade Prompted the Decision to make Puerto Rico a Colony", *Washington Post*, 3 October 2017.

challenges in the quest for global primacy against the Soviet Union during the Cold War, on transnational terror networks since 2001, and more recently on the evolving strategic competition in Asia and the Pacific.

The widespread discursive downgrading of territorial significance to US power in the post-war years also reflects attempts to come to terms with technologically enhanced tectonic shifts in the post-war international system. The introduction of nuclear and thermonuclear weapons, missiles, and networked computing fundamentally challenged traditional understandings of time and space as categories of international relations and warfare. The vastly enhanced destructive potential of these technological quantum leaps emphasized the vulnerabilities of territory and inspired a transnational drive to supersede national sovereignties with global governance.[124]

In addition, the sheer scale, spectrum, and geographic extent of US influence during the Cold War further enhanced this sense of historical rupture and the frequent dismissal of its topography of power. After all, the United States utilized a wide range of "imperial repertoires" to simultaneously prevent Soviet expansion and prohibit the possible resurgence of German and Japanese imperial ambitions for half a century.[125] In part, this strategy of containment rested on a multilayered, historically informed approach that combined institutional internationalism as well as economic and military integration with ideological and cultural appeal. It was advanced through extensive economic and military aid, an interlocking partially global system of security alliances, the integration of industrial economies, and the extensive use of cultural diplomacy and propaganda in the struggle for world opinion.

The manifestations of this strategy differed across world regions; in Europe, it encompassed military occupations and troop deployments, economic stabilization, political integration, and cultural attraction. In this context, US influence has been described as hegemonic, an "empire by invitation", with "soft power" and not territorial control as its most enduring feature.[126] In the Global South, the approach was often heavy-handed and not only relied on the

---

[124] O. Rosenboim, *The Emergence of Globalism: Visions of World Order in Britain and the United States, 1939–1950*, Princeton: Princeton University Press, 2017.
[125] The term "imperial repertoires" is from Burbank and Cooper, *Empires in World History*, p. 3.
[126] Norwegian historian Geir Lundestad has been a leading proponent of this interpretation: G. Lundestad "Empire by Invitation? The United States and Western Europe, 1945–1952", *Journal of Peace Research* 23 (1986) 3, pp. 263–277; G. Lundestad, *"Empire" by Integration: The United States and European Integration, 1945–1997*, Oxford: Oxford University Press, 1998; the term "soft power" as a descriptor of US hegemony was introduced by political scientist Joseph S. Nye Jr. in the 1980 (J.S. Nye, *Bound to Lead: The Changing Nature of American Power*, New York: Basic Books, 1990).

attraction of regional political and security alliances and modernization offers, but also encompassed support for authoritarian regimes, extensive territorial wars, and frequent covert interventions.[127]

But these configurations of US influence in international affairs during the Cold War not only inspired the analytical marginalization of territorialized power but also underwrote its continued relevance to the American Empire in geographical imaginations, policy repertoires, and spatial formats. The potential repercussions of revolutionary military technology for territorial sovereignty were frequently integrated into pre-Cold War "mental maps" and inspired policy responses along coordinates of historically validated spatial trajectories.[128] In this context, the utility of colonial empire persisted and frequently intersected with the quest for global primacy as a platform for the simultaneous projection of US force and access denial to power competitors. The territorial grounding of US global reach informed the spatial logic of containment, its appreciation of empire, and the development of a worldwide network of military bases and imperial outposts.

Containment was informed by the work of various Anglo-American geopolitical thinkers during the first half of the twentieth century, such as Alfred Thayer Mahan, Halford Mackinder, Isaiah Bowman, and Nicholas Spykman.[129] Their writings grappled with the interconnectedness of geography and power in international relations and delineated territories and oceanic spaces, whose

---

127 O.A. Westad, *The Global Cold War: Third World Interventions and the Making of Our Times*, Cambridge: Cambridge University Press, 2006; for a compendium on US military interventions, see B. Salazar Torreon, "Instances of Use of United States Armed Forces Abroad", Congressional Research Service Report R42738, 12 October 2017; the number of covert operations between 1945 and 1991 is estimated at more than 80, see: J.W. Dower, *The Violent American Century: War and Terror since World War Two*, Chicago: Haymarket Books, 2017, p. 51.

128 Mental maps provide a cognitive framework for understanding the world and acting within it: A.K. Henrikson, "The Geographical 'Mental Maps' of American Foreign Policy Makers", *International Political Science Review* 1 (1980) 4, pp. 495–530; A.K. Henrikson, "Mental Maps", in: M.J. Hogan and T.G. Paterson (eds.), *Explaining the History of American Foreign Relations*, Cambridge: Cambridge University Press, 1991, pp. 177–192.

129 On US Cold War geostrategic thought, see S. Fröhlich, *Zwischen selektiver Verteidigung und globaler Eindämmung: Geostategisches Denken in der amerikanischen Außen- und Sicherheitspolitik während des Kalten Krieges*, Baden-Baden: Nomos, 1998; J.L. Gaddis, *Strategies of Containment: A Critical Appraisal of Postwar American Security Policy*, Oxford: Oxford University Press, 1982; on intellectual antecedents and a comparison of Mackinder and Spykman, see S. Fröhlich, *Amerikanische Geopolitik: Von den Anfängen bis zum Ende des Zweiten Weltkrieges*, Landsberg am Lech: Olzog Verlag, 1998; more recently, see G. Sloan, *Geopolitics, Geography and Strategic History*, Abingdon: Routledge, 2017, pp. 38–61 and 114–188; on Bowman, see Smith, *American Empire*.

control might either secure global dominance or threaten the survival of the United States. In contrast to British geographer Mackinder, who before World War I identified control over the heartland of Eurasia as the key to international primacy, his American colleague Spykman argued during World War II that control over the edges of Eurasia, the "Rimland", and its circumferential seaways was fundamental to global dominance. His "imperial view of world order" envisioned that the United States would replace the empires of the Old World and reinforced the desire for extensive US bases in the Pacific to contain the potential expansion of Russia and China.[130]

Both views significantly shaped US Cold War geostrategic perspectives and the evolution of containment. This approach filtered threat perceptions and policy responses and allocated priority to securing control over much of the "Rimland" to neutralize Soviet globalist designs, establish a security parameter for the imperial core, and enable protected access to resource rich world regions. In this geopolitical discourse, itself a practice of "epistemological imperialism", territorial control of prime strategic "real estate" quickly overrode extra-spatial considerations.[131] These discourses also perpetuated anxieties, which not only shored up the national security state in the metropole but also accelerated its outreach to the global frontiers. Geopolitics was used to maintain a threat horizon that exaggerated strategic challenges of a single hostile Eurasian power that would outman, outproduce, and outgun the United States. Such anxieties served as an important rationale for America's continued engagement of the global frontiers just as fear of European imperial powers in North America had discursively accompanied the creation of a transcontinental settler empire more than a century before.[132]

The prominence of spatial discourses during World War II accustomed Americans to view global affairs through the lens of geopolitics and its highly

---

130 O. Rosenboim, "Geopolitics and Empire: Visions of Regional World Order in the 1940s", *Modern Intellectual History* 12 (2015) 2, pp. 353–381, at 366.
131 G.Ó. Tuathail, *Critical Geopolitics*, Minneapolis: University of Minnesota Press, 1996, p. 55; on geographic knowledge and power in American Cold War discourses, see M. Farish, *The Contours of America's Cold War*, Minneapolis: University of Minnesota Press, 2010.
132 On World War II discourses, see T. Barney, *Mapping the Cold War: Cartography and the Framing of America's International Power*, Chapel Hill: University of North Carolina Press, 2015, p. 26; on US map-making and popularity during the war, see S. Schulten, *The Geographical Imagination in America, 1880–1950*, Chicago: University of Chicago Press, 2001, pp. 204–238; on anxieties and geopolitical discourse in the Cold War, see J.A. Thompson, "The Geopolitical Vision: The Myth of an Outmatched USA", in: J. Isaac and D. Bell (eds.), *Uncertain Empire: American History and the Idea of the Cold War*, Oxford: Oxford University Press, 2012, pp. 91–114.

popular visualizations. Despite their intellectual association with German expansionism, the influence of spatial logics on understanding the East-West confrontation remained strong.[133] In addition to highly popular catch phrases (Iron Curtain), it also infused the Cold War lexicon with its geostrategic terminology (spheres of influence, strong points, perimeters, lines, and bloc), concepts (land power versus sea power, heartland, and rim area, and domino theory), and its geographic denominations and distinctions (Eurasia, population centres, and production centres).

But such geopolitical perspectives also contained fundamental policy contradictions, especially between Washington's rhetorical endorsement for decolonization since the early 1940s and its simultaneous reliance on imperial territoriality in the post-war world.[134] Once engaged with the Soviet Union in a struggle for global influence, the United States shifted its course and stabilized selected European colonies. This shift followed geopolitically informed policy descriptions such as NSC-68 is the commonly accepted title of this document. (NSC-68, 1950), which highlighted the need for the United States to not only maintain allies and client states in support of global Soviet containment but to deny the USSR access to vast regions from Africa to Asia.[135] While the selective maintenance of European imperialism challenged American credibility, it also provided a cost-effective surrogate for Washington's continued reliance on imperial territoriality by providing raw materials, intelligence data, and secure spaces for the deployment of US forces abroad.

These troop deployments relied on a global network of military bases and imperial outposts and represented a trusted spatial format of the American Empire since the early nineteenth century. During the first Cold War, from the late 1940s to the 1960s, as many as 70 per cent of those bases were located in colonies.[136] Washington also leased access to military bases around the world through legal agreements that often subverted local sovereignty reminiscent of

---

133 For a critique of this continuity thesis, see L. Hepple, "The Revival of Geopolitics", *Political Geography Quarterly* (Supplement) 5 (1986) 4, pp. 521–536; on US perceptions of German geopolitical discourses during World War II, see Tuathail, *Critical Geopolitics*, pp. 111–140.
134 On US wartime planning for British decolonization, see W.R. Louis, *Imperialism at Bay 1941–1945: The United States and the Decolonization of the British Empire*, Oxford: Oxford University Press, 1977; on Southeast Asia: M. Frey, *Dekolonisierung in Südostasien: Die Vereinigten Staaten und die Auflösung der europäischen Kolonialreiche*, Munich: Oldenbourg Verlag, 2006; R.J. McMahon, *The Limits of Empire: The United States and Southeast Asia since World War Two*, New York: Columbia University Press, 1999.
135 E.R. May (ed.), *American Cold War Strategy: Interpreting NSC-68*, Boston: Bedford Books, 1993.
136 Go, *Patterns of Empire*, p. 142.

nineteenth century "unequal treaties" in the quest for imperial extraterritoriality.[137] After the Cold War, this network contracted to about 800 installations of various sizes and functions, which still accounts for 95 per cent of the world's foreign bases.[138] These bases "delimited a vast new area of de facto American sovereignty. They were/are the territorial nodes of the American post-war empire."[139]

This vast global network of military bases highlights the continued reliance of the American polity on spatially tangible formats of empire as well as underlines that imperial territoriality was never uncontested. From Diego Garcia in the Indian Ocean to Okinawa in Japan to Vieques in Puerto Rico across the spatial arc of overseas empire and its global frontiers, bases often served either as focal points for anti-colonial protest or potential political fault lines in bi- and multilateral relations with allies and client states.[140]

Furthermore, the end of the Cold War and the subsequent decade of unrivalled US power steadily obscured the spatial formats of this preponderance, thus simultaneously affirming its utility. The effects of this global reach of imperial territoriality were often discursively subsumed under globalization and its protective force of a *Pax Americana*, which appeared no longer based on spatial rule "but through involvement in and control over networks, be they financial, informational, or technological."[141]

Finally, this emphasis on deterritorialized networks of power masked not only America's continued reliance on territory but also obscured the spatial aspirations of rising power competitors in Europe and Asia. Although the Cold War had been "the great age of American expansion", the United States increasingly struggled to maintain its purported unipolarity in the new millennium by "deploying power differentials [...] to freeze

---

[137] Raustiala, *Does the Constitution Follow the Flag*, pp. 138–160; see also K. Raustiala "Empire and Extraterritoriality in Twentieth-Century America", *Southwestern Law Review* 40 (2011), pp. 605–615, at 612–613.
[138] D. Vine, *Base Nation: How U.S. Military Bases Abroad Harm America and the World*, New York: Henry Holt & Co., 2015.
[139] P.S. Golub, *Power, Profit & Prestige: History of American Imperial Expansion*, London: Pluto Press, 2010, p. 66.
[140] C. Lutz (ed.), *The Bases of Empire: The Global Struggle against U.S. Military Posts*, New York: New York University Press, 2009; on Vieques, see also K.T. McCaffrey, *Military Power and Popular Protest: The U.S. Navy in Vieques, Puerto Rico*, Rutgers: Rutgers University Press, 2002.
[141] T.J. Biersteker, "State, Sovereignty, and Territory", in: W. Carlsnaes, T. Risse and B.A. Simmons (eds.), *Handbook of International Relations*, London: Sage, 2002, pp. 157–176, at 166.

the global balance of power".[142] This proved elusive as China and Russia both applied the lessons of US imperial spatial modalities to challenge American dominance in many world regions. China's Belt and Road Initiative to integrate the "Rimland" and its accompanying maritime strategy's reliance on insular strong points highlight such appropriation of American geostrategic thought and practice since the days of Alfred Thayer Mahan.[143] Faced with territorial competition and spatial fault lines across the planet, the return of flag plantings and annexations, and the struggle for control over the "Rimland" and its oceanic spaces, former US National Security Advisor H.R. McMaster remarked in 2017 that "[g]eopolitics are back, and back with a vengeance, after the holiday from history we took in the so-called post-Cold War period."[144]

But geopolitical imaginations and practices were never far from the American Empire's remarkably consistent reliance on a great variety of spatial formats of rule at home and abroad. This chapter's analytical emphasis on territorialized power has explored the history, contours, and spatial tangibility of this empire in its global contexts. It has also suggested alternative temporal-spatial arcs of empire to reframe widely accepted interpretative segmentations of the polity's historical trajectory. Finally, this chapter has challenged traditional understandings of the developmental stages of the US nation-state by foregrounding the oscillating but always present composite and hybrid character of this polity as empire and nation. The cumulative effect of this focus on imperial territoriality has thus complicated standard historical narratives; it has also offered conceptual trajectories and a potentially synthesizing analytical framework to replace exceptionalist obfuscations with spatially informed interpretations of empire, nation, and the global in the history of the United States.

---

[142] J. Darwin, *After Tamerlane: The Rise & Fall of Global Empires, 1400–2000*, New York: Penguin Books, 2007, p. 480.

[143] J.-M.F. Blanchard and C. Flint, "The Geopolitics of China's Maritime Silk Road Initiative", *Geopolitics* 22 (2017) 2, pp. 223–245; J.R. Holmes, "Strategic Features of the South China Sea: A Tough Neighborhood for Hegemons", *Naval War College Review* 67 (2014) 2, pp. 30–51; W. Mayborn, "The Pivot to Asia: The Persistent Logic of Geopolitics and the Rise of China", *Journal of Military and Strategic Studies* 15 (2014) 4, pp. 76–101.

[144] McMaster quoted in: U. Friedman, "The World According to H. R. McMaster", *The Atlantic*, 9 January 2018, https://www.theatlantic.com/international/archive/2018/01/hr-mcmaster-trump-north-korea/549341/ (accessed 20 January 2018).

John Breuilly
Modern Territoriality, the Nation-State, and Nationalism

Introduction

This chapter began life as a commentary on a paper that was to be given by Charles Maier at a workshop at the German Historical Institute London on "The Territorial State after 1989" in June 2013. Maier was unable to make the workshop, so my commentary became the keynote paper. I have reworked it to relate to the theme of the present volume, which is to do with the specific modern historical form assumed by such concepts as state, territory, boundaries, and sovereignty and how these have shaped nationalist ideology. However, this does remain more an extended critique of the arguments of Maier than the presentation of an alternative argument. In this critique, I consider not just Maier's unpublished paper of 2013 but also publications in which he sets out his arguments about modern territoriality at greater length and in a broader context.[1]

First, let me historicize what is at stake here. Territoriality has been a key aspect of organized coercive power – often what we might also call state power – at least since the era of sedentary agriculture. Furthermore, territoriality will continue to be central to such power for the foreseeable future. So the issue is not about territoriality as an aspect of state power generally but about a specifically modern form of territoriality and its associated modern state power. This in turn I will relate to arguments about the modernity of nationalist ideology.

Second, I agree with Maier about locating the origins of modern territoriality – both conceptual and institutional – in early modern Europe.[2] I also agree that the specific hallmarks of this territoriality are the idea of the state as unmediated sovereign power exercised over the subjects/citizens of a sharply bounded territory and that the inhabited land mass of the world is completely covered by

---

[1] C.S. Maier, "Transformations of Territoriality: 1600–2000", in: G. Budde, S. Conrad, and O. Janz, *Transnationale Geschichte. Themen, Tendenzen und Theorien*, Göttingen: Vandenhoeck & Ruprecht, 2005, pp. 32–55; C.S. Maier, "Leviathan 2.0: Inventing Modern Statehood", in: E. Rosenberg (ed.), *A World Connecting, 1870–1945*, Cambridge: Harvard University Press, 2012, pp. 29–282; C. S. Maier, *Once within borders. Territories of power, wealth, and belonging since 1500*, Cambridge, Massachusetts 2016.
[2] I distinguish between the concept of territory and the practice of territoriality. On the former, which can be traced back at least to classical Greece and Rome, see S. Elden, *The Birth of Territory*, Chicago: University of Chicago Press, 2013.

a number of such states. It is these attributes of unmediated sovereignty, sharp boundaries, and global political geography that are specifically modern.

Third, I agree with much of the way in which Maier characterizes typical phases in the development of territoriality since the sixteenth century. One can select three major transformations in sixteenth-century Europe that help explain the emergence of new forms of territoriality associated with the formulation of concepts such as sovereignty and frontiers.

First, there is the breakdown of the unity of Latin Christianity and the plunging of much of Europe into fierce religious conflict. This created a new form of what Maier calls "identity space", especially with the "confessionalization" of the state.[3] Second, the discovery and the early settlement and exploitation of the "New World" gave access to resources and encouraged new ideas and practices of imperial rule. Third, both these transformations were channelled through a few competing regimes occupying a small space on the Atlantic seaboard of Europe, framing their religious and imperial ambitions in universalist terms and innovating militarily to pursue those ambitions.

It is this dialectic between the small space of Europe and the apparently unbounded space of the world beyond that shapes the initial modern concepts of territoriality – combining in a specific way Maier's points about the bounded landmass and the unbounded high seas.[4] As boundaries are contested and enforced through war in Europe, so are they projected, often fantastically, on to the still unknown land masses abroad.

What makes early modern Europe distinct apart from these three transformations is that modern territoriality in Europe involved symmetry. Frontiers have always mattered (e.g. the Roman *limes*[5] or the Habsburg military borders), and control of space and the people within those frontiers has always been crucial. However, before the early modern period, the usual pattern is of one dominant imperial power confronting other and different kinds of polities: China and tributary kingdoms, Persia and assorted Greek city states, or Rome and the tribes of northern Europe.[6] The language of universal empire still matters in sixteenth-

---

[3] Although recently various historians of the Reformation and Counter-Reformation have suggested that the "confessionalization" thesis of Heinz Schilling and others has been exaggerated.

[4] Carl Schmitt, as Maier mentions, develops an argument along these lines in *Der Nomos der Erde*.

[5] See P. Parker, *The Empire Stops Here: A Journey Along the Frontiers of the Roman World*, London: Pimlico, 2010,

[6] These are never simple distinctions, culturally or spatially. The "barbarians" and the "civilized" mix and interpenetrate and, indeed, the contrasting stereotypes we inherit from writers

century Europe but increasingly, whether it is Charles V or Louis XIV, is deployed by a ruler who looks increasingly similar to other rulers. That is not to set aside the great differences between England/Britain, Castille/Spain, France, the United Provinces, etc., but it is possible to conceptualize them as similar units engaged in power struggles, especially when coalitions can be deployed to counter the power of any one unit threatening hegemony.

However, modern territoriality goes through further transformations, which Maier enumerates. One is the Enlightenment notion that societies under sovereign control are not fixed, unchanging units whereby state power can only be increased as a zero-sum game, either conquering other lands or seizing more resources from one's own subjects, but instead malleable arrangements that, by the forceful use of reason, can be made more productive. This was a project rather than an achievement in the eighteenth century, but it did produce changes in how territoriality and rule were understood.

For complex and much debated reasons, changes that increased productivity did start to transform societies. "Society" came to be regarded no longer as an object of old or new style, unenlightened or enlightened rulers, but as a dynamic and autonomous force, indeed one that might reshape the state rather than the other way round. It is no accident that the first historians to write of class struggle as the motor of history are not Marx and Engels but the "bourgeois" historians of the French Revolution, such as Guizot. That takes us to revolution, democracy, and the transformation of the concept of sovereignty as flowing from God, embodied in monarchy and hierarchy, to that of popular sovereignty, with its implications of equality and participation. At its most stark, the Jacobins outlined a unitary concept of France and the French, expressed not just in the proclamation of new arrangements of time and space but also in the abolition of corporations, privileges, and "intermediate powers".

There is therefore little to dispute over the major phases of the development of modern territoriality: from the centralizing monarchies with their project of confessional unity in the early modern period, through the processes of change associated with Enlightened reform, commercial society, and popular revolution in the eighteenth and early nineteenth centuries; on to the revolutions in technologies of production, communication, and transportation in the nineteenth and early twentieth centuries; through the global wars and

---

who identify as "civilized" (e.g. Tacitus writing about "Germans" or Walter Scott writing about Highland Scots) are ways of responding to that interpenetration.

the rise and decline of imperial blocs in the twentieth century to the collapse of the Union of Soviet Socialist Republics (USSR) and the survival of currently one world power (though by no means hegemonic), along with the most modern forms of globalization in communications, finance, transport, military, and other spheres. In this last phase, much of what might be regarded as the debate over territoriality has typically taken the form of debates over the future of the nation-state – whether relatively unchanged as the major "power container",[7] or disappearing in the face of supranational forms of power, or continuing but in some transformed way.

Maier brings a particular twist to this history. The title of his contribution to *A World Connecting* is "Leviathan 2.0", as contrasted with Leviathan 1.0, which belongs to what one might call the era of Thomas Hobbes: the age of absolutism in Europe and imperialism in the New World.[8] Maier then conceptualizes a Leviathan 2.0, focusing on the period c. 1850–1880 as a "moment" that witnessed a cluster of global political transformations, ushering in a new stage of territoriality and type of state. Maier also suggests that from the mid-1960s to the early 1980s, we can discern a shift to a third stage that, amongst other things, deterritorializes state power.

A central idea concerning the Leviathan 2.0 is that events such as the Meiji Restoration, German and Italian unification, and the US Civil War led to the formation of a new kind of territoriality in which, to use two very useful terms deployed by Maier, there was a convergence between decision space and identity space. This convergence is implied in the very term "nation-state". Such states formed the core of the global imperial powers and their conflicts from the late nineteenth century through the two world wars. Following imperial collapse (in much of Europe after 1918, beyond Europe after 1945), this nation-state form was generalized to the colonial subjects of imperial rule. The collapse of the USSR largely completed the process whereby the inhabited land mass of the world was divided up in to a series of such nation-states.[9]

It is key elements of these arguments that Maier puts forward about territoriality that I want to critique.

---

[7] I take the phrase from Michael Mann in his volumes on the "sources of social power".
[8] This book consists of five book-length chapters that take different approaches to the "global history" of the world between 1870 and 1945. I reviewed this extensively: J. Breuilly, "Strategies for Writing Global History", *The Journal of Global History* 9 (2014), pp. 314–332.
[9] There remain a few polities such as Singapore, the Sultanate of Brunei, and the Gulf oil kingdoms, where the term "nation-state" would not apply.

Critique

Introductory Points

My critique can be summarized in the following points:
1. The development of territoriality is a more general process than nation-state formation.
2. Territorialization is not a linear trend but alternates with phases of deterritorialization, both within and between different places.
3. It is necessary to distinguish between territoriality as coercive power and the largely non-territorial features of ideological and economic power and to consider how they can in some way be combined in the nation-state form.
4. It is necessary to distinguish between the progressive universalization of the *concept* of territoriality and the necessarily partial institutionalized realization of territoriality as organized coercive power.
5. The key condition of modern territoriality is the transformation from subject to citizen towards mass politics, which changes both the functions and symbolic meaning of territoriality.
6. These critiques have implications for current and near future territoriality.

Territoriality is Distinct From Nation-state Formation

Maier argues that new forms of territoriality developed in the early modern period before nation-state formation.[10] Some were associated with monarchical centralization and can be linked to the kinds of boundary claims made by a ruler such as Louis XIV. Even when national terminology appears in the justifications for these boundary claims, they are essentially monarchical, as with the so-called "reunion" arguments used to justify war to take over territory on France's northern and eastern frontiers. Following successful expansion, more effective fortifications were constructed and French laws and systems of

---

10 I assume that although we call monarchical France and England "national" states before the eighteenth century, this is not to be regarded as the same as the claims made about those states, especially after the French Revolution and the moves towards parliamentary government based on a widening franchise in what was now Britain after the late eighteenth century. It would appear Maier would accept this distinction as, in his own argument, the USA acquires some additional "nation-state" quality as a result of the Civil War, just as more obviously did the political arrangements in the German, Italian, and Japanese lands.

administration introduced. Military as well as dynastic ambitions gave substance to territoriality, for example in the special military border districts of the early modern Habsburg Empire.

In the New World, the European powers also made precise boundary claims, starting with the Papal "division" of territory between Portugal and Spain along an east-west line that basically granted Portugal Africa and Spain America. However, given the ignorance of global geography at the time, no one actually knew this, and such territorial divisions were expressions of European aspiration. The institutionalization of such boundaries arose only in a process of negotiation and conflict, both between the imperial powers and – something that is often neglected – indigenous elites.

Much depended not only on how balanced or one-sided were power relationships but also on what interests were at stake and what place territory had in the economy and culture of the contending groups. For example, there were specific problems when European societies, practising sedentary agriculture (whether large or small scale, farm or plantation), encountered pastoral societies, as one can see with the treaties the British and French concluded with Native American societies in North America, later the British with indigenous groups in Australia and New Zealand, as well as a whole range of European powers with sub-Saharan African polities. European claims were often justified on the grounds that a "civilized" society was one which cultivates clearly bounded portions of land and that by contrast pastoral and other kinds of nomadic societies cannot be said to "own" land.

The practices through which such attitudes were implemented can be linked back to the processes Maier describes in continental Europe of cadastral surveys and subsequently the individualization of property rights in land – whether described as "enclosure" in mainland Britain or "peasant emancipation" in continental Europe. The clear drawing of boundaries around "private" property matches the clear drawing of boundaries around the "public" territory of the state. We can see the close relationship between these two processes in the expansion of the USA as well as in the way Napoleon imposed definite state boundaries in conquered central Europe along with the introduction of a civil code named after him, which was centred on the idea of absolute, individual property rights in demarcated parcels of land.

However, there is a gap in Maier's account of the progress of territoriality in Europe for the period 1792 to 1815, a crucial period both for the nationalization of territorial claims and also in realizing various functional forms of territorial power.

The Girondins who led France into war with *ancien régime* Europe in 1792 made novel claims that overrode earlier conceptions of territoriality by insisting that there could be no overlaps or blurring of France's frontiers. The tangled jurisdictions on the eastern frontier whereby inhabitants of a single territory owed different obligations to the French crown and to the Holy Roman Empire were rhetorically and then militarily swept aside by revolutionary France. Just as territory was clearly demarcated internally with the construction of a system of departments, so was it also clearly demarcated against "non-France".

Various of these new features of territoriality also came to operate in the expanding area conquered by French armies, sometimes with but more often without any national justification. Tangled and overlapping jurisdictions were swept aside, for example in the new republics, later princely states, set up in the Italian and German lands and elsewhere. These might be designated as parts of greater France (e.g. left bank of the Rhine territories formerly within the Holy Roman Empire), as "model" states under rulers chosen by Napoleon (usually relatives) or in the expanded states granted to existing native princes. In almost all cases, the governments of these territories removed, at least legally, the privileges and corporations associated with substate forms of territorial autonomy (e.g. urban guild powers or rural noble powers). There were admittedly limits to such territorialization, above all because they were dependent upon an external power: France. Thus an "archaic" practice that undermined territoriality, indeed often the viability, of some of these states was Napoleon's policy of making privileged land grants in order to endow a new imperial nobility.[11]

These advances in territoriality were maintained, even reinforced, after 1815. The Vienna Settlement may have been "restoration" so far as Prussia, Austria, and Russia were concerned but not in relation to the myriad overlapping jurisdictions of pre-revolutionary central and southern Europe. The territorial simplification of the German and Italian lands, in which a series of medium-sized states had been granted "internal" sovereignty by Napoleon was maintained.[12] That was qualified by the Metternichian policy of reserving the

---

[11] This demonstrates the non-linear development of modern territoriality and the conflicts between different interests and values. These could even exist within the mind of a single person, most notably Napoleon who seemed undecided between self-images of a new Charlemagne, enlightened European despot, or architect of a pluralist system of states based on shared principles of reason and freedom.

[12] In the case of the *Deutsche Bund*, set up in 1814/15, the ingenious solution, adopted from the Holy Roman Empire and in effect continued by Napoleon as "Protector" of the *Rheinbund*, was to state that members of the *Bund* could not engage in diplomatic or military action independently. As Prussia and Austria also had territory outside the *Bund*, they were exempt from this rule. There were some interesting intermediate cases such as Hannover until 1837 and Schleswig-Holstein until 1864 where a member state of the *Bund* was ruled by a prince with territories outside the *Bund* but the *Bund* territory was kept distinct from the non-*Bund* territory.

right to intervene in the internal affairs of these states, although usually this was legitimized by getting the ruler of the state to make an appeal for such intervention.

These medium states, as well as larger ones, including Bourbon France, built on the Napoleonic legacy of tougher, territorially sharply defined and bureaucratically centralized states. German and Italian unification finished this process. Bismarck did not pursue "German unification" so much as a clear territorial distinction between one zone controlled from Berlin and another from Vienna. Why his creation was then called "Germany" raises questions about the need to legitimize territorial sovereignty in national terms, which I consider later.

In the nineteenth and early twentieth centuries, the major European powers projected a set of distinct boundaries upon low population zones, most notably in relation to much of Africa at the Berlin Conference (1884/85).[13] Even if one considers these boundaries both symbolically and functionally meaningless at the time (often the territory in question was unexplored and unmapped by Europeans), they still acquired meaning with the further penetration of imperial power in the twentieth century and then in the way in which postcolonial states sought, with the support of the major powers, to project their power to the state boundaries.[14]

Much of this territorialization was a projection of more powerful states upon less powerful regions, even if disguised in the form of treaties that presented the arrangement as negotiation between equals. Here, we must distinguish between conceptual and institutional territorialization. The power of the major European states (both within and then beyond Europe), and latterly the USA and the USSR, made it possible for them to project favoured concepts of territoriality across various parts of the world. However, only under certain conditions would these concepts be realized institutionally, and yet again only under other conditions would both these concepts and institutions be represented as those of nation-states. In the first instance, for example, many colonial territories with notionally clear boundaries were left to pre-colonial practices in which such boundaries were of little importance. Only when the

---

[13] Though even this apparently "arbitrary" carve-up of African lands between European states has been questioned; see S. Katzenellenbogen, "'It Didn't Happen in Berlin': Politics, Economics and Ignorance in the Setting of Africa's Colonial Boundaries", in: P. Nugent and A. I. Asiwaju (eds.), *African Boundaries: Barriers, Conduits and Opportunities*, London: Pinter, 1997, pp. 21–31.

[14] On the role of state boundaries in the new states of Africa, see J. Herbst, *States and Power in Africa: Comparative Lessons in Authority and Control*, Princeton: Princeton University Press, 2000; P. Englebert, *Africa: Unity, Sovereignty and Sorrow*, Boulder: Lynne Rienner, 2009.

imperial powers sought to "develop" such territories or to defend them against other such powers were the boundaries institutionalized through such practices as border posts and patrols as well as documentation procedures, which defined which people "belonged" to one or another colonial territory. In the second instance, even if colonial territories or, in the case of the USSR, the non-Russian republics, were given a "national" designation, they clearly were not envisioned at the time as becoming nation-states. That was a concept later devised as one way of justifying the break-up of empires.

Phases and Zones of "Territorialization" Alternate and Combine With Those of "Deterritorialization"

Much of early modern overseas European imperial expansion did not take a territorial form. Portuguese and, following that, Dutch imperialism often took the form of trade whereby the Europeans were satisfied to establish coastal footholds, leaving control of the hinterland to indigenous rulers, provided only that they were willing and able to engage in the desired commerce.

Those indigenous rulers might well preside over a "deterritorialization" as part of this transaction, most notably with the impact of the Atlantic slave trade upon those African hinterlands from which the slaves were drawn. New forms of rule emerged but not necessarily as control of clearly demarcated territory, indeed often undermining such forms of territorial control that had previously existed.

One might expect such "deterritorialization" to decline globally with the abolition of the slave trade and the creation of "empires of settlement" in North America, Australia, New Zealand, and South Africa, or "administered empires" in tropical zones where plantations were established with a small and changeable European population, or in zones combining elements of these two features. Yet the greatest phase of "non-territorial imperialism" was still to come, namely with British extra-European hegemony after 1815.

Maier justifiably debunks the claim by the late nineteenth-century British historian Sir John Seeley that the British Empire was established in a "fit of absence of mind", but Seeley has a point, or rather two points.

First, the "informal" empire, about which Gallagher and Robinson wrote the seminal pioneering account, was not established in any deliberate, long-term way.[15] John Darwin, in his recent book on the British imperial project,

---

15 R. E. Robinson and J. Gallagher, *Africa and the Victorians*, New York: St. Martin's Press, 1961.

makes it clear that it was not in fact a single project but a patchwork assemblage of different modes of influence in which direct territorial rule was just one element.[16] Even as formal imperial rule was established, most notably in British-controlled India in 1858, at the same time British officials were retreating from some of the modes of direct rule practised by the East India Company, which, amongst other things, was held responsible for the revolution of 1857.[17]

Arguably, British imperial control was bound to become increasingly territorial. Henry Maine, who did so much to develop the historical justification and administrative models for "indirect rule", regarded the Raj as, to deploy his distinction, a "legislating" and not a "taxing" empire. "Traditional" law codified and enforced by British officials and soldiers was a contradiction in terms. Territoriality was institutionalized by the process of defining zones of control, drawing up cadastral surveys, and seeking to individualize property rights (even when villages were designated collective owners). This was even more the case in those Indian coastal cities and other zones where capitalist penetration was most rapidly advancing. Nevertheless, informal empire, linked to the doctrine of free trade – which proclaimed and, in practice, sought to institutionalize the separation of economic from coercive power – was significant through much of the nineteenth century, where the British had the greatest influence. Did the British need indigenous territorial sovereigns with whom to negotiate "informal" empire?

In high population zones with existing sophisticated systems of rule, most notably imperial China, there was no attempt even to challenge existing modes of coercive power but only to enforce trading from coastal enclaves such as the great eastern seaboard cities and Hong Kong. This did undermine the territorial power of the imperial state in various ways. First, the imperial powers insisted that their citizens be subject to their own, not Chinese, laws, a status tellingly named "extra-territoriality". Second, zones were created in cities, such as Shanghai, that were beyond *all* imperial control. Finally, more indirectly but also more significantly, imperial exactions and incursions undermined what pre-modern territorial imperial power existed. The Taiping Rebellion destroyed central control, and the regionally commanded forces raised to repress it laid the basis for widespread local coercive power (the so-called "warlords"), which

---

16 J. Darwin, *The Empire Project: The Rise and Fall of the British World System 1830–1970*, Cambridge: Cambridge University Press, 2009.
17 This is a central argument in K. Mantena, *Alibis of Empire: Social Theories and Ideologies of Late Imperialism*, Princeton: Princeton University Press, 2009, focusing on the work and thought of Henry Maine.

characterized both the late imperial and much of the republican period from the mid-nineteenth to mid-twentieth century.

The second justification for Seeley's claim is that what compelled the British to move towards clearer forms of territorial rule ("formal empire") was not a clearer sense of an imperial project but short-term responses to new challenges. Gladstone, an ardent anti-imperialist and believer in informal influence and free trade, took Britain into a formal occupation of Egypt because of internal challenges that threatened existing commercial relations as well as the vital Suez Canal. Challenges from a recovering France, and the new powers of Germany, Japan, and the USA more generally, triggered the formal division of extra-European territories. The same process was at work in the territorialization of the Americas both as an outcome of inter-imperial conflict and conflict between imperial power and white settler–led insurgencies.

This phase of nineteenth-century informal British Empire – with one, albeit quite weak hegemonic power – resembles US global power since 1990. Just as the term "empire" is considered problematic for the USA and often rejected by Americans, so too one should be cautious about referring to the British "Empire" for much of the nineteenth century. The defeat of France in 1815 was in a way the equivalent of the collapse of the USSR in 1989–1991. It meant that the remaining hegemonic power did not need to clearly demarcate its zones of imperial power from those of competing powers. The major difference, of course, is that British imperialism did not confront a system of legally defined, territorial nation-states in the way that the USA did.

One should not think that there was any resumption of a long-term secular "rise of territoriality" once British imperial power was challenged. War shattered territoriality: in Central Europe and the Middle East between 1914 and 1923, in China from 1937 until 1949, in Southeast Asia after 1941, and in parts of Europe after 1939/1941. The fact that clear lines were drawn on maps after these wars – whether in terms of new imperial claims (e.g. the Sykes-Picot Agreement between Britain and France in the Middle East) or the designation of new nation-states in Central Europe in 1919 or in Asia immediately after 1945 or in much of sub-Saharan Africa between 1958 and 1970 – should not blind us to the fact that this was often no more than a conceptual, not an institutional, achievement.[18] What is more, such "territorialization" was only possible on the basis of a violent destruction of an earlier territorial order. It would be a while

---

[18] For a cogent critique of the conventional view that Sykes-Picot was both definitive and arbitrary with respect to certain Middle East state boundaries, especially the one between Syria and Iraq, see S. Pursley, "'Lines Drawn on an Empty Map': Iraq's Borders and the Legend of the Artificial State", *Jadaliyya*, 2015, http://www.jadaliyya.com/Details/32140

after such a process of "reterritorialization" that the new boundaries would acquire some institutional substance and ideological force, often becoming the basis on which colonial nationalist movements claimed independence.

Even in the more "settled" zones, which for a time were known as the First World or Second World, it is difficult to see how "territoriality" in national terms was advanced for states that willingly or unwillingly belonged to suprastate military alliances such as the Warsaw Pact and North Atlantic Treaty Organization. We are again confronted with a de facto if not de jure distinction between internal and external sovereignty of the kind Metternich enforced in the German and Italian lands and the East India Company and later the Raj in non-British India.[19] Later, Carl Schmitt would make a similar point about how the Monroe Doctrine, an early nineteenth-century US claim to hegemony in South America, was incorporated into the post–World War I agreement that established the League of Nations, thereby enshrining a contradiction between hegemony and sovereignty, a contradiction that for Schmitt was in turn an expression of the hypocrisy of that institution.

This complex combination of territorial and non-territorial, national and non-national power can be found even within the same state. The Soviet Union insisted on national territoriality in the non-Russian republics and institutionalized national identity in a series of "affirmative action" policies.[20] Yet, at the same time, it institutionally combined coercive, economic, and ideological power at the level of the "imperial" state and enforced boundary control much more effectively at the border between communist and non-communist regimes than it did between the Soviet Union and its nominally sovereign communist neighbours. Meanwhile, in the two major communist powers, China and the USSR, state territoriality as free movement by citizens was undermined by the requirement for internal passports, the denial of rights to rural immigrants in urban areas (still current Chinese practice), the wholesale forced movements of populations and the designation of certain territories within the state as places of exile where normal rule of law did not apply. If we associate territoriality and the doctrine of popular sovereignty as entailing the right of free movement of citizens throughout state territory, clearly such practices undermine such aspects of modern territoriality.

I cannot therefore discern any linear trend towards greater "territoriality", whether in imperial or national form, but instead opposing trends in various

---

19 This was a point made by Partha Chatterjee in his contribution to the above mentioned GHIL conference.
20 T. Martin, *The Affirmative Action Empire: Nations and Nationalism in the Soviet Union, 1923–1939*, Ithaca: Cornell University Press, 2001.

places and periods. Territoriality is a useful concept but only in conjunction with its negation. I will return to this theme later when I argue that globalization – not itself a recent development even if associated with new features since 1990 – necessarily involves both "more" and "less" territoriality.

Distinguishing Between the Territoriality of Coercive Power and That of Ideological and Economic Power

Maier's key moment in the shift to a distinctively modern form of territoriality is 1850–1880, precisely the time when the conditions for a series of global challenges to British hegemony were being formed. This was most obviously the case with the "national unifications" of Germany, Italy, Japan, and the USA – all involving inter-state and/or civil war. It was also a time when other empires (Romanov, Ottoman, Qing, Persian), with a greater or lesser degree of success, sought to reform themselves by borrowing from the more successful cases (first Britain and France, and later increasingly Japan, Germany, and the USA).

Maier's "moment" has two key elements: it is seen as *national* and it is about the transformation of coercive power. However, following various political theorists (Max Weber, Ernest Gellner, and Gianfranco Poggi, with modifications Michael Mann) I distinguish three forms of power, ideological, and economic power in addition to coercive or military-political power, characterized by the typical sanctions that are used to enforce such power. The point about these forms of power is that they are not necessarily transformed at the same time or along the same lines as coercive power.

Ideological Power

Very broadly one can distinguish a range of ideologies that have the capacity to stimulate, channel, and focus human action. First, and most important, is religion. It is at the heart of many resistances to modern imperialism and the attempt to impose a particular kind of territorial order. At times, it threatens to destroy such an order, as in China in the late 1850s and early 1860s or in India in 1857. Even when animating imperial expansion, it often does so in transterritorial ways, as one sees in much Christian missionary effort, which was not circumscribed, let alone directed, by territorial states. The interaction between dominating and resisting religious movements can produce especially explosive results, such as the Boxer Uprising of 1900, which included the killing of many Christian missionaries and their families.

There are also secular ideologies with great influence that are not territorially circumscribed. Race ideology, for example, plays an increasingly strong role in animating and justifying imperialist projects. Its most powerful expression is that of white race superiority claims, in such forms as Seeley's arguments about global Anglo-Saxon imperial rule or in justifying immigration controls on Chinese labour. In turn, it elicits responses on behalf of non-white groups, most notably in the plethora of pan-nationalisms (pan-Asian, pan-African, pan-Islam, pan-Arab), which often accept the division of the world into separate races while challenging the particular hierarchy preached by white race apologists.[21] It is also entangled with the rather distinct category of ethnicity, which is used to distinguish allegedly inherited (biological or cultural) differences between groups of the same race – whether Sun Yat-sen's diatribes against the Manchu (and his claims about the "five races of China" argument) or radical anti-Semitism or the ethno-national claims made within the Habsburg, Romanov, and Ottoman empires.

Furthermore, there are the two secular progressive ideologies of liberalism and socialism. Arguably liberalism was the founding ideology of modernity, with its justifications for the removal of privileged distinctions, group hierarchy, and the view of the state as a servant of "society". What is interesting about both these broad ideologies is their neglect of territoriality and of state power as something distinct, derived either from relationships between individuals (e.g. the social contract as the basis of states) or classes. The main reason is that both ideologies, so far as inequalities of power were concerned, were fixated on the dramatic fortunes of capital as a restless, global force, and rather less on the other two components of classical political economy – land and labour – which are territorially less mobile and which require some kind of territorial control.[22]

There remains nationalism that appears to be the ideological expression of state as territoriality (national homeland) and as identity (the nation) par excellence. However, I think it is misleading to think of nationalism as an ideology in the same way as religion, race, ethnicity, liberalism, socialism, and conservatism. I also think it is wrong to tie the development of nationalism to national history or, at least initially, nation-state formation and development. However, these are matters I will

---

21 For an introduction to the burgeoning work on pan-nationalism, see C. Aydin, "Beyond Civilisation: Pan-Islam, Pan Asianism and the Revolt Against the West", *Journal of Modern European History* 4 (2006) 2, pp. 204–223.
22 I leave aside conservatism as a parasitic ideology, raised from implicit defence of custom to explicit advocacy of tradition through challenges to the status quo.

take up later in the section on the relationship between identity and decision space.[23]

For the moment, my provisional conclusion is that these forms of ideological power, although they can be harnessed to justify the coercive transformation we call nation-state formation, are not themselves territorially delimited forms of power and the moment of *formation* as coercive power is not to be equated with the *foundation* of the nation-state as a particular combination of coercive, ideological, and economic power.

Economic Power

The economic basis of modern imperialism is capitalism. Maier's moment of coercive nation-state formation is also the heyday of free trade. The principal German and Italian states, along with Britain and France and various smaller European states, were in the process of negotiating lower tariffs virtually at the same time as steps towards national unification were being taken. Even the moves to protectionism taken from the late 1870s have been exaggerated as they covered a small range of goods, and the tariffs were not especially high, certainly by later standards. Furthermore, internally within continental Europe (Britain and the USA were exceptional in this regard) – linked to the advance of the inner dimensions of territoriality – we find the sweeping away of guilds, privileged forms of landownership, separate legal codes for town and country, and restrictions on free movement and settlement, as well as the making of stricter distinctions between public and private sources of revenue (e.g. with regard to monarchies) along with distinguishing between the proper objects of public and private expenditure.

Most significant of all, and generally neglected in discussions of modern state-building, is peasant emancipation. This began with reforms on some royal properties (e.g. in the Prussia of Frederick the Great), was decreed in revolutionary fashion in France in August 1789, was extended by Napoleon beyond France, was haltingly continued after 1815, was virtually completed in much of central Europe during the 1848–1849 revolutions, and finally serfdom was

---

[23] I consider the relationship between modern territoriality and nationalist ideology in more detail in an article devoted to the theme of modernization theory and historical writing: J. Breuilly, "Modernisation and Nationalist Ideology", *Archiv für Sozialgeschichte* 57 (2017) special issue, pp. 131–154.

legally abolished in Russia in 1863. On this basis, whether to the benefit of small holding farmers (as in France) or to formerly privileged landowners (as in much of Prussia) or some combination of these, land was increasingly defined as private property and agricultural labour as waged. To put it sweepingly, on this transformation was laid the basis of modern mass politics and the formation of peasant, elite conservative, and worker parties. This in turn disseminated a territorial political system through the electoral politics of a parliament that covered the state territory and broke down that territory into a series of constituencies.

The emergent system of territorial states also empowered international forms of cooperation, which can be regarded as essential conditions for interactions between states, such as agreements on the measurement of time, the use of gold as the basis of currency exchanges, and standardized forms of communication (e.g. postal and telegraphic). There was a school of "national economy" – especially important in the USA and Germany – but it was of far less importance than classical political economy or marginal utility economics, which superseded classical political economy. Economic transactions were more important across imperial blocs than within them; for example, patterns of capital investment and government borrowing do not largely fit within the zones of formal imperial control (Britain invested more heavily in independent Latin American states than in its African colonies, with the possible exception of South Africa). Even some aggressive German imperialists, confronted with the inability to make headway against Britain in terms of naval power, began to see the merits of a *Pax Britannica* as creating an integrated economic zone where capital from all over the world can easily move. Challenged by popular and regime resistance to imperialism in China, six imperial powers allied to crush the Boxer Uprising in 1900. There was no simple congruency between the patterns of state coercive power and of economic power.

So as with ideological power, there is a great deal that is non-territorial about trends in economic power. Nation-state formation is a very particular kind of territorially focused coercive power, which defined the internal order of the core of the major imperial powers increasingly but which cannot be projected beyond those territories before 1918.

The Conceptual and the Institutional Diffusion of Territoriality

One can trace a series of institutional changes that amounted to an increasingly distinct projection of state sovereignty over those occupying a demarcated territory. For example, the sovereign removed significant forms of coercive power from "overmighty" subjects such as fortresses, stockpiles of weapons, and followings of armed men and sought to insulate its frontiers from armed incursions from outside, whether by states or other entities. In this way, the classic Weberian state with a monopoly of large-scale coercive power is formed. However, it is not clear how widely this was diffused beyond the cores of the major imperial powers by the end of the nineteenth century.

Such a *concept* of sovereign power over a demarcated territory was increasingly projected on to many parts of the world, but the requisite institutional changes to realize this concept did not take place. China from the mid-nineteenth to mid-twentieth century is a good example. On the one hand, China was diplomatically recognized by the major powers, even if they also recognized territorial losses as in the form of Japanese annexations and conceding special zones of control to all the major imperial powers. After 1919, China was a recognized sovereign state in the League of Nations. Nevertheless, the central state lacked coercive power over its whole territory. Conversely, certain forms of territoriality were achieved by non-state means. The Imperial (from 1912 Chinese) Maritime Customs Service, which operated from 1854 until 1949, treated China as a single economic territory so far as the control of trade across its borders was concerned. However, this was a "private" institution run largely by Europeans and some Americans who nevertheless displayed a good deal of loyalty towards "China".

Yet there were also strict limits to its institutional achievements, as the Customs Service operated in areas where it was difficult, if not impossible, to carry out its designated functions. The Taiping Rebellion undermined central imperial control and was crushed with the use of armed forces raised under local officials, which in turn formed the basis for regional "warlord" power in the late imperial period and throughout the life of the republic (1912–1949). The nationalists were busy reconstituting sovereign territorial power between 1926 and 1937, but this project was abruptly reversed with the Japanese invasion and then the civil war from 1945 until 1949. Chinese groups, in particular the nationalists and the communists, had the modern concept of territoriality as a goal, and various events, such as the popularization of Woodrow Wilson's Fourteen Points and the idea of "national self-determination", probably made the concept an increasingly important one to a growing number of people. Nevertheless, China, if anything, saw a "deterritorializing" trend from the mid-nineteenth to mid-twentieth century.[24]

---

[24] On the impact of Wilson's doctrine of national self-determination, see E. Manela, *The Wilsonian Moment: Self-Determination and the International Origins of Anti-Colonial Nationalism*, Oxford: Oxford University Press, 2007; F. Dikötter, *The Age of Openness: China before Mao*, Hong Kong: Hong Kong University Press, 2008.

In other areas more directly under the control of imperialist nation-states, there were also conceptual projections of territoriality but again not given much in the way of institutional form. This had begun piecemeal in certain European zones with the recognition of new states such as Serbia and Greece in the early nineteenth century. Later other Balkan regions broke away from Ottoman control. As a procedure of international agreement and recognition, the conceptual requisites for a "modern" state were elaborated: a constitution, a princely ruler (usually drawn from a cadet branch of an established European royal family), a commitment to rule of law and respect for various individual and/or group rights, and a clearly demarcated boundary. This trend was generalized through much of Central Europe after 1918, mightily assisted by the US doctrine of national self-determination backed by elaborate data built up by teams of academics. In the form of colonial rather than sovereign territories, this was also projected on to much of sub-Saharan Africa and the Middle East, for example with the establishment of League of Nation "mandates".

Furthermore, political elites in the states in question took the issue of territoriality very seriously, often by insisting that the state did not control all the territory it should – as embodied, for example, in a series of conflicting claims to Greater Serbia, Greater Bulgaria, and Greater Greece. In colonial territories, pan-nationalism declined as nationalist elites concluded that the best prospect of gaining independence was to focus on that self-contradictory concept: the "colonial state". The main difference between the form taken by "self-determination" in European nineteenth-century and post-1918 small state formations and post-1945 extra-European colonies was that generally it had been ethno-nationality (based on some combination of language and religion) that defined the territory of the nation-state in the first set of cases, while it was the colonial territory that defined the "nationality" of the state in the second set. The third great wave of small nation-state formation following the collapse of the USSR and Yugoslavia combined elements of the two earlier phases, in that the new states were largely based on the territory of the constituent republics of the former states, but these had already been defined in ethno-national terms.

In part, the formation of small nation-states out of larger imperial states was linked to the emergence of nationalist movements with territorial forms matching that of the new state. However, often they were as much, if not more, an international solution dictated by the major external powers who wished to liquidate one formal imperial power (sometimes even including their own) but not by transferring the territory and its inhabitants to the formal rule of another imperial power.

Undoubtedly in some cases, especially where a territorial-wide nationalism played a major role in achieving independence, there was a substantial institutional and political base for the new state.²⁵ Roeder argues that the non-Russian republics had become sufficiently real so that those in charge of its institutions had a greater capacity to achieve independence and wield power in the new situation than any other elites. It is also argued that the "ethnic affirmative action" policy of the USSR had created a national identity space that could match republican decision space. However, clearly this varies regionally: broadly speaking, the fates of the West, South, and Central Asian republican zones have taken very different forms based on the degree to which national identity and republican institutions had developed before the Soviet collapse.

Elsewhere, little of this had happened. The Soviet ethno-national programme was exceptional, going against the usual trend for the core – as state power, economic interest, and national identity – to discriminate in favour of itself, often at the expense of inhibiting any genuinely territorial power or identity forming in the peripheries. The modern concepts were often little more than rhetoric – even if important rhetoric because the major powers subscribed to this and insisted that periphery elites do so too – superimposed upon distinctly non-territorial forms of power and identity. In such cases, "territorial nationalism" too was just an elite response to an "outer" form rather than representing anything more popular or deeply believed.²⁶

This combination of conceptual without institutional territoriality continues to this day, for example in the patronizing language of "failed states" and "neo-patrimonialism" applied to various regions of Africa and Asia. In some cases, the conceptual project arguably produces the opposite of institutional territoriality. Arnold Toynbee argues that the projection of the nation-state model on to parts of Central Europe and the Balkans after 1918 was a disaster for the region, breaking up natural economic unities (e.g. along the Danube), forming weak and non-viable states whose elites engaged in petty and vicious conflicts with one another. The Austro-Marxist Karl Renner, who had argued, along with Otto Bauer, for combining genuine national cultural autonomy with a multiethnic state, also canvassed the idea of a Danubian Federation.

---

25 However, in the most impressive case of organized mass nationalism – India – the fact that there were two competing movements caused the failure of the "territorial" solution and led to the massive violence associated with partition.

26 Partha Chatterjee has consistently distinguished adaptive "outer" from more distinctive and authentic "inner" nationalism, and many nationalist writers have made distinctions such as that between "civilization" and "culture" to try to capture the way nationalism both adapted to the universally projected concept of the nation-state and the claim to uniqueness for the particular nation.

Broadly speaking, the nationalist programme, as it had taken shape in the nineteenth century, had projected national independence as a process of creating larger and more progressive state forms such as Germany, Italy, Austria-Hungary, and Poland. There often was recognition of "small nations" but not taking the form of sovereign territorial states. The identification of the territorial state with the nation-state and of the nation-state with post-imperial constructions – whether ethno-national (as in Central Europe after 1918) or territorial (as in extra-European empire after 1945) or as a combination (as with the non-Russian republics of the USSR) – in many ways undermined the move towards a genuine territorialization of the world where the separate states each wielded effective power internally and in their relations with each other. It also tended to divide internal coercive from ideological and economic power more sharply, which in turn rendered that coercive power increasingly incoherent and weak.

Yet, so long as the concept of the sovereign, territorial nation-state was defended by the most powerful states, it acquired a life of its own. Englebert argues that, despite their weakness and failure to make a reality of sovereign power in a demarcated territory, African states have rarely been subject to significant secessionist or irredentist challenges. He attributes this to the way in which external forces (more powerful states but also powerful non-state entities such as business corporations and international charities) continue to buttress the "idea of the state" such that even those who contest the power of the existing government claim to do so in the name of the state.

In all these ways, the universalization of the concept of the territorial state is not only not accompanied by its institutional generalization but in fact the conceptual projection actually helps maintain and even create the lack of real territoriality. Indeed, one might go further and argue that the simultaneous existence of territorialization and deterritorialization are necessary to one another, in a dialectic in which one produces the other, indeed where territoriality is advanced in some states precisely through inhibiting or even reversing it in other states.

Territoriality and Democracy

Territoriality acquires a special significance when the subjects of the state identify themselves with that state and this usually, although not always, is associated with the development of citizenship, both in terms of the proportion of the population who become citizens and the range of rights and obligations of that citizenship.

I begin with a neglected aspect of the Treaty of Westphalia (1648). This, of course, is deployed as a founding myth for the study of international relations, with the claims that in the agreement was embodied the idea of the sovereign, clearly demarcated territorial state subject to no higher form of authority and each juridically equal to all the others.[27] Empirically one might question some of these points. How territorial was the Holy Roman Empire? How could equality be squared with making three of the signatory states guarantors for the agreement as a whole? However, I want to draw attention to another feature of the treaty. It identified three legitimate confessional forms of Christianity: Catholic, Lutheran, and Reformed (we often use the term Calvinism). It established the territorial distribution of the adherents of the three confessions at a particular date. It declared that, in the event of boundary changes between states, the existing territorial distribution of faiths be observed. Whereas the Peace of Augsburg (1555) had declared that the religion of the prince was the religion of the people, this provision in the Treaty of Westphalia reversed that principle. The reason was clear: it appeared that the constant attempt to force people to change their religion had led to the bloody conflicts of the last century or so. By separating the confessional identity of subjects from that of their rulers, it was hoped to avoid one major reason for conflict. It was intended to mean that if the ruler changed his faith, he could not impose it on his subjects (a great relief to Protestant Saxons, whose hereditary king was constantly taking the elective kingship Poland and converting to Catholicism!). It also meant that any territorial changes following a war should not be accompanied by efforts at mass conversion. Interestingly, the most important single instance of conversion was that of the prince falling in line with the majority of his subjects, not the other way round. Henry IV of France recognized that, out of necessity, "Paris is worth a mass".

Admittedly, this limited principle of toleration was not always observed, as when Louis XIV revoked Henry's Edict of Nantes, but it was established. So already, even before modern citizenship and democracy was granted, some princes were compelled to recognize that the identity space, which would reinforce the authority of the territorial monarchy, in an age when confessional identity counted for more than national identity, had in part to come "from below".

Still, what counts most for securing a subject/state link in the modern territorial state is citizenship. This is a complex term and one needs to distinguish between particular functions (rights and obligations) and their practical

---

[27] For a critique of this "myth", see B. Teschke, *The Myth of 1648: Class, Geopolitics and the Making of International Relations*, New York: Verso, 2003.

realization, on the one hand, and the role of citizenship in establishing identity, usually called nationality, in the modern state, on the other.

The most dramatic changes in citizenship were associated with the American and French revolutions. The French Declaration of the Rights of Man and of the Citizen stipulated that power proceeded from the people; the US Declaration of Independence insisted that governments must rest upon the "consent of the governed". Of course, the rhetoric alone does not suffice, and until citizenship is institutionalized into a range of rights and obligations, it can mask many kinds of undemocratic rule.

T.H. Marshall usefully distinguishes between legal, political, and social citizenship.[28] The first was associated with equality before the law and involved the removal of privilege. The second was associated with the right to vote in and stand for election to a sovereign parliament. The third was associated with the right to welfare of various kinds, such as medical care or income support in unemployment or old age. Marshall tends to focus on rights rather than obligations (such as jury and military service, or the making of tax and other public payments) and to see the three forms of citizenship coming in successive phases – arguably a generalization from the English/British experience, but the functional distinctions are valuable nonetheless.

Interestingly, Marshall does not consider the essential condition for all these and any other forms of citizenship, namely *state membership*. Yet, without this concept taking a territorial form, it is difficult to see how any modern citizenship can exist. Let me take one well-documented example of how this might come about. On one day in October 1842, the Prussian state for the first time defined who was a Prussian subject.[29] On that same day, other laws were passed that modified the current system of poor relief. Hitherto, a subject was only eligible for poor relief in the parish of his or her birth. With a state-wide labour market developing along with cyclical unemployment typical of capitalism, this was becoming an impractical provision. Under the new law, residence in a place for three years qualified someone for poor relief. However, that meant one could no longer depend upon the parish to make the decision as to who was entitled to relief; it had become a matter for the state. Until then, Prussia, so far as claims to poor relief were concerned, could be treated as the sum of its parishes, and the boundary that mattered was the parish boundary. Now, in order to avoid free riders from outside Prussia claiming such relief, one

---

[28] T.H. Marshall, *Class, Citizenship and Social Development*, New York: Doubleday, 1964.
[29] *Staatsangehöriger*, literally member of the state, as opposed to the German term for citizen, which is *Staatsbürger*. On the link of territory to citizenship, see A. Fahrmeir, *Citizenship: The Rise and Fall of a Modern Concept*, New Haven, Yale University Press, 2008.

had to define who was a Prussian. State membership mattered for many poor people. In a way, it was what Marshall would call a form of social citizenship, which triggered the state definition of subject membership in the Prussian case.

The history of citizenship as a bundle of rights and obligations enforced by the state, and the different stages and forms it takes in different places, is yet to be written, but I would argue that it is at the heart of modern territoriality and is key to the foundation as opposed to the formation of the nation-state. Many of the surveillance techniques we associate with the "growth of the modern state" are not so much impositions upon a passive population but necessary, often popular instruments for the enforcement of citizenship. Universal conscription requires a register of eligible males of the appropriate age groups – to this end, Napoleonic France was the first to establish the necessary bureaucracy that enabled Napoleon to raise mass armies year after year. Prevention of benefit claims by foreigners requires not just a clear distinction between citizen and foreigner but also that this be documented for each individual.[30] Not only that, if only particular categories of citizens had certain rights or obligations (old-age benefits, military service, and level of income for taxation), then mass data on the relevant information had to be gathered, maintained, and retrieved by specialist agencies of the state. Inevitably, the bounded state and those defined as its subjects/citizens increased its salience both as institutional reality and social experience.

The modern "iron cage" (Max Weber) was being constructed, not as a top-down process but a broader social process. To return to my distinction between "forming" and "founding" a nation-state, it may be that Italy was formed as a nation-state between 1861 and 1871 as part of the coercive "moment" Maier describes, but arguably France was "founded" as a nation-state during the peacetime period of the Third Republic from 1871 to 1914, when, in Eugen Weber's famous formulation, peasants were made into Frenchmen. Again, Weber's book arguably does not describe so much a deliberate top-down project (though there were such elements involved) but the complex outcome of internal migration (national labour market, railway travel, and growth of urban-industrial centres), mass literacy in a standardized French vernacular, and adult manhood suffrage for elections to a sovereign parliament. All these changes had a clear territorial focus.

Even those who came to question identifying nationality with membership of the existing territorial state were forced to adopt some of its territorial

---

30 For a long time, the available technology did not allow one to check this documentation at the state boundary, but the requirement that everyone have such documentation available for inspection by state officials could serve the same purpose by enabling deportation.

features. An interesting attempt to resist this was made by Otto Bauer and Karl Renner, the Austrian Marxist theorists and socialist politicians, with their idea of nationality as a personal rather than territorial attribute. But nationality politics in the Habsburg Empire expressed itself in territorial terms as nationalists claimed a majority in one place or another, which in turn meant the election of a deputy or the confirmation of claims to a school. Not only that, the Habsburg state itself went through various stages of projecting nationality upon its subjects – usually giving this territorial form, such as in regional parliaments – as one way of making closer connections between citizens and their state. When Lenin and Stalin turned their attention to the nationality question in the Romanov Empire, they explicitly rejected Bauer and opted for a territorial definition of nationality, even though Stalin's definition of ethno-nationality focused on "personal" attributes. The approach would eventually justify the formation of non-Russian republics, territorial entities but each designated with a "titular" nationality and associated name.

Which brings me back to nationalism. Like most political ideas, this starts off as an affair of intellectual minorities, usually taking the form of a radical, even utopian idea pitted against existing political forms of mainly sprawling dynastic empires and petty princedoms. What is more, it is a transnational movement often developed by exiles who have more to do with similar figures from other "nations" than with most of their fellow nationals.

I suggest that it is not so much the growing influence of these small groups that pushes politics in a national direction but rather the growing importance of territoriality combined with the advance of citizenship that makes the national idea seem so persuasive. Once peasants were made into Frenchmen (French women have to wait longer!), a process in which explicit nationalism was just one element (especially at those moments of war), then a political idea that turned Frenchness from an identity into a value and a programme acquired increasing appeal. By the time we get to a mass electorate and society within such a state, we find that all political groupings are stressing their national qualities as well as that their particular constituents constitute the heart of the nation and their policies are best suited to serve the national interest. One can perhaps continue to identify a specific political position that might be called nationalist as one that focuses on purging the nation of impure or alien elements (such as the Jew, or ethnic or racial minorities) or extending state territory to include places and peoples that are part of the "nation", but in fact such political positions rarely attract much popular support. That goes to parties that focus on either economic power (class and occupational and economic sector interests, such as unionization or tariff protection) or non-national ideological questions (e.g. secular as opposed to religious education). Nationalism is not so much a particular value position then but rather the claim by all such parties to be focused on control of the existing territorial state, a state that is now credited with a national character and a national history that backs that up.[31]

The same arguments apply to citizenship law in terms of who automatically acquires citizenship, which, in the modern world, is usually equated with national citizenship. Again, it is important to distinguish between identity and function. An influential distinction in modern nationalism studies is between civic and ethnic. Brubaker associates this distinction with that between the two basic principles of automatic citizenship: place of birth or parentage (ius solis/the law of the soil and jus sanguinis/law of the blood).[32] The first characterized citizenship law in the French Third Republic and the second in the German Second Empire. Civic nationality could be seen as open to outsiders and ethnic nationality as closed. Many other contrasting attributes could be added.

Once again, however, we must make the distinction between decision and identity space and look at the range of functions that link citizenship to territoriality.[33] The first thing to note is that the distinction is of no significance for that part of the population born on the national territory of the parents (father in most cases; mother when an illegitimate child) who hold national citizenship. The second is to note that people are no freer in their choice of birthplace as in their parents, so there is no distinction in terms of freedom. A third point to note is that seeing the law of the soil as stimulating immigration and the law of the blood as discouraging it might be getting the causality the wrong way round.

The French government after 1871 was haunted by the threat that low demographic growth would condemn France to declining power, including the capacity

---

[31] I have elaborated this argument in various publications, such as J. Breuilly "On the Principle of Nationality", in: G.S. Jones and G. Claeys (eds.), *The Cambridge History of Nineteenth-Century Political Thought*, Cambridge: Cambridge University Press, 2011, pp. 77–109; J. Breuilly, "What Does It mean to Say that Nationalism is Popular?" in: M. van Ginderachter and M. Beyen (eds.), *Nationhood from Below: Europe in the Long Nineteenth Century*, Basingstoke: Palgrave Macmillan, 2012, pp. 23–43. Mark Hewitson has recently argued that the preparedness of Germans to fight in the wars of unification has more to do with citizenship and acceptance of the legitimacy of the state demand to participate in wars against other states than with enthusiasm for nationalist ideology. M.Hewitson, *The People's Wars: Histories of Violence in the German Lands, 1820-1888*, Oxford: Oxford University Press, 2017.
[32] R. Brubaker, *Citizenship and Nationhood in France and Germany*, Cambridge: Havard University Press, 1992.
[33] This argument is closely related to the distinction Oliver Zimmer makes between national symbols and their uses. For example, language can symbolize nationality but can be used either to exclude or assimilate immigrants. See O. Zimmer, "Boundary Mechanisms and Symbolic Resources: Towards a Process Oriented Approach to National Identity". *Nations and Nationalism 9* (2003) 2, pp. 173–193.

to take revenge for defeat in the Franco-Prussian war and to recover Alsace-Lorraine. A law of the soil would encourage immigration and boost demographic growth and in addition would mean the male children of immigrants would be liable to military service. By contrast, Germany was a country of fast population growth and had a particular concern to discourage permanent immigration from Russia. Its legal tradition, emanating from a number of often small states where there was a greater likelihood than in a larger state that a child would be born outside the state of its parents, was naturally inclined to the law of the blood. However, that "blood" was parental, not race or ethnic "blood". Ethnic or race homogeneity would only be secured if the stock of parents was already homogenous; otherwise, it would perpetuate whatever ethnic or racial diversity already existed.

Finally, citizenship law is always liable to modification if powerful interests demand that. Once Muslim immigration from Algeria increased, the French government took steps to ensure that these racially and religiously distinct immigrants could not automatically acquire citizenship for children born to them in France. Conversely, the German government became very concerned that male colonists in German African colonies would automatically confer German citizenship upon the children they had from marriages to black African women. Two different principles led to unintended consequences that triggered the same prejudice. The result was the same abandonment of the original principle. What we see here is how the national territory is becoming associated with various identities that cannot be coded as either civic or ethnic but which rather combine pre-political claims (a nation existed here before there was a nation-state and indeed it is that prior existence that justifies this state) with political claims (this state should be a republic or a monarchy, liberal or illiberal, secular or religious, etc.). These then become crystallized, usually in contested ways, into different notions as to what is "truly national". Increasingly, competitions for power associated with such conflicting claims are focused on the national territory and key institutions such as parliament. In this sense, identity space becomes national space, not so much through the power of nationalism as through the power of the increasing link between territoriality and citizenship as well as the multiple national claims, all of which are territorially focused.[34]

---

[34] Citizenship becomes contentious when there are specific pressures such as a particular flow of immigration. It also becomes contentious when boundaries rather than people move, for example in India after 1947 or when there is a move to mass expulsion or even worse of designated minorities. In each case it is the sudden disjuncture between decision and identity space that creates the problem.

There are two further steps in this process, although they are not inevitable or irreversible or final.

The first is that the modern territorial state fuses the range of different functional boundaries. The abolition of internal tariff barriers (between town and country, or between provinces), coupled with the raising of effective tariff controls at the state boundary, creates a common economic space. Indeed, it has been argued that the vision of achieving this – as in the work of Friedrich List, himself deeply influenced by the US "economic nationalist" Alexander Hamilton – helps one imagine the nation as an economic unit.[35] Welfare benefits extend beyond poor relief and are no longer the responsibility of parishes but are managed by state agencies. For a period in the nineteenth and early twentieth centuries, a number of modern states obliged all young male citizens to military service, another national responsibility and nationalizing experience. That, of course, is one step that has been reversed with the shift to professional armed forces and often long-distance, "indirect" modes of warfare, which, in a different way, threaten to undermine accepted notions of state territoriality. Freedom of movement within the state territory might be said to embody a particularly liberal concept of territoriality, one that was never achieved in the USSR and which is heavily qualified in contemporary China. But even liberal state territoriality imposes restrictions on such movement beyond state territory. Even in cases where movement is unimpeded (e.g. under the Schengen Agreement for certain EU countries) both in law and practice, people are required to carry documentation proving their national citizenship and the destination state can insist on its production – the EU queue in airports might appear privileged compared to the non-EU queue but it is a queue nevertheless.

As the different functional boundaries all come to converge on the national frontier, so does that frontier come to figure more prominently in the experiences of the citizenry. Michael Billig's seminal work *Banal Nationalism* shows how the nation-state is distinguished from the world beyond, through such devices as the distinction in newspapers between "home" and "foreign" news. For example, one can also note how "local" news is relegated to a lower position; when the BBC TV's "national and international news" broadcast, which lasts about 30 minutes, is finished, the announcer declares that "we" will now be going to the news "where you are", and then there are 10-minute local news broadcasts. Weather forecasts popularize maps of the nation-state; British

---

[35] For List's influence beyond Germany, see M. Metzler, "The Cosmopolitanism of National Economics: Friedrich List in a Japanese Mirror", in: A.G. Hopkins (ed.), *Global History: Interactions Between the Universal and the Local*, Basingstoke: Palgrave Macmillan, 2006, pp. 98–130.

weather forecasts even manage very often to block out most of the territory of the Republic of Ireland. There is a common set of everyday signs and symbols that constantly and subconsciously transmit "nation-stateness", such as a particular style of road signs, railway timetables, or flags. Sometimes state and national signs and symbols get separated, as in Wales or Catalonia, which can have important consequences for a sense of popular national identity.

Such national projections are not just neutral or "banal". Boundaries can be invested with sacred qualities. After the German Second Empire annexed Alsace-Lorraine, there was mass publicity in France about the humiliation involved and the need to revenge and reverse this act. For a long time, I was sceptical about the popular impact of this. However, research by Martyn Lyons, based on the letters written home between 1914 and 1918 by French soldiers in that small part of Alsace that France militarily occupied for part of the war, not only confirms but also qualifies that impact.[36] These were men with low levels of literacy drawn from all over France and often in their letters more preoccupied with how their farms and families were faring than with the war. Yet again and again, it turns out that they were very conscious of the loss of Alsace. Many had read or knew of the mass-selling story of two boys cycling round France, *Le Tour de France par deux enfants: Devoir et Patrie* (1877). What was interesting here was the puzzlement many expressed that, when they finally found themselves in this place that essentially was part of France, the inhabitants, when they spoke to them, were foreigners, indeed Germans! However, most national citizens only perceive national boundaries as imagined, not as real in this way.

One can find numerous ways in which such sacralization takes place: geography and history and other lessons in the mass schools that the modern nation-state sets up, popular atlases, later in radio and television broadcasts, or the speeches of democratically elected politicians. In this way, the mythical stories nationalism tells about a sacred land and a special people become felt experiences. That in turn feeds back to the functional boundaries. Immigration controls, for example, cease to be just about calculations of costs and benefits but are framed in terms of the invasion of national space.[37] Sometimes the "rational" part of a government knows that certain immigration streams are

---

[36] The army command, as also those in Britain, Germany, and Austria-Hungary, used a random sample of such correspondence as a way of gauging popular opinion amongst the rank and file, and this invaluable source survives. See his essay M. Lyons, "France: National Identity from Below, 1914–1919", in: M. Lyons, *The Writing Culture of Ordinary People in Europe, c. 1860–1920*, Cambridge: Cambridge University Press, 2013, pp. 91–112.

[37] Only thus can one in part explain the British vote to leave the European Union in the referendum of 2016.

positively beneficial, indeed virtually essential, for the national economy but another, "emotional" part has to brandish controls and restrictions in order to prove that it is rebuffing the "invasion".

For these reasons, I would focus on nation-state foundation rather than formation, and I would stress that it is the functional expansion of the size of the citizenry and their range of rights and obligations that is most important in that foundational process, along with a set of modernizing changes, more so initially than wars and the symbolic declarations of national independence. However, once the process of sacralizing boundaries gathers momentum that becomes a force in its own right – a key component of certain kinds of populist nationalism and sometimes even a threat to the functional adjustment of boundaries and their controls for particular ends.

Implications for the Present and Future of Territoriality

The powerful nation-state of the modern era has managed to bring together decision space, in the sense of sovereign power able to monopolize coercive power within its own clearly demarcated boundaries, with identity space, in the sense of infusing the majority of citizens with the sense that this is "their" nation-state. At the same time, it has fused together a range of functionally defined spaces and boundaries and managed to impose some state restraints upon transnational economic and ideological power, in part by directly incorporating these as forms of national power (e.g. giving a national twist to liberal or socialist or conservative or religious ideologies). The powerful modern nation-state embodies institutionally distinctive forms of territoriality of the kind Maier analyses. However, the stress here is on *powerful* and *institutional*. The story is very different for regions where the state is not powerful, either in its external relations and/or in its capacity institutionally to enforce modern forms of sovereignty and territoriality. Here modern territoriality may well have been projected as a concept but not as an institutionalized set of practices.

There are three issues I want to consider in relation to the probable future of modern territoriality.

The first is the argument that new forms of power are likely to erode territoriality, even of the most powerful and institutionally realized nation-states. I will not repeat a set of arguments that one constantly encounters about the power of multinational corporations, international banks and hedge funds, the Internet, etc. I would only note in passing that very often the powerful nation-state appears able to bend some of these global developments to its control. The most recent revelations about how US and UK security agencies monitor Internet traffic, especially when it crosses into territorial space, or the ways in which the Chinese and other governments monitor and close down websites, suggest that the powerful nation-state still is perhaps the major player in the exercise of these forms of power.

The second is that territoriality is not a linear process that "rises" and then "declines" but rather a partial and multiple set of processes. Partial in the sense that the advance of modern territoriality in one place might well be associated with its regression in another, and indeed there may well be a close relationship between the two processes. Multiple in the sense that functional territoriality might grow stronger in one dimension (say, immigration control) but weaker in another (say, control of financial flows).

The third, and the main point I want to make, is that the creation of identity space in the sense of mass citizen identification with the nation-state, which in turn is associated with institutionalizing various functional forms of territoriality as well as infusing the boundary and sovereignty with sacral qualities, imposes strict limits on future possibilities. We see that even quite weak states where such identity space has been formed put up significant resistance to threats to existing state sovereignty, as the mass indignation in small Southern European member states of EU policies demonstrates.

Once this has crystallized in a particular form, it can appear very difficult to restructure. Making peasants into Frenchmen was one thing; making Frenchmen into Europeans, let alone cosmopolitans, is something completely different. Peasant identity is a different kind of identity from national identity. One can combine them without difficulty. However, where national identity means state identity, and the state is seen as a sovereign space in which one either does or does not belong, it is difficult to see how it can be combined with a European identity that makes some of the same claims. Some analysts think there can be a gradual undermining of this identity space, first by stressing that people can see themselves in multiple identities, which can reinforce rather than conflict with one another, and second by arguing that the different functional identities can once more become disentangled from each other and we can enter some "neo-medieval" world where the "parcellized sovereignty" of the feudal era is reproduced.

I am sceptical of this. First, that earlier world was a non-democratic world, a world of distinct privileges and levels of power, which could therefore tolerate degrees of separate (collective) identities that even the most ardent advocate of multiculturalism today could not imagine.[38] Second, especially at times of crisis

---

38 See J. Breuilly, "The Historical Conditions for Multiculturalism", in: J. Eade et al. (eds.), *Advancing Multiculturalism*, Post 7/7, Newcastle: Cambridge Scholars Publishing, 2008, pp. 7–28.

the theoretically available repertoire of identities available to the modern citizen do become zero-sum games. Is "my" currency to be controlled by the territorial state or some transnational central bank? "My" tax rates or welfare benefits? The command structure over "my" armed forces. Democratic identity space means that that notion of "my" has a particular form and force.

Of course, things do change. But if they do so, I think it will be in a crisis, with violence, undermining existing forms of territoriality before any alternative might, if ever, become clear. This, of course, has been the "normal" experience of much of the world, which has not had the good fortune to live as a secure citizen in a powerful modern nation-state, in part because precisely those states have imposed such conditions upon other parts of the world. Modern territoriality is not so much an inexorable and universal process, which is now under threat, as it is the good fortune of some parts of the world, which proceeds in a partial, multiple, and discontinuous manner.

―――
Part III: **Portals**

Geert Castryck
Disentangling the Colonial City: Spatial Separations and Entanglements inside Towns and across the Empire in Colonial Africa and Europe

It has been argued that the first places of genuine global integration, where people, capital, goods, and ideas from across the world came together, were colonial cities.[1] When looking more closely, it appears that the argument primarily targets port cities in Asia, Africa, and the Americas. In these places, more than in many European towns in early colonial times, people from different parts of the world lived, worked, and traded. Furthermore, exchange between unevenly developed economic zones took place and maritime and terrestrial worlds met. These connections and entanglements had a fundamental impact on the shape, significance, and even existence of these towns. "They were 'global pivots of change' [...], instrumental in creating the space in which today's capitalist world-economy operates [...] long before the phenomenon occurred in the metropolitan capitals".[2] Nevertheless, it was only a matter of time until the direct colonial and urban encounter would also apply to cities in Europe and beyond the coast. Colonial connections are still visible in cities today, either in the diversity of people walking the streets, in buildings or monuments marking colonial rule, or in a town's spatial layout and symbolic markers.

Although the term "colonial city" usually refers to cities in colonies,[3] the features that make a city colonial also apply to cities in the colonial metropole. Connections and entanglements between the colony and the metropole, a core corollary of colonialism, ipso facto shape both sides of the equation. Colonialism implicates the metropole not only as an emitter of colonial domination, but also as a constituent part of an asymmetrical power relation, which by definition is a reciprocal relation. Mobility of people in a colonial context included colonial settlers moving from metropole to colony, colonial subjects moving within and between colonies (e.g. in processes of labour migration or urbanization), as well

---
[1] A.D. King, *Urbanism, Colonialism and the World-Economy: Cultural and Spatial Foundations of the World Urban System*, Abingdon: Routledge, 1991, pp. 6–7.
[2] Ibid., 7.
[3] See, e.g., H. Gründer and P. Johanek, *Kolonialstädte, Europäische Enklaven oder Schmelztiegel der Kulturen?*, Münster: LIT Verlag, 2001.

as migrants from the colonies to the metropoles. The predicate "colonial" should therefore not be confined to areas under colonial administration but can better be applied to those phenomena that characterize colonialism and that are the result of colonial relations, wherever they manifest themselves. In this understanding, Paris, Hamburg, and Oxford bear attributes of the colonial city in them as much as the port cities of Dakar, Mumbai, and Dar es Salaam, or as the inland cities of Lubumbashi, Kigoma, or Nairobi.

By reconstructing (re)constellations of local and global connections inside colonial cities, this chapter offers an essentially spatial analysis of how colonialism worked in towns. The chapter shows that the colonial city was characterized by a high concentration of connections, both in town and across the colonial world. The city, as a whole, was not connected, but different parts of town each had their relations in different directions. The colonial attempt to obtain control over cities, as shown in numerous projects of colonial urban planning and segregation, was thus at least in part a spatial project, locally disentangling and severing the manifold global connections in the colonial city.

Our approach took inspiration from the analytical category "portal of globalization", which provides a way to localize with precision where global connections and relations are produced, paying attention to the development of practices or institutions for dealing with global connectedness.[4] Some places are more vibrant in the production of global connectedness and in stimulating qualitative changes in the nature of global connectedness than others, but it is worthwhile to keep the eyes open in every place on earth to uncover possible pathbreaking ways of shaping globalization – or connectedness, which is the primary interest of this chapter. Locally available assets, such as a tradition of connectedness, creative or innovative actors, a diverse population interacting locally and globally, the physical presence of infrastructure of transportation or communication (or the local historical quality to attract such infrastructure), etc. are crucial in this regard, and they are not only at work in the big imperial metropoles or powerhouses of globalization. The category "portal of globalization" provides an analytical entry point to interpret globalization in a multicentred, heterogeneous, actor-oriented, space-sensitive, and historically contingent fashion while, at the

---

[4] Cf. M. Middell and K. Naumann, "Global History and the Spatial Turn: From the Impact of Area Studies to the Study of Critical Junctures Of Globalization", *Journal of Global History* 5 (2010) 1, pp. 149–170; G. Castryck, "Introduction – From Railway Juncture to Portal of Globalization: Making Globalization Work in African and South Asian Railway Towns", *Comparativ* 25 (2015) 4, pp. 7–16; C. Baumann, A. Dietze and M. Maruschke, *Portals of Globalization in Africa, Asia, and Latin America*, Leipzig: Leipziger Universitätsverlag, 2017, especially "Portals of Globalization – An Introduction".

same time, acknowledging the thrust, with ups and downs, of intensifying and accelerating interactions and interdependencies on a global scale. Even though our concern is not so much globalization per se, we adopt this analytical entry point for our reconstruction and spatial interpretation of connections and separations within and between cities in a colonial context.

The empirical basis for this chapter lies in Berlin's Africa, that is to say the parts of Africa included in the free trade zone determined at the Berlin Congo Conference (1884/85) as well as the European (and North American) lands involved in this initially one-sided space-making imposition. After situating our approach in relation to the existing literature, we will make an analysis of colonial cities, empirically drawing on four East and Central African examples: Dar es Salaam, Kigoma, Bujumbura, and Lubumbashi. We gauge the colonial origin and role of these cities as well as the colonial imprint on these towns' spatial layout and relations. We then move on to ask the same questions about European colonial cities such as London, Paris, and Brussels.

Overall, we argue that colonial cities are marked by and mark manifold connections and entanglements as well as asymmetries and separations premised on the unequal power relations of colonialism, both within the metaphorical "city walls" and across the globe. Global connections are not a flat maze but a power relation of connections in different directions and with different magnitudes of force. Such connections typically are highly concentrated in cities – colonial cities when it comes to the era of the essentially asymmetric colonial spatial order we focus upon.

African Urban History

In African urban history, two narratives coexist and collide. One, empirically rather thin, assumes that, except for some coastal towns, cities hardly existed in pre-colonial Africa.[5] The other, painstakingly, piles up evidence that Africa has places that can be called towns since time immemorial.[6] A similar dissonance

---

[5] For a balanced assessment of this view, see A. Jones, *Afrika bis 1850*, Frankfurt/Main: S. Fischer, 2016, pp. 170–171.

[6] D.M. Anderson and R. Rathbone (eds.), *Africa's Urban Past*, Oxford: James Currey, 2000; A. Burton (ed.), *The Urban Experience in Eastern Africa c. 1750–2000*, Nairobi: British Institute in Eastern Africa, 2002; S.J. Salm, and T. Falola (eds.), *African Urban Spaces in Historical Perspective*, Rochester: University of Rochester Press, 2005; B. Freund, *The African City: A History*, Cambridge: Cambridge University Press, 2007; C. Coquery-Vidrovitch, *The History of African Cities South of the Sahara: From the Origins to Colonization*, Princeton: Markus Wiener,

exists between narratives of colonialism as an overwhelming European imposition of absolute domination[7] versus African resilience,[8] long-lasting negotiations and compromises,[9] the colonizers' inescapable colonial situation,[10] and everyday tensions of empire.[11] The claim for either a strong or a weak colonialism, for either African cities or externally introduced urbanization, reflects different views on the position and integration of Africa in the world. Cities as places of concentration and connection allow us to escape these binaries and to reconstruct the complexity and diversity of colonial connectedness.

When looking at African colonial cities, it is not our main concern whether or not these places were urban before the colonial era, but what matters is how the past affects the colonial city: its location, connections, and significance. Likewise, it is spatially visible that different groups with agency as well as different directions and intensities of connectedness are at play in

---

2009; G. Myers, *African Cities: Alternative Visions Of Urban Theory And Practice*, London: Zed Books, 2011.

7 The narrative of overwhelming colonial almightiness is no longer prominent in state-of-the-art historiography but still is in circles propagating moral indignation and mobilizing for reparations. To give but one example of a book that caused an overly justified outcry against colonial abuse and atrocities, yet reduced Africans to passive victims, thereby completely reproducing the colonial bias that denied any agency to Africans, see A. Hochschild, *King Leopold's Ghost: A Story of Greed, Terror, and Heroism in Colonial Africa*, Boston: Houghton Mifflin, 1998.

8 A focus on resistance has been prominent in African history ever since the nation-building narratives of decolonization in the 1950s and 1960s, illustrated by the seminal article by T.O. Ranger, "Connexions between 'Primary Resistance' Movements and Modern Mass Nationalism In East and Central Africa", *Journal of African History* 9 (1968) 3, pp. 437–453 and 631–641. For a critique of this "connection" between primary resistance and modern nationalism, see C.M. Young, "Nationalism, Ethnicity, and Class in Africa: A Retrospective (Nationalisme, ethnicité et classe en Afrique: une rétrospective)", *Cahiers d'Études Africaines* 26 (1986) 103, pp. 421–495.

9 A critical yet sympathetic overview of the focus on the long and winding road of struggles, negotiations, and compromises in the making of African history can be found in the special issue of the *Journal of African Cultural Studies* in honour of Terence Ranger: J. Lonsdale, "Agency in Tight Corners: Narrative and Initiative in African History", *Journal of African Cultural Studies* 13 (2000), pp. 5–16. For a self-critical assessment of the tensions between the narrative of resistance and nationalism versus small-scale stories of the personal, social, and political initiatives of historical actors in the historiography on Africa's (colonial) past, see also T. Ranger, "The Invention of Tradition Revisited: The Case of Colonial Africa", in: T. Ranger and O. Vaughan (eds.): *Legitimacy and the State in Twentieth-Century Africa. Essays in honour of A.H.M. Kirk-Greene*, Basingstoke: Palgrave Macmillan, 1993, pp. 62–111.

10 The idea stems from the article written in the late colonial period by G. Balandier, "La situation coloniale: approche théorique", *Cahiers internationaux de sociologie* 11 (1951), pp. 44–79.

11 The wording is derived from F. Cooper and A.L. Stoler (eds.) *Tensions of Empire: Colonial Cultures in a Bourgeois World*, Berkeley: University of California Press, 1997.

every colonial city, thus shaping the historically contingent spatial positions and layouts of these cities.

It should be noted that colonial cities have been researched before. Limiting this overview to African colonial cities, three strands of colonial urban history exist side by side. First of all, there is a wide range of literature on colonial urban planning.[12] Either focusing on the spatial layout of colonial cities, on policies of control and containment through spatial engineering, or on the role of individual actors, this approach explains both the colonial character and the particular shape of cities across the colonial world. Apart from being part of a colonial project, though, this approach pays little attention to a town's global connections – or, if at all, these connections are meant, and believed, to be controlled or curtailed.

Reflecting tendencies in African history in general, a second strand in colonial urban history substantiates that African city dwellers circumvented, undermined, and confronted colonial urban planning and control measures, turning colonial cities into spaces quite different from what the colonial administrations had envisaged.[13] Instead of spaces of control, many a colonial city became a space of contestation. Here as well, most of the existing research limits its focus to one city, or sometimes to the symbiosis between a few cities within one colonial realm.

A third strand, invoked in the opening sentence of this chapter, approaches colonial cities as pivots of global change, prominently highlighting global connections.[14] However, in this approach the micro level in town and the variations between different parts of town are often overlooked; put otherwise, the attention remains limited to selected sites of global connectedness that are understood as characterizing the town as a whole. They often also pay more attention to the long-distance connections than to the entanglements with the hinterland.

---

12 Cf. P.D. Curtin, "Medical Knowledge and Urban Planning in Tropical Africa", *The American Historical Review* 90 (1985) 3, pp. 594–613; G.A. Myers, *Verandahs of Power: Colonialism and Space in Urban Africa*, Syracuse: Syracuse University Press, 2003; L. Beeckmans, "Editing the African City: Reading Colonial Planning in Africa from a Comparative Perspective", *Planning Perspectives* 28 (2013) 4, pp. 615–627.
13 L. White, *The Comforts of Home: Prostitution in Colonial Nairobi*, Chicago: University of Chicago Press, 1990; P. Martin, *Leisure and Society in Colonial Brazzaville*, Cambridge: Cambridge University Press, 1995.
14 See, e.g., N. Worden, "VOC Cape Town as an Indian Ocean Port", in: H.P. Ray and E.A. Alpers (eds.), *Cross Currents and Community Networks: The History of the Indian Ocean World*, Oxford: Oxford University Press, 2007, pp. 142–162; K.R. Hall (ed.), *Secondary Cities and Urban Networking in the Indian Ocean Realm, c. 1400–1800*, Lanham: Lexington Books, 2008; R. Mukherjee (ed.), *Oceans Connect: Reflections on Water Worlds across Time and Space*, Delhi: Primus Books, 2013.

This chapter makes a plea to overcome this pars pro toto view on the globally connected colonial city. Some scholars have already undertaken similar efforts, either by explicitly focusing on one neighbourhood and its connections[15] or by being precise in localizing connections on neighbourhood, street, or house level. The latter has so far primarily been done for European or metropolitan colonial cities.[16] In this chapter, we want to draw upon this meticulous localization of connections, on the one hand, and combine it with the older research strand that reconstructed colonial urban planning, on the other hand.

We call for a spatial reading of the colonial city as a space where connections in different directions coexist and interact, each having their spaces in town, which together shape the colonial city. The spatial shape of the colonial city, thus, lies at the same time in the layout and separations in town, in the variety of spatial connections in different parts of town, and in the interactions – or lack thereof – between these different parts. We argue that it is these connections and interactions, both across the colonial world and in town, both facilitated and confined by colonialism, that make a city colonial.

Colonial Cities in Berlin's Africa

In this section, we introduce Dar es Salaam, Kigoma, Bujumbura, and Lubumbashi as well as London, Paris, and Brussels as colonial cities, each in a different way positioned, connected and internally structured within a colonial spatial order.

---

[15] Cf. L. Bigon, "'Garden City' in the Tropics? French Dakar in Comparative Perspective", *Journal of Historical Geography* 38 (2012) (1), pp. 35–44; S. Baller, "Urban Football Performances: Playing for the Neighbourhood in Senegal, 1950s–2000s", *Africa* 84 (2014) (1), pp. 17–35; L. Beeckmans and L. Bigon, "The Making of the Central Markets of Dakar and Kinshasa: From Colonial Origins to the Post-colonial Period", *Urban History* 43 (2016) (3), pp. 412–434; N. Carrier, *Little Mogadishu: Eastleigh, Nairobi's Global Somali Hub*, New York: Oxford University Press, 2016.

[16] M. Matera, *Black London: The Imperial Metropolis and Decolonization in the Twentieth Century*, Berkley: University of California Press, 2015; M. Goebel, *Anti-Imperial Metropolis: Interwar Paris and the Seeds of Third World Nationalism*, Cambridge: Cambridge University Press, 2015. For a meticulous reconstruction of the affiliations of owners or tenants on the level of cadastral parcels in colonial Elisabethville (today Lubumbashi), see S. Boonen and J. Lagae, "A City Constructed by 'des gens d'ailleurs': Urban Development and Migration Policies in Colonial Lubumbashi, 1910–1930", *Comparativ* 25 (2015) (4), pp. 52–70.

Dar es Salaam, the Colonial Capital on the Indian Ocean Shore

Dar es Salaam became a colonial city under German colonial rule. However, it was the sultan of Zanzibar who decided to build Dar es Salaam in the 1860s as a refuge from the hectic life in the bustling town of Zanzibar.[17] When the town was founded, there were already several thriving towns on the East African coast, which was then part of the realm of the sultan. Dar es Salaam (literally "Haven of Peace") was intended to be quiet and relaxed, and, at least from that point of view, the history of the town turned out a failure. Cities change and perform different functions over time. It is important to notice that the town was founded as part of a regional spatial order in East Africa, centred around Zanzibar and connected to the Indian Ocean world and as such to the world economy at large.

In the wake of European colonization, Dar es Salaam became the colonial capital of German East Africa in 1891. At first sight, it may seem to be a rupture to change a site of relaxation into an administrative centre, but this is only partly true. What the German colonial rulers actually did was remove their operations from Bagamoyo, one of the bustling towns on the coast, where the old order was too strong and too hostile for the European colonizers.[18] Dar es Salaam was still to some extent the "Haven of Peace" for the ruling elite, as it had been in the sultan's times, yet now for a new elite with a new imperial and metropolitan reference. The direction and the magnitude of force of the town's connections changed, but the old function as safe and quiet haven lived on as well.

When looking at the inhabitants of the town, a similar instance of simultaneous continuity and change can be seen. The town grew from an estimated 3,000 inhabitants at the end of the 1880s to roughly 13,000 a decade later.[19] This population consisted of only a handful of Germans and primarily three broadly defined other groups, each embedding their own connections: people from the surrounding coastal areas who were attracted by the opportunities to make a living in town, people from the East and Central

---

[17] This section contains a cursory historical and spatial sketch of Dar es Salaam. For more thorough information, see J.R. Brennan and A. Burton, "Introduction", in: J.R. Brennan, A. Burton and Y. Lawi (eds.): *Dar es Salaam: Histories from an Emerging African Metropolis*, Dar es Salaam: Mkuki Na Nyota Publishers, 2007, pp. 1–75.
[18] For an analysis of anti-colonial resistance in Bagamoyo around 1890, see J. Glassman, *Feasts and Riot: Revelry, Rebellion, and Popular Consciousness on the Swahili Coast, 1856–1888*, Portsmouth: Heinemann, 1995.
[19] Brennan and Burton, "Introduction", p. 26.

African interior, and people from across the Indian Ocean. The composition of the population tells us something about the entanglement of pre-existing spaces of connection. Indians had played a role in the Zanzibari trade system of the nineteenth century, but the rise of Indian inhabitants in Dar es Salaam from 100 in 1891 to 2,600 in 1913 and 8,800 in 1938 (of a total urban population of 33,500, i.e. more than a quarter) took place in the context of the Indian Ocean world, by then incorporated into a British imperial order. People of the East and Central African interior had already travelled to and from the coast and settled on the coast, either as slaves or caravan porters, within the context of the nineteenth-century trade system centred on Zanzibar, and they continued to do so in the colonial era. The coastal people, previously concentrated in other coastal towns, had taken part in the Zanzibari trade system as well. Considered together, we notice that the German retreat to the sultan of Zanzibar's resort led to a colonial town inhabited by people connected in different ways across East and Central Africa and the Indian Ocean world. For these people, Dar es Salaam was a different town, with different functions, directions, and references, than for the German and later British colonial rulers – or for the later Tanzanian national rulers for that matter.[20]

This not only is observable if we look at the spatial functions and hierarchical position (positionality) of the town in relation to a global colonial spatial order in the making, but also is manifested in the spatialization processes inside the town. In the course of the colonial period, urban planning measures implemented a spatial separation of the population groups mentioned above. As mentioned before, research on colonial urban planning has primarily researched colonial motivations and legitimations for segregation measures, on the one hand, and the failures of urban regulation in the face of popular resistance or resilience, on the other hand. From a local perspective, there is a wealth of rigorous historical research on "regulation and its failures in colonial Dar es Salaam". This chapter does not add much to the analysis of the local politics of "administering urbanization" and the motivations, strategies, practices, and policies regarding issues like land use, housing, and

---

[20] There are, of course, also differences and tensions amongst the population groups just mentioned. See J. R. Brennan, "Between Segregation and Gentrification: Africans, Indians, and the Struggle for Housing in Dar es Salaam, 1920–1950", in: J.R. Brennan, A. Burton and Y. Lawi (eds.): *Dar es Salaam: Histories from an Emerging African Metropolis*, Dar es Salaam: Mkuki Na Nyota Publishers, 2007, pp. 118–135. For identity strategies and tensions in nearby Zanzibar, see L. Fair, *Pastimes and Politics: Culture, Community, and Identity in Post-abolition Urban Zanzibar, 1890–1945*, Athens: Ohio University Press, 2001.

policing in town.[21] Our main concerns, though, are the connections and separations in town and how they relate to connections over longer distances and attempted colonial control.

The setting for our argument is the well-known spatial organization of the centre of Dar es Salaam, consisting of an area of Indian residence in the commercial part of town, the neighbourhood of Kariakoo (and numerous later extensions of the city) meant for African inhabitants, the Mnazi Mmoja Grounds separating these zones, and an area of European residence, still most resembling the lush and green atmosphere of the sultan's "Haven of Peace". This has been interpreted as a separation of population groups – and rightly so. Yet, we can also read the spatializations inside the town as a local separation of areas with different connections – across the Indian Ocean, with the interior, and with the European metropole, respectively. These different areas of operation and connection were spatially separated in town but also entangled in the form of exchanges between people from different neighbourhoods. Mobility and exchanges within Dar es Salaam were at the same time movements and connections between different spatial frames of reference.

Hence, colonial policies of controlling and containing groups of people – or trying to do so – was as much a matter of controlling space as of controlling people. By separating groups of people in town, also their manifold connections could be disentangled and – to some extent – controlled or contained. Nevertheless, Indians, coastal people, and people stemming from the interior – which is, admittedly, an arbitrary category, gradually overlapping and merging with coastal people – made a living and made their town, drawing on their respective vested connections, while concurrently making use of the infrastructures and opportunities provided by colonialism. For sure, there were also Europeans making a living in town and likewise contributing to the urban environment and its connections and separations. In short, there were multiple Dar es Salaams, each with its distinct connectivity, not only consecutively but also simultaneously.

---

21 Cf. J.R. Brennan, A. Burton and Y. Lawi (eds.), *Dar es Salaam: Histories from an Emerging African Metropolis*, Dar es Salaam: Mkuki Na Nyota Publishers, 2007. Part 1 of this volume is entitled "Administering urbanization".

Kigoma-Ujiji and Bujumbura, Colonial Cities at Lake Tanganyika

We now move some 1,200 kilometres inland, symbolically taking the train the German colonial government – or the African workforce – had built at the beginning of the twentieth century, and incidentally following the same trajectory of the nineteenth-century, Zanzibar-centred caravan route. Kigoma and Bujumbura are two towns on Lake Tanganyika, which have also been created as colonial towns by the German colonizers, but which are moreover much more than just towns made by the colonizer.

Bujumbura is now the capital city of Burundi and lies at the north-eastern tip of the lake. It had been a regional market in pre-colonial times, a militarily strategic place under German rule, and capital of the Belgian-led mandate territory of Ruanda-Urundi. The urban area of Kigoma-Ujiji lies some 200 kilometres more to the south, in the present-day state of Tanzania. Ujiji was important in late pre-colonial times; German rulers chose nearby Kigoma as the endpoint of the railroad linking East and Central Africa with the Indian Ocean, and after a short Belgian interlude, Kigoma-Ujiji became part of the British-governed Tanganyika Territory.

When considering the urban planning of Kigoma-Ujiji, we observe the typical three-tier division of colonial towns in East Africa, which we also encountered in Dar es Salaam. The old urban centre of Ujiji serves as an African settlement, including a few inhabitants of Arab origin, perpetuating connections with east Congo and the East African area dating from the pre-colonial period. Remarkably, in colonial times Ujiji was predominantly inhabited by people with connections around and across Lake Tanganyika and not so much by people stemming from the immediate surrounding rural area of Buha. By then, these Ha people had become an important part of the urban population as well.[22] A tiny European residential strip in Kigoma, close to the port and the railway station, lies 7 kilometres to the north-west of Ujiji. Different from many colonial urban planning projects, but somehow comparable to the move from Bagamoyo to Dar es Salaam mentioned before, the Europeans moved away from the "old" centre of the

---

22 Cf. G. Castryck, "Bordering the Lake: Transcending Spatial Orders in Kigoma-Ujiji", *International Journal of African Historical Studies* 52, 1 (2019). Ujiji, of course, has its own more sophisticated internal spatial organization, which we do not reconstruct in this chapter for lack of place. See S. Hino, "Neighborhood Groups in African Urban Society: Social Relations and Consciousness of Swahili People of Ujiji, a Small Town of Tanzania, East Africa", *Kyoto University African Studies* 6 (1971), pp. 1–30.

urban area, creating a "new" centre – which had already been the site of an important regional market in pre-colonial times – for the purpose of colonial rule and trade. The important Indian presence in town, complemented with a few Arab and Greek entrepreneurs,[23] was located adjacent to the European strip. Furthermore, a neighbourhood called Mwanga, where the African personnel of European and Indian employers lived, is situated between Kigoma and Ujiji. Over the years, the space between Kigoma and Ujiji has gradually urbanized as well, turning Kigoma-Ujiji into a contiguous urban area. A racial and socioeconomic reading of this spatial organization can be found in colonial sources.[24] This urban planning reflected attempted colonial control through the separation of population groups and coincidingly served economic needs of all groups concerned – albeit under unequal conditions. Yet, we can also read this spatially, calling attention to the connections these different parts of town had, both over short and long distances. Thus, colonial urban planning was not only about separating people but also about locally disconnecting manifold global connections.

Like in Kigoma-Ujiji, urban planning and segregation was also applied to Bujumbura. Here as well, we witness a separation of neighbourhoods and people during the colonial period, which again is not only spatialization or segregation within this town, but is also in relation to the spaces surrounding this town and regarding long-distance spatial connections. The situation of today is in fact the spatial layout created in the 1930s and undoing the situation in which all non-Europeans (including some Greek merchants) inhabited one neighbourhood in the heart of town, between the colonial administrative centre and the lake.

---

[23] Obviously, Greeks are also Europeans. Yet, occasionally dubbed "second rate whites", they occupied an intermediary position between the colonizer and the colonized, both socially and spatially. The three-tier structure "European"-"Asian"-"African", in fact, hid a much more complex stratification, having hierarchies amongst Europeans, between Indians and Arabs, and amongst Africans as well. For a historical situation of the label "second rate whites", see Boonen and Lagae, "A City Constructed", pp. 60–64.

[24] Tanzania National Archives (TNA), Tanganyika Territory – District Officer's Reports, Kigoma District, Annual Report 1931, p. 25; TNA, 63. Western Province (Regional Office Tabora), File T.2/41, Kigoma Township – General, 1921–1950; TNA, Native Affairs General – Tanganyika Secretariat, File 41622, Minor Settlements – Western Province, 1951. Also see D.E. McHenry, Jr., "Reorganization: an Administrative History of Kigoma District", *Tanzania Notes and Records* 84 (1980) 85, pp. 65–76; S. Hino, "Social stratification of a Swahili town", *Kyoto University African Studies* 2 (1968), pp. 51–74; S. McCurdy, "Transforming Associations: Fertility, Therapy, and the Manyema Diaspora in Urban Kigoma, Tanzania, c. 1850–1993", PhD dissertation, Columbia University, 2000.

The spatial reorganization of Bujumbura was both necessary, because of the growth of the urban population, and politically welcome in order to contain and control different population groups. We can distinguish five areas in town, and all five are destined for people who differed from the surrounding Burundian population in one way or another: permanent Swahili residents, Asian settlers, (the workplace for) colonial administrators, Europeans (mainly Belgians and Greeks), and temporary Congolese staff. Towards the end of the colonial period, the number of Burundians moving to town, and thereby not or no longer integrating in the Swahili community, rapidly increased.[25]

We now move on to a reconstruction of how different groups of people appropriated these towns in different ways and with different connections. Based on archival and field research in both towns, we particularly demonstrate the connections of the Indian and Swahili communities in Bujumbura and Kigoma-Ujiji. Although Indians were already active in the Zanzibar-centred East and Central African caravan system of the nineteenth century, the connections of the Indian communities of colonial Kigoma and Bujumbura relied on the spatial framework and infrastructures of European colonialism in general and of the British Empire in particular. Notwithstanding, the direction and intensity of their connections differed significantly from those of European imperial connectedness.

In 1931, the Indian community in Kigoma consisted of almost 400 people, and in Bujumbura approximately 80. By 1955, the number in Kigoma had risen to more than a 1,000 Asians (most of them Indians) and in Bujumbura to almost 700 Indians. Also of importance is the change in gender and age balance. In 1931, both in Bujumbura and in Kigoma, there were only half as many women than men, and even fewer children. After the Second World War, there were more Indian children than adults in Bujumbura, and females made up 45 per cent of the Indians in Kigoma.[26] Furthermore, by the end of the 1930s the population lists contain a growing number of elderly widowed mothers who came over from India or the East African coast to spend their old age with their children at Lake Tanganyika. By 1946, at least 8 Indian widows of between 54 and 61 years lived with their children in Bujumbura. There are also examples

---

25 Cf. G. Castryck, "Moslims in Usumbura (1897–1962): Sociale geschiedenis van de islamitische gemeenschappen van Usumbura in de koloniale tijd", PhD dissertation, Universiteit Gent, 2006, pp. 83–90 and 118–159.
26 TNA, Tanganyika Territory – District Officer's Reports, Kigoma District, Annual Report 1931 & 1935; Castryck, "Moslims in Usumbura", pp. 123–126.

of a sick father who came to live with his son, or a 70-year-old man who came over to live with his younger brother.

These data indicate that the Indians were increasingly intent on remaining in the area and on building their lives there. Indians in Bujumbura and Kigoma developed their professional and family lives locally but kept long-distance relations alive. In broad strokes, these connections took place within the realm of the British Empire, and at the same time they crossed the borders of the empire, as can be seen in the intensive business relations between Kigoma and Bujumbura as well as reaching into the Belgian Congo. In fact, many Indian traders in Bujumbura operated from Kigoma-Ujiji. They maintained long-distance connections with places of origin, short-distance connections between both urban centres and with surrounding markets, and on top of that relations with other communities within both towns.[27]

The British Empire, or colonialism in general, provided the historical, political, and spatial order within which these Indian communities deployed their agency, but in so doing they also went beyond and bended this order. The multilevel connections spread across the globe, had decisive Kigoma-Bujumbura and Indian Ocean-Lake Tanganyika axes, and radiated outwards to include markets in the region and neighbourhoods inside town. Nevertheless, the precise loci of connection were not the colonial cities as a whole but only specific quarters and even particular businesses and families inside these town quarters.

For the second example, the focus is on a group of people who were the backbone of urbanization in the region. I call them "Swahili", based on the language, religious, and cultural identity these people acquired parallel to their process of urbanization.[28] At least until the 1930s, both Bujumbura and Kigoma-Ujiji were primarily Swahili towns. Swahili newcomers in the emerging urban centres along Lake Tanganyika partly stemmed from the surrounding area, but a significant part also came from the eastern part of the present-day Democratic Republic of Congo.[29] They started arriving before European colonialism, as part of a historical

---

[27] Cf. Castryck, "Moslims in Usumbura", pp. 163–182.
[28] Cf. P. Gooding, "Slavery, 'Respectability,' and being 'Freeborn' on the Shores of Nineteenth-century Lake Tanganyika", *Slavery & Abolition* 40, 1 (2019), pp. 147–167; G. Castryck, "Living Islam in Colonial Bujumbura: The Historical Trans-locality of Muslim Life between East and Central Africa", *History in Africa* 46 (2019). Henceforth, Swahili without quotation marks.
[29] Castryck, "Bordering the Lake".

order connected to the caravan trade with the coast.[30] This order enabled spatial connections and mobility and included the ability to have local influence, either based on relations within local political contexts or based on references to the epicentre of the caravan trade system on the Indian Ocean coast.

It is precisely this reference to the east or to the coast that made Swahili the dominant culture for people who in fact came from the west but did so within and drawing upon a locally embedded and translocally connected historical order that provided the framework and the spatial connections for settlement. Moreover, these spatial connections remained operational and relevant as well as even further developed long after that transient order had been overtaken by European colonialism. Family relations, religious learning, mobility for professional reasons, exchange of political ideas, the travelling of fashion and music styles, as well as imaginary, symbolic, and ritual connections with places of origin or cultural reference continued to flourish between and within Swahili cities. Swahili cities dating back to the Zanzibari period remained "familiar" places, and lines of communication between these cities remained open, partly making use of the connections and mobility enabled by the colonial order that had supplanted the preceding one.

Despite the pulling apart of connections, which were oriented differently, in the urban layout of colonial cities, interactions in town continued. Swahili, Arab, Indian, Congolese, Burundian, Rwandan, and Ha people interacted significantly, thus again tying together multidirectional connections, which the colonial authorities attempted to prevent, limit, or control. These cities not only existed parallel to and circumvented colonialism, they also bore the clear imprint of colonialism in their spatial layout. In both urban areas being examined, the Swahili connections were actively removed from the heart of town, either by moving the Swahili out of the original city centre, as was the case in Bujumbura, or by moving the heart of the city itself, leaving the Swahili behind in a part of town (Ujiji), which gradually became marginalized in comparison to Kigoma. Connections in different directions and with different magnitude of force thus were pulled apart inside colonial towns, making colonialism a project of disconnection as much as of connection.

---

30 Cf. S.J. Rockel, *Carriers of Culture: Labor on the Road in Nineteenth-century East Africa*, Portsmouth: Heinemann, 2006; B. Brown, "Ujiji: the History of a Lakeside Town, c. 1800–1914", PhD dissertation, Boston University, 1973, pp. 1–271

Lubumbashi, the Capital of Minerals, Mining and Merchants

Highlighting, in a succinct manner, the economic capital of the Democratic Republic of the Congo, Lubumbashi (in colonial times Elisabethville), we can similarly depict a globally connected town, which is both locally segregated and intertwined. Different from the previous examples, this city did not build on precolonial urbanization but on rich mineral deposits in the area.[31] The so-called geological scandal of Katanga, which is extremely rich in mineral resources, attracted European colonial powers and led to an Anglo-Belgian exploitation of the region, including the founding of the city of Elisabethville, named after the then Belgian queen, but run by the company Union Minière du Haut Katanga (UMHK). Founded as part of a mining enterprise, the conception of this town was different from the colonial cities primarily functioning in a territorial-administrative logic. The spatial layout of the city was and stil is oriented towards the mines. In town, the typical separation between European residential areas and quarters for African workers, separated by a neutral zone, formed the basis of the urban grid. However, when having a closer look, a large part of the urban population was neither part of the European colonizers nor of the African workforce. Greek, Italian, Portuguese, Jewish, and Indian merchants, petty traders, and shopkeepers formed a middle ground – both socioeconomically and spatially – between the European and African neighbourhoods. Breaking up the separations in town, they also brought in their own long-distance connections of commercial and family networks. Boonen and Lagae show how housing politics were used to enforce the separation of population groups, which only met with mixed success. In this economically conceived colonial city, unforeseen urban areas were carved out through the daily practices of connecting and exchanging.[32]

A Greek, Jewish, and Indian part of town emerged from the connecting practices in town while also drawing on connections with their respective networks stretching across Central and Southern Africa and beyond. Connections

---

[31] For our spatial depiction of Lubumbashi, we primarily draw on the spatial analysis by Boonen and Lagae, "A City Constructed". Also see S. Boonen, "Une ville construite par des 'gens d'ailleurs': Développements urbains à Élisabethville, Congo belge (actuellement Lubumbashi, RDC)", PhD dissertation, Universiteit Gent, 2019.

[32] Also see S. Boonen and J. Lagae, "Scenes from a Changing Colonial 'Far West': Picturing the Early Urban Landscape and Colonial Society of Cosmopolitan Lubumbashi, 1910–1931", *Stichproben* 15 (2015) 28, pp. 11–54; J. Lagae, S. Boonen and S. Lanckriet, "Navigating 'Off Radar': The Heritage of Liminal Spaces in the City Center of Colonial/Postcolonial Lubumbashi, DR Congo", in: R. Lee et al. (eds.), *Things Don't Really Exist Until You Give Them a Name: Unpacking Urban Heritage*, Dar es Salaam: Mkuki Na Nyota Publishers, 2017, pp. 86–93.

in colonial towns were clearly not limited to colonial connections in the narrow sense, and the colonial city was only viable because of in-town and long-distance connections, bypassing, undermining, and, paradoxically, also facilitating colonial policies and colonialism as such. Without these intermediaries, the sterile fully segregated model of the colonial city would have been a complete failure. Colonialism was premised on its own dysfunctionality in order to function, yet it also provided the arena for all kinds of differently connected – both locally and globally – groups of people.

The paradox of colonial urban planning and segregation lies in the fact that the colonial city is characterized by the dysfunctionality of its urban planning or by the only partial and diminishing efficacy of segregation. The colonial character lies in the asymmetries and obstacles to connectedness as much as it lies in the inevitability of these connections, which make productive use of colonial infrastructures and imperial spaces of mobility and interaction. Indians, in particular, were as much hindered as they were facilitated by the British Empire. The same goes, mutatis mutandis, for other population groups, which explains the scattered spatial layout as well as the both separated and interrelated spatial connections of cities in East and Central Africa. Thus, the different strands in the literature come together. The African agency to circumvent urban segregation measures, notwithstanding the real effect of the spatial grid and attempted control, complemented a variety of idiosyncratic and resilient global connections in different neighbourhoods, which, despite spatial segregation, led to patterns of interaction in town, and are the constituent elements of the colonial city.

European Colonial Cities

We push our argument one step further by applying the same logic to European cities during the colonial period. As colonialism was not only contradictory per se but also worked because of and premised on its inherent contradictions, it is worthwhile to consider this insight in relation to the metropolitan capitals, asking what the place of Paris, London, or Brussels had in this colonial constellation, which worked despite, not because of, its principles of divided worlds on local and global scales. For lack of space, we did not include cities that were not the seat of an imperial capital (e.g. Hamburg, Oxford, Marseilles, etc.), although we could, without any doubt, apply the analysis to these cities as well. We could also extend the argument to the present day, as colonialism has been decisive in producing both enabling and inhibiting asymmetries, which characterize the global constellation of connections and separations within and between cities until today.

For this section, we limit ourselves to three former colonial metropoles in Europe, which we only briefly touch upon in order to make our point that understanding the colonial city should include how the colonial city is also at work in the European colonial metropoles. We primarily draw on the empirical work of Marc Matera on London and Michael Goebel on Paris as well as on own observations of Brussels, which together underpin our overall argument.[33] In these European colonial towns, similar mechanisms as in Africa were at play. The obvious connection of the colony to the metropole produced unanticipated connections in the metropole, in turn having an impact on the colonies and on colonialism and making the metropolitan city a colonial city as well, being shaped by and dependent upon colonial connections.

Even though in the conceived political order of imperial rule the metropolitan capital is the place where decisions over the colonial world are taken, in reality this conception inevitably shapes the metropole as well. Not only is there a direction and magnitude of force from the decision-making centre to the colonial world, the colonial world also manifests itself in the metropole, bringing and making connections in town as well as redefining these cities as colonial cities – not unlike Dar es Salaam, Kigoma, Bujumbura, or Lubumbashi. This means that colonial imperialism manifests itself in metropolitan spaces in two ways: first, the sites of colonial rule and the self-glorification of imperial posturing in the form of monuments[34] (which we will not discuss in this chapter); and, second, the activities and connections made by and between migrants from across the colonial world.

For interwar Paris, Goebel reconstructs connections between African (especially North African), East Asian, and Latin American migrants and traces the spread and development of anti-imperial, nationalistic, communist, and eventually also fascist ideas within both the Parisian local and transcolonial networks of these migrants. His analysis of the networking and political awakening of students is particularly relevant for our argument. Whereas the French imperial government hoped to instil Francophilia by attracting an intellectual elite to French universities, an unanticipated side effect was the circulation and maturing of anti-imperial ideas. He highlights the importance of networks of relatives or acquaintances, who welcomed newcomers, and even

---

33 Matera, *Black London*; Goebel, *Anti-Imperial Metropolis*.
34 Cf. D. Cannadine, *Ornamentalism: How the British saw their Empire*, Oxford: Oxford University Press, 2001.

more importantly the very dense space where most of them lived and were active. Paris not as a whole but in and around the Quartier latin, and within that neighbourhood the rue Cujas in particular, was at the heart of the globally connected and increasingly anti-imperial student activity. Goebel pays special attention to national student associations from China, Latin America, Vietnam, and North Africa and to how they politically and organizationally inspired each other. Many of the protagonists would become intellectual and political leaders of decolonization and national liberation in their countries of origin (e.g. Ho Chi Minh, Léopold Senghor, Habib Bourguiba, and Deng Xiaoping). He narrows his focus even further by stressing the high concentration of exchange in the house numbers 16 to 20 at rue Cujas, being home to several cheap hotels housing students from all over – what would later be called – the Third World, including French colonies like Vietnam, Congo, and Algeria (although strictly speaking, the latter was not a colony according to the French).[35] The rare interaction with labour migrants, especially from Algeria, indicates that the anti-imperial student networks were an elite affair, despite socialist leanings in many student associations. The Algerian workers stood not only socially apart from the studying elite-in-the-making, but also spatially, living in the Parisian banlieues instead of the Quartier latin.[36]

Locating precisely where a decisive concentration of global connectedness was produced, including paying attention to specific actors and associations, is a fine example of the "portals of globalization" approach introduced at the beginning of this chapter. It should be noted that in this case it was not the French imperial rulers that turned Paris into a "portal of globalization" but rather students from the colonized or otherwise globally peripheral world, who made a specific and relatively small part of Paris into an anti-imperial portal, deeply imbued with colonial connections.

Matera undertakes a similar analysis of imperial London. He particularly reconstructs the networks of people of African descent, including people from West and East African British colonies as well as Afro-Caribbean and African American migrants. Tracing people back to the exact addresses where they lived, with whom they lived or whom they met, and where they could take a shower provides a very precise picture of the social geography and topography of "Black Londoners" in the interwar period. Here as well, the imperial capital was the site where anti-imperial, socialist, and pan-African ideas could develop, and here as well a plethora of later African and Caribbean political

---

35 Goebel, *Anti-Imperial Metropolis*, p. 116.
36 Ibid., p. 145.

leaders came to fruition in the imperial capital (e.g. Jomo Kenyatta, Kwame Nkrumah, and George Padmore). Just like Goebel, Matera localizes the sites where intercolonial connections are concentrated, and identifies Camden Town and the area around Soho and Russell Square as the centre of Black London.[37] Within the imperial metropole, the colonial city – the city based on colonial connections, separations, asymmetries, and contestations – is not everywhere, but it is prominent and relevant in specific spaces within the imperial metropole.

Acknowledging that the metropolitan city is in itself also a colonial city shaped by colonialism and influences from the colonies turns the metropole into an anti-colonial city as well, both ipso facto by thwarting the spatial divide upon which colonialism is premised and because of the anti-imperial networks, organizations, and ideas colonial subjects developed in the metropole. The separations that characterize colonialism were both overcome by intense entanglements between metropolitan spaces, the colonized world, and beyond as well as reproduced in the heart of the metropolitan (capital) cities.

Turning to Brussels, the city from where colonial Lubumbashi (then Elisabethville), Bujumbura (then Usumbura), and for a short period of time Kigoma (1916–1921, under military occupation) were colonially governed, we see extremely little presence of colonial subjects until the very end of the colonial period, when the World Exposition in Brussels in 1958 provided an occasion for Congolese to meet in Brussels, with a noted concentration in the Centre d'Accueil du Personnel Africain in Tervuren.[38] Nevertheless, the city was the focal point of anti-imperialism when the League Against Imperialism held its inauguration conference in Brussels in 1927, having a tremendous impact on the students in Paris rather than in Brussels itself.[39] Brussels only became a colonial city after the colonial period, having its main Congolese neighbourhood, Matonge, almost in the backyard of the royal palace, practically stared at by an equestrian statue of King Leopold II, the notorious founding father of Belgian colonialism. Until today – or increasingly in recent times – colonial space in Belgium, and in Brussels in particular, has been a contentious issue, reflected in red paint ("blood") attacks on royal statues and in campaigns to dedicate a street or square or to erect a statue in honour of Congo's first – and assassinated – prime minister, Patrice Lumumba. Brussels is today more a (post-) colonial city than it was during the colonial period.

---

37 Matera, *Black London*, pp. 6–11.
38 Z.A. Etambala, *De teloorgang van een modelkolonie, Belgisch Congo 1958–1960*, Leuven: Acco, 2008.
39 Goebel, *Anti-Imperial Metropolis*, pp. 136–137.

The spatial layout of African cities shows a continuity with the colonial period, although the population groups inhabiting the respective quarters in town have changed, now reflecting socioeconomic (class) rather than colonial (race) differences. Colonialism left its traces in the street grids but not so much in the people living in the city. In European colonial cities, the opposite is true. In Paris, the Quartier latin no longer has the status it used to have in colonial times. In London, Notting Hill and Brixton rather than Camden Town and Soho are the quarters with a high concentration of people of African descent. And in Brussels, the Congolese quarter of Matonge, remarkably situated between the centre of Belgian political life and Brussels' European district, only came into being from the very end of the colonial period onwards. The spatial logic changed, but the people of African descent or from the former colonies are more present than ever. In short, the colonial city left its spatial imprint on African towns, but it is in the former colonial metropole that the colonial city lives on.

Conclusion

To sum up, focusing on colonial cities in Africa and Europe we saw how the interplay of local and global as well as of connection and disconnection underpins the spatial relations both between and within cities in colonial Africa and Europe. On a more conceptual level, this empirically illustrated attempt to make sense of how urban, colonial, and global relate to each other in colonial cities can also be explained as an analytical exercise organized around the categories "spatial format", "spatial order", and "portal of globalization". "Spatial formats" are widely shared and firmly established abstractions or imaginations of space, which structure spatial practices and perceptions thereof.[40] The common understanding of particular types of spaces as "cities", for instance, presupposes a set of characteristics that are considered to be applicable to all "urban" spaces and that underpin the behaviour of actors in these cities, thus shaping the city after that common understanding. This common understanding – which is both an abstraction of observed, experienced, or perceived realities as well as a strong reference that informs action and shapes the city after its own image – is a spatial format. The spatial format "city" is not a tangible

---

40 Cf. U. Engel, *Regionalismen*, Berlin: De Gruyter, 2018, pp. 3–5; M. Middell, "Raumformate – Überlegungen zu einer unvollständigen Liste historischer Phänomene" (preliminary notes).

place but an abstraction that allows us to group places as different as Brussels, Kigoma, and Dar es Salaam under one umbrella. This is more than just performativity of language or semantics, as the common use of the term "colonial city" for cities in the colonies demonstrates. Signified like this, the labelling is used to distinguish between cities, to ungroup cities like London and Dar es Salaam, based on whether or not they are in areas under colonial administration. Notwithstanding, we demonstrated in this chapter that there is no qualitative difference in spatial practices and connections depending on whether or not a city is situated in the colonies or in the metropole. Colonial city, therefore, is not a spatial format but merely draws our attention to the positionality or the hierarchical position of a given city within a spatial order, to the fundamental asymmetric agenda of colonialism as such.

Spatial order, then, refers to the constellation of spatial formats at a particular time in history. The difference between colonial Lubumbashi, Bujumbura, and Paris is not so much a qualitative difference on the level of the spatial format "city", but instead a different positionality in the constellation of several spatial formats, of which city, territorial state, and empire are probably the most relevant ones in our analysis. In other words, a colonial city is a city within a colonial spatial order. The fact that the colonial city is a category of asymmetric power relations makes it imperative to include cities in the imperial metropole in an analysis of the colonial city. Otherwise, if historians would adopt the strict separation between colonial cities in parts of the world under colonial administration, on the one hand, and colonial cities in parts of the world exercising colonial domination, on the other, they would heedlessly reproduce the essentially asymmetric power relations within the colonial spatial order. The colonial "denial of coevalness"[41] can be the object or outcome of study but must never be an unconsidered premise leading to a research design that reproduces the colonial separations. The differences between the cities under scrutiny are, without a doubt, undeniable, but they are differences of degree, differences of power, differences of positionality within a colonial spatial order; they are not categorical differences between types of cities.

At the cross section or urban spatial format, colonial spatial order, and "portal of globalization", we narrated how relations between and within urban spaces epitomize the colonial city. The historical specificities of colonial cities, asymmetric perspectives on them, and the relations between and within them make differently qualified cities into similarly functioning building blocks within a colonial

---

[41] Cf. J. Fabian, *Time and the Other: How Anthropology makes its Object*, New York: Columbia University Press, 1983.

spatial order. Colonial cities have the combination of urbanness and coloniality, of concentration and separation, of connectedness and disconnection, and of interaction and entanglement between all of these factors in common. The spatial format "city" informed the spatial practices of urbanites as much as the colonial spatial order underpinned the connections and their asymmetries on local and global levels. Yet, the concrete and idiosyncratic processes of spatialization within and between colonial cities lays bare the complicated dynamics of connection and disconnection, of flow and control, and of local interactions and global entanglements that make the global condition as well as the colonial order tangible and relevant.

Colonial cities marked entanglement and separation, which is a crucial factor of colonialism, and they did so in a highly concentrated way, spatially reproducing the colonial entanglements and separations within the areas of each of these towns. These cities continue to do so until today. The colonial period may be over, but the colonial city, as one way to make sense of urban spatializations until the present day, is not.

Holger Weiss
Hamburg, 8 Rothesoodstrasse: From a Global Space to a Non-place

Introduction

Rothesoodstrasse is a small street situated in the Venusberg area, one of Hamburg's former notorious working-class and harbour districts, only a few steps from St. Pauli Piers. Today, the street is lined with residential buildings, some built in the historicist style of the late nineteenth century, others were erected after the Second World War. If you would stop in front of house number 8, you would see a typical façade of a 4-storey post-war building. The anonymity of the site is telling: the historical past is absent and for anyone who does not live in the house, the site is a non-place, a spot with no memory nor meaning. Nevertheless, before the Bomb War and destruction of Hamburg in 1943, a late nineteenth-century building stood at the premises. In 1924, the building had been bought by a certain Albert Walter. This person was one of the leading persons in the Communist agitation and propaganda work among seamen and harbour worker. The address 8 Rothesoodstrasse was the premises for his worldwide communication network. Officially, it housed the Hamburg Port Bureau and International Seamen's Club (or Interclub). After 1930, the headquarters of the International of Seamen and Harbour Workers (ISH) as well as those of the International Trade Union Committee of Negro Workers (ITUCNW), two radical umbrella organizations that had been established by the Red International of Labour Unions (RILU, also known as Profintern), were located in the same building.

The objective of this chapter is to use the site (8 Rothesoodstrasse) as a lens for a spatial analysis of radical transnational solidarity during the late 1920s and early 1930s. Focus will be on activities planned and orchestrated in the building as well as on the possibilities and constraints that affected the operations in Hamburg. A similar approach was used by Constance Margain in her "multiscalar" analysis of the International of Seamen and Harbour Workers. Magain identified three operational levels. At the local level, there were the Interclubs, which were connected at a national level to national trade union sections or Communist parties, while at a global level the Interclubs were linked to the RILU and the Communist International (Comintern) in Moscow.[1]

---

[1] C. Margain, "The International Union of Seamen and Harbour Workers (ISH) 1930–1937: Interclubs and Transnational Aspects", *Twentieth Century Communism* 8 (2015) 8, pp. 133–144.

https://doi.org/10.1515/9783110643008-008

However, the organizational structure of the ISH was much more complicated as it was not only multiscalar but also of a multidimensional character. Established as an umbrella organization for radical, that is to say Communist-controlled or -dominated labour unions, it was the ambition of the ISH to have national sections in all countries in the world. In theory, a national union of maritime workers would cut its ties with the International Transport Workers' Federation (ITF) and vote for joining the ISH. In praxis, however, apart from the Danish stokers' union, this was unrealistic as the Communists never constituted a majority in the various national unions, and the leadership of the unions was usually firmly in the hands of the reformist, socialist, and/or syndicalist majority. Also, the Interclubs were not planned to be part of the national unions but to be under operational surveillance of the ISH Secretariat in Hamburg. Thus, the operations of the Communists among seamen and harbour workers applied a dual structure. The national sections were to establish themselves as counterparts to the reformist/socialist/syndicalist-dominated unions in each country. Their central unit for agitation and propaganda were the Communist-led cells on board the ships and in the harbours. On the other hand, the Interclubs, as will be outlined in the first part of the chapter, were to focus on work among foreign seamen.[2]

A multiscalar analysis of the activities that evolved from 8 Rothesoodstrasse does not necessarily include the national level. This is due to fact that the headquarters of the German national section, the Einheitsverband der Seefahrer, Hafenarbeiter und Binnenschiffer, was not located at 8 Rothesoodstrasse but at 19/20 Kohlhöfen in the Gängeviertel quarters, close to the Hamburg headquarters of the German Communist Party. The Einheitsverband, in turn, was the maritime unit of the German Revolutionary Trade Union Opposition (Revolutionäre Gewerkschaftsopposition, RGO). Consequently, the RGO and, by extension, the German Communist Party tried as much as possible to monitor and supervise the activities of the Einheitsverband, especially via the Communist faction within the union. However, influencing and steering trade union activities among seamen and harbour workers through the Party was never an easy task, especially due to the usually earlier syndicalist background of seamen. Consequently, the leadership of the Einheitsverband, especially its leader Ernst Wollweber, highlighted their independence from the Party and the RGO by consolidating

---

[2] H. Weiss, "The International of Seamen and Harbour Workers – A Radical Global Labour Union of the Waterfront or a Subversive World-Wide Web?", in: H. Weiss (ed.), *International Communism and Transnational Solidarity: Radical Networks, Mass Movements and Global Politics, 1919–1939*, Leiden: Brill, 2017, pp. 256–317.

a political space of their own.³ Thus, as will be discussed in the second part of the chapter, the leadership at the ISH Secretariat, especially ISH President George Hardy and ISH Secretary Albert Walter, had little means at their disposal to interfere in the activities of the national sections, including the German one.

Nevertheless, as will be discussed in the third part of the chapter, 8 Rothesoodstrasse emerged as a global space not least through the activities of the ISH Secretariat and the International Trade Union Committee of Negro Workers. In theory, the two units operated independently of each other. In praxis, their activities overlapped, which would result in friction between the leading figures of the two units. Both organizations operated within two circuits: the first one being in control of the RILU and Comintern apparatus based in Moscow and Berlin, and the second one being the global communication network, which each of the organizations was capable of establishing and in turn tried to monitor and direct from its headquarters in Hamburg. Two parallel organizational hierarchies existed: in the first circuit, the ISH and the ITUCNW were at the bottom of the of the RILU/Comintern Apparatus, whereas in the second circuit, the secretariats of both organizations were at the centre of their respective global networks.

The theoretical perspective for analysing 8 Rothesoodstrasse as a site of "the global in the local-cum-local in the global" is inspired by a modified territories (T), places (P), scales (S), and networks (N) framework.⁴ The activities in the building targeted and operated at *places* and *scales*. The Interclub focused on foreign seamen visiting Hamburg, thus the activists of the Club had to visit the ships in the harbour and tried to invite crew members to come to the Club. The ISH sought to coordinate international campaigns in support of national strikes, whereas the ITUCNW envisioned itself as the spearhead of a radical, anti-colonial, and anti-imperialist movement for "black toilers" in the African Atlantic. Both the ISH and the ITUCNW operated as a *network* between individuals rather than groups or organizations. Last, but not least, *territory* was both a constraint as well as an opportunity. Communist and anti-colonial activities were closely monitored if not prohibited by national governments. In the Hamburg area, paramilitary units of

---

3 L. Eiber, *Arbeiter und Arbeiterbewegung in der Hansestadt Hamburg in den Jahren 1929 bis 1939 – Werftarbeiter, Hafenarbeiter und Seeleute: Konformität, Opposition, Widerstand*, Frankfurt/Main: Peter Lang, 2000, pp. 186–188.

4 See B. Jessop, N. Brenner and M.R. Jones, "Theorizing Socio-spatial Relations", *Environment and Planning D: Society and Space* 26 (2008) 3, pp. 389–401. Equally inspiring are the discussion about "moderate relationalism" and "phase space" in M. Jones, "Phase Space: Geography, Relational Thinking, and Beyond", *Progress in Human Geography* 33 (2009) 4, pp. 487–506.

the Communists fought with those of the Social Democrats or the National Socialists and the police, usually resulting in bloody clashes, among others the "Battle at the Round Mountain" (Schlacht am Runden Berge) in Geesthacht in 1927 or the "Bloody Sunday" in Altona in 1932.[5] In some of the working-class areas of Hamburg, such as the Gängeviertel of Hamburg Neustadt, Barmbek, or Schiffbek, the Communists controlled the local political space and were able to create "free-zones" dominated by the Party and its organizations.[6] Depicted as "Little Moscows" and known for their "small-place communism and counter-communities", they existed in several places in inter-war Western Europe.[7]

Background: The "Third Period" and the "Class-Against-Class" Tactic

The International of Seamen and Harbour Workers was a short-lived transnational radical umbrella organization for Communist-dominated/-controlled trade unions of maritime transport workers established in 1930 during the "Third Period" of Comintern. Officially presented as a radical and independent platform, the ISH was in reality a masked continuation of the Comintern's mari-time section, the International Propaganda and Action Committee of Transport Workers (IPAC Transport, originally established as the International Propaganda Committee of Transport Workers [IPC Transport] in 1922 and reorganized and renamed in 1928), and was financed through subsidies from Moscow. Starting with the Fourth World Congress of the RILU in July 1928, the Comintern shifted to the "Class-Against-Class" tactic, which was officially proclaimed at the Sixth World Congress of the Comintern in August 1928. The Comintern's reading of the current situation was that the class struggle was entering a new phase, and a new wave of revolutionary activity was expected. RILU General Secretary Alexander

---

5 W-R. Busch (ed.), *"Klein-Moskau" – Geesthacht 1919–1933*, Münster: Lit Verlag, 1999; J. C. Häberlein, "Scope for Agency and Political Options: The German Working-Class Movement and the Rise of Nazism", *Politics, Religion & Ideology* 14 (2013) 3, pp. 377–394.
6 E. Pape and L. Barghorn, "'Klein Moskau wurde die Gegend genannt' – Nachbarschaft und Politik im Hamburger Gängeviertel", pp. 1–49, http://asg-hh.de/download.html?&filename=g__ngeviertel_perfekt.pdf (accessed 3 December 2018).
7 A. Knotter, "'Little Moscows' in Western Europe: The Ecology of Small-Place Communism", *International Review of Social History* 56 (2011) 3, pp. 475–510; K. Morgan, "Bastions, Black Spots and Other Variations in and Beyond the Specificities of the Little Moscow", *Twentieth Century Communism* 5 (2013) 5, pp. 193–209.

Lozovsky called for a rapid formation of red unions and a break with mainstream unions that were blocking the worker's path to revolutionary consciousness.[8]

The change in strategy of the RILU signalled the break with the Communists' previous attempts to cooperate with reformist elements within the trade unions. The ISH's aim was to challenge the hegemony of the International Transport Workers' Federation as well as the various national waterfront labour unions. The rationale behind this policy was the belief in Moscow that the former policy of a "unity front from below", where the Communists had formed so-called revolutionary opposition groups within labour unions dominated by the Social Democrats, had to be replaced with a new approach. The main idea was to transform existing opposition groups into independent radical unions and to establish independent radical platforms for these organizations. This new strategy focused on establishing revolutionary trade unions, taking an extremely hostile stance towards reformist unions and the Social Democratic parties, branding them as "social fascists".[9]

However, as Dieter Nelles outlines in his study on the ITF, work among the maritime transport workers was difficult, not least due to regulations about when to strike and their long period at sea when they were cut off from organized labour unions. Another handicap was that both Social Democratic and Communist parties and labour leaders regarded the waterfront as a secondary field of work – in sheer numbers, the maritime workers constituted but a small portion of the work force.[10] Also, as Peter Cole and David Featherstone underline, apart from the Marine Transport Workers Industrial Union, the official maritime trade unions in the USA, Britain, and elsewhere were preominantly exclusionary and segregationist.[11] Similar calls for multiracial spaces and organizations by ISH activists faced similar problems in the early 1930s.[12]

---

8 See J. Manley, "Moscow Rules? 'Red' Unionism and 'Class Against Class' in Britain, Canada and the United States, 1928–1935", *Labour/Le Travail* 56 (2005), p. 23; R. Tosstorff, *Profintern: Die Rote Gewerkschaftsinternationale 1920–1937*, Paderborn: Schoenigh, 2004.
9 Tosstorff, *Profintern*, pp. 657–661.
10 D. Nelles, *Widerstand und internationale Solidarität: Die Internationale Transportarbeiter-Föderation (ITF) im Widerstand gegen den Nationalsozialismus*, Essen: Klartext-Verlag, 2001; on the ITF, see B. Reinalda (ed.), *The International Transport-Workers Federation 1914–1945: The Edo Fimmen Years*, Amsterdam: Stichting beheer IISG, 1997.
11 See P. Cole, *Wobblies on the Waterfront: Interracial Unionism in Progressive-Era Philadelphia*, Champaign: University of Illinois Press, 2007; D. Featherstone, *Resistance, Space and Political Identities: The Making of Counter-Global Networks*, Hoboken: Wiley-Blackwell, 2008, pp. 124–125.
12 See also D. Featherstone, "Maritime Labour and Subaltern Geographies of Internationalism: Black Internationalist Seafarers' Organising in the Interwar Period", *Political Geography* 49 (2015), pp. 7–16; for a critical discussion on local reactions of the instructions from Moscow, see J.C.

Local Nodes in a Global Network: The International Seamen's Clubs

The first International Seamen's Club was established in Leningrad in 1922. It was located at 15 Prospect Ogorodnikova and solely directed its activities towards foreign seamen that arrived at the port. The Interclub was located in an old palace of the Russian nobility, surrounded by a large garden. Although the interior of the palace was a witness of its former grandeur, it had been transformed into a political space by the Bolsheviks by placing a large bronze statue of Lenin in the vestibule. Large signposts on the doors oriented a visiting seaman to a specific section, such as the German, French, Anglo-American, Scandinavian, or Colonial, which were in charge of work among various national seamen. Other rooms contained a library, a gym, and a large dining hall.[13] One year later, a similar club was established in Vladivostok, followed by others in most major Soviet ports.

However, as direct connections with Soviet Russia were limited during the early part of the 1920s and the Soviet Interclubs had been branded by Western shipowners and government authorities as sources of the "Bolshevik pest", the International Propaganda Committee of Transport Workers decided to move its centre of activity among seamen and harbour workers to Hamburg and other ports where Communist activities were legal and to establish Port Bureaus, which were to serve as centres for communication and information.[14] The plan was to establish centres in the most imporant ports of the world, that is to say in New York, San Francisco, Sydney, Liverpool, Hamburg, Buenos Aires, and Marseilles.[15] The person in charge of this operation was Albert Walter, an ex-seaman who was one of the leaders of the German maritime union, the Deutscher Schiffahrtsbund, which had joined the RILU in 1922.[16] Walter was thereafter commissioned by RILU President Alexander Losovsky to

---

Häberlein, "Between Global Aspirations and Local Realities: The Global Dimensions of Interwar Communism", *Journal of Global History* 7 (2012) 3, pp. 415–437.
13 "Eröffnung des Internationalen Seemannsklubs in Leningrad, Deutsche Botschaft", 8.6.1932, German Federal Archives, Berlin-Lichterfelde, R1501/20224, fol. 126.
14 "The Most Urgent Task of the International Committee of Propaganda of the Transport Workers", no date (ca. 1921), Russian State Archive of Social and Political History, Moscow, 534/5/149, fol. 61–63.
15 T. Barker, "Proposition for Marine Transport Bureaus", no date (ca. 1921), Russian State Archive of Social and Political History, 534/5/149, fol. 96–97.
16 H. Weber and Andreas H., "Walter, Albert Paul", in: H. Weber and A. Herbst, *Deutsche Kommunisten: Biographisches Handbuch 1918 bis 1945*, Berlin: Dietz-Verlag, 2008, p. 988.

develop the IPC Transport into a global platform.[17] This was achieved through Walter's second unit, the International Port Bureaus. In 1924, he bought a house at 8 Rothesoodstrasse, close to Hamburg's waterfront, which became the headquarters of the Hamburg Port Bureau. Officially, Port Bureau activities were ca-mouflaged under the guise of visiting locales for harbour workers and visiting seamen of the Interclub. From here, he developed his global communication network.[18] According to an advertisement in the Danish journal *Laternen*, six Interclubs existed outside the Soviet Union in 1927, namely in Hamburg, Bordeaux, Marseilles, Copenhagen, Rotterdam, and New York.[19] In early 1930, already 23 Interclubs existed in various ports outside the Soviet Union,[20] followed by 11 new clubs established in the USA during the second half of the year.[21]

The rationale of an Interclub was its legal and official status. An Interclub could only be established in a location if Communist activity had not been banned and declared illegal by the national authorities. Consequently, a location that was constantly raided by the police or closed by the local authorities was of little value. Of similar importance was the possibility for Communist activity in the maritime labour unions. Therefore, the objective of the International Propaganda Committee of Transport Workers was to establish International Port Bureaus, which, together with the Interclubs, were to serve as centres for Communist agitation and propaganda among seamen and harbour workers. In addition, their task was to combat the "false" message of the Christian Seamen's Homes and Missions and Reformist leadership of the maritime unions as well as to support the maritime workers in their struggle for better working conditions and salaries.[22] Objectives were publicized in magazines and leaflets and were thus known to both the target groups as well as the authorities. For example, the Interclub in Copenhagen published an advertisement in its magazine, *Laternen*, calling class-conscious seamen to visit the Interclub instead of the Christian Seamen's Missions.[23] The New York Interclub was strategically located close to the Seamen's

---

[17] H. Knüfken, *Von Kiel bis Leningrad: Erinnerungen eines revolutionären Matrosen von 1917 bis 1930*, Berlin: BasisDruck, 2008, pp. 210–211.
[18] J. Valtin, *Out of the Night*, New York: Alliance Book Corporation, 1941, pp. 38–39, 103–104.
[19] See list of Interclubs in *Laternen* 2 (1927).
[20] "Abschrift: Internationaler Seemannsklub in/Adressen der Internationalen Seemannsklubs", no date (ca. 1930), German Federal Archives, Berlin-Lichterfelde, R1501/20224, fol. 7.
[21] V.L. Pedersen, "George Mink, the Marine Workers Industrial Union, and the Comintern in America", *Labor History* 41 (2000) 3, p. 312.
[22] "Hampurin merimiesklubi 10-vuotias", *Majakka* 6 (1932), p. 21.
[23] *Laternen* 2 (1927) 6.

Church Institute.[24] Leaflets distributed in the latter premises invited the seamen to visit the Interclub: "DONT [sic] EAT IN DIRTY STEW POT JOINTS / THE GRUB IS BAD ENOUGH ABOARD SHIP / TRY THE CLEANEST PLACE ON SOUTH ST. INTERNATIONAL SEAMEN'S CLUB RESTAURANT."[25]

The Western authorites, the reformist, syndicalist, and Catholic labour unions, as well as the shipowners and Christian Seamen's Missions regarded the Interclubs as dangerous "counter spaces" that radicalized seamen and lured them to adopt the Communist credo. Press cuttings collected by the German police testify to the fear of these radical establishments or "free spaces", which neither the authories, the union leadership, nor the Christian mission were able to control. The Catholic newspaper *Germania* warned its readers that the Interclubs were perilous sites where seamen were radicalized and revolutionized.[26] The Industrial Workers of the World's magazine *Marine Worker* branded the Interclubs as "scratch-a-way-Inn" that were used by the Communists to "lure penniless seamen, especially in the winter months, to come in and partake of watery stew and political propaganda."[27] The Australian government authorities as well as the national seamen's union viewed the Interclubs with suspicion and regarded them to be nothing less than the clandestine agitation centres of the RILU: "The Club in Sydney was full of Communist literature and prominence is given to a photograph of Lenin."[28] In the USA, the syndicalist *Seamen's Journal* warned its readership that the only task of the Interclubs was "to make use of the world's seamen as the shock troops for communism."[29]

Each Interclub contained a library with Communist and radical newspapers and journals on display as well as a restaurant or bar where cheap food was served. During the evening, the Interclub staged theatre or film shows or organized other cultural events.[30] More important was its function as a rallying point for radical seamen and Communist agitators. According to a report sent to the Swedish secret service, the Port Bureaus and Interclubs had three main tasks: to agitate among seamen, to serve as gateways for illegal Communist

---

[24] S. Schwartz, *Brotherhood of the Sea: A History of the Sailors' Union of the Pacific, 1885– 1985*, New Brunswick: Transaction Books, 1986, p. 70.
[25] Seamen's Church Institute, "Hospital Flyer", 2 March 1933, *Seamen's Church Institute Digital Archives*, http://seamenschurch-archives.org/sci/items/show/1828
[26] "Sowjetpropaganda auf dem Seewege", *Germania* 5, 7 January 1931.
[27] *Marine Worker*, 15 Ocotber 1928, quoted in Schwartz, *Brotherhood of the Sea*, p. 71.
[28] *Canberra Times*, 3 May 1928.
[29] *Seamen's Journal*, September 1928, quoted in Bruce Nelson, *Workers on the Waterfront: Seamen, Longshoremen, and Unionism in the 1930s*, Champaign: University of Illinois Press 1990, p. 76.
[30] Knüfken, *Von Kiel bis Leningrad*, pp. 211–212.

literature, and to provide a safe place for the meetings of the international propaganda committees.[31]

The establishment of the ISH in October 1930 resulted in a reorgaization of the activities of the Interclubs and Port Bureaus. The former agitation and propaganda centres of IPAC Transport were to be transformed and developed into the "political-organizational centres" of seamen and harbour workers. Their main task was mass agitation for political campaigns to strengthen the global outreach of the ISH.[32] The Interclubs were to be monitored and directed by the ISH Secretariat as a means to further effectivate and coordinate their work.[33] In addition, a special committee ("bureau") at the ISH Secretariat in Hamburg was put in charge to produce information and propaganda material for the Interclubs, such as the *ISH Information Bulletin*, which was published in several languages and directed at the fuctionaries of the Interclubs.[34] Every Interclub was to be divided into national sections, each of them to concentrate on work among seamen from their home countries or language group.[35] In praxis, however, only the larger Interclubs listed several sections.

The Hamburg Interclub: Place, Network, and Territory

Albert Walter was successful in establishing a global communication network by making use of the Hamburg Interclub. His strategy was to establish small cells onboard ships, which could take care of the illegal transportation of printed agitation and propaganda material, of the illegal transfer of cash

---

[31] "Internationella hamnbyråer", 1 November 1928, Swedish National Archives, Stockholm, HP 1459 32D.
[32] "Draft Decision: Basic Principles" (of the work of the ISH), no date (ca. 1930), Russian State Archive of Social and Political History, Moscow, 534/5/219, fol. 81–84.
[33] "An alle Interclubs und sämtliche angeschlossene Organisationen" (ISH instructions), 4 April 1931, Russian State Archive of Social and Political History, Moscow, 534/5/221, fol. 1–4; "Resolution über die Tätigkeit des Hamburger Internationalen Klubs", no date, 15 April 1931, Russian State Archive of Social and Political History, Moscow, 534/5/220, fol. 155–161; "Decisions of the II. Plenary Session of the Executive Committee of the ISH on the Activity and Tasks of the International Seamen's Clubs", September 1931, Russian State Archive of Social and Political History, Moscow, 534/5/224, fol. 191–203.
[34] "Seeleute und Hafenarbeiter hissen die rote Fahne!", *Rotes Gewerkschafts-Bulletin (R.G.B.)* 68 (special issue), 18 October 1930, German Federal Archives, Berlin-Lichterfelde, R1501/20224, fol. 19.
[35] "Internationale Seemannsklubs", *Internationale Gewerkschafts-Pressekorrespondenz* 76, 8 October 1931, p. 7; "Hampurin Merimiesklubi 10-vuotias", *Majakka* 6 (1932), p. 21.

subsidies to parties and unions, as well as of the hiding of stowaways, including couriers and emissaries. This was achieved by the so-called Hamburg method. The core idea was to establish a personal contact between an agitator and a seaman when a new ship arrived in Hamburg. A small group of Interclub functionaries and harbour activists boarded a ship in order to distribute leaflets and pamphlets among the crew. In addition, the crew members were invited to come to the Interclub and participate in its evening programmes. Most importantly, a report was written after every visit, listing reliable contacts and identifying potential partners for future cooperation. The names of individuals, cells, and ships were thereafter collected in a catalogue. This database, which already by the late 1920s included hundreds of individual seamen and ships, was the core of Albert Walter's communication network.[36] However, as Peter Huber and Niels Erik Rosenfeldt emphasize in their work, the core unit directing the Comintern's clandestine communication networks was its International Communications Office (OMS), including the operations of the courier service and the transfer of money to parties.[37] Consequently, Walter's ships units were but cogs in a larger apparatus over which he and his bureau in Hamburg had no influence. Instead, the nodal point was the OMS office in Berlin.

The Hamburg Interclub was a contested territory. On the one hand, its premises were controlled by the functionaries of the club, who, in turn, had to deliver monthly reports on their activities to Walter. Apart from organizing the evening programme at the club and running the restaurant, the person in charge of the club was also responsible for the financial balance of the activities. Nevertheless, the main objective was to create an "open space" for foreign seamen and local visitors, one that was not controlled by "bourgeoise" and "capitalist" autorities. On the other hand, as the Communists in Germany were at loggerheads not only with the local state and police authorities but also Social Democratic and National Socialist organizations, the Interclub became a contested territory. A rather common feature were fist fights in the restaurant if Nazi finks tried to interrupt a meeting at the club, which usually resulted in the arrival of a police commando to calm down the situation. In general, however, police raids were politically sanctioned and occurred either for internal or

---

36 Eiber, *Arbeiter und Arbeiterbewegung*, p. 186.
37 P. Huber, "The Cadre Department, the OMS and the 'Dimitrov' and 'Manuil'sky' Secretariats during the Phase of Terror", in: M. Narinsky and J. Rojahn (eds.), *Centre and Periphery: The History of the Comintern in Light of New Documents*, Amsterdam: International Institute of Social History, 1996, p. 129; N.E. Rosenfeldt, *The "Special" World: Stalin's Power Apparatus and the Soviet System's Secret Structures of Communication, I–II*, Copenhagen: Museum Tusculanum Press, 2009.

exteral reasons. Seamen and dockers' strikes were accompanied by police raids against 8 Rothesoodstrasse as both the shipowners and the bourgeoise politicians (rightly) claimed that they were organized by the Interclub. Occasionally, foreign authorities put pressure on German authorities for their "lax" attitude towards Communist agitation and propaganda orchestrated by international Communist agencies based in Germany, notably the Port Bureau and Interclub in Hamburg. However, as long as Communist activities were legal in Germany, a police raid and closure of the Interclub was seldom a protracted affair.[38]

One who was not impressed with the work in Hamburg was ISH President George Hardy. Despite some early successes in the reorganization of the Interclub, Hardy rapidly became dissatisfied with the conditions in Hamburg. Although being one of the largest ports in the world, Hamburg had, according to Hardy, several severe disadvantages. The first one was that very few colonial seamen called at Hamburg and none of them had the port as his place of residence. The second hindrance was tied to the first: few British, Dutch, and American ships called at Hamburg and, among the Scandinavians, the Norwegian merchant fleet – which itself was one of the largest in the world during the early 1930s – called in at British rather than at German ports. Hamburg, Hardy reasoned, was not the ideal hub for the ISH and therefore proposed that ISH headquarters be moved to London.[39] However, neither the leadership of the ISH nor the RILU supported his plan. The main reason for the negative decision was strategic: the Interclub in London was not functioning very well and the national section of the ISH in the United Kingdom, the Seamen's Minority Movement, was in constant disarray and had a chronic lack of funding.[40]

Transnational Work of the Hamburg Interclub

Starting in 1924, the Hamburg Interclub focused on agitation and propaganda work among domestic as well as foreign seamen. One of its prime target groups

---

38 For vivid descriptions about police raids against the Interclub, see Valtin, *Out of the Night*. Police raids were often reported in the internal reports, for example the raid on 1 February 1930, from: "Bericht Februar 1930" (Internationales Hafenbüro für Seeleute, Hamburg), Russian State Archive of Social and Political History, Moscow, 534/5/216, fol. 14–15.
39 "Hardy to Lozovsky, Hamburg", 30 March 1931, 534/5/220, fol. 139–142.
40 "The Situation, the Work and the Tasks of the ISH – Resolution on the Report of Comrade Hardy and Walter", 12 July 1931, Russian State Archive of Social and Political History, Moscow, 534/5/221, fol. 114–123.

were seamen onboard Scandinavian freighters. The reason for this were obvious: Communist activities were legal in the Scandinavian countries but the trade fleet of the Scandinavian countries, especially the Norwegian one, seldom called at their home ports. Thus, work among Scandinavian seamen had to be conducted outside Scandinavia, and Hamburg was one of the major ports for Scandinavian shipping. The utlimate task of the Scandinavian section of the Hamburg Interclub was to establish a transnational link between the Scandinavian seamen and their maritime labour unions at home.[41] Therefore, members of the section were usually functionaries who had been sent to Hamburg from the Communist faction of a Danish, Norwegian, or Swedish maritime union.

The first person in charge of the Scandinavian section was the Norwegian Arthur Samsing, whose main task was to organize a local unit of the Communist faction of Norsk Matros- og Fyrbøterunionen, the Norwegian seamen's union, at the Interclub. This was of strategic importance as the Norwegian trade fleet was the fourth largest in the world during the 1920s and Norwegian ships sailed all over the world. Samsing's activities ended abruptly after a police raid on the Interclub in 1929, resulting in his expulsion from Germany.[42] He was replaced by two Norwegians, Fred Nilssen and Leif O. Foss. Much to the dismay of the functionaries, work among Norwegian seamen was challenging and provided little reward; many of them were unemployed and stranded in Hamburg and were most of the time drunk.[43] Another drawback was Hamburg's peripheral position as a stopover for Norwegian freighters; it was not the German harbour but those in the British Isles that were the central places for agitation and propaganda among Norwegian seamen.[44] This was also highlighted by George Hardy in his critique of work among foreign seamen in Hamburg and his proposal to move the centre of activities to London.[45] Consequently, after the reorganization of the Hamburg Interclub in 1931, the Scandinavian section broadened its activities and focused on work among seamen from all Scandinavian countries.[46]

---

41 "Army Counter Intelligence Corps (CIC) Interrogation Report (R-G44-50), Richard Krebs", 1950, National Archives, Washington DC, FO 10501, fol. 6, 52.
42 A. Samsing, *Autobiography*, Leningrad, 10 February1935, Russian State Archive of Social and Political History, Moscow, 495/247/540, fol. 50–51.
43 "Bericht August-September 1930" (Internationales Hafenbüro für Seeleute, Hamburg), Russian State Archive of Social and Political History, Moscow, 534/5/216, fol. 67–69.
44 "Bericht März 1930" (Internationales Hafenbüro für Seeleute, Hamburg), Russian State Archive of Social and Political History, Moscow, 534/5/216, fol. 17–18.
45 "Hardy to Lozovsky", fol. 139–142.
46 "Resolution über die Tätigkeit des Hamburger Internationalen Klubs", no date (ca. 1931), Russian State Archive of Social and Political History, Moscow, 534/5/220, fol. 159.

The reorganization of work at the Interclub in 1931 also resulted in the establishment of two new sections: a Finnish and a Baltic one. Little is known about their activities apart from each publishing a monthly journal, *Majakka* in Finnish and *Majakas* in Estonian. Agitation and propaganda work among seamen from Finland and the Baltic countries was complicated as Communist activities were illegal in these countries. Communist activities were underground and clandestine operations or were conducted under the guise of legal organizations. The journals produced at the Interclub therefore served as the main agitation and propaganda vehicles; visiting seamen were enlisted as liaisons and couriers who tried to disseminate the journals in their home countries.[47]

Work among so-called colonial seamen was of equal strategic importance. Initially, the main focus was on Chinese and Japanese seamen.[48] The key person was Comrade Leo, or Liao Chenghzi, who was in charge of the work among Chinese seamen from 1928 to 1932. His main task was to produce Communist leaflets in Chinese and to develop an international Communist network between China and European port cities.[49] At first, he was quite successful and Albert Walter boasted in his communication to Moscow that numerous new cells had been established and direct communications had been secured with China.[50] However, the impact was superficial and fragile, and the Communist impact on Chinese seamen remained limited, with the majority sticking to a mixture of nationalist and anti-colonial sentiments.[51] In January 1931, Liao started to cooperate with the African-American trade union functionary James W. Ford. He had been sent from Moscow to establish the secretariat of the International Trade Union Committee of Negro Workers (see part below on "Between Two Circuits: The ITUCNW"). He was ordered to cooperate with Albert Walter, the ISH, and the Interclub and was immediately assigned by Walter to work among African and Caribbean seamen. Ford was rather successful and half a year later he had already been able to establish cells on more than a dozen ships. However, Ford was critical of the workload; instead of concentrating on his work as ITUCNW secretary, he spent most of his time assisting the

---

47 J. Mihkelsen, "Sjöfolket i Estland", *Merimies – Sjömannen* 4 (1935), pp. 12–13.
48 "Jahresbericht 1930" (Internationales Hafenbüro für Seeleute, Hamburg), Russian State Archive of Social and Political History, Moscow, 534/5/216, fol. 77–87.
49 Lars Amenda, "Between Southern China and the North Sea: Maritime Labour and Chinese Migration in Continental Europe, 1890–1950", in: Sylvia Hahn and Stan Nadel (eds.), *Asian Migrants in Europe: Transcultural Connections*, Göttingen: V&R Unipress, 2014, p. 69.
50 "Bericht über die Arbeit unter den chinesischen Seeleuten" (1–31 March1930 & 3–28 April 1930), April 1930, Russian State Archive of Social and Political History, Moscow, 534/5/216, fol. 36, 37.
51 Amenda, "Between Southern China", p. 69.

Interclub in its agitation and propaganda work. Ford's poignant criticism reached Moscow and resulted in a reorganization of work in the colonial section in September 1931. Thereafter, the Interclub, together with the Einheitsverein, focused on the Indian and Chinese seamen, whereas the organization of African and Caribbean seamen was the joint responsibility of the Interclub and the ITUCNW.[52]

Aspiring to Become a Global Actor: The ISH Secretariat

Established in late 1930, the ISH Secretariat had its office in rooms adjoining the Interclub at 8 Rothesoodstrasse and initially consisted of three members. George Hardy, chair, was editor of the *ISH Information Bulletin* as well as in charge of the contacts with the anglophone countries, India, and the Far East. Albert Walter, secretary, was in charge of the technical apparatus as well as work in the Nordic, Baltic, and German-speaking countries. The third member, Auguste Dumay, was in charge of connections with France, the Iberian and Mediterrannean countries, as well as work in the French colonies in Africa and mandated territories in the Near East and in Latin America.[53] A reorganization of work at the headquarters in Hamburg followed sometime during the first half of 1931. Hardy was transferred to the United Kingdom and Dumay to France while Walter took over the secretariat in Hamburg. In addition, a new parallel unit was established, the so-called "illegal secretariat", which was manned by Comrade Adolf.[54] The person was Alfred Bem (alias Adolf Shelley), sent by Moscow to monitor the activities of the ISH (legal) Secretariat of Albert Walter. Strategically, Shelley's secret office was located in an (unknown) location in Hamburg.[55]

---

[52] "Decisions of the II Plenary Session of the Executive Committee of the ISH on the Activity and Tasks of the International Seamen's Clubs", September 1931, Russian State Archive of Social and Political History, Moscow, 534/5/224, fol. 197–198.
[53] "Duties and Tasks of Secretariat Members", 17 March 1931, Russian State Archive of Social and Political History, Moscow, 534/5/220, fol. 128–129.
[54] See the correspondence between "Henry" (Luigi Polano) and Adolf Shelley, Russian State Archive of Social and Political History, Moscow, 534/5/221, fol. 162–174.
[55] "CIC interrogation report, Richard Krebs", fol. 2; R. Jensen, *En omtumlet tilværelse*, Copenhagen: Fremad, 1957, p. 103.

In accordance with the hierarchical rules of the Comintern Apparatus, the various national units and its activities were to be coordinated, monitored, and controlled by the centre. This was to be achieved by sending written instructions by couriers, by receiving written monthly reports on activities, and by visits of national functionaries to the ISH headquarters. "Travelling instructors" were sent to the national sections when they were to be reorganized or in order to coordinate actions during a national strike. For example, Comrade Henry (Luigi Polano) was sent on a mission to Norway and Sweden in May 1931 with a mandate to co-manage the strike of the dockworkers in Oslo.[56]

One of the ISH's main structural problems was its dual position as both an independent and a Communist-controlled union. Its links to the Party apparatus were generally weak; this was not only the case in Hamburg but also characterized the relationship between the Party and the various national ISH sections throughout the world. While most, if not all, of the leading comrades were party members, the majority of the rank-and-file were syndicalists rather than Communists. At times, in Hamburg, the ISH was even in disagreement with other Communist organizations, such as the Red Marine or even the local branch of the German Communist Party. On the other hand, the independent position of the organization was advantageous from a strategic and tactical perspective; it was not controlled by the local German Communist Party or the German Revolutionary Trade Union Opposition apparatus in Hamburg and neither were its sections taking any directives from the leadserhip of either the national parties or the Red International of Labour Unions. Nevertheless, the weak relationship between the ISH and both its sections and the Party was time and again considered to be a handicap, especially when the ISH Secretariat tried to direct affairs in the sections. If Hamburg failed to influence the affairs of one section, ISH Secretary Walter tried to ask the Party leadership to interfere – sometimes successfully but more often not and the only avenue left was to ask the RILU and Comintern Apparatus to intervene and settle the case.

Another challenge for communication – and control – was language. Only German and English were in use at the ISH Secretariat and the non-German-speaking and non-English-speaking sections continuously complained about not receiving material in Spanish, Portuguese, or French, or about having trouble in translating German and English directives. Similarly, the ISH headquarters was in trouble when receiving messages and reports from its sections – it took days if not weeks to have them translated into German and vice versa. For Adolf Shelley

---

56 "Arbeitsbericht des Sekretariats der ISH", Hamburg, 16 June 1931, Russian State Archive of Social and Political History, Moscow, 534/5/221, fol. 186.

this was a major problem, and he urged Moscow to find a solution to it and declared, "we should not be a German-English International!"[57]

A Global Moment: The 1932 ISH World Congress

The visible manifestation of any organization aspiring to be a global player is to organize a world congress. Already the terminology used – world congress – distinuishes the event from a local, regional, or national affair. Calling for a world congress is to make a territorial claim and statement: representatives from all over the world are summoned to a particular location for a common, unifying goal. This was also the case for the ISH. Although it had been established as an outcome of an international summit at the Hamburg Interclub in October 1930, it was to be a provisional organization to be officially established at a future world congress. The first plan was to arrange the congress in Copenhagen but due to the negative attitude of the Danish authorities, a new place had to be found for the venue. The Hamburg Interclub was out of question: its meeting hall was too small for the congress. In addition, the police authorities vetoed a Communist summit to be organized in the city. Eventually, the organizers managed to convince the local authorities in Altona, one of Hamburg's suburbs, but administratively part of Prussia, to give backing to the new congress venue.[58] Despite police harassment and all sorts of difficulties, some 173 delegates from 30 nations finally made it to Altona, where the congress was convened 21–24 May 1932.[59]

A central theme discussed at the plenary sessions concerned living conditions onboard and demands for seven-hour working days, unjust working conditions, and demands for a fair salary. Another theme was the right to form unions and the right to strike onboard ships, their techniques, and under what circumstances one was to pursue a certain tactic. A third general theme was what positions the seamen were to take in a future conflict or even war; a fourth theme was the potential of the radicals to gain more influence in unions that were controlled by the Social Democrats.[60] In public, the congress downplayed the revolutionary aim of

---

57 "Letter from Adolf (Shelley) to 'Werte Genossen'", Hamburg, 24 November 1931, Russian State Archive of Social and Political History, Moscow, 534/5/223, fol. 88.
58 L. Braun, "Über den Kongress der Seeleute", 2 June 1932, Russian State Archive of Social and Political History, Moscow, 534/4/405, fol. 241–242.
59 "Kongress der ISH", Russian State Archive of Social and Political History, Moscow, 534/5/232, fol. 75–76.
60 Eiber, *Arbeiter und Arbeiterbewegung*, pp. 183–184.

the ISH and the organizers were strictly ordered to make sure that the vocabulary of the proclamations and presentations did not arouse the suspicion of the police.[61] On the other hand, far away from the public, meetings and conferences of various commissions were held behind the scenes, in which only the inner circle of the Communists and trusted activists participated.[62]

Between Two Circuits: The ITUCNW

The third unit operating at 8 Rothesoodstrasse was the International Trade Union Committee of Negro Workers (or the Hamburg Committee as it was referred to in the internal communications of the RILU and Comintern). The ITUCNW was the brainchild of the combined efforts of the Comintern, the RILU, and a handful of African Caribbean/American activists. Initially established as the International Trade Union Committee of Negro Workers of the RILU in July 1928, the organization had been officially inaugurated at the First World Negro Workers Congress in July 1930. The original plan was to organize the congress in London.[63] However, due to the rather cryptic response from the British government, that is to say not an outright rejection but neither an acceptance, the Interclub in Hamburg was chosen as the new venue for the congress. The congress itself was hailed by the organizers as a success: Approximately 19 participants from the USA, the Caribbean, and sub-Saharan Africa gathered in Hamburg and laid the foundation of a new radical network in the African Atlantic.[64]

As other RILU Trade Union Committees, the ITUCNW was more of a coordinating Secretariat than a membership organization and it was never planned to become a radical trade union platform for the black toilers in the African Atlantic.[65] The "Class-Against-Class" policy laid out the guidelines of both the

---

61 §14 from: "Instruktionen für die Kommission zur Leitung des Internationalen Kongresses der ISH", 11 May 1932, Russian State Archive of Social and Political History, Moscow, 534/5/232, fol. 35.
62 E. Nørgaard, *Revolutionen der udeblev: Komintenrs vikrsomhed med Ernst Wollweber og Richard Jensen i forgrunden*, Copenhagen: Fremad, 1975, pp. 94–95.
63 "An Appeal to Negro Workers of the World", *The Negro Worker* 3 (1930) 1, p. 1.
64 "Report of Proceedings and Decisions of the First International Conference of Negro Workers", Hamburg: International Trade Union Committee of Negro Workers, 1930, p. 1; see also H. Adi, *Pan-Africanism and Communism: The Communist International, Africa and the Diaspora, 1919–1939*, Trenton: Africa World Press, 2013.
65 See H. Weiss, *Framing a Radical African Atlantic: African American Agency, West African Intellectuals and the International Trade Union Committee of Negro Workers*, Leiden: Brill, 2014.

ITUCNW and of its predecessor: it was never to link up with political Pan-Africanism or even to emerge as a "Black International". Instead, the agenda and objectives of the organization had an exclusive class-based rather than an inclusive race-based character: it was to be an organization only for the black toilers, not for the black bourgeois. Its task was to develop class-conscious (proletarian) international solidarity among the black toilers in their struggle against colonial and imperial exploitation.[66]

The RILU never planned that the ITUCNW would emerge as an independent actor. Instead, the Hamburg Committee was to discuss and outline work with the European Bureau of the RILU in accordance with instructions that were prepared by the RILU Secretariat, the RILU Negro Bureau, or the Executive Committee of the Comintern. In addition, the Hamburg Committee was to cooperate with the ISH Secretariat, the Hamburg bureaus of both the German Communist Party and of the RGO, as well as with the Party headquarters in Berlin.[67]

The intimate structural connections between the ISH and the Hamburg Committee were part and parcel of the grand strategy designed in Moscow. As noted in first part of this chapter, the ISH Secretariat and the local Interclub were to be assisted by the Hamburg Committee in their "special work" among African and Caribbean seamen. In terms of planning for activities concerning the African Atlantic, the ISH, the Hamburg Committee, and the RILU Negro Bureau were to cooperate.[68] Both organizations received funding from Moscow via the same relay station in Berlin, namely the European Bureau of the RILU. Monthly payments were transferred from the Comintern via Berlin to the ISH account in Hamburg; the activities and the salaries of the personnel of the Hamburg Committee were paid from the ISH account. The transfer of funds from Moscow to Germany neatly reveals the positions of the various organizations in the solar system of the Comintern: on top the Comintern centre in Moscow, next the RILU Secretariat, then the RILU European Bureau, and then the ISH and the Hamburg Committee.[69]

---

[66] "What is the International Trade Union Committee of Negro Workers?", *The Negro Worker* 1 (1931) 10–11, p. 45. Also M. Barek (ed.), *What is the International Trade Union Committee of Negro Workers? A Trade Union Programme of Action*, Hamburg: Graphische Industrie Hamburg GmbH, no date (ca. 1931).
[67] "Plan of Work and Immediate Tasks of the International Trade Union Committee of Negro Workers at Hamburg", no date (ca. 1931), Russian State Archive of Social and Political History, Moscow, 534/3/668, fol. 6–7.
[68] "Letter from Padmore to Walter", 21 July 1931, Russian State Archive of Social and Political History, Moscow, 534/3/668, fol. 96.
[69] "Ausgaben der ISH für das ITUCNW, April 1931 – Mai 1932", Russian State Archive of Social and Political History, Moscow, 534/4/407, fol. 145–146; for a detailed discussion, see Weiss, *Framing a Radical African Atlantic*, Chapter 7.2.2.6.

The realization and fulfilment of the planned cooperation, however, proved to be far more difficult. During Ford's period as secretary of the Hamburg Committee, the leadership of the ISH regarded the Hamburg Committee merely as a branch of the ISH rather than an independent organization. For example, the readers of the ITUCNW's journal, *The Negro Worker*, were notified about the planned demonstration on the International Day of Struggle Against Imperialist War on 1 August. Therefore, Ford highlighted that the campaign "must be utilized with a view of organizationally strengthening the I.S.H. among the colonial seamen, the recruiting of new members from among the colonial seamen must be in the forefront of our work of mobilizing these seamen against war preparations and for the fight to better their living conditions and for the defense of the Soviet Union."[70]

Ford's time as secretary ended in September 1931 when he was recalled to Moscow. A few months later, George Padmore, born in Trinidad and member of the Communist Party of the USA took over the operations of the Hamburg Committee. At first, the relationship between these two organizations became more balanced, although the Hamburg Committee was still expected to assist the ISH in its agitation and propaganda work among seamen. Soon, however, the relationship again reached its nadir as Padmore regarded work among Black seamen in European ports to be done in the name of the Hamburg Committee, an idea that was opposed by Albert Walter, the secretary of the ISH, who (rightly) claimed that work among seamen was aimed to strengthen the national sections of the ISH, not to establish subcommittees of the ITUCNW. Padmore even presented the ITUCNW as the spearhead of black seamen in the October–November 1931 issue of *The Negro Worker*. It is likely that the ISH Secretariat must have dismissed such a claim as dissident. Be as it may, five months later, the April 1932 issue of the journal held as its front cover a photomontage highlighting a class-conscious message to the reader: A "White", a "Black", and a "Yellow" worker (i.e. seaman) pointed united towards the catchword "Strike!", standing in front of a red flag carrying the badge of the International of Seamen and Harbour Workers. An "Appeal to the Negro Seamen and Dockers" by the ISH further urged the Black seamen "to join ship and dock committees of the International Seamen and Harbour Workers Union which are fighting for the [...] demands of the Negro seamen and the sailors of other races and colours."[71]

---

[70] "August First and Negro Workers", *The Negro Worker* 1 (1931) 7, pp. 4–6. See H. Weiss, "Between Moscow and the African Atlantic: The Comintern Networks of Negro Workers", *monde(s) histoire, espaces, relations* 10 (2016), pp. 89–108.
[71] "Appeal to the Negro Seamen and Dockers", *The Negro Worker* 2 (1932) 4, p. 24.

Despite the frictions between the Hamburg Committee and the ISH Secretariat, the former was dependent upon the latter in its ambition to establish a radical network in the African Atlantic. *The Negro Worker*, as well as the pamphlets and booklets published by the ITUCNW, was disseminated in two ways in the African Atlantic. It was sent by postal services to countries where Communist activities had not been banned by the authorities, such as the USA or the United Kingdom. In the Caribbean and African colonies, however, the colonial authorities had banned subversive and anti-colonial activities, including Communist agitation and propaganda. Therefore, the journal was smuggled into these countries by making use of the courier system of the ISH, namely its covert network through the ship cells that had been established on German, British, and other vessels, which were docking at ports in the Atlantic, Indian, and Pacific oceans.[72]

Visible and Non-visible Radical Black Activists in Hamburg

The premises at 8 Rothesoodstrasse became at the turn of the 1930s a hotspot for political activists in the African Atlantic. Some of them attended the Interclub and the ITUCNW headquarters as visible guests, while others participated in meetings behind closed doors. Among the former were the African and Caribbean delegates who participated at the World Congress of Negro Workers in July 1930. Garan Kouyaté, a radical political activist from the French Sudan and leader of the Ligue de défense de la Race Nègre in France, had been cooperating with Ford already in 1929, but the French police authorities had prevented him attending the 1930 Hamburg conference. However, he managed to visit Hamburg in June 1931 when he had a "conference" with Ford and the ISH Secretariat, where he delivered a report on work among colonial seamen in France. The outcome of the meeting was that Kouyaté was to be sent to Marseilles to jointly work among seamen for the ISH and the ITUCNW as well as to establish a subcommittee within the ITUCNW.[73] One year later, he attended the ISH World Congress as one of the keynote speakers and presented a report on the organization of the colonial maritime transport workers' fight for economic justice.[74] Shortly after the World Congress, Padmore and Kouyaté

---

72 See Weiss, *Framing a Radical African Atlantic*, ch. 8.5.
73 "NN (Adolf Shelley) to Pechmann (head of the RILU Bureau in Berlin)", 13 June 1931, Russian State Archive of Social and Political History, Moscow, 534/5/221, fol. 155–161.
74 ISH, "De internationale Søtransportarbejderes Verdens-Enhedskongres og dens Beslutninger!", Copenhagen, no date (ca. 1932), p. 4.

held a four-day meeting about the practical organization of the ITUCNW, probably at the bureau of the Hamburg Committee. Not surprisingly, both supported a more independent position of the ITUCNW vis-â-vis the ISH; among others, they called for the organization to have its own budget.[75]

Another African visitor at 8 Rothesoodstrasse was the Sierra Leonean seamen E.F. Foster Jones. He had called at Hamburg several times in 1931 and 1932. Ford, and later Padmore, had given him the task to turn the Kroomen Seamen's Club in Freetown, Sierra Leone, into an Interclub. Foster Jones was enlisted both by the ISH and the Hamburg Committee as a courier and for special, that is to say clandestine, tasks in West Africa.[76] Most of his meetings at 8 Rothesoodstrasse must have been held behind closed doors. However, at least on one occasion, he was used by the ISH as a speaker at one of their rallies in Hamburg.[77]

Postscript: 1933 and After or Turning 8 Rothesoodstrasse into a Non-place

Communist agitation and propaganda activities at 8 Rothesoodstrasse ended abruptly in early March 1933. Political tension gained momentum when the Nazis came to power in Germany in January 1933. Anticipating a prolonged period of political turmoil and increased police attacks, the leadership of the Hamburg Interclub had already moved its printing press to a secret location in the harbour area in late 1932.[78] In early February, the police arrested George Padmore during a raid on his apartment in Altona and held him in detention for two weeks. The ISH, together with the local branch of the German Red Aid, tried in vain to arrange for his release. Instead, the local police authorities decided to deport him to England on 21 February.[79] A few days later, the German Reichstag building stood in flames, followed by the emergency decree and the mass arrest of German Communists, among others Albert Walter, on 28 March.

---

75 "Practical Decisions on the Discussions of the Int. Tr. Un. Comm.", 23–26 May 32, Russian State Archive of Social and Political History, Moscow, 534/3/753, fol. 111.
76 Weiss, *Framing a Radical African*, pp. 386–388.
77 Weiss, "Between Moscow and the African Atlantic", p. 90.
78 Eiber, *Arbeiter und Arbeiterbewegung*, p. 186.
79 Bill, "Über die Verhaftung und Ausweisung des Gen(ossen) Padmore", no date (ca. February 1932), Russian State Archive of Social and Political History, Moscow, 534/4/461, fol. 123–125; on the deportation of Padmore, see Weiss, *Framing a Radical African Atlantic*, pp. 578–582.

On 5 March 1933, Nazi stormtroopers (Sturmabteilung, SA) attacked the facilities of the Interclub, and on 16 March, the local police closed the Interclub and the ISH office.[80]

However, the activities of the ISH and the Interclub were at first not paralysed by the assault. Anticipating an imminent period of illegality, the ISH archives and Albert Walter's catalogue of ship cells and contact persons had been transferred to a secure hiding place already on 27 February. After the crackdown on the Communists in Hamburg, operations were moved underground and Ernst Wollweber tried to reorganize work on an illegal basis. After the raid on 8 Rothesoodstrasse, it was decided to relocate the ISH headquarters, including its archive, to Copenhagen. Here, Adolf Shelley's illegal secretariat continued its operations in the office building Vesterport at Vesterbrogade, under the guise of being the office of the engineering company A. Selvo & Co.[81] Officially and in public, the ISH headquarters were claimed to be at Toldbodgade 16 – the address of the Copenhagen Interclub.[82] The activities of the ITUCNW were also not badly shaken. Padmore moved to Paris in early March 1933, where he continued to publish *The Negro Worker* – albeit informing his readers that the post box of the journal was at 16 Toldbodgade in Copenhagen![83]

The Nazi takeover in Germany in 1933 marked the end of Communist and anti-colonial activities at 8 Rothesoodstrasse. The building was stripped of its radical political significance and turned into a non-political space, housing a Christian dormitory of young females from 1934. Nevertheless, the Nazi whitewashing of former radical and red spaces was initially not entirely successful. The Hamburg Interclub had been a "free space" for radical-minded seamen and was portrayed by them as a positive place of memory. One of the few public reactions was by Franz Tetrowitz, who publicly protested when the former Interclub was turned into a dormitory. "We paid the house with our own money", he shouted outside the building one evening and accused the authorities for having illegally grabbed it. "I will seek revenge when I am abroad; the SA men are all rags," he continued. Not surprisingly, Tretrowitz was immediately assaulted by some bystanders and handed over to the police, who put him in jail. One year later, he was condemned for public mockery of

---

80 Weiss, *Framing a Radical African Atlantic*, p. 575.
81 "Richard Jensen personal file", 19 April 1933, The National Archives, London, KV 2/2158; N.E. Rosenfelt, *Verdensrevolutionens generalstad: Komintern og det hemmelige apparat*, Copenhagen: Gads forlag, 2011, pp. 203–204.
82 Weiss, *Framing a Radical African Atlantic*, p. 577, at fn. 8.
83 Ibid., p. 588.

the SA and sentenced to six months in jail.[84] If Tretrowitz' public outcry marked the beginning transformation of a former radical global space into a political non-place, the destruction of the building at 8 Rothesoodstrasse during the bombing of Hamburg in 1943 marked the end of the process.

---

[84] "Staatsanwaltschaft Landgericht – Strafsachen Franz Tetrowitz", no date (ca. 1934), Staatsarchiv Hamburg, 213-11_00142/36.

Antje Dietze
Visions of the World. Transnational Connections of the Panorama Industry in Leipzig at the Turn of the Twentieth Century

Entertainment industries played a significant role in the wave of globalization that marked the turn of the twentieth century. At that time, the cultural sector in most large cities of the Western world and beyond underwent a profound transformation. With new forms of profit-oriented businesses – like panoramas, music halls, variety theatres, amusement parks, and cinemas – having been established over the course of the nineteenth century, they now reached mass audiences and increasingly shaped urban public spheres and economies. These evolving industries relied on intense contacts and exchanges across urban networks and wide-ranging touring circuits, providing city dwellers with cosmopolitan experiences. The entertainment industries became an important element in the function of modern cities as entrance points for cultural transfers – or portals of globalization.[1]

As part of a transnational turn in the historiography of popular culture, urban leisure, and entertainment industries, scholars have started to uncover a broad spectrum of cross-border connections in this sector. Recent studies have emphasized the fundamental role of city networks, transimperial entanglements, transnational and transregional production networks, and cultural circulations and brokers. These studies have traced the specific patterns and spaces of interaction that played a role in the rapid expansion of art and entertainment at the time.[2] Investigating the different nodes and hubs of the sector

---

[1] See the definitions in M. Middell and K. Naumann, "Global History and the Spatial Turn: from the Impact of Area Studies to the Study of Critical Junctures of Globalization", *Journal of Global History* 5 (2010) 1, pp. 149–170, at 162; M. Geyer, "Portals of Globalisation", in: W. Eberhard and C. Lübke (eds.), *The Plurality of Europe. Identities and Spaces*, Leipzig: Leipziger Universitätsverlag, 2010, pp. 509–520, at 509.
[2] C. Charle (ed.), *Le temps des capitales culturelles: XVIIIe-XXe siècles*, Seyssel: Champ Vallon, 2009; J. Osterhammel, "Globale Horizonte europäischer Kunstmusik, 1860–1930", *Geschichte und Gesellschaft* 38 (2012) 1, pp. 86–132; L. Platt, T. Becker and D. Linton (eds.), *Popular Musical Theatre in London and Berlin, 1890 to 1939*, Cambridge: Cambridge University Press, 2014; T. DaCosta Kaufmann, C. Dossin and B. Joyeux-Prunel (eds.), *Circulations in the Global History of Art*, Farnham: Ashgate, 2015; C. Balme and N. Leonhardt, "Introduction: Theatrical

as portals of globalization can be a productive avenue to further analyse the differentiated and uneven geographies of modern entertainment industries. This perspective builds on, among many other things, insights from cultural transfer studies, which have increasingly focused on understanding the particular spaces and multiple scales of cultural interaction. These include not only sites and channels of concentrated exchanges and contact, but also areas that remain excluded, shielded, or disconnected from these processes.[3] In a similar vein, researchers of imperial, colonial, and transnational history have called for a closer look at the scope, mechanisms, and effects of particular connections and circulations in order to overcome some unproductive abstractions and generalizations in globalization studies.[4]

The concept of portals of globalization adds an interesting approach to these global interactions and how they are anchored and managed at various locations. The proposal is not to revive global-local dichotomies but, on the contrary, to focus on sites of concentrated interaction where mediating agents foster, steer, or restrict connections on multiple scales; on the way they build up knowledge, practices, and institutions to deal with global connectedness; and on the long-term transformations and historical reflections of these interactions.[5] This approach has been used in case studies to investigate, for instance, how different forms of connectedness are produced in a variety of world regions and to conduct long-term analyses on how different stakeholders adapt or make use of portals in shifting spatial orders.[6] In this view,

---

Trade Routes", *Journal of Global Theatre History* 1 (2016) 1, pp. 1–9; M. Rempe and C. Torp, "Cultural Brokers and the Making of Glocal Soundscapes, 1880s to 1930s", *Itinerario* 41 (2017) 2, pp. 223–233.

3 M. Espagne, "La notion de transfert culturel", *Revue Sciences/Lettres* 1 (2013), https://journals.openedition.org/rsl/219; A. Dietze and M. Middell, "Methods in Transregional Studies: Intercultural Transfers", in: M. Middell (ed.), *The Routledge Handbook of Transregional Studies*, Abingdon: Routledge, 2018, pp. 58–66.

4 F. Cooper, "What is the Concept of Globalization Good For? An African Historian's Perspective", *African Affairs* 100 (2001) 399, pp. 189–213; P.-Y. Saunier, "Globalisation", in: A. Iriye and P.-Y. Saunier (eds.), *The Palgrave Dictionary of Transnational History*, Basingstoke: Palgrave Macmillan, 2009, pp. 456–462.

5 Middell and Naumann, "Global History and the Spatial Turn", pp. 162–163; Geyer, "Portals of Globalisation"; C. Baumann, A. Dietze and M. Maruschke (eds.), "Portals of Globalization in Africa, Asia, and Latin America", *Comparativ* 27 (2017) 3–4.

6 G. Castryck (ed.), "From Railway Juncture to Portal of Globalization: Making Globalization work in African and South Asian Railway Towns", *Comparativ* 25 (2015) 4; M. Maruschke, *Portals of Globalization: Repositioning Mumbai's Ports and Zones, 1833–2014*, Berlin: De Gruyter, 2019.

portals play a crucial role for the production, challenging, and recombination of spatial formats under the global condition.

Against this background, this chapter reviews the emergence and evolution of the panorama industry in Leipzig, with a special focus on the era from 1871 to the turn of the twentieth century. At that time, panoramas were among the leading forms of visual mass entertainment. The panorama industry is especially interesting for the study of portals of globalization because it not only linked urban spheres with transnational production networks, but panoramas also served as entry points for shifting spatial imaginations in an era of radically intensifying global interconnections. They are closely linked to the emergence of a modern visual culture that profoundly transformed the way audiences related to the world at large.[7]

The global expansion of this entertainment genre is considered here from the perspective of a city that was an important centre of culture and trade both in the Kingdom of Saxony and in the German Empire, but did not belong to the first tier of global cultural metropolises. Much academic attention has been dedicated to popular culture in leading Western metropolises like Paris, London, and New York. Those cities functioned as "labs of modernity" – pioneers, hubs, and control centres of modern entertainment industries.[8] But there is insufficient knowledge about how exactly the corresponding circuits operated in relation to the interplay of different spatial formats. Looking at these networks from various angles reveals how and why new forms of entertainment "travelled", helping to better unpack the complexity of the exchanges in question. My analysis therefore does not remain limited to the city

---

[7] See the classic argument on the transformed experience of space through panoramic travel: W. Schivelbusch, *The Railway Journey: The Industrialization of Time and Space in the Nineteenth Century*, Berkeley: University of California Press, 1987, pp. 52–69. In a similar vein, literary scholars have traced panoramic perspectives and shifts in the way reality is constructed in texts, see A. Byerly, *Are We There Yet? Virtual Travel and Victorian Realism*, Ann Arbor: University of Michigan Press, 2012; V. Byrd, *A Pedagogy of Observation: Nineteenth-Century Panoramas, German Literature, and Reading Culture*, Lewisburg: Bucknell University Press, 2017. Panoramas and nineteenth-century visual culture have been analysed in terms of a modernization of perception with profound effects on knowledge and power relations, see T. Bennett, "The Exhibitionary Complex", *New Formations* 4 (1988), pp. 73–102; J. Crary, *Techniques of the Observer: On Vision and Modernity in the Nineteenth Century*, Cambridge: Massachusetts Institute of Technology Press, 1992.

[8] On the exceptional character of the metropolises, see H. Reif, "Metropolen. Geschichte, Begriffe, Methoden", *CMS Working Paper Series* 1 (2006); F. Lenger, *European Cities in the Modern Era, 1850–1914*, Leiden: Brill, 2012, pp. 7–8 and chapter I.

space but presents the entertainment industries in Leipzig in relation to profound shifts in large-scale production networks and spatial imaginations.

The first section introduces the city of Leipzig as a traditional centre of long-distance exchanges and gives an initial overview of the role the cultural sector played in its changing patterns of interconnections. The subsequent sections are devoted to the example of the panorama industry, outlining its general production and distribution structures, how forms of business organization changed over time and circulated transnationally, and how and by whom panoramas were established in Leipzig. The central question is to what extent a regional metropolis like Leipzig was integrated into uneven large-scale networks of the entertainment industries as well as how local institutions and agents fostered and used this integration for their own purposes, thereby shaping the logics of this portal in reimagining and recombining relevant spatial formats at the time.

Transnational Networks and the Entertainment Sector in Leipzig

The city of Leipzig has long been a regional metropolis and centre for long-distance exchanges and transfers. Since the Middle Ages, it has hosted an important trade fair, connecting routes and markets in Western, Central, and Eastern Europe. The city grew and prospered tremendously during the nineteenth century.[9] Leipzig became a premier transport hub with the first long-distance railroad line in Germany (Leipzig-Dresden, 1837–1839). It developed into a centre for trade as well as the publishing, printmaking, mechanical engineering, building, chemical, and textile industries. Its regional importance and transnational connections became a prominent feature in representations of Leipzig as a cosmopolitan city and aspiring modern metropolis. The city guide for visitors of the 1913 International Building Trade Exhibition provides a typical example of the city's public self-image:

---

9 The city's population rose above 100,000 in 1871, exceeded the half million mark in 1905, and reached almost 625,000 inhabitants in 1914. The population growth was partially based on the incorporation of surrounding villages. See A. Müller, "Großstadtwerdung", in S. Schötz (ed.), *Geschichte der Stadt Leipzig, vol. 3, Vom Wiener Kongress bis zum Ersten Weltkrieg*, Leipzig: Leipziger Universitätsverlag, 2018, pp. 451–459. However, the city was not a political centre – the king of Saxony resided in Dresden and in 1871 Berlin became the capital of the German Empire.

> Leipzig, the biggest and possibly also the oldest city of Saxony [...], is known to every German as the seat of the Imperial Court of Justice, as the arena of the Battle of the Nations, as a famous university. A city of trade and music, it enjoys a worldwide reputation: since it is the metropolis of the book trade, the leading city of the fur trade on the Continent. Its conservatory and its Gewandhaus concerts are held in high esteem overseas. Its industry is gaining increasing importance, and a number of factories [...] have become global companies.[10]

As this description shows, the cultural sector played a prominent role not only in the web of economic and cultural interconnections the city maintained, but also in local identity-building. Besides the book trade and university, Leipzig's cultural prestige relied primarily on institutions of "high culture" like the Conservatory of Music or the Gewandhaus Orchestra, founded and supported by the city's middle-class civil society.

Most previous research has focused on these cultural ventures and has in part also explored their transnational connections.[11] However, the city of Leipzig also developed into an important centre of commercial entertainment for mass audiences in the German Empire. In the late nineteenth century, the business expanded significantly, connecting the city to growing national and transnational circuits of the entertainment industries. Despite playing a major role in the cultural entanglements and transfers in Leipzig, this sector has thus far been scarcely examined. There are different reasons for this. Many entertainment venues in Leipzig were destroyed in World War II and never rebuilt, mainly because socialist cultural policies in the German Democratic Republic were rather unfavourable towards private enterprises and commercial

---

10 My translation from *Offizieller Führer durch die Internationale Baufach-Ausstellung mit Sonderausstellungen Leipzig 1913 und durch Leipzig und Umgebung mit einem Plan von Leipzig*, Leipzig: C.F. Müller, 1913, p. 71.

11 For studies that focus on middle-class culture in Leipzig in transnational perspective, see, e.g., T. Adam (ed.), *Philanthropy, Patronage, and Civil Society. Experiences from Germany, Great Britain, and North America*, Bloomington: Indiana University Press, 2004; T. Höpel and S. Sammler (eds.), *Kulturpolitik und Stadtkultur in Leipzig und Lyon (18.–20. Jahrhundert)*, Leipzig: Leipziger Universitätsverlag, 2004; Y. Wasserloos, *Das Leipziger Konservatorium der Musik im 19. Jahrhundert: Anziehungs- und Ausstrahlungskraft eines musikpädagogischen Modells auf das internationale Musikleben*, Hildesheim: Olms, 2004; A. Pieper, *Music and the Making of Middle-Class Culture: A Comparative History of Nineteenth Century Leipzig and Birmingham*, Basingstoke: Palgrave Macmillan, 2008; W. Weber, *The Great Transformation of Musical Taste: Concert Programming from Haydn to Brahms*, Cambridge: Cambridge University Press, 2008; S. Keym and K. Stöck (eds.), *Musik-Stadt, vol. 3, Musik in Leipzig, Wien und anderen Städten im 19. und 20. Jahrhundert*, Leipzig: Schröder, 2011; and the contributions in S. Schötz (ed.), *Geschichte der Stadt Leipzig, vol. 3, Vom Wiener Kongress bis zum Ersten Weltkrieg*, Leipzig: Leipziger Universitätsverlag, 2018.

entertainment.¹² Moreover, scholars long preferred to study prestigious forms of "high art" as opposed to "lowbrow" commercial culture. Popular entertainment has, however, gradually been rediscovered as a relevant driving force of cultural interconnections and change.

Against this background, the purpose of this contribution is to show how modern entertainment enterprises were established in Leipzig and how they gained greater significance in the city's web of transnational exchanges. Commercial entertainment, in general, depends heavily on mass audiences to realize profits. As a consequence, it was mainly the big metropolises – as well as industry and trade exhibitions – that leveraged the breakthrough of these new formats in the second half of the nineteenth century. Leipzig, despite being among the largest cities in the German states as well as empire, was still too small to make many of the new entertainments profitable on a regular basis. The city had less than 100,000 inhabitants in 1870, compared to several million in Paris and greater London at the same time, while Berlin and Vienna were fast approaching the one million mark. So at first, it was primarily Leipzig's trade fairs and exhibitions that facilitated the emergence of entertainment industries there.

Up until the 1870s, traveling shows came to Leipzig mainly during the big trade fairs in spring and fall in order to benefit from the visiting traders, tourists, and day trippers.¹³ The city strongly controlled the access of itinerant traders and performers, but issued concessions more readily during fair seasons to increase the attractiveness of the fair.¹⁴ The performers consisted of small impresarios, artist-entrepreneurs, and family businesses bringing all kinds of entertainments and curiosities to the city. Among these amusements were acrobats, magicians, music acts, puppet theatre, magic lantern shows,

---

12 How and to what extent they have been replaced by new cultural institutions and transnational interconnections under the conditions of the emerging Cold War is beyond the scope of this article, but it would be an important part of a long-term analysis of Leipzig as a portal of globalization in changing spatial orders.

13 For a detailed study of cultural offerings by traveling show people at Leipzig's fairs ca. 1800–1918, see G. Klunkert, *Schaustellungen und Volksbelustigungen auf Leipziger Messen des 19. Jahrhunderts*, Göttingen: Cuvillier, 2010, pp. 21–37, which the following historical overview is based on.

14 Funfairs were allowed during the main Jubilate (Easter) and Michaelmas trade fairs, which each lasted three weeks. Traveling shows in general were dependent on concessions and privileges from the state and city. Strong supervision and censorship persisted even after freedom of trade was granted in Saxony and the German Empire. See Klunkert, *Schaustellungen*, pp. 23–24, 37–40; K. Hauffe, I. Höer and Y. Klüglich, "Messevergnügungen", in: H. Zwahr, T. Topfstedt and G. Bentele (eds.), *Leipzigs Messen 1497–1997. Gestaltwandel – Umbrüche – Neubeginn*, vol. I, Cologne: Böhlau Verlag, 1999, pp. 301–316.

exhibitions of "exotic" or unusual people and animals, wax museums, amusement rides, shooting galleries, and so on. These shows took place in and near the city centre – in guesthouses, booths, attics, and public places, accompanying and mingling with the trade fair business.

Gradually, permanent spaces of entertainment were established in the city: first in restaurants, beer gardens, ballrooms, and club houses and then in special representative premises that were often run by corporations: a zoo was opened in 1878; a variety theatre, the Krystall-Palast Varieté, replaced the older Schützenhaus entertainment venue in 1882; a permanent panorama rotunda was constructed in 1884; permanent movie theatres opened in 1906; and an amusement park was opened in 1913/14. These enterprises relied on the enormous population growth of the last decades of the nineteenth century as well as on the freedom of trade, which was introduced in Saxony in 1861 and helped to further stimulate commercial and industrial development. By the end of the nineteenth century, the entertainment sector within the city had undergone a profound structural change: it had transitioned from seasonal offerings by traveling shows at the fairs to permanent venues owned and managed by private corporations.

The Emergence of the Panorama Business and Early Panoramas at the Leipzig Fairs

In order to give a more detailed account of what these institutional changes in the entertainment sector meant for the city and its spatial interconnections, I will limit my further analysis to the example of the panorama industry. Panoramas are a form of visual entertainment that became hugely popular following the late eighteenth century and made images of the world accessible for greater segments of the population at a time when visual representations were not yet ubiquitous.[15] Panorama exhibitions were introduced in most of the

---

15 General information on panoramas is based on F. Robichon, "Le Panorama, spectacle de l'histoire", *Le Mouvement Social* 131 (1985), pp. 65–86; R. Hyde, *Panoramania! The Art and Entertainment of the 'All-embracing' View*, London: Trefoil, 1988; M.-L. von Plessen and U. Giersch (eds.), *Sehsucht. Das Panorama als Massenunterhaltung des 19. Jahrhunderts*, Frankfurt/Main: Stroemfeld/Roter Stern, 1993; S. Oettermann, *The Panorama: History of a Mass Medium*, New York: Zone Books, 1997; E. Huhtamo, *Illusions in Motion: Media Archaeology of the Moving Panorama and Related Spectacles*, Cambridge: Massachusetts Institute of Technology Press, 2013; L. Garrison (ed.), *Panoramas 1787–1900: Texts and Contexts*, 5 vols., London: Pickering & Chatto, 2013.

major cities in Europe, North America, and Australia, and in some cities in Asia and South America, and the paintings circulated widely.

The general term "panorama" refers to a wide variety of exhibition formats. Panoramas in the narrower sense (also called cycloramas in North America) were monumental circular paintings exhibited in special round buildings, with a visitor platform in the middle. They offered 360-degree views of big cities, landscapes, or major battles, creating the illusion of being immersed in the scenery. The panorama was invented by the painter Robert Barker in Edinburgh, and he obtained a patent for it in 1787. Panoramas achieved international success after Barker built the first permanent panorama rotunda in London in 1793. Soon after, other entrepreneurs joined the business. During a first wave of panorama enthusiasm in the early nineteenth century, permanent rotundas were constructed in London, Paris (1799), and New York (1804). The only permanent panorama building in the German-speaking world at the time was at the Prater, the amusement park in Vienna (1801/1804). These cities functioned as production centres of the panorama business. From there, the paintings were also sent on tours to other cities where they were usually shown in temporary wooden constructions.

Moving panoramas consisted of very long painted canvases that were gradually rolled out in front of the audience, unfolding views of a passing landscape and creating the impression of a railway or boat trip, often accompanied by lectures and music. They were especially popular in the United States, as they could be transported easily and thus were more suitable for a frontier society. Dioramas were large flat or semicircular paintings on transparent canvas, commonly displayed behind a stage-like frame with a light show that suggested, for example, the change from day to night. The diorama was invented by Louis Daguerre, a renowned theatre designer, who would later invent daguerreotype photography, and the painter Charles Bouton. They opened a diorama exhibition in Paris in 1822 as well as a branch in London the following year. Dioramas were also shown in other European and North American cities. In Germany, the term diorama mostly referred to regular but monumental paintings exhibited in niches with special lighting and false terrain.

All these types of panoramas were exhibited during the Leipzig trade fairs. Circular panoramas that had been sent on tour from London, Vienna, and Paris, as well as panoramas from traveling entrepreneurs, came to the city early on. For example, Barker's panorama of London was shown in Leipzig in 1800 on its continental tour.[16] The panorama of Toulon – painted by Pierre Prévost,

---

[16] For a detailed list of all sorts of panoramas exhibited during Leipzig's trade fairs, see Klunkert, *Schaustellungen*, pp. 338–358 and CD.

Constant Bourgeois, and Charles-Marie Bouton – produced and first shown in Paris, was exhibited in Leipzig in 1802. William Barton's panorama of Vienna was displayed in 1806 and 1834 and that of Paris in 1833; and his panorama of Gibraltar in 1815 and 1828 – they had first been exhibited in the rotunda at Vienna's Prater. Augustin Siegert's panorama of the Etna volcano came to Leipzig in the 1820s. The traveling artist-entrepreneur Johann Michael Sattler from Salzburg, who toured Europe with a panorama of his home town between 1829 and 1838, came to Leipzig in 1833. Dioramas, some moving panoramas from the US of the rivers Ohio and Mississippi and other forms of panoramas were also shown in Leipzig during the fairs. However, audiences in Leipzig remained dependent on the initiative of individual agents and entrepreneurs, most of them from outside the city, who decided to come and install temporary exhibitions there. Leipzig had the trade fair to attract the new visual spectacles, but, like most cities at the time, it was still too small to make permanent commercial exhibitions profitable. However, temporary panorama exhibitions continued to be exhibited during the fairs all throughout the nineteenth and into the twentieth centuries.

How the Second Panorama Wave Came to Germany: A Franco-German Transfer via Brussels

By the late 1870s, a second wave of panorama enthusiasm had begun and the business boomed in an unprecedented manner. In addition to the temporary exhibitions, permanent panorama rotundas were now built, not only in the large metropolises but also in most major cities in Europe; in Germany alone, six rotundas were constructed in Berlin, three each in Munich and Hamburg, two in Frankfurt/Main, and one each in Leipzig, Cologne, Dresden, Breslau, Bremen, Düsseldorf, and in other cities.[17] Panoramas also became a regular sight at industry and trade exhibitions. This was the result of a profound reorganization of the panorama business as it was consolidated into a transnational industry. This section will first provide a general overview of the new business structures that were introduced in German cities as the result of a Franco-German cultural transfer. The next section will then outline more precisely how entrepreneurs in Leipzig became involved.

---

17 See Oettermann, *The Panorama*, pp. 235–285.

The second panorama craze was initiated in Paris. Painter and military officer Jean-Charles Langlois had been producing panoramas and running panorama rotundas there since the 1830s. With a focus on patriotic motifs of France's military battles – from the Napoleonic Wars to more recent battles in Algeria, the Greek War of Independence, and the Crimean War – and with financial support by Napoleon III and the city, he was able to suport his work despite the generally diminishing interest in large circular panoramas.[18] Langlois developed many of the artistic and economic standards that would define the panorama industry in the last third of the nineteenth century, running his business through a stock company and an elegant rotunda at the Champs-Elysées. After Langlois' death in 1870, investors founded a new company that exhibited a panorama of the Siege of Paris, from the Franco-Prussian War (1870/71), by historical painter Félix Philippoteaux. In 1878, it was included in the French national exhibit at the Parisian Universal Exhibition and became an enormous success, accruing immense profits. In the 1880s, the company was able to expand its business transnationally, producing panoramas for foreign markets and sending its own paintings on tours through Europe and North America.[19]

The Universal Exhibition had served as an intensifier, and now the new success formula for a profitable panorama business was appropriated by others: stock companies raising the vast quantities of money needed for the giant paintings, buildings, and innercity real estate, combined with patriotic paintings of recent military battles to draw on the collective enthusiasm in an era of nationalism and imperial expansion while providing monumental visual spectacles for mass audiences. Panoramas played an important role in the construction of national cultures during the nineteenth century, not least by serving as sites of memory for important battles.[20] At the same time, they presented

---

18 Among the panoramas produced by Langlois were the Battle of Navarino (1827), opened 1831; the Battle of Algiers, opened 1833; and the Battle of Borodino (1812), opened 1834 (Ibid., pp. 158–163; C. Joubert and F. Robichon (eds.), *Jean-Charles Langlois (1789–1870). Le Spectacle de l'Histoire*, Paris: Somogy, 2005).
19 See F. Robichon, *Die Illusion eines Jahrhunderts – Panoramen in Frankreich*, in: M.-L. von Plessen and U. Giersch (eds.), *Sehsucht. Das Panorama als Massenunterhaltung des 19. Jahrhunderts*, Frankfurt/Main: Stroemfeld/Roter Stern, 1993, pp. 52–63; Oettermann, *The Panorama*, pp. 163–167.
20 G. Koller, "Panoramen als Orte bürgerlicher Schaulust und Bildung im Deutschen Kaiserreich", in: B. Huberl (ed.), *Kunst, Nation und nationale Repräsentation*, Bönen: Kettler, 2008, pp. 87–100; F. Becker, "Augen-Blicke der Größe. Das Panorama als nationaler Erlebnisraum nach dem Krieg von 1870/71", in: J. Requate (ed.), *Das 19. Jahrhundert als Mediengesellschaft*, Munich: Oldenbourg, 2009, pp. 178–191; A. Bartetzky, "Das Panorama als kommerzieller Vergnügungsort und nationale Weihestätte", in: A. Bartetzky and R. Jaworski

visions of the wider world – of long-distance trade and travel, exotic places and landscapes, as well as explorations and conquests – which were imbued with imperial or colonial imaginations and often promoting such endeavours.[21]

An immense wave of investment started and the boom in panorama production lasted roughly until 1900. While London had been the pioneering centre of the first panorama wave, this time the city was not as influential. The new centres of panorama production and enthusiasm were in Francophone and German-speaking Europe and the US. In the wake of the Universal Exhibition (1878), several rotundas were built in Paris, and panorama stock companies were founded in many cities. Brussels became one of the hubs of this industry – in the year 1880 alone, Franco-Belgian investors registered more than twenty panorama companies at the Brussels stock exchange.[22] These consortia organized and financed panoramas in different cities – including London, Berlin, Madrid, Rome, Moscow, and New York – establishing standardized transnational production and distribution networks. Many of the companies founded during the post-1878 panorama fever were short-lived, but markets continued to expand. Via the United States, the business model was transferred to Canada, Australia, and Japan.[23] Panorama historian Stephan

---

(eds.), *Geschichte im Rundumblick. Panoramabilder im östlichen Europa*, Cologne: Böhlau, 2014, pp. 13–26.

21 D.B. Oleksijczuk, *The First Panoramas: Visions of British Imperialism*, Minneapolis: University of Minnesota Press, 2011; J.P. Short, *Magic Lantern Empire: Colonialism and Society in German*, Ithaca: Cornell University Press, 2012; R. Benjamin, "Colonial Panoramania", in: M. Jay and S. Ramaswamy (eds.), *Empires of Vision: A Reader*, Durham: Duke University Press, 2014, pp. 111–137; J. Plunkett, "The Overland Mail: Moving Panoramas and the Imagining of Trade and Communication Networks", in: S. Chaudhuri et al. (eds.), *Commodities and Culture in the Colonial World*, Abingdon: Routledge, 2017, pp. 58–74.

22 I. Leroy, "Belgische Panoramagesellschaften 1879–1889. Modelle des internationalen Kapitalismus", in: M.-L. von Plessen and U. Giersch (eds.), *Sehsucht. Das Panorama als Massenunterhaltung des 19. Jahrhunderts*, Frankfurt/Main: Stroemfeld/Roter Stern, 1993, pp. 74–83; I. Leroy, *Le Panorama de la Bataille de Waterloo. Témoin Exceptionnel de la Saga des Panoramas*, Brussels: Pire, 2009, pp. 39–49. For a historical account, see S. Hausmann, "Die neueste Entwicklung der deutschen Panoramenmalerei", *Die Kunst für Alle* 5 (1 June 1890) 17, pp. 257–263.

23 On the worldwide expansion of the panorama business, see von Plessen and Giersch, *Sehsucht*; Oettermann, *The Panorama*; M. Colligan, *Canvas Documentaries: Panoramic Entertainments in Nineteenth-Century Australia and New Zealand*, Melbourne: Melbourne University Press, 2002; G. Koller (ed.), *Die Welt der Panoramen*, Amberg: Büro Wilhelm, 2003; G. Streicher (ed.), *Panorama: Virtuality and Realities*, Amberg: Büro Wilhelm, 2005; T. Rombout (ed.), *The Panorama Phenomenon: The World Round!*, The Hague: Panorama Mesdag, 2006; G. Koller (ed.), *The Panorama in the Old World and the New*, Amberg: Büro Wilhelm, 2010; Bartetzky and Jaworski, *Geschichte im Rundumblick*.

Oettermann estimated the numbers of visitors of 360-degree panoramas between 1870 and 1900 to be about 10 million in Germany and about 100 million in Europe and North America.[24]

Within a few years, a new transnational panorama network had emerged. It was based on interconnected cities with different functions that served as portals of the global industry – some were production and financing centres, others were merely sites of exhibition. While actors in the major hubs had more power to shape and control the business, no one city was independent from the wider networks, as the profitability of panoramas could only be secured by exhibiting them in several cities to increase the number of visitors.

It was by way of the Belgian companies that the new panorama business model came to Germany. They first exhibited panoramas of battles from the Franco-Prussian War, capitalizing on patriotic sentiments after the German states won the war and unified to form the German Empire. The companies commissioned paintings from celebrated German historical painters: for example, from Louis Braun in Munich and Anton von Werner, director of the Academy of Arts in Berlin. Both had been to France to study historical painting. They had never painted a panorama before, but they succeeded with the help of French and Belgian specialists.[25] Braun, who had been a war correspondent during the Franco-Prussian War, became the most prolific and prominent panorama painter in Germany. Panorama workshops were established in Berlin and Munich, and Munich soon became one of the major panorama production centres in Europe. Their production relied on the prestige and talent provided by the art academies and their professors and students.[26]

The French-Belgian parent companies mostly hid behind local subsidiaries and relied on local managers and investors. This was essential in a business that was heavily based on national and imperial propaganda. While technical standards and transnational business cooperation were developed to facilitate the circulation of the paintings for higher profits, the patriotic content, especially of the battle paintings, often obstructed cross-cultural exchange.[27] This

---

24 Oettermann, *The Panorama*, p. 240.
25 H. Siebenmorgen, *Louis Braun (1836–1916). Panoramen von Krieg und Frieden aus dem Deutschen Kaiserreich*, Schwäbisch Hall: Hällisch-Fränkisches Museum, 1986; P. Alexandre and H. Beutter (eds.), *Der Panoramamaler Louis Braun (1836–1916). Vom Skizzenblatt zum Riesenrundbild*, Schwäbisch Hall: Hällisch-Fränkisches Museum, 2012; D. Bartmann (ed.), *Anton von Werner: Geschichte in Bildern*, Munich: Hirmer, 1997.
26 A. Weidauer, *Berliner Panoramen der Kaiserzeit*, Berlin: Gebr. Mann, 1996; F. Schiermeier, *Panorama München. Illusion und Wirklichkeit. München als Zentrum der Panoramenherstellung*, Munich: Schiermeier, 2009.
27 Weidauer, *Berliner Panoramen*, p. 16; Oettermann, *The Panorama*, pp. 236–239.

led to largely segregated distribution circuits – different paintings of the Franco-Prussian War circulated in German-speaking countries as opposed to France and Belgium. Paintings of British or Scottish battles or of the American Civil War were produced for export in the studios in Munich or Berlin.[28]

At the turn of the twentieth century, the second panorama wave ebbed in most countries. Several explanations have been put forth for this. It seems that the end of the panorama boom was brought about both by internal and external factors: the decline of the medium itself as well as new competitors in the realm of visual entertainment. Oettermann highlights the exhaustion of war themes, especially those of the Franco-Prussian War, which by then was 30 years in the past.[29] Formerly popular depictions of cavalry battles had become more and more anachronistic in view of new military technology, and aesthetically, realistic historical painting had passed its zenith. Entrepreneurs struggled to find new themes and styles to revive audience interest, but they succeeded only partially. At the same time, the whole media landscape had started to change dramatically. New forms of visual entertainment became available for mass audiences that offered fresh images more quickly and easily. In addition to advances in photomechanical printing, cinematography was on the rise. The lack of movement and dynamism in panorama presentations became a growing concern – it still took weeks or months to produce new canvases, and the images remained static. The First World War accelerated the collapse of the transnational business networks. Most panorama exhibitions were closed, production came to a halt, and the rotundas were torn down or turned into warehouses, cinemas, skating rinks, and the like. However, the end of the second panorama wave had complex and various causes as well as mixed impacts across uneven business networks, as surviving panorama exhibitions and studios in different countries and the recent renaissance of the panorama phenomenon indicate.[30]

---

28 For example, in the 1880s, Philipp Ernst Fleischer painted panoramas of the battles of Omdurman, Bannockburn, Trafalgar, and Waterloo for the British market in one of the Munich panorama studios – see Schiermeier, *Panorama München*, p. 16. In Berlin, Bracht painted two panoramas of the Battle of Chattanooga for the cities of Philadelphia and Chicago – see Weidauer, *Berliner Panoramen*, pp. 28–29.
29 Oettermann, *The Panorama*, p. 241. On the end of the panorama boom, see also G. Koller, "Panoramas und Film. Die Anfänge des Kinos und die Folgen für das Panorama um 1900", in: G. Koller (ed.), Die Welt der Panoramen, Amberg: Büro Wilhelm, 2003, pp. 76–84.
30 See the website of the International Panorama Council for a database of surviving panoramas and for recent developments: International Panorama Council, "Home", https://panoramacouncil.org (accessed 14 December 2018).

Second-wave Panoramas in Leipzig: The Panorama am Roßplatz and the Krystall-Palast

The two most important permanent exhibition venues for panoramas and dioramas in Leipzig were the Panorama am Roßplatz and the Krystall-Palast.[31] These examples show how local businesspeople from the trade, finance, and catering sectors learned to make use of commercial entertainments and built the appropriate business connections and institutional framework. They transferred business models established in other, often much bigger cities, to Leipzig and adapted them to local conditions. They can be seen as mediating agents, integrating the city of Leipzig into the second-wave panorama industry and controlling the quality and the extent of these transnational connections. Their enterprises and exhibition sites served as entry points for cultural transfers, not only bringing more images of the world to the city, but also establishing new institutions and practices to channel and exploit cross-border cultural and economic entanglements.

Leipzig's only permanent rotunda for 360-degree panoramas opened at Roßplatz in 1884.[32] It was an iron and stone rotunda built for circular panorama paintings measuring approximately 16 by 118 meters. The building housed a large restaurant with a garden on the ground floor, wine cellars, tasting rooms, and shops in the basement, and the panorama exhibition on the first floor. The Leipziger Panorama-Gesellschaft (Leipzig Panorama Company), which owned and managed the site, was not directly linked to the French-Belgian companies, and its shares were not traded publicly. It was one of the local initiatives that were formed in many German cities, inspired by the French-Belgian model. The company decided to link up with the existing production and distribution networks. The rotunda building matched the

---

[31] More panoramas and dioramas were exhibited as part of the Saxon and Thuringian Industry and Trade Exhibition (1897). See L. Fraenkel (ed.), *Officieller Führer der Sächsisch Thüringischen Industrie und Gewerbe Ausstellung*, Leipzig: G.L. Daube & Co., 1897. A Kaiserpanorama opened in the city in 1886. Kaiserpanoramas were multistation viewing apparatuses for stereoscopic glass slides, invented by August Fuhrmann. First introduced in 1880 in Breslau, they soon opened all over Europe, either as branches of Fuhrmann's enterprise or run by competitors. See D. Lorenz, *Das Kaiser-Panorama. Ein Unternehmen des August Fuhrmann*, Munich: Münchener Stadtmuseum, 2010.

[32] Oettermann, *The Panorama*, pp. 247–250; H.-J. Böhme, "Panoramen in Leipzig – Seh-Lust im Großformat", *Leipziger Blätter* 56 (2010), pp. 28–31.

transnational standard measures, thereby allowing canvases to be circulated, and the majority of the panoramas exhibited there from 1884 to 1910 were patriotic battle paintings showing scenes from the Franco-Prussian War.

An overview of the paintings and their origins gives a clear picture of the particular production and distribution networks in which the Panorama am Roßplatz was integrated.[33] The first panorama exhibited there showed the Battle of Mars-la-Tour, a cavalry battle from the Franco-Prussian War. It was painted in Munich by Louis Braun and was commissioned directly for Leipzig. It remained on display until 1886 and later went on to Hamburg and Zurich.[34] The next one, showing the Battle of Villiers from the same war, was also commissioned for Leipzig. It had been produced under the direction of Berlin-based painter Eugen Bracht and later went to Dresden.[35] Another panorama produced specifically for Leipzig featured the Battle of the Nations that had occurred around the city in 1813. It was painted under the direction of Norwegian painter Otto Sinding, who had strong ties to Berlin and Munich.[36] Other panoramas exhibited in Leipzig had been produced on behalf of French-Belgian panorama companies and had previously been shown in other German cities. All of them featured battles from the Franco-Prussian War: the Battle of Gravelotte-St. Privat, painted by Emil Hünten and Wilhelm Simmler, first shown in Berlin from 1881 to 1883[37]; a second Battle of of Gravelotte-St. Privat painted by Louis

---

[33] Brochures for most of the panoramas and dioramas exhibited there can be found in the library of the Stadtgeschichtliches Museum, Leipzig. Further information on the panorama and diorama exhibitions in Leipzig has been gathered from the local newspaper *Leipziger Tageblatt und Anzeiger* (since 1905: *Leipziger Tageblatt und Handelszeitung*).

[34] "Die Schlacht bei Mars-la-Tour oder der Todesritt der Brigade von Bredow", exhibited 1884–1886. Around 200,000 visitors allegedly came to see it within nine months. See: P. Stein, "Das Leipziger Schlacht-Panorama. Die Schlacht bei Mars la Tour", in: *Gartenlaube* 45 (1884), pp. 738–740; Schiermeier, *Panorama München*, p. 49; Alexandre and Beutter, *Der Panoramamaler Louis Braun*, pp. 24, 129–131.

[35] "Vor Paris. Die Sachsen am 2. December 1870", shown 1887–1890. See M. Großkinsky, *Eugen Bracht (1842–1921). Landschaftsmaler im wilhelminischen Kaiserreich*, Darmstadt: Mathildenhöhe, 1992, pp. 39, 91–92.

[36] "Völkerschlacht bei Leipzig 1813", on display 1895–1898. See also G. Koller, "Otto Sindings panorama i Leipzig", in: T. Sinding Steinsvik (ed.), *Kunstnerbrødrene: Maleren Otto Sinding, Billedhuggeren Stephan Sinding, Komponisten Christian Sinding*, Modum: Blaafarveværket, 2000, pp. 120–126.

[37] "Gravelotte. Sturm der Garden und Sachsen auf St. Privat", exhibited 1892–1894. See Weidauer, *Berliner Panoramen*, pp. 17–18.

Braun in Munich and first shown 1883 in Dresden for the opening of the rotunda there[38]; and the Battle of Weissenburg, also by Louis Braun, painted and first shown in Munich from 1883 to 1884.[39]

From 1890 to 1892, the rotunda at Roßplatz housed a semicircular panorama showing a reconstruction of the ancient city of Pergamon by Alexander Kips and Max Koch, based on German archaeological excavations at the time, and a series of dioramas that featured German and British-American explorations of Africa and celebrated Emperor Wilhelm I.[40] All of these had first been exhibited at the jubilee exhibition of the Royal Academy of Arts in Berlin in 1886.[41] The last panorama exhibited at Roßplatz, from 1905 to 1910, was an exception as it had been imported from France. Painted by Charles Édouard Armand-Dumaresq, it showed a French view of the Battle of Bapaume from the Franco-Prussian War.[42] Some of the panoramas were accompanied by diorama exhibitions with more geographically diverse contents but still with a strong emphasis on recent military battles: among them were dioramas of the defeat of the Commune uprising in Paris in 1871 by French panorama painter Félix Philippoteaux, the Second Boer War, and the Battle of Port Arthur from the Russo-Japanese War.[43]

While the panorama entrepreneurs in Leipzig linked up with globally interconnected production networks, this integration remained highly selective and regionally limited. The majority of the paintings exhibited in Leipzig were produced in Munich and Berlin and circulated mainly within German-speaking

---

[38] "Sturm der Sachsen unter Kronprinz Albert auf St. Privat", exhibited 1898–1901. See Schiermeier, *Panorama München*, p. 49; Alexandre and Beutter, *Der Panoramamaler Louis Braun*, pp. 115–117.

[39] "Sturm der Preußen und Bayern auf Weissenburg am 4. August 1870", exhibited 1901–1905. See Schiermeier, *Panorama München*, p. 46; Alexandre and Beutter, *Der Panoramamaler Louis Braun*, pp. 103–105.

[40] These included "Stanley an den Congo-Fällen" by Wilhelm Gentz and Ernst Körner, showing Henry Morton Stanley's Congo exploration in the mid-1870s; "Wißmann auf der Elephantenjagd" by Eugen Bracht et al. showing an elephant hunt during a German expedition to Africa; "Kaiser Wilhelm I. auf der Fahrt nach dem Kriegsschauplatze" and "Das historische Eckfenster", showing German Emperor Wilhelm I, by Berlin painter Franz Skarbina.

[41] See Großkinsky, *Eugen Bracht*, p. 92; Oettermann, *The Panorama*, pp. 257–258.

[42] '"Die Schlacht von Bapaume am 3. Januar 1871", painted in Lille in 1882 and also shown in Paris.

[43] "Der Todeskampf der Pariser Commune. Vor/Nach der Erstürmung des Friedhofes Père-la-Chaise im Mai 1871", two dioramas by Félix Philippoteaux and exhibited in 1893–1894; "Der Heldenkampf der Buren. Drei Dioramen", painter unknown and exhibited in 1902–1903; "Die Seeschlacht von Port Arthur", diorama by German painter Robert Gleich and exhibited in 1905–1906.

countries. Moreover, most of the panoramas and the texts in the accompanying brochures openly propagated German nationalism and imperialism. They celebrated the bravery and sacrifice of German troops and the defeat of the French both in the Napoleonic Wars and in the Franco-Prussian War, expressed admiration for Emperor Wilhelm I, and supported German colonial enterprises and archaeological expeditions. The panoramas and dioramas were dedicated to nation and empire-building, collective memory, and patriotic education. They also included a strong emphasis on regional identity and pride, often featuring crown prince and later King Albert of Saxony and Saxon troops.[44] The patriotic themes as well as the gestures of loyalty to the Saxon king helped to legitimize the commercial panorama enterprise and connect it to "higher" values and interests, all while offering popular attractions for mass audiences. At the same time, occasional exhibitions of panoramas and dioramas by prestigious French artists such as Armand-Dumaresq and Philippoteaux paid homage to the pioneering influence of French historical painting and panorama production. Patriotic imagery and rhetoric, on the one hand, and transnational entanglements and emulation, on the other, were not mutually exclusive but complementary.

Nationalism clearly served as a marketing tool that was used to strengthen the panorama industry and to embed it more effectively at the local and regional scale. The integration went as far as using panoramas to boost economic development in the city of Leipzig, which is evidenced when focusing on the owners of the Panorama am Roßplatz and the business strategies they pursued. The rotunda was built by Friedrich August Nietzschmann, a master carpenter, in 1884. After 1886, the Leipziger Panorama-Gesellschaft was listed as the owner of the property. A major shareholder was the Leipziger Immobiliengesellschaft (Leipzig Real Estate Company), a local stock company engaged in property acquisition and management. The successive operators of the panorama restaurant also ran the panorama exhibitions and acquired the paintings. In 1898, a new company, the German limited liability company, Leipziger Panorama GmbH, was founded and took over the site. While the Leipziger Immobiliengesellschaft remained involved, another major shareholder came in – the Leipziger Bierbrauerei zu Reudnitz, Riebeck & Co. AG (Leipzig Beer Brewery of Reudnitz, Riebeck & Co.), one of the biggest breweries in Saxony. After 1903, it was the sole shareholder of the Leipziger Panorama GmbH. This arrangement survived the end of panorama exhibitions at the premises and remained in place until Riebeck finally absorbed

---

44 Panoramas showing crown prince Albert von Sachsen and Saxon troops included Louis Braun's Battle of Mars-la-Tour, Eugen Bracht's Battle of Villiers, Hünten and Simmler's Battle of Gravelotte-St. Privat, and Louis Braun's Battle of Gravelotte-St. Privat.

the Leipziger Panorama GmbH in 1937.[45] The rotunda at Roßplatz was destroyed in the bombings of World War II.

But why did these companies engage in the panorama business? It was not uncommon for real estate developers to invest in representative cultural venues that helped increase the value of the surrounding land. The Roßplatz had long been an important market and trade fair site with restaurants, guest houses, and hotels. It was remodelled in the late nineteenth century with a series of prestigious building projects, the panorama rotunda being only one of them: for example, the Hôtel de Prusse was rebuilt from 1881 to 1883; the house of the exclusive philanthropic society Harmonie opened in 1887; the elegant Café Bauer opened in 1890; and the Markthalle, near Roßplatz, opened in 1891. The Leipziger Immobiliengesellschaft was deeply involved in the redevelopment of the Roßplatz at the time.[46] Its holdings of the panorama premises became part of a larger real estate development process.

In the course of the nineteenth century, not only real estate developers but also brewery, restaurant, pub, and beer hall owners increasingly used the entertainment business for their own profit – the shows attracted crowds and helped sell more food and beverages. To ensure and enhance sales, the Riebeck brewery had pursued an expansion strategy and gradually acquired more and more breweries and restaurants in the region.[47] From this perspective, the panorama paintings helped to promote the panorama restaurant and the sale of Riebeck beer, which was also advertised on the rotunda building and in the panorama brochures sold for each exhibition. The first panorama painting exhibited at Roßplatz attracted more than 2,000 visitors on some days.[48] Many of them also visited the restaurant, which offered matching concerts of military

---

[45] See *Leipziger Adreß-Buch, 1884–1911*; Sächsisches Staatsarchiv Leipzig (SStAL), Amtsgericht Leipzig, Handelsregister, file no. 21096, Fol. 10079 (Leipziger Panorama, GmbH); SStAL, Amtsgericht Leipzig, Handelsregister, file no. 21064, Fol. 6821 and HRB 293 (Riebeck-Brauerei Aktiengesellschaft Leipzig); R. Börner (ed.), *Die Sächsischen Actien-Gesellschaften und die an sächsischen Börsen courshabenden auswärtigen Industriewerthe. Jahrbuch der Dresdner, Leipziger und Zwickauer Börse*, 7th edition, Riesa: Börner, 1897; *Handbuch der Deutschen Aktien-Gesellschaften. Das Spezial-Archiv der Deutschen Wirtschaft*, Darmstadt: Hoppenstedt, 1898–1940. See also G. Wustmann, *Leipzig und die Leipziger Immobiliengesellschaft. Ein Beitrag zur Geschichte der Stadt im letzten Drittel des neunzehnten Jahrhunderts*, Leipzig: Verlag der Leipziger Immobiliengesellschaft, 1899, p. 162.
[46] Wustmann, *Leipzig und die Leipziger Immobiliengesellschaft*, pp. 46–61, 87–99.
[47] See *Handbuch der Deutschen Aktiengesellschaften*, and the company's articles of association (Statut) in SStAL, Amtsgericht Leipzig, HRB 293, vol. 4, 26/4, pp. 26, 87.
[48] "Leipzig, 25. October. Das vor kurzer Zeit eröffnete Schlachten-Panorama...", *Sechste Beilage zum Leipziger Tageblatt und Anzeiger* 78 (26 October 1884) 300, p. 5707.

bands in the garden and became a popular location in Leipzig. Consequentially, Riebeck acquired all shares in the Leipziger Panorama GmbH in 1903 in order to secure its hold on the flourishing restaurant.[49] The restaurant was in fact able to continue on its own even after the end of panorama exhibitions in 1910 and took over the first floor. After 1911, the former exhibition hall was used for billiards, and in 1926, the Panorama-Künstlerspiele opened there, offering concerts and theatre. The end of diorama and panorama exhibitions at Roßplatz coincided not only with the end of the wider panorama boom, but also with local dynamics – both the Leipziger Immobiliengesellschaft and Riebeck exited the panorama business some years after the exhibitions had fulfilled their purpose of stimulating local economic development.

Another important location of the panorama business in Leipzig was the Krystall-Palast, the city's biggest entertainment complex, which included a diorama exhibition. The Krystall-Palast was founded by local merchant Eduard Berthold, who was an enthusiast and promoter of commercial entertainments.[50] In 1881, he purchased the defunct Schützenhaus, the former clubhouse of the Leipzig shooting association. The premises, which were located just outside of the city centre, had been developed by the former owners into an entertainment venue influenced by Parisian trends – with the Trianon, a spectacular amusement garden, and a big restaurant and event hall used for diverse festivities, concerts, and shows. With the help of bank loans, Berthold converted the whole site in accordance with the most up-to-date standards of show business. He added a crystal hall construction modelled after the Crystal Palace that had first made waves at the Great Exhibition in London in 1851 and was later rebuilt as an exhibition hall in Sydenham. The adapted version of the Leipzig Krystall-Palast took into consideration the specific requirements of a city much smaller than London. It included a variety of entertainment, with something for everyone: theatre and concert halls, club rooms, a winter garden, bowling alleys, a restaurant and cafe, and exhibition spaces.[51] Berthold also tried to accommodate the widespread

---

49 See *Jahres-Bericht der Leipziger Bierbrauerei zu Reudnitz, Riebeck & Co., Aktiengesellschaft für das achtzehnte Geschäftsjahr vom 1. Oktober 1903 bis 30. September 1904*, in: SStAL, Amtsgericht Leipzig, HRB 293, vol. 4, 26/4, pp. 249.
50 Berthold owned a clothing store in the city centre. See *Leipziger Adreß-Buch, 1869–1890*.
51 On the Krystall-Palast, see "Der neue Krystallpalast in Leipzig", in: *Leipziger Illustrirte Zeitung* 2027 (6 May 1882), pp. 365–368; O. Moser, *Entwickelungsgeschichte des Krystall-Palastes vormals Schützenhaus-Etablissement zu Leipzig*, Leipzig: Frankenstein & Wagner, 1887; P. Daehne, *Festschrift der Leipziger Krystall-Palast Aktiengesellschaft aus Anlaß des fünfundsiebzigjährigen Bestehens des früheren Schützenhaus-Etablissements, gegründet 1834, und des fünfundzwanzigjährigen Bestehens der Krystall-Palast-Aktiengesellschaft gegründet 1884*, Leipzig: J.J. Weber, 1909; E.W. Schmidt, *50 Jahre Krystall-Palast, 100 Jahre Bestehen des früheren*

interests of the city's elites in a representative and modern location for social events, providing rooms for private festivities as well as for meetings of clubs, associations, and professional organizations.

This strategy became even more pronounced when Berthold added a huge multifunctional hall to the premises in 1887. The Alberthalle was named after King Albert of Saxony. The name was probably also a tip of the hat, so to say, to the Royal Albert Hall in London, the concert hall that had opened in 1871 and was named after the deceased prince consort of Queen Victoria. With the Alberthalle, Berthold's initial aim was to construct a permanent circus hall in Leipzig, but circuses visited the city only irregularly. So he came up with a plan that permitted various uses and was regarded as a real innovation at the time. He envisioned the Alberthalle as a multifunctional event hall that could serve not only as a circus but also as a concert hall, a ballroom, an exhibition hall, and a theatre and could accommodate 3,000 to 4,000 visitors. On the upper floor, right above the big event hall, Berthold planned an additional exhibition room for dioramas. With a panorama, concert hall, municipal theatre, and his own variety theatre and club rooms already in place in Leipzig, it was economically reasonable to choose a flexible structure that included all kinds of cultural offerings.[52] Based on Berthold's vision, Arwed Roßbach, an architect from Leipzig who would later construct some of the most prestigious buildings in the city, designed the Alberthalle.[53] The hall opened at the time of the trade fair in spring 1887, with a series of guest performances by Circus Renz.[54] The Krystall-Palast complex was one of the biggest entertainment venues in Germany, claiming in its advertisements that it could accommodate 15,000 visitors at the same time.

Berthold decided not to install a second circular panorama in Leipzig. Instead, he opted for dioramas that could be changed more easily and, by

---

Schützenhauses. Eine Erinnerungsbeigabe zum Jubiläums-Festprogramm vom 16. bis 31. März 1936, Leipzig: Krystall-Palast, 1936; A. Busse, *Saltos, Stars und Sekt auf Marken: Krystallpalast-Varieté-Geschichten*, Leipzig: Stoneart-Verlag, 1998; T. Bitterlich, "Variétégeschichte um 1900. Studien zum Vergesellschaftungsprozeß einer sozialen Figuration im Bereich der Freizeit", MA thesis, Universität Leipzig, Institut für Theaterwissenschaft, 2002.

52 See Moser, *Entwickelungsgeschichte*, pp. 38–40.
53 A. Rossbach, "Der Zirkus- und Diorama-Bau im Crystallpalast zu Leipzig", *Deutsche Bauzeitung* 22 (31 March 1888) 26, pp. 153–154; B.M. Kaun, *Arwed Rossbach 1844–1902. Ein Architekt im Geiste Sempers. Das Gesamtwerk*, Wettin-Löbejün: Stekovics, 2011.
54 O. Moser, "Die neue Albert-Halle des Krystallpalastes zu Leipzig", *Leipziger Illustrirte Zeitung* 2284 (9 April 1887), p. 377.

showcasing several paintings, would offer something to suit all tastes.⁵⁵ He got connected to the same panorama and diorama distribution networks the owners of the rotunda at Roßplatz had worked with. Celebrated Munich panorama and diorama artists Louis Braun and Hans Petersen were in charge of setting up the exhibition. It opened in 1887 with seven monumental paintings by different painters from Munich. The dioramas covered a wide range of subjects – from Monaco, the Alps, and Cameroon to a harem scene, a German naval exercise, and Napoleon I in Leipzig – combining the typical range of popular orientalist, colonialist, historicist, and nationalist topics at the time.⁵⁶ In 1890, the exhibition was replaced by a so-called "concert and restaurant panorama", envisioned by Berthold and executed under the direction of Leipzig-based painter Ernst Kiesling. It featured an ideal Italian landscape as a picturesque backdrop for a wine restaurant and Viennese café, but it only remained open until the end of the year.⁵⁷ From 1893 to 1896, the Krystall-Palast exhibited three marine panoramas, all by Hans Petersen. They showcased a German steamboat entering New York harbour (first shown in Bremen in 1890, then in Frankfurt/Main and Berlin), the island of Heligoland, which had just been handed over to Germany by the British in 1890, and a naval review in front of the German emperor.⁵⁸ These panoramas were in fact advertising the North German Lloyd steamship lines and reflected German public enthusiasm for the navy.

The dioramas at the Krystall-Palast reveal an interesting shift in the spatial imaginations produced by the panorama industry as well as other segments of the world that the portal now gave access to. These smaller formats were not as suitable for monumental and spectacular battle scenes. They had always been

---

55 Moser, *Entwickelungsgeschichte*, pp. 46–47.

56 The dioramas shown at the opening in 1887 were "Monte Carlo und Monaco" and "Alpenglühen" (alpenglow) by Edmund Berninger; "Frauenleben im Orient" (a harem scene) by Franz Simm; "Bad einer römischen Kaiserin" (bathing Roman empress) by Hermann Schneider; "Deutsche Truppen an der Ostsee" (naval exercise by German troops in the Danzig Bay) by Braun and Petersen; the colonial scene "Aqua-Stadt von Kamerun" by Petersen and Leopold Schönchen; and Braun's "Die Flucht Napoleon I. aus Leipzig am 19. October 1813" (Napoleon's flight from Leipzig after losing the Battle of the Nations). See "Aus dem Diorama des Krystallpalastes zu Leipzig", *Leipziger Illustrirte Zeitung* 2302 (13 August 1887), p. 159; Moser, *Entwickelungsgeschichte*, pp. 46–49; Daehne, *Festschrift*, pp. xxxi–xxxv; Schmidt, *50 Jahre Krystall-Palast*, p. 6.

57 See A. Weiske, "Das Concert- und Restaurant-Panorama im Leipziger Krystallpaläste", *7. Beilage zum Leipziger Tageblatt und Anzeiger* 131 (11 May 1890), p. 3124.

58 1893 "Einfahrt des Lloyd-Dampfers 'Lahn' in den Hafen von New-York"; 1893 "Helgoland mit sturmdurchwühlter See und Rettung Schiffbrüchiger"; 1894–1896 "Flottenparade vor Sr. Majestät dem Kaiser im Kieler Kriegshafen". See Weidauer, *Berliner Panoramen*, pp. 32–33; Oettermann, *The Panorama*, pp. 271–273.

characterized by a larger variety of subject matters, allowing for more experimentation and quicker change. However, the choices of paintings in the Krystall-Palast also highlight new orientations that came to the forefront as the century closed. New locations were added to the imaginary geography of modern Germans through the development of tourism (especially the Alps and Italy), the peak of mass migration (to North America), German colonialism, and a focus on naval expansion in the rising competition with Britain. Some of the paintings also show an ambition to "elevate" the entertainment format through themes more typical in academic painting, reflecting the social range of patrons at the Krystall-Palast, many of them belonging to the city's elite.

Despite various efforts, the diorama exhibitions were not successful enough and ended.[59] However, it was exactly Berthold's initial decision to combine different forms of entertainment that helped to stabilize the Krystall-Palast in the long term and made it flexible enough to adapt to local conditions and changing trends. After the end of the diorama and panorama exhibitions, the Krystall-Palast offered film screenings. The Alberthalle was turned into a cinema in 1918 and the Krystall-Palast housed several film production companies.[60] The complex as a whole remained in business until it was destroyed in World War II.

Just like the Panorama am Roßplatz, the Krystall-Palast exhibitions relied heavily on national production and distribution networks. Following the same trends as panorama and diorama exhibitions in other German cities, the Krystall-Palast offered patriotic topics and a German view on global entanglements painted by German artists. At the same time, the Krystall-Palast company itself became closely integrated into transnational business networks. Berthold's business plan had seemed so promising that even while the Alberthalle was still under construction, investors became interested in the venture. In March 1887, the Krystall-Palast was converted into a stock company with the help of Edmund Becker, of the local bank house Becker & Co.[61] The Leipziger Krystall-Palast, AG (Leipzig Crystal Palace Company, Limited) had its seat in London, with a branch in Leipzig. Berthold remained the managing director of the Krystall-Palast until 1890 but was no longer its sole owner. The company's board of directors consisted almost exclusively of bankers, merchants, industrialists, and jurists from

---

59 Daehne, *Festschrift*, p. xxxi; Schmidt, *50 Jahre Krystall-Palast*, p. 6.
60 The cinema was renovated and became property of the Ufa in 1924, see *Ufa-Theaterhalle. Festschrift herausgegeben zur Wieder-Eröffnung am 11. November 1924*, Leipzig 1924.
61 Moser, *Entwickelungsgeschichte*, pp. 40–41, 52.

Leipzig.⁶² The innovative business plan of an enthusiast of modern entertainments had convinced the local economic elite to join and eventually take over the business. They discovered commercial entertainment as an attractive investment opportunity and then integrated Berthold's venture into the structures of transnational finance. In the era of German nationalism and imperialism, this was a delicate move. While modern cities functioned as portals of economic entanglement and global imaginations, it was still crucial that ownership remained in local hands and fantasies of the world bound by cultural and political affiliations.⁶³

Conclusions

Investigating the dynamics of modern entertainment industries through the lens of portals of globalization is part of a wider tendency in globalization research to focus on the particular mechanisms and geographies of cross-border exchanges as well as on their historical transformations in shifting spatial orders. Accordingly, the aim here was to examine the particular role the panorama enterprises in the city of Leipzig occupied within transnational production networks and to identify the mediating agents who devised practices and institutional frameworks to profit from and steer these interconnections. This in turn adds insights into the interplay of different spatial scales and formats in the development of modern entertainment industries under the global condition. The last decades of the nineteenth century were a critical phase in the formation of these industries, with the consolidation of large-scale business networks that rested upon an increasing number of permanent production and exhibition facilities in various locations and tapped into spatial imaginations that envisioned the relationship between city, region, nation-empire, and world.

The transition from seasonal offerings was gradual – initially, new venues and shows opened during fair season to increase the number of visitors. At the same time, older formats remained in existence – smaller panoramas were still exhibited during the fairs. But in 1907, the city relocated the Kleinmesse – sales

---

62 See SStAL, Amtsgericht Leipzig, Handelsregister, file no. 21066, Fol. 6967 (Leipzig Crystal Palace Company, Limited). Roßbach and Berthold left the board of directors in 1888 and 1890, respectively.

63 In his brochure presenting the new Krystall-Palast in 1887, publicist Otto Moser made efforts to downplay the London connection in order to remove existing doubts of the locals and encourage them to buy shares in the company. Moser, *Entwickelungsgeschichte*, pp. 4, 52–54. In 1926, the company closed the London location and moved its headquarters to Leipzig.

and amusement stands – to the Platz vor dem Frankfurter Tor, a place outside of the city gates, separating the retail and show trade from the growing sample fair businesses in the centre. This spatial separation amplified the larger structural changes in the entertainment business that profoundly reshaped the urban cultural landscape. At the turn of the twentieth century, private corporations operating representative permanent venues dominated the entertainment sector in the city.

The transformation of Leipzig's cultural sector played out in close interaction with a reorganization of the entertainment industries on a larger scale. The second panorama boom propelled extensive shifts in the spatial organization and mechanisms of panorama production and distribution. New financial and production centres as well as transnational standards and circuits were established. These changes enabled entrepreneurs in Leipzig to construct permanent exhibition venues, as they could rely on a successful business model and a steady supply of panoramas and dioramas. While they did not exercise decisive influence on the panorama industry as a whole and remained dependent on production and distribution structures established by others, they were able to decide what panoramas were being exhibited in Leipzig, and some of the paintings they commissioned later went on to other cities.

Viewing Leipzig as a portal of globalization, these shifts reveal a changed position of the city within transnational entertainment networks as well as the emergence of new actors and institutions that fostered and controlled these interconnections. Economic and cultural exchanges and transfers were introduced and regulated differently over time. During the first panorama wave, exhibition offerings in Leipzig depended on the initiative of itinerant performers and on concessions from the city and state. During the second wave, local companies operating permanent panorama exhibitions took over some of these functions. The new panorama and diorama venues were established in Leipzig, not as part of transnational business expansion from the pioneering centres of metropolitan culture, but rather on the initiative of entrepreneurs from the city. They introduced new visual spectacles in the city that drew crowds and could be used as profit opportunities and marketing tools. Moreover, they increasingly influenced the city's public sphere and modes of relating to the world – a mediating function they were able to retain even after the decline of the panorama business.

The city of Leipzig occupied a particular position within these transnational networks of the second-wave panorama industry. The industry consisted of loosely linked circuits based on the interplay of various production sites, distribution channels, and locations for display. Apart from the global metropolises, corporate headquarters in Brussels and production facilities in Munich and

Berlin played an essential role. The Leipziger Panorama-Gesellschaft and the Krystall-Palast acquired most of their panoramas and dioramas directly from the producers in Berlin and Munich or from distribution networks that connected German-speaking cities in Europe. These were part of intersecting panorama circuits worldwide, and some of the paintings travelled as far as the United States, Australia, and Japan. But Leipzig remained largely disconnected from those other areas. Apart from a few exceptions, the panoramas and dioramas exhibited in Leipzig were patriotic paintings produced in Germany. The visions of the world they offered focused on the role and claims of Germans and the German Empire in the world, sometimes with a regional or local twist. This makes the panorama business a good example of how portals of globalization are not only transfer points fostering new connections but are also filtering to what extent these affect the location and how they are perceived. They hence play a crucial role in creating uneven and fragmented geographies of production networks and spatial imaginations under the global condition.

This uneven integration of panorama networks and markets was in part the result of an interesting tension in the industry – a play of scales between transnationally entangled business structures, national or imperial imaginations, and local or regional cultural and economic agendas. The entrepreneurs of the second panorama wave had aimed to foster transnational standards and touring of the paintings in order to increase their profits. At the same time, they had discovered nationalism and imperialism as a powerful marketing tool to draw crowds, legitimate their businesses, and secure support by political elites. Their focus on patriotic imagery had some adverse side effects: it became a barrier for the wide circulation of the canvases and led to largely separated distribution circuits in different countries or cultural spheres. Moreover, panoramas and dioramas were used as instruments of real estate speculation and the promotion of breweries and restaurants (as in the case of the panorama rotunda) or as part of a diversification strategy for an urban entertainment complex (in the case of the Krystall-Palast). Consequentially, the transnational panorama business also became integrated into diverse local and regional development projects.

Analysing the entertainment industries from the perspective of portals of globalization opens up a more nuanced understanding of a city's integration into global networks. By looking at specific transfer agents and the way they influenced changing patterns of interconnection, the city appears not as a bounded place affected by global flows, but as a dynamic interaction site. It is then possible to evaluate not only the quality and range of a city's spatial interconnections, but also the agency different kinds of actors had when managing them, and the capacities and institutions that they built up over time. This way, we can get a more refined picture of how cultural formats "travelled" from place to place and how complex multiscale networks were established, operated, and transformed. Moreover, analysing a regional metropolis can help to better grasp the unevenness of transnational cultural and economic integration and to understand how various spatial formats, functional specializations, and logics of action come into play in different segments of the networks.

Part IV: **International Spaces**

Glenda Sluga
The International History of (International) Sovereignty

> In a plastic period like this it seems as though anything could happen.
> Emily Greene Balch, *Nobel lecture, 1947.*

Historians have all but dispensed with a conventional chronology that marks the Treaty of Westphalia (1648) as the origin of a modern state-centric territorial sovereignty. Instead, they are accumulating evidence that, since at least the early nineteenth century, sovereignty stretches back to the imperial practice of intervention into polities elsewhere on humanitarian grounds.[1] Imperial sovereignty was less uniform than imperial officials and cartographers asserted; instead, as Lauren Benton has argued, it was (and is) usually "more myth than reality, more a story that polities [told] about their own power than a definite quality that they possess[ed]".[2] Then there is the increasing number of historical examples of non-normative, quasi-invisible forms of extra-territoriality that shaped the global imperial political architecture of the late nineteenth century: from the remaining principalities of the Holy Roman empire, and the conceptually distinctive practices of the Habsburgs as they separated cultural sovereignty from political sovereignty within their imperial territory, to the European claims to commercial and municipal authority in the treaty ports that dotted China's seaboard and river system, carving out the spoils of war.[3]

In this chapter, my aim is to move this new history of sovereignty more firmly into the twentieth century. During that century, imperial sovereignties came under increased pressure from the privileging of national-state sovereignty, on the one hand, and, less consistently, the (imagined) authority of intergovernmental institutions and practices, and the universalist ambitions inscribed in international law as being representative of mankind, on the other. My focus is on those less consistent moments, at the end of the two world wars,

---

[1] See B. Simms and D.J.B. Trim (eds.), *Humanitarian Intervention: A History*, Cambridge: Cambridge University Press, 2011.
[2] L. Benton, *A Search for Sovereignty: Law and Geography in European Empires, 1400–1900*, Cambridge: Cambridge University Press, 2009, p. 279.
[3] See, e.g., N. Wheatley, "Spectral Legal Personality in Interwar International Law: On New Ways of Not Being a State", *Law and History Review* 35 (2017) 3, pp. 753–787; cf. C. Schmitt's anti-League text, "The Nomos of the Earth in the International Law of the Jus Publicum Europaem", *Telos* (2006); as well as the voices of the nationalists of Danzig.

and the Cold War decades of decolonization. In 1919 and 1945, the concept of sovereignty was tackled as an international problem by statesmen establishing international world orders and by thinkers, many of them Nobel Prize winners. Throughout both these periods, we find the relevance of an "international" sovereignty articulated as international territory. From the 1950s to the 1970s, decolonization, working through the United Nations (UN), involved the reinvention of the world's nation-state-scape around the concept of "permanent sovereignty" and the commercial benefits of "natural resources". These diverse strands were brought together in the UN's Moon Agreement (1979), which stipulated international sovereignty over the "natural resources" of outer space in the interests of "mankind". They extend across a spectrum of twentieth-century national and international sovereignty, imagined in legal, really existing, and visible and invisible forms. In what follows, I work my way along this spectrum, singling out the peculiar place of *economic* sovereignty in this (international) history.[4]

1919: National Utopia

The arrival of nation-state sovereignty has long shaped historical narratives surrounding the end of the First World War. As the delegates of the victorious powers – Britain, US, France, Australia, Italy, Japan, China, the Maharaja of Bijkaner – assembled in Paris in 1919 to confront the problem of contested territories in the former European and non-European lands of defeated and collapsed empires, they utilized their war-won collective moral and military authority to impose the principle of nationality as the determinant of political and territorial sovereignty. That principle, also known as "self-determination", implied that political borders would coincide with the national identification of a population and territorial sovereignty with the sovereign status of the national people.[5]

Here, historians have long told us, was the inevitability of territorial nation-state sovereignty at work. To be sure, even before the war's end, the victorious governments had gathered experts to mobilize the authority of

---

[4] A. Cameron and R. Palan, *The Imagined Economies of Globalization*, London: Sage, 2004, p. 8; see also G. Simpson, "Something to Do with States", in: A. Orford and F. Hoffmann (eds.), *The Oxford Handbook of the Theory of International Law*, Oxford: Oxford University Press, 2016; also N. Schrijver, *Sovereignty over Natural Resources: Balancing Rights and Duties*, Cambridge: Cambridge University Press, 2008, p. 368.

[5] G. Sluga, *The Nation, Psychology and International Politics 1870–1919*, Basingstoke: Palgrave Macmillan, 2006. This had been the thrust of Woodrow Wilson's famous Fourteen Points presented in 1918.

"scientific facts" in order to determine the true borders of (Central) Europe's nation-states. This move was intended to underline the "scientific" authority of sovereignty as much as its political or international legitimacy. However, there was no agreement among the experts about the appropriate scientific method. Instead, in Paris in 1919, politicians and experts alike – many of them classicists, historians, and geographers – found themselves debating an older question: What is a nation?

Their answers were surprising. In the international context of peace-making in 1919, peace-makers confirmed the view that the status of women and of race were defining prerogatives of nation-state sovereignty. Therefore, they could not be subject to any international agreement.[6] They also agreed that it was appropriate to move whole populations across newly established political borders in the defeated Habsburg and Ottoman empires in order to make the reality fit the principle, namely that sovereignty represented individuals who shared an intrinsic nationality.[7] Even in these cases, where the geographical location of people had to be adjusted in order to make the principle of nationality work, historians preferred to fault the backwardness of the "eastern" parts of Europe, rather than the principle at stake.[8]

In practice, then, even national sovereignty could be an imperfect practice mediated through the League of Nations' fragile international authority. The most obvious sites of that authority were the Hague-based Permanent Court of International Justice, the International Labour Office, and the International Health Organization.[9] The introduction of minority rights in some post-war European treaties also gave the League symbolic authority over the security of racial or

---

[6] The majority of the peace-makers had accepted the inclusion of race equality as a principle to be included in the League's covenant, but Wilson took the decision that the lack of unanimity meant it could not be passed. By contrast, peace-makers agreed unanimously that the status of women was definitive for national sovereignty – despite demands of feminists for making it an international/universal issue. See Sluga, *The Nation, Psychology and International Politics*; also G. Sluga, "What is National Self-Determination? Nationality and Psychology during the Apogee of Nationalism", *Nations and Nationalism*, 11 (2005) 1, pp. 1–20.

[7] For all the conventional commentary on the problematic relationship of national identities to national spaces in the territories of the former Habsburg and Ottoman empires, as the American philosopher John Dewey noted at the time, even in the territories of the US, France, and Britain there was no simple equation of national identification and national spaces. For more on all this history, see Sluga, *The Nation, Psychology and International Politics*.

[8] See G. Sluga, *The Problem of Trieste and the Italo-Yugoslav Border: Difference, Identity and Sovereignty in Twentieth-Century Europe*, Albany: State University of New York Press, 2001.

[9] The Permanent Court of International Justice had its physical home in the Carnegie-funded Hague Peace Palace, completed in 1913. See G. Sluga, *Internationalism in the Age of Nationalism*, Philadelphia: University of Pennsylvania Press, 2013, pp. 11–78.

ethnic minorities (rather than individuals) that remained within the borders of former Habsburg territories granted national self-determination.[10] When peacemakers agreed to deploy alternative forms of sovereignty in a few contested borderlands, League bodies also assumed "international" responsibility. This was particularly the case in the Free City of Danzig – contested between Germany and Poland – a semi-autonomous city state in existence between 1920 and 1939 under actual League of Nations supervision, embodied in appointed high commissioners that included a series of English, Irish, Italian, and Swiss men.[11]

When it came to contested colonial spaces, the League was also given responsibility, obliquely, for a completely new concept of international imperial oversight rationalized in the language of national sovereignty. The mandate system, as it was known, was a distorted manifestation of the principle of nationality, imposed on the colonial territories of the defeated Ottoman, Austro-Hungarian, and German empires in Africa, the Middle East, and the Pacific. On the argument that these territories were not yet biologically, psychologically, or politically capable of exercising national self-determination, they were subjected to a logic of delayed sovereignty and placed in the trust of mandate powers: Britain, France, Australia, New Zealand, South Africa, or Belgium.[12]

The League mandate system exhibited the tensions between national and international sovereignty as well as territorial and non-territorial practices of sovereignty in this new international system. Most notably, empires and aspiring imperial powers could exercise economic sovereignty without territorial sovereignty. As Susan Pedersen argues, mandates created "spaces from which sovereignty was banished altogether" by allowing – on imperial precedent – the decoupling of legal territorial sovereignty and economic control.[13] So, Belgium

---

[10] Cf. D. Whitehall, "Hannah Arendt and International Law", in: A. Orford and F. Hoffmann (eds.), *The Oxford Handbook of the Theory of International Law*, Oxford: Oxford University Press, 2016, pp. 231–256; Arendt argues that the minority treaties transformed the state from an instrument of the law into an instrument of the nation, granting supremacy to the will of nation over all legal and abstract institutions.

[11] Danzig is currently known by its Polish name, Gdańsk. The "free city" idea had also been experimented with under Napoleon as well as the European powers determining a post-Napoleonic order in 1815. The case of the Free State of Fiume (currently Croatian Rijeka), an international polity invented as a resolution to the competing territorial claims of the Kingdom of Italy and a new Kingdom of Serbs, Croats and Slovenes, is another example; the "free state" existed for only one year de facto and four years de jure, but it held League membership and its own currency, the Fiume Krone, stamped over Habsburg notes.

[12] Sluga, *The Nation, Psychology and International Politics*.

[13] S. Pedersen, *The Guardians: The League of Nations and the Crisis of Empire*, Oxford: Oxford University Press, 2016, pp. 203, 232.

was not allowed to absorb its mandate Ruanda-Urundi into its colonial Congo administration, but when, in 1928, Ruanda experienced famine, Belgians were given room to justify labour practices for cultivation, portage, and roadwork, even though the League forbade forced labour. In the case of Iraq, a different scenario was deployed by the mandate power. Britain decided to grant Iraq political independence, while maintaining imperial control over its economic and military sovereignty. Britain avoided international oversight (such as it was) while still making use of the League as a forum in which Iraq could claim its transition from mandate to the status of an independent territorial state. Pedersen argues that the Permanent Mandates Commission became a bureaucratic procedural body that "helped make the end of empire imaginable and normative statehood possible" and confirmed that territorial control was not "essential to the maintenance of global power".[14]

Imperial adaptations of sovereignty were further adapted in an era that privileged both the language of internationalism and nationalism. The United States had already learnt that the relatively invisible economic forms of extra-territorial sovereignty could be deployed outside of the League context. Woodrow Wilson – a League enthusiast – reasoned the United States had no interest in the imperial connotations of mandates, even though American experts were crucial to the scheme's conceptualization. Instead, the United States government favoured the exercise of political and economic influence through the less visible precedents of extra-territorial economic sovereignty, including protectorates and concessions, as well as overt military occupation.[15]

1945: International Utopia

The League's replacement, the United Nations, relied for its authority on a charter that reflected the expanded spectrum of wartime thinking on the political significance of the international, including the possibilities of internationalization. In the traumatic wake of a second world war, even the doyen of realpolitik, Hans Morgenthau, spoke of the obsolescence of the nation-state. Territorial sovereignty was up for debate, most often in the frame of federalism, even as anti-colonial movements called on their own right to nation-state forms of sovereignty, as based on the promise of the Atlantic Charter (1941).[16]

---

14 Ibid., p. 203.
15 Sluga, *The Nation, Psychology and International Politics*, pp. 5, 129, 131, 157.
16 Sluga, *Internationalism in the Age of Nationalism*, pp. 1–10, 79–117.

The Charter of the UN (1945), exacerbated the existing tensions in the concept of sovereignty: it affirmed the sovereign status of nation-states; lent enhanced status to non-governmental organizations (NGOs); and it aligned the international authority and legitimacy of the UN itself with a new language of universal human rights.[17] National sovereignty was still not assumed to be a universal right, and in 1945, the mandate system made its return, in a revised form, as "trusteeship". The trusteeship regime was applied to the colonies that had remained in the mandate system – the majority in Africa and the Pacific – and those colonial territories taken from defeated Japan. In contrast with the mandate requirements, this time trustee international obligations were overseen more actively by the UN Trusteeship Council and its bureaucratic arm, the Trusteeship department.[18] The race-inflected civilizational narratives of 1919 that undergirded the delay of claims to national sovereignty by colonies were replaced with the hierarchical logic of modernity and relative economic development – measured in the language and images of industrialization and urbanization.[19]

As before, international sovereignty was brought into play in contested borderlands. In the port town of Trieste, where the post-fascist Italian republic and the new communist Yugoslav government both claimed authority, and British-American forces actually occupied the territory, an international "free territory" seemed to be the answer.[20] The Free Territory of Trieste (FTT), 738 square kilometres of land governed by a UN Security Council-approved governor, was authorized by the Paris Peace Treaty (10 February 1947). Its international status was underlined in the curious way it was meant to be "free" of "race/ethnicity/ and nationality"; even the governor could not be a citizen of the territory so as to avoid possible national bias.[21] Nevertheless, the FTT was promised all the symbolic trappings of national sovereignty: its own currency, official flag, stamps, passport, and coat of arms, and produce from the region was to be marked "Made in the Free Territory".[22] Its "free" status was most explicitly constituted through the designation of its port as a free customs zone. The FTT was also propped up by a less visible economic rationalization. The United States and

---

17 United Nations, *Charter of the United Nations*, 1 UNTS XVI, 24 October 1945.
18 Sluga, *Internationalism in the Age of Nationalism*, pp. 79–117.
19 A. Anghie, *Imperialism, Sovereignty and the Making of International Law*, Cambridge: Cambridge University Press, 2005.
20 G. Sluga, "Inventing Ethnic Spaces: 'Free Territory', Sovereignty and the 1947 Peace Treaty", *Acta Histriae*, 4 (1998), pp. 173–186; and Sluga, *The Problem of Trieste*, pp. 83–110.
21 See Sluga, "Inventing Ethnic Spaces".
22 For the interim British and American military government (in control until 1954 as it turned out), the FTT was neither a state nor a nation, although it did recognize three local languages: Italian, Slovene, and Croatian.

Britain portrayed the FTT as an extension of the transnational ideology of the developing Marshall Plan for a "unified Western European economy".

By 1945, the FTT had in its favour a groundswell of popular support in Trieste for anti-nationalist solutions to the question of its political sovereignty – as an antidote to the decades of violence unleashed in the context of interwar nationalism. European intellectuals and social scientists also saw in the "free territory" idea a possible model for alternatives to national sovereignty as a basis for political progress and peace. For the British historian A.J.P. Taylor, Trieste was "one symbol of the way things are going" – away from nationally defined sovereignty towards greater internationalization.[23] When the plan for the FTT was officially abandoned on 20 March 1948, on the authority of an agreement between the United States, Britain, and France, the three powers blamed the Soviet Union for rejecting all governors they nominated, and the local residents, who, they stated, were incapable of identifying with a "free territory". We might also argue it was the British and American overseers who lacked imagination.

International Imaginaries

In 1919, the League's status, even in the mandate question, such as it was, had been coddled in pre-war and wartime international imaginaries – imaginaries that conventionally relied on the symbolic landscape and motifs of the national territorial state.[24] Publications such as *Das Internationale Leben der Gegenwart* (International Life Today) the work of the prominent German pacifist Alfred Hermann Fried – awarded the Nobel Peace Prize in 1911 – mapped a new international landscape. This Baedeker for "International Land" comprised the lines that connected intergovernmental networks, including the ever – increasing number of public international unions, such as the Universal Postal Union or the International Telegraph Union, or the growing corpus of international law represented by the Hague Tribunal.[25] On this map, the authority of the sovereign state was significantly interrupted by actually existing international law

---

23 PRO: FO371/48949, R16674/14935/92, General News Talk, World Affairs by AJP Taylor/ GVM (From the Home Service) Pt. II. The Trieste Issue 24/9/45; quoted in Sluga, *The Problem of Trieste*, p. 136..
24 For more on the conceptual relevance of imaginaries in the international context, see Sluga and Clavin, *Internationalisms: A Twentieth-Century History*, Cambridge: Cambridge University Press 2017, pp. 1–10; Sluga, *Internationalism in the Age of Nationalism*, pp. 150–160.
25 A.H. Fried, *Das internationale Leben der Gegenwart*, Leipzig: Teubner, 1908.

and multilateral institutions, which, as Fried saw it, had begun to emulate national forms of governance on an international scale.[26]

At the end of the Second World War – a period that the 1946 Nobel Peace Prize winner Emily Greene Balch described as "plastic" – the parameters and possibilities of international sovereignty were stretched even further by new ways of imagining territorial boundaries and political citizenship.[27] Balch was well known for her activism and writing on "immigrants, international economics, international cooperation, colonialism, and the development of international law in the global commons of air, sea and the polar regions".[28] Against the background of the Second World War, she insisted on the urgency of internationalizing "waste spaces", which could not be walled off by frontiers and were not bound by human collective affinities, and which "by their nature [...] would seem destined to be brought under international control".[29] She particularly had in mind the southern polar regions, which, although "hardly worth the cost of a struggle to possess it", was already subject to conflicting claims, "which are likely to grow extensively and intensively".[30] It was precisely for that reason, Balch maintained, that the Antarctic should be given "the new status of an international territory". Balch conceptualized this international territory in ways that were significantly different from the Allies' FTT; it was to be administered "by authorities set up by the community of nations for purposes in which all are interested".[31]

Balch's wartime op-ed pieces in the *New York Times* took up the concept of international territory in the context of the rapidly changing landscape of the

---

[26] M. Herren, "'They Already Exist': Don't They? Conjuring Global Networks Along the Flow of Money", in: I. Löhr and R. Wenzlheumer (eds.), *The Nation State and Beyond: Governing Globalization Processes in the Nineteenth and Early Twentieth Centuries*, Berlin: Springer, 2013, pp. 43–62.

[27] Balch, herself, an economist and veteran of World War I pacifist and feminist movements, by then in her 70s, did her best to push "things" in that international direction. In a recent extensive study, Roger P. Alford portrays Fried and Emily Greene Balch as exemplary of Nobel Laureate "international norm entrepreneurs", who, by virtue of their prizes, facilitated the "emergence, cascading, and internalization of norms" (R.P. Alford, "The Nobel Effect: Nobel Peace Prize Laureates as International Norm Entrepreneurs", *Virginia Journal of International Law*, 2008, pp. 61–153).

[28] As an economist teaching at Wellesley, Balch was forced to resign because of her politics.

[29] E.G. Balch, "UN and the Waters of the World", *Survey Graphic* 36 (1947), pp. 529–530, 554–557.

[30] E.G. Balch, "The Polar Regions as a Site for an Experiment in Internationalism", *WILPF Int. Circ. Letter* 1 (1945); E.G. Balch "A Consortium of All, Rules for Waste Space", *New York Times*, 3 March 1940; R.L. Buell, *Isolated America*, New York: Alfred E. Knopf, 1940.

[31] E.G. Balch, "The Polar Regions", in: *Papers of Emily Greene Balch, 1875–1961*, Swarthmore College Peace Collection, Scholarly Resources microfilm edition, reel 23, pp. 18–19.

southern polar regions. She argued for the internationalization of the Antarctic on the grounds that there was no "native population" or settlement, it held limited economic value (although she admitted sometime in the future the region's mineral resources might be attractive), and its meteorological stations were integral to the international work of scientists. To these arguments, she added the claim that the internationalization of the Antarctic would offer an instructive experiment and stimulus for the internationalization of colonial administration. It would even endow the UN with an actual material piece of "real estate" and "a territorial foothold".[32] In all these cases, she promoted internationalization as a method of conflict containment in areas that might invite contestation over sovereignty, in order to encourage "all-human use of the resources of our little planet".

Permanent Sovereignty

Balch's formula for thinking sovereignty by emphasizing resources and "deep" territory returned throughout the 1950s in the context of decolonization and reconceptualizations of national sovereignty as "permanent sovereignty". More specifically, permanent sovereignty was the flagpole under which post-colonial states reacted to a growing awareness that (European) international law protected foreign investors with existing stakes in the natural resources of their territories. It added to territorial sovereignty the significance of claims over "natural resources" on economic grounds, even though the borders of actually existing forms of economic sovereignty were increasingly invisible and difficult to see.[33] In another paradox, the idea of permanent sovereignty as national sovereignty over natural resources was legally conceptualized in the international fora of the UN as part of its universalist human rights agenda.

Viewed in the form of a timeline, this international legal history presents a series of steps that was given legitimacy by the UN's quasi-lawmaker role.[34]

---

32 Ibid.
33 S. Pahuja, *Decolonising International Law: Development, Economic Growth and the Politics of Universality*, Cambridge: Cambridge University Press, 2011, p. 93; see also B. Rajagopal, *International Law from Below Development, Social Movements and Third World Resistance*, Cambridge: Cambridge University Press, 2003, pp. 50–72.
34 Schrijver, *Sovereignty over Natural Resources*, p. 377. Schrijver argues that the UN is a quasi-law-maker and that "certain categories of UN resolutions can have legal effects beyond their status as mere recommendations" (Ibid., p. 373).

- In 1952, permanent sovereignty was laid out in a UN General Assembly resolution as "the right of peoples to use and exploit their natural wealth and resources is inherent in their sovereignty".[35]
- In 1958, the UN General Assembly established the UN Commission on Permanent Sovereignty over Natural Resources as part of its enquiry into the right of peoples and nations to self-determination.
- In 1962, in the early stages of the UN's "Decade of Development", the UN General Assembly affirmed with a "declaration" "the right of peoples and nations to permanent sovereignty over their natural wealth and resources" as well as to exercise that right "in the national interest of their economic development and of the well-being of the people of the state concerned".[36]
- In 1966, the principle of permanent sovereignty appeared in the final version of the International Covenant of Human Rights, as Article 1:

    All peoples may, for their own ends, freely dispose of their natural wealth and resources without prejudice to any obligations arising out of international economic co-operation, based upon the principle of mutual benefit, and international law. In no case may a people be deprived of its own means of subsistence.[37]

As Sundhya Pahuja explains, the international legitimations of permanent sovereignty encoded in the UN from the 1950s onwards add up to "an attempt to assert political control over the economic sphere via the deployment of national sovereignty [...which] occurred via the projection and stabilisation of a particular meaning for the 'international' sphere".[38] This was evident in the "global 1970s" when UN attempts to address economic inequality between the North and South culminated in a programme for a New International

---

[35] United Nations, "Right to Exploit Freely Natural Resources", General Assembly Resolution 626 (VII), 21 December 1952, http://www.un.org/en/ga/search/view_doc.asp?symbol=A/RES/626(VII).

[36] United Nations, "Permanent Sovereignty over Natural Resources", General Assembly Resolution 1803 (XVII), 14 December 1962, http://www.ohchr.org/EN/ProfessionalInterest/Pages/NaturalResources.aspx

[37] United Nations, *Vienna Convention on Succession of States in Respect of Treaties*, UN Doc. A/CONF.80/31, 27 October 1978; African Commission on Human and Peoples' Rights, *African Charter on Human and Peoples' Rights*, CAB/LEG/63/3, 27 June 1981.

[38] United Nations, "Permanent Sovereignty over Natural Resources"; Pahuja, *Decolonizing International Law*, p. 96. "[D]espite its economic hue, the claim to PSNR [Permanent Sovereignty over Natural Resources] was understood by the Third World as a political claim [...] cast in terms of sovereignty, an avenue available to the nascent Third World precisely because of the universal promise of international law – In this instance, the promise of equal recognition to particular sovereigns" (Ibid., p. 99).

Economic Order (NIEO) put to the UN General Assembly.[39] The aim of the NIEO programme (1974) was to address economic inequality between the North and South, in part by asserting the principle of "permanent sovereignty over natural resources and the right to expropriation – as well as control over foreign investment, raw material prices, commodity exports, and their indexation to manufacturer prices".[40]

These same debates within the UN – among its bureaucracy and member states – were impelled by a growing sense among analysts of the international order that permanent sovereignty was not only set against the remnants of an imperial legacy, but also against the relatively invisible economic agency of "transnational" or "multinational" corporations. It was no coincidence that in this same period the figure of the multinational corporation appeared in social scientific assessments of the contemporary situation, spectre-like, standing in for radically changing forms of economic activity that marked a new epoch of "casino capitalism", or what we now think of as the collateral damage of neoliberalism: from the rise of tax havens to the explosion of transnational flows of money through the operation of unregulated private banks, often taking fiscal advantage of the internationally sanctioned era of development projects in the Third World.[41] Throughout the 1970s, as existing European-founded international law protected foreign investment, splitting political and economic sovereignty, the permanent sovereignty debates made state control of natural resources a part of the struggle against the liquid flow of money – as private capital – and reinforced the view of international sovereignty as a constituent dimension of economic globalization.[42]

---

[39] Pahuja, *Decolonizing International Law*, pp. 102, 111.

[40] This principle was immanent in the Charter of Economic Rights and Duties of States, adopted by the General Assembly that same year. Self-determination as nation-state sovereignty was demanded as a human right, along with economic progress or development (United Nations, *Charter of Economic Rights and Duties of States*, General Assembly Resolution 3281 (XXIX), 12 December 1974).

[41] Schrijver, *Sovereignty over Natural Resources*, pp. 333, 347; see S. Strange, *Casino Capitalism*, Manchester: Manchester University Press, 2015. As Vanessa Ogle's work is now following up, this was also the period that saw the rise of tax havens: V. Ogle, Archipelago Capitalism: Tax Havens, Offshore Money, and the State, 1950s–1970s, in: *The American Historical Review* 122 (2017), pp. 1431–1458.

[42] Strange, *Casino Capitalism*, p. 125. Strange says national sovereignty "can never deliver on its promise to demarcate a sphere of political control prior to 'international' intervention. This is because it is not a pre-constituted entity but rather the *outcome* of a struggle over the meanings of the 'national' and the 'international' which already implies relations of domination, subordination, oppression and power" (Ibid., p. 123).

When, in 1986, the UN passed the Declaration on the Right to Development, which included the rights of peoples to exercise "sovereignty over all their natural wealth and resources", it was already behind the times, given the extent to which economic trends transgressed the traditional conception of state sovereignty defined through territorial borders.[43] By then, the international setting in which permanent (national) sovereignty gained its political legitimacy and traction was also the space in which alternative conceptions of international sovereignty were pursued, again. As the anthropologist Felicity C. Scott argues, some of the newly emboldened (mainly Californian) environmental NGOs dreamed of eradicating nation state sovereignty altogether in "new paradigms of sovereignty".[44]

New modes of imagining international sovereignty in the "global 1970s" returns us to the role of Nobel Prize winners.[45] In 1976, the recipient of the 1969 Nobel Prize in Economic Sciences (the first year it was awarded), Dutch economist Jan Tinbergen was hired by the Club of Rome to coordinate a "second World Project model": the "Reimagining International Order".[46] Tinbergen's brief was to bring the economic facts of interdependence into alignment with a "reinterpretation of national sovereignty". For his purposes, Tinbergen drew on the principle of "functional sovereignty" determined by "optimum decisions

---

[43] Schrijver, *Sovereignty over Natural Resources*, p. 378. Schrijver argues that permanent sovereignty became an important basis for insisting on duties to the environment, duty of care, and the observation of international agreements such as the World Charter of Nature, Convention on Biological Diversity, and the African Charter on Human and Peoples' Rights.

[44] F. D. E. Scott, *Outlaw territories. Environments of insecurity/architectures of counterinsurgency*, New York: Zone Books, 2016.

[45] The section in which Alford focuses on unifying strands such as liberty, democracy, humaneness, public spirit repudiation of violence, and spiritual universalism, as well as the institutional apparatus that was fostering the organization of "world society" comprises nearly 100 pages. He admits that the history of international law does have an influence, especially on the elite norm entrepreneurs he focuses on. In the same direction, he accepts that the laureates' norms have different narratives in different periods, that is to say that international norms have a life cycle. Apparently, Balch belongs to a mid-century Nobel "humanitarian" school of pacifists, although her unique institutional focus on "social and economic justice" connects her to the early twentieth-century populist pacifism represented by Fried's generation Alford, "The Nobel Effect", pp. 99–100.

[46] Tinbergen received the prize for his work on model-building in the interest of "specifying optimum socio-economic orders". The first World Project model was also commissioned by the Club of Rome, from MIT systems theory specialists, who gave life to a new international imaginary by mapping an "international land" visualized as flowcharts (J. Tinbergen, "Lecture to the Memory of Alfred Nobel", 12 December 1969, http://www.nobelprize.org/nobel_prizes/economic-sciences/laureates/1969/tinbergen-lecture.html).

levels", that is, the level at which decisions should be made for different kinds of problems/issues. At stake was the welfare of the present and future world population – in particular the poor – and averting environmental and social catastrophe. In this view, for example, permanent sovereignty was still relevant, although only until the economic status of the specific developing country improved; later on "natural and intellectual resources should be considered a common heritage of mankind". Tinbergen's report was multifaceted and echoed recommendations of the kind that supported the ambitions of earlier Nobel Peace Prize winners: from the "management of the oceans in the interest of mankind", to international taxation and the beginnings of a global planning system. But its necessary innovations are obvious, including the need for "a code of conduct of transnational enterprises with legally enforceable elements".

Somewhat appositely, the report would not have come about without the instigation or funding of a new kind of NGO, the Club of Rome itself: an elite collective of scientists, economists, businesspeople, international civil servants, and politicians. According to its founder Aurelio Peccei, the club operated as a "collegio invisible"; Peccei, himself a multinational "industrialist" (working with Fiat and Olivetti), and transnational investment banker dabbling in developmental funding (the creator of the ADELA private bank operating in Latin America) was keen to establish a "new paradigm of sovereignty" reflective of interdependent international/global realities, particularly exponential population growth and its effects on the environment.[47] System theory, to quote MIT's Jay Forrester, at the time was built on expectations that the "invisible" would be visualized "by conjuring up a coherent picture of an unseen order" made available through different kinds of international imaginary. On this cyber model, it was possible to imagine an economic and environmental post-sovereign future, as Scott describes, "a future for Western notions of progress and multinational corporations in a global, system-based, managerial form of governance and a marketplace no longer constrained by the nation-state".[48]

---

47 A. Peccei, *The Human Quality*, Oxford: Pergamon Press, 1977.
48 Scott, *Outlaw Territories*, pp. 221, 223. Under the supervision of Jay Forrester, the group used "an early computer-generated world system model to map the association between population, resource depletion, pollution, industrial output, and food" (although not the movement of private investment). The 1972 bestseller that came out of this study, *Limits to Growth*, sold 9 million copies, in 29 countries, and was a defining influence on the UN environment conference. It also established a model for other "cyber"-generated studies, such as Buckminster Fuller's celebrated "World Game", from that same year, which used computers and data to simulate a football field–sized map with viewing balconies, 8 to 10 stories high, to present an undistorted picture of the entire Earth built out of resources, climate weather conditions, population, and demographic trends as well as the entire range of environmental information

In the later decades of the twentieth century, we find conceptions of sovereignty – national and international – mediated through the idea of international life as the product of economic interdependence, increasingly identified as globalization. International institutions were often imagined as the means by which the quasi-invisible flows of a globalized economy might be better governed, in the overlapping, as well as competing, interests of nations and humankind. Tinbergen's "Reimagining the International Order" report and the Club of Rome are evidence of the extent to which questions of economic equality and social justice revolved around the problem of sovereignty and around repertoires that had accumulated layers of historically specific conceptions of territory.[49]

Conclusion

> [T]he imagined community of the territorial nation-state, the dominant and perhaps constitutive imagery of political life in the past two centuries, is very rapidly giving way to a series of imagined *economies* [original emphasis] which maintain the fiction of the state – and indeed perpetuate it as a legal entity – but situate it within a radically different set of boundaries and notions of social space.[50]

> It is a curious phenomenon, then, that the legitimacy of economic globalization is today being so passionately challenged by so many prominent voices claiming to speak for the interests of both a common humanity and national sovereignty.[51]

In 1974, Aurelio Peccei noted that economists were observing how, "for the first time [...] political unit, i.e. territory, and economic unit are no longer congruent. This, understandably, appears as a threat to national governments".[52] His

---

from the memories of the multimillion-bit capacity digital computers. The aim was to predict the myriad consequences of any sorts of actions that can have environmental consequences.

49 Tinbergen's report reflected developments in the social sciences more broadly, including the rise of economics as a respected scientific discipline with its own Nobel Prize. The fact that Tinbergen won the Nobel in Economic Sciences the same year that International Labour Organization won the Nobel Peace Prize is testimony to the importance in this international domain of economic thinking of a *longue durée* international social justice vision of economic equality.

50 R. Palan and A. Cameron, *The Imagined Economies of Globalization*, London: Sage, 2004, p. 8; see also F. Johns, "Theorizing the Corporation in International Law", in: A. Orford and F. Hoffmann (eds.), *The Oxford Handbook of the Theory of International Law*, Oxford: Oxford University Press, 2016, p. 737.

51 B. Steil and M. Hinds, *Money Markets and Sovereignty*, New Haven: Yale University Press, 2009, p. 240.

52 Peccei, *The Human Quality*, p. 46.

observation echoed the imperial status quo a century earlier, which included practices that separated territorial control from "the maintenance of global power".[53] If we look back over the twentieth-century international history of sovereignty, tensions across national/international, extra-territorial/economic, and territorial/legal political forms of sovereignty were in evidence even though they were not particularly "visible" in scientific representations of sovereignty as a problem. These tensions disturbed the authority of mandates, trusteeships, protectorates, concessions, and international settlements. They also reverberated through the less-well-known economic functions of the League of Nations, and in the post-1945 international system, from the International Monetary Fund and World Bank to the General Agreement on Tariffs and Trade and the World Trade Organization.[54] The late nineteenth-century public international unions, which were so important to Fried's international landscape, can also be characterized as transnational economic bodies (see Charles Alexandrowicz's avant-garde 1950 study of international economic organizations), and Fried's map could as well have been marked by the trails of transnational money flows, whether in the pre-war imperial setting or in the interwar operations of the League-connected Bank for International Settlements.[55] In the late 1940s, even the FTT was imagined as an extension of the Marshall Plan, and "free markets" as the ideal territorial form – although, significantly, such a liberal economic vision was not enough to displace prevalent Cold War imaginaries that supported ethno-national imagined communities as the basis of territorial sovereignty instead.

The UN treaties agreed upon at the end of the 1960s and the end of the 1970s regarding outer space and the moon practised what were by this time familiar reimagined sovereignties. They drew on "the ideas of the use and exploitation of nature that underpinned the longer legal understanding of property". The United States and the Soviet Union "worried about whether it could be possible to claim sovereignty, for example, over the moon simply by sticking a flag into its surface [...] a ceremony that colonial powers had considered many

---

53 Ibid.
54 Schrijver, *Sovereignty over Natural Resources*, p. 368.
55 In the early 1920s, the newly national Austria became the focus of an austerity experiment under the supervision of a League-imposed (and Dutch) commissioner and influence of the same bankers who ran the (Basel-based) Bank of International Settlements (BIS). The BIS was a financial institution created under the sign of the League of Nations' international authority, as a forum for cooperation between central banks. It had privileged extra-territorial status, providing services for international organizations but holding no supranational functions. However, for the socialist party, the terms of the League intervention were viewed as a form of economic colonialism (Herren, "They Already Exist").

times before to be sufficient to claim sovereignty over various regions of the globe".[56] However, Americans insisted that they raised their flag not as a sign of a national territorial claim, but rather as recognition of their national achievement.

The 1979 Moon Agreement also invoked a new "deep" or "thick" territorial conception sovereignty, replete with economic control of natural resources as a "human right", as fundamental to both nation-statehood, and as the sovereign claims and responsibilities of "humankind". Even as the UN discussions aimed to "prevent the moon from becoming an area of international conflict", the agreement recognized "the benefits which may be derived from the exploitation of the natural resources of the moon and other celestial bodies".[57] It even allowed for special provisions that declared the Moon's natural resources the common heritage of humankind.[58] The moon was "not subject to national appropriation by any claim of sovereignty, by means of use or occupation, or by any other means; neither the surface nor the subsurface of the moon, nor any part therefor or natural resources in place", but states could agree to establish an international regime "to govern the exploitation of the natural resources of the moon". If this occurred, developing countries were to have special consideration in sharing the benefits derived from those resources.[59] These international discussions about the moon's sovereignty read like older chapters in the longer history of the overlapping and competing international, imperial, and national imaginaries. They also exhibited the shifting weight given to the natural resources that were seen as fundamental to the new industrial/technology industries. Natural resources were used as a way to measure the development of more advanced human societies and as an answer to the vulnerability of national sovereignty to the invisible forms of economic interdependence that technology was meant to reveal.

Unlike the social scientists Steil and Hinds, who declare the twenty-first century opposition of economic globalization, on the one hand, and common humanity aligned with national sovereignty, on the other, a "curious phenomenon",

---

[56] A. Fitzmaurice, *Sovereignty, Property and Empire, 1500–2000*, Cambridge: Cambridge University Press, 2014, p. 324.

[57] United Nations, "Agreement Governing the Activities of States on the Moon and Other Celestial Bodies", General Assembly Resolution 34/68, 11 July 1984, http://disarmament.un.org/treaties/t/moon/text

[58] See also the UN Committee on Peaceful Uses of Outer Space (United Nations Office for Outer Space Affairs, "UN Committee on Peaceful Uses of Outer Space", http://www.unoosa.org/oosa/en/ourwork/copuos/index.html (accessed 3 December 2018)).

[59] United Nations, "Agreement Governing the Activities of States on the Moon".

I have tried to show how these themes were mutually reinforcing throughout the twentieth century. In the 1970s, the new language of a global commons took hold in the context of permanent sovereignty, imagined as national control over natural resources. I also disagree with the political economists Palan and Cameron, who argue (from an ideologically and methodologically opposed position to Steil and Hinds, with which I am on the whole not only sympathetic but admiring) that "the imagined community of the territorial nation-state, the dominant and perhaps constitutive imagery of political life in the past two centuries, is very rapidly giving way to a series of imagined *economies* which maintain the fiction of the state – and indeed perpetuate it as a legal entity – but situate it within a radically different set of boundaries and notions of social space". Instead, as explained above, that shift had already begun to impact on the ways of thinking about sovereignty in the 1970s, largely through the spectre of the multinational/transnational state.

The visibility of this otherwise relatively invisible movement of money and commerce was in part the contribution of economists such as Tinbergen, who deployed a computer-generated data set imagination. In the latter decades of the twentieth century, new paradigms of sovereignty were negotiated in the context of these competing and intersecting visions of international/global life, such as new large-scale world visions built on the foundations of cybernetics and systems theory, which pursued data on population numbers and resource depletion and ignored the movement of dollars. Sovereignty also took other forms, such as in depoliticized (although not unideological) views of "international life", imagined as a space where territory now mattered as the site of "natural resources" while commerce itself was the optimal force for establishing the globe's interdependence.

There is a certain dearth to the stories historians have told about the territorial nation-state version of sovereignty, as if extra-territoriality and international imaginaries had no place in them, or existed only as their antitheses. The current research climate is pushing both cultural and economic framings of historical narratives closer together. Reconnecting them, I would argue, is allowing us to give more specificity to the history of the transformation of an imperial world order to an international world order, and to capture the choices that were available as well as those that were made. It offers us a way of historicizing globalization as an idea and phenomenon as well as the relative political significance of imaginaries, what they hide, and what they reveal. I have tried to track a spectrum of twentieth-century sovereignty thinking, including the changing significance of the international as a site for determining territorial nation-state sovereignty and as a form of sovereignty itself, imagined on a territorial template. This same history exposes the shifting parameters of relatively invisible economic imperatives and economic distortions of sovereignty – in imperial, international, and global contexts, but with varying visibility.

Steffi Marung, Uwe Müller and Stefan Troebst
Monolith or Experiment?
The Bloc as a Spatial Format

Introduction: The Bloc as a Political and as an Analytical Concept

Discussing the "bloc" as a spatial format is both an obvious and a problematic undertaking. The term bloc suggests a rather coherent configuration, either dominated from a centre or held together by a series of characteristics shared by the parts comprising the bloc. But interestingly enough, there has not been very much reflection about the bloc as a specific geographical or geopolitical formation. Certainly, there is an abundant amount of literature addressing the Soviet bloc, the socialist camp, or Cold War Eastern Europe more specifically, which has – without reaching a consensus – investigated and problematized the nature and histories of this particular bloc.[1] Competing narratives present this spatial formation either as an effect of a geopolitical strategy, as an imperial experiment of the Soviet Union, or as the spatialized outcome of a common ideology that identified global capitalism as the main opponent. Some of these narratives emphasize the failures, ruptures, and weaknesses of the bloc's

---

[1] To name but a few overviews produced both in East and West before and after the end of the Cold War: Z. K. Brzezinski, *The Soviet Bloc. Unity and Conflict. Revised Edition*, New York, NY: Praeger, 1960; R. Löwenthal, *Der geborstene Monolith. Von Stalins Weltpartei zum kommunistischen Pluralismus*, Berlin ² 1967; *Geschichte der sozialistischen Gemeinschaft. Herausbildung des realen Sozialismus von 1917 bis zur Gegenwart*. Von einem Autorenkollektiv unter Leitung von E. Kalbe, Berlin (Ost): VEB Deutscher Verlag der Wissenschaften, 1981; J. K. Hoensch, *Sowjetische Osteuropa-Politik 1945–1975*, Kronberg Ts., Düsseldorf: Athenäum, 1977; J. Hacker, *Der Ostblock. Entstehung, Entwicklung und Struktur, 1939–1980*, Baden-Baden: Nomos, 1983; M. Hausleitner, *Die sowjetische Osteuropapolitik in den Jahren der Perestrojka*, Frankfurt am Main and New York: Campus Verlag, 1994; V. K. Volkov, "U istokov koncepcii 'socialističeskogo lagerja'" ["At the beginning of the concept of a socialist camp"], in: *U istokov "socialističeskogo sodružestva": SSSR i vostočnoevropejskie strany v 1944–1949 gg*, Red. L. Ja. Gibianskij. Moskva: Nauka, 1995, pp. 11–22; S. Pons and F. Gori (eds.), *The Soviet Union and Europe in the Cold War, 1943–53*, London: Macmillan, 1996; L. Gibianskij, "Die Bildung des Sowjetblocks in Osteuropa. Ziele, Strukturen, Mechanismen (1944–1949)", *Forum für osteuropäische Ideen- und Zeitgeschichte* 1 (1997) 2, pp. 204–225; J. M. Faraldo, P. Gulińska-Jurgiel, and Ch. Domnitz (eds.): *Europa im Ostblock. Vorstellungen und Diskurse (1945–1991)* (= Zeithistorische Studien, 44), Köln et al.: Böhlau 2008; S. Bottoni, *Long Awaited West. Eastern Europe since 1944*, Bloomington, IN: Indiana University Press, 2017.

institutionalization, while others investigate the specific transnationality within the camp,[2] together with its relation to its Western counterpart as well as to the Global South and the worlds of Western globalization.[3] Summarizing this literature in its entirety and translating all of it into the conceptual framework of this volume is neither possible nor sound.

On the other hand, far from being an analytical term – into which concepts of nation-state or empire introduced in this volume have been developed over decades of research on modern territoriality at least in part – this Cold War offspring nevertheless had been a joint obsession for plenty of the academic, political, and popular literature written during the second half of the twentieth century. This literature aimed to provide a common denominator for a seemingly coherent geographic area as well as for an ideological, political, economic, and military community of states while attaching meaning to a complex and – as authors from both sides of the Iron Curtain tirelessly emphasized – *new* spatialization. Even without its attributive adjectives – "Soviet" or "Eastern" – bloc almost exclusively referred to the group of socialist states, more often specifically those in Europe and less frequent, or in a more qualified way, those outside. Understood as being part of a Soviet sphere of influence, the group was considered to be cut off from ties to Western Europe, the Western world, and the world economy more broadly. The employment of the term took off in the mid-1940s, reflecting the tides of the Cold War, with peaks in use in the first half of the 1960s, massive decline during the years of détente during the 1970s, and upswings in the 1980s,[4] which demonstrates the close link between this spatial semantic with the dynamics of the Cold War logic itself.

---

2 P. Babiracki, "Interfacing the Soviet Bloc", *Ab Imperio* 4/2011, pp. 376–407; P. Babiracki and A. Jersild (eds.), *Socialist Internationalism in the Cold War*, Cham: Springer International Publishing, 2016; P. Babiracki, K. Zimmer, and M. David-Fox (eds.), *Cold War Crossings: International Travel and Exchange across the Soviet Bloc, 1940s–1960s*, Arlington: College Station, Texas A & M University Press, 2014.

3 D. Jajeśniak-Quast, "Conclusions: The Multiple International Dimensions of Comecon. New Interpretations of an Old Phenomena", *Comparativ* 27 (2017) 5/6, pp. 140–149; O. A. Westad, The *Global Cold War: Third World Interventions and the Making of our Times*, Cambridge, New York Cambridge University Press, 2005; J. Mark, A. Kalinovsky, and S. Marung, *Alternative Globalizations: Encounters Between the Eastern Bloc and the Postcolonial World*, Bloomington, Indiana University Press (in print).

4 Ngram Viewer for "Soviet bloc" (https://books.google.com/ngrams/graph?content=soviet+bloc&year_start=1800&year_end=2008&corpus=0&smoothing=3&share=&direct_url=t1%3B%2Csoviet%20bloc%3B%2Cc0). Interestingly enough, the term "socialist camp" shows a similar rise, starting from the early 1940s, peaking in the early 1960s, and rapidly declining afterwards (https://books.google.com/ngrams/graph?content=socialist+camp&year_start=1800&year_end=2008&corpus=0&smoothing=3&share=&direct_url=t1%3B%2Csocialist%20camp%3B%2Cc0).

In addition, the bloc metaphor, designed to emphasize the monolithic nature of a Soviet-dominated realm, became prominent among Western observers, while from inside the area this language was either never used or completely rejected. Rather, alternate proposals were introduced such as the "socialist camp" or the "socialist world system", which despite being easily misunderstood as translations of this spatiality into a "socialist language" made competing claims about the structure and functioning of the constituted space. And although it should have invited a complementary talk about a "Western bloc", this never occurred, even though in Eastern European debates a sort of Western bloc was at times addressed by hinting at the hegemonic role of US imperialism around which the capitalist West was arranged in bondage. The bloc term had been popularized by Western observers less due to an analytical interest and more because of political motivation, claiming homogeneity of a hermetic space firmly organized around a Soviet centre, thereby allowing the ruptures within to be identified in a triumphalist manner. To make matters worse, the bloc imaginary had proliferated so much that it merged with "Eastern Europe" – spanning from east of the Elbe River to Vladivostok – a legacy that continues to shape the dynamics of eastward enlargement of the European Union until today.

Yet, an investigation into the question, if – or rather *how* – the bloc can be qualified as a spatial format, turns out to be exceptionally productive to gain a better understanding of the twentieth century as a particular period of experimentation with processes of respatializations under the global condition. As explicated by Richard Löwenthal,

> [i]f we describe the relations of the Soviet Union to its allied states under communist rule in East Central and South Eastern Europe with the term 'Soviet Bloc', rather than using the term 'Soviet system of alliances' from international law or talk more pointedly and critically of a 'Soviet empire', we do so because these other designations do not characterize fully the originality of these relations. Subsuming this definitely *novel* formation under concepts, that have been coined to describe familiar political and legal phenomena, says either too little or too much.[5]

In this way, the influential German political scientist – born in 1908, himself embodying the complexities of European socialisms during the twentieth century and being a leading expert in the West German discussion on the

---

5 R. Löwenthal, "Vormachtkontrolle und Autonomie in der Entwicklung des Sowjetblocks", in: *Der Sowjetblock zwischen Vormachtkontrolle und Autonomie*, ed. R. Löwenthal and B. Meissner, Köln: Markus Verlag, 1984, p. 11 (translation and emphasis ours).

"burst monolith" of the bloc[6] – highlights both the dilemma and the productivity of the concept in investigating respatializations during the twentieth century. The bloc concept was an effort to translate experiences from the world of empires into a new spatial order that was both characterized by an (attempted) universalization of international law and by competing claims made by the two Cold War superpowers of how these new nation-states as well as this new international community should be organized.

This translation was particularly intricate in and for a region that had been undergoing repeated experiments of respatialization since the nineteenth century.[7] With an overlapping of four competing empires – German, Russian, Habsburg, and Ottoman – both the rise of and resistance against the imperial order as well as modernizing attempts within the empires had ushered in numerous proposals and ambitions – often in a transnational or transimperial practice – to reorganize the region, which after the Second World War would be addressed as the (European) Soviet bloc. In this context, the nation-state was not the only model that critics of these empires could think of.

Historical References

The "Slavic idea", imaginations of a specific Slavic unity and solidarity across space and time, was one of the most dynamic lenses through which actors from within and outside the region started to rethink its spatiality beyond the nation and the empire since the mid of the nineteenth century. The assumption that there is a specific Slavic space organized around a common identity – constructed around ethnicity and/or language and/or religion – providing a home for the family of all Slavs has taken on multiple forms since the nineteenth century, undergoing numerous transformations up until the 1950s and with remobilizations today.[8] Such forms ranged from Austro-Slavism in the Habsburg

---

6 Löwenthal, *Der geborstene Monolith*.
7 S. Marung, M. Middell, and U. Müller, "Territorialisierung in Ostmitteleuropa bis zum Ersten Weltkrieg", in: F. Hadler and M. Middell (eds.), *Handbuch einer transnationalen Geschichte Ostmitteleuropas*, vol. 1: *Von der Mitte des 19. Jahrhunderts bis zum Ersten Weltkrieg*, Göttingen: Vandenhoeck & Ruprecht 2017, pp. 37–130; S. Marung, M. Middell, and U. Müller, "Multiple Territorialisierungsprozesse in Ostmitteleuropa", in: Hadler and Middell, *Handbuch*, pp. 425–456.
8 S. Troebst, "Slavizität. Identitätsmuster, Analyserahmen, Mythos", *Osteuropa* 59 (2009) 12, pp. 7–19; idem, "Post-Panslavism? Political Connotations of Slavicness in 21st Century Europe", in: A. Gąsior, L. Karl, and S. Troebst (eds.), *Post-Panslavismus: Slavizität, Slavische Idee und Antislavismus im 20. und 21. Jahrhundert*, Göttingen: Wallstein Verlag 2014, pp. 17–21.

monarchy – mainly promoted by liberal Czechs that aimed at a democratization and federalization of the empire – to pan-Slavism in the Russian Empire – promoted mainly by Russian critics of the elites' autocracy and its negative Poland policy while still adopting a leading role for Russia in the region – to Illyrism and Yugoslavism in Southeastern Europe, to variants of neo-Slavism in Western and Southeastern Europe in the early twentieth century with varying degrees of Russophobia, to the mobilization of the Slavic idea by Soviet elites from the 1940s to the early 1950s. These imaginations and projects not only resulted in increased productivity in the arts and literature but also fed into a political symbolic reservoir utilized to create legitimacy for varying projects: from nation-building after the end of empire, to the formation of international alliances, to the mobilization of support during war times against a common enemy – and including the creation of academic disciplines and institutions.

Although all these variants of the Slavic idea aimed at redefining the Slavic space transnationally, the proposals were not congruent, and they often fragmented the region into different puzzle pieces of Eastern, Western, and Southern Europe, imagining different geographies of the respective pan-Slavic project. Furthermore, all of them were characterized by a complex intertwinement of national, imperial, regional, and transnational spatialization and spatial imaginations. The pan-Slavic card, such as neo-Slavism or Yugoslavism, was often played to legitimize a particular nationalism (or multiple nationalisms) against an empire or against a threat from outside: such as the Russian variant during the First World War against the German, Habsburg, and Ottoman empires; the Soviet variant during the Second World War against Nazi Germany; or the Polish variant since the nineteenth century.

Even more frequent, pan-Slavism appeared to be crucial to establishing a claim to leadership for a particular national group in the region. That was true, for example, for Czech imaginations of their role as modernizers and democratizers of the region, for the Polish mission as a bridge between East and West,[9] for the Russian mission in the East, and for the Soviet mission in the socialist camp. And similar to the bloc, pan-Slavism was the result of the anxieties and perceptions of outside observers, which often overemphasized the homogeneity of the Slavic space and constructed it as a threat to competing

---

9 M. Krzoska, "Historische Mission und Pragmatismus. Die slawische Idee in Polen im 20. Jahrhundert", *Osteuropa* 59 (2009) 12, pp. 77–94.

claims for hegemony in the region, in particular from German, Italian, Greek,[10] or Ottoman[11] perspectives.

And although the Slavic idea did not survive long during the Cold War,[12] it had been reactivated by Stalin, after the German attack on the Soviet Union, to bring together all potential anti-German and anti-fascist allies in the region as well as to mobilize support among the Slavic diaspora in the West and overseas.[13] Lenin had rejected pan-Slavism as an ideology of Russian imperialism, yet ideas of Slavic unity and transnational cooperation returned as a tool to mediate relations between communist parties of the region with the Communist International (Comintern).[14] Most prominently, the communist Balkan Federation, founded in 1920, united the communist parties of Bulgaria, Yugoslavia, and Greece, which were joined later by Romania. With Stalin blaming such initiatives as detrimental expressions of nationalism, it was marginalized and ended its activities around 1931.

Within the Soviet Union, however, pan-Slavism of a different kind was officially promoted as a method to legitimize Russian nationalism as the leading force during the 1930s within the first socialist state. The concept was turned outward in the 1940s, when Stalin tried to gather Slavic allies against the German enemy. In this context, the Bulgarian communist Georgi Dimitrov and the Russian writer Aleksandr Fadeev prepared in 1941 the establishment of an All-Slavic Committee, which would bring together writers, composers, artists, and other intellectuals from all over (Slavic) Eastern Europe and engage – through radio and print media, most prominently its journal *Slavjane*, as well as in congresses – in the mobilization of support for the Soviet war effort, condemning

---

10 S. Adamantios "Vom 'großrussischen Panslavismus' zum 'sowjetischen Slawokommunismus'. Das Slaventum als Feindbild bei Deutschen, Österreichern, Italienern und Griechen", in: Gąsior, Karl, and Troebst, *Post-Panslavismus*, pp. 388–426.

11 Z. Gasimov, "Vom Panslavismus über den Panturkismus zum Eurasismus. Die russisch-türkische Ideenzirkulation und Verflechtung der Ordnungsvorstellungen im 20. Jahrhundert", in: Gąsior, Karl, and Troebst, *Post-Panslavismus*, pp. 448–472.

12 J. C. Behrends, "Die 'sowjetische Rus' und ihre Brüder. Die slawische Idee in Russlands langem 20. Jh.", *Osteuropa* 59 (2009) 12, pp. 95–114; idem, "Stalins slavischer Volkskrieg. Mobilisierung und Propaganda zwischen Weltkrieg und Kaltem Krieg (1941–1949)", in: Gąsior, Karl, Troebst, and Helm, *Post-Panslavismus*, pp. 79–108.

13 S. Fertacz, "Von Brüdern und Schwestern. Das Allslawische Komitee in Moskau 1941–1947", *Osteuropa* 59 (2009) 12, pp. 139–152; V. C. Fišera, "Kommunismus und slawische Idee. Von der Kommunistischen Balkanföderation zum gesamtslawischen Komitee (1920–1946)", *Osteuropa* 59 (2009) 12, pp. 125–138.

14 Fišera, "Kommunismus und slawische Idee".

German and Italian fascism as well as imperialism.[15] It not only connected intellectually as well as through the methods of its activities to interwar traditions of transnational Slavic movements, but it also translated these perspectives and activities into a socialist internationalism under Soviet leadership, intending to serve as a transmission belt for Soviet propaganda. This perspective, however, was taken up – and not simply forced upon – non-communist actors such as Edward Beneš, who supported this type of solidarity after the frustration of the Munich Agreement (1938) while emphasizing the role of Czechs as a modernizing and democratizing force in the region. This neo-Slavic rhetoric was also taken up by Polish and Czech communists in their founding documents – the Lublin Manifesto (1944) and the Košice Programme (1945).[16] This initiative reached its zenith shortly before it fell apart. The All-Slav Congress in 1946 in Belgrade was meant to mediate the long-standing competition between the Russian and South Slavic versions of how to play the "Slavic card", and it not only brought together delegates from the region but also representatives of Slavic communities from the US, Canada, South America, and Australia – including non-communist groups but not anti-communist ones – hence further developing the geography of Slavic solidarity after the Second World War. Institutionalizing this shift, the short-lived Pan-Slavic Committee was founded, with a Yugoslav as its chairman and a Russian, a Pole, a Czech, and a Bulgarian as vice-presidents, and Belgrade being defined as its headquarters. In 1947, the All-Slav Committee, based in Moscow, was reorganized as the Slav Committee of the Union of Soviet Socialist Republics (USSR), uniting Russians, Ukrainians, and Belorussians.[17] However, the split between Tito and Stalin in 1948 marked the failure of these efforts, in the wake of which experiments with Slavic solidarity as a founding myth for communist alliances across the region in the confining Cold War context were soon to be marginalized. Furthermore, these efforts had not provided an answer to the triple challenge facing international and Soviet socialism against the background of the emergence of multiple respatializations from empire to nation more globally: how to integrate the non-Slavic communities of the Soviet Union into the socialist project, let alone the non-Slavic parts of the emerging bloc, and not to mention the decolonizing societies in Africa and Asia, which would receive enormous attention during the 1960s. The emergence of the bloc has to be read

---

[15] Fertacz, "Von Brüdern und Schwestern".

[16] Behrends, "Die 'sowjetische Rus'".

[17] H. Kohn, "Pan-Slavism and World War II", *The American Political Science Review* 46 (1952) 3, pp. 699–722, here 708–710; S. Troebst, "Schwanengesang gesamtslavischer 'Einheit und Brüderlichkeit'. Der Slavenkongress in Belgrad 1946", in: Gąsior, Karl, and Troebst, *Post-Panslavismus*, pp. 43–68.

against the background of these crucial problems the new socialist elites in the region had to solve.

A Novel Spatial Format?

Accordingly, in this chapter we start from the assumption that a focus on the question of how the multiple processes of respatialization in the second half of the twentieth century inspired the imagination of a novel spatial format helps to both break away from and historicize the Cold War lens, which has been so influential in shaping the concept of the bloc. From such a conceptual starting point, questions of the failure or success of the bloc – either with regard to Cold War competition; to it becoming an international actor in its own right, emancipating itself from the Soviet Union; or by imitating Western regionalisms – appear less important, by turning the "if" into a historically more productive "how". Which actors have participated in which way in these multiple respatializations, guided by which spatial imaginations, developing which specific practices, institutionalizations, and routines, and with which effects to shape, challenge, and transform what has become known – yet in different ways accepted and appropriated – as the (Soviet) bloc?

We will use the bloc as an analytical term while historicizing its emergence as a concept and as a spatializing practice. Investigating the bloc as a possible spatial format means to zoom in on a period. Matthias Middell identifies the years between 1918 and 1961 as a historical period of major transformations of spatial orders, when traditional spatial formats came increasingly under pressure for various reasons. Not only did the race for new colonies reach its limits, due to the rise of anti-colonial national and transnational movements since the early twentieth century,[18] Western European metropolitan elites tried to react, for example, by attempting to reorganize the empire.[19] Moreover, in the wake of the First World

---

18 M. P. Bradley, "Decolonization, the Global South, and the Cold War, 1919–1962", in: M. P. Leffler and O. A. Westad (eds.), *Cambridge History of the Cold War 1*, Cambridge: Cambridge University Press 2010, pp. 464–485; M. Frey and J. Dülffer (eds.), *Elites and Decolonization in the Twentieth Century*, Houndmills, Basingstoke: Palgrave Macmillan 2011; M. Goebel, *Anti-Imperial Metropolis: Interwar Paris and the Seeds of Third World Nationalism*, New York: Cambridge University Press, 2015; H. Weiß, *Framing a Radical African Atlantic: African American Agency, West African Intellectuals, and the International Trade Union Committee of Negro Workers*, Leiden: Brill 2014.
19 F. Cooper, *Citizenship between Empire and Nation: Remaking France and French Africa, 1945–1960*, Princeton: Princeton University Press, 2014; R. Davis, "Perspectives on The End of

War, it became exceedingly clear for most national elites that their states would not be able to compete in a world characterized by ever more dense entanglement and connectivity in the political, cultural, and economic realms, motivating them to find new answers by experimenting with regional and transnational alliances.[20] Finally, Lenin's and Wilson's insistence on the right to self-determination of peoples (for very different reasons)[21] became a fundamental challenge for most empires while in the newly emerging nation-states in Eastern Europe imperial(ist) expansion was perceived as a necessity to secure raw material provision for national industries and was hence combined with an ambition to be involved in world affairs.[22] New spatial formats emerged and hence highly dynamic respatializations occured, of which the emergence of the Soviet Union, the fascist expansion in Europe, processes of decolonization, the emergence of new regionalisms in the East, West, and South of the world, as well as the proliferation of special economic zones and enclaves appear to be the most prominent ones.[23]

To question to what extent the bloc can be seen as a specific spatial format is at the same time a test if the characteristics of such a format, as the more durable result of multiple practices and processes of respatialization,[24] can be identified when investigating the bloc, namely routinization, institutionalization, performance, and reflexivity. At its foundational moment, the bloc was specific because it started its career as a spatial concept as a Western – that is to say, outside – imagination applied to a geopolitical alliance in the East of

---

The British Empire. The Historiographical Debate", *Cercles* 28 (2013), pp. 3–25; A. G. Hopkins, "Rethinking Decolonization", *Past & Present* 200 (2008), pp. 211–247; S. Marung, M. Middell, and U. Müller, "Territorialisierung in Ostmitteleuropa bis zum Ersten Weltkrieg", pp. 37–130; S. Marung, M. Middell, and U. Müller, Multiple Territorialisierungsprozesse, pp. 425–456.

20 G. Sluga and P. Clavin (eds.), *Internationalisms: A Twentieth-Century History*, Cambridge, New York: Cambridge University Press 2017; M. Herren (ed.), *Networking the International System. Global Histories of International Organizations*, Cham: Springer International Publishing 2014.

21 E. Manela, *The Wilsonian Moment: Self-determination and the International Origins of Anticolonial Nationalism*, Oxford: Oxford University Press 2014; A. J. Mayer, *Wilson vs: Lenin: Political Origins of the New Diplomacy, 1917–1918*, Cleveland, New York: Meridian Books 1967.

22 M. A. Kowalski, *Dyskurs Kolonialny w Drugiej Rzeczypospolitej [Colonial Discourse in the Second Polish Republic]*, Warszawa: DiG 2009; S. Lemmen, "The 'Return to Europe': Intellectual Debates on the Global Place of Czechoslovakia in the Interwar Period", *European Review of History* 23 (2015) 4, pp. 613–614; P. Puchalski, "The Polish Mission to Liberia. Constructing Poland's Colonial Identity", *The Historical Journal* 60 (2017) 4, pp. 1–26; B. Thorpe, "Eurafrica: A Pan-European Vehicle for Central European Colonialism (1923–1939)", *European Review* 26 (2018) 3, pp. 503–513.

23 M. Middell, *Raumformate – Bausteine in Prozessen der Neuverräumlichung* (=Working paper series SFB 1199 at Leipzig University, Nr. 14), p. 20.

24 Ibid.

Europe under the hegemony of the Soviet Union. Nevertheless, this imagination not only inspired comprehensive reflection by Western observers – and among their Eastern counterparts rejecting the notion of a bloc – on the very nature of the "camp" (as another of these circulating metaphors), but it also corresponded to a series of practices and institutionalizations aiming at stabilizing what the West called a bloc. Here, spatial entrepreneurs as particularly capable actors navigating the overlapping processes of respatialization came to the fore.

Tensions and conflicts seem to have been the defining features of these practices and imaginations, which have often been interpreted as indicators for the failures and weaknesses of the bloc. However, they could rather be historicized as a key feature of the respatializations of the particular transition moment in the global spatial order Matthias Middell has described. The fact that the Soviet bloc quickly dissolved when the Cold War came to an end has probably been interpreted too quickly as proof of its shortfalls. Still, during the four decades of its existence the actors involved did not seem to have been all the time too convinced of these failures, and instead invested enormous efforts to either expand and stabilize or to compete, contain, or change the bloc. These empirical practices and strategies seem to rather indicate that the second half of the twentieth century was a crucial moment of experimenting with new spatial formats, the outcomes of which are still hard to theorize beyond post-Cold War triumphalism.

Competing Conceptual Claims: Theorizing the Bloc from Within and Outside

As the Second World War came to an end, a new political geography for the European continent and the world more broadly – prepared in negotiations in Teheran, Yalta, and Potsdam – began to shape the spatial imaginaries of political elites of the soon to be dissolving anti-German alliance. Warning the American President Harry S. Truman of the Soviet expansionist agenda, the British Prime Minister Winston Churchill in May 1945 most prominently articulated the emergence of a split of the continent, a divide that would break up the old imperial and national order:

> From Stettin in the Baltic to Trieste in the Adriatic, an iron curtain has descended across the Continent. Behind that line lie all the capitals of the ancient states of Central and Eastern Europe. Warsaw, Berlin, Prague, Vienna, Budapest, Belgrade, Bucharest and

Sofia, all these famous cities and the populations around them lie in what I must call the Soviet sphere, and all are subject in one form or another, not only to Soviet influence but to a very high and, in many cases, increasing measure of control from Moscow.[25]

Without mentioning the main competitor – the Soviet Union – but focusing on Poland, Romania, and Bulgaria as its captives as well as Greece and Turkey as contested frontier states, two years later Truman translated this diagnosis into the key rationale of the future American foreign policy, conceptualizing the global order as being divided between a "free world" – whose protection the United States would see themselves as being responsible for – and a world of "totalitarian regimes",[26] thereby expressing the new spatial logic as a combination of geopolitical and ideological rationales. As is well known, this argument not only provided the legitimation for the launching of the Marshall Plan, but was also replicated – and refined – a few months later by Andrei Zhdanov at the founding meeting of the Communist Information Bureau (Cominform), identifying the emergence of an "imperialist and anti-democratic camp, on the one hand, and the anti-imperialist and democratic camp, on the other", with the first being led by the United States and the second by the Soviet Union, comprising in his view not only the "new democracies" of Eastern Europe but also Finland as well as Indonesia, Egypt, Syria, India, and Vietnam as associates.[27] Zhdanov further developed Truman's less specific notion of "worlds" and Churchill's geopolitical term of "sphere of influence" into the concept of the "camp", which not only suggested a specific way of internal organization and hierarchy but also typified both in terms of political and ideological nature and in relation to another spatial format: the empire. Much less focused on Europe than Churchill, Zhdanov more explicitly than Truman envisioned the formation of the camp as a potentially planetary process, referring not only to the reorganization of the European political geography, but also to a world of empires coming increasingly under pressure.

This new spatial vocabulary was soon translated into a multitude of still fluid and productive institutionalization projects in the political, economic, and military realms on both sides of what became known as the Iron Curtain: from

---

25 W. S. Churchill, "The Sinews of Peace", in: *Winston S. Churchill. His Complete Speeches 1897–1963*, vol. VII: 1943–1949, ed. R. R. James, New York: Chelsea House Publishers 1974, pp. 7285–7293, here 7289.
26 Truman, Speech delivered before a Joint Session of Congress, 12 March 1947, https://www.americanrhetoric.com/speeches/harrystrumantrumandoctrine.html.
27 Speech by Andrei Zhdanov (member of the Soviet Politburo) at the founding of the Cominform in September 1947, http://educ.jmu.edu/~vannorwc/assets/ghist%20102-150/pages/readings/zhdanovspeech.html

the Cominform[28] (1947–1956) to the Warsaw Pact (1955–1991)[29] and the Council for Mutual Economic Assistance (COMECON, 1949–1991),[30] on the one hand, and the Marshall Plan (1948–1952), the Organisation for European Economic Co-operation/Organisation for Economic Co-operation and Development (OEEC/OECD, 1948), the European Coal and Steel Community (1951–2002) and the European Economic Community (EEC, 1957), as well as North Atlantic Treaty Organization (NATO, 1949) on the other. Yet, even though these institutional infrastructures soon provided – in different forms and logics – the governmental nerve system for the emerging bloc(s), their delimitation and nature remained far from widely accepted as a new spatial format. The sceptical voices were plenty, and they surged during encounters across the East-West divide in particular. Intervening in the production of United Nations Educational, Scientific and Cultural Organization's *History of Mankind* in 1959, Konstantin V. Ostrovityanov, vice president of the Soviet Academy of Sciences, fiercely rejected all conceptualizations in the draft manuscript of the 6th volume, which took up Truman's framing: "Ignoring the undeniable emergence and intensive development of a new, socialist camp in the twentieth century, the authors advance an utterly fallacious concept based on the existence of two worlds: 'the world of democracies headed by the USA' and 'the world of totalitarian states'" into which the Soviet Union had been included together with fascist Italy and Nazi Germany. He demanded to "form a special group of industrially-developed capitalist countries of Western Europe, North America and Australia" as well as

---

[28] G. M. Adibekov, *Kominform i poslevoennaja Evropa*, Moskau: Rossija molodaja, 1994; G. Procacci (ed.), *The* Cominform. Minutes *of the Three Conferences 1947/1948/1949*, Milano: Fondatione Feltrinelli, 1994.

[29] T. Diedrich, W. Heinemann, and Ch. F. Ostermann (eds.), *Der Warschauer Pakt. Von der Gründung bis zum Zusammenbruch 1955 bis 1991*, Berlin: BPB, 2009; V. Mastny, M. Byrne (eds.), *A Cardboard Castle? An Inside History of the Warsaw Pact, 1955–1991*, Budapest, New York: Central European University Press, 2005; F. Umbach, *Das rote Bündnis. Entwicklung und Zerfall des Warschauer Pakts, 1955–1991*, Berlin: Christoph Links, 2005.

[30] U. Müller and D. Jajeśniak-Quast (eds.), *Comecon Revisited. Integration in the Eastern Bloc and Entanglements with the Global Economy* (= Comparativ 27 [2017] 5/6); R. Ahrens, *Gegenseitige Wirtschaftshilfe? Die DDR im RGW – Strukturen und handelspolitische Strategien 1963–1976*, Köln et al.: Böhlau Verlag, 2000; L. K. Metcalf, *The Council of Mutual Economic Assistance. The Failure of Reform*, New York: Columbia University Press, 1997; G. Neumann, "Probleme der osteuropäischen Wirtschaftsintegration", in: J. Wysocki (ed.), *Wirtschaftliche Integration und Wandel von Raumstrukturen im 19. und 20. Jahrhundert*, Berlin: Duncker&Humblot 1994, pp. 159–187; R. W. Stone, *Satellites and Commissars: Strategy and Conflict in the Politics of Soviet-Bloc Trade*, Princeton: Princeton University Press, 1996. See also A. Steiner, "The Council of Mutual Economic Assistance. An Example of Failed Economic Integration?", *Geschichte und Gesellschaft* 39 (2013), pp. 240–258.

"to give due space to the socialist countries, bringing out the features which they have in common and which distinguish them from the other countries, as well as the national characteristics of each country" and "to give special, more profound treatment to the countries and peoples of Asia, Africa and Latin America which all have in common the struggle against colonialism".[31] While Ostrovityanov echoed Zhdanov's notion of the newness and the dynamic openness of the socialist camp – fuelled by the optimism during the Khrushchev thaw in the Soviet Union, which coincided with the globalization of the socialist claim against the backdrop of swelling decolonization – he hinted at the parallel logic shared between the three worlds in transition: the capitalist West, the socialist East, and the decolonizing South. The relation between these two approaches to conceptualizing the global spatial order remained vague until the end of the Cold War, repeatedly resulting in tensions within the socialist camp.

Nevertheless, Western observers from the other side of the Atlantic struggled with making sense of the Soviet bloc well into the 1960s. In a 1964 study on COMECON undertaken by the Carnegie Endowment for International Peace, the editor-in chief succinctly claimed in her introductory note: "The Council of Mutual Economic Assistance is the least known of all the regional organisations."[32] The study's author, the Polish emigrant Andrzej Korbonski, professor of political science at University of California, Los Angeles and a specialist on Polish economic history, wondered,

> [e]ven today, it is difficult to pinpoint exactly the reason for the creation of COMECON at that particular time. Presumably the organization was designed as an instrument of Soviet control over the East Central European economies in response to the Marshall Plan, the establishment of the Organization for European Economic Cooperation, and the division of Europe into two camps. It is actually rather surprising that the organization was not formed even earlier, simultaneously with the Cominform.[33]

Another Polish emigrant, political scientist and presidential advisor Zbigniew Brzeziński, who had popularized the concept of the "Soviet bloc" a few years earlier,[34] immediately questioned its uniformity. One of the book's reviewer,

---

[31] Information Paper No. 25: Communication from Dr. K. V. Ostrovityanov, acting president USSR Academy of Sciences on Volume VI, UNESCO archives, SCHM 2, File 0.30, Information Papers 1-33, 1951–1966.
[32] Anne Winslow in Andrzej Korbonski, "COMECON", *International Conciliation* No. 549, September 1964, p. 1.
[33] Korbonski, "COMECON", p. 5.
[34] Brzeziński, *Soviet Bloc*.

publishing in 1965 in the *American Historical Journal*, revealed the fluidity as well as the effectiveness of this spatial concept. While claiming that it "is probably accepted today by most [...] observers of Soviet affairs, that the monolithic bloc of Communist states of Stalin's day has given way to a more loosely organized system in which various forms of autonomy are practiced", he merged it quickly with another geographical and historical region of similar fragility: Eastern Europe. He stated,

> [o]ne of the problems of any assessment of East Europe, past or present, is that there is really no such area, save as a geographical expression. [...] The only bond of unity has been external force, be it from the Ottoman empire, the Habsburgs, or the Red Army. Thus while unity has often been imposed from above, diversity has more often been the natural activity of the nationalities involved.[35]

Paralleling the Soviet practices of his present with imperial spatializations of the region in the past, the reviewer identified the – ahistorically claimed – nations of the region as contenders both in imperial and Soviet hegemony.

Although emerging as a powerful concept, Western observers grappled into the 1960s with defining the new quality of the "Soviet bloc": it was claimed to be monolithic *and* fragmented, clearly delimited *and* fluid, organized around a strong centre *and* shattered by multiple internal power struggles, powerful as an international player *and* weakly institutionalized as such. In the struggle to make sense of this paradox, analysts often had to refer to spatial formats they seemed to know: the empire and the nation-state. Löwenthal's warning cited above demonstrates that they probably missed the point: that is to say, the novelty of a formation that went beyond the mere changing of empires or nation-states with imperial complementary spaces into new – socialist – garb.

In this struggle to make sense of the newness of this spatialization, Western European observers were also, unsurprisingly, involved. As the emergence of the bloc was not only a geopolitical reaction to a changing global geography after the Second World War, but also a process of economic regionalization in competition to Western dynamics, advisors to agencies driving Western European integration seemed to be mostly interested in how to develop relations with this neighbouring economic region and had to likewise resort to spatial concepts they were familiar with: in their case supranational integration. A leaflet from July 1963 underlined that the development of the COMECON made it "impossible de juger de l'activité économique de ces pays et de leur politique

---

35 W. Lerner, "Review of The Soviet Bloc: Unity and Conflict by Zbigniew K. Brzezinski", *The American Historical Review* 70 (1965) 2, pp. 463–464.

commerciale sans connaître les structures, les objectifs et les problèmes de cet organisme". And while the report admitted that "Les promoteurs du Conseil insistent à cette époque sur le principe de l'égalité souveraine de tous ces membres. Il n'y a pas d'organisme supranational", it interpreted the institutional reforms of the organisation after 1962 as a "mutation [...] profonde. On s'oriente vers un organisme supra-national".[36] In early 1970, an analysis by the Directorate-General for Press and Communication of the European Commission identified a "zone économique unique" in the making but concluded that the aim and direction of the transformations that COMECON had undergone during the past decade could not be plainly established. Still, the analysis clearly identified a reciprocal relation between the integration process unfolding in Western Europe and economic processes in the continent's Eastern half, not only due to a mutual interest in trade relations across the East-West divide, but also because the EEC had been very influential acting as a model for future integration processes in the East.[37]

Indeed, there had been efforts made by COMECON to develop trade relations with the EEC as well as with the European Free Trade Association on a multilateral basis, but led as well as the Soviet initiative to become member of NATO in 1954 not to success, also due to the distrust on the Western side.[38] The intensifying dynamic of Western European integration provided an important incentive within COMECON to push for innovative forms of the economic organization within the bloc.[39] In addition, economic relations with neutral countries in

---

36 Unspecified, Structures et Objectifs du COMECON. La correspondance européenne, Quotidien d'Information et de Documentation sur l'Europe, 5 juillet 1963 (= Structure and Objectives of Comecon. The European Correspondence, Daily Information and European Documentation, July 5, 1963). Archive of European Integration, University of Pittsburgh, http://aei.pitt.edu/73851/.
37 B. Rudpolph, Le Conseil de l'Aide Économique Mutuelle, COMECON, Conception de Base et Transformation du COMECON. Etudes et Analyses No 88, Direction Generale Presse et Information, Bruxelles, le 12 janvier 1970 (= The Council of Economic Mutual Aid, Comecon, Base Design and Transformation of Comecon. Studies and Analyses No. 88, Directorate General Press and Information, Brussels, 12 January 1970 [EU Commission – Press Notice]), Archive of European Integration, University of Pittsburgh, http://aei.pitt.edu/73846/.
38 M. A. Lipkin, *Sovetskij Sojuz i integracionnye processy v Evrope: seredina 1940-x – konec 1960-s godov* [*The Societ Union and the Integration Process in Europe: Mid-1940s – End 1960s*], Moscow Universitet Dmitrija Požarskogo, 2016.
39 S. Kansikas, "The Council for Mutual Economic Assistance – A Restricted Cold War Actor", Comparativ 27 (2017) 5/6, pp. 84–100.

Northern Europe were promoted at the COMECON level.[40] Hence, not only in the Western observers' perceptions but also in projects developed inside the bloc, the intimate relation between the emergence of this spatial format and other diachronic and synchronic formations was reflected: the concept of the bloc seemed to be unthinkable without empire, nation-state, and regionalisms emerging (not only) on the continent.

An Attempt to Respatialize Political, Economic, and Cultural Interactions

Consequently, the Soviet bloc became, as we have seen, a powerful spatial concept to characterize the novelty and relevance of a number of respatializations that Western observers witnessed and placed themselves in relation to. A lack of consensus on its nature lingered and this has often been interpreted as a failure, a fragmentation, or a weakness of the bloc. Such debates in the West were complemented by clashes within the socialist camp, among politicians and theoreticians, to define the newness and rationales of these respatializations. While the bloc metaphor was rejected, the "camp" – as popularized by Zhdanov – became, after Stalin's death, increasingly refined and redefined. One key challenge to articulating the features of the camp as a specific spatial format seemed to lie in the reconciliation between three logics, which were rooted in different historical experiences in the region: How to reconcile socialist internationalism with the emphasis on – or obsession with – national sovereignty (and hence national diversity) and the transnational networks of communist parties? While the tensions between these three logics are until today interpreted as the Achilles heel of the bloc – preventing it from developing in a more similar manner to Western integration – it may be more fruitful to conceptualize the efforts to theoretically and practically solve them as productive and flexible spatial experiments, as reactions to profound transformations of the spatial order of the continent as well as in other parts of the world. The permanent balancing of the international, the national,

---

40 D. Jajeśniak-Quast, "Reaktionen auf westeuropäische Wirtschaftsintegration in Ostmitteleuropa: Die Tschechoslowakei und Polen von den fünfziger bis zu den siebziger Jahren", in: *JEIH Journal of European Integration History* 13 (2007) 2, pp. 69– 84 G. Enderle-Burcel, P. Franaszek, D. Stiefel, and A. Teichova (eds.), *Gaps in the Iron Curtain. Economic relations between neutral and socialist countries in Cold War Europe*, Kraków: Wydawnictwo Uniwersytetu Jagiellońskiego, 2009.

and the transnational logics of interaction between societies, parties, and states was probably *the* defining feature of the bloc, not its flaw.

Although during the first decade and a half of the emergence of the bloc had admittedly been mostly dominated by Soviet ambitions to fortify a monolithic bloc, these were still accompanied by fierce intra-Soviet debates about the nature of and contradictions in the camp[41] as well as on the nature of capitalism and its relations to the socialist camp, most prominently during the so-called Varga debate[42] of the 1940s, in which the above-cited Ostrovityanov had played a prominent role as both prosecutor and judge of Eugen Varga's "errors". The decade after Stalin's death saw not only the rehabilitation of Varga's more nuanced analysis of capitalist-socialist relations and differentiations within the socialist camp, but also remarkable efforts of "inventing socialist cooperation".[43] As a result of these efforts, COMECON declared in June 1962 the Basic Principles of the International Socialist Division of Labour, which defined a "community of socialist countries" as being composed of "free, sovereign peoples striding towards socialism and communism, united through their common ground of their interests and objectives, through the indissoluble ties of international socialist solidarity". The elements of this community were not only sovereign nation-states, but those with similar[44] – socialist – economic and political systems, as "equal" and "fraternal" members with their own "vital interests", voluntarily cooperating with each other.[45] Furthermore, the nation-state principle was complemented by actors that would be able to act transnationally: "The communist and workers' parties of the socialist countries emerge as initiators and organizers of the international socialist division of labour." And while this document was often interpreted by Western observers as an indicator for an intensified integration or a step towards the supranationality of the organization, it cautiously did not make use of these terms – which did not mean that attempts towards supranationalization had not been made, for example with plans for a supranational planning agency. Yet, they had failed due to the resistance of the one or the other member state, as in the case of the planning agency, for example, Romania.

---

41 J. C. Valdez, *Internationalism and the Ideology of Soviet Influence in Eastern Europe*, Cambridge, New York: Cambridge University Press, 1993.
42 K. D. Roh, *Stalin's Economic Advisors: The Varga Institute and the making of Soviet Foreign Policy*, London: Tauris, 2018.
43 E. Radisch, "The Struggle of the Soviet Conception of Comecon", *Comparativ* 27 (2017) 5/6, pp. 26–47, at p. 31.
44 Aleksandrov, Amvrosov, Anufriev et al (eds.), *Naučnyj kommunizm: Slovar' [Scientific Communism: Glossary]*, Moscow: Polizdat 1983.
45 German History in Documents, vol. 9, Two Germanies, 1961–1989. http://germanhistorydocs.ghi-dc.org/sub_document.cfm?document_id=1163.

Planning remained a national affair, and the "principles" were only the minimal consensus that could be reached. The key mode of holding the thus defined community together was rather "coordination", which also better expressed the reality of interactions.[46] It was only in 1971 that COMECON, with the Comprehensive Programme, set "socialist economic integration" as its goal,[47] while the revised charter of COMECON in 1974 was formulated in a more robust language, with "cooperation" and "integration" as the modes in which states and societies in the economic realms would interact.[48] The "camp" terminology and the elaboration of the "socialist division of labour" as the guiding rationale of making it coherent were complemented by the concept of a (global) "socialist community" – the Russian term *sodruzhestvo*, often translated as commonwealth or community, derived from the Russian term for friendship, hinted at a specific (claimed) quality of relations. The 1983 edition of the *Soviet Dictionary of Scientific Communism* defined this by emphasizing three elements: first, it is formed by economically and politically similar states; second, it is an international union of a new type, resting on a specific kind of international relations, that differ from the "bourgeois" variant; and third, it does so by not only promoting "socialist integration" but also pursuing a joint political and economic agenda of spreading socialism and communism worldwide. Based on the key principles of national sovereignty and non-interference, bilateral and multilateral cooperation and integration would be motivated by reaping mutual benefits and practicing socialist internationalism. Such a community would manifest itself in a joint foreign policy of the respective states in the United Nations, the Warsaw Pact, and COMECON as well as in the ideological and cultural ties shared between the societies. The authors explicitly referred to the Comprehensive Programme for further socialist integration of COMECON and the Political Consultative Committee of the Warsaw Pact as further institutionalization of this community and materialization of this revised understanding of the rationales within the bloc. And while interaction with the capitalist states on the basis of peaceful coexistence was presented as expedient and possible, the community was clearly established as the "avant-garde" of further revolutionary transformations in the world, providing a model for socialist

---

[46] U. Müller, Introduction: Failed and Forgotten? New Perspectives on the History of the Council for Mutual Economic Assistance, in: Müller, Jajeśniak-Quast (eds.), *Comecon Revisited*, pp. 7–25, at 13 f.

[47] J. M. van Brabant, *Economic Integration in Eastern Europe: A Handbook*, New York: Routledge, 1989, pp. 81–101.

[48] German History in Documents, vol 9, Two Germanies, 1961–1989, http://germanhistory docs.ghi-dc.org/sub_document.cfm?document_id=1166.

transformations that originated in the historical experience of the Soviet Union.[49]

This combination of a historical narrative of the transformation of the global spatial order with the positioning of the socialist community – the Soviet Union at the centre of otherwise equal states[50] – as the driver of these transformations was confirmed in mainstream theorizations across the bloc. An authors' collective in the German Democratic Republic (GDR) periodized the emergence of the socialist community of states – more narrowly defined as the members of COMECON and the Warsaw Pact[51] – after the October Revolution (1917) and identified the close alliance of its members with the Soviet Union as its main feature.[52] Introducing the "socialist world system" as a broader term, a system that the authors saw emerging after the Second World War,[53] they specified its geographical makeup in 1981 as comprising Albania, Bulgaria, China, the GDR, Yugoslavia, North Korea, Cuba, Laos, Mongolia, Poland, Czechoslovakia, Hungary, the Soviet Union, and Vietnam,[54] thereby not only glossing over the many ruptures and tensions within the socialist camp since the 1940s, but also uniting the different memberships and positions of states in the diverse organizations forming the infrastructures of the camp. The prominence of the term "world system of socialism" had already been growing in Soviet discussions during the 1970s,[55] and it seemed to be increasingly replacing the concept of a socialist commonwealth.

While both within and outside the bloc had been defined through its confrontational relation to the capitalist West, its peculiarity manifested itself in several ways: firstly, in the co-presence of national, international, and transnational rationales of spatialization; secondly, in the historicization of the emergence of a new spatial order, with the October Revolution and the Second World War being presented as the most important caesuras; and thirdly, in the hierarchization of actors. In the latter, this hierarchy placed the Soviet Union at the centre, with the community of socialist states being organized in concentric circles that spanned from Eastern Europe to the Global South to form an ever-expanding socialist

---

49 Aleksandrov, Amvrosov, Anufriev et al (eds.), *Naučnyj kommunizm*.
50 *Geschichte der sozialistischen Gemeinschaft*, p. 40.
51 Ibid.
52 Ibid., p. 5.
53 Art. "Weltsystem", in: *Philosophisches Wörterbuch*, ed. G. Klaus and M. Buhr, 11th ed., Leipzig: VEB Bibliographisches Institut, 1975, vol. II, pp. 1290–1291.
54 *Geschichte der sozialistischen Gemeinschaft*, p. 39.
55 Art. "Mirovaja sistema socializma" ["World-System of Socialism"], in: *Bol'šaja sovetskaja ènciklopedija*, 3. Aufl., vol. 16: Mëzija – Moršansk. Moskva: Izd. "Sovetskaja ènciklopedija", 1974, pp. 939–943, here 939.

world system. Historicization, hierarchization, and opposition characterized what we could conceptualize as the spatial script of socialism – an interplay of spatial imaginations and practices of spatialization that were defined by escalating tensions between internationalism and the territorializing obsession with the nation-state; between a socialist universalism and specific interests; and between quasi-imperial ambitions and geopolitical anxieties of Soviet elites and a socialist cosmopolitanism.

It is these tensions and the co-presence of the national-international-transnational logics that makes attempts futile to conceptualize the respatialization within the socialist camp in relation to a terminology that has been developed for other historical processes, such as supranationality, subsidiarity, or multilevel governance. One might rather argue that this complexity has for more than 40 years opened up multiple rooms for manoeuvre for different groups of actors – experts, intellectuals, politicians, factory managers, artists, or members of the youth – on a multitude of fields – economy, military, international relations, the arts, or societal movements – to pursue their own specific agendas. At the same time, it required extremely capable spatial entrepreneurs with the respective spatial literacy to manage these overlapping logics. In the second part of this chapter, we will shed light on some of these efforts to create infrastructures and institutions as well as to navigate the emerging complex spatiality of the bloc.

Constructing the Bloc: Infrastructures, Institutions, and Actors

While analysts and theoreticians on both sides of the Iron Curtain struggled to define the nature of the "camp", the "bloc", or the "commonwealth", a multitude of infrastructures, institutionalizations, and networks emerged as the result of the activities of a wide spectrum of actors – both inside and outside the bloc. One of the most prominent was certainly COMECON,[56] whose founding is often interpreted as a reaction to the implementation of the Marshall Plan by the US as a competing offer of economic regionalization. However, there had been other, non-Soviet ideas how to organize economic cooperation in the

---

[56] U. Müller, and D. Jajeśniak-Quast (ed.), *Comecon Revisited*; R. Bideleux, I. Jeffries, *A History of Eastern Europe. Crisis and Change*, London, New York: Routledge, 1998, pp. 534–543; L. Crump, S. Godard, "Reassessing Communist International Organizations: A Comparative Analysis of COMECON and the Warsaw Pact in Relation to their Cold War Competitors", *Contemporary European History* 27 (2018) 1, pp. 85–109.

region. For example, the Yugoslav-Bulgarian treaty of 1947, based on an initiative by Dimitrov and Tito, had further developed the format of the Balkan Federation (introduced above) by adding an economic dimension. Furthermore, as most of the post-war states in the region found themselves in a relatively precarious position in the global economy – adopting the strategy of import substitution to bolster economic development while defending state control of foreign trade in the planned economy and being mostly interested in technology transfer and technical assistance free of charge, which the Soviet Union would provide – the integration into the General Agreement on Tariffs and Trade or other Western economic international regimes was highly unattractive for them.[57] Nevertheless, they would, most of the time, not react to these challenges by promoting economic integration in the sense of classical economics: "The CMEA was never intended to maximize integration through trade, but rather to provide a protected environment within which to maximize the power, stability and economic growth of the socialist states."[58] COMECON differed from historical precursors of trade and tariffs integration, such as the German Customs Union of the nineteenth century or within the Habsburg monarchy, as well as from more current structures, such as the European Communities (EC), since it was not designed to maximize trade by benefitting from comparative cost advantages, but it aimed at providing the basis for joint investment projects.[59] The lack of supranational institutions is often identified as a flaw or the reason for the failure of the bloc,[60] yet this translates the standards of Western market economies to centrally planned economies[61] and therefore fails to grasp its specific flexibility.

When Nikita Khrushchev suggested the establishment of a joint CMEA Central Planning Office to introduce a supranational planning system,[62] this idea was

---

[57] E. Dragomir, "The Creation of the Council for Mutual Economic Assistance as seen from the Romanian Archives", *Historical Research* 88 (2015) 240, pp. 35–379.
[58] Bideleux, I. Jeffries, *History of Eastern Europe*, p. 538.
[59] L. Csaba, "Joint Investments and Mutual Advantages in the CMEA – Retrospection and Prognosis", *Soviet Studies* XXXVII (1985), pp. 227–247; D. R. Stone, "CMEA's International Investment Bank and the Crisis of Developed Socialism", *Journal of Cold War Studies* 10 (2008), pp. 48–77.
[60] A. Steiner, The Council of Mutual Economic Assistance: An Example of Failed Economic Integration?, *Geschichte und Gesellschaft* 39 (2013), pp. 240–258.
[61] M. Dangerfield, "Sozialistische Ökonomische Integration. Der Rat für gegenseitige Wirtschaftshilfe (RGW)", in: B. Greiner, Ch. Th. Müller, C. Weber (eds.), *Ökonomie im Kalten Krieg*, Hamburg: Hamburger Edition, 2010, pp. 348–369, here 364–368; U. Müller, "Introduction. Failed and Forgotten?", pp. 10–14.
[62] Ahrens, *Gegenseitige Wirtschaftshilfe*, p. 12. The seriousness of Khrushchev's proposal is assessed differently in the literature. See M. Simai, "A Case Study of Economic Cooperation in

rejected by Romania – acting probably in the interests of other small members – for fear of Soviet domination and of degradation to the producer of agricultural goods for the Eastern bloc. Planning of the economy was regarded as an essential part of national sovereignty, and Romania wanted to uphold its national industrialization policy.[63] Polish fears of the Federal Republic of Germany (FRG) and mistrust of East Germany's privileged status vis-à-vis the FRG in turn brought a temporary alliance of convenience with Moscow, supporting a further centralization of economic organization around Moscow. Leading economists from Czechoslovakia and Hungary in contrast believed that integration should be fostered by more rational pricing, a convertible CMEA currency, and a free socialist market. Therefore, they rejected a stronger centralization in Moscow.[64] The Comprehensive Programme can be interpreted as a compromise between these two visions The programme aimed to coordinate medium-term economic plans. This, however, was limited in practice to the exchange of goods and to specialization in the manufacture of certain goods. Joint planning by the CMEA was not foreseen. Consequently, the structure and investment policy was not coordinated but remained the full responsibility of the member states. Closer cooperation was possible with the implementation of individual projects, in which only interested countries could participate.[65]

The back and forth between different attempts to supranationalize the bloc, at least in its economic dimension, can likewise be interpreted with regard to its competing regionalization project in Western Europe, the reactions to which also revealed the flexibility of the bloc. When the EC introduced at the end of the 1960s the common market as well as a common foreign economic policy,

---

Eastern Europe", in: D. Nicol, L. Echevarria and A. Peccei (eds.), *Regionalism and the New International Economic Order*, New York: Pergamon Press, 1981, p. 126; Stone, *Satellites and Commissars*, p. 34.

63 E. Dragomir, "New Explanations for Romania's Detachment from Moscow at the Beginning of the 1960s", *Valahian Journal of Historical Studies* 13 (2010), pp. 51–82. For Poland see W. Jarząbek, "Polish Economic Policy at the Time of Détente, 1966–78", *European Review of History*, 21 (2014) 2, pp. 293–309.

64 J. Kučera, "Zwischen 'kapitalistischem' und 'sozialistischem' Weltmarkt: Die tschechoslowakische Wirtschaftsreform der 1960er Jahre und der RGW", in: C. Boyer (ed.), *Zur Physiognomie sozialistischer Wirtschaftsreformen: Die Sowjetunion, Polen, die Tschechoslowakei, Ungarn, die DDR und Jugoslawien im Vergleich*, Frankfurt am Main: Klostermann, 2007, pp. 179–200; See also Ahrens, *Gegenseitige Wirtschaftshilfe*, pp. 213–225, Stone, "CMEA's International Investment Bank".

65 H. Machowski, Der Rat für gegenseitige Wirtschaftshilfe. Ziele, Formen und Probleme der Zusammenarbeit, in: Rat für gegenseitige Wirtschaftshilfe. Strukturen und Probleme, Bonn: Ostkolleg der Bundeszentrale für politische Bildung, 1987, p. 20.

both the Soviet Union and smaller Eastern European states had to deal with a massive regional power, with which they could only hope to successfully negotiate if they were able to cooperate more effectively with their own socialist brothers. When, in 1962, Soviet plans to strengthen COMECON had failed due to the resistance of smaller states, the competing Western European economic integration motivated them to give up their reservations at least in part. The Comprehensive Programme was the compromise that could be reached. Even though official trade relations between COMECON and the EC were established only in the mid-1980s, this manoeuvring seems to be not only a failure but also an indicator for a certain flexibility of the spatial format of the bloc.[66]

The bloc was, furthermore, crucially formed through technological infrastructures, which included the Organization for Cooperation in the Field of Post and Telecommunication, founded in 1957. Its members were Bulgaria, China, Czechoslovakia, the GDR, Hungary, Mongolia, North Korea, Poland, Romania, the Soviet Union, and Vietnam.[67] This was complemented by a number of organizations for cooperation in different fields of industry[68] and agriculture,[69] cosmic communication,[70] transport,[71] banking,[72] radio and television,[73] as well as science and technology.[74] The varying geographies of their memberships –

---

[66] S. Kansikas, *Socialist Countries Face the European Community. Soviet-Bloc Controversies over East-West Trade*, Frankfurt am Main: Peter Lang, 2014.

[67] Art. "Organisation für die Zusammenarbeit auf dem Gebiet des Post- und Fernmeldewesens (OSS)", in: Kleines politisches Wörterbuch. Berlin (Ost): Dietz Verlag, 1973, 625.

[68] Art. "Organisation für die Zusammenarbeit auf dem Gebiet kleintonnagiger chemischer Erzeugnisse (Interchim)", ibid., pp. 625–626; Art. "Organisation für die Zusammenarbeit der Wälzlagerindustrie (OZWI)", ibid., p. 627; Art. "Organisation für die Zusammenarbeit in der Schwarzmetallurgie (Intermetall)", ibid., pp. 627–628.

[69] D. Jajeśniak-Quast: "'Hidden Integration'" – RGW-Wirtschaftsexperten in europäischen Netzwerken", in: *Jahrbuch für Wirtschaftsgeschichte*, 2014/1, pp. 179–195.

[70] Art. "Organisation für kosmische Nachrichtenverbindungen (Intersputnik)", in: *Kleines politisches Wörterbuch*, Berlin (Ost): Dietz Verlag, 1973, pp. 628–629.

[71] R. Roth, H. Jacolin (eds.): *Eastern European Railways in Transition. Nineteenth to Twenty-first Centuries*, Farnham et al: Ashgate, 2013; U. Müller, "Verkehrspolitik im RGW zwischen Integration und Desintegration", in: G. Schulz, and M. Spoerer (eds.): *Integration und Desintegration Europas. Wirtschafts- und sozialhistorische Beiträge*, Stuttgart: Franz Steiner Verlag, 2019, pp. 99–124.

[72] Art. "Internationale Bank für Wirtschaftliche Zusammenarbeit (IBWZ)", in: *Kleines politisches Wörterbuch*, Berlin (Ost): Dietz Verlag, 1973, pp. 366–368; Art. "Internationale Investitionsbank (IIB), ibid., pp. 369–371.

[73] Art. "Internationale Rundfunk- und Fernsehorganisation (OIRT)", ibid., p. 373.

[74] Art. "Internationales Zentrum für wissenschaftliche und technische Zusammenarbeit", ibid., pp. 377–378; D. Jajeśniak-Quast: "Ein lokaler 'Rat für gegenseitige Wirtschaftshilfe': Eisenhüttenstadt, Kraków Nowa Huta und Ostrava Kunčice", in: Ch. Bernhardt, H. Reif (eds.):

often being smaller or larger than COMECON – reflected the dynamic nature of the bloc, which still seemed to revolve around notions of socialist development as well as opposition to and competition with other forms of economic and technological integration.

Most prominently, the regional electricity grid Mir had been created through the bottom-up combination of individual cross-border linkages, including those across the East-West divide, in an effort to satisfy the growing energy demand for the ambitious industrialization programmes at the heart of the socialist model of development.[75] Requiring not only the resolving of technological problems but also administrative and political ones, the energy sector had been key and the most productive in implementing the principles of a socialist division of labour, after 1962, and in the context of the COMECON's Comprehensive Programme, after 1971. The global energy crisis of the mid-1970s, in addition to the reorientation of the Soviet energy policy towards an intensification of multilateral, bloc-wide cooperation, led to further investments into new energy technologies, such as nuclear power, as well as promoted increasing cooperation with the West. During the 1980s, however, these efforts finally hit the wall.[76] While Falk Flade emphasizes the centrality of COMECON as an actor promoting East-West cooperation, Sonja D. Schmid equally underlines the outstanding success of nuclear power cooperation in COMECON in particular.[77] This, on the one hand, was related to the interplay between Soviet interests in economic – and hence political – stability in the region, which made the USSR willing to provide technological, scientific, and financial support for the creation of the respective infrastructure in the COMECON member states, which, in turn, learned to exploit Soviet anxieties in their favour. At the same time, Schmid argues, "the emphasis on

---

Sozialistische Städte zwischen Herrschaft und Selbstbehauptung. Kommunalpolitik, Stadtplanung und Alltag in der DDR, Stuttgart: Franz Steiner Verlag 2009 (=Beiträge zur Stadtgeschichte und Urbanisierungsforschung, Bd. 5), pp. 95–114.

[75] J. Perović (ed.), *Cold War Energy: A Transnational History of Soviet Oil and Gas*, London: Palgrave Macmillan, 2017; P. Högselius, A. Hommels, A. Kaijser, E. van der Vleuten (eds.), *The Making of Europe's Critical Infrastructure. Common Connections and Shared Vulnerabilities*, Houndmills, Basingstoke: Palgrave 2013; P. Högselius, A. Kaijser, E. van der Vleuten (eds.), *Europe's Infrastructure Transition. Economy, War, Nature*, London, New York: Routledge, 2016; F. Flade: *Energy Infrastructures in the Eastern Bloc. Poland and the Construction of Transnational Electricity, Oil, and Gas Transmission Systems*, Wiesbaden: Harrassowitz 2017.

[76] F. Flade, "The Role of the Council for Mutual Economic Assistance in the Construction of the Transnational Electricity Grid Mir", *Comparativ* 27 (2017) 5/6, pp. 48–64.

[77] S. D. Schmid, "Nuclear Colonization? Soviet Technopolitics in the Second World", in: G. Hecht, *Entangled Geographies: Empire and Technopolitics in the Global Cold War*. Cambridge, MA: MIT Press, 2011, pp. 125–154.

modernization through scientific and technological progress was the one part of the Soviet civilizing mission that was compatible with other ideologies"[78] and therefore was productive in forging transnational ties among a community of experts across and beyond the bloc.

These experts seem to have been some of the most capable spatial entrepreneurs pursuing an agenda of shaping the bloc through institutionalizations. Simon Godard's work is particularly instructive in this respect. Investigating mid-ranking staff of the COMECON agencies, he investigates how they navigated their competing loyalties as national and international actors.[79] Not only had their number grown following the strengthening of the organization's agencies after the 1960s, but they had also increasingly become competent in mediating the different levels and logics of the organization between Party-related so-called "basic organizations", (their) national governments, and what they identified as being economically rational in the interest of the bloc as a whole. Expertise became the main currency for investment, which these traveling experts supplied through these multiple arenas under the single umbrella of COMECON.

A Learning System?

The organizational dynamics of COMECON and the Warsaw Pact that gathered speed after Stalin's death while Soviet elites abandoned their resistance to strengthening the resources for these organizations,[80] both cornerstones of the socialist camp developed their "actoreness" as international organizations and "went through a process of institutionalisation, multilateralisation, integration and foreign policy coordination", in particular in moments of crisis in which "both organisations [...] learnt to cope with dissent and diverging national interests, and which developed the potential to operate as collective actors."[81] Conflict, as Crump and Godard underline, "was neither their weakness nor a sign of malfunction of an imperial system, but their strength, and as such can be considered a learning moment, which made them resemble their Western counterparts".[82] This learning not only concerned the agencies of the

---

78 Ibid., p. 144.
79 S. Godard, "Creative Tension: The Role of Conflict in Shaping Transnational Identity at Comecon", *Comparativ* 27 (2017) 5/6, pp. 65–83.
80 Radisch, "The Struggle of the Soviet Conception of Comecon".
81 L. Crump, S. Godard: "Reassessing Communist International Organisations" p. 88.
82 Ibid., p. 108.

institution – the Secretariat and the Standing Commissions in particular – but also the members of the organizations learning to mobilize both COMECON and the Warsaw Pact to pursue their own national interests. In this regard, e.g. Polish and Hungarian initiatives to reform COMECON in the 1960s and 1970s can be interpreted as a strategy to counter the challenges of the global economy and implement national development plans.

While COMECON and the Warsaw Pact may have defined the nucleus of this web of networks and organizations, these institutionalizations were far from being the only ones. What could be characterized as transnational organizations – and were during the Cold War often dismissed as Soviet front organizations – amounted to an impressive number, covering a large variety of social, political, and cultural fields.[83] These ranged from the International Student Union (founded in Prague in 1946) and the World Federation of Democratic Youth (founded in London in 1945), with its World Festivals of Youth and Students (founded in Prague in 1947, followed by Budapest in 1949, Berlin in 1951, Bucharest in 1953, Warsaw in 1955, Moscow in 1957, Vienna in 1959, Helsinki in 1962, Sofia in 1968,[84] Berlin in 1973, Havana in 1978, Moscow in 1985, and Pyongyang in 1989), to the International Organization of Journalists (founded in Prague in 1946), the International Federation of Resistance Fighters (founded in Vienna in 1951), and the World Federation of Trade Unions (founded in Prague in 1945). These webs were spun through the meetings and conferences of communist and workers' parties on a global scale – most prominently the meetings in Moscow (1957, 1960, 1969, and 1987) – and varying regional scales: pan-European (1958, 1961, and 1976 in Berlin, 1961 in Karlovy Vary, Moscow in 1970); Eastern European (1957 and 1958 in Moscow); Western European (1959, 1963, and 1965 in Brussels; 1959 in Rome; 1966 in Vienna, and 1970 in Paris); and Northern European (1957 in Helsinki; 1959 in Stockholm).[85]

---

[83] B. Morris, "Communist International Front Organizations. Their Nature and Function", *World Politics* 9 (1956) 1, pp. 76–87.
[84] E. Breßlein, *Drushba! Freundschaft? Von der Kommunistischen Jugendinternationale zu den Weltjugendfestspielen*, Frankfurt am Main: Fischer Taschenbuchverlag, 1973; Art. "Weltfestspiele der Jugend und Studenten", in: *Kleines politisches Lexikon*, Berlin (Ost): Dietz Verlag, 1973, pp. 954–955; P. Koivunen, *Performing Peace and Friendship. The World Youth Festival as a Tool of Soviet Cultural Diplomacy, 1947–1957*, PhD University of Tampere, 2013.
[85] Art. "Sovesčanija kommunističeskich i rabočich partij", in: *Bol'saja sovetskaja enciklopedija*, t. 24, kn. I: Sobaki – struna, Moscow Izd. "Sovetskaja enciklopedija", 3th ed., 1976, pp. 144–160.

Often, these organizations and their trajectories and members reflected the protracted relation between pre-war internationalism, rising Cold War tensions, and surging clashes for national liberation and decolonization in the Global South, which became increasingly entangled with the logics of communist internationalism dating back to the interwar period and Cold War competition during the 1950s and 1960s. The Women's International Democratic Federation (WIDF) was a particular case in point, as not only its activists engaged in an emerging international legal order of human rights and humanitarianism, but also its national affiliates developed both on a global and on a national scale feminist agendas in the context of socialist societies – an often complicated intervention.[86] Established in Paris in 1945 at a meeting organized by the Union of French Women (the mass women's organization of the French communist party), the WIDF was, on the one hand, designed as a rival to the International Council of Women, which had been founded at the end of the nineteenth century and was an expression of the competing universalisms during the early post-war decades. However, as Celia Donert argues, "it is crucial to remember that the WIDF emerged from local circumstances at the grass roots of the communist and wider labour, radical and anti-colonial movements after 1945",[87] with its first cohort of members being intellectuals, artists, and activists who were politicized by the rise of fascism and the Spanish Civil War (1936–1939) as well as through their participation in anti-colonial conflicts. Their biographies often exhibit the diversity of experiences and engagements with communist and feminist agendas, which, particularly during the early decades of the organization's existence, were frequently at odds with a Cold War logic – in which the US dismissed it as a Soviet front organization when it became a Soviet-sponsored movement, such as the case with the World Peace Council

---

[86] L. J. Rupp, *Worlds of Women: The Making of an International Women's Movement*, Princeton: Princeton University Press, 1997; F. de Haan, "Introduction" to "Forum: 'After Ten Years: Communism and Feminism Revisited'", *Aspasia* 10 (2016), pp. 102–111; Ch. Bonfiglioli, *Cold War Internationalisms, Nationalisms and the Yugoslav-Soviet Split*; R. Popa, "Translating Equality between Cold War Divides Women Activists from Hungary and Romania and the Creation of International Women's Year", in: *Gender Politics and everyday Life in State Socialist Eastern and Central Europa*, ed. Sh. Penn, J. Massino, New York: Palgrave, 2009, pp. 59–74; K. Ghodsee, "Rethinking State Socialist Mass Women's Organizations: The Committee of the Bulgarian Womens Movement and the United Nations Decade for Women, 1975–1985", *Journal of Women's History* 24 (2012) 4, pp. 49–73; K. Ghodsee, *Second world, Second Sex: Socialist Women's Activism and Global Solidarity during the Cold War*, Durham: Duke University Press, 2019.
[87] C. Donert, "From Communist Internationalism to Human Rights: Gender, Violence and International Law in the Women's International Democratic Federation Mission to North Korea, 1951", *Contemporary European History* 25 (2016) 2, pp. 313–333, here p. 317.

and the World Congress of Youth. Yet, its membership originated not only from Europe, but also from Asia, Africa, and Latin America, which made this network a crucial interface for relations between the Cold War's Second and Third Worlds. Accordingly, the "communist internationalism espoused by the WIDF in the early Cold War was premised on the existence of nations linked by working-class solidarity across borders and on supporting revolutionary struggle if necessary to achieve national liberation from colonial or capitalist oppression."[88]

This entanglement between internationalism, nationalism, Cold War logics, and a universalist agenda for the protection of women's rights shaped the mindsets of the activists from Africa, Asia, and Europe, whose trajectories reflected the diversity of leftist female intellectuals and activists, who were part of a longer history of women's peace activism. Connecting human rights discourses with national liberation and socialist agendas, these activists linked national liberation movements and demands for gender equality to a global struggle against imperialism. While these actors challenged simplistic narratives of an East-West divide and expressed the much more complex spatialities of communist internationalism, the WIDF's split in 1956 was an effect of the unresolved tensions between these divergent logics. When the Berlin-based secretariat of the organization refused to condemn the Soviet invasion of Hungary and instead focused only on the Suez crisis in 1956, the Western-affiliated activists would no longer join their Eastern European fellows. Yet, "[i]nternational development, humanitarian relief and technical assistance programmes in North Korea and Vietnam represented one of the many ways in which socialist internationalism became part of everyday life in the socialist bloc throughout the 1950s and 1960s, along with international congresses for students, women or workers, sporting events [...] students exchanges and scholarships for African, Asian and Latin American students at Soviet and East European universities or bilateral agreements on contract labour between socialist countries in Eastern Europe, Africa, and Asia."[89]

---

[88] Ibid., p. 320.
[89] Donert, "From Communist Internationalism to Human Rights", p. 332, on labour and educational mobility, see: A. K. Alamgir, "Labor and Labor Migration in State Socialism", *Labor History* 59 (2018) 3, pp. 271–276; Idem, "From the Field to the Factory Floor Vietnamese Government's Defense of Migrant Workers' Interests in State-Socialist Czechoslovakia", *Journal of Vietnamese Studies* 12 (2017) 1, pp. 10–41; Q. Slobodian, *Comrades of Color: East Germany in the Cold War World*, New York, Oxford: Berghahn, 2015; Ch. Schwenkel, "Rethinking Asian Mobilities", *Critical Asian Studies* 46 (2014) 2, pp. 235–258; C. Katsakioris, "Creating a Socialist Intelligentsia: Soviet Educational Aid and its Impact on Africa (1960–1991)", *Cahiers d'études africaines* 2 (2017) 226, pp. 259–288; E. Burton (ed.), "Journeys of Education and Struggle: African Mobility in Times of Decolonization and the Cold War" (Special Issue), *Stichproben: Wiener Zeitschrift für kritische*

The Cultural Dimension of Bloc-Building

The complicated relation between the emergence of the bloc as a spatial format with parallel processes of respatialization in the context of the Cold War and decolonization is also apparent with regard to many of the ambitious initiatives of Soviet cultural diplomacy of these decades. The First Film Festival of African and Asian Cinema, held in 1968 in Tashkent, is a prominent case in point.[90] Taking place shortly after the violent abolition of the Prague Spring, this meeting gathered 240 filmmakers from 49 African and Asian countries, among them the Senegalese novelist and director Ousmane Sembène; the Indian actor, director, and producer Raj Kapoor, the Japanese filmmaker Fumio Kamei, and the Kyrgyz director Tolomush Okeev, many of whom had previously studied the Soviet Union.[91] This event was crucially shaped by the overlap of Cold War competition and a socialist internationalism in the realm of art, at which Third World artists were provided with a room to connect and lobby for their agenda and to compete with the dominating cinema industries of Hollywood and Western Europe. While Rossen Djagalov and Masha Salazkina conceptualize it as a "contact zone", borrowing the term from Marie Louise Pratt, they further underline that "the Soviet terrain is much more multifaceted and more utopian than Pratt's colonial 'contact zone'", highlighting the "polyvalence of Soviet interactions with the non-Soviet world".[92] The extensive process for selecting delegates to the festival alone demonstrates the challenges that the Soviet organizing committee had to solve, navigating the tensions not only between geopolitical, artistic, and commercial interest of the Soviet organizers and audience but also between the official rhetoric of countering the global dominance of Hollywood with a "cultural colonialist agenda on part of the Soviet organizers".[93] This complexity increased through the discussions of the participants coming together in Central Asia, in which two meanings of Third World cinema could not be reconciled: one referring to the

---

Afrikastudien 34 (2018); M. Schenck, *Socialist Solidarities and their Afterlives: Histories and Memories of Angolan and Mozambican Migrants in the German Democratic Republic, 1975–2015*, PhD dissertation, Princeton University 2017.

90 R. Djagalov and M. Salazkina, "Tashkent 68: A cinematic contact zone", *Slavic Review* 75 (2016) 2, pp. 279–298.
91 G. Chomentowski, "L'expérience soviétique des cinémas africains au lendemain des indépendances", *Le temps des médias* 26 (2016) 1, p. 111; J. Woll, "The Russian Connection: Soviet Cinema and the Cinema of Francophone Africa," in: F. Pfaff (ed.), *Focus on African Films*, Bloomington: Indiana University Press, 2004, pp. 223–240.
92 Djagalov and Salazkina, "Tashkent 68", p. 280–81.
93 Ibid., p. 284.

cinema of "developing nations" of the Global South – a perspective in which the Cold War's second world was placed above their Southern partners – and one referring to an emancipatory artistic agenda more globally, which would address a transformation of Eastern European culture and cinema as well. Hence, both the themes of the festival and the practices of shaping it demonstrate the overlapping and partly incongruent spatialities of the bloc in its relation to the Cold War's Third World, which had emerged since the 1950s as another powerful spatial imagination in an effort to reduce the complexity of the Cold War's multiple repatializations,[94] including the translated institutionalizations.[95]

Such tensions also materialized in the economic realm. The ambitious principles of a socialist division of labour, as formulated in 1962, were in theory also meant for interactions with the so-called developing countries in what many call today the Global South. However, the application of this logic, soon after the mid-1960s, faced profound constraints during moments of rising economic crisis on a global scale and in Eastern Europe more specifically.[96] The tension between internationalism and nationalism reduced the ambitious geography of the socialist world system as well as it provoked a reorientation to the West when searching for economic partners. This occurred not only by keeping aspiring Southern countries, such as Mozambique and Angola, at a distance as associate members (or refusing association per se, while Cuba and Vietnam had gained membership status in 1972 and 1978 respectively),[97] but also by being unable to coordinate the bloc economic relations with the Global South on a multilateral scale[98] as well as by struggling with taking up the calls for a New International Economic Order.[99]

---

[94] C. Kalter, *The Discovery of the Third World. Decolonization and the Rise of the New Left in France, c. 1950–1976*, Cambridge: Cambridge University Press, 2016.

[95] J. Dinkel, *The Non-Aligned Movement: Genesis, Organization and Politics (1927–1992) (New Perspectives on the Cold War 5)*, Leiden/Boston: Brill 2019.

[96] S. Lorenzini, "Comecon and the South in the Years of Détente: A Study on East-South Economic Relations", *European Review of History* 21 (2014) 2, pp. 183–199.

[97] Z. Laidi, "L'URSS et l'Afrique. Vers une extension du système socialiste mondial?", *Politique étrangère* 48 (1983) 3, pp. 679–699.

[98] Ch. Coker, "Adventurism and Pragmatism: The Soviet Union, Comecon, and Relations with African States", *International Affairs (Royal Institute of International Affairs)* 57 (1981) 4, pp. 618–633; M. Trecker, *Red Money for the Global South: The Council for Mutual Economic Assistance (CMEA) and the Economic Side of the Cold War in the Third World*, phil. Diss., München 2017.

[99] J. Oxenham, "The Comecon Group of European States and the NIEO", *International Review of Education* 28 (1982) 4, pp. 434–438; B. Kocsev, "Fighting Global Inequalities. The Institute for World Economics and its Analysis of Underdevelopment", in: M. Middell (ed.), *Kommunismus jenseits des Eurozentrismus (= Jahrbuch für Historische Kommunismusforschung)*, Berlin:

Contemporary Western observers did not miss this opportunity to fiercely criticize the bloc in this regard as an "alternative system of exploitation".[100]

The bloc's position as a whole was contrasted by the much more diversified dynamics in the bilateral relations between Eastern European countries and newly emerging states in the Global South. Here not only economic and military relations expanded,[101] but also societal interactions as a result of flourishing mobilities of students, academics, and workers.[102] These encounters again reveal the tension between internationalism and nationalism, materializing in conflicts and misperceptions, which often had to do with marginalizations due to race and gender.[103]

With regard to dynamics within the bloc, more recent studies on transnational networks and encounters inside the more narrowly defined European socialist camp have challenged simplifying narratives about "unity and diversity" in the camp. While the recurring political crisis in the camp in the 1950s and 1960s[104] has

---

Metropol Verlag, 2019, pp. 173–187; Idem, "The Unwealth of Nations: How Economists Conquered the Field of Area Studies in Hungary", in: K. Naumann, T. Loschke, S. Marung and M. Middell (eds.), *In Search of Other Worlds. Essays towards a Cross-Regional History of Area Studies*, Leipzig: Universitätsverlag, 2019, pp. 169–197.
100 S. J. Noumoff, "COMECON and the Third World", *Economic and Political Weekly* 15 (1980) 34, pp. 1443–1454.
101 Ph. Mühlenbeck, *Czechoslovakia in Africa, 1945–1968*, Houndmills Palgrave, 2016; A. Hilger, *Sowjetisch-indische Beziehungen 1941–1966: Imperiale Agenda und nationale Identitat in der Ära von Dekolonisierung und kaltem Krieg*, Köln et al.: Böhlau, 2018, A. Iandolo, "De-Stalinizing Growth: Decolonization and the Development of Development Economics in the Soviet Union", in: S. J. Macekura and E. Manela (eds.), *The Development Century: A Global History*, Cambridge, Cambridge University Press, 2018, pp. 197–219; Ph. Muehlenbeck and N. Telepneva, *Warsaw Pact Intervention in the Third World: Aid and Influence in the Cold War*, London et al.: Bloomsbury, 2018; N. Telepneva, *Our Sacred Duty: The Soviet Union, the Liberation Movements in the Portuguese Colonies, and the Cold War, 1961–1975*, PhD Thesis, London School of Economics and Political Science (University of London), 2014.
102 Schwenkel, "Rethinking Asian Mobilities"; Katsakioris, "Creating a Socialist Intelligentsia"; Burton (ed.), "Journeys of Education and Struggle"; Schenck, *Socialist Solidarities;* S. Marung, "The Provocation of Empirical Evidence: Soviet African Studies between Enthusiasm and Discomfort", *African Identities* 16 (2018) 2, pp. 176–190.
103 M. Matusevich, "Black in the U.S.S.R: Africans, African Americans, and the Soviet society", *Transition* 100 (2008), pp. 56–75; P. Davis, "'Coulibaly' Cosmopolitanism in Moscow: Mamadou Somé Coulibaly and the Surikov Academy Paintings, 1960s–1970s", in: E. Rosenhaft and R. Aitken (eds.), *Africa in Europe: Studies in Transnational Practice in the Long Twentieth Century*, Liverpool: Liverpool University Press, 2013, pp. 142–161.
104 J. Perović, "The Tito-Stalin Split: A Reassessment in Light of New Evidence", *Journal of Cold War Studies* 9 (2007) 2; L. Gibianskii, "The Soviet-Yugoslav Split and the Cominform", in: *The Establishment of Communist Regimes in Eastern Europe, 1944–1949*, ed. N. Naimark and

prompted contemporary Western observers to "prove" its fragmentation, others, such as Rachel Applebaum, have recently argued that

> [d]uring these decades, contact between the Soviet Union and its satellite states, far from declining, actually became more pervasive, and the lives of ordinary Soviet and eastern European citizens became more intertwined. Furthermore, these interactions became more dynamic, as Soviet imperialism was gradually replaced by a new policy of transnational 'friendship' in the realm of everyday life.[105]

This "friendship" was reflected in the founding of friendship societies, the expansion of mass tourism across the bloc,[106] the spreading of pen-pal correspondences, as well as trade of mass media and consumer goods. These exchanges "were supposed to help build a transnational socialist community, which would serve as both a counter to and competitor with the capitalist west".[107] The investigation into this peculiar kind of transnationality has turned out to be extremely productive in recent years, helping to re-evaluate the nature of the camp beyond narratives of "Sovietization" of the region or the formation of a Soviet "empire".[108] Patryck Babiracki, in this respect, argues that

> the former Soviet bloc was a web of multiple, overlapping spaces, geographies, political and intellectual projects, and identities rather than a clearly circumscribed and isolated system of state communisms. Now the Soviet bloc can be seen as a nexus of competing systems of power that often crisscross the formal political boundaries; power, more than before, appears to result from a good fit, compatibility, or 'synergy' between these various systems and networks and different actors' ability to compromise. Concerned with problems of mobility, compatibility, and stability of networks, the new analytic framework complements the hitherto dominant pattern of interpretation without necessarily invalidating all its premises or usefulness in answering important questions.[109]

L. Gibianskii, Boulder, CO: Westview Press, 1997, pp. 291–312; L. M. Lüthi, *Sino-Soviet Split: Cold War in the Communist World*, Princeton: Princeton University Press, 2008; S. Radchenko, *Two Suns in the Heavens. The Sino-Soviet Struggle for Supremacy, 1962–1967*, Washington, D.C.: Woodrow Wilson Center Press, 2009; M. Retegan, *In the Shadow of the Prague Spring: Romanian Foreign Policy and the Crisis in Czechoslovakia, 1968*, Iasi: The Center for Romanian Studies, 2000; K. Dawisha, *The Kremlin and the Prague Spring*, Berkeley: University of California Press, 1984; Ch. Gati, *Failed Illusions: Moscow, Washington, Budapest, and the 1956 Hungarian Revolt*, Washington, D.C.: Woodrow Wilson Center Press, 2008.
105 R. Applebaum, "The Friendship Project: Socialist Internationalism in the Soviet Union and Czechoslovakia in the 1950s and 1960s", *Slavic Review* 74 (2015) (3), pp. 484–507, here p. 485.
106 A. E. Gorsuch, *All this is Your World: Soviet Tourism at Home and Abroad After Stalin*, Oxford: Oxford University Press, 2013.
107 Applebaum, "The Friendship Project", p. 486.
108 Babiracki, "Interfacing the Soviet Bloc".
109 Ibid., p. 381.

Capable spatial entrepreneurs, accordingly, had to navigate a complex web of interactions and spatialities, webs that were spun, for example, by soldiers and refugees during and in the wake of the Second World War, by Soviet advisors travelling the region during the 1950s, and by students and youth or tourists and adventurers visiting universities, recreational centres, and festivals, respectively, across the region. Consequently, although the

> Soviet interest was initially focused on the creation of a secure buffer zone against a future attack from the West [...] Soviet and East European communists also thoroughly transformed their countries' landscapes, languages, fashions, rhythms of industrial production, identities, and values. By the 1970s, the inhabitants of the Second World came to share a distinct culture, which eventually outlived socialist political systems; it is also a culture that has been rarely acknowledged, much less 'theorized.'[110]

Against the background of these findings, what has shaped the bloc have not only been the tensions between different forms of proletarian and socialist internationalism, geopolitical interests of the Soviet Union, and territorializing ambitions of the bloc constituting states but also the tensions between officially promoted transnational ties and the appropriation of the emerging transnational networks to challenge the core logic of the bloc as a system of socialist states.[111] This is also demonstrated by research about the socialist World Youth Festivals, as Pia Koivunen argues: "Despite this strong linkage to the regime, however, using the World Youth Festival for the purposes of Soviet cultural diplomacy was not entirely in the hands of the establishment, but was dependent on its target audience: youth",[112] as an effect of which "Soviet authorities failed to make the World Youth Festival an agreed field, a global institution that would have been recognized not only by the socialist but also by the capitalist world."[113] It were these transnational arenas – officially promoted and appropriated by a variety of actors from within and outside the region – like the World Youth Festivals, that "could offer various purposes and means for cross-cultural encounters, even if the context was more often than not politicized.

---

110 Babiracki, Jersild (eds.), *Socialist Internationalism in the Cold War*, p. 2.
111 R. Gildea, J. Mark, and N. Pas, "European Radicals and the 'Third World'. Imagined Solidarities and Radical Networks 1958–73", *Cultural and Social History* 8 (2011) 4, pp. 449–472; J. Mark, P. Apor, "Socialism goes Global: Decolonization and the Making of a New Culture of Internationalism in Socialist Hungary, 1956–1989", *Journal of Modern History* 87 (2015) 4, pp. 852–891; K. Christiaens and I. Goddeeris: "Competing Solidarities? Solidarność and the Global South during the 1980s", in: Mark, Kalinovsky, Marung (eds.), *Alternative Globalizations* (in print).
112 Koivunen, *Performing Peace*, p. 6.
113 Ibid., p. 28.

Instead of one performance designed 'from above' by the organisers, festival youth created several ways to perform international friendship and discuss matters of peace."[114]

Conclusion

The multiple efforts to conceptualize the bloc from within and outside the socialist camp as well as the great variety of strategies to put this spatial concept into practice make it difficult to dismiss the bloc simply as either a Cold War invention to discredit the "enemy" or as failed Soviet attempts to create a unique empire, or as a detour in history finally confirming the superiority of Western (European) regionalization. That spatial formats are characterized as relatively stable and durable outcomes of processes of spatialization does not mean that they have to be eternal to qualify as such nor could this be found historically. Rather, different temporalities of spatial formats could provide a way to develop a typology. The multitude of fields in which the bloc materialized – often with varying geographies – appears as a remarkable feature, which it again shared spatial formats emerging in parallel, most prominently the results of the Western European integration process. While the latter has been described with the help of concepts such as supranational or multilevel governance, the multiscalar logic of bloc formation seems to be more complicated, as it was shaped by entwined logics of territorial states and (trans)national parties.

Owing to the fact that the bloc was shaped by the permanent tension – or maybe rather dialectic – between the logics of the national, the transnational, and the international, it required particularly competent spatial entrepreneurs navigating these unruly waters. They were not necessarily found at the higher ranks of political parties and government agencies but often among mid-ranking experts, artists or students, or activists for a universal cause, often mobile enough to learn about the diversity of realms. The legacies of their practices and the translation of their experiences into the post-socialist world are still to be investigated.

Socialist internationalism, the fight for national autonomy at the semi-periphery of the global economy, Soviet geopolitics, as well as a common ideology were encouraging the formation of the bloc in multiple ways, leading to outcomes that are often interpreted still today as contradictory, whereas for

---

[114] Ibid., p. 358.

contemporaries of that time they seemed to have been perceived rather as opening up different arenas in which they would be able to pursue their specific interests. The historicization of the bloc as being rooted in the effects of the October Revolution provided a further legitimization for the hierarchy inside the camp, yet it was appropriated by diverse actors in the bloc to challenge exactly the assumed dominance of the Soviet Union. To this end, for example, the stability of the region provided leverage for political elites in the so-called Soviet satellites, or for participants at youth or cultural festivals, to question official narratives of what socialist internationalism was about. These rooms for manoeuvre were also opening up for spatial entrepreneurs because the bloc had emerged in a very positive or negative relation to synchronous projects of respatialization – such as Western and Southern regionalisms as well as decolonization – as well as to previous ones – such as empire and communist internationalism. Accordingly, its legitimation was greatly intertwined with observing, interpreting, and relating to these synchronic and diachronic partners or competitors. Some might interpret this as a pitfall, while for those interested in how spatial formats have been shaped by spatial entrepreneurs in a period of extreme volatility the four decades of balancing these contradictions rather appear to be impressive, awaiting further empirical investigation. This is an agenda not only for historians of the twentieth century and its multiple globalizations projects, but also for those interested in the legacies of the respatializations that were presented here, even if the bloc's institutions dissolved very quickly. Still, Soviet and Czech military equipment, for example, plays a prominent role in violent conflicts worldwide until today; the Eurasian Economic Union and the Commonwealth of Independent States have emerged to reorganize the post-Soviet space; the "near abroad" is a key concept in the Russian geopolitical vocabulary; the Visegrád Four played a prominent role as an East-Central European lobby group during the eastward enlargement of the European Union; and Polish and Hungarian elites have mobilized arguments about the specificity of the region vis à vis the Western European half of the continent to develop new ties with China. Hence, understanding the complexities of the bloc as a spatial format and its multiple transformations provides a fruitful field for inter disciplinary communication.

Ulf Engel
Regionalisms and Regional Organizations

Introduction

Since the 1950s – with the rise, and despite the financial, the refugee, and the identity crises, of the European Union (EU)[1] – regional organizations have been firmly rooted in the collective memory of the Global North. In contrast, attention to regional identity and integration processes also in the Global South has been more recent and dates back to the years following the end of the Cold War. The academic debate on the phenomena, often described as *regionalisms*, is characterized by the assumption that they have greatly increased in numbers since 1989/90.[2] It remains open whether this perception is caused by terminological insecurity or by a real growth in numbers. Empirical observations about regionalisms and their signification may differ considerably, as can be demonstrated by a short analysis of the difference between the emergence of a specific spatial vocabulary, on the one hand, and its academic interpretation, on the other. According to the Google Ngram Viewer, which allows ca. 5 million books scanned by Google to be searched for the usage of certain terms (currently for the period 1800–2008), "international organization" can be dated back to the 1850s.[3] Depending on language selection – English, British English, American English, German, French, etc. – specific results may differ slightly. While books written in British English or French the combination "international" + "organization" already appears around 1850, in American English books it only appears for the first time around 1868, and in German books around 1910. "International organization" reaches its peak in all

---

1 K. K. Patel, *Projekt Europa. Eine kritische Geschichte*, München: C.H. Beck 2018.
2 E.D. Mansfield and H.V. Milner, "The New Wave of Regionalism", *International Organization* 53 (1999) 3, pp. 589–627.
3 Here and in the following Google Ngram Viewer 2017, "International Organization", "Regional Organizations", etc., <https://books.google.com/ngrams/> (accessed 25 September 2017).

Note: This chapter is an and updated translation of U. Engel, *Regionalorganisationen und Regionalismen*, Berlin: De Gruyter (2018). An early version of this text was published in K. Larres and R. Wittlinge (eds.), *Global Politics: Actors and Themes, Understanding International Affairs*, Abingdon: Routledge, 2019, pp. 170–187. I am grateful to Matthias Middell (Centre for Area Studies, Leipzig) and Ute Wardenga (Leibniz Institute for Regional Geography, Leipzig) for critical comments. Responsibility for the information and views set out in this chapter lies entirely with the author.

https://doi.org/10.1515/9783110643008-012

four academic languages around 1960, after which the frequency settles back to the level of the 1930s.

The term "regional organization", however, only appears considerably later, exactly during the first decade of the twentieth century, and more frequently after the end of World War I. So semantically two different phases can be identified: one period starting around 1860, in which people started writing about "international organizations" and a shorter period after around 1910, in which people also thought about "regional organizations". Evidently, this says little about the existence in practice of regional organizations before 1910. For many years, the interpretational sovereignty over the question what regional and international organizations, respectively, are and when this spatial format[4] historically came into being was within the domain of political science – and more concretely, its subdiscipline International Relations (IR) – a scientific field that emerged after World War II to become the main interpretational actor in this field.

Accordingly, the history of international organizations traditionally dates back to the League of Nations, founded on 10 January 1920.[5] In contrast, regional organizations are said only to have entered the global stage after World War II. However, some prehistory of international organization is acknowledged by mainstream political science, sometimes dating back to the Congress of Vienna in 1814/15. Although political science makes a difference between *intergovernmental organizations* (IGOs) and *international non-governmental organizations* (INGOs), the majority of IR literature is state-centric and, by and large, ignores, for instance, networks, companies, movements, etc. Usually IGOs are classified according to their membership: universal (all sovereign states), global (worldwide), regional (proximity), multilateral (more than two), or bilateral (two), respectively.[6] This IR majority view has been disputed by two perspectives that grew in popularity during the 1990s: urban studies and global history. The former uses the terms region and regionalization at subnational levels of analysis, including the identification of other types of relevant actors, whereas the latter questions the IR periodization of international organizations, also including an interest in actors that do not match the imagination of a Westphalian system of sovereign nations states, such as empires or networks.

---

4 For the term see below.
5 D. Armstrong et al., *International Organisation in World Politics*, 3rd ed., Basingstoke: Palgrave Macmillan, 2004 (1982); as well as V. Rittberger and B. Zangl, *International Organization: Polity, Politics and Policies*. Basingstoke: Palgrave Macmillan, 2006 (first German edition 1994).
6 D. Armstrong et al., *International Organisation*, p. 8. An exception is the Community of Portuguese Language Countries (Comunidade dos Países de Língua Portuguesa, CPLP), the organization of former Portuguese colonies, whose core member in fact do not share any borders.

For this chapter, the global history perspective is of particular interest because it focuses on international organizations during the period 1815 to 1945. The Dutch historian Bob Reinalda, for instance, integrates the Congress of Vienna, which had reordered Europe's political landscape after Napoleon's defeat, on an equal footing with the United Nations into a global history of international organizations. The early part of this global history also includes the Central Commission for the Navigation of the Rhine (1815) or the Zollverein, the German customs union (1834–1871).[7] In contrast to its usage of the term "international organization", global history contributions do not make analytical use of the terms "region", "regionalism", or "regional organization": In the 13 volumes of the leading journal of *Global History*, only one article has been published on this field.[8] There is not one single monograph or edited collection mentioned in the review section in which these terms play a central role.

This chapter will provide a summary of the debate about regionalisms and regional organizations. In the following part, an unavoidably incomplete overview will be given on the empirical phenomenon "regional organization", largely from an IR perspective. In the third part, a theoretical vocabulary for the analysis of regional organizations in past and contemporary processes of globalization will be introduced, centred around notions of "spatial format" and processes of "ordering space". In the fourth part, two major IR debates around the epistemology and the periodization of regionalisms will be recapped, inter alia with a focus on the distinction introduced in the 1990s between "old" regionalism in Europe and a "new" regionalism" in the Global South. These perspectives will then be juxtaposed in opposition to the state of the art in global history. Against the background of this discussion, in part five the functioning of regional organizations will be deepened by analysing the African Union (AU) in three fields: (1) The construction of regional order; (2) the establishment of distinct regional policy architecture, with regard to peace and security as well as democracy and governance; and (3) the emergence of interregional and transregional practices between the AU, on the one hand, and the United Nations as well as the European Union, on the other. This will be followed by conclusions.

---

7 B. Reinalda, *Routledge History of International Organizations: From 1815 to the Present Day*, Abingdon: Routledge, 2009; and B. Reinalda (ed.), *Routledge Handbook of International Organizations*, Abingdon: Routledge, 2013.

8 See *Journal of Global History* (2006–2018); for an exception, see M. Winkler "Another America: Russian Mental Discoveries of the North-west Pacific Region in the Eighteenth and Early Nineteenth Centuries", *Global History* 7 (2012) 1, pp. 27–51. The same almost holds true for the journal *Globalizations* (2004–2018), whose authors use the category just slightly more often.

Empirical Overview

Because the field of international organizations is extremely dynamic, the exact number of regional organizations existing today is very difficult to tell. Only a few institutions regularly try to offer overviews. The spectrum ranges from aspirations to be comprehensive to measurments of, however defined, political relevance. At one end of the spectrum is the *Yearbook of International Organizations*, edited by the Union of International Associations, which by mandate goes beyond regional organizations. Here there is detailed information on 38,000 active and another 32,000 dormant international organizations in 300 states and territories, including intergovernmental organizations and international non-governmental organizations. Every year another 1,200 organizations are added to the yearbook.[9] At the other end of the spectrum is the annual report of the UN secretary-general on cooperation between the United Nations and regional organizations: It only lists 26 "important" regional organizations that actively participate in the work of the United Nations – from the African Union to the Organization for the Prohibition of Chemical Weapons.[10] Somewhat between these two positions, the *Europa Directory of International Organizations*, in addition to the United Nations and its five regional commissions, counts a further 15 UN organizations and 18 specialized UN agencies. It further lists 65 "important" international organizations outside the United Nations and a variety of other international organizations.[11]

To give an impression of the regional embeddedness and functional scope of regional organizations, the following part focuses on world regions and their regional organizations. In Europe, the field stretches from the European Economic Community (EEC, 1957), which later was developed into the political European Union (EU, 1993), to the European Free Trade Association (EFTA, 1960), to the European Patent Office (EPO, 1977), to the European Science Foundation (ESF, 1974) and the European Space Agency (ESA, 1975), to the Organization for Security and Co-operation in Europe (OSCE, 1975). Below this European space, subregional groups of EU member states have been formed, for instance in the finance sector with the Nordic Investment Bank (NIB, 1976)

---

9 See Union of International Associations (ed.), *Yearbook of International Organizations*, Leiden: Brill Academic Publishers, <http://www.uia.org/yearbook> (accessed 15 April 2019). The yearbook is published by Brill, and the entries allegedly are updated every six to eight weeks.
10 United Nations Secretary-General, *Cooperation Between the United Nations and Regional and Other Organizations* (A/71/160 and S/2016/621), New York: United Nations, 2016.
11 Europa Publications, *The Europa Directory of International Organizations*, London: Europa Publications, 1999.

or the political/cultural alliance of the Visegrád Group (V4, 1991), with its central East European members: Poland, Czech Republic, Slovakia, and Hungary. Among the more prominent transatlantic regional organizations is the North Atlantic Treaty Organization (NATO, 1949) and the South Atlantic Peace and Cooperation Zone (ZPCAS, 1986).

Yet what has been at the heart of the debate in the past 25 years is the launch, or revival, of regional organizations in the Global South – though some academics claim that the peak of this dynamic is already over.[12] On the African continent, this includes the African Union (which emerged in 2001 from the transformation of its predecessor, the Organization of African Unity, 1963), and eight officially recognized regional economic communities (or RECs): the Communauté des Etats Sahélo-Sahariens (CEN-SAD, 1998), the Common Market for Eastern and Southern Africa (COMESA, 1994), the East African Community (EAC, 1967–1977, revived in 2000), the Communauté Economique des États de l'Afrique Centrale (CEEAC, 1981), the Economic Community of West African States (ECOWAS, 1975), the Intergovernmental Authority on Development (IGAD, 1986) at the Horn of Africa, the Southern African Development Community (SADC, founded in 1979 and relaunched in 1992), as well as the Union Maghreb Arabe (UMA, 1989).

In Asia, among the more prominent regional organizations are the Asian Development Bank (ADB, 1966), the Association of Southeast Asian Nations (ASEAN, 1967), and the Mekong River Commission (MRC, 1995). In the Arab world, there are the Arab League (1945) and the Saudi-dominated Gulf Cooperation Council (GCC, 1981). Important Eurasian regional organizations include the Collective Security Treaty Organization (CSTO, 1992); the Commonwealth of Independent States (CIS, 1991), states that formerly belonged to the Soviet Union; as well as the Shanghai Cooperation Organization on Security and Trade (SCO, 1996), of which Russia, China, and India are members. In the Americas, "relevant" regionalism projects include the Organization of American States (OAS, 1948); the Southern Common Market (MERCOSUR, 1991), with Argentina, Brazil, Paraguay and Uruguay; the Andean Community (CAN, 1996, founded as the Andean Pact, 1969); the Caribbean Community (CARICOM, 1973); and the Bolivarian Alliance for the Peoples of Our America (ALBA, 2004). Around the Indian Ocean, there is the Commission de l'Océan Indien (COI, 1982) and for the Arctic neighbours the Arctic Council (1996), which also includes as permanent participants so-called identitarian NGOs, such as the Aleut International Association or the Saami Council. In the Pacific, there are the Australia, New Zealand, United States Security Treaty (ANZUS,

---

[12] A. Malamud and G.L. Gardini, "Has Regionalism Peaked? The Latin American Quagmire and its Lessons", *International Spectator* 47 (2012) 1, pp. 116–133.

1951) and the economic Pacific Islands Forum (1991, founded as the South Pacific Forum, 1971).

In IR, this trend of geographical extension and functional proliferation of regional organizations is discussed in terms of diffusion theories: the idea of regionalism "travels".[13] Critics of this approach argue that diffusion theories generally overlook concrete actors and processes of hybridization. As an alternative to linear or staged cases of diffusion, culture studies approaches of cultural transfer have emphasized that the active search of societies, organizations, etc. for finding solutions elsewhere, their active and often transnational transfer, as well as the process of appropriation of out-of-own-context models and their subsequent hybridization should take centre stage.[14]

Regionalisms and Regional Organizations in Processes of Globalization

In this part of the chapter, the role of regionalisms and regional organizations in past and contemporary processes of globalization is discussed. First, a theoretical vocabulary will be introduced that is based on the work of the Leipzig-based Collaborative Research Centre (SFB) 1199: "Processes of Spatialization under the Global Condition", which was launched in January 2016.[15] Second, it will recap how regionalisms and regional organizations so far have been discussed by mainstream IR in order to, finally, confront these viewpoints in a global history perspective.

---

[13] See A. Jetschke and T. Lenz, "Does Regionalism Diffuse? A New Research Agenda for the Study of Regional Organizations", *Journal of European Public Policy* 20 (2013) 4, pp. 626–637; and A. Jetschke and P. Murray, "Diffusing Regional Integration: The EU and Southeast Asia", *West European Politics* 35 (2012) 1, pp. 174–191. But also see A. Acharya, "How Ideas Spread: Whose Norms Matter? Norm Localization and Institutional Change in Asian Regionalism", *International Organization* 58 (2004) 2, pp. 239–275.

[14] See M. Middell, "Kulturtransfer und historische Komparatistik – Thesen zu ihrem Verhältnis", *Comparativ* 10 (2000) 1, pp. 7–41; and M. Middell, "Kulturtransfer, Transferts culturels, Version: 1.0", *Docupedia-Zeitgeschichte*, 28 January 2016, <http://docupedia.de/zg/Kulturtransfer>.

[15] See Collaborative Research Centre (SFB) 1199: "Processes of Spatialization under the Global Condition", <http://research.uni-leipzig.de/~sfb1199/index.php?id=7> (accessed 15 April 2019).

The spatial turn in the humanities and social sciences has generated a consensus that space is not simply a given but is actively constructed through social interactions – hence, the talk about "social spaces".[16] These social spaces are based on the historical sedimentation of other social spaces; they can be territorialized, but they do not have to be. In case of the former, distinct regimes of territorialization emerge. Social spaces exist in parallel and at various, entangled scales, and they are utilized accordingly by various actors. This is so far the conventional wisdom of the spatial turn. Against this background, the SFB 1199 is now trying to further develop this line of reasoning by introducing the category of "spatial formats" and fine-tuning the relation between spatial formats, the practice of spatial by spatial entrepreneurs, and the resulting emergence of spatial orders. At the centre of this endeavour is the signification of spatial imaginations of specific social actors in intersubjective processes that lead to tangible spatial order.

First and foremost, spatial formats are attributes based on a spatial semantic by which things are named by actor Y as X (apparently, some actors are more successful than others in framing spatial formats). Examples of spatial formats could be "empire", "value chain", or "regionalism". The SFB 1199 assumes that references to spatial formats have increased since the end of the Cold War (the SFB is, of course, also enquiring into the historicity of this observation). This increase also seems to be linked to the fact that actors are not yet in a position to clearly identify and unequivocally classify their various activities, and it seems that the use of spatial semantics makes spatial formats appear more stable. The increase of semantic references to space, secondly, also means that actions become more diverse in terms of scales, networks, etc. – though obviously it may very well be that simply the number of significations has increased, rather than the number of empirical observations.

Spatial formats, as such, are not material; they are not "social spaces". Instead, they are patterns out which actors recognize and name those that seem to be relevant to them at a given moment in time because they correspond to their particular political projects. In this sense, spatial formats are patterns,

---

16 In general, see H. Lefebvre, *The Production of Space*, Oxford: Blackwell Publishing, 1991 (1974); E.W. Soja, *Postmodern Geographies: The Reassertion of Space in Critical Social Theory*, London: Verso, 1989; D. Massey, J. Allen and P. Sarre (eds.), *Human Geography Today*, Cambridge: Polity, 2005 (1999); and G.Ó'Tuathail and S. Dalby (eds.), *Rethinking Geopolitics*, Abingdon: Routledge, 1999. For a proposed typology, see B. Jessop, N. Brenner and M. Jones, "Theorizing Sociospatial Relations", *Environment and Planning D: Society and Space* 26 (2008) 3, pp. 389–401; and also their updated version: "Territory, Politics, Governance and Multispatial Metagovernance", *Territory, Politics, Governance* 4 (2016) 1, pp. 8–32.

templates, models, or standards. They can also be memories about past real-world spatial orders – for instance, the Cold War order with "the wall" or the "racial order" of apartheid as well as the resurgence of India or China to global greatness.

Secondly, the SFB employs the term "spatial order" by focusing on the practice of space ordering by rendering "accepted", "valid", or "important" spatial formats visible. Ordering space is a cognitive process involving discursive interpretation and social negotiation of what in the past has been described as "social space". Ordering, or signifying, space both means to make something visible and to charge it with meaning.[17] Spatial formats are a lens through which the otherwise only metaphorically existing space can be intersubjectively communicated. For this to happen, it takes entrepreneurs of signification and a respective audience to resonate these significations. And it also takes instruments, media, and strategies of signification: speaking, symbolizing, and doing, for instance by establishing financial flows, practising violence, etc. The successful ordering of space depends on the fact that something can be labelled and institutionalized. This in turn depends on the existence of an actor Y, a spatial entrepreneur, with an interest in labelling and institutionalizing, often in competition with other actors. In the process of ordering space, charging it with meaning becomes central as well as imaginations of "adequacy", "relevance", or "appropriateness" of specific spatial formats – nota bene successful spatial orders in turn produce spatial formats. In the end, spatial orders emerge that have material expressions.

A current example of this nexus, though not exactly concerning a regional organization, is the "One Belt, One Road" vision of an open regionalism – the "new silk road" – which is currently implemented by China.[18] Starting in 2013 and pushed forward by considerable financial, trade, and geostrategic interests, the global remembrance of a spatial format – the "old silk road" – is invoked; eventually, it will lead to the construction of a mega region between China and Europe and a new phase in a Chinese-controlled phase of globalization.

Spatial orders not necessarily "speak" to everyone: actors see, read, experience, translate, and/or understand spatial orders – or do not. Spatial orders are replicable. They can be politicized, be loaded with meaning, be hierarchized,

---

[17] As a "sensitizing concept", the term signification played a central role in the research programme DFG Priority Programme (SPP) 1448: "Adaptation and Creativity: Technologies and Significations in the Production of Order and Disorder", which was coordinated by the universities of Halle and Leipzig: <http://www.spp1448.de> (accessed 15 April 2019).
[18] See "Belt and Road Initiative", *South China Morning Post*, <http://www.scmp.com/topics/belt-and-road-initiative> (accessed 15 April 2019).

and although they may be of a temporary nature only, they usually last a rather long time. Spatial orders enable or produce hierarchical or non-hierarchical relations between spatial formats. They provide an influential framework for the signification of specific spatial formats. This includes the possibility that the meaning of spatial formats can change within a spatial order. These significations are the reason why specific spatial formats are asserted over others. With reference to regionalisms and regional organizations, it can be observed that time and again regions are measured through speaking or acting. If successful, this leads to calls for the political organization of a regional project. Thus, the question is why, and for whom, during the past 25 years "the regional" has become more important.

To make a second point in this part of the chapter: for political science, IR regional organizations first and foremost are geographically defined subtypes of international organizations (IOs) and in this sense bureaucracies that exercise different types of authority: "(1) [to] classify the world, creating categories of problems, actors, and action; (2) fix meanings in the social world; and (3) articulate and diffuse new norms and rules".[19] Thus, they are territorialized subtypes of intergovernmental organizations in which regional cooperation among states leads to the establishment of regional interstate regimes in various policy fields.[20]

The academic debate has often focused on undirected processes of regionalization, discussed in terms of economic and/or political integration of societies.[21] Regional organizations are also discussed in terms of "regionalisms", seen as transnational interactions and interdependencies.[22] Regionalism projects usually go hand-in-hand with the development of regional awareness or regional identities, that is to say the construction of different forms of "cognitive regionalism".[23] While in the past the academic debate concentrated on the role of specific regional organizations in global politics, more recent contributions to the debate have highlighted the need to address the interactions between different regional

---

19 M. Barnett and M. Finnemore, *Rules for the World: International Organizations in Global Politics*, Ithaca: Cornell University Press, 2004, p. 31.
20 A. Hurrell, "One World? Many Worlds? The Place of Regions in the Study of International Society", *International Affairs* 83 (2007) 1, pp. 127–146, at 128.
21 See M.F. Schultz, F. Söderbaum and J. Öjendal, "Introduction: A Framework for Understanding Regionalization", in: M.F. Schultz, F. Söderbaum and J. Öjendal (eds.) *Regionalization in a Globalizing World*, London: Zed Books, 2001, pp. 1–17.
22 F.Söderbaum, *The Political Economy of Regionalisms: The Case of Southern Africa*, Basingstoke: Palgrave Macmillan, 2004, p.16.
23 Hurrell, "One World? Many Worlds?", p. 128. See also B.Hettne and F.Söderbaum, "Theorising the Rise of Regionness", *New Political Economy* 5 (2000) 3, pp. 457–474.

organizations. In this case, empirical reconstruction and the quests for theory-building revolves around "interregionalism".[24] From a non-IR perspective, it is remarkable that in this debate "regionalism" is universalized and treated as a distinct spatial format that is given significance in a specific spatial order. Some, though not all, actors that participate in the debate over regionalisms take a social-constructivist position, which allows them to discuss the constructed character of regions. "There are no 'natural' regions, and definitions of 'region' and indicators of 'regionness' vary according to the particular problem or question under investigation", argues the Oxford-based British political scientist Andrew Hurrell.[25] Accordingly, on the one hand, regions, regionalisms, and regional organizations can be studied as "containers for culture and for value diversity; poles and powers; one level in a system of multi-level governance; and/or harbingers of change and possible transformation".[26]

On the other, those academics that are influenced by the spatial turn in the humanities and social sciences treat regional organizations as concrete spatializations of specific social fields under the *global condition*, that is to say the historic transformation towards modern forms of globalization in the period 1840 to 1880.[27] They look both at discursively constructed "regions" as well as at the political, cultural, economic, or social integration practices at the heart of these processes.[28] Arguably, since the end of the Cold War an increase in regionalization projects can be observed because actors want to regain sovereignty and control that they have lost in processes of deterritorialization.[29]

---

24 See F. Söderbaum and L. van Langenhove (eds.), *The EU as a Global Player: The Politics of Interregionalism*, Abingdon: Routledge, 2006; H. Hänggi, R. Roloff and J. Rüland (eds.), *Interregionalism and International Relations*, Abingdon: Routledge, 2006; F. Baert, T. Scaramagli and F. Söderbaum (eds.), *Intersecting Interregionalism: Regions, Global Governance and the EU*, Dordrecht: Springer, 2014; as well as P. de Lombaerde, F. Söderbaum and J.-U. Wunderlich, "Interregionalism", in: K.E. Jorgensen et al. (eds.), *The SAGE Handbook of European Foreign Policy*, vol. II, London: Sage, 2015, pp. 750–761.
25 A. Hurrell, "Regionalism in Theoretical Perspective", in: L. Fawcett and A. Hurrell (eds.), *Regionalism in World Politics*, Oxford: Oxford University Press, 1995, pp. 37–73, at 38.
26 Hurrell, "One World? Many Worlds?", p. 136.
27 See R. Robinson, "Mapping the Global Condition: Globalization as the Central Concept", *Theory, Culture & Society* 7 (1990) 2, pp. 15–30; and M. Geyer and C. Bright, "World History in a Global Age", *The American Historical Review* 100 (1995) 4, pp. 1034–1060.
28 From an urban studies perspective, see J.-P.D. Addie and R. Keil, "Real Existing Regionalism: The Region between Talk, Territory and Technology", *International Journal of Urban and Regional Research* 39 (2015) 2, pp. 407–417.
29 On the theoretical foundations and the underlying notion of sovereignty, see N. Brenner, "Beyond State-Centrism? Space, Territoriality, and Geographical Scale in Globalization Studies",

With the development of a debate in politics and academia on the nature of the world order emerging after the end of the Cold War,[30] it has been increasingly discussed how regionalisms and regional organizations both theoretically and practically relate to current processes of globalization.[31] On the relation between the "one world of the international system and the many worlds of the different regionalisms", Hurrell provides four arguments that try to explain the attractiveness of regionalisms for states of the Global South. First, to many "the region is the most appropriate and viable level to reconcile the changing and intensifying pressures of global capitalist competition on the one hand with the need for political regulation and management on the other". Second, he holds, for these countries "it is easier to negotiate 'deep integration' and the sorts of profoundly intrusive rules needed to manage globalization at the regional rather than the global level." Third, Hurrell also finds that regionalism – "given that value and societal consensus are likely to be bigger and the practical problems of governance beyond the state more manageable at that level" – for many countries of the Global South "can be part of a process of controlled or negotiated integration into the global economy". And, fourth, in particular for countries of the Global North, regionalism "offers a favourable level at which to recast the post-1945 bargain between market liberalization and social protection".[32]

Theory and Society 28 (1999) 1, pp. 39–78; A. Acharya, "Regionalism and the Emerging World Orders: Sovereignty, Autonomy, Identity", in: S. Breslin et al. (eds.), *New Regionalism in the Global Political Economy: Theories and Cases*, Abingdon: Routledge, 2002, pp. 20–32; and J. Agnew, "Sovereignty Regimes: Territoriality and State Authority in Contemporary World Politics", *Annals of the Association of American Geographers* 95 (2005) 2, pp. 437–461.

30 See G. Sørensen, "What Kind of World Order? The International System in the New Millennium", *Cooperation and Conflict* 41 (2006) 2, pp. 343–363; and S. Chaturvedi and J. Painter, "Whose World, Whose Order? Spatiality, Geopolitics and the Limits of the World Order Concept", *Cooperation and Conflict* 42 (2007) 2, pp. 375–395.

31 See A. Gamble and A. Payne (eds.), *Regionalism and World Order*, Basingstoke: Palgrave Macmillan, 1996; J.H. Mittelman, "Rethinking the 'New Regionalism' in the Context of Globalization", *Global Governance* 2 (1996) 2, pp. 189–213; B. Hettne, "Globalization and the New Regionalism: The Second Great Transformation", in: B. Hettne, A. Inotai and O. Sunkel (eds.) *Globalism and the New Regionalism*, Basingstoke: Palgrave Macmillan, 1999, pp. 1–24; as well as B, Hettne, "Reconstructing World Order", in: M. Farrell, B. Hettne and L. van Langenhove (eds.), *Global Politics of Regionalism*, London: Pluto Press, 2005, pp. 269–286.

32 See Hurrell, "One World? Many Worlds?", p. 131.

Regionalisms and the establishment of regional organizations can be seen as "sovereignty-boosting" practices of the Global South.[33] They are characterized by a specific form of political rationality: actors are taking deliberate decisions about the spatial dimension (or *scale*) that they want to achieve a specific aim with. [34] With reference to the French historian Jacques Revel, this can be called a *jeux d'échelles* (a play with the scales).[35] In the different world regions, this is playing out in different ways. Because of selective integration practices in Latin America and Asia and also overlapping membership in African regional organizations, some authors talk about "modular", "loose", or "bifurcated" regionalism, respectively.[36]

Sometimes these sovereignty strategies may work against established international norms and their territorialization regimes,[37] as the current debate about impunity for African heads of state and government in cases of gross human rights violations illustrates. The African Union decided – though not unanimously – at its 28th summit on 30–31 January 2017, held in Addis Ababa, Ethiopia upon a withdrawal strategy from the International Court of Justice. To summarize, because "the West", allegedly for imperialist and racist reasons, is instrumentalizing the Court against acting African heads of state and government, the 34 African signatories of the Rome Statute should withdrawal from this agreement. Instead, the African Union, in principle, wants to bring perpetrators of genocide, crime against humanity, or war crimes only *after* their term of offices has ended before the not yet ratified African Court of Justice and Human and Peoples' Rights.[38]

---

[33] See F. Söderbaum, "Modes of Regional Governance in Africa: Neoliberalism, Sovereignty Boosting, and Shadow Networks", *Global Governance* 10 (2004) 4, pp. 419–436; and F. Söderbaum, *Rethinking Regionalism*, Basingstoke: Palgrave Macmillan, 2015.
[34] U. Engel et al. (eds.), "Introduction: The Challenge of Emerging Regionalisms Outside Europe", in: U. Engel et al. (eds.), *The New Politics of Regionalism: Perspectives from Africa, Latin America and Asia-Pacific*, Abingdon: Routledge, 2016, pp. 1–15, at 5.
[35] See J. Revel, *Jeux d'échelles: La micro-analyse à l'expérience*, Paris: Gallimard, 1996.
[36] See G.L. Gardini, "Towards Modular regionalism: The Proliferation of Latin American Cooperation", in: U. Engel et al., *The New Politics of Regionalism*, pp. 19–36; R. Mushkat, "'Loose' Regionalism and Global Governance: The Association of Southeast Asian Nations (ASEAN) Factor", *Melbourne Journal of International Law* 17 (2016) 1, pp. 238–256; and F. Mattheis, "Towards Bifurcated Regionalism: The Production of Regional Overlaps in Central Africa", in: U. Engel et al., *The New Politics of Regionalism*, pp. 37–51.
[37] On the term sovereignty strategy, see Agnew, "Sovereignty Regimes".
[38] African Union, "Decision on the International Criminal Court", Assembly/AU/Dec.622 (XXVIII), Addis Ababa, Ethiopia, 30–31 January 2017.

Debates on Epistemology and Periodization of Regional Organizations

The academic debate over regionalisms and regional organizations started in the 1940s, mainly within the relatively young discipline of political science. Since, controversial discussions have been held, first, about "the right" epistemological approach to the study of the nature and development of regionalisms and, second, about the periodization and historical depth of the phenomenon. Traditional rational choice-based approaches from International Relations, for instance, have turned to the subfield of regional security politics, with a focus on states that face a so-called security dilemma (that is to say at risk of an arms race in case that they are arming themselves) and those who engage in regional security cooperation to reduce opportunity costs.[39] Neo-functional approaches have tried to demonstrate how states become members of forms of security cooperation as a result of spillover effects.[40] And intergovernmental approaches have stressed that the establishment of regions is the result of deliberate government decisions taken during negotiations.[41] These positions have become mainstream in political science. But because of their, often only implicit, metatheoretical assumptions, they are also facing critique.

First, all three approaches mentioned above are grounded in methodological nationalism, that is to say they are privileging the state as the only unit of analysis.[42] Second, they are deeply rooted in modernization theory: successful regional integration can only be based in societies that function according to a constructed "European model". Third, they are sharing a skewed vocabulary. The term "region", for instance, is equated with the process of "regionalization"; the focus is merely on economic and political organizations and the results of integration, rather than on processes of spatialization and the ordering of space. And, fourth, this orthodoxy has been criticized because of its underlying conceptual Eurocentrism.[43] A contingent post-World War II West European experience, which

---

[39] K. Waltz, *Theory of International Politics*, New York: McGraw-Hill, 1979.
[40] For two classics, see D. Mitrany, "The Functional Approach to World Organization", *International Affairs* 24 (1948) 3, pp. 350–363; and E.B. Haas, *The Uniting of Europe*, London: Stevens & Sons, 1958.
[41] As a representative take of this approach, see A. Moravcsik, "Negotiating the Single European Act: National Interests and Conventional Statecraft in the European Community", *International Organization* 45 (1991) 1, pp. 19–56.
[42] On the term, see J.Agnew, "The Territorial Trap: The Geographical Assumptions of International Relations Theory", *Review of International Political Economy* 1 (1994) 1, pp. 53–80.
[43] Engel et al., "Introduction", pp. 2, 6.

finally led to the establishment of the European Union, is universalized and serves as a role model for regional integration everywhere. At least until the 2016 referendum on Brexit, the planned withdrawal of the United Kingdom from the EU,[44] most theories of regional integration assumed a linear "European model" that consists of five consecutive stages. The removal of tariff and non-tariff trade barriers is followed by a free trade zone, which is followed by a customs union with a single external tariff. This is followed by a common market based on the free traffic of goods, services, labour, and capital; then the common market grows into an economic and monetary union. Finally, this integration model reaches its peak with the formation of a political union.[45]

In contrast to this orthodoxy, new approaches in regionalism research have turned to the study of the non-European world. They also focus on cases of informal regionalism, non-state regionalisms, and dynamic regionalisms. In view of a post-Cold War increase in research on regionalisms in Africa, Asia, and Latin America,[46] a group of Scandinavian academics at the University of

---

[44] For one of many alarmist discussions, see L. Scuira, "Brexit Beyond Borders: Beginning of the EU Collapse and Return to Nationalism", *Journal of International Affairs* 70 (2017) 2, pp. 109–123. But also see B. Jessop "The Organic Crisis of the British State: Putting Brexit in its Place", *Globalizations* 14 (2017) 1, pp. 133–141.

[45] For a typical, more recent example of this kind of argumentation, see R. Baldwin, "Sequencing Asian Regionalism: Theory and Lessons from Europe", *Journal of Economic Integration* 27 (2012) 1, pp. 1–32.

[46] In general, see S. Breslin et al. (eds.), *New Regionalisms in the Global Political Economy*, Abingdon: Routledge, 2002; and F. Söderbaum and T.M. Shaw (eds.), *Theories of New Regionalism: A Palgrave Reader*, Basingstoke: Palgrave Macmillan, 2003. Also see M. Telò (ed.), *European Union and New Regionalism: Regional Actors and Global Governance in a Post-hegemonic Era*, Farnham: Ashgate, 1999. On Africa see D. Bach, "Regionalism & Globalization in Sub-Saharan Africa: Revisiting a Paradigm", in D. Bach (ed.), *Regionalisation in Africa: Integration and Disintegration*, Oxford: James Currey, 1999, pp. 1–13; M. Bøås, M.H. Marchand and T.M. Shaw, "The Political Economy of New Regionalisms", *Third World Quarterly* 20 (1999) 5, pp. 897–910; J.A. Grant and F. Söderbaum (eds.), *The New Regionalism in Africa*, Farnham: Ashgate 2003; and U. Lorenz and M. Rempe (eds.), *Mapping Agency: Comparing Regionalisms in Africa*, Farnham: Ashgate, 2013. On the Middle East, see M.-M.O. Mohamedou, "Arab Agency and the UN Project: The League of Arab States between Universality and Regionalism", *Third World Quarterly* 37 (2016) 7, pp. 1219–1233. On Asia, see M. Beeson, *Regionalism and Globalization in East Asia: Politics, Security and Economic Development*, Basingstoke: Palgrave Macmillan, 2007; M. Beeson (ed.), *Routledge Handbook of Asian Regionalism*, Abingdon: Routledge, 2012; C.M. Dent, *East Asian Regionalism*, Abingdon: Routledge, 2008; E.L. Frost, *Asia's New Regionalisms*, Boulder: Lynne Rienner, 2008; and N. Thomas (ed.), *Governance and Regionalism in Asia*, Abingdon: Routledge, 2009. And on Latin America, see J.W. Cason, *The Political Economy of Integration: The Experience of Mercosur*, Abingdon: Routledge, 2011; O. Dabène, *The Politics of Regional Integration in Latin*

Gothenburg around 2000 proclaimed a new paradigm: the *New Regionalism Approach* (NRA).⁴⁷ Dissociating itself from neo-functionalism, this approach claims to be reflexive, process-oriented and multidimensional (meaning, going beyond politics and economics).⁴⁸ Epistemologically, the NRA is based on a "new", "critical", or "heterodox" reading of International Political Economy, as coined by the Canadian political scientist Robert W. Cox.⁴⁹

Quite successfully, the NRA has constructed a contrast between the "old regionalism" and the "new regionalism". This is based, first, on the temporal juxtaposition of developments after 1945 and those after 1989; second, on a geographical differentiation between Europe and the Global South; and, third, on the claim that regionalisms in the Global South are different from regionalisms in Europe in number and scope ("narrow vs. broad"). In addition, the NRA stresses the social construction of new regions. At least rhetorically, this invokes a spatial turn dimension. However, in most cases this pledge is not honoured by systematic spatial reasoning. This may be explained by the fact that most NRA authors consider regionalization processes to be quasi-natural – although, first and foremost, one should ask who and why has an interest to utilize the spatial format regionalism.

The NRA debate thus far can be separated into six overlapping periods, starting with the late 1990s in which the "new regionalisms" were identified as the reason for fundamental social change of the international system.⁵⁰ Around the same time, some NRA authors started to locate the "new regionalisms" in "globalization", mainly conceiving globalization as a single economic process

---

America, Basingstoke: Palgrave Macmillan, 2009; L. Gómez-Mera, *Power and Regionalism in Latin America*, Notre Dame: University of Notre Dame Press, 2013; and P. Riggirozzi and D. Tussie (eds.), *The Rise of Post-Hegemonic Regionalism: The Case of Latin America*, Dordrecht: Springer, 2012.

47 See R. Väyrynen, "Regionalism: Old and New", *International Studies Review* 5 (2003) 1, pp. 25–51.

48 Söderbaum, *The Political Economy of Regionalisms*, p. 16.

49 R.W. Cox, "Social Forces, States and World Orders: Beyond International Relations Theory", *Millennium: Journal of International Studies* 10 (1981) 2, pp. 126–155; and R.W. Cox, *Approaches to World Order*, Cambridge: Cambridge University Press, 1996. Also see the appreciation of his oeuvre in *Globalizations* 13 (2016) 5.

50 See Hettne, "Globalization and the New Regionalism"; and F. Söderbaum and T.M. Shaw (eds.), *Theories of New Regionalism*. This periodization is inspired by N. Bisley, *Rethinking Globalization*, Basingstoke: Palgrave Macmillan, 2007.

that has a geographic centre and can objectively be measured, etc.[51] This was followed by a third phase in which this relationship was theoretically reflected upon.[52] In the 2000s, NRA authors tried to empirically ground the analytical category "new regionalisms".[53] In the fifth phase, starting in the early 2010s, the NRA has been consolidated into an academic field, which can be seen with the institutionalization of this knowledge order, for instance through the editing of a "companion" as well as through the retransfer of knowledge from the NRA debate to the field of European studies.[54] A sixth phase started when some NRA authors began to transcend the boundaries of NRA by provincializing the NRA as just one discourse formation among many. They admitted that some discourse entrepreneurs have initiated a specific talk about regional phenomena, which, no doubt, became rather influential – but they state that this talk represents only one of many ways to signify the spatial format "regionalism".

The critiques of the NRA is that it is based on methodological nationalism and that the empirical recognition of "new regionalisms" beyond the state is not paralleled by a theoretical debate. And also, despite the assumption that regions are the result of cultural constructions, these very regions are equated with the states that are constituting the regions.[55]

In the late 2000s, some scholars started to discuss the concept of "comparative regionalism" as an alternative to the NRA.[56] Although this has produced some interesting ideas,[57] substantial empirical contributions to this debate are

---

[51] L. Fawcett and A. Hurrell (eds.), *Regionalism in World Politics*, Oxford: Oxford University Press, 1995; and Gamble and Payne, *Regionalism and World Order*.

[52] See S. Breslin and G. Hook (eds.), *Microregionalism and World Order*, Basingstoke: Palgrave Macmillan, 2002; and Hurrell, "One World? Many Worlds?".

[53] See, e.g., F. Söderbaum and I. Taylor (eds.), *Afro-Regions: The Dynamics of Cross-Border Micro-Regionalism in Africa*, Uppsala: Nordiska Afrikainstitutet, 2008.

[54] See T.M. Shaw, J.A. Grant and S. Cornelissen, "Introduction and Overview: The Study of New Regionalism(s) at the Start of the Second Decade of the Twenty-First Century", in: T.M. Shaw, J.A. Grant and S. Cornelissen (eds.), *The Ashgate Research Companion to Regionalisms*, Farnham: Ashgate, 2011, pp. 3–30; A. Sbragia and F. Söderbaum, "EU-Studies and the 'New Regionalism': What can be Gained from Dialogue?", *Journal of European Integration* 32 (2010) 6, pp. 563–582; and A. Warleigh-Lack, N. Robinson and B. Rosamund (eds.), *New Regionalism and the European Union: Dialogues, Comparisons and New Research Directions*, Abingdon: Routledge, 2011.

[55] Engel et al., "Introduction", pp. 1–10.

[56] F. Söderbaum, "Old, New and Comparative Regionalism: The History and Scholarly Development of the Field", in T.A. Börzel and T. Risse (eds.), *The Oxford Handbook of Comparative Regionalism*, Oxford: Oxford University Press, 2016, pp. 16–37, at 31.

[57] In chronological order, see A. Warleigh-Lack, "Studying Regionalisation Comparatively: A Conceptual Framework" in A.F. Cooper, C.W.H. Hughes and P. de Lombaerde (eds.), *Regionalisation and Global Governance: The Taming of Globalisation?*, Abingdon: Routledge,

yet to come – partly because methodologically they are fairly demanding and call for multilingualism and familiarity with the research traditions of more than just one discipline.[58]

With regard to the second major debate in research on regionalisms and regional organizations, periodization, and historicization, mainly two competing narratives have been developed in political science. According to the first, the history of regionalisms and regional organizations starts in the 1920s with the League of Nations, while the second narrative begins with the end of World War II. Representing the first strand of reasoning, the Italian political scientist Mario Tèlo has developed a *longue durée* of regionalism marked by four "epochs" between 1900 and 2016.[59] The first epoch stretches from World War I to the Great Depression years of 1929 to 1936. It is characterized by an authoritarian and hierarchical regionalism (e.g. the British Commonwealth). The second epoch of "the regionalism" starts with World War II and is marked by the bipolar world order during the Cold War. During the 1950s to 1980s, it was determined by US hegemony and a myriad of multilateral institutions (e.g. NATO, ASEAN, etc.). After a brief historical moment of US hegemony after the decline of the Soviet Union in the post-1989 years, the third epoch of regionalisms has also seen the demise of

---

2008, pp. 43–60; A. Acharya, "Comparative Regionalism: A Field Whose Time Has Come?", *International Spectator* 47 (2012) 1, pp. 3–15; T.A. Börzel, "Comparative Regionalism: European Integration and Beyond", in: W. Carlsnaes, T. Risse and B. Simmons (eds.), *Handbook of International Relations*, London: Sage, 2013, pp. 503–530; T.A. Börzel and T. Risse (eds.), *The Oxford Handbook of Comparative Regionalism*; F. Söderbaum, *Rethinking Regionalism*, Basingstoke: Palgrave Macmillan, 2015; L. Fioramonti (ed.), *Regions and Crises: New Challenges for Contemporary Regionalisms*, Basingstoke: Palgrave Macmillan, 2012; L. Fioramonti (ed.), *Regionalism in a Changing World: Comparative Perspectives in the New Global Order*, Abingdon: Routledge, 2012; L. Fioramonti and F. Mattheis, "Is Africa Really Following Europe? An Integrated Framework for Comparative Regionalism", *Journal of Common Market Studies* 54 (2016) 3, pp. 674–690; and E. Solingen, *Comparative Regionalism: Economics and Security*, Abingdon: Routledge, 2015.

58 For an exception, see F. Mattheis, *New Regionalism in the South: Mercosur and SADC in a Comparative and Interregional Perspective*, Leipzig: Leipziger Universitätsverlag, 2015. On the methodological challenge, see P. de Lombaerde et al., "The Problem of Comparison in Comparative Regionalism", *Review of International Studies* 36 (2010), pp. 731–753.

59 M. Telò, *Regionalism in Hard Times: Competitive and post-liberal trends in Europe, Asia, Africa, and the Americas*, Abingdon: Routledge, 2017, p. 67. Arguing in a similar way, see also L. Fawcett, "Regionalism from an Historical Perspective", in M. Farrell, B. Hettne and L. van Langenhove (eds.), *Global Politics of Regionalism: An Introduction*, London: Pluto Press, 2005, pp. 21–37; and D. Rodogno, S. Gaunthier and F. Piana, "What does Transnational History Tell Us about a World with International Organizations? The Historians' Point Of View", in: B. Reinalda (ed.), *Routledge Handbook of International Organizations*, Abingdon: Routledge, 2013, pp. 94–105.

the US during what Tèlo calls "globalization". This epoch is described as belle époque; it is dominated by regional organizations such as ASEAN, MERCOSUR, the African Union, and SADC. The contemporary epoch starts with the global financial crisis 2007/08; it is characterized by fragmentation and the emergence of a multipolar world order with competing regionalisms and interregionalisms, "instrumental regionalism", trade that mainly is focusing on allies, and the securitization of many realms (e.g. the 2000 Russian project of the Eurasian Economic Community, which became the Eurasian Economic Union in 2015, or the Transatlantic Trade and Investment Partnership, which has been being negotiated between the United States and the EU since 2013).

In contrast, the Gothenburg-based political scientist Fredrik Söderbaum proposes a shorter periodization, starting with the end of World War II.[60] Initially the important world order context is bipolarity during the Cold War in Europe and the decolonization of the countries in the Global South. The connections between national, regional, and global forms of governance emerge in the context of European integration beyond the nation-state, on the one hand, and the development of post-colonial states in the Global South, on the other. The actors of this first phase of (an essentialized) "regionalism" are organized as sector-specific, with regionalisms driven by states being organized in regional organizations. A second phase of regionalism then began with the end of the Cold War, around 1989. The world order context was characterized by "globalization" and "neo-liberalism". Different forms of multilateralism became instable, and at the same time nation-states were transformed. During this period, regionalisms served as a means to "resist" or "tame" "globalization", or to "advance" it. Dominant regionalisms are described as multisectoral or specialized. The importance of non-state actors has increased; there is a contrast between formal and informal regionalisms. Söderbaum also observes a difference between regionalisms and process of regionalization. And during the 2000s, with the "war on terror", the global financial crisis, as well as the rise of the BRICS (i.e. Brazil, Russia, India, China, and South Africa) and other "emerging powers", a multipolar or multiplex world order has arisen. Regional governance has become an important element of global governance, with states and non-state actors, both formal and informal, act in a growing number of sectors.

In contrast to political science, global history writing has developed a different periodization of regionalisms. However, global history scholars are not using the

---

60 Here and in the following, see Söderbaum, "Old, New and Comparative Regionalism", p. 31.

term "regional organization", but they consistently talk about "international organizations", even when they look at regional organizations. Despite this difference in signification, global history has developed rich empirical evidence of regional organizations, whose origins date well before 1919[61] – although they, too, differ on the question when exactly the history of regionalisms started. While Reinalda in his *Routledge History of International Organizations* has the history of regional organizations begin with the Vienna Congress (1814/15) and the Central Commission for the Navigation of the Rhine (1815 – clearly is a distinctively regional organization), the Basel-based historian Madeleine Herren, in a global history of the international order, chooses the International Committee of the Red Cross (1863/64) and the International Telecommunication Union (1865) as the starting point – according to her, everything between 1815 and 1865 is considered to be a prehistory of the international order of the nineteenth and twentieth centuries.[62]

Regional Practices in Africa

In this section, three fundamental practices of regional organizations will be discussed based on the example of the African Union: The making of a regional spatial order during the transformation of the Organization of African Unity to the AU in 1999–20002; the establishment of regional policy architectures in the fields of peace and security and democracy and governance; and the emergence of interregional routines, for instance the strategic partnerships between the AU and the United Nations as well as the AU and the European Union.

First, the foundation of the African Union in 2001 as a supranational organization with little delegation of member states' sovereignty to the AU Commission (AUC) was a compromise. The conventional wisdom of academia argues that negotiations were held between a "minimalist" camp, led by South Africa's then president Thabo Mbeki and Nigeria's Olusegun Obasanjo, and "maximalists", spearheaded by Libya's Muammar al-Gaddafi.[63] The Frankfurt-based political scientist Antonia Witt has developed a more nuanced understanding of the

---

[61] See K. Dykmann, "The History of International Organizations – What is New?", *Journal of International Organizations Studies* 2 (2011) 2, pp. 79–82.
[62] Reinalda, *Routledge History of International Organizations*, pp. 17–21, 28–30; as well as Madeleine Herren, *Internationale Organisationen seit 1865: Eine Globalgeschichte der Internationen Ordnung*, Darmstadt: Wissenschaftliche Buchgesellschaft, 2009, p. 15.
[63] See T.K. Tieku, "Explaining the Clash and Accommodation of Interests of Major Actors in the Creation of the African Union", *African Affairs* 103 (2004) 411, pp. 249–267.

various interests and identities. She identifies three positions: a "defence union", a "people's union" and a "manager-states' union".[64] The first version was proposed by Libya and supported, at a certain moment in time, by states such as Chad, Ghana, Liberia, Mali, Malawi, Senegal, and Sudan. They regarded "the globalization" as a hostile environment and wanted to protect themselves, with recourse to a pan-African tradition, by establishing the "United States of Africa". This regionalism would be a union without any state boundaries and based on a complete transfer of sovereignty of AU member states to the new centre. The nature of integration and unity of the African continent has indeed been subject to decades of intellectual and political debates, though the sequencing – gradual incrementalism vs. accelerated implementation – was always controversial.[65] In any case, in 2009 Gaddafi pushed the African Union to adopt a roadmap for the implementation of the United States of Africa by the year 2017. According to this plan, the AU Commission should have been replaced by an AU Authority that would take over from member states the sole international representation in the fields of peace and security, regional integration, development assistance, as well as "shared values" and institution- and capacity-building.[66] The project collapsed with the violent death of Gaddafi in 2011.[67]

The second position regarding the future of the African Union was supported by South Africa and Ghana (after a change of government), and later also by the AU Commission and the Pan-African Parliament. The concept of a *people's union* aimed at providing public goods (e.g. security) and democratic participation. In contrast, the *manager-states' union* only regarded states as actors of African unity; this vision was supported, among others, by regional heavyweights such as Egypt, Nigeria, Senegal, and Uganda. As a result of these

---

[64] Here and in the following, see A. Witt, "The African Union and Contested Political Order(s)", in: U. Engel and J. Gomes Porto (eds.), *Towards an African Peace and Security Regim: Continental Embeddedness, Transnational Linkages, Strategic Relevance*, Farnham: Ashgate, 2013, pp. 11–30.

[65] See K. van Walraven, *Dreams of Power: The Role of the Organization of African Unity in the Politics of Africa 1963–1993*, Farnham: Ashgate, 1999.

[66] See African Union Assembly, *Special Session of the 12th Ordinary Session of the Assembly. Report on the Outcome of the Special Session on Follow Up to the Sharm El Sheikh Assembly Decision AU/Dec. 206 (XI) on the Union Government* [Sp/Assembly/AU/Draft/Rpt(1)], Addis Ababa: African Union, 2009.

[67] See U. Engel, "The Changing Role of the AU Commission in Inter-African Relations – The Case of APSA and AGA", in: J.W. Harbeson and D. Rothchild (eds.), *Africa in World Politics: Engaging a Changing Global Order*, 5th ed., Boulder: Westview Press, 2013, pp. 186–206, at 188–194.

competing visions of a spatial format, the African Union is a compromise of supranational regionalism, in which member states have ceded little sovereignty. Nevertheless, the Union – and especially the AUC – has developed into an influential actor in its own right.[68]

Second, and opposite to its predecessor – the OAU, which was mainly concerned with decolonization and the struggle against apartheid – the African Union had to deal with violent conflict, terrorism, and extremism (e.g. forms of jihadism), as well as cases of unconstitutional changes of government, including coups d'etats, electoral violence, and controversial debates about presidential term limits. Based on the same political principles as the OAU – most importantly sovereignty of member states and non-interference in each other's internal affairs – the Union has introduced an innovative new principle to inter-African relations: the right to intervene in member states, pursuant to a decision of the AU Assembly of Heads and Government, in cases of "grave circumstances, namely war crimes, genocide and crimes against humanity".[69] In order to meet the various challenges the African Union is implementing, an ambitious African Peace and Security Architecture (APSA), comprising a Peace and Security Council (PSC), a Continental Early Warning System (CEWS) to anticipate and mitigate potential violent conflicts, a military African Standby Force (ASF) for short-term deployment in cases of conflict, an advisory Panel of the Wise, and a Peace Fund to finance respective interventions.[70] Most elements of APSA have been implemented (initially 2010 was the target), although, when comparing the five AU-defined meta-regions (North, Central, West, East, and South), with different speed and efficiency.[71] At the same time, this reorientation has increased the pressure to coordinate and harmonize AU activities with those of the Regional Economic Communities (RECs). The division of labour between the Union and the eight officially recognized partner RECs is still a work in progress.

In addition, the African Union is implementing a complimentary African Governance Architecture (AGA).[72] It is based on universal values, democratic aspirations, and respect for human rights as well as principles of rule of law,

---

68 Engel, "The Changing Role of the AU Commission"; and U. Engel, "The African Union's Peace and Security Architecture. From aspiration to operationalization", in: J.W. Harbeson and D. Rothchild (eds.), *Africa in World Politics: Constructing Political and Economic Order*, 6TH ed., Boulder: Westview Press, 2016, pp. 262–282.
69 See Organisation of African Unity, *Constitutive Act of the African Union*, Lomé: Organization of African Unity, 2000, § 4 (a, g-h).
70 See African Union, *Protocol Relating to the Establishment of the Peace and Security Council*, Durban: African Union, 2002.
71 See Engel, "The African Union's Peace and Security Architecture".
72 See African Union, *African Charter on Democracy, Elections and Governance*, 30 January 2007.

constitutional order, regular free and fair elections, the independence of the judiciary, etc. However, ratification of the relevant legal document, the African Charter on Democracy, Elections and Governance (2007), took five years. By 6 February 2019, only 32 out of 54 member states had ratified the charter, and only Togo had tabled the mandatory report on the state of democracy and human rights in its country. The further integration of APSA and AGA within the AUC, between the AUC and member states and RECs, as well as between RECs remains a huge challenge.[73]

Third, the African Union pursues a specific form of sovereignty-boosting – interregionalism – by developing strategic partnerships with both the United Nations and the European Union in the field of peace and security.[74] Both institutions play an important role in financing respective interventions in Africa, especially in the terms of peace-keeping operations and police missions. Beginning in the mid-2000s, the partnerships are based on a dense network of institutional connections that has led to closer policy coordination and the enhancement of the institutional capacities of the Union. Since 2006, there are annual consultations between the AU PSC and the UN Security Council (UNSC), there is a permanent working group on conflict prevention and resolution, and twice a year there are meetings at working level (desk-to-desk meetings). In 2009, a Permanent Mission at the United Nations was opened, and the following year a Joint Task Force on Peace and Security was established. In the same year the UN Office to the African Union was established. And since 2014, cooperation has been facilitated through annual Joint UN-AU Frameworks for an Enhanced Partnership in Peace and Security.

The partnership between the African Union and the European Union is based on the Joint Africa Strategy and its Plan of Action (2007). Institutionally, there are regular meetings at the level of summits of heads of state and government, ministers, and the commissions (college-to-college), as well as the PSC and the EU Political and Security Committee, the AU Military Committee and the AU Military Staff Committee, and the Joint Africa Expert Groups. Both partnerships are considered to be vital to the African Union to increase its room to

---

[73] Engel, "The African Union's Peace and Security Architecture".
[74] Here and in the following, see U. Engel, "The African Union and the United Nations: Crafting international partnerships in the field of peace and security", in: T. Karbo and T. Murithi (eds.), *The African Union: Autocracy, Diplomacy and Peacebuilding in Africa*, London, New York: I.B. Tauris 2017, pp. 265–281.; and U. Engel, "An Emerging Inter-Regional Peace and Security Partnership: The African Union and the European Union", in: S. Aris, A. Snetkov and A. Wenger (eds.) *Inter-organizational Relations in International Security. Cooperation and Competition*. London and New York: Routledge, 170–187.

manoeuvre – in this sense the partnerships are a core sovereignty strategy. This is despite the fact that political disagreement continues within important issues, for instance the question of the UNSC reform and stronger representation of African states (including a veto right); the NATO intervention in Libya in 2011 that led to regime change and the dissolution of the state; the international policy on Mali in 2013 in view of an armed jihadist insurgency and a coup d'etat; as well as various hegemonic agendas driven by the P3 (France, United Kingdom, and United States). The Union, therefore, argues that the respective partnerships should be based on stronger African ownership and recognition of its priorities.[75]

The three examples drawn from the practices of the African Union demonstrate how regional organizations establish distinct functional policy architectures and how they try to increase their sovereignty through interregional partnerships. Politically, African regionalism remains contested by member states, the RECs, or international partners. This also illustrates that regionalisms are characterized by processes of negotiation over interests and identities. This example shows the spatial format of regionalism can only be implemented in collaboration with other spatial formats. At the same time, it increases the options of member states to boost or reclaim some of their sovereignty. Regionalisms play a central role in ordering space and producing a continental spatial order. For the creation of a global spatial order, regionalisms have gained influence during the last three decades – so much so that some authors envisage a fragmented system of multilevel governance, a global governance run by regional organizations.[76]

Conclusions

Regional organizations play an important role in regional and global processes, in almost all policy fields. Since the end of the Cold War, they have grown in number and relevance. In academic debates on regional organizations and the processes of regionalization and region-building, a number of fundamental

---

[75] African Union Commission Chairperson, *Report of the Chairperson of the Commission on the Partnership between the African Union and the United Nations on Peace and Security: Towards Greater Political Coherence*, Tabled at the 307th meeting of the AU Peace and Security Council held in Addis Ababa, Ethiopia. PSC/PR/2. (CCCVII), Addis Ababa: African Union, 9 January 2012, §§ 94–97.

[76] See A. Acharya, "The Future of Global Governance: Fragmentation May Be Inevitable and Creative", *Global Governance* 22 (2016) 4, pp. 453–460.

intellectual challenges remain. This holds true for the active role of regional organizations in contemporary processes of globalization, the periodization of regionalisms during the past 200 years, and comparative research on regionalisms and regional organizations. Empirically, there is still a need for detailed case studies on the internal dynamics and decision-making processes of regional organizations, but also with regard to inter-regional practices. This also goes for the reconstruction of often undocumented national interests in regional organizations, the interplay between state and non-state organization, or the finances of regional organizations.[77] Today, the actorness of regional organizations is rarely disputed; however, there is a lack of empirical studies that reconstruct this agency vis-à-vis member states or with regard to the "international system" and other regional organizations. And, finally, there is a wide open space to analyse the professionalization and institutionalization of regional organizations from the Global South, their internal processes of learning, and the cultural transfers among different regional organizations.

---

[77] On the last point, see U. Engel and F. Mattheis (eds.), *The finances of regional organisations in the Global South – Follow the money*, Abingdon: Routledge (in print).

Sarah Ruth Sippel and Michaela Böhme
Dis/Articulating Agri-food Spaces: The Multifaceted Logics of Agro-investments

Introduction

Global agri-food spaces are constantly in flux. Understood as a product of the spatial practices of distinct groups of actors within the food system, global agri-food spaces form temporary stable patterns of agricultural production and consumption relations, producing connections as well as interruptions across different locations, places, and geographies. At the same time, there are periods in time that are perceived as critical moments where new actors emerge that start to challenge established patterns within the food system. This chapter focuses on one of such transformational moments: the emergence of new types of agro-investments over the past ten years. Conceptualizing such investments as projects that reshape existing spatialities within agricultural commodity chains, this chapter demonstrates how the varying motives under which investment capital operates give rise to diverse and partly diverging respatializations of agricultural commodity chains. These respatializations, we argue, furthermore have the potential to challenge the dominant patterns within the agri-food system.

Our analysis starts with the food price hikes in 2007/08 and 2011, which many observers have considered as a transformative moment in global agri-food relations.[1] After two decades of volatile and overall declining food prices, there was a sudden increase in food prices as a result of a special and unprecedented combination of factors with short- and mid-term aspects: the temporary decline of agricultural production and food stocks coupled with rising demand, export restrictions, new agro-fuel policies, as well as financial speculation on commodity markets.[2] These factors were further embedded within long-term developments, such as declining investments in rural areas and state-led reregulation of agricultural and financial policies.

---

[1] See, e.g., J. Clapp and M.J. Cohen (eds.), *The Global Food Crisis: Governance Challenges and Opportunities*, Waterloo: Wilfrid Laurier University Press, 2009; C. Rosin et al. (eds.), *Food Systems Failure: The Global Food Crisis and the Future of Agriculture*, Abingdon: Routledge, 2014.

[2] J. Gertel and S.R. Sippel, "The Financialisation of Agriculture and Food", in: M. Shucksmith and D.L. Brown (eds.), *International Handbook of Rural Studies*, Abingdon: Routledge, 2016, pp. 215–226.

Together, these events were considered as signalling a structural crisis in agriculture and its organizational and institutional frameworks.[3] Food price hikes particularly affected the livelihoods of those groups of people who already need to spend a major part of their income on food, leading to "food riots" in numerous urban centres across the Global South. At the same time, this conjunction of events also triggered a renewed interest in agricultural production and farmland, as different groups of actors – including private and state-owned companies, sovereign wealth funds and agricultural investment funds – sought to respond to the new pressures arising from a broader restructuring of the global food system as well as to benefit from the new identified investment opportunities.

A large body of literature has emerged in critical agri-food studies that examines the new types of capital permeating agri-food around the globe.[4] While this literature has made important contributions to uncover the commonalities of current agro-investments, relatively less emphasis has been placed on the contradictions and discrepancies involved and resulting from the great diversity and heterogeneity of the underlying logics that characterize current investments in food and farming. Indeed, within the same investment location, we often find a multiplicity of investors from different geographies and institutional contexts at work, which, while all investing in agricultural resources, pursue substantially different investment strategies that have highly varied outcomes for the agricultural contexts in which investments take place. In other words, the widely shared perception amongst scholars that the 2007/08 food price crisis represents a sort of turning point for investor interest in farmland runs the risk of essentializing the current wave of agro-investments as an internally coherent and operationally congruent phenomenon.[5] In an effort to de-essentialize our understanding of agro-investments, we suggest that a spatial

---

[3] P. McMichael and M. Schneider, "Food Security Politics and the Millennium Development Goals", *Third World Quarterly* 32 (2011) 1, pp. 119–39.

[4] See, e.g., B. White et al., "The New Enclosures: Critical Perspectives on Corporate Land Deals", *The Journal of Peasant Studies* 39 (2012) 3–4, pp. 619–647; M. Edelman, C. Oya and S. M. Borras Jr., "Global Land Grabs: Historical Processes, Theoretical and Methodological Implications, and Current Trajectories", *Third World Quarterly* 34 (2013) 9, pp. 1517–31; I. Scoones et al., "The Politics of Evidence: Methodologies for Understanding the Global Land Rush", *The Journal of Peasant Studies* 40 (2013) 3, pp. 469–483; P. McMichael, "Land Grabbing as Security Mercantilism in International Relations", *Globalizations* 10 (2013) 1, pp. 47–64.

[5] S. Ouma, "From Financialization to Operations of Capital: Historicizing and Disentangling the Finance-Farmland-Nexus", *Geoforum* 72 (2016), pp. 82–93; R. Pedersen and L. Buur, "Beyond Land Grabbing: Old Morals and New Perspectives on Contemporary Investments", *Geoforum* 72 (2016), pp. 77–81; J.E. Goldstein and J.S. Yates, "Introduction: Rendering Land Investable", *Geoforum* 82 (2017), pp. 209–211.

lens is helpful to tease out the differences in investment logics and strategies that different groups of actors pursue as well as to better comprehend their broader implications for the reconfiguration of global agri-food relationships.

Starting with Australia as an example of one particular investment geography, this chapter explores and contrasts the investment dynamics of two groupings of actors that have been in the spotlight of the debate on the new wave of global agro-investments: companies from China, on the one hand, and "Western" actors backed by financial capital, on the other. Both groups of actors have become important sources of foreign capital in Australia over the past ten years and, within this context, have acquired substantial amounts of farmland. Although both types of actors target similar assets in food production – especially large-scale farm holdings in the areas of grain and livestock production – there are fundamental differences in the motives that inspire their investment strategies. The chapter, firstly, identifies the varying motives behind the respective capital flows, together with the interest in acquiring agricultural resources. Secondly, the chapter considers how investments decisions are part of, and integrated into, a global agri-food strategy the actors pursue. Based on this, the multifaceted logics are uncovered that underpin Chinese and finance-backed agricultural investments, which produce variegated commodity chain respatializations that entail simultaneous but fundamentally different processes of "dis/articulating" agri-food spaces.

To be clear, we do not wish to present the two groups of actors we examine here as clear-cut or natural "categories" of investors. Indeed, the logics behind the current wave of agro-investments are often fuzzy and fluid and, following Visser,[6] should rather be conceptualized as continuum, ranging from practices that turn farmland into a commodity and resource to practices that render it as a financial "asset". Even though we acknowledge the empirical complexity and "fuzziness" of agro-investments and their multilayered, opaque, as well as shifting characteristics, which are often difficult to disentangle, the prototypical presentation of Chinese and finance-backed investment logics is appropriate inasmuch it allows us to flesh out our theoretical argument with more clarity.

We frame our analysis conceptually by taking the notion of the "commodity chain" as an analytical lens to examine the spatial reconfigurations of global agri-food relationships, combining this with a relational perspective on space. Following Doreen Massey,[7] we understand space as a "product of interrelations"

---

[6] O. Visser, "Running out of Farmland? Investment Discourses, Unstable Land Values and the Sluggishness of Asset Making", *Agriculture and Human Values* 34 (2017) 1, pp. 185–198.
[7] D. Massey, *For Space*, London: Sage, 2005.

that is made up of interactions. Conceptualized in this way, space becomes "the sphere of the possibility of the existence of multiplicity in the sense of contemporaneous plurality", and thus is never finished or closed but always in the process of being made.[8] Agri-food spatialities, then, are not fixed container-like territories but are the result of production-consumption linkages, which are articulated with each other and in constant flux while at the same time becoming manifest in individual territorial scopes.[9]

We, furthermore, take up two inspirations from authors who have sought to spatialize commodity chains analysis.[10] Global commodity chains approaches have emerged as a widely used perspective to study global agri-food relations. Drawing on the work of Wallerstein, Hopkins, and Gereffi and colleagues,[11] the global commodity chain emerged as a popular means to follow agricultural products from "farm to fork", thereby conceptually linking production in one part of the world to consumption in another. While being the "appropriate organizational field to use in studying economic globalization",[12] with regard to their underlying conceptualization of space, as Berndt and Boeckler note, global commodity chains approaches are marked by a certain methodological territorialism.[13] Conceptually, authors either ask how individual "locations" (such as cities, regions, or nation-states) influence commodity production or follow the

---

8 Ibid., p. 9.
9 J. Gertel and S.R. Sippel, "Introduction: Seasonality and Temporality in Intensive Agriculture", in: J. Gertel and S.R. Sippel (eds.), *Seasonal Workers in Mediterranean Agriculture: The Social Costs of Eating Fresh*, Abingdon: Routledge, 2014, pp. 3–22, at 12.
10 D. Leslie and S. Reimer, "Spatializing Commodity Chains", *Progress in Human Geography* 23 (1999) 3, pp. 401–420; J. Bair and M. Werner, "Commodity Chains and the Uneven Geographies of Global Capitalism: A Disarticulations Perspective", *Environment and Planning A* 43 (2011) 5, pp. 988–997; J. Bair and M. Werner, "The Place of Disarticulations: Global Commodity Production in La Laguna, Mexico", *Environment and Planning A* 43 (2011) 5, pp. 998–1015; C. Berndt and M. Boeckler, "Performative Regional (Dis)Integration: Transnational Markets, Mobile Commodities, and Bordered North–South Differences", *Environment and Planning A* 43 (2011) 5, pp. 1057–1078; J. Bair et al., "Dis/Articulating Producers, Markets, and Regions: New Directions in Critical Studies of Commodity Chains", *Environment and Planning A* 45 (2013), pp. 2544–2552.
11 For a comprehensive overview, see J. Bair, "Global Capitalism and Commodity Chains: Looking Back, Going Forward", *Competition & Change* 9 (2005) 2, pp. 153–180.
12 G. Gereffi, "International Trade and Industrial Upgrading in the Apparel Commodity Chain", *Journal of International Economics* 48 (1999), pp. 37–70, quoted in: C. Berndt and M. Boeckler, "Performative Regional (Dis) Integration: Transnational Markets, Mobile Commodities, and Bordered North–South Differences", *Environment and Planning A* 43 (2011) 5, pp. 1057–1078.
13 Berndt and Boeckler, "Performative Regional (Dis)Integration", pp. 1057–1078.

trajectories of commodities from one such location to the other. In both cases, locations appear as a pregiven as goods, people, ideas, and capital are investigated as they move *between* places. Instead, Berndt and Boeckler suggest to turn the "territorial logic upside down" by asking how these mobilities (re)produce locations.[14] Following this reversed logic, we take the mobilities of investment flows as our starting point and explore how they connect locations and people in new ways, thereby reshaping the existing spatialities within agri-food chains.

A second inspiration comes from the notion of "dis/articulation" as introduced by Bair and Werner.[15] Focusing on "dis/articulations" within commodity chains, Bair and Werner emphasize the reproduction of uneven geographies that are both constitutive of, as well as constituted by, the configurations of global productions.[16] Disarticulations are presented as a way to "explicate the layered histories of dispossession, disinvestment, and accumulation" that shape a location's position in global circuits of commodity production.[17] Drawing on Hall's concept of articulation as a process of forging unity out of difference, articulations are in turn understood as an ongoing material and ideological work to link up relations of production and complexly structured social formations. Adding a spatial component to this work of linking, Bair and Werner elaborate:

> It is not only the work of linking up constructions of social difference with processes of valuation and capital accumulation, but also that of reproducing geographical difference by linking and delinking places to commodity chains that are formed and reformed through these moments of connection and severance.[18]

Following Bair and Werner, we explore the dynamics of linking/delinking and connection/severance within agri-food chains. Instead of addressing the implications of disinvestments, however, we focus on new forms of investments, which, as we argue, can equally include important moments of delinking agri-food spaces. Our aim in using the notion of dis/articulation is thus to highlight the dual and simultaneous dynamic of de/linking introduced by the two groupings of actors and their investment motives, which either sever existing linkages by

---

14 Ibid., p. 1061.
15 Bair and Werner, "Commodity Chains and the Uneven Geographies of Global Capitalism", pp. 988–997; Bair and Werner, "The Place of Disarticulations", pp. 998–1015.
16 Bair and Werner, "Commodity Chains and the Uneven Geographies of Global Capitalism", p. 989.
17 Bair and Werner, "The Place of Disarticulations", p. 1001.
18 Bair and Werner, "Commodity Chains and the Uneven Geographies of Global Capitalism", p. 993.

breaking up agri-food productions into investible units or forge connections by linking up production steps in integrated supply chains. In sum, developing a spatial lens on current food system dynamics thus means to start from the practices of actors within the agri-food system and to explore how these practices constantly produce new agri-food spatialities and, in doing so, refer to as well as challenge existing spatialities. Spatially reframed, the commodity chain thereby becomes an important analytical lens – a "spatial format" – to explore these projects of respatialization pursued by various actors, along with their implications for the dominant patterns, or "spatial order", of the food system.

Empirically, the chapter draws on several months of qualitative fieldwork conducted by the authors between 2016 and 2018. Whereas Böhme's research has focused on the Chinese companies that are active in Australia's agri-food sectors and took place in Australia and China, Sippel has investigated financial actors and their activities in the Australian context. In what follows, we first outline the respective backgrounds, motives, and resulting investment strategies of Chinese actors and financial actors individually. Based on that, we position them towards one another with regard to the respatializations they advance within global agri-food commodity chains.

Articulating Agri-Food Spaces: Chinese Investment in Australian Agriculture

Since the beginning of the decade, Australia has experienced a growing inflow of capital originating from China in its food and agriculture sector. Chinese companies from both the private and the state-owned sector have been acquiring agricultural assets along the entire agricultural supply chain, from farms to processing plants to logistics facilities to branding. Australia is not unique but part of a broader trend in Chinese companies looking to invest in food and agriculture in different regions all over the world. Linked to a policy evolution in the way Chinese officials think about national food security, the current trend in overseas investments in food and agriculture marks a decisive shift from China's long-favoured preference for self-sufficiency towards more engagement with global markets and the deepening of food trade relationships. The reasons behind this departure from self-sufficiency are complex and mutually reinforcing. They include natural resource constraints, environmental degradation resulting from rapid industrialization, and dietary shifts linked to rising incomes and urbanization.[19] The greater international engagement of Chinese agri-businesses also reflects the growing competitive pressures China's domestic agriculture sector has been facing since its accession to the World Trade Organization in 2001 and the subsequent liberalization of agricultural imports.[20] Constrained by fragmented farming areas, the existence of a still sizeable small-scale peasantry together with rising costs for inputs, many agricultural products are not competitive in face of cheap imports from large agricultural export nations such as the US, Brazil, or Canada. These combined factors have resulted in a drastic increase in imports, turning China into the world's largest importer of agricultural products.[21]

Although the new vision for "feeding China" calls for giving imports and international markets a greater role, it would be a mistake to assume that the Chinese state is prepared to relinquish control over national food security to global market forces or to the interests of Western-dominated agri-food traders. As Ye explains,[22] two pillars characterize China's new food security strategy. One is a continued effort to promote domestic agro-industrial development, aimed at increasing output, productivity, and efficiency. The other is to gain better control over the flow and supply of China's food imports. To this latter end, the Chinese government has designed a set of policy measures that encourage Chinese companies to "go out" and actively participate in global agri-food production and trade. The aims of China's agricultural "going out" strategy are multidimensional and include the diversification of China's current import sources, for example by forging new agricultural ties with newly emerging agricultural exporters such as

---

[19] F. Gale, J. Hansen and M. Jewison, "China's Growing Demand for Agricultural Imports", EIB-136. US Department of Agriculture, Economic Research Service (2015), https://www.ers.usda.gov/webdocs/publications/43939/eib-136.pdf?v=0; Australian Government, "Feeding the Future: A Joint Australia-China Report on Strengthening Investment and Technological Cooperation in Agriculture to Enhance Food Security", Australia-China Joint Working Group, https://dfat.gov.au/about-us/publications/trade-investment/feeding-future/Documents/feeding-the-future.pdf (accessed 21 May 2018).
[20] F. Gale, J. Hansen and M. Jewison, "China's Growing Demand for Agricultural Imports", EIB-136. US Department of Agriculture, Economic Research Service (2015), https://www.ers.usda.gov/webdocs/publications/43939/eib-136.pdf?v=0
[21] J. Dong et al., "Kuoda Nongchanpin Jinkou Manzu Duoyan Xiaofei Xuqiu" [Expand Imports of Agricultural Products to Meet Diverse Consumer Needs], *Farmer's Daily*, 23 May 2018, http://www.xinhuanet.com/politics/2018-05/23/c_1122876313.htm
[22] X. Ye, "Zhunque Bawo Guojia Liangshi Anquan Zhanlüe de si ge Xin Bianhua" [Correctly Grasping Four New Changes in the National Food Security Strategy], *People's Daily*, 14 January 2014, http://theory.people.com.cn/n/2014/0117/c83865-24152538.html

Russia or Ukraine; the promotion of technological and diplomatic cooperation in agriculture; and the expansion of agricultural investments in different commodity sectors and along the entire agricultural supply chain.[23]

Within China's emerging global food strategy, Australia is valued for its abundant natural resources, its "clean and green" image, as well as its advantage in the production and export of dairy, sheep, and beef products.[24] Take the beef industry as an example; Australia is now China's largest source of imported beef, accounting for 34 per cent of China's official beef imports.[25] While China's beef market is highly competitive, with players such as Brazil, Uruguay, New Zealand or the US all contending for market share, Australia is in a relatively advantageous position due to a number of market access and trade agreements it signed with China. The China-Australia Free Trade Agreement (ChAFTA), coming into force in 2015, will eliminate import tariffs on frozen beef products by 2024. In addition, Australia and China signed protocols for the export of chilled beef, which goes into premium retail channels such as high-end restaurants and supermarkets and commands higher prices than frozen beef products. Furthermore, in 2015, Australia became the first country worldwide to be granted access to export live cattle to China for slaughter.[26]

The case of beef provides an instructive example how the context from which investment capital emerges has a decisive impact on the way in which investors respatialize agricultural commodity chains. As the examples below will show, the political decision to promote China's integration into global

---

[23] H. Zhang and Q. Cheng, "China's Food Security Strategy Reform: An Emerging Global Agricultural Policy", in: F. Wu and H. Zhang (eds.), *China's Global Quest for Resources: Energy, Food and Water*, Abingdon: Routledge, China Policy Series, 46, 2016, pp. 23–41; X. Lü et al., "Kuaguo Liangshang Fazhan Zhanlüe dui Zhongguo Nongye 'Zouchuqu' de Qishi" [Development Strategies of Transnational Grain Traders and their Significance for China's Agricultural "Going Global" Strategy], *Shijie Nongye* [World Agriculture] 11 (2014), pp. 15–17; X. Ye, "Zhunque Bawo Guojia Liangshi Anquan Zhanlüe de si ge Xin Bianhua" [Correctly Grasping Four New Changes in the National Food Security Strategy], *People's Daily*, 14 January 2014, http://theory.people.com.cn/n/2014/0117/c83865-24152538.html; X. Di and W. Zhang, "Zhongguo Nongye 'Zouchuqu': Tedian, Wenti ji Fazhan Silu" [China's Agricultural "Going Global": Characteristics, Issues, and Development Ideas], *Guoji Jingji Hezuo* [International Economic Cooperation] 7 (2013), pp. 43–46.

[24] E. Gooch and F. Gale, "China's Foreign Agriculture Investments", EIB-192, US Department of Agriculture, Economic Research Service (2018), https://www.ers.usda.gov/webdocs/publications/88572/eib-192.pdf?v.

[25] Meat & Livestock Australia (MLA), "Market Snapshot China Beef: Australian Trade Overview", (2015), https://www.mla.com.au/globalassets/mla-corporate/prices–markets/documents/os-markets/red-meat-market-snapshots/mla_china-market-snapshot_may-2015.pdf.

[26] Ibid.

agricultural markets has opened a new frontier for access to resources abroad. In their efforts to navigate this frontier and to enhance their control and power over the increasingly global flow of food into China, Chinese agricultural entrepreneurs, investors, and businessmen seek to build integrated supply chains that produce new articulations across a multiplicity of agrarian spaces, from cattle farms in Australian ruralities to the dinner tables of Chinese middle-class families.

Internationalizing China's Beef Sector

The internationalization of China's beef sector is in many ways emblematic of the goals as well as contradictions of China's agricultural development trajectory since the beginning of the reform era in the late 1970s. Encouraged by development policy and increased marketization, China has experienced strong growth in its domestic beef industry over the past decades. China's cattle herd is now the world's third largest, after India and Brazil.[27] While small-scale peasant farmers continue to produce the majority of China's beef, the government has made great efforts to promote the concentration and intensification of the industry. Modern-style factory farms are seen as an answer to issues of quality assurance and output constraints.[28] Yet, the Chinese beef industry is not able to keep up with the explosive growth in domestic demand. The year 2010 marked a turning point for the industry as a combination of high domestic demand and rapidly increasing production costs pushed domestic beef prices up, with imports now being cheaper than domestically produced beef.[29] Since 2012, China has been a net importer of beef, with imports increasing 15-fold in 5 years, which are forecast to remain so in the foreseeable future due to persisting constraints in land, feed, water, and supply chain development.[30]

---

27 Ibid.
28 T. DuBois and A. Gao, "Big Meat: The Rise and Impact of Mega-Farming in China's Beef, Sheep and Dairy Industries", *Global Research* (2017), https://www.globalresearch.ca/big-meat-mega-farming-in-chinas-beef-sheep-and-dairy-industries/5607796.
29 Q. He and N. Wang, "Fuhe Xiaofei Shengji Qushi, Kanhao Jinkou Niurou Qianjing" [Optimism About the Prospects of Imported Beef Based on Trend Towards Upgrading Consumption], *Huatai Zhengjuan Yanjiu Baogao* [Huatai Equity Research], 11 September 2016, https://crm.htsc.com.cn/doc/2016/101208/40c2f977-abb6-46a1-ae3b-13717ca577cc.pdf.
30 Agriculture and Agri-Food Canada (AAFC), "Sector Trend Analysis: Inside China Beef Trade", (2017), http://www.agr.gc.ca/resources/prod/Internet-Internet/MISB-DGSIM/ATS-SEA/PDF/6863-eng.pdf.

With beef imports now constituting a sizeable share of China's domestic beef consumption, the beef import industry has turned into a lucrative business for Chinese companies attempting to capitalize on the anticipated growing demand for beef by Chinese consumers. Since 2010, interest in the sector has skyrocketed, driven not only by Chinese firms with established operations in the domestic beef sector but also by investors and entrepreneurs from other areas attracted by high profit margins. These players have been trying to establish a dominant position in China's emerging international beef cattle trade by looking for secure, long-term supply relationships, for example via supply agreements with foreign producers and partnerships. Direct investments into the beef cattle supply chain overseas are another important avenue by which economic actors attempt to capitalize on China's growing beef demand. In Australia, much of China's investment interest has concentrated on the acquisition of primary production assets. Chinese investors have acquired cattle farms across all of Australia, from northern Australia's extensive cattle farming through to southern Australia's intensive cattle systems characterized by higher stocking rates and land productivity. Whereas farm acquisitions have generated considerable political debate, Chinese investments further down the supply chain have received relatively less attention. Next to cattle farming, Chinese capital is now involved along the entire beef supply chain, including the feedlot, processing, and transportation sectors. While some investors are involved in China's domestic beef production or own distribution and retail networks in China, other investments come from unrelated industries such as real estate or industrial manufacturing.

Although the Chinese beef sector promises profit opportunities for those firms able to secure stable supplies from the international market, it is at the same time characterized by fierce competition over price and the constant arrival of new domestic and foreign players.[31] In response to these pressures, the Chinese beef industry has seen increasing vertical integration along the beef supply chain. According to Heffernan, "vertical integration occurs when a firm increases ownership and control of a number of stages in a commodity system".[32] Table 1 illustrates this process, with 10 out of 15 companies owning assets at multiple points in the supply chain. Most investors own assets at the production stage. A smaller number of investors have begun building their supply chains from the processing stage without ownership of farms further upstream.

---

31 DuBois and Gao, "Big Meat".
32 W.D. Heffernan, "Concentration of Ownership and Control in Agriculture", in: F. Magdoff, J.B. Foster and F.H. Buttel (eds.), *Hungry for Profit: The Agribusiness Threat to Farmers, Food, and the Environment*, New York: Monthly Review Press, 2000, pp. 68–69.

Table 1: Companies wholly owned or backed by Chinese investment with operations in the Australian beef sector, 2011–2018.

Company	Australia				China	
	Production	Feedlot	Processing	Transport	Processing	Distribution
ABL Red Meat		X				X
Australia Aulong Auniu Wang (AAAW)	X					X
Hengyang Group[a]			X		X	
Fucheng Group	X				X	X
Hailiang Group	X					X
Harmony Agriculture and Food (HAAFCO)	X	X	X	X	X	X
New Hope Group			X		X[b]	X[c]
Rifa Salutary Pastoral	X					
Shanghai CRED	X	X				
Consolidated Australian Pastoral Holdings (CAPH)	X		X			
Taihua Foods			X		X	X
Tianma Bearings Group	X					
Union Agriculture	X					

Yang Xiang Assets		X
Xinyangfeng Fertilizer Company		X

Compiled from company materials and news reports.
[a] In early 2018, Hengyang divested from one of the two slaughterhouses it owns in Australia. The processing facility was acquired by Harmony Agriculture and Food (HAAFCO), a Sino-Australian joint venture with Chinese majority ownership.
[b] New Hope Group also owns beef processing facilities the US.
[c] New Hope Group also owns beef distribution channels in the US.

Discussions with investors and industry insiders have shown that a complex set of factors determines at which point of the supply chain an investor will enter, including overall business strategy, size and industry background of the acquiring firm, as well as acquisition opportunities and market cycles. As one investor told us, reflecting on the flexibility with which investors have begun to integrate supply chains:

> [S]ome of them own farms, some don't, and some of them own the cattle from the feedlot but have contracted growers. It's a bit like building Lego, you can almost do it anyway you want. (Interview, Shanghai, 2018)

It is also important to note that vertical integration is not necessarily achieved only by acquiring assets at different stages of the chain but also via contracts with operators further downstream regarding the feeding, slaughtering, and packaging of beef cattle according to the grower's specification. Especially for smaller investment projects, the goal is to retain possibilities of control over the beef product all the way through to the Chinese consumer rather than to own the supply chain itself.

Backward, Forward, and Multidimensional Strategies of Integration

Even though many investors aim to achieve vertical integration, the strategies these actors use exhibit some fundamental differences. As our research shows, vertical integration strategies fall into at least three broad categories, which we term backward integration, forward integration, and multidimensional strategies of integration. While backward and forward integration focuses on the rearticulation of bilateral agri-food relationships between China and Australia, multidimensional strategies of integration are underpinned by a global vision of the agri-food system, seeking to link agri-food production and consumption across multiple geographies.

Starting with backward integration strategies, these are used by Chinese firms that invest in Australian agriculture to support the supply of products into their existing distribution channels:

Australia Aulong Auniu Wang (AAAW) represents a typical backward integration strategy. AAAW is owned by Dashang Group, a large Chinese retailer that operates department stores and supermarkets across China's north-east. Since 2015, Dashang Group has acquired five cattle stations in the Hunter Region in New South Wales as well as Queensland, where the company breeds

Australian beef. AAAW has contract arrangements with feedlot and processing firms in Australia and exports chilled and frozen beef products under its "Hunter Valley" brand to the retail stores it operates in China. To complement its beef line, the company also owns and operates vineyards in France and Australia. Backward integration strategies like that of AAAW are spurred by a need to secure a consistent supply of beef products at stable prices for an existing retail operation. To be profitable in China's challenging market environment, Chinese retailers need to ensure they can offer beef products at competitive prices. Owning one's own source of beef supply is hence often seen as a way to control the beef price and, consequently, the profit margin. In the words of a managing director of a Chinese-invested beef producer in Australia:

> Retail is tough because there's so much competition. So, the margins generally are quite similar and transparent. If you're only going to be able to sell a product for so much, for you to extract more profit out of it, what do you do? You have to reduce your cost of input. And the best way for you to do that is for you to be able to own and control that. (Interview, Sydney, 2017)

Investors engaged in forward vertical integration, in contrast, do not have existing distribution channels in China. Their business background is often outside the agriculture sector, but they see increasing beef demand as an investment opportunity and attempt to grow their existing business by diversifying into the beef sector.

Harmony Agriculture and Food (HAAFCO) provides a typical example of a forward integration strategy. In 2016, HAAFCO was set up as a joint venture between Australian interests and Chinese majority shareholder Dalian Hesheng Holdings. Hesheng is a diversified business conglomerate with interests in numerous industries, including chemicals, financial services, and real estate. Since its inception, HAAFCO has acquired two grazing properties in Western Australia and Victoria, respectively, as well as two feedlot facilities and a slaughterhouse. In addition, HAAFCO's majority owner, Hesheng, is involved in a joint venture with Chinese state-owned logistics companies Sinotrans Group and China Merchants Group, which own and operate two ships approved for the live cattle export trade between Australia and China. In December 2017, HAAFCO was amongst the first Australian beef companies to send a live cattle consignment from Australia to the port of Qingdao, a government-designated development zone for the import of meat products, where Hesheng also recently acquired quarantine and processing facilities. Finally, HAAFCO has gained access to distribution networks in China via Hesheng's acquisition of Chinese iconic meat brand "Qingdao Snowdragon". Having achieved a fully integrated vertical supply chain, the company aims to increase total production capacity to 100,000 heads of cattle per year. Forward integration strategies endeavour to connect Australian beef supply and the Chinese consumer market, but unlike backward-integrated businesses, the starting point is not an existing retail or distribution business in China operating on fixed margins. Rather, forward-integrated investors aim to capture the full value along the supply chain. With the efficiencies of large-scale operations and the removal of intermediary agents in the supply chain, a vertically integrated model offers investors the opportunity to gain more control over price as well as quality assurance, thereby strengthening their position in China's fiercely competitive market place.

Lastly, a small group of Chinese investors pursues multidimensional integration strategies, seeking to link various locations of production with multiple consumer markets within the global agri-food system. While central governmental policy has been advocating Chinese companies to "go global" and develop into internationally competitive agribusinesses since 2006, few Chinese companies to date have established themselves as true global players. One of China's domestic agribusinesses poised to become such a global player is the New Hope Group, China's largest private agriculture group and a significant overseas investor.

New Hope started its business as an animal feed company in 1982, but since then has moved into higher value-added sectors in poultry, pork, and dairy production. A merger with Chinese poultry producer Liuhe Group in 2005 significantly enhanced the company's integration into China's domestic protein production chain, where it operates along all stages from feed production, breeding, slaughtering, and processing to fully cooked meals. Although the New Hope Group has been engaged in overseas investment projects since the late 1990s, recent investments have shifted the focus from greenfield projects in developing countries to acquisitions of processing and technology assets in countries with modern, agro-industrial sectors. In 2013, New Hope, in conjunction with its private equity arm Hosen Capital, acquired Australian beef processor Kilcoy Pastoral Company. Kilcoy is Queensland's largest dedicated feed grain beef processor, producing beef products for more than 20 markets globally. Since then, New Hope has made further strategic investments to transform Kilcoy from a slaughterhouse into what the company refers to as a "global premium protein provider". Key acquisitions that have been added since include the Ruprecht Company, a US-based producer of value-added beef products and Kilcoy's largest US customer as well as Weidao Food Company, a Chinese producer and supplier of meat protein-based products to high-end restaurants in China. These acquisitions have not only enabled New Hope to strengthen its distribution channels in some of the world's key beef markets, but also to access advanced product research and development capabilities. New Hope's global beef business will be run by a newly formed entity, Kilcoy Global Foods, headquartered in Australia, which integrates company operations and supply chain stages in Australia, the US, and China. New Hope is eager to capitalize on China's dietary transition to higher value-added protein products; however, its ambitions go beyond the Chinese market. Rather than narrowing its focus on how to connect foreign resources with Chinese demand, New Hope's leaders think of beef production as a global industry that is increasingly interlinked with emerging economies such as China. By connecting markets and technologies and developing its supply chains across three strategic locations, the ultimate goal is to become a competitive player in a global industry.

Disarticulating Agri-Food Spaces: Finance-Backed Investment in Australian Agriculture

A second category of recent capital inflows into Australian agriculture comes from the financial sector. The way in which agricultural resources are being reconceptualized in this context can be considered as a second way of reorganizing the sociospatial relationships within agri-food commodity chains. This reorganization, at its core, aims to create new "asset geographies",[33] that is to say to construct assets that deliver reliable income streams.[34] Against the backdrop of the conjunction of short- and long-term events in 2007/08 outlined in the introduction, financial actors have shown a heightened interest in agricultural assets, and more recently expanded their investments to encompass further elements of agricultural supply chains. As with Chinese investments, this process is not unique to Australia but part of a broader dynamic identified in the literature as "financialization" of agriculture and food.[35] Social studies of financialization investigate how finance exceeds its traditional role of providing capital and starts to reshape the underlying

---

[33] A. Leyshon and N. Thrift, "The Capitalization of Almost Everything: The Future of Finance and Capitalism", *Theory, Culture and Society* 24 (2007) 7–8, p. 109.
[34] A. Leyshon and N. Thrift, "The Capitalization of Almost Everything: The Future of Finance and Capitalism", *Theory, Culture and Society*, 24 (2007) 7–8, pp. 97–115; K. Birch, "Rethinking Value in the Bio-Economy: Finance, Assetization, and the Management of Value", *Science, Technology, & Human Values* 42 (2017) 3, pp. 460–490.
[35] See, e.g., J. Clapp, "Financialization, Distance and Global Food Politics", *Journal of Peasant Studies* 41 (2014) 5, pp. 797–814; S.R. Isakson, "Food and Finance: The Financial Transformation of Agro-food Supply Chains", *Journal of Peasant Studies* 41 (2014) 5, pp. 749–775; J. Gertel and S. R. Sippel, "The Financialisation of Agriculture and Food", in: M. Shucksmith and D.L. Brown (eds.), *International Handbook of Rural Studies*, Abingdon: Routledge, 2016, pp. 215–226; H.

logics of the economy and society more generally.[36] Agri-food scholars have observed such processes of financialization across various levels of the agri-food system, with one entry point being agricultural resources and their assetization, that is to say their construction as financial asset classes.[37]

Based on, but distinct from, commodification, "assetization" refers to the transformation of things into revenue-generating and tradable resources.[38] The interest in "tangible assets" such as agricultural resources has to be seen within the broader context of the search for, and corresponding expansion of, reliable income-yielding assets, which Leyshon and Thrift identify as a key driver of the 2000s international financial system.[39] This search was rooted in the macroeconomic conditions of low interest rates and low inflation across large parts of the world since the mid-1990s, leading to flat yield curves and abundant liquidity. Within this context, infrastructures such as highways, airports, or public water supply networks have served as one area for the construction of new income streams based on "tangible" or "real assets". The interest in agricultural resources stems from the same context, coupled with assumptions regarding the impact of agricultural resources on financial portfolios as well as assessments of risk-return relationships and how these play out within different regional contexts.

At the global level, farmland investments were notably spurred by the rise in commodity prices in 2007/08 and 2011. Investor discourses furthermore promoted agricultural resources as alternative assets by advancing neo-Malthusian arguments of resource scarcity (i.e. finite availability of land versus rising global demand for food),[40] on the one hand, and by constructing food (in)security narratives as both legitimizing and incentivizing investments, on the other.[41] Within this global context, Australia appeared as a highly profitable low-risk environment for investments, while, at the same time, large portions of

---

Bjørkhaug et al., *The Financialization of Agri-food Systems: Contested Transformations*, Abingdon: Routledge, 2018.

[36] N.A.J. van der Zwan, "Making Sense of Financialization", *Socio-Economic Review* 12 (2014) 1, pp. 99–129.

[37] J. Clapp, S.R. Isakson and O. Visser, "The Complex Dynamics of Agriculture as a Financial Asset: Introduction to Symposium", *Agriculture and Human Values* 34 (2017) 1, pp. 179–183.

[38] K. Birch, "Rethinking Value in the Bio-Economy: Finance, Assetization, and the Management of Value", *Science, Technology, & Human Values* 42 (2017) 3, pp. 460–490.

[39] A. Leyshon and N. Thrift, "The Capitalization of Almost Everything: The Future of Finance and Capitalism", *Theory, Culture and Society* 24 (2007) 7–8, p. 100.

[40] M. Fairbairn, "'Like Gold with Yield': Evolving Intersections Between Farmland and Finance", *Journal of Peasant Studies* 41 (2014) 5, pp. 777–795.

[41] N. Larder, S.R. Sippel and G. Lawrence, "Finance Capital, Food Security Narratives and Australian Agricultural Land", *Journal of Agrarian Change* 15 (2015) 4, pp. 592–603.

land came on the market as major landowners divested their holdings following a prolonged period of drought in the 2000s.[42] Similar to the Chinese investments outlined above, however, the finance-driven respatialization of agri-food relationships does not refer to land exclusively but is also applied to further elements of agricultural productions, such as water or livestock. Below, three brief examples illustrate how actors have started to construct agriculture-based income streams in the Australian context.

Constructing Agriculture-Based Income Streams

The creation of income streams based on agricultural productions is closely connected with a number of assumptions regarding the performance of farmland in financial portfolios, as grounded in financial theory. Simply put, farmland returns consist of two parts, the income return, defined as the portion of the farm revenues or profits attributed to the land as opposed to labour and management, and the capital return, being the change in the market value of the land from year-to-year.[43] Thus, farmland is seen as both productive and appreciating. Based on these calculations, income streams are constructed in various ways by combining the (anticipated) appreciation of farmland values with the returns gained from the associated production in a so-called "own-operate" model, or based on the (anticipated) land appreciation only, in combination with the rent (received from leasing out the land) in an "own-lease out" model.

The US-based asset management company Westchester, which manages retirements saving for Teachers Insurance and Annuity Association – College Retirement Equities Fund (TIAA-CREF), is a prominent example of the application of the "own-lease out" model where the acquired farmland is subsequently leased to tenants that pay a certain price for the lease depending on the value of the land. Westchester manages a global farmland portfolio with some USD 8 billion assets and commitments under management across 7 countries, including the US, Brazil, and Poland.[44] In Australia, Westchester started acquiring

---

[42] N. Larder, S.R. Sippel and N. Argent, "The Redefined Role of Finance in Australian Agriculture", *Australian Geographer* 49 (2018) 3, pp. 397–418.
[43] M. Painter and C. Eves, "The Financial Gains from Adding Farmland to an International Investment Portfolio", *Journal of Real Estate Portfolio Management* 14 (2008) 1, pp. 66.
[44] Westchester Agriculture Asset Management, "Company Profile", http://www.wgimglobal.com/company-profile.

farmland in 2007[45] and has continuously increased their holdings since, amounting to at least 200,000 hectares of farmland owned across New South Wales, Western Australia, Queensland, and Victoria.[46]

The approach of Macquarie Group's investments in primary production in turn represents the own-operate model. The Sydney-based Macquarie Group is a global investment bank and financial services provider and, among others, was a pioneer in infrastructure investments, operating private and public infrastructure funds spread across a multitude of sectors (including toll roads, airports, and energy and communication) and geographies.[47] Currently, Macquarie Infrastructure and Real Assets runs two agricultural funds (Macquarie Pastoral Fund and Macquarie Crop Fund), which manage some 4.5 million hectares of farmland, mostly located in Australia and some investments in Brazil.[48]

Limiting "investment risks" for investors is a key element of successful income stream generation as the goal is not only to create an income stream, as such, but also one that delivers the desired returns for investors while contributing aspects such as non-correlation with other asset classes. Various strategies are employed to limit the investment risks and to realize the desired returns for investors while "asset geographies", based on agricultural productions, are being created. One strategy is the creation of diversity in regard to the investment regions. Regional diversity is mostly based on assumptions about climatic factors, such as rainfall patterns, in different regions or across the northern/southern hemisphere. This means that financial investors attempt to acquire farms across different climatic regions within Australia as well as at a global scale. For example, Westchester's pursues the "goal of owning farmland in all the major grain exporting countries around the world".[49] A second key strategy is to establish economies of scale to balance the risks associated with individual agricultural productions; as one interviewee stated:

---

[45] Westchester Agriculture Asset Management, "Global Thoughts", Newsletter 1 (Winter 2011) 2, pp. 1–4, http://www.wgimglobal.com/sites/default/files/assets/newsletter/final-nwsltr-12-5-11-1-revised.pdf
[46] A. Magnan, "The Financialization of Agri-food in Canada and Australia: Corporate Farmland and Farm Ownership in the Grains and Oilseed Sector", *Journal of Rural Studies* 41 (2015), pp. 1–12.
[47] M.I. Torrance, "Forging Glocal Governance? Urban Infrastructures as Networked Financial Products", *International Journal of Urban and Regional Research* 32 (2008) 1, pp. 1–21.
[48] Macquarie Infrastructure and Real Assets, "Credentials", 31 March 2018, http://static.macquarie.com/dafiles/Internet/mgl/com/mirafunds/about-mira/docs/mira-credentials.pdf?v=8
[49] Westchester Agriculture Asset Management, "Global Thoughts".

You need to design a portfolio that smooths the volatility of those returns. Because you're going to have one farm which is failing and one is doing very well. If you're not big enough to create that scale, then yes, you will expose yourself to a high degree of volatility. (Interview 2017)

Within the "own-lease out" model, this volatility can be smoothed out to certain extent, with the operational risk being shifted to the tenant. At the same time, however, the tenant relationship itself can present a potential risk as "you may have a year where there's no tenant, you can't find a farmer, then you must farm that farm yourself" (Interview 2017). The tenant risk can be minimized in the operation model. Therefore, the different models are associated with different risk characteristics.

A similar income stream construction based on an "own-lease out" relationship has recently emerged for irrigation water.[50] The construction of income streams based on irrigation water relies on a unique and highly complex system of water markets that has been created in Australia over the past twenty years as part of the broader neo-liberal restructuring following the belief that markets are best placed to solve environmental problems. Even though the anticipated positive environmental effects of water trading have not been achieved, the water market has opened up the possibility to construct income streams based on the acquisition and subsequent lease out of water entitlements by financial investors. Asset management firms such as Blue Sky Alternative Investments Limited and Kilter Rural have identified this opportunity and started to purchase and then lease out water entitlements on behalf of their investors.[51] In addition to the immediate income stream achieved from lease incomes, the rationale behind investments equals the case of farmland, namely that water entitlements will appreciate over time and thereby deliver long-term capital growth as water is becoming increasingly scarce.

Lastly, during our research we found a third way of establishing an agriculture-based income stream, illustrating the creativity employed by actors in constructing such income possibilities for investors. In this case, the investor uses capital flows to acquire cattle that are being raised on "host farms". While the host farmer receives a fixed amount of capital to raise the cattle as well as potentially undertake farm improvements, the investor receives the income that is

---

[50] N. Larder, S.R. Sippel and N. Argent, "The Redefined Role of Finance in Australian Agriculture", *Australian Geographer* 49 (2018) 3, pp. 397–418.
[51] Blue Sky Alternative Thinking, "Our Real Assets", (2018), https://blueskyfunds.com.au/what-we-do/real-assets/; Kilter Rural, "Welcome to Kilter Rural", (2017), http://www.kilterrural.com/

realized from selling the cattle. In this way, the investor receives a predictable income stream within a short turn over of 12 months without needing to commit to a long-term investment of buying one particular farm in a specific location and taking on the associated risks around farm management:

> They [the investors] don't have to buy the farm, so they haven't got a big equity layout. They're effectively getting what they want. They're getting the beef, not the farm, while they're getting the produce from the farm. It's still the same as running a farm. They're getting a diversity of spread, because they're not fixed on the one location. If they bought the farm and tried to raise beef, they would be in a position where they effectively would be fixed to that farm. (Interview, 2017)

As our interviewee explained, for the host farmer this works as "a release of capital":

> It's very rarely that you'll find a farm where they have a 100 per cent equity, and they have a surplus of cash to run the operation. In most cases, even if they have a 100 per cent equity, they will borrow against that equity to draw down the cash to run their operations, including buying the livestock. [...] The way that we sell it to our farmers is we're saying, "Look, you don't have to go and borrow that AU$2.5 million to buy livestock. We will give you the livestock, and we will give you an AU$1.50 a kilo for every kilo that you put on. And you can then go to the bank and borrow that, put improvements on here, which is a capital improvement, which will give you value". (Interview 2017)

The provision of such new sources of equity capital to farmers is a common argument also often made by farmland and water investors, which, given the high levels of debt among Australian farmers, responds to the need for alternative capital sources to maintain farming.[52] Hence, in a nutshell, the cattle income stream also relies on a certain division and distribution of activities, capital flows, and benefits as well as mechanisms of risk sharing between the different parties. The interests between the parties align with the aim of receiving equity capital – non-debt cash flow – on the side of the "host" as well as the income stream derived from the benefits that can be made, or are anticipated to be made, from agricultural production on the side of the investor. Contrary to farmland and water investments, however, investment decisions do not include appreciation of the asset but are purely grounded in certain assumptions regarding the development of commodity markets, in this case the development of global cattle markets. At the same time, economies of scale are

---

[52] N. Larder, S.R. Sippel and N. Argent, "The Redefined Role of Finance in Australian Agriculture", *Australian Geographer* 49 (2018) 3, pp. 397–418.

a crucial component as the investment is structured around a network of a large number of some 170 host farms gathered by the intermediary.

Dis/Articulating Agri-Food Spaces

How are current investment activities respatializing the existing patterns within agricultural commodity chains? After having presented the two groupings of actors and their investment activities individually, the last section draws them together and sums up the processes of dis/articulation as well as associated respatializations of agri-food relationships they entail.

First, we have shown that investment flows by Chinese companies, on the one hand, and financial actors, on the other, are incentivized in substantially different ways, leading to two fundamentally different logics applied to agricultural commodity chains (as illustrated in Figure 1). Chinese companies have invested in Australia against the backdrop of the interest of "feeding China", and thereby integrate primary production activities into a broader agri-business strategy to supply Chinese markets, or rather certain consumer groups within Chinese markets, with specific high-quality "premium" products. The direct acquisition of primary productions as a part of the "feeding China" strategy is a new dynamic that did not exist until recently. In order to realize the anticipated benefits from growing Chinese demand for beef and high-quality protein products, the mere ownership of overseas farmland for beef production, however, is considered insufficient by many Chinese investors. Rather, what is required is the construction of a "paddock-to-plate story", through which investors pursue connecting their primary production activities in Australia with market demand in China. Hence, strategies of vertical integration constitute an essential part of the investment logic driving agro-investments from Chinese actors. By increasing ownership or control over various stages of the commodity chain, from production to processing to retail and marketing, investors endeavour to strengthen their influence over commodity prices, ensure stability of supply, and enhance control over product quality – a key factor given the recent history of Chinese food scandals and low levels of consumer trust in domestic food production. Crucially, and in stark contrast to agro-investments by finance-backed actors, investment value can only be realized by forging new articulations within commodity chains that allow Chinese investors to control the supply of agricultural commodities from the Australian rural spaces of production to the geographies of demand emerging in China.

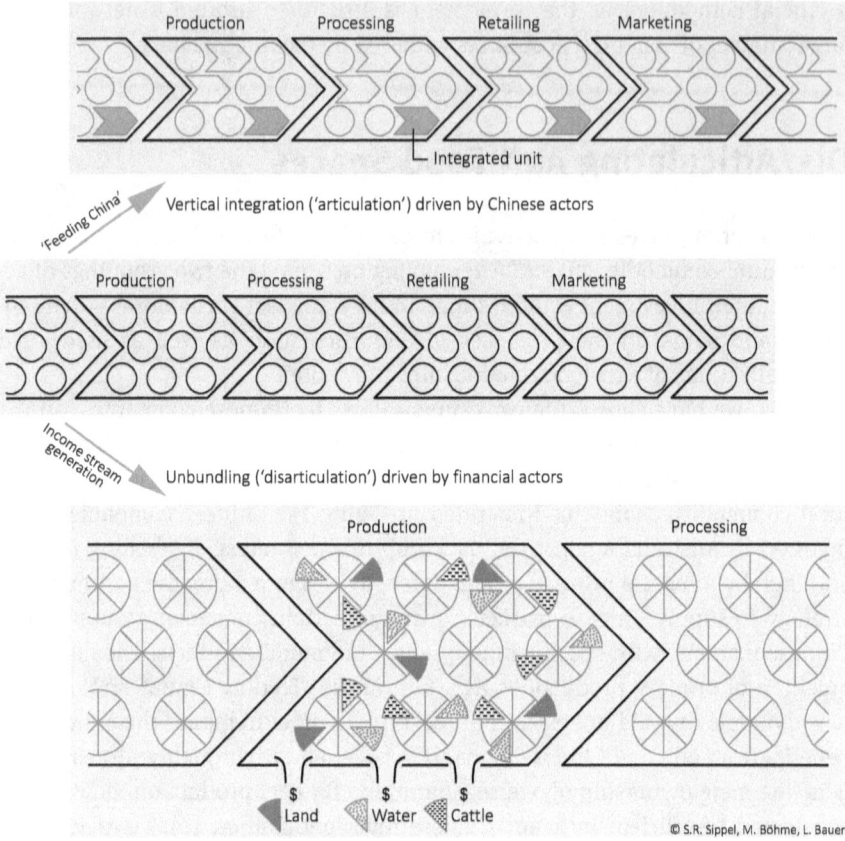

Figure 1: Respatializations of agri-food relationships.

Capital inflows from the financial sector in turn reconceptualize agricultural resources as "assets", namely as things that are able to deliver reliable income streams for investors in the future. The main goal is the investment of money for the creation of more money with agriculture serving as the "vehicle" through which this multiplication process takes place. It is therefore not the agricultural product itself nor considerations of food security, food safety, or quality of the produce that are of concern to investors but rather the question whether the capital invested will increase within the respective timeframe and to the expected degree. "Real facts" concerning the agricultural production and the quality of the food are still important as they determine the return that can be achieved. However, they are placed at the second rank as they are necessary for the reliability of the income stream but do not constitute a primary goal in itself. As demonstrated, income streams can be based on rental payments, commodity sales, and resource appreciation, either in separate or combined ways. This process entails disarticulations within agricultural commodity chains because agricultural elements and activities need to be conceptually unbundled to deliver such income streams. The construction of agriculture-based income streams relies on specific prerequisites, namely the possibility to acquire agricultural components in an individual fashion that is detached from the rest of the farming activity as a whole. The conceptual step that is undertaken here is to compartmentalize and divide farm elements instead of imagining them as being tied or belonging together. In other words, disarticulating agricultural elements and activities within the commodity chain is a key component in the construction of income streams. These disarticulations do not just happen by themselves but require active work to change the social and institutional fabric within commodity chains, including the establishment of new markets, the promotion of a "tenant culture" in farming, or the setting up of respective legal instruments to allow for capital in- and outflows to take place.

Secondly, both Chinese and financial investments in Australia are part of global strategies pursued by the actors. Both groups of actors employ a "global gaze" at the planet, where every region is – at least hypothetically – assessed in terms of the potential value it can provide to the respective goals pursued. However, this global gaze is again motivated by different goals and associated assessment criteria. Since the official promulgation of the agricultural "going out" strategy, the Chinese government has encouraged overseas agricultural investment in a number of regions and countries. Virtually any country can be targeted for investment according to a wide range of criteria. These include the abundance of land, water, and other agricultural resources; the presence of developed commodity chains linking production, processing, and logistics; the possibility to set up technical assistance and agricultural cooperation projects with less-developed countries within China's South-South cooperation framework; as well as countries or regions where agricultural investment can be tied to broader diplomatic initiatives, such as China's "One Belt, One Road" (OBOR) initiative.[53] In the case of Australia, investment opportunities are constructed around the vision of mobilizing investment to unlock Australia's potential for becoming the "food bowl" of Asia.[54] Australia's proximity to the Asian market and its reputation as a producer of high-quality protein foods such as beef,

---

53 E. Gooch and F. Gale, "China's Foreign Agriculture Investments", EIB-192, US Department of Agriculture, Economic Research Service (2018), https://www.ers.usda.gov/webdocs/publications/88572/eib-192.pdf?, p. 21.
54 C. Ma, *Fu Aodaliya Touzi Zhinan* [How to Invest in Australia], Beijing: Zhongguo Shangwu ChubanShe [China Commerce and Trade Press], 2014.

dairy, and sheep, which enjoy a growing demand amongst Chinese consumers, are key components shaping investor interest.

In principal, financial investors equally consider any regional context worldwide as a potential "asset geography". In line with the goal of generating reliable income streams, investment decisions are determined by an assessment of the risk-return characteristics of investment contexts, where potential risks involved with investments are weighed against the anticipated chances for return. Limiting investment risks, that is to say reducing the risk of low or negative returns, is hence a key component in assessing and compiling investment contexts for portfolios. The potential of new asset geographies is assessed according to assumptions in regard to complementarity and correlation with other investment regions and potential political and economic risks while aiming at achieving economies of scale across regionally diverse contexts. Thus, although the agricultural strategies of the two groupings of actors investigated in this chapter are global in terms of their outlook, our research highlights that investment processes, strategies, and interactions always need to be considered in light of the specific combinations of global and regional aspects shaping them.

Lastly, both types of investments have the potential to challenge the currently dominant spatial patterns – the spatial order – within the agri-food system. New spatialities emerge that connect Australian farms and food industries with Chinese producers in new ways via integrated supply chains controlled by Chinese companies. These emerging spatialities counter existing spatial patterns within the agri-food system as they challenge the historically dominant "North-South" direction of capital flows. Moreover, players such as the New Hope Group seek to challenge the hegemony of large Western-based agri-businesses such as Cargill. The flow of finance capital into agricultural productions equally challenges existing spatialities within agricultural commodity chains. As capital from private individuals in North America and Europe is being channelled into agricultural productions, not only are new actors – savers and asset managers – becoming enmeshed in agricultural commodity chains in new ways, producing new linkages between producers and savers in different parts of the world. Financial capital also comes with new logics and rationales and thereby reconfigures the existing power geometries between commodity chain actors.

To conclude, the conjunction of events in 2007/08 can be interpreted as a transformative moment in global agri-food relationships that has renewed the interest in agricultural production and farmland from diverse groups of actors. As a result, new forms of capital have flowed into agricultural resources around the world, which involve multiple and contradictory processes of respatialization of agri-food relationships. As we have demonstrated with Australia, these agro-investments crystallize distinct investment logics: control over agricultural resources to cater to changing consumer demands on the one hand and the construction of agriculture as a financial asset class to provide investors with a reliable income stream on the one hand and. Being at play simultaneously, these investment logics produce fundamentally different spatial outcomes, giving rise to conflicting dynamics of articulation and disarticulation within agri-food chains. Bringing these simultaneous but fundamentally different respatializations to the fore is an important step towards de-essentializing debates on global agro-investments. At the same time, while these investment logics need to be analytically separated, they cannot be treated in isolation if we are to gain a better understanding of the multi-layered transformations reshaping global agri-food spaces. The focus on the spatial transformations within commodity chains allows for this diversity of aligning as well as diverging dynamics within agri-food relationships to be captured.

Hannes Warnecke-Berger
The Spatial Turn and Economics: Migration, Remittances, and Transnational Economic Space

Introduction

Space has become an all-pervasive topic. Particularly in the humanities and social sciences, the spatial turn propelled a rethinking of the influence of space and different spatialities on human behaviour and vice versa. However, it seems like that the reverse took place in economics. Space – as a still prominent trend of classical economics – remains rather unreflected. Mainstream economics treat space as state-based, essentially capitalist, and as internally as well as externally homogenous. Economics are the last but still very powerful bastion of so-called "methodological nationalism"[1] and "methodological territorialism".[2] Definitions of economics include a rather strong but unquestioned notion of space, territory, and state. Economics are about supply, demand, and the market as well as about production, consumption, and transaction within a *given* space. International economics, then, is about economic transactions among these *given* spaces.

Three empirical interventions indicate, however, that "methodological nationalism" and "methodological territorialism" are becoming increasingly difficult to defend. Firstly, in recent decades, foreign direct investment has grown faster than world trade, and world trade has grown faster than world production.[3] In a nutshell, more and more places have been integrated to produce the same world economic output. This trend both reflects capital exports as well as commodity trade. Second, financial markets have continued to grow even stronger than the real economy, and the financial crisis of 2008 highlighted that the production of financial value is becoming increasingly disconnected from spaces where

---

[1] A. Wimmer and N. Glick Schiller, "Methodological Nationalism and Beyond: Nation-State Building, Migration and the Social Sciences", *Global Networks* 2 (2002) 4, pp. 301–334.
[2] E. Sheppard, "Geography, Nature, and the Question of Development", *Dialogues in Human Geography* 1 (2011) 1, pp. 46–75.
[3] P. Dicken, *Global Shift: Mapping the Changing Contours of the World Economy*, New York: Guilford, 2011.

real economic production has been taking place.[4] Third, the strength of global migration flows highlight that labour markets are far from homogenous and unlikely to remain in equilibrium. The great majority of migrants come from or are in the Global South, and in recent decades, especially South-North migration has been increasing.[5] Reflecting these issues, recent discussions on commodity and value chains,[6] transnational corporations and production networks,[7] financialization,[8] and finally migration and remittances have made important claims in redefining the notion of economic space.

Remittances by international migrants are particularly informative in this regard. Remittances are monetary transfers and thus part of a financial circuit. Remittances connect the places where migrants work and earn money with the faraway places where family members spend this money. Since the late 1990s, remittances exceed official development aid, portfolio investments, and in some parts of the world even foreign direct investments.[9] While the entire flow of remittances remains stable and even increases, it only does so as migrants continue to send a veritable share of income to their home families.

I argue that remittances are initially the result of translocal relations among migrants and their family members. My primary focus lies on migrants living and working in the Global North and maintaining these relations through remittances to their families living in the Global South. Remittances interlink different places that are asymmetrically integrated in the world economy. As an expanding financial circuit, however, remittances create a transnational economic space. Remittances therefore posit an ideal starting point in rethinking economic space.

This chapter first problematizes the notion of space in economics and then continues by offering an alternative political economy approach to space as being

---

[4] M. Heires and A. Nölke (eds.), *Politische Ökonomie der Finanzialisierung*, Wiesbaden: VS Verlag für Sozialwissenschaften, 2014.
[5] M. Czaika and H. de Haas, "The Globalization of Migration: Has the World Become More Migratory?", *International Migration Review* 48 (2014) 2, pp. 283–323; E. Dickinson, *Globalization and Migration: A World in Motion*, Lanham: Rowman & Littlefield, 2017.
[6] G. Gereffi and M. Korzeniewicz (eds.), *Commodity Chains and Global Capitalism*, Westport: Greenwood Press, 1994; B. Selwyn, "Global Value Chains and Human Development: A Class-Relational Framework", *Third World Quarterly* 37 (2016) 10, pp. 1768–1786.
[7] Dicken, *Global Shift*; J. Henderson et al., "Global Production Networks and the Analysis of Economic Development", *Review of International Political Economy* 9 (2002) 3, pp. 436–464.
[8] G.A. Epstein (ed.), *Financialization and the World Economy*, Cheltenham: Edward Elgar, 2005; E. Helleiner, "Explaining the Globalization of Financial Markets: Bringing States Back In", *Review of International Political Economy* 2 (1995) 2, pp. 379–389.
[9] World Bank, *Migration and Remittances Factbook 2016*, Washington DC: World Bank, 2016.

produced through economic practices. This chapter argues that this leads us to an understanding of space in economics that combines the topography of economic places and the relationality of these places. Bringing these two perspectives – on topographies and relationalities – together, the chapter finally shows how remittances produce transnational economic spaces.

Economics and the Indifference towards Space: A Deconstruction

Standard economic textbooks either focus on individual choices on the background of scarcity in the case of neo-classical microeconomics or on national accounts in the case of macroeconomics. David Ricardo's classic text on foreign trade is a good illustration. He justifies his theory of foreign trade in stating:

> Thus England would give the produce of the labour of 100 men, for the produce of the labour of 80. Such an exchange could not take place between the individuals of the same country. The labour of 100 Englishmen cannot be given for that of 80 Englishmen, but the produce of the labour of 100 Englishmen may be given for the produce of the labour of 80 Portuguese, 60 Russians, or 120 East Indians.[10]

Three things come together in this conception of space in Ricardo's work. Firstly, space is internally homogenous since factors of production are completely mobile within the same country. Secondly, other spaces demarcate this space externally. Between these spaces, factors of production are immobile and only the produce of labour, commodities, as well as money and gold circulate. Thirdly, in between these spaces, a national border maintains the distinction between internal mobility and external immobility. As the other classics, Ricardo does not make a difference between micro- and macroeconomics. Nevertheless, his text illustrates that economics is essentially about the relation among different homogenous spaces. These three criteria still define the core of economic space as the system of national accounts highlights. This convention of world statistical data defines economic space as the "geographic territory administered by a government within which persons, goods, and capital circulate freely".[11]

---

10 D. Ricardo, *On the Principles of Political Economy and Taxation*, London: John Murray, 1817, ch. 7.17.
11 Commission of the European Communities et al., "System of National Accounts 1993", (1993), p. 402.

In addition to national economic spaces, the same perspective describes economic spaces beyond the national territory as homogenous spatialities encompassing more than one single state, such as currency areas, free trade zones, tax unions, or common markets.[12] Recently, notions such as regions[13] and industrial clusters[14] have received increasing attention. However, these concepts rely on a spatial homology. While these concepts subvert the centrality of state space, they tend to replace state by region, cluster, or network. Nonetheless, each of these spatialities remain in symmetrical order in relation to each other. Even though the importance of state space has been reduced, economic space is still theoretically interpreted "like a set of Russian dolls: moving thought the various levels reveals no specificity, but in the contrary process the duplication of identical operating systems".[15]

While the classics of economic thought have been keen defenders of the national economy, the neo-classic revolution intended to abolish this national foundation of economics. By focusing on rational choice decision-making of individuals, microlevel analysis has gained greater consideration. Maintaining the spatial homology, neo-classic economics treat spaces as singular places.[16] Neo-classic authors thus tend to neglect economic macrodynamics, which are an economic order of emergence apart from the sum of its different singular parts. Even critical authors share this neo-classical assumption in acknowledging that "the totality of economic activities is so unstructured and complex that it cannot be an object of effective calculation, management, governance, or guidance".[17]

Economic space becomes a "global mosaic", as Scott paradigmatically claims in his writing on regions. Interestingly, he continues in stating that this mosaic

---

[12] See, e.g., B. Balassa, "Towards a Theory of Economic Integration", *Kyklos* 14 (1961) 1, pp. 1–17; R.A. Mundell, "A Theory of Optimum Currency Areas", *American Economic Review* 51 (1961) 4, pp. 657–665.

[13] P.R. Krugman et al., *The Spatial Economy: Cities, Regions and International Trade*, Cambridge: Massachusetts Institute of Technology Press, 1999; J.D. Sachs, "Institutions Matter, but Not for Everything: The Role of Geography and Resource Endowments in Development Shouldn't be Underestimated", *Finance & Development* 40 (2003) 2, pp. 38–41.

[14] H. Schmitz and K. Nadvi, "Clustering and Industrialization: Introduction", *World Development* 27 (1999) 9, pp. 1503–1514; M.E. Porter, "Clusters and the New Economics of Competition", *Harvard Business Review* 76 (1998) 6, pp. 77–90.

[15] B. Lepetit, *The Pre-Industrial Urban System: France, 1740–1840*, Cambridge: Cambridge University Press, 1994, p. 403.

[16] E. Sheppard, "Geographical Political Economy", *Journal of Economic Geography* 11 (2011) 2, pp. 319–331.

[17] B. Jessop and S. Oosterlynck, "Cultural Political Economy: On Making the Cultural Turn Without Falling into Soft Economic Dociology", *Geoforum* 39 (2008) 3, p. 1157, pp. 1155–1169.

"is beginning to override the core-periphery relationships that have hitherto characterized much of the macro geography of capitalist development".[18] Because of global economic interactions, and following neo-classical thought based on equilibrium models, mainstream economics expects global convergence towards a perfect functioning of market forces and "a homogenous economic space without borders and frictions".[19] In this perspective, the world consists of one singular economic space, one single world market, and one single capitalist space. In this perspective, economics are about capitalist space, since other economic spaces would not even exist. Economics then tend to fall into "capitalocentrism".[20] Non-capitalistic economic spaces remain outside the research scope.

While large parts of economics do not approach economic space as an object of investigation, but take it for granted, the same authors construct economic space implicitly. In sum, space is still prominently treated in economics as state-based, essentially capitalist, and as internally as well as externally homogenous. The spatial turn, in contrary, provides compelling arguments to rethink these rather strong assumptions as it widens the view on the permeable nature of state borders, the existence of other-than-capitalist economies with specific spatialities, as well as on the possibility of structural heterogeneities.

Towards a Political Economy of Economic Space

The question of what is an economic space – or rather space as a result of economic practices and interaction – reaches deep into the core of economic *and* spatial theorizing. A possible answer furthermore should be able to both develop a general understanding of economic space and at the same time to differentiate between varying forms of economic space. The following idea integrates both dimensions into a proper political economy approach of processes of spatialization that are mainly driven forward by economic interaction and practices.

---

18 A.J. Scott, "Global City-Regions and the New World System", in: S. Yusuf et al. (eds.), *Local Dynamics in an Era of Globalization: 21st Century Catalysts for Development*, Oxford: Oxford University Press, 2000, pp. 84–91, at 87.
19 C. Berndt and M. Boeckler, "Performative Regional (Dis)Integration: Transnational Markets, Mobile Commodities, and Bordered North-South Differences", *Environment and Planning A* 43 (2011) 5, pp. 1057–1078, at 1057.
20 K. Gibson and J. Graham, *The End of Capitalism (As We Knew It): A Feminist Critique of Political Economy*, Minneapolis: University of Minnesota Press, 2006, p. 6.

I argue that the birth of economic space is related to the evolution of economic surplus. On the one hand, to enhance and manage economic surplus societies need to create economic topographies that interlink production, exchange, and consumption. On the other hand, economic surplus generates questions of distribution, the use of political power, and hence respatialization. Both issues are interwoven, and as a relation to each other, result in specific economic spatialities.

Topographies of Economic Space

In a Marxist perspective, it is argued that humans appropriate nature in a metabolic relation with their external world.[21] With existing economic surplus, humans emancipate themselves from nature and begin to develop a built environment.[22] As soon as economic surplus evolves, a social division of labour arises, and an initial rise in productivity leads to the diversification of places of production, places of consumption, and places of exchange.[23] In the process of sedentarization, a place-based economy develops into a spatialized economy. Following this, societies need to relate diverging places of production, consumption, and exchange to each other. I call this horizontal relationship between production, consumption, and exchange *economic topography*.

Three particular issues regarding this relationship are crucial. The first issue consists in the substitutability of places where economic practices take place.[24] A place of production is fully substitutable if the same product can be produced at the same costs without involving transaction costs at any other place. In contrast, an economic place is non-substitutable if the good can exclusively be produced at one specific place. Economic spaces thus interlink various places of differing substitutability. These spaces are neither fully

---

[21] N. Smith, *Uneven Development: Nature, Capital and the Production of Space*, Oxford: Basil Blackwell, 1984.
[22] D. Christian, *Maps of Time: An Introduction to Big History*, Berkeley: University of California Press, 2004; V.G. Childe, "The Urban Revolution", *The Town Planning Review* 21 (1950) 1, pp. 3–17.
[23] D. Massey, "Uneven Development: Social Change and Spatial Divisions of Labor", in: T.J. Barnes et al. (eds.), *Reading Economic Geography*, Oxford: Blackwell, 2004, pp. 111–124; R.A. Walker, "Class, Division of Labour and Employment in Space", in: D. Gregory and J. Urry (eds.), *Social Relations and Spatial Structures* (Critical Human Geography), Basingstoke: Palgrave Macmillan, 1985, pp. 164–189.
[24] M. Storper, "Territories, Flows, and Hierarchies in the Global Economy", in: K.R. Cox (ed.), *Spaces of Globalization: Reasserting the Power of the Local* (Perspectives on Economic Change), New York: Guilford, 1997, pp. 19–44.

territorialized nor completely deterritorialized. Such economic spaces often rather take the form of networks. I focus here on this kind of economic spaces that are networks of related places.[25]

Second, such economic spaces are composed of three interlinked spheres: production, exchange, and consumption. Each of these spheres follow its own logic.[26] In the sphere of production, labour fabricates goods. In the sphere of consumption, on the other side, humans use up these goods and a single person is connected with a single good. Both spheres create their microspatialities, such as the manufacturing plant, the factory, the supermarket, the shopping mall, etc. Finally, the sphere of exchange connects both production and consumption. This sphere links places of production with places of consumption as well as internally to each sphere, such as labour with capital in production as well as consumers with goods in the sphere of consumption. Value comes into circulation through exchange, which involves the circulation of either humans or artefacts and goods.

Third, there is a time lag between production and consumption. Once a good is produced, it has to be exchanged and brought to the consumer, who then consumes the good. The time between these different steps – that is to say, between the production process, exchange, and consumption – involves circulation costs.[27] Simultaneously, this time lag attempts to control time and therefore to minimize circulation costs. The invention of money, for instance, is one mechanism to control the time lag.[28] Therefore, economic

---

[25] The concept of networks gained significance in describing a multiple and simultaneous existence of forms, modes, sets of social relations, institutions, as well as regulations. The trend of confronting nation-state rule with networks of simultaneous modes of control is even more far-reaching since the discussion on networks is in a way endemic. Networks topologically interlink and relate different places on a horizontal level in producing links, nodes, and ties. See H. Leitner and E. Sheppard, "The City is Dead, Long Live the Net: Harnessing European Interurban Networks for a Neoliberal Agenda", *Antipode* 34 (2002) 3, pp. 495–518. While the discussion on economic networks shows that capital, labour, and commodities are crossing national borders by moving from one place to another, this discussion does not consider that the same processes account for converging economic spaces towards a unifying homogenous economic entity, in fact creating new borders as well as profound asymmetries. The concept of networks is thus an important step towards modelling economic spaces. However, the same concept tends to flatten hierarchies and power differentials.

[26] M. Storper and R. Walker, *The Capitalist Imperative: Territory, Technology, and Industrial Growth*, Malden: Blackwell, 1989.

[27] This was early on discovered by K. Marx, *Grundrisse der Kritik der politischen Ökonomie*, MEW 42, Berlin: Dietz Verlag, 1972 (1857/1858), p. 430; And again highlighted by D. Harvey, *Spaces of Capital: Towards a Critical Geography*, Abingdon: Routledge, 2001.

[28] M. Binswanger, "Money Creation, Profits, and Growth: Monetary Aspects of Economic Evolution", in: E. Helmstädter and M. Perlman (eds.), *Behavioral Norms, Technological Progress,*

spaces are costly in the sense that they require the investment of costs to overcome distances through transportation.[29] Therefore, actors aim to find solutions to reduce the distance in time and space between production and consumption, which results in diverse forms of respatialization.

While in a static model economic spaces are networks of interlinked places, in a dynamic model these spaces function as time-dependent circuits of value and thus of labour, goods, and money.[30] In this rather substantivist perspective, I define economic topographies as an outcome of the people's struggle for survival and the management of economic surplus.[31] Economic topographies constitute circuits of value across space and time. They reflect how people make a living through production, exchange, and consumption of goods and artefacts produced by humans. Economic spaces are hence networked formations of places of production, exchange, and consumption, functioning in time as circuits of production and social reproduction.

Relationality of Economic Space

Maintaining the division of labour and the (re)distribution of economic surplus necessarily involves political power.[32] In this perspective, it is (almost) impossible to describe autonomous and static economic spaces because they obviously do not exist on their own. Spaces produced through economic practices are

---

and Economic Dynamics: Studies in Schumpeterian Economics, Ann Arbor: University of Michigan Press, 1996, pp. 413–438, at 415; A.T. Paul, *Die Gesellschaft des Geldes: Entwurf einer monetären Theorie der Moderne*, Wiesbaden: VS Verlag für Sozialwissenschaften, 2012, p. 156.

29 E. Sheppard, "Transportation in a Capitalist Space-Economy: Transportation Demand, Circulation Time, and Transportation Innovations", *Environment and Planning A* 22 (1990) 8, pp. 1007–1024; E. Sheppard and T. Barnes, *The Capitalist Space Economy: Geographical Analysis after Ricardo, Marx and Sraffa*, London: Unwin Hyman, 1990.

30 R. Lee, "'Nice Maps, Shame About the Theory?' Thinking Geographically About the Economic", *Progress in Human Geography* 26 (2002) 3, pp. 333–355; R. Lee, "The Ordinary Economy: Tangled up in Values and Geography", *Transactions of the Institute of British Geographers* 31 (2006) 4, pp. 413–432.

31 In arguing not to forget the physical nature of the economy, hence survival, I maintain a substantivist position associated with the work of both Marx as well as K. Polanyi, "The Economy As Instituted Process", in: K. Polanyi et al. (eds.), *Trade and Market in the Early Empires: Economies in History and Theory*, Glencoe: Free Press, 1957, pp. 243–269; for an overview on the substantivist/formalist debate, see, e.g., R.R. Wilk, *Economies and Cultures: Foundations of Economic Anthropology*, Boulder: Westview Press, 1996.

32 H. Bernstein, *Class Dynamics of Agrarian Change*, Nova Scotia: Fernwood, 2010.

related to those produced through political practices and interaction as well as imagination. Introducing political power into seemingly flat economic topographies thus broadens the perspective on the vertical relational character of such spaces, which comprises relations among human beings and artefacts, as well as of relations among objects and subjects. People create this relation through respatialization, which can be more specifically understood as the "ordering of living entities and social goods" and the "positioning in relation to other positionings".[33]

I argue that for these processes of respatialization to become effective or even dominant the availability of and actors' access to economic surplus is crucial. While economic topographies evolve out of the division of labour on a horizontal level between production, exchange, and consumption, the relational character of space is rooted in the actors' strategies in confining and managing this topography. Respatialization, in this regard, means to establish borders, define inflows and outflows, allocate labour and capital, access economic surplus, impose property rights, and therefore bring topographically chaotic and potentially boundless economic practices "in order". Through respatialization, actors create vertical links between and among themselves and other actors and places, and they create these ties and links with different intensity.

Respatialization hence involve the use of political power in arranging and shaping space, redefining links among places where economic practices take place, making some of these links more possible than others, and in turn imposing costly barriers on other links. Respatialization therefore introduces a vertical level to the horizontal topographical layer.

Different strategies of respatialization relate to different economic spheres. In the sphere of exchange, for instance, respatialization as confining interlinkages of economic places becomes most apparent in the formation of monetary systems, ultimately controlled by centralized state apparatuses.[34] Currency areas are spaces confined by the availability of a legal tender, in which respatialization minimizes transaction costs between places located within this space. At the same time, transaction costs beyond the space created in this way increase. In this regard, respatialization involves political power and enables economic

---

33 M. Löw, "The Constitution of Space: The Structuration of Spaces through the Simultaneity of Effect and Perception", *European Journal of Social Theory* 11 (2008) 1, pp. 25–49, at 35.
34 B.J. Cohen, *The Geography of Money*, Ithaca: Cornell University Press, 1998; E. Helleiner, *The Making of National Money: Territorial Currencies in Historical Perspective*, Ithaca: Cornell University Press, 2003; N. Dodd, "Money and the Nation-State: Contested Boundaries of Monetary Sovereignty in Geopolitics", *International Sociology* 10 (1995) 2, pp. 139–154; G.K. Ingham, *The Nature of Money*, Cambridge: Polity, 2004.

practices and interaction among economic places within this space as well as restrains economic practices beyond and across other spaces. Likewise, the spheres of production and consumption receive their vertical dimension through processes of respatialization. Accordingly, class relations among workers and entrepreneurs come into being also as spatialized power relations. The "fabrication of labour"[35] as a class can be interpreted as a struggle over collective goods, in which labour eventually accepts to focus on social struggles within certain boundaries. Finally, in the sphere of consumption, respatialization enables and fixes social practices as well as produces further spatialities, such as the supermarket, the shopping mall, etc.[36] Consumption then expresses needs and desires as "an ongoing process rather than a momentary act of purchase".[37] As an effect of ordering economic practices and places where these practices are located, economic life becomes organized.

By focusing on political power as the inherent process of respatialization, inequalities, power differentials, and asymmetries come to the fore. Different strategies of respatialization create variable depths of horizontal as well as vertical linkages and ties. Eventually, the metaphor of a topographical economic network gains a third dimension by expanding and growing in depth.

The relationality of economic spaces, which emerges from processes of spatialization, further differentiates the notion of economic space. While the topography of places on a horizontal axis, the separation of different economic spheres, and the rise of linkages of places in the form of networks refers to the horizontal dimension of economic space, the relationality of economic space refers to the vertical dimension of economic space. The creation of connections among different places simultaneously leads to the relative ignoring of other places, which is based not only on economic but also on political power relations. In this sense, economic space then is always politico-economic.

Analytically, these layers of space can be analysed independently from one another. In reality, they overlap and a veritable struggle over the "bringing into congruence" and the "synchronization" of both layers of space evolves as there are clearly tensions between both spatial layers. A place-based economic network tends to be expansive, following the logic of comparative advantage, whereas other actors might focus on fixing places and imposing borders.

---

[35] R. Biernacki, *The Fabrication of Labor: Germany and Britain, 1640–1914*, Berkeley: University of California Press, 1995; R. Biernacki, "Labor as an Imagined Commodity", *Politics & Society* 29 (2001) 2, pp. 173–206.
[36] R. Hudson, *Economic Geographies: Circuits, Flows and Spaces*, London: Sage, 2005, p. 167.
[37] L. Crewe, "Geographies of Retailing and Consumption", *Progress in Human Geography* 24 (2000) 2, pp. 275–290, at 280.

Different results of economic respatialization – such as a national economy within politically established boundaries or a transnational economic space interlinking, merging, and even overcoming yet established economic spaces – then evolves out of processes through which spatialized social practices at specific places are increasingly condensed, synchronized, and structured. In turn, they might emerge into stabilized spatial format. Such a perspective broadens the analysis to include agency, social conflict, and social change.

Economic Globalization and the Subversive Role of Migration and Remittances

The impressive advances during the nineteenth century in technology and transportation, among other things, led for the first time in world history to a "global condition" – to "entanglement on a global scale".[38] This was also the "age of mass migration".[39] Even though human mobility is part of human life,[40] the reduction of transportation costs globally increased the propensity to migrate. Many migrants during the nineteenth century sent money back home to improve living conditions of relatives left behind[41] or paid for overseas tickets to finance family reunifications.[42] Migration, potential migrant savings, as well as remittances thus go hand in hand.

However, further improvements in technology and communications in the last quarter of the twentieth century again led to an impressive reduction in transaction costs. In contrast to the age of mass migration, where the decrease in costs was related to transportation of goods and people, today, this reduction is primarily related to financial transactions and money.

---

38 C. Bright and M. Geyer, "Benchmarks of Globalization: The Global Condition, 1850–2010", in: D. Northrop (ed.), *A Companion to World History*, Hoboken: Wiley-Blackwell, 2012, pp. 285–300, at 288.
39 T.J. Hatton and J.G. Williamson, *The Age of Mass Migration: Causes and Economic Impact*, Oxford: Oxford University Press, 1998; T.J. Hatton and J.G. Williamson, *Global Migration and the World Economy: Two Centuries of Policy and Performance*, Cambridge: Massachusetts Institute of Technology Press, 2005.
40 Christian, *Maps of Time*.
41 R. Esteves and D. Khoudour-Castéras, "Remittances, Capital Flows and Financial Development during the Mass Migration Period, 1870–1913", *European Review of Economic History* 15 (2011) 3, pp. 443–474; G.B. Magee and A.S. Thompson, "'Lines of Credit, Debts of Obligation': Migrant Remittances to Britain, c.1875–1913", *The Economic History Review* 59 (2006) 3, pp. 539–577.
42 Hatton and Williamson, *The Age of Mass Migration*, p. 14.

Remittances are one specific outcome of this process. Since the late 1990s, remittances exceed official development aid, portfolio investments, and in some parts of the world even foreign direct investments. Global remittances accounted for USD 601 billion in 2015.[43] As with migration, remittances are unequally distributed: a stable share of 73 per cent of migrant dollars flows to developing societies. In some cases, developing societies are even dependent on these inflows.

In analytical terms, the disruptive role of migration and remittances consists of enlarging economic circuits of production and social reproduction. Migration and remittances affect both layers of economic space: First, migration and remittances necessarily change factor endowments of economic places. This leads to a shifting substitutability of places and consequently shapes economic topographies.[44] Second, both migration and remittances cross political borders that are yet established and therefore provoke the respatialization of this particular order. Since different actors as well as different places are integrated into these expanding circuits – and each of those actors and places with different strengths *and* towards different depths – specific places and nodes gain more importance in contrast to others. Some places of remittances are integrated, others not, and others finally are even excluded. Some actors strategically intervene in these circuits, others not, and others again are even actively excluded. Consequently, spatial tensions and frictions arise, eventually provoking the redefinition of established borders, the challenging of already effective spatializations, as well as future access to circuits of production and social reproduction.

In the following, I show how this subversive role of migration and remittances tends to produce transnational economies. Thereby, I argue that the way in which remittances are produced is a particular form of respatialization, resulting in the emergence of transnational economic spaces.

---

43 World Bank, *Migration and Remittances Factbook 2016*, p. 23.
44 In economic models, they are both a balancing mechanism, as labour should move from low paid to high paid and capital from less to more productive areas and countries. See J.R. Harris and M.P. Todaro, "Migration, Unemployment and Development: A Two-Sector Analysis", *The American Economic Review* 60 (1970) 1, pp. 126–142. However, even though migration and remittances continue, the North-South divergence remained stable, as W.R. Thompson and R. Reuveny, *Limits to Globalization: North-South Divergence*, Abingdon: Routledge, 2010 convincingly argue.

The Decision to Remit: The Emergence of Translocal Moral Economies

I argue that remittances originate from translocal moral economies, which connect specific places from where migrants send money with specific places to where migrants send this money. As discussions on migrant transnationalism show, migrants do not simply emigrate and immigrate, leave their culture behind, and assimilate into new cultural contexts. Quite on the contrary, migrants maintain social relationships with their home families.[45] This relationship is translocal as it connects specific places of migrant experiences.[46] This translocal social relationship among remittance senders and receivers combines a whole set of forms of communication[47]; moral expectations[48]; emotions of guilt, shame, and obligations[49]; economic calculations such as the propensity to save or to consume; as well as intentions to maintain control over money.[50]

I call this relationship a translocal moral economy. The notion of moral economy suggests that rather than fixed economic interests, such as financial altruism or risk diversification, actors need to mobilize and promote remittance payments.[51] Even though the migrant ultimately needs to command the transfer, the mobilization of remittances involves both the migrant *and* the home family. These actors can manipulate, cultivate, and economize family bonds through communication. The specific ways in which remittances are produced and circulate are negotiated outcomes of translocal moral economies. As

---

[45] For an overview, see, e.g., S. Vertovec, *Transnationalism*, Abingdon: Routledge, 2009.

[46] C. Greiner and P. Sakdapolrak, "Translocality: Concepts, Applications and Emerging Research Perspectives", *Geography Compass* 7 (2013) 5, pp. 373–384.

[47] R. Dekker et al., "The Use of Online Media in Migration Networks", *Population, Space and Place* 22 (2016) 6, pp. 539–551.

[48] K. Wright, "Constructing Human Wellbeing across Spatial Boundaries: Negotiating Meanings in Transnational Migration", *Global Networks* 12 (2012) 4, pp. 467–484; E.O. Katigbark, "Moralizing Emotional Remittances: Transnational Familyhood and Translocal Moral Economy in the Philippines' 'Little Italy'", *Global Networks* 15 (2015) 4, pp. 519–535.

[49] J.K. Bernhard et al., "Transnationalizing Families: Canadian Immigration Policy and the Spatial Fragmentation of Care-giving among Latin American Newcomers", *International Migration* 47 (2009) 2, pp. 3–31.

[50] J. Carling, "Scripting Remittances: Making Sense of Money Transfers in Transnational Relationships", *International Migration Review* 48 (2014) 1, pp. 218–262.

[51] The concept of the moral economy captures social situations in which economic behaviour is embedded in non-economic landscapes of knowledge and ideas or rather a moral universe that is characterized by moral values about justice and other expectations on rights and obligations. For an overview on the concept, see W.J. Booth, "On the Idea of the Moral Economy", *American Political Science Review* 88 (1994) 3, pp. 653–667.

social arenas, these translocal moral economies simultaneously impose strain and facilitate the actors' struggle to advance and/or to restrain the money transfers of migrants.

Gaining From Remittances: Towards a Transnational Economic Space

As soon as remittances proved to be a valuable global resource in terms of money compared to foreign direct investments and to official development aid, states, development agencies, transfer operators, hometown associations (HTA), banks, and other institutions interested in accessing and managing remittances have been promoting means to leverage remittances for development.[52] While individual remittance transfers originate from an intrafamily translocal relationship, these actors rather focus on the macro remittance flow. Increasingly, they become parasitic on the translocal moral economy. Without direct access to the migrants' savings, the real source of remittances, these secondary actors are obliged to create an institutional remittance architecture in both places of money remitters and places of money receivers to enable the channelling of the macro remittance flow. I interpret these political attempts to construct a "global remittances agenda"[53] as a process of respatialization to gain access to migrants' savings and private money transfers.

Apart from the translocal moral economy, possibilities to access and control remittances are limited. The "parasitic" actors introduced above can access the place of migrant savings, the place of the spending of these savings, or the exchange between both places.[54] For instances, diaspora

---

[52] M. Bakker, *Migrating into Financial Markets: How Remittances Became a Development Tool*, Berkeley: University of California Press, 2015.

[53] H. Cross, "Finance, Development, and Remittances: Extending the Scale of Accumulation in Migrant Labour Regimes", *Globalizations* 12 (2015) 3, pp. 306, 305–321.

[54] Theoretically, the appropriation of remittances is oriented either directly towards accessing the migrant or the home family, or indirectly towards approaching the social context in which remittances appear. The indirect access is usually carried out by (1) approaching the destination of remittances and channelling remittances into "productive" purposes; (2) approaching the transaction with the objective to increase transaction costs; (3) imposing indirect taxes, such as value-added tax, which do not tax remittances directly but demand structure that arises out of remittances; (4) approaching the migrant abroad aiming at influencing the extent of remittance transactions. It is, however, almost impossible to institutionalize the direct appropriation of remittances as the cause for remittances, the family bond between migrant and home family, remains private and thus outside the direct control of secondary actors.

bonds,[55] the securitization of remittances,[56] remittances as a means to make a gain from financial inclusion and from microcredits,[57] etc. are opportunities to capitalize on remittances from outside of the translocal moral economy.

Through remittances, the local intrafamily as well as place-based nature of remittances moves from an exclusive local scale and eventually includes issues of national and international relations.[58] The remittance issue is elevated to a transnational scale, and the translocal moral economy moves beyond its initial context. As an effect of this process, a transnational economic space emerges that ties migrants to their home families, relatives, and friends, as well as these to and between actors outside the moral economy. Based on remittances, an enlarged circuit of social and economic production and reproduction emerges. Depending on the positionality of the actors involved, including the migrant and the home family, this transnational space exposes frictions, social conflicts, asymmetries, and power differentials. Furthermore, depending on the positionality of each actor within this economic space, different strategies of respatialization arise.

Respatializing Transnational Economies: Social Conflicts and the Rescaling of Political Power

Remittances are a clear signifier of "transnationalism from below"[59] and the very expression of "transnational living".[60] Remittances are private in the sense of belonging to a family as well as public in the sense of a development tool for political actors.[61] I argue that remittances give rise to a transnational

---

[55] S.L. Ketkar and D. Ratha, "Diaspora Bonds for Funding Education", *Migration Letters* 8 (2011) 2, pp. 153–172.

[56] D. Hudson, "Developing Geographies of Financialisation: Banking the Poor and Remittance Securitisation", *Contemporary Politics* 14 (2008) 3, pp. 315–333.

[57] M. Orozco, *Migrant Remittances and Development in the Global Economy*, Boulder: Lynne Rienner, 2013.

[58] M.A. Paarlberg, "Diaspora Outreach by Latin American Parties", PhD thesis., Georgetown University, 2017.

[59] M.P. Smith and L.E. Guarnizo (eds.), *Transnationalism From Below*, New Brunswick: Transaction Publishers, 1998.

[60] L.E. Guarnizo, "The Economics of Transnational Living", *International Migration Review* 37 (2003) 3, pp. 666–699.

[61] C. Horst et al., "Private Money, Public Scrutiny? Contrasting Perspectives on Remittances", *Global Networks* 14 (2014) 4, pp. 514–532.

economic space that incorporates both societies in the Global North as well as in the Global South. Remittances (re)produce political, social, and economic inequalities within this economic space. Remittances not only entangle a set of actors who are engaged in producing remittances, they also have potential effects at different scales.

On the one hand, the inflow of remittances may result in renewed external economic dependencies as well as may have similar effects like the so-called "Dutch disease".[62] However, remittance-receiving societies in the Global South often are able to gain and to maintain relative autonomy in certain policy domains. In contrast to pure dependency put into discussion by authors of dependency theory, actors in these societies engage in the respatialization of this transnational economic space and thus struggle for agency. Even though the transnational economic space seems to privilege transnational political actors at first glance, aspects of (re)nationalization and at the same time (re)localization are crucial in understanding this process.

On the other hand, at specific places where remittances are produced or appropriated actors gain autonomy from local economic conditions.[63] Due to remittances, subaltern groups in fact have at their disposal larger amounts of money. Notwithstanding, the same groups are obliged to securing the future flow of remittances by maintaining localized means of access and control of the migrant living abroad. A crucial issue then is that places are interwoven in different depths in a network that not only relates migrants and home families but also even entails entire remittance-sending and -receiving societies.

Remittances cause a shift in political accountability from remittance-receiving societies and political regimes in the Global South towards remittance-sending societies in the Global North.[64] The political importance of foreign migrants, remittances, as well as institutions capable of channelling remittances increases owing to the fact that these are essential parts of a spatial format *in the making*. Accordingly, these different dimensions are able to (re)define nodes of local, national, as well as transnational ties, eventually, redefining borders and creating profound frictions. Increasingly, governments, lobby groups, and business enterprises try to become part of the negotiation over how

---

[62] P. Acosta et al., "Remittances and the Dutch Disease", *Journal of International Economics* 79 (2009) 1, pp. 102–116.
[63] P. Athukorala, "The Use of Migrant Remittances in Development: Lessons from the Asian Experience", *Journal of International Development* 4 (1992) 5, pp. 511–529.
[64] Cross, "Finance, Development, and Remittances".

to design and to (re)organize transnational economic spaces. The discussion on residence permission in the US,[65] or the increasing importance of HTAs,[66] for instance, are instructive in this regard.

HTAs institutionally link migrant communities in remittance-sending societies and local communities in receiving societies. They improve the flow of information and formalize personal and economic bonds among migrant and home family.[67] HTAs emerge as political actors, which do not exclusively monitor and manage remittances but create local hierarchies as well as aim at respatialization by alternating established ties among local, national, and transnational scales of social action. The discussion about integrating migrants in national elections in remittance-receiving societies furthermore exemplifies that governing remittances has major impacts on established political regimes.[68] Although translocal communities appear in remittance-sending societies based on new identities, as well as politicized social conflicts rooted in experiences of transnational migration, these very mechanisms produce reverse effects in remittance-receiving societies. Here, remittances tend to depoliticize social conflicts, sometimes even negatively affecting local capabilities to organize.[69] These examples suggest that local actors in remittance-receiving societies tend to rely on translocal strategies of strengthening ties between specific places. National governments as well as transnational actors such as banks or HTAs, in contrast, seem to intervene in the translocal moral economy by fostering transnational ties, thereby disguising the meaning of specific places.

Strategies of transnationalization then may conflict with strategies of localization economic space. I further argue that these different strategies are distributed unequally within the transnational economic space. Elites intend to create and to foster transnational ties in this economic space, thereby minimizing local opportunities for migrant family members in gaining control over remittances. In contrast to elites and although low-income remittance-receiving households are engaged in a transnational economic topography, they are

---

[65] D.M. Moloney, *National Insecurities: Immigrants and U.S. Deportation Policy since 1882*, Chapel Hill: University of North Carolina Press, 2012.
[66] On hometown associations, see T. Lacroix, "Conceptualizing Transnational Engagements: A Structure and Agency Perspective on (Hometown) Transnationalism", *International Migration Review* 48 (2014) 3, pp. 643–679.
[67] Orozco, *Migrant Remittances and Development in the Global Economy*.
[68] B.E. Whitaker, "The Politics of Home: Dual Citizenship and the African Diaspora", *International Migration Review* 45 (2011) 4, pp. 755–783.
[69] A. Garni and F.L. Weyher, "Dollars, 'Free Trade', and Migration: The Combined Forces of Alienation in Postwar El Salvador", *Latin American Perspectives* 40 (2013) 5, pp. 62–77.

likely to prefer strategies of respatialization as a localizing of economic space in order to maintain opportunities to attract and channel remittances and eventually to control their use and expenditure.

Consequently, the emerging transnational economic space has a contradictory effect: remittances financially empower subaltern groups. At the same time, remittances reduce the ability of these groups to produce or format economic space beyond the local and close socioeconomic environment. In this manner, remittances moderate economic hardship on a local level but erode political agency to influence economic hardship in larger global or transnational arenas.

Conclusion

Economic space is one of the most fundamental categories of "the economy". All the more astonishing is that economics rather treat economic space implicitly or even tend to ignore space as a proper research issue. Mainstream economics often treat economic space as state space, as homogenous space, and as essentially capitalist space. Economics thus often perpetuates methodological nationalism and territorialism.

In this chapter, I proposed an alternative political economy approach to space and processes of respatialization under the global condition, namely economic space as consisting of two interrelated dimensions: topographies of places and the relationality of these places. Both dimensions depend on the availability of economic surplus. Economic spaces entangle political and economic realms. Therefore, these spaces are, as a direct result, politico-economic spaces. As such, analytically, economic spaces are networks of economic places that are created in processes of respatialization. And economic spaces function as circuits of production and social reproduction.

Using this political economy approach for the analysis of remittances, I showed that remittances tend to produce transnational economic spaces. Remittances bring about social change by substituting power relations that are yet established and by challenging existing strategies of respatialization. Remittances produce enlarged monetary circuits of production and social reproduction. In this regard, new actors gain access to new forms of economic surplus. In turn, accessing economic surplus enables these actors to implement their own strategies of respatialization. At the same time, remittances transnationalize the scope of influence of actors.

Remittances locally and transnationally overcome previously dominant economic spaces, which economic actors once created based on other forms of economic surplus and strategies of respatialization. These new patterns result in transnational economic spaces that entangle remittance-sending and remittance-receiving societies.

However, the analysis of transnational economic space, emerging as a result of increasing remittances and the respective efforts to manage and control them, challenges earlier conceptions of economic spaces long dominant in economics as these remain embedded in a flat social order. Instead, processes of respatialization are essentially contested processes, and once established spatial formats are continuously (re)negotiated. The relation between remittances and processes of respatialization demonstrates that spatial formats are neither homogenous nor stable, but instead a result of social conflicts, in which asymmetries and power differentials are steadily produced and reproduced.

Authors

Böhme, Michaela, PhD candidate, Leipzig University, SFB 1199 "Processes of Spatialization under the Global Condition", michaelaboehme@uni-leipzig.de. Recent publications: (with Sarah R. Sippel and Cynthia Gharios) "Strategic Financialization? The Emergence of Sovereign Wealth Funds in the Global Food System", in: *Financialisation, Food Systems and Rural Transformation*, eds. H. Bjørkhaug, A. Magnan, and G. Lawrence, London: Routledge, 2018.

Breuilly, John, Emeritus Professor of Nationalism and Ethnicity, London School of Economics, j.breuilly@lse.ac.uk. Recent publications: "Modern Empires and nation-states", *Thesis Eleven* 139 (2017) 1; "Modernisation and Nationalist Ideology", *Archiv für Sozialgeschichte* 57 (2017); "Popular Nationalism, State Forms and Modernity", in: *Nations, Identities and the First World War: Shifting Loyalties to the Fatherland*, eds. Nico Wouters and Laurence van Ypersele, London: Bloomsbury Academic, 2018.

Castryck, Geert, Senior Researcher in African and Global History, Leipzig University, SFB 1199 "Processes of Spatialization under the Global Condition", geert.castryck@uni-leipzig.de. Recent publications: "Introduction – The Bounds of Berlin's Africa: Space-making and Multiple Territorialities in East and Central Africa", *International Journal of African Historical Studies* 52 (2019) 1; "Bordering the Lake: Transcending spatial orders in Kigoma-Ujiji", *International Journal of African Historical Studies* 52 (2019) 1; "Living Islam in Colonial Bujumbura: The Historical Translocality of Muslim Life between East and Central Africa", *History in Africa* 46 (2019).

Dietze, Antje, Senior Researcher, Leipzig University, SFB 1199 "Processes of Spatialization under the Global Condition", adietze@uni-leipzig.de. Recent publications: (ed. with Claudia Baumann and Megan Maruschke) *Portals of Globalization in Africa, Asia, and Latin America*, special issue *Comparativ* 27 (2017) 3–4; (ed. with Katja Naumann) *Situating Transnational Actors*, special issue *European Review of History* 25 (2018) 3–4.

Engel, Ulf, Professor for "Politics in Africa", Institute of African Studies, Leipzig University, uengel@uni-leipzig.de. Recent publications: (ed. with M. Boeckler and D. Müller-Mahn) *Spatial Practices: Territory, Border and Infrastructure in Africa*, Leiden and Boston MA: Brill Academic Publishers, 2018; "The African Union's twin APSA and AGA agenda – Moving beyond donor dependence and member states' resistance?", *Stichproben. Wiener Zeitschrift für kritische Afrikastudien* 2019 (35); "Knowledge production at the African Union on conflict early warning", *South African Journal of International Affairs* 25 (2018) 1.

Jessop, Bob, Distinguished Professor of Sociology, Lancaster University, b.jessop@lancaster.ac.uk. Recent publications: (with N.L. Sum) *Towards a Cultural Political Economy: Putting Culture in its Place in Political Economy*, Cheltenham: Edward Elgar, 2013; *The State: Past, Present, Future*, Cambridge: Polity Press, 2015.

Marung, Steffi, Senior Researcher, Leipzig University, SFB 1199 "Processes of Spatialization under the Global Condition", marung@uni-leipzig.de. Recent publications: (ed. with Katja Naumann, Torsten Loschke, and Matthias Middell) *In Search of Other Worlds: Essays towards a Cross-Regional History of Area Studies*, Leipzig: Leipziger Universitätsverlag, 2019; "The provocation of empirical evidence: Soviet African Studies between enthusiasm and discomfort", *African Identities* 16 (2018) 2.

Middell, Matthias, Professor of Cultural History, Director of the Global and European Studies Institute, Leipzig University, middell@uni-leipzig.de. Recent publications: (ed. with Frank Hadler) *Handbuch einer transnationalen Geschichte Ostmitteleuropas 1750–1918,* Göttingen: Vandenhoeck & Ruprecht 2017; (with Torsten Loschke, Steffi Marung, and Katja Naumann) *In Search of Other Worlds. Towards a Cross-regional History of Area Studies,* Leipzig: Leipziger Universitätsverlag, 2018; (ed.) *Kommunismus jenseits des Eurozentrismus* (= Jahrbuch für historische Kommunismusforschung 2019), Berlin: Metropol-Verlag, 2019; (ed.) *The Routledge Handbook of Transregional Studies,* London: Routledge, 2018; (ed. with Konstanze Klemm) *The many Facets of Global Studies. Perspectives from the Erasmus Mundus Global Studies Programme,* Leipzig: Leipziger Universitätsverlag 2019.

Miggelbrink, Judith, Chair of Human Geography, TU Dresden, judith.miggelbrink@tu-dresden.de. Recent publications: (with Frank Meyer) "Politics of withdrawal and communities' responses. On the contested nature of post-secular rapprochement in a declining region", *Geographica Helvetica* 72 (2017); (with Rhys Jones, Sami Moisio, Mikko Weckroth, Michael Woods, Juho Luukkonen, and Frank Meyer) "Re-conceptualising Territorial Cohesion Through the Prism of Spatial Justice: Critical Perspectives on Academic and Policy Discourses", in: *Regional and Local Development in Times of Polarisation. Re-thinking Spatial Policies in Europe,* eds. Thilo Lang and Franziska Görmar, Singapur: Palgrave Macmillan, 2019; (ed. with Frank Meyer and Kristine Beurskens) *Ins Feld und zurück. Praktische Probleme qualitativer Forschung in der Sozialgeographie,* Wiesbaden: Springer VS, 2018.

Müller, Uwe, Senior Researcher, Leibniz Institute for the History and Culture of Eastern Europe in Leipzig, uwe.mueller@leibniz-gwzo.de. Recent publications: "Verkehrspolitik im RGW zwischen Integration und Desintegration", in: *Integration und Desintegration Europas. Wirtschafts- und sozialhistorische Beiträge,* eds. Günther Schulz and Mark Spoerer, Stuttgart: Steiner, 2019; (ed. with Dagmara Jajeśniak-Quast) *Comecon revisited. Integration in the Eastern Bloc and Entanglements with the Global Economy,* special issue *Comparativ* 27 (2017) 5–6; "Transnationale Verflechtungen der Wirtschaft in Ostmitteleuropa", in: *Handbuch einer transnationalen Geschichte Ostmitteleuropas,* vol. 1: *Von der Mitte des 19. Jahrhunderts bis zum Ersten Weltkrieg,* eds. Frank Hadler and Matthias Middell, Göttingen: Vandenhoeck & Ruprecht 2017.

Schumacher, Frank, Professor of International History at the University of Western Ontario, Canada, fschuma@uwo.ca. He has published widely on the role of the United States in world affairs and the history of colonialism; he is currently at work on two books: Embedded Empire: The Spatial Contours of American History and Theodore Roosevelt: Cosmopolitan Nationalist.

Sippel, Sarah Ruth, Lecturer at the Institute of Anthropology and Principal Investigator of C04/SFB 1199 "Processes of Spatialization under the Global Condition", Leipzig University, sippel@uni-leipzig.de. Recent publications: "Financialising Farming as a Moral Imperative? Renegotiating the Legitimacy of Land Investments in Australia", *Environment and Planning* A, 50 (2018) 3; (with Nicolette Larder and Geoffrey Lawrence) "Grounding the Financialization of Farmland: Perspectives on Financial Actors as New Land Owners in Rural Australia", *Agriculture and Human Values* 34 (2017).

Sluga, Glenda, Kathleen Fitzpatrick Laureate Fellow, Professor of International History, University of Sydney, glenda.sluga@sydney.edu.au. Recent publications: (ed. with Patricia Clavin) *Internationalisms: A Twentieth Century History,* Cambridge: Cambridge University

Press, 2017; "1919, international organizations, and the future of international order", special issue *International Affairs* 2019; "'Who Hold the Balance of the World?' Bankers at the Congress of Vienna, and in International History", *American Historical Review* 122 (2017) 5.

Troebst, Stefan, Professor of East European Cultural History, Leipzig University, troebst@uni-leipzig.de. Recent publications: "Storage medium of conflict memory: The East European imprint on modern international law", in: *History and International Law: An Intertwined Relationship*, ed. Annalisa Ciampi, Cheltenham: Edward Elgar, 2019; "1667 – A Threshold Year? Debating the 'Breakthrough of the Modern Age' in Muscovite Russia", *Revue de Synthèse* 139 (2018) 1–2; "Historical Mesoregions and Transregionalism", in: *The Routledge Handbook of Transregional Studies*, ed. Matthias Middell, London: Routledge, 2018.

Warnecke-Berger, Hannes, Senior Researcher at the Department of International and Inter-Societal Relations at University of Kassel, hwarneckeberger@uni-kassel.de. Recent publications: *Politics and Violence in Central America and the Caribbean*, London and New York: Palgrave Macmillan, 2018; (ed. with G. Pisarz-Ramirez) *Processes of Spatialization in the Americas: Configurations and Narratives*, Frankfurt a. M. and New York: Peter Lang, 2018; "La globalisation de la rente et la montée de la violence", *Naqd: Revue d'études et de critique sociale* (2018) 36.

Weiss, Holger, Professor, Åbo Akademi University, holger.weiss@abo.fi. Recent publications: "'Boycott the Nazi Flagg': Antifascist Agendas of the International of Seamen and Harbour Workers and Its Activities in Northern Europe During the First Half of the 1930s", in: *Antifascism in the Nordic Countries: New Perspectives, Comparisons and Transnational Connections*, eds. Kasper Braskén, Nigel Copsey, and Johan Lundin, London and New York: Routledge 2018; "'Vereinigt in der internationalen Solidarität'. Der Aufruf der Internationale der Seeleute und Hafenarbeiter an die 'Kolonial'- und 'Neger'-Seeleute in den frühen 1930er-Jahren", *Jahrbuch für historische Kommunismusforschung* (2019); *För kampen internationellt! Transportarbetarnas globala kampinternational och dess verksamhet i Nordeuropa under 1930-talet*, Helsinki: Työväen historian ja perinteen tutkimuksen seura, 2019.

Index

Addis Ababa 321
Africa 1, 7, 8, 27, 30, 32, 43, 116, 122, 135, 146, 154, 156, 157, 167, 169, 183, 185, 243, 245, 260, 262, 281, 287, 302, 323, 328, 331
– Central 185, 190, 192, 194, 198
– East 185, 190, 192, 194, 198
– South Africa 62, 157, 164, 260, 327, 328, 329
– sub-Saharan 159, 166
– West Africa 132
African Charter on Democracy, Elections and Governance (2007) 331
African Court of Justice and Human and Peoples' Rights 321
African Union (AU) 312, 313, 314, 321, 327, 328, 329, 330, 331, 332
– African Governance Architecture (AGA) 330, 331
– African Peace and Security Architecture (APSA) 330, 331
– African Peace and Security Council (PSC) 330, 331
– African Standby Force (ASF) 330
– African Union Commission (AUC) 328, 330, 331
– Continental Early Warning System (CEWS) 330
agriculture 41, 149, 154, 297, 337, 339–341, 344–349, 351, 353, 356, 357, 359
Alaska 113, 120, 126, 137, 139
Albania 293
Albert, King of Saxony 244, 247
Alexandrowicz, Charles 271
Algeria 174, 200, 237
Allen, John 79, 99, 101
Alsace 174, 176
Alsace-Lorraine 174, 176
America 118, 131, 136, 139, 147, 154
– the Americas 1, 2, 116, 132, 159, 183, 314
– Central 117, 118, 126, 131, 132
– Latin America 31, 41, 164, 199, 200, 218, 269, 287, 302, 321, 323

– North 40, 69, 111, 112, 113, 115, 121, 135, 145, 154, 157, 185, 235, 237, 239, 249, 286
– South 40, 117, 160, 235, 281
Andean Community (CAN) 314
Applebaum, Rachel 306
Arab League 314
Arctic Council 314
Argentina 27, 314
Armand-Dumaresq, Charles Édouard 243, 244
Asia 8, 115, 116, 117, 118, 121, 127, 131, 135, 141, 143, 146, 147, 159, 167, 183, 235, 281, 287, 302, 314, 321, 323, 357
– Central 167, 303
– East 31, 69, 73, 117
– South 69, 167
– Southeast 159
– West 117, 167
Asian Development Bank (ADB) 314
Association of Southeast Asian Nations (ASEAN) 314, 326, 327
Atlantic Charter (1941) 261
Australia 9, 69, 154, 157, 212, 235, 238, 252, 258, 260, 281, 286, 315, 336, 339, 341–349, 350–353, 355, 357, 358
– Queensland 346, 348, 352
– Victoria 347, 352
– Western 347, 352
Australia, New Zealand, United States Security Treaty (ANZUS) 315
Austria 155, 271
Austria-Hungary 168, 176

Babiracki, Patryck 306
Bair, Jennifer 338
Balch, Emilie Greene 257, 264, 265
Barker, Robert 235
Barry, Andrew 83
Barton, William 236
Bayly, Christopher 31, 32
Bear, C. 96, 98
Becker, Edmund 249
Beck, Ulrich 35

Belgium 2, 201, 240, 260
Belgrade 281, 284
Bem, Alfred 218
Beneš, Edward 281
Berlin 7, 8, 27, 43, 156, 185, 188, 207, 214, 222, 233, 236, 238–240, 242, 243, 248, 252, 284, 300, 302
– Berlin Afrika/Congo Conference (1884/85) 27, 43, 156, 185
– Berlin's Africa 7, 8, 43, 185, 188
Berndt, Christian 337
Berthold, Eduard 246–250
Billig, Michael 175
Black, Jeremy 113
Boeckler, Marc 337
Böhme, Michaela 9, 10, 339
Bolivarian Alliance for the Peoples of Our America (ALBA) 314
Bordeaux 211
Bourgeois, Constantin 236
Bourguiba, Habib 200
Bouton, Charles-Marie 235, 236
Bowman, Isaiah 144
Bracht, Eugen 242
Braun, Bruce 96, 98
Braun, Louis 242, 243, 248
Brazil 41, 62, 118, 314, 327, 340–342, 351, 352
Brenner, Neil 21, 34, 60, 64
Breuilly, John 7
Brookings Institution 45
Brussels 185, 188, 198, 199, 201–203, 236, 238, 251, 300
– as colonial city 185, 188–192, 199, 203
– World Exposition (1958) 201
Brzeziński, Zbigniew 287
Bucharest 284, 300
Budapest 284, 300
Buenos Aires 116, 210
Bujumbura 185, 188, 192–196, 199, 201, 203
Bulgaria 166, 280, 281, 285, 293, 295, 297
Burbank, Jane 107
Burundi 192, 194, 196

California 114, 268
– UCLA 287
Cameron, Angus 273

Caribbean 40, 120, 126, 127, 131, 132, 133, 140, 221, 224
Caribbean Basin 112, 115, 118, 132, 134
Caribbean Community (CARICOM) 314
Carnegie Endowment for International Peace 133, 287
Cass, Lewis 119
Castryck, Geert 8
Catalonia 176
Central Commission for the Navigation of the Rhine 312, 328
Chad 329
Charles V 151
Chatterjee, Partha 167
Chenghzi, Leo (Liao) 217
China 39, 46, 62, 69, 117, 145, 148, 150, 158–162, 164, 165, 175, 200, 217, 257, 258, 293, 297, 309, 314, 317, 327, 336, 339–344, 346, 347, 348, 349, 355, 356, 357
China-Australia Free Trade Agreement (ChAFTA) 341
Churchill, Winston 284, 285
Club of Rome 268, 269, 270
Cold War 9, 26, 43, 46, 137, 138, 143, 144, 145, 146, 147, 148, 258, 271, 275, 276, 278, 280–282, 284, 287, 300–304, 308, 310, 316, 317, 319, 320, 323, 326, 327, 332
Cole, Peter 209
Collective Security Treaty Organization (CSTO) 314
Collier, Stephen J. 78, 86, 87
colonial cities 183–204
colonialism 7, 8, 40, 76, 109, 129, 133, 136, 138, 139, 142, 183–186, 188, 191, 194–196, 198, 199, 201–204, 249, 264, 287
– nuclear 7, 136, 138, 141
colonies 7, 10, 56, 59, 109, 110, 118, 126, 146, 166, 183, 184, 199, 201, 202, 203, 262, 282
– African 164, 174, 224
– American 32, 110
– British 200
– European 130, 146
– French 200, 218

– Japanese 130
– Portuguese 311
– settler, plantation 41
– Spanish 127, 129
– US 130, 131, 132, 135, 140
Comintern. See *Communist International (Comintern)*
Commission de l'Ocean Indien (COI) 314
Commonwealth of Independent States (CIS) 309, 314
Communauté des États Sahélo-Sahariens (CEN-SAD) 314
Communauté Économique des États de l'Afrique Centrale (CEEAC) 314
Communist Information Bureau (Cominform) 285, 286, 287
Communist International (Comintern) 205, 207, 208, 214, 219, 221, 222, 280
Congo 185, 192, 195, 196, 197, 200, 201, 243
Cooper, Frederick 107
Copenhagen 211, 220, 226
Council for Mutual Economic Assistance (CMEA, COMECON) 286–300
Cox, Robert W. 324
Crimean War 237
Crump, Laurien 299
Cuba 118, 127, 129, 133, 139, 293, 304
Currier, Dianne 84, 85
Czechoslovakia 279, 281, 293, 296, 297, 309, 314

Danzig/Gdańsk 248, 260
Dar es Salaam 184, 185, 188, 189, 191, 203
de Certeau, Michel 76
DeLanda, Manuel 78, 80, 81, 93, 95, 96, 97, 98
Deleuze, Gilles 79, 80, 81, 95, 96, 97
Dewey, John 259
Diego Garcia 147
Dierks, Konstantin 115
Dietze, Antje 8
Dimitrov, Georgi 280, 295
Djagalov, Rossen 303
Dominican Republic 127, 133
Donert, Celia 301
Dresden 231, 236, 242, 243
Dumay, Auguste 218

East African Community (EAC) 314
East India Company 158, 160
Economic Community of West African States (ECOWAS) 314
Ecuador 118
Edict of Nantes 169
Edinburgh 235
Egypt 159, 285, 329
Elisabethville 188, 197, 201
Empires
– American 127, 136, 146
– Austro-Hungarian 260
– British 2, 159
– Caribbean 119
– Chinese 41
– colonial 128, 140, 141, 143, 144
– Ethiopian 41
– German 7, 19, 41, 173, 234, 254, 262, 279
– Habsburg 41, 261, 279
– Holy Roman 155, 169, 259
– Japanese 41
– Mongol 75
– Ottoman 161, 162, 259, 260, 278, 279, 288
– Persian 161
– Quing 161
– Roman 16
– Romanov 161
– Russian 41, 280
– Spanish 118
Engel, Ulf 9
Ethiopia 41, 323
Eurasia 27, 32, 62, 69, 75, 145, 146, 314
Eurasian Economic Union 309, 327
Eurocentrism 5, 21, 29, 38, 323
Europe 1, 2, 3, 7, 8, 22, 36, 69, 71, 72, 73, 118, 120, 131, 135, 143, 147, 149, 150, 152, 154–156, 159, 163, 181, 259, 276, 283, 285, 302, 312, 313, 317, 322–324, 327, 358
– Central 3, 7, 159, 166, 167, 168, 231, 284
– East Central 277, 279
– Eastern 9, 231, 275, 277, 279, 280, 283–285, 288, 293, 297, 300, 302, 304–307
– Northern 290, 300
– Southeastern 277, 279
– Southern 279

– Western 69, 210, 231, 265, 276, 279, 282, 286, 288, 289, 296, 297, 300, 303, 308, 309
European Coal and Steel Community 286
European Economic Community (EEC) 286, 289, 313
European Free Trade Association (EFTA) 289, 313
European Patent Office 313
European Science Foundation (ESF) 313
European Space Agency (ESA) 313
European Union (EU) 46, 48, 71, 72, 73, 175, 277, 309, 310, 312, 313, 323, 327, 328, 331

Fadeev, Aleksandr 280
Featherstone, David 209
Federal Republic of Germany (FRG) 296
Finland 217, 285
Flade, Falk 298
Ford, James W. 8, 217, 218, 223–225
Forrester, Jay 269
Foss, Leif O. 216
Foucault, Michel 23, 82, 83, 87, 93
France 2, 32, 33, 41, 111, 113, 151, 153–156, 159, 161, 163, 164, 169, 171, 173, 174, 176, 218, 224, 237, 239, 240, 243, 258, 259, 260, 263, 332, 347
– Bourbon France 156
– French Revolution 153
– Napoleonic France 171
– Third Republic 2, 171, 173
Franco-Prussian War (1870/71) 174, 237, 239, 240, 242–244
Frederick II 163
Free State of Fiume/Rijeka 260
Free Territory of Trieste (FTT) 262, 263, 264, 271
Fried, Alfred Hermann 263, 264, 271

Gaddafi, Muammar al 328, 329
GDR. See *German Democratic Republic*
Gellner, Ernest 161
General Agreement on Tariffs and Trade 271, 295
Gentz, Wilhelm 243
Gereffi, Gary 337

German Democratic Republic (GDR) 29, 232, 293, 297. See also Germany, East Germany
German Historical Institute, London 149
Germany 127, 135, 156, 159, 161, 164, 168, 174, 216–218, 224, 227, 228, 233, 237, 238, 241, 249, 250, 254, 262, 288
– East Germany 298
– Second Empire 176
Ghana 331
Gladstone, William Ewart 159
global condition 2–6, 8, 18, 25, 27, 28, 36, 37, 47, 79, 135, 204, 230, 250, 252, 277, 315, 319, 370, 377
globalization 1, 2, 4, 5, 6, 11, 16, 21, 26, 31, 32, 33, 34, 35, 39, 45, 46, 47, 57, 78, 80, 86–88, 129, 136, 147, 152, 161, 184, 228, 250, 270, 273, 287, 309, 317, 319, 324, 327, 329
– economic 267, 270, 272, 337, 370
– portal(s) of 7, 45, 184, 200, 202, 203, 228, 229, 230, 233, 250–253
– processes of 18, 25, 312, 315, 320, 333
– Western 276
Global North 310, 320, 361, 375
Global South 9, 143, 276, 293, 301, 304, 305, 310, 312, 314, 320, 321, 324, 327, 333, 335, 361, 375
Godard, Simon 301
Goebel, Michael 199–201
Gothenburg 323, 327
Great Britain 41, 110–112, 151, 153, 154, 159, 161, 163, 164, 176, 209, 249, 258, 260, 261, 263
Greece 73, 166, 280, 285
Greek War of Independence 237
Grosz, Elizabeth 84
Guam 129
Guano Islands Act (1856) 127
Guantanamo Bay 139
Guattari, Felix 79, 80, 95, 96, 97
Gulf Cooperation Council (GCC) 314

Haiti 133
Hall, Stuart 338
Hamburg 8, 184, 205–208, 210, 211, 213–216, 218–226, 242

– Hamburg Port Bureau and International Seamen's Club (Interclub) 205
Hamilton, Alexander 175
Hannover 155
Haraway, Donna J. 85
Hardy, George 207, 215, 216, 218
Hawaii 127, 129, 139
Helsinki 300
Henry IV 169
Herren, Madeleine 328
Hinds, Manuel 272, 273
Hirschman, Daniel 90
Hobbes, Thomas 152
Ho Chi Minh 200
hometown associations (HTA) 373, 376
Honduras 118
Hong Kong 158
Hopkins, Terence K. 337
Huber, Peter 214
Hungary 168, 176, 293, 296, 297, 302, 314
Hünten, Emil 242, 244
Hurrell, Andrew 319, 320

immigration 124, 136, 162, 173, 174, 176, 178
imperialism 76, 107, 108, 114–116, 118, 126, 133, 138, 145, 146, 152, 157, 159, 161, 163, 164, 199, 201, 223, 244, 250, 252, 277, 280, 281, 302, 306
India 32, 39, 62, 114, 158, 160, 161, 167, 174, 194, 218, 285, 314, 317, 327, 342
Indonesia 285
industrialization 2, 262, 296, 298, 339
Intergovernmental Authority on Development (IGAD) 316
International Committee of the Red Cross 328
International Health Organization 259
International Labour Office 259
International Monetary Fund 271
International of Seamen and Harbour Workers (ISH) 205–209, 213, 215, 217–226
International Organization of Journalists 300
International Organization of Resistance Fighters 300
International Organization of the Francophonie 43

international organization(s) 2, 3, 42, 301, 310, 311, 312, 313, 318, 328
International Propaganda and Action Committee of Transport Workers (IPAC) 208, 213
International Student Union 300
International Telecommunication Union 328
International Telegraph Union 263
International Trade Union Committee of Negro Workers (ITUCNW) 205, 207, 217, 218, 221–226
International Transport Workers' Federation (ITF) 206, 209
Iron Curtain 146, 276, 284, 285, 294
Italy 73, 135, 161, 168, 171, 249, 258, 286
– Kingdom of 41, 260

Japan 41, 69, 117, 127, 130, 135, 137, 143, 147, 153, 159, 161, 165, 217, 238, 243, 252, 258, 262, 303
Jessop, Bob 6, 21, 34, 60
Jones, E. Foster 225
Jones, M. R. 21, 34, 60, 102

Kamei, Fumio 303
Kapoor, Raj 303
Karlovy Vary 302
Kenyatta, Jomo 201
Khrushchev, Nikita 287, 295
Kiesling, Ernst 248
Kigoma 184, 185, 188, 192–196, 199, 203
Kingdom of Serbs, Croats and Slovenes 260
Kips, Alexander 243
Kissinger, Henry A. 42
Koch, Max 243
Koivunen, Pia 307
Korbonski, Andrzej 287
Korea 126
Körner, Ernst 243
Koselleck, Reinhart 5, 36
Košice Programme (1945) 281
Kouyaté, Garan 224

Langlois, Jean-Charles 237
Laos 295
Latham, Robert Gordon 100

Latin America. See under *America*
Latour, Bruno 83, 99
Law, John 91
League of Nations 3, 160, 165, 166, 259, 260, 271, 311, 326
Lefebvre, Henri 15
Leipzig 6, 8, 48, 51, 53, 75, 77, 228, 230–236, 241–252, 315
Leipzig University 4
– Collaborative Research Centre (SFB 1199) 4, 6, 28, 315–317
Leningrad 210
Lenin, Vladimir I. 172, 210, 212, 280, 283
Leopold II 201
Leyshon, Andrew 350
Liberia 133, 329
Libya 328, 329, 332
Li, Murray 94, 95
Lippmann, Walter 107, 109
List, Friedrich 175
Liverpool 210
London 110, 185, 201, 217, 218, 223, 232, 235, 237, 240, 248, 249, 251, 302
– Black London 200, 201
– as colonial city 185, 188, 198, 199, 201, 202, 203
– Great Exhibition (1851) 246
– imperial London 200
Losovsky, Alexander 210
Louis XIV 151, 153, 169
Löwenthal, Richard 277, 288
Lublin Manifesto (1944) 281
Lubumbashi 184, 185, 188, 197, 199, 201, 203. See also Elisabethville
Lumumba, Patrice 201
Lyons, Martin 176

Mackinder, Halford 144, 145
Mahan, Alfred Thayer 144, 148
Maier, Charles 8, 23, 107, 149–154, 157, 161, 163, 171, 177
Maine, Henry 158
Malawi 329
Mali 329, 332
Manchu 162
Mann, Michael 161
Marcus, G. E. 93

Margain, Constance 205
Marine Transport Workers Industrial Union 209
Marseilles 198, 210, 211, 224
Marshall Plan 263, 271, 285, 286, 287, 294
Marshall, Thomas H. 170, 171
Marung, Steffi 9
Massey, Doreen 50, 51, 98
Matera, Marc 199–201
Mather, C. 87
Mbeki, Thabo 328
McMaster, Herbert Raymond 148
Meiji Restoration 152
Mekong River Commission (MRC) 314
Metternich, Wenzeslaus 160
Metzger, Jacob 68
Mexico 118, 119
Mexico City 118
Michigan 119
Micronesia 139, 141, 142
– Federated States of Micronesia 139
Middell, Matthias 6, 75, 76, 282, 284
Middle East 159, 166, 260
Miggelbrink, Judith 6
migration 6, 7, 30, 42, 57, 66, 131, 171, 251, 361, 370, 371
– labour 10, 183
– mass 57, 249, 370
– South-North 361
– transnational 376
Miller, Peter 83
modernization 144, 230, 299
modernization theory 23, 163, 322
Mol, Annemarie 91
Mongolia 293, 297
Monroe, James 115
Montesquieu, Charles Secondat baron de 119
Morgenthau, Hans 261
Moscow 8, 205, 207, 208, 209, 217, 218, 220, 222, 223, 238, 281, 285, 296, 300
Mozambique 304
Müller, M. 99
Müller, Uwe 9
Mumbai 184
Munich 236, 239, 240, 242, 243, 248, 251, 252

Munich Agreement (1938) 281
Murdoch, John 102

Nairobi 184
Napoleon I 32, 154, 155, 156, 163, 171, 248, 262, 312
Napoleon III 237
nationalism 31, 57, 122, 124, 125, 162, 166, 167, 172–174, 176, 177, 237, 244, 250, 252, 261, 263, 279, 280, 302, 304, 305
– cultural, ideological 121
– methodological 21, 57, 58, 322, 325, 360, 377
nation-state(s) 2, 3, 6, 7, 9, 10, 19, 29, 30, 31, 33, 37, 40, 41, 42, 44, 71, 96, 100, 101, 107–109, 120, 121, 136, 139, 140, 148, 149, 152, 153, 156, 157, 159, 162–164, 166–168, 171, 174–179, 258, 259, 261, 262, 267, 269, 270, 272, 273, 276, 278, 283, 288, 290, 291, 294, 327, 337, 366
Nelles, Dieter 209
New International Economic Order (NIEO) 266, 267, 304
New South Wales 346, 352
New York 210, 211, 230, 235, 238, 248, 264
New Zealand 54, 157, 260, 315, 341
Nicaragua 118
Nietzschmann, Friedrich August 244
Nigeria 331
Nilssen, Fred 216
Ninkovich, Frank 118
Nkrumah, Kwame 201
non-aligned movement 43
North Atlantic Treaty Organization (NATO) 160, 286, 289, 314, 326, 332
Northern Mariana Islands 139
North Korea 293, 297, 302

Obasanjo, Olusegun 328
Ocean
– Atlantic 116, 224
– Caribbean 127
– Indian 147, 189, 190, 224, 314
– Pacific 127, 132, 224
Oettermann, Stephan 239
Okeev, Tolomush 303

Okinawa 147
Oklahoma 114
Ong, Aihwa 78, 86, 87
Organization for European Economic Cooperation/Organization for Economic Co-operation and Development (OEEC/OECD) 286
Organization for Security and Co-operation in Europe (OSCE) 313
Organization of African Unity (OAU) 314, 318, 328, 330
Organization of American States (OAS) 314
Ostrovityanov, Konstantin V. 286, 287, 291
Oxford 184

Paasi, Ansi 68
Pacific Islands Forum 315
Padmore, George 8, 201, 223–226
Pahuja, Sundhya 266
Palan, Ronen 273
Panama 132, 133
Panama Canal 129, 131, 132, 139
Paris 2, 169, 184, 199, 200, 201, 202, 203, 226, 230, 233, 235, 236, 237, 238, 243, 258, 259, 300, 301
– as colonial city 185, 188, 198
Paris Colonial Exposition (1931) 133
Paris Peace Treaty (1947) 262
Peace of Augsburg (1555) 169
Peccei, Aurelio 269, 270
Pedersen, Susan 260, 261
Permanent Court of International Justice, Hague 259, 263
Petersen, Hans 248
Philippines 129, 139
Philippoteaux, Félix 237, 243, 244
Poggi, Gianfranco 161
Poland 168, 169, 260, 279, 285, 287, 293, 297, 314, 351
Polano, Luigi 219
Portugal 41, 73, 154
Prague 86, 284, 300
Prague Spring 303
Pratt, Marie Louise 303
Prévost, Pierre 37
Prussia 2, 155, 163, 164, 170, 171, 220
Puerto Rico 129, 147

Rabinow, Paul 90
Red International of Labour Unions (RILU) 205, 207–210, 212, 215, 219, 221, 222
Reed, L. A. 90
regionalization 9, 31, 71, 296, 308, 311, 318, 319, 322, 324, 327, 332
– economic 288, 294
Reinalda, Bob 312, 328
Renner, Karl 167
Republic of Ireland 176
Republic of Palau 139
Republic of the Marshall Islands 139, 141
respatialization(s) 4, 5, 6, 10, 11, 127, 129, 134, 139, 277, 278, 290, 294, 303, 309, 334, 336, 339, 351, 355, 358, 359, 365, 367–371, 373–378
Revel, Jacques 321
Ricardo, David 362
Rijeka 260
Robertson, Roland 34
Roeder, Philip 167
Romania 280, 285, 291, 296, 297
Rome 150, 238, 300
Rome Statute 321
Rosenfeldt, Niels Erik 214
Rose, Nikolas S. 83
Roßbach, Arwed 247
Rotterdam 211
Ruanda 261
Russia 2, 62, 72, 111, 113, 126, 145, 148, 155, 164, 167, 174, 210, 278, 279, 280, 281, 292, 309, 314, 327, 341, 362
– October Revolution (1917) 293, 309
– Soviet Russia 210

Saka, E. 93
Salazkina, Masha 303
Samsing, Arthur 216
San Francisco 210
Sassen, Saskia 86, 87
Sayer, Andrew 53
Schleswig-Holstein 155
Schmid, Sonja D. 298
Schmitt, Carl 160
Schumacher, Frank 6
Scott, Allen J. 363
Scott, Felicity C. 268, 269

Scott, James Brown 133
Seeley, Sir John 157, 159, 162
Sembène, Ousmane 303
Senegal 303, 329
Senghor, Léopold 200
Serbia 166
Serres, Michel 99
Seven Years' War 39
Seward, William Henry 118
Shanghai Cooperation Organization on Security and Trade (SCO) 314
Shelley, Adolf 218, 220, 226
Siegert, Augustin 236
Simmler, Wilhelm 242
Sinding, Otto 242
Sippel, Sarah Ruth 9, 10, 339
Skarbina, Franz 243
Slovakia 314
Sluga, Glenda 9
Smith, Neil 55
Söderbaum, Fredrik 327
Sofia 285, 300
South Atlantic Peace and Cooperation Zone (ZPCAS) 314
Southern African Development Community (SADC) 314, 327
Southern Common Market (MERCOSUR) 314, 327
South Pacific Forum 315
Soviet Union. See *USSR*
Spain 41, 111, 151, 154
Spanish-American War (1898) 127
Spanish Civil War 301
spatialization(s) 4, 8, 9, 16, 17, 22, 28, 47, 48, 51, 54, 55, 63, 65, 66, 75, 77, 79, 80, 103, 190–193, 204, 276, 279, 281–284, 288, 293, 294, 308, 315, 319, 322, 364, 369
spatial turn 4, 16, 24, 25, 48, 49, 51, 57, 316, 319, 324, 360, 364
Spykman, Nicholas John 144, 145
Stalin, Joseph 172, 280, 281, 288, 290, 291, 299
Stanley, Henry Morton 243
Steil, Benn 272, 273
Stettin 284
Stockholm 300

Sudan 224, 329
Suez Canal 159
Suez crisis 302
Sun Yat-sen 162
Swanton, Dan 93
Sydney 210, 212, 347, 352
Syria 285

Tanzania 190, 192
Tashkent 303
Taylor, A. J. P. 263
Teachers Insurance and Annuity Association – College Retirement Equities Fund (TIAA–CREF) 351
Tèlo, M. 326, 327
Tetrowitz, Franz 226
Thrift, Nigel 350
Tinbergen, Jan 268, 269, 270, 273
Tito, Josip Broz 281, 295
Togo 331
Toynbee, Arnold 167
TPSN (Territory, place, scale, and networks framework) 21, 22, 34, 35, 38, 48, 60–71, 74–77
Trieste 262, 263, 284
Troebst, Stephan 9
Truman, Harry S. 284, 285, 286
Turkey 285
Turner, Frederick Jackson 124, 125

Uganda 329
Ujiji 192–196
Ukraine 281, 341
UN. See *United Nations*
Union Maghreb Arabe (UMA) 314
Union of Soviet Socialist Republics 42, 69, 72, 143, 146, 152, 156, 157, 159, 160, 166–168, 175, 211, 223, 263, 271, 275, 277, 280–287, 293, 295, 297, 303, 306, 307, 309, 314, 326
United Kingdom 215, 218, 224, 323, 332
United Nations 46, 139, 258, 261, 262, 265–268, 286, 292, 312, 313, 328, 331
– Moon Agreement (1979) 258, 272
– UN Charter (1945) 262
– UN Educational, Scientific and Cultural Organization (UNESCO) 286

– UN General Assembly 266, 267
– UN Security Council (UNSC) 262, 331, 332
United States of Africa 329
United States of America 2, 3, 6–8, 33, 41, 46, 72, 74, 107–109, 113–122, 124, 126, 127, 129, 130–148, 153, 154, 156, 159, 161, 163, 164, 166, 175, 211, 213, 214, 223, 226, 235, 238, 252, 261–263, 271, 281, 285, 286, 294, 301, 315, 327, 332, 340, 341, 345, 351
– Civil Rights Act (1964) 138
– Civil War 6, 152, 153, 240
– Declaration of Independence 170
– Supreme Court 138
– United States Objectives and Programs for National Security 146
– Voting Rights Act (1965) 138
United States of Europe 72
Universal Postal Union 263
urbanization 2, 41, 61, 183, 186, 190, 195, 197, 262, 340
Uruguay 314, 341
USA. See *United States of America*
USSR. See *Union of Soviet Socialist Republics*

value chains 3, 10, 42, 64, 316, 357, 361
Varga, Eugen 291
Victoria, Queen 247
Vienna 156, 233, 235, 236, 284, 300
Vienna Congress 311, 213, 328
Vietnam 23, 200, 285, 293, 297, 302, 304
Visser, Oane 336
Vladivostok 210, 277

Wake Island 129
Wales 176
Walker, William 118
Wallerstein, Immanuel 337
Walter, Albert 8, 205, 207, 210, 211, 213, 214, 217–219, 223, 225, 226
Warnecke-Berger, Hannes 10
Warsaw 284, 300
Warsaw Pact 160, 286, 292, 293, 299, 300
Washington 113, 118, 135, 139, 141, 146
Weber, Eugen 171
Weber, Max 21, 53, 161, 165, 171

Weiß, Holger 8
Werlen, Benno 24
Werner, Anton von 239
Werner, Marion 338
West Indies 116
Westphalia
– Peace of Westphalia (1648) 35, 56
– Treaty of Westphalia 169, 257
– Westphalian system 311
White, Richard 36
Wilhelm I., Emperor 243, 244, 248
Wilson, Woodrow 134, 165, 261, 283
Witt, Antonia 328
Wollweber, Ernst 206, 226
Womens's International Democratic Federation (WIDF) 301, 302
World Bank 271
World Congress of Youth 302
World Federation of Democratic Youth 300
World Federation of Trade Unions 300
World Festivals of Youth and Students 300, 307
– Prague, Budapest, Berlin, Bucharest, Warsaw, Moscow, Vienna, Helsinki, Sofia, Havana, Pyongyang 300
World Peace Council 301
World Trade Organization (WTO) 271, 340
World War I 3, 120, 123, 145, 240, 268, 279, 285, 311, 326
World War II 120, 124, 135, 137, 145, 194, 205, 232, 245, 249, 261, 264, 278, 279, 281, 284, 288, 293, 307, 311, 323, 326, 327

Xiaoping, Deng 200

Yokohama 116
Yugoslavia 166, 262, 280, 293

Zanzibar 189, 190, 192, 194, 196
Zhdanov, Andrei 285, 287, 290
Zurich 242

www.ingramcontent.com/pod-product-compliance
Lightning Source LLC
Chambersburg PA
CBHW031324230426
43670CB00006B/235